6-15-62

GROWTH OF INDUSTRIAL PRODUCTION
IN THE SOVIET UNION

NATIONAL BUREAU OF ECONOMIC RESEARCH
NUMBER 75, GENERAL SERIES

Growth of
Industrial Production
in the Soviet Union

BY

G. WARREN NUTTER
UNIVERSITY OF VIRGINIA

ASSISTED BY

ISRAEL BORENSTEIN
AND
ADAM KAUFMAN

A STUDY BY THE
NATIONAL BUREAU OF ECONOMIC RESEARCH

PUBLISHED BY
PRINCETON UNIVERSITY PRESS
PRINCETON, NEW JERSEY
1962

Printed in the United States of America

This study, one of a series dealing with Soviet economic growth, was made possible by funds granted by the Rockefeller Foundation. The Rockefeller Foundation is, however, not to be understood as approving or disapproving by virtue of its grant any of the statements made or views expressed herein

To Jane, my wife
For her sympathy and understanding

Contents

CONTENTS

CONTENTS

Tables

Charts

Preface

THIS is the second in a series of reports setting forth results of the study of Soviet economic growth begun in 1954 under a grant from the Rockefeller Foundation. It deals with industry and appropriately appears after Professor Gregory Grossman's appraisal of official Soviet statistics on industrial output.

Our work has been based ultimately on official Soviet sources, and it has been complicated by the changes in Soviet policy on publishing statistics that have taken place during our six years of research. As new statistics appeared beginning in 1956, we revised our analysis to take account of them, at least of those published through 1959. An older sample of data still provides the basis for one or two subsidiary statistical analyses noted in the text, where complete revision would have taken more time than the minor refinement in results warranted. As for the new Soviet data appearing in 1960, we have been able to incorporate only selected items because of the advanced stage of our work at the time of their release.

The basic data used in this study are given in our appendixes. Additional materials from Soviet sources of different types and dates have been compiled into a six-part abstract (*Statistical Abstract of Industrial Output in the Soviet Union, 1913–1955*, Parts 1–5, New York, National Bureau of Economic Research, 1956; and *Supplement* to same, 1957), which supplements the present volume. Many of the figures in our appendixes are given more precisely than their accuracy warrants, the extra places being provided to reduce the rounding error in statistics that others may wish to derive. For example, the production indexes in Appendix D are generally given to four or more significant places, but in the text we have usually rounded them to the nearest percentage point and annual average rates of growth derived from them to the nearest tenth of a point. As is always the case in working with figures of varying and essentially unknown degrees of accuracy, it is neither possible nor desirable to be entirely consistent in assigning significant places to basic or derived statistics. Rounding rules are necessarily rather arbitrary.

In transcribing Russian words into the Roman alphabet, we have used the Library of Congress transliteration system, except that diphthong marks have been eliminated and the apostrophe has been used for the hard as well as the soft sign. We have deviated from this system only where common usage has established a different transliteration, as the names of some well-known persons, or where a transliteration made by others is cited, as the names of Russian authors of books translated by others. Russian words are followed by an English translation the first time they appear in a chapter. For publications in Russian, our translation of the title is given in brackets following the title in Russian. For publications originally in Russian but translated into another language, the title is given only in the language of translation.

In working with Russian materials, I was almost a blind man seeing through the eyes of others, who fortunately had not only full command of the language and the literature but also exceptional competence in economic statistics. Israel Borenstein and Adam Kaufman were my principal colleagues, and the study owes much to them.

Many others also participated. Professor Alexander Erlich and Dr. Nestor Terleckyj both made substantial contributions to our research work at an early stage. Professor John H. Young prepared a valuable report on Soviet military production, and Nicholas DeWitt on the Soviet cement industry. Professor Stanley Zyzniewski was very helpful in supplying information on Soviet reparations and various historical matters, Maude Pech in calculating the statistics we have used on industrial productivity in the United States, and Harold Wool in preparing a report on Soviet population and labor force. None of these persons can, of course, be held responsible for the use made of their work. Marie-Christine Culbert has been an ideal editor and general assistant, aided by Julia Kamermacher. Charlotte Wasserman and Murray Feshbach handled statistical operations during part of the study, Martha Jones managed the many IBM computations, and Robert S. Johnson indexed the book. Finally, H. Irving Forman has done his usual fine job of preparing charts.

I am indebted to many of the Bureau Board and staff for detailed comments and suggestions: Moses Abramovitz, Arthur F. Burns, Solomon Fabricant, Raymond W. Goldsmith, Albert J. Hettinger, Jr., F. Thomas Juster, Hal B. Lary, Geoffrey H. Moore, Harry Scherman, George J. Stigler, and Leo Wolman. Drafts were widely circulated among scholars, particularly specialists in Soviet studies, and helpful comments were received from Edward L. Allen, James M. Buchanan, John M. Cassels, Ronald Coase, Gregory Grossman, Naum Jasny, Alec Nove, James R. Schlesinger, and John

H. Young. These reviewers have helped us to repair many mistakes and to make many improvements, though each undoubtedly still has his own reservations about, and objections to, the final result. We regret that other scholars in the Soviet field whose views we solicited did not find it possible to give similar help to the study.

Finally, the University of Virginia, through the Wilson Gee Institute for Research in the Social Sciences and the Thomas Jefferson Center for Studies in Political Economy, has been generous in its support in the form of facilities, personnel, and financial aid, relieving somewhat the heavy burden borne by the National Bureau.

G. WARREN NUTTER

London, England
January 1961

GROWTH OF INDUSTRIAL PRODUCTION
IN THE SOVIET UNION

CHAPTER 1

Introduction

FOUR centuries of Tsarist rule in Russia came to an end in mid-March 1917. The succeeding provisional government stayed in power only a few months, and by mid-November the precursor of the Communist Party, under the leadership of Lenin, had assumed control of the central government, marking the origin of a new political order later named the Union of Soviet Socialist Republics. Our purpose is to study the record of industrial growth in that political order over the forty-odd years that have passed since its founding.

A Sketch of Developments

At the outset the country endured a civil war lasting through 1920 and accompanied by a precipitous decline in economic activity: industrial production contracted by 80 per cent, agricultural production by perhaps 50 per cent. The population shrank by five million as war losses were compounded by famine and pestilence. The existing economic order was supplanted by a disorganized and quasi-military system later called "War Communism," which was in turn replaced by the interim New Economic Policy (NEP) when social and economic conditions became chaotic. After eight years of recovery, economic activity approached once again, with notable exceptions, its prerevolutionary level.

Late in 1928 the economic order took on its now characteristic nature with the introduction of the First Five Year Plan, aimed primarily at accelerating industrial growth. Within the first year of its operation, agriculture was collectivized with the resultant disruption in the rural economy accompanied by famine and large-scale destruction of agricultural capital. Against this background, industry grew rapidly through 1933,[1] persons engaged increasing by about 60 per cent, man-hours of work by about 40 per cent, and output by about 50 per cent.

The already rapid industrial growth accelerated during the Second Five Year Plan, which began in 1933, output approximately doubling. Over the four years 1933–1937, persons engaged increased by about 40 per cent, man-hours worked by about 45 per cent, and output by about 85 per cent.

NOTE: Industry will be defined throughout in accord with Soviet usage, including manufacturing, mining, logging, fishing, and generating of electricity.

[1] The year 1933 is used as a terminal date here instead of 1932, because employment in the latter year is not accurately known.

3

In the face of a widespread political purge that depleted administrative and technical leadership, growth slackened in the short-lived Third Five Year Plan, terminated by World War II. The growth in industrial output in this period, 1937–1940, was no larger than can be attributed to territorial gains growing out of the Hitler-Stalin pact.

World War II brought with it enormous losses in property and human life. While Lend-Lease deliveries helped offset the losses in production, industrial output stood in 1945, after German-occupied territories had been regained, at some 80 per cent of the prewar level, and this figure is probably too high because of the tendency to overstate wartime output in production indexes. In 1946, after a rapid reconversion, output stood at less than 60 per cent of its prewar level. Recovery was swift in the Fourth Five Year Plan, begun in 1946, so that the prewar level of industrial output was apparently regained by 1948 or 1949. In the Fifth Five Year Plan, beset by new disturbances in the form of the Korean War and the political succession after Stalin's death, industrial expansion continued at a rapid pace: over the five years, persons engaged increased by about 20 per cent, man-hours worked by about 10 per cent, and output by about 60 per cent. Since 1955 the rate of expansion has retarded somewhat, though output has apparently continued to grow at an average rate of 7.1 per cent a year compared with 9.6 per cent over 1950–1955.

Which Period to Study

In view of this history of spurts of growth interspersed with major disturbances, one may wonder whether it makes sense to study industrial growth over the entire Soviet period. Perhaps it would be best to eliminate years of disturbance and consider only periods of sustained growth, on the ground that economic performance may be misrepresented if growth is attributed to years of stagnation and decline as well as to years of expansion. This view is persuasive, but it implies a limited objective in studying Soviet industrial history.

How we study history depends on what we wish to learn from it. We could never list all the things we wish to learn, or design a specific historical study to meet truly general interests. Every investigator is inevitably motivated more by some interests than by others, but two basic approaches to history may be distinguished. A study may aim at getting the record straight, at describing events "as they really happened." Or it may aim at drawing lessons from history, to be utilized in some way or other in dealing with the future. It is trite to say that neither approach can stand by itself: the facts to be set straight must be selected from a boundless volume; they must be relevant to something, and this usually means that they must bear on lessons sought from history. Similarly, useful lessons must be derived from an accurate record.

There is, nevertheless, a distinction to be drawn, if only of degree rather than kind. Lesson-seeking sheds light on a narrower set of issues than fact-seeking, and they tend to be more ephemeral, reflecting topical questions of the day. Studies should, of course, be oriented to matters of importance today, but not so much that they lose worth as their importance fades.

Because of the tragic political conflict the West has had thrust upon it, there is at present deep concern over the immediate prospect that the industrial base of power may expand more rapidly in the Soviet Union than in the West. This has had much to do with attracting our attention to the best years of Soviet industrial growth and away from the worst. Most specialists on the Soviet economy start their studies with the year 1928, when comprehensive centralized planning was introduced. Some go further and argue that the period of war and postwar recovery should be eliminated from consideration, leaving the years 1928–1940 and 1948–1958 for study. All growth should be attributed to those years alone, according to this view;[2] otherwise predictions of future growth rates are likely to be in serious error.

Even from this restricted point of view, one may doubt whether our eyes should be fixed solely on the best years of Soviet growth. Rapid expansion was favored in those times by unique circumstances not likely to be encountered again. At the beginning of the Plan period, the Soviet Union had a large idle labor force to draw upon in expanding industry. It also had at its disposal a large pool of as yet unutilized Western technology, available at relatively low cost because of depressed business conditions in the industrialized world. The Russian people were prepared to work hard and undergo sacrifices in order to make up for lost time. The government made them work even harder by methods that could not be used indefinitely.

After World War II there was again a willingness on the part of the people to endure, and the government to impose, abnormal hardships in order to make a rapid recovery and to achieve the level of economic

[2] For examples of these attitudes, see *Soviet Economic Growth: A Comparison with the United States*, Joint Economic Committee, Congress of the United States, Washington, 1957, p. 22, footnote 9; Gregory Grossman in *American Economic Review*, May 1957, pp. 643 ff; and Hans Heyman, Jr., in *idem*, May 1958, pp. 423 ff, and in *Comparisons of the United States and Soviet Economies*, Joint Economic Committee, Congress of the United States, Washington, 1959, Part I, p. 8.

acuvity that would have obtained in the absence of war. War losses were very heavy, and they placed a big handicap on postwar economic growth. But there were also factors helping offset this handicap: expansion of territory and resources, extension of political control over the so-called satellite countries, receipt of Western economic aid during and immediately after the war, employment of prisoners of war and other forced labor, and collection of reparations from defeated countries. There was, in addition, a second wave of technological innovation from the outside following wartime contact with the West and acquisition of Western goods on a large scale in the form of economic aid and reparations.

Prediction of future growth is always precarious, and one seldom knows in advance what kind of evidence on past performance will be most helpful. While nature may make a political leap through revolution, it seldom makes an economic leap. Economies do not rise phoenix-like from their own ashes; they grow out of the past. Hence, the production record of the future cannot be fully disconnected from the "trend" of the past. It would be as unwise to project as yet short-lived spurts of growth in a mechanical manner as simply to project the long "trend." The wisest course would seem to be to weigh evidence from both short and long periods of growth before making judgments on the future, the weight given to each depending on the problem at hand. Each person will do this in his own way.

When one is interested in more than predicting future growth, the long historical record becomes even more relevant. Often it is critical. We are, for example, interested in finding out how a Soviet-type economy performs over the course of history. For this purpose we wish to know how it responds to crises, generated both internally and externally, as well as how it performs under normal conditions. We also wish to know whether the economy generates its own disturbances. If we ignore bad years of growth merely because they are bad years, we beg matters at issue.

On a more concrete level, we may be misled about the forces responsible for growth by ignoring years of disturbance. As we shall see later, Soviet industrial output has apparently multiplied between six and seven times since the revolution. Let us attribute this growth entirely to the years in which aggregate output rose beyond a previous peak—that is, to the period 1928–1940 and 1948–1958. We then say that the 1958 level—and presumably a comparable composition—of output could have been reached by 1939: output could have multiplied six to seven times between 1917 and 1939 under "normal" circumstances.

This conclusion seems unreasonable on its face, and reflection shows why. Aside from the fact that time was required to consolidate the revolution and to develop a working economic system, things were happening over the period 1917–1928 that contributed to later economic growth. Population increased by nine million people, or 6 per cent. Output grew substantially in some industrial sectors, even though not in the aggregate: by 50 per cent in fuel and electricity; by 46 per cent in chemicals; by 151 per cent in agricultural equipment; and 58 per cent in consumer durables. Progress was made in eliminating widespread illiteracy.[3] And, probably most important, great technological advances were being made in the outside world, advances that the Soviet Union inherited with the inauguration of the Plan period. In short, productive capacity was expanding over these years even though actual output was not. Some of these same factors were operating similarly during World War II, though it is much more doubtful, because of very heavy war losses, that on balance they raised productive capacity.

We know, of course, only what has been, not what might have been. Things would have been different had the Soviet Union not suffered a civil war, political instabilities, and a major world war. But we shall never know in what specific respects they would have been different. The weight we give to "abnormal" elements must ultimately be a matter of judgment, depending on the issue at hand.

We have tried to make this a fact-seeking study, useful for many different purposes, and have therefore examined Soviet industrial performance over the long as well as the short run. As each topic is taken up, long-run performance is generally discussed first, and shorter-run performance is then viewed within this perspective. There are drawbacks to this approach from some points of view, but it has seemed to us best all round.

Periods and Subperiods

Except for brief discussions of the Tsarist period and the last few years, our study covers the period 1913–1955, or 42 years.[4] We shall often refer to this as the "entire Soviet period," though that is obviously not

[3] See, e.g., W. H. Chamberlin, *Soviet Russia*, Boston, 1931, pp. 286 ff.
[4] The period beginning at the end of 1913 and continuing through 42 years can be designated as either 1914–1955 or 1913–1955. The first must be read as meaning "from the beginning of 1914 to the end of 1955," the second as "from the end of 1913 to the end of 1955." Neither form seems to be firmly established in usage, and both have shortcomings. We have chosen the second as more convenient for two reasons: first, the number of years of growth in a period is easily found by subtracting the beginning year from the last; and second, the terminal years of each period correspond to benchmark dates. The primary drawback is the confusion that may be caused about the beginning year for a five year plan. Thus, when the Second Five Year Plan is referred to as the period 1932–1937, it must be remembered that the initial year of the plan was 1933.

strictly correct. The use of 1913 as the prerevolutionary benchmark accords with general practice, which can be justified on the ground that this was the last normal year before World War I. In any case, use of other prerevolutionary benchmarks is precluded for most purposes since some output data are available only for Tsarist territory, whereas the data for 1913 have been generally adjusted by Soviet statisticians to the interwar Soviet territory. The closing date for most analysis had to be 1955 because of the time spent on the study. That year also marked the end of the Fifth Five Year Plan, the last completed plan to date.

The Soviet period divides naturally into two major parts: the pre-Plan period, covering 1913–1928, and the Plan period, covering 1928–1955. The former may be subdivided into the periods of World War I and War Communism (1913–1920) and the NEP (1920–1928); the latter, into the periods for the component five year plans, with an interruption for World War II (1940–1945). These plans were as follows:

First: 1928–1932
Second: 1932–1937
Third: 1937–1940
Fourth: 1945–1950
Fifth: 1950–1955

This breakdown of periods and subperiods has an obvious advantage in that it corresponds to well-known chronology. We follow it not so much for this reason, but because Soviet statistics are organized to cover these periods—particularly the plans—and therefore are more plentiful for the terminal dates than for intermediate years. While it might be desirable to date some periods differently for purposes of economic analysis, we are limited in doing so by shortage of data.

Nature and Plan of the Study

The basic purpose of this study is to describe the historical record of Soviet industrial production. An economist's job has, of course, only

---

On another matter of dating, we have generally sacrificed accuracy for simplicity. Beginning with the fall of 1921, a fiscal year was established in the Soviet Union for economic accounting, the year starting on October 1. This practice was continued until the fall of 1930, when the calendar year was re-established as the accounting unit. We have made no effort to adjust data for fiscal years to a calendar year basis since any adjustment would be essentially arbitrary without improving analysis. We have, nevertheless, followed the practice of designating a fiscal year by the calendar year in which it ended, unless greater precision is called for in the nature of the discussion. Hence, the year 1927/28 is generally referred to as 1928, 1928/29 as 1929, and so on.

begun when he describes events in a manner relevant to causal analysis, but we have limited ourselves primarily to this task in order to put first things first. We hope to provide raw materials for analysis to the extent allowed by the scope of our study, by the shortcomings of Soviet statistics, and by the limits to our own capabilities.

It has been said that the Soviet Union is more than a mystery: it is a secret. The greatest handicap to study of the Soviet economy is the absence of a coherent body of relevant and reliable statistics. The weaknesses of the data are outlined in the second chapter and to some extent in the third, although the latter is primarily concerned with qualitative aspects of industrial growth. This rather lengthy background discussion presents the necessary qualifications against which the statistical analysis of the remainder of the book should be continually viewed. In this sense, the second and third chapters are as essential to a proper understanding of Soviet industrial growth as the quantitative measures developed later.

The difficulties with data also account in part for the organization of topics. We proceed from simple to more and more complex methods of describing growth, starting with an analysis of growth in physical output of individual industries and ending with an analysis of growth in aggregative output as measured by production indexes. This procedure of leading up to aggregates seems to be justified on other counts as well, in particular because the discontinuous nature and shifting structure of Soviet industrial growth create difficult problems of measurement if we use conventional index numbers, to say nothing of the difficulty of finding appropriate weighting factors.

Statistical and measurement problems being so central, we have tended to place more discussion of technical issues in the text than might ordinarily be called for, particularly in Chapter 5, in which the data and techniques underlying our production indexes are discussed and our indexes are compared with those computed by others. We have felt it necessary to provide meticulous explanations there and at several other points in the book at the expense, perhaps, of readability. The general reader may often find this annoying if not plain boring, and he may find it more tasteful to skip such sections, at least at first reading. Technical details may generally be omitted without breaking the continuity of discussion.

After setting out the aggregative measures and defining their limitations, we move on in the next two chapters to some interpretative discussion, intended as a rather introductory analysis of industrial growth. A broad view is given first, followed by a focusing on selected details.

We make liberal comparisons of Soviet and U.S. industrial growth, particularly in Chapter 8, not only to give perspective but also to supplement the inferences that can be drawn about Soviet growth from the limited data available. That is to say, there is something to be gained by reasoning through an expanded analogy. We know much more about U.S. industry than we do about Soviet industry, and we are therefore in a position to judge indirectly the adequacy of our knowledge of Soviet industry, and perhaps to extend our knowledge, by taking advantage of relevant analogies. Both for this purpose and to provide a perspective against which Soviet growth can be appraised, it would have been preferable to make comparative studies involving other countries as well. We have not done this because of the need to publish the basic findings of our study within a reasonable time limit. Relevant data for the United States are readily available; they are more difficult to find for other countries. We leave these important comparative studies to other scholars, with the assurance that they will not be neglected.

Since a study of this magnitude and complexity does not lend itself to a simple summary of findings, we do not attempt to provide one at this point. Instead, the last chapter is designed to be a more or less self-contained summary. Those readers who prefer an advance perspective may wish to read this last chapter at the start as well as the end.

It is suitable to conclude these introductory comments by acknowledging the heavy debt we owe to scholars who have devoted themselves to study of the Soviet economy. Their contribution to our work is pervasive and cannot be singled out or summarized. Nor is it fully reflected in the numerous citations throughout the book. This study falls within the stream of expanding knowledge about the Soviet economy, drawing heavily on what has come before and, we hope, adding something to it.

CHAPTER 2

The Data: Knowns and Unknowns

A STATISTICAL study naturally begins with an appraisal of the underlying data, in this case, official Soviet statistics. Discussion tends to get focused on defects, more easily seen than virtues, and this carries with it the danger that the basic statistics may seem to be worse than they are. Almost every economist in no matter what field of empirical research soon becomes convinced, as he gets familiar with his materials, that no data could be as bad as those he is forced to work with. He has explored the defects more thoroughly than others have. Heeding this lesson, we should weigh the good features with the bad before passing judgment. As we shall see, Soviet statistics, despite their serious shortcomings, do form a basis for studying industrial growth when used with care.

The statistics relevant to a study of industrial growth fall into several categories: output of individual industries, prices and related cost data, labor and capital inputs, and aggregative measures. The discussion here will center on only the first of these, namely, output of individual industries expressed in physical terms. The other types of data will be discussed at appropriate points in other chapters.

The discussion cannot be exhaustive but will concentrate on some of the more significant points. Fortunately, the subject has already been treated very carefully and thoroughly by Professor Gregory Grossman in an earlier report in this series,[1] which should be consulted by those interested in a more detailed analysis. That excellent study is, in fact, the basis of much that will be said here.

Introductory Remarks

The defects of Soviet statistics on physical output are important and must be understood if the data are not to be misused. There are three major shortcomings, all deriving from the nature of the Soviet political and economic orders. The first is the selectivity of published data, a factor that works in two opposing directions. On the one hand, some areas of poor performance are shielded from view, causing the published data to underrepresent slower-growing sectors of industry. On the other hand, some of the more rapidly expanding economic activities associated with the military sector are also not reported on. It is impossible to determine

---

[1] Gregory Grossman, *Soviet Statistics of Physical Output of Industrial Commodities: Their Compilation and Quality*, Princeton for National Bureau of Economic Research, 1960.

11

whether the net effect is to promote an overstatement or an understatement of growth. As we shall see, the degree of selectivity has varied considerably over the years. For a long stretch of time, from 1938 to 1956, almost no data were published on the absolute level of output in any sectors of industry.

The second shortcoming is ambiguity. Primary sources generally do not contain adequate definitions of industries in terms of administrative and territorial coverage, product coverage, and stage of fabrication at which output is being measured. Titles given to industries can be misleading—for example, "silk fabrics" are chiefly rayon—and slight verbal changes may signify a basic change in definition not otherwise described. Things are not always what they seem to be, and the user of Soviet data should beware. In the end, he still will have to use many data whose meaning he does not fully comprehend, and conclusions should be qualified on this account.

The third shortcoming is the general overstatement of absolute levels of output within the Plan period for the sample of industries reported on. The lower the priority of an industry from the Soviet point of view and the less precisely its output can be measured, the greater the overstatement is likely to be, for reasons to be developed later. That much can be said, but no more; we cannot now place an order of magnitude on the overstatement, in the large or in the small. The tendency toward overstatement needs to be taken into account most when levels of output are being compared between the Soviet Union and other countries. It has less bearing on internal measures of growth, since it is doubtful that relative overstatement of output has increased systematically with time, except with respect to prerevolutionary and early Soviet years. Hence growth will, on this count, be overstated relative to, say, 1913 or 1928 but not necessarily relative to later base years. Over later spans of years growth may be overstated, understated, or more or less accurately reflected by the available output data, the effect depending on specific circumstances, some of which cannot now be adequately known.

Offsetting these shortcomings is another feature of the Soviet system: the large volume of economic statistics collected and processed. As Professor Devons has tersely put it, "Without statistics there can be no planning."[2] It is a curious fact that the United States, lying more or less at the opposite pole from centralized planning, is probably the only other country as figure-minded as the Soviet Union—for quite different

---

[2] Ely Devons, *Planning in Practice: Essays in Aircraft Planning in Wartime*, Cambridge, Eng., 1950, p. 133.

reasons, of course. The question of quality and reliability aside, the volume of output data flowing out of the Soviet Union during interwar years and since 1956 has been large by normal standards, despite the policy of selective publication. Quantity substitutes to some extent for quality.

When all is said, Soviet data, with their many faults, do provide a basis for assessing Soviet industrial performance and growth, if carefully used and interpreted. This is shown most convincingly by the fact that growth patterns derived from using these data make economic sense. There is a basic internal consistency in the figures; differential rates of growth conform in direction with developments that can be directly observed; certain phenomena appear that are characteristic of economic growth everywhere, such as retardation in growth of individual industries; and changes in industrial structure are shown that are otherwise known to have occurred. These and other lines of evidence on the reliability of the data will be developed more fully at later points in this and other chapters.

But the faults remain to affect the accuracy of measures of growth, and we turn now to discuss them more fully. Since most of the difficulties stem from the nature of the Soviet system and its statistical apparatus, we begin with a review of their salient features as they affect the reliability of statistics.

General Characteristics of Soviet Statistics

Fault can be found with the economic statistics of every country. They represent, in the first place, a mere sampling of the unbounded volume of data that might be recorded. They have been collected with specific objectives in mind—more varied and far-reaching in some countries than in others— and will therefore be of varying use depending on the purposes they are made to serve. They contain, in the second place, errors introduced at different stages of observation and assemblage. These will depend on the state of statistical literacy among the collectors and suppliers of data, on the effort expended on record-keeping, and on the degree of active competition in gathering and analyzing data. They are, finally, subject to manipulation and distortion by parties with a stake in the figures, checked only to the extent that there are independent fact-seekers and fact-gatherers with competing interests. No government or other statistical agency can be relied upon to resist the temptation to stretch figures to its own account if it feels it can get away with it.

Progress in economic statistics has been driven in the West by two

13

engines: competition and technical sophistication. An extreme example is perhaps provided by the United States, a country unique in its long tradition of figure-gathering. Thumbnail histories usually mislead, particularly when they treat the causes of some institutional development, but we may perhaps be allowed to speculate very briefly on the evolution of the American statistical system in order to illustrate its basic characteristics and how they differ from those of the Soviet system.

The habit of collecting statistics was formed early, with a constitutional requirement of a decadal census for the purpose of apportioning political representation. Existence of a large market economy led to demands for expanding economic intelligence on the part of legislators who made the laws defining the economy, businessmen who organized it, and scholars who studied it. The government census gradually expanded to cover an increasing area of economic statistics, and special censuses ultimately evolved. At the same time, private agencies arose engaging in a host of specialized activities in economic statistics, each serving the particular interests of its consumers. The long history of statistical activity, together with its competitive nature, provided the experience and pragmatic testing that in turn promoted improvements in technical procedures and competence.

A critical feature of the American statistical system, as it has evolved, is the multiplicity of statistical sources. While the government plays an important role in collecting and disseminating statistics, there is no sustained unity of interest among the governing because of the nature of the political system: federalism, representative government, governmental checks and balances, and the two-party system. No sanctity attaches to the official statistics of the moment; they are subject to challenge and are continually challenged by both ins and outs; they are subject to revision and are frequently revised. There are not only these internal checks, but also the external checks of private statistical organizations and researchers, pursuing their own work as they see it.

Similar conditions prevail in other Western countries in varying degrees. At bottom, representative government, competitive scholarship, and free public discourse are the Western institutions that have counteracted error and misrepresentation in statistics, imperfectly to be sure but at least to an important extent.[3]

[3] The Soviet image of Western statistics is rather different: "It is said that under capitalism comprehensive and truthful economic statistics are not to be expected because of the secretiveness of private firms, the lack of centralized coordination in and authority over the generation and collection of data, the class interests of the governments in power and the mendacity of their statisticians, etc." (Grossman, *Soviet Statistics*, p. 22). Some of

The importance of these institutions is shown by the generally unsatisfactory nature of the statistics gathered and issued during wartime, when public discussion is curbed and large segments of the economy are centrally directed. Devons, in his informative little book on the British experiences of aircraft planning in World War II, concluded his chapter on the role of statistics in planning by saying:[4]

> The pseudo-scientific atmosphere which the use of charts and statistics created gave great power to the statisticians. For it was fairly easy by the manipulation of statistics and charts to "prove" a particular case; and the statisticians soon came to realize that many of the officials not used to handling figures were both impressed by this manipulative power and incapable of acquiring it themselves. The department or directorate which had a skilled statistician always had a great initial advantage in any inter-departmental or inter-directorate dispute. And any statistician who was concerned with issues of policy was bound to find himself, sooner or later, selecting and manipulating statistics in such a way as to guide policy along the lines which he had decided, on quite general grounds, were the right ones.
>
> Attempts were made to avoid this danger, by separating the collection and issue of statistics from decisions and discussions of policy. But such attempts invariably failed in M.A.P. [the Ministry of Aircraft Production]. First, because the analysis of data about the past is so intimately concerned with the planning of the future, that any attempt to separate the two functions usually resulted either in the planners paying little attention to the past and so making the most unrealistic plans, or in the planners setting up their own fact-finding staff which by-passed the statistical division and so deprived it of any influence. Secondly, life in a statistics division which was separated from policy was apt to be dull, and there was great difficulty in attracting efficient staff to such a division. In any case, unless the staff of the statistics division were closely concerned with policy decisions, they had no easy means of knowing which were the most significant statistics to collect and analyze; and they had the greatest difficulty in ensuring that some notice was taken of the results of their analyses. The danger that the planners who have a monopoly of the statistics might distort the figures

---

the real shortcomings of American government statistics are discussed in Geoffrey H. Moore, "Accuracy of Government Statistics," *Harvard Business Review*, Spring 1947, pp. 306–317.

[4] Devons, *Planning in Practice*, pp. 163 f.

to prove their case cannot be avoided. Where planning is necessary, great power must inevitably fall into the hands of the statisticians.

These words might well have been written about the Soviet statistical system. The troubles with Soviet statistics stem, in the first instance, from the system of centralized authoritarian planning—from the nature of what Grossman, following others, has called the "command economy." Statistics are collected, processed, and issued by only one agency: the state. There are no independent sources to restrain each other or to be used as checks on each other, except to the extent that related figures published by different state agencies might not be fully coordinated before issuance. From the nature of the planning system, everybody seems to have a stake in the figures—those who report them as well as those who process and use them—since performance is judged by them.

One finds in the Soviet responses to difficulties the same dilemmas pictured by Devons under less trying circumstances: statistical and planning agencies are separated, united, and then separated again; internal checks are evolved through a dual reporting system with the administrative and statistical hierarchies supposedly cross-checking each other, later to be abandoned in favor of consolidated reporting through the statistical hierarchy alone; and so on. As Grossman has emphasized:[5]

> ... one must not exaggerate the specifically Russian or communist elements in these problems. Rather, given the way human beings react in the face of authority and in their quest for material well-being, the problems discussed here arise by and large from the logic of a command economy and a sellers' market. To be sure, many of the details, aspects, and nuances are peculiar to the Soviet scene, and some perhaps even to the Russian "national character," if there be such a thing. But the broader outlines of these problems can be easily recognized in other authoritarian organizations, especially in other command economies, and in sellers' markets in other countries and at other times.

There is, at the same time, a second set of difficulties with Soviet statistics that originates in circumstances rather specific to communism and the Russian case. The Soviet system embodies an international crusade, and statistics are grist for the propaganda mill. Knowing the ideological views of Soviet leaders, one finds it hard to picture them

[5] Grossman, *Soviet Statistics*, pp. 4 f.

dispensing facts in a passive and detached manner. The official doctrinal concept of statistics as a discipline is considerably at variance with the traditional Western view, statistics being considered "a social science, the theoretical base of which is formed by historical materialism and Marxist-Leninist political economy."[6]

Another set of quite different endemic difficulties, especially in the formative period of Soviet statistics, may be traced to the meager heritage from the Tsarist era of experience and competence in statistical work. The staff conducting statistical work in agencies of the central Tsarist government was notoriously inefficient, and censuses were infrequent and narrow in scope—the first complete population census was taken in 1897. Industrial statistics were largely the by-product of the factory inspection and tax collection systems. Though private trade associations engaged in some statistical activities, they were limited in scope and came into existence late in the nineteenth century, when industrialization first surged forward in Russia. Statistical investigations of high quality were conducted throughout the last four decades of the nineteenth century by professionals working (voluntarily, for the most part) with the *zemstva*, or local and provincial councils; and out of this activity there emerged a nucleus of well-qualified statisticians, particularly in agriculture. But the range of activities and the number of people involved were small. Coupled with this was the crucial fact that educational levels were low in the bulk of the population, around 60 per cent being illiterate in 1914 and most of the rest not far above the threshold.[7] These factors must have had an adverse effect on the quality of statistics at least in the earlier Soviet years, despite the rapidity with which statistical activities grew and illiteracy declined.

Counteracting these detrimental features has been the urgent internal need for reliable statistics to run the economy. In the Soviet economic system, statistics form the basis for making plans, checking on their fulfillment, allocating resources, making technical managerial decisions, assessing performance, and dispensing rewards and punishments—in

[6] A. Yezhov [Ezhov], "Soviet Statistics in the Last Forty Years," *Problems of Economics* (authorized English translation of *Voprosy ekonomiki*), May 1958, p. 34. For further citations, see Grossman, *Soviet Statistics*, p. 23.

[7] The information on statistics is from Bernard Pares, *A History of Russia*, rev. ed., New York, 1944, pp. 402 ff; and A. Yezhov [Ezhov], *Soviet Statistics* (translated from the Russian), Moscow, 1957, pp. 5 ff. As to illiteracy, the census of 1897 listed 79 per cent of the population as illiterate, varying from 20 per cent in the Baltic provinces to 94 per cent in Central Asia. This had apparently fallen to just under 60 per cent by 1914. See M. T. Florinsky, *Russia: A History and an Interpretation*, New York, 1953, Volume II, pp. 1256 f; G. Vernadsky, *A History of Russia*, New Haven, 1951, p. 398; and S. Harcave, *Russia: A History*, 3rd ed., Philadelphia, 1956, pp. 313 ff.

short, for performing virtually every economic function. The pressure for trustworthy statistics comes, so to speak, from the top downward: every agency in the political and administrative hierarchy strives to get truthful reports from subordinate units.

Centralized authoritarian direction of the economy thus generates forces with opposing effects on the reliability of statistics. On the one side, there is a pressure for misreporting moving from the bottom upward: self-interest motivates each subordinate unit to try to mislead its superior, the central government finally being motivated to mislead the outside world. On the other side, there is a pressure for accuracy moving from the top downward, similarly motivated by self-interest. Which force gains the upper hand?

The answer is misreporting, since it does occur—as we shall see—even though it is certainly restricted by the pressure for accuracy. But before moving to the evidence, we may conclude these general remarks by noting the concern of Soviet officials themselves over the question of reliability of statistics. In the words of Grossman once more:[8]

> Even a cursory reading of the Soviet literature reveals that the central statistical authorities have been well aware of the imperfect reliability of the data submitted to them. A closer study leaves no doubt that they have been gravely concerned over the problem, and that the question of accuracy of physical output data occupies the very center of this concern. It is also clear that the main source of inaccuracy is believed to be distortion of reported data by interested parties, aided by the negligence, if not abetted by the connivance, of the lower statistical agencies.

The basis of this concern will emerge from the details of the statistical system and the statistics themselves.

The Statistical System: A Brief Summary[9]

During early Soviet years the statistical apparatus, called the Central Statistical Administration (*Tsentral'noe statisticheskoe upravlenie*, abbreviated *TsSU*), had an independent status, containing within it a special agency, the Division of Census and Statistics of the Supreme Council of the Economy (*Vysshii sovet narodnogo khoziaistva*, abbreviated *VSNKh*), concerned primarily with large-scale state industry. With the advent of

---

[8] Grossman, *Soviet Statistics*, p. 49.
[9] This section is a condensation of *ibid.*, Part One.

centralized planning, dissatisfaction arose over the separation of planning and statistical agencies, and in 1930 *TsSU* was made a part of the State Planning Commission (*Gosplan*). The name of the statistical arm was soon changed, in line with its new status, to the lengthy title Central Administration of Economic Record-Keeping Attached to the *Gosplan* of the USSR (*Tsentral'noe upravlenie narodnokhoziaistvennogo ucheta pri Gosplane SSSR*, abbreviated *TsUNKhU*). The merger of the central agencies was strengthened in 1938,[10] after a series of purges associated with the ill-fated population census of 1937, and it was extended to subordinate units late in 1943. The unified structure continued until 1948, when the statistical organization, which had been renamed *TsSU* in 1941, was separated from the *Gosplan* at all levels. It has retained its independent position up to the present.

During its affiliation with the *Gosplan*, the statistical organization was developed into a hierarchical structure on a regional basis. A chain of subordination became established with the central administration at the top, followed by administrations at the level of the republic, territory (*krai*), province (*oblast'*), major city, district (*raion*), and lesser city.[11] This hierarchy has remained in force, apparently being unaffected by the economic and administrative reorganization of 1957, which will be commented on briefly below.

The basic simplicity of this statistical organization belies the complex system of reporting that existed until the reforms of 1957. Data originating in economic enterprises flowed upward through two parallel channels: on the one side, the statistical hierarchy already described and, on the other side, the economic-administrative hierarchy (see Chart 1).[12] The system also provided for cross-reporting and for simultaneous reporting at different levels in the hierarchy. Thus, the enterprise reported in three directions at once: to the local statistical unit, to the next higher statistical unit (at the provincial level if existent, otherwise at the republic level), and to its immediate superior in the economic-administrative hierarchy, typically a chief administration (*glavk*). The chief administration in turn submitted a consolidated report to both its ministry and the central statistical office, and the ministry did the same to the central statistical office. Finally, the statistical offices at every level submitted separate

[10] In this connection, the name was altered to read "of the *Gosplan*" from "attached to the *Gosplan*."

[11] For a short period, these were also subdistrict inspectorates. The "chain of command" given here is simplified. For example, the so-called autonomous republics are subordinate to the union republics to which they are assigned. Major cities are the capital cities of union republics, plus Leningrad.

[12] This chart is also simplified. See the cited source.

consolidated reports to the corresponding level of the Communist Party, the government, and the planning organization—a flow not shown in our chart.

This complex system could have arisen for a number of reasons, not the least being the desire of every agency to have the most up-to-date figures at its disposal. Whatever its origins, the system abounded in possible

CHART I

The Soviet Statistical System Until Mid-1957

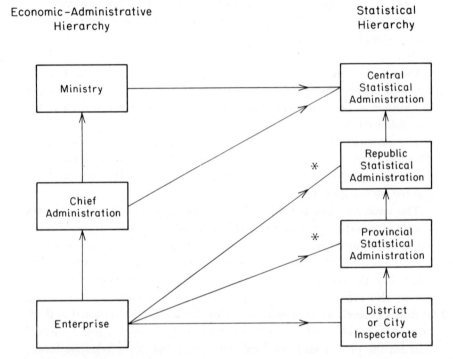

Arrows indicate direction of reporting.
* For republics without provinces, reports were made directly to the republic; otherwise, to the province.
Source: Adapted from Grossman, *Soviet Statistics*, p. 37

cross checks. Sums could be checked at almost every level in five different places: the ministerial, statistical, Party, government, and planning organizations. The only figures whose accuracy was not subject to direct checking were the basic data reported by the enterprise itself. Despite the many opportunities for checking figures, it is doubtful that the system did much more than multiply paperwork. The main obstacle to effective auditing is the enormous volume of data that must be rapidly processed by the Soviet statistical system. Given this fact—discussed more fully below—and the strong incentives to misreport, the interlacing of agencies in the statistical network may have worked in the opposite direction, aiding cooperative misreporting.

The system of parallel reporting was abandoned with the reforms of 1957, occasioned by the administrative reorganization of industry into regional economic councils (*sovnarkhozy*). The details of the new reporting system need not detain us, since it does not generally apply to the period of this study.[13] We may merely note that the upward flow of data to the central government now seems to proceed solely through the statistical apparatus. In line with this change, Starovskii, head of *TsSU*, remarked that "whereas up to now the checking of accounting data has been done by the respective subdivisions of chief administrations and ministries, now this most responsible work will be entirely entrusted to *TsSU* agencies."[14]

In a more lengthy comment, Starovskii says:[15]

In addition to the state statistical agencies, to which enterprises reported data (on state accounting forms), ministries, departments, and their chief administrations required a tremendous number of different tables, questionnaires, and estimates. Parallel accounts were also sent to financial and banking agencies and to a number of local organizations, and often so-called "wild" accounts (i.e., those not prescribed by law) were compiled. One of the managers of the former Ministry of Heavy Machine Building considered it essential to have, for example, data on the height at which electric light bulbs were hung in factories and other such information without which he thought it was impossible to administer from the center the enterprises under his jurisdiction.

The administrative reorganization of industry and construction enables us to eliminate existing defects. Now the receipt and processing of accounting statistics for these branches of the national economy is centralized in the state statistical agencies. Industrial enterprises, construction works, and economic organizations present their accounts to the appropriate province, territory, or republic statistical agencies. Further processing of statistical data is done by agencies of the USSR Central Statistical Administration. Beginning with the accounts for June 1957, the regional economic councils, the Party and Soviet administrative agencies, and the planning committees will receive the

[13] For the details, see Grossman, *Soviet Statistics*, pp. 38 ff.
[14] V. Starovskii, "Novye zadachi sovetskoi statistiki" [New Tasks for Soviet Statistics], *Kommunist* [The Communist], 1957, No. 14, p. 70.
[15] *Ibid.*, pp. 62 f.

statistical material they need directly from the local agencies of the Central Statistical Administration. Within *TsSU* the summary accounts will come not from the ministries but from the local agencies of *TsSU* and *TsSU* will process them and present them to the USSR government, the *Gosplan*, and other central organizations . . . .

The size of the statistical apparatus is indicated by Soviet estimates that nearly two and a half million persons are employed directly in keeping and processing records.[16] Reporting is done on a current basis.[17] All enterprises (except the very smallest producing for local markets) must submit monthly telegraphic reports on physical output, followed by a mailed report sent within three days of the end of the month; they must submit comprehensive monthly and quarterly reports, covering other economic data as well as output, within fifteen days. For products considered particularly important (e.g., fuel, steel, electricity), additional telegraphic reports must be submitted daily or every ten days. Each echelon in the statistical structure must then process within ten to fifteen days the data it receives. With such a flood of data, it is doubtful that much could be done beyond summing and tabulating in this brief period even if the statistical operations were fully mechanized; but only 3 to 4 per cent of those engaged in statistical work had the use of electrical adding and computing machines as late as 1953.[18]

So much for the flow of data into the system. The flow out of it, in the form of published statistics, has been less steady and voluminous. In some respects, the high point of published industrial statistics was reached in the late 1920's. The data, published in many sources, were comprehensive and detailed, and their processing was directed by competent economists and statisticians. Concurrently with the five year plans, the flow of published statistics gradually diminished, the low point being

[16] See Grossman, *Soviet Statistics*, p. 30, n. 21. According to *Pravda*, May 12, 1958, the number engaged in this work was put at "about three million, of whom almost 80 per cent are engaged in so-called primary record-keeping." For the United States, the 1950 census of occupations lists about 376,000 accountants and auditors and 721,000 bookkeepers in the employed labor force, a total of 1.1 million. Many of these are engaged in activities not covered by the Soviet concept of record-keeping.

[17] Small-scale enterprises are excepted, their output being estimated through periodic censuses and sample surveys. Current reporting was tried during the period 1949–1954 and then abandoned. Until 1930 all enterprises, large-scale as well as small-scale, were covered by comprehensive periodic censuses. Before the 1957 reforms, each enterprise reported currently on more than a hundred forms, sixty to seventy of them flowing into the centralized reporting system. Even after the reforms, centralized current reporting was in force (in 1957) for more than 10,000 commodities. For details, see Grossman, *Soviet Statistics*, p. 35, n. 15.

[18] Most do have the abacus, a valuable computational aid. For more details on mechanization, see *ibid.*, pp. 55 ff.

reached after 1937 and continuing as late as 1956, when a striking improvement took place. Since then, published statistics have moved toward the coverage characteristic of the late 1920's and early 1930's, but they have not regained that stage yet.

During the First and Second Five Year Plans, published statistics came to be concentrated almost exclusively in a set of annual statistical abstracts, setting the practice for later years. The most important volumes are those bearing the title *Socialist Construction of the USSR* (*Sotsialisticheskoe stroitel'stvo SSSR*), the first being published in 1934 and the last in 1938. These collections of data are roughly comparable in coverage, detail, and amount of explanatory material with summarizing abstracts published in Western countries. They are not comparable with Western primary statistical sources, such as the various census publications of the United States and the United Kingdom.

The most comprehensive of these Soviet abstract-like publications is the volume that appeared in 1936, containing data through 1935. From this peak, the amount of published statistical material fell off sharply. The abstract appearing in 1938, the last of this series, covered only the period of the Second Five Year Plan and a selective group of industries. It was not until 1956, or eighteen years later, that a similar abstract again appeared.

During the years intervening between 1938 and 1956, the only published statistics were those contained in official announcements and directives, political speeches, occasional articles in specialized journals, textbooks, and a handful of books written by Soviet authorities and largely descriptive or polemical in nature. Annual summaries of industrial performance were generally presented in less than a page of the newspaper. Statistics were limited in nature as well as amount: absolute data on output were given out very rarely and for only a very small sample of products; data were usually stated in relative terms, as a percentage of some base figure, itself unknown or obscure. The cryptic information given out during this period caused economic research in the West to take on the characteristics of archaeology.

The appearance in 1956 of a small statistical abstract, *The National Economy of the USSR* (*Narodnoe khoziaistvo SSSR*), markedly improved the statistical picture. Even so, the volume contains only fifty to sixty pages with basic data for industry.[19] More significant additions to industrial

---

[19] In one English translation, these pages are reduced by more than half without materially affecting readability (*Statistical Handbook of the USSR*, Harry Schwartz, ed., New York, 1957).

statistics were made with the publication of several abstracts in 1957 and 1958, the most important being *Industry of the USSR* (*Promyshlennost' SSSR*).[20] This volume contains 447 pages, with about 168 presenting data on physical output. Virtually all the data on industry in *The National Economy of the USSR* (1956) are repeated in *Industry of the USSR*, while the latter contains many data not in the former.

These recent Soviet abstracts may be compared with statistical sources for the United States. The 1956 edition of the *Statistical Abstract of the United States* contains some 100 pages of industrial data in small type; the *Product Supplement* to the census of manufactures for 1954 contains 259 pages, twice the size of those in the Soviet abstract, of physical output data. If we move to primary sources, the basic volumes of the latter census contain about 3,600 pages, and the *Minerals Yearbook* for any recent year is equally large, though the pages are smaller.

The scope of the most recent Soviet statistical abstracts is perhaps better indicated by the number of industrial products covered. Output data are given for about 90 products in *The National Economy of the USSR* (1956) and 212 in *Industry of the USSR*, in most cases for benchmark years.[21] The product coverage of these recent Soviet abstracts is generally less comprehensive than that of *Socialist Construction* (1936), particularly for chemicals, nonferrous metals, and minerals. In the *Product Supplement* to the U.S. census of manufactures for 1947, physical output data are given for some 6,000 products; the census for 1954 covers about the same number. In the U.S. census of mineral industries for 1954, physical output data are given for more than 750 products. These product coverages are, of course, larger than for earlier years, but in every industrial census of the United States since the turn of the century, the count of products would run at least to many hundred—in most, to several thousand. At the same time, it should be recognized that such counts describe detail more than breadth of coverage. That is to say, the products summarized in the recent Soviet abstracts would be broken down into hundreds of subproducts in U.S. statistics.

[20] For a list of recent statistical handbooks, see *Soviet Studies*, January 1959, pp. 312 ff, and January 1960, pp. 348 ff. The volumes discussed in the text have been followed by steadily improved handbooks, particularly by new editions of *The National Economy of the USSR* appearing in 1959 and 1960.

[21] For the industries covered by *Industry of the USSR*, data are given for every year over 1913–1955, except 1941–1944 inclusive, in the case of 59; only for benchmark years in the case of 76; and only for selected benchmark years in the case of 77. Benchmark years are taken as 1913, 1928, 1932, 1937, 1940, 1945, 1950, and 1955.

In addition to the official Soviet compendiums of statistics, there are a number of secondary sources containing information of one sort or another bearing on industrial output. These range from articles and monographs, such as are found in various professional journals, to general reference books, such as the *Great Soviet Encyclopedia* (*Bol'shaia sovetskaia entsiklopediia*). From the late 1930's to 1956, these sources contained only scattered information on output in relative terms, as mentioned above. Occasionally, an absolute figure might be given. Products were seldom defined and references were not made to related collections of data. Such information is useful only to fill in gaps in other data.

The dearth of statistics in secondary sources reflects the control exercised at the center over release of information internally as well as externally. At the Twentieth Party Congress in February 1956, Mikoyan complained of the absence of large-scale statistical studies in the Soviet Union and remarked that "unfortunately, Comrade Starovsky had these statistical data under lock and key in the Central Statistical Administration. Economists are still deprived of the opportunity of working with them and are condemned to recite and repeat old formulas, old data. This is one reason we do not see creative work from our economists."[22] This statement, it later turned out, was a clue to the forthcoming change in statistical policy. The volume of data has expanded in secondary sources along with official statistical publications, but there still seems to be little available there that is not also in primary sources.

The statistical publications of the Soviet period generally do not reproduce data for the Tsarist period, except for the year 1913, which is used as a basis of comparison for later developments. The only exception to date is the most recent abstract, *Industry of the USSR*, which contains prerevolutionary output series for eight industries. Most data for the Tsarist period must be drawn from the statistical sources of those times. These sources have important shortcomings, primarily traceable to their limited coverage and to the circumstances under which the data were collected (mainly as a by-product of the factory inspection system and as an aid in the administration of taxes). However, there is no indication of widespread distortion or suppression of statistics, either by those providing the primary entries or by those processing the data. The data for the Tsarist period are deficient mainly by virtue of errors, omissions, and poor coverage.

[22] *Current Digest of the Soviet Press*, VIII, 8, p. 10 (original text in *Pravda* and *Izvestia*, February 18, 1956).

Evidence on Reliability of Data[23]

Reliability in a statistical context generally means the accuracy with which quantitative magnitudes measure the things they are purported to measure. Put another way, a statistic is reliable if it is an accurate magnitude for a definite thing. Inaccuracy or ambiguity may be the result of error, distortion, or fabrication, and, needless to say, the distinction between ambiguity and inaccuracy fades at the margins. As an example, consider a magnitude given as the output of coal. Even if the output is measured as accurately as possible, it cannot be adjudged a reliable datum unless we know how the term "coal" is being used.

Ambiguity is a general characteristic of Soviet output data, increasing in degree as the data become more aggregative. At one extreme stands the official Soviet index of industrial production. This index is the result of a set of actual calculations on actual data; but we have only a rough notion of the data and calculations, and hence cannot reproduce the index or fully understand its meaning. Enough is known, however, to be able to say, as almost all Western scholars do, that the index does not represent any of the concepts of aggregate production utilized in Western statistics, though it goes by the same name.

The disparity in these statistical constructs may be shown by tracing

[23] There is an extensive Western literature on this subject, and the discussion here draws much from it. The following is a partial list of specialized monographs and articles: Abram Bergson, "A Problem in Soviet Statistics," *Review of Economic Statistics*, November 1947, 234–242; *idem*, "Reliability and Usability of Soviet Statistics," *The American Statistician*, June–July 1953, 13–16; Colin Clark, *A Critique of Russian Statistics*, London, 1939; Maurice Dobb, "Further Appraisals of Russian Economic Statistics— A Comment on Soviet Statistics," *Review of Economics and Statistics*, February 1948, 34–38; Alexander Gerschenkron, "The Soviet Indices of Industrial Production," *Review of Economic Statistics*, November 1947, 217–226; *idem*, "Comment on Naum Jasny's 'Soviet Statistics,'" *Review of Economics and Statistics*, August 1950, 250–251; *idem*, "Reliability of Soviet Industrial and National Income Statistics," *The American Statistician*, June–July 1953, 18–21; Gregory Grossman, *Soviet Statistics*; Naum Jasny, "Intricacies of Russian National Income Statistics," *Journal of Political Economy*, August 1947, 299–322; *idem*, "Soviet Statistics," *Review of Economics and Statistics*, February 1950, 92–99; *idem*, "International Organizations and Soviet Statistics," *Journal of the America . Statistical Association*, March 1950, 48–64; *idem*, *The Soviet 1956 Statistical Handbook: A Commentary*, East Lansing, 1957; Stuart A. Rice, "Statistical Concepts in the Soviet Union Examined from Generally Accepted Scientific Viewpoints," *Review of Economic Statistics*, February 1952, 82–86; *idem*, "Statistics in the Soviet Union," *Bulletin of the Atomic Scientists*, June 1952, 159–162; Harry Schwartz, "On the Use of Soviet Statistics," *Journal of the American Statistical Association*, September 1947, 401–406; *idem*, "The Organization and Operation of the Soviet Statistical Apparatus," *The American Statistician*, April–May 1952, 9–13; V. Tsonev, "Falsification of Soviet Industrial Statistics" (unpublished manuscript), Research Program on the USSR, New York, 1953; and Lynn Turgeon, "On the Reliability of Soviet Statistics," *Review of Economics and Statistics*, February 1952, 75–76.

through the consequences of accepting the Soviet index at face value. According to the official Soviet index, industrial production multiplied 27 times between 1913 and 1955. Over the same period, industrial production in the United States multiplied 4.7 times, according to a standard Western-type index (see Table 61). If these indexes were both taken to measure the same kind of growth, one would conclude that Soviet industrial production had grown almost six times as much as American production. This would imply in turn that Soviet industrial production in 1955 was about 80 per cent of the American level, since in 1913 it was about 14 per cent. In fact, Soviet production in 1955 was, by our calculations, only about 23 per cent of the American level (see Table 63) and, by recent Soviet pronouncements, 36 per cent.[24] One concludes that the Soviet index of industrial production exaggerates growth as that concept is typically measured in the West.

Every industry is a mixture of heterogeneous elements to some degree, and what we call "physical output" is an index number in miniature, even for the more narrowly defined industries. Ambiguity is dispelled only to the extent that product coverage and aggregating methods are described in detail. As we have already noted, Soviet statistical sources are lax in this regard, and the data one must work with are correspondingly ambiguous.

On the other side, the numerical accuracy of many Soviet output data also comes under question, no matter how the industries to which they

[24] Until recently, Soviet statisticians had not fallen into inconsistencies on this score. As late as 1957, a Soviet statistical source (Ia. Ioffe, ed., *Strany sotsializma i kapitalizma v tsifrakh* [Socialist and Capitalist Countries in Figures], Moscow, 1957, p. 8) gave the fractions as 6.8 per cent for 1913 and 47.6 per cent for 1955. Similar fractions for 1913 are given in *Ekonomika sotsialisticheskikh promyshlennykh predpriiatii* [Economics of Socialist Industrial Enterprises], Moscow, 1956, p. 7; *Ekonomika promyshlennosti SSSR* [Economics of Industry of the USSR], Moscow, 1956, p. 21; and *Spravochnik komsomol'skogo propagandista i agitatora* [Reference Book for the Young Communist Propagandist and Agitator], Moscow, 1957, p. 126. These figures, though wrong, are at least consistent with comparative growth of the official Soviet index and the American index employed in Soviet sources. For an intriguing sketch of the gyrations followed to preserve such internal consistency, see A. Nove, " '1926/7' and All That," *Soviet Studies*, October 1957, pp. 127 ff.

Recently, the picture has changed completely, and the fractions of output claimed are no longer consistent with the official Soviet index. Briefly stated, the latest Soviet position, announced in 1959 by no less an authority than Khrushchev, is that output was 12.5 per cent of the American level in 1913 and 50 per cent in 1958 (*Vestnik statistiki* [Statistical Bulletin], 1959, No. 11, pp. 17 ff). These fractions would imply that Soviet industrial production multiplied 18 times over 1913–1958, not 36 times as shown by the official index. The official claim is thus cut in half at one blow, and it still remains much too large, as we shall see.

Incidentally, the last-mentioned source states that the figure of 7 per cent for 1913 was never given official recognition, merely being an estimate of private Soviet economists. This is contrary to fact, as may be seen by examining the sources cited above.

apply are defined. These inaccuracies result in the main from misreporting—mostly overreporting—generated within the statistical system.

It is difficult for an outsider to appraise the reliability of Soviet statistics, since he must rely almost entirely on reports of émigrés[25] or on internal evidence, in the manner of the historian. With minor exceptions, public discussion of statistics is not allowed within the Soviet Union: they must be accepted without open question. And, since the government has a monopoly of statistics, it is not possible to check independently derived and published figures against each other.

In the discussion that follows, we shall consider, first, elements in the statistical system that promote distortion at various levels; second, examples of published statistical information that must be considered unreliable, by virtue of either distortion or ambiguity; and, third, the inferences about reliability that can be drawn from internal evidence presented by the statistics themselves. The discussion will be only suggestive, for, as Grossman remarks, "It would be futile to attempt to list all the pitfalls in the interpretation of Soviet statistics, even of only the industrial physical output data. In the final analysis each figure must be tested separately and on its own ground for possible descriptive distortion, always bearing in mind what it is that the statistics are 'trying to prove.' "[26]

MISREPORTING

Misreporting starts with the enterprise itself. The incentive reaches down to the worker and up to the manager. The worker's incentive derives, in the first place, from the piece-rate system of pay, which applies to almost every job where activity can be measured in physical units. As early as 1928, piece rates applied to more than half the hours worked by all persons engaged (excluding plant managers and superior echelons) in large-scale industry; the percentage rose to 70 by 1935. A comparable statistic is not available for later years, but in 1955 more than three-quarters of persons engaged in *all* industry were paid on a piece-rate basis. Piece rates tend to be progressive: the higher the output, the larger the pay per piece. In addition, special premiums are paid to some workers for economical use of inputs and other savings in unit costs, and non-pecuniary perquisites—such as vacations, better housing, and preferential

---

[25] The most comprehensive summary and thorough analysis of émigrés' views on this subject is contained in Joseph Berliner, *Factory and Manager in the USSR*, Cambridge, Mass., 1957.

[26] Grossman, *Soviet Statistics*, pp. 117 f.

rations of other types, where rationing is in force—accrue to workers with superior output records. Foremen and other overseers receive similar rewards, based on the performance of those under their supervision.[27] These factors all motivate the worker to exaggerate his output.

Overreporting by workers seems to be widespread.[28] Much of it applies to intermediate activities rather than to the final output of an enterprise, but this may indirectly force management to overreport final output to make it consistent with inflated wage costs. Direct overreporting of final output generally requires the cooperation of management and the independent inspectors. Since there is no conflict of interest between worker and management in this matter, such cooperation may be forthcoming wherever detection is difficult, as in the case of output measured in bulk. Moreover, the pervasive piece-rate system apparently extends in some instances to those who record final output. Thus, one example is known of a clerk whose job was weighing and recording the output of coal and who was paid a piece rate for the amount of coal recorded.[29] This case is perhaps extreme, but one can imagine similar jobs where a worker would be in a position to inflate finished output and where it would be in his interests to do so.

Management's incentive to inflate output derives from the fact that the system of rewards and penalties is geared primarily to its success in meeting or overfulfilling its output quotas. Other goals (such as planned profits) are important, but the manager receives special benefits and privileges to the extent that he accomplishes the output targets set for him—and special penalties to the extent that he fails to do so.[30] His foremost concern is, therefore, with the recorded output, and one would expect the representative manager to be tempted to improve on the actual record by one means or another. This incentive is strengthened by the fact that other indexes by which his performance is judged are improved step by step with the output record. The manager may react by writing up output or skimping on quality, a matter discussed in more detail in the next chapter.

One consequence is a tendency for the product mix to get arranged so

[27] This paragraph is based on *ibid.*, pp. 59 ff.
[28] See, e.g., Berliner, *Factory and Manager*, pp. 172 ff.
[29] Grossman, *Soviet Statistics*, p. 63.
[30] See Berliner, *Factory and Manager*, Chapter III; and A. Nove, "The Problem of Success Indicators in Soviet Industry," *Economica*, February 1958, 1–13. For a description of similar conditions in Hungary, see Bela Balassa, *The Hungarian Experience in Economic Planning*, New Haven, 1959, pp. 132 ff.

that it reflects the highest possible output in terms of the units of measure designated in the planned goal. Alec Nove cites a classic, if apocryphal, example of a nail factory:[31]

> ... When the plan was established in *numbers*, only small nails were made; so the basis of the plan was changed to weight, and then there were only *large* nails. If the plan is expressed in money, then only those which are cheapest to make will be produced, and probably all of the same size; if each type of nail is to be separately specified in the plan, this would be a glaring case of bureaucratic over-centralization. If the price of nails reflected supply-and-demand conditions, of course, things would be different; but this verges on heresy. Meanwhile, there are repeated appeals to the managers to provide a proper assortment of products.

A number of similar examples are documented by Grossman,[32] and need not be repeated here. The point to be made is that a shift in the unit of measure or an expansion in the coverage of a product category provides an opportunity for the skillful manager to "create" additional output without productive effort, merely by adjusting the product mix. This can be done only over a relatively short period of time, but the fictitious increase in output can occur each time there is a change-over in unit of measure or an expansion in coverage. When output series in different physical units are spliced together—as in the case of flat glass, leather, linen fabrics, and so on—the result may be a substantial exaggeration of the growth in output.

Where such opportunities as these are not present, the manager may resort to simulation. The techniques of simulation are too varied and complex to discuss at length here.[33] It should be noted, however, that devices have been found for "losing" simulated output in inventory and for "passing it on" to customers. While the economic system abounds with seeming built-in checks, these do not prevent widespread misreporting. Officials within an enterprise who are liable for inaccurate records—the

---

[31] A. Nove, "The Pace of Soviet Economic Development," *Lloyds Bank Review*, April 1956, p. 10.

[32] Grossman, *Soviet Statistics*, pp. 73 ff. For the situation in Hungary, see Balassa, *The Hungarian Experience*, pp. 140 ff.

[33] On them, see Berliner, *Factory and Manager*, Chapters VIII–X; and Grossman, *Soviet Statistics*, pp. 65 ff. Grossman comments (p. 66, n. 23): "Although Berliner's data refer primarily to the thirties, there seems to have been little fundamental change in this regard." This seems to be confirmed by Hungarian experience as related by Balassa (*The Hungarian Experience*, pp. 140 ff).

chief accountant, the head of the planning department, and so on—seem to be dominated by the plant manager and enmeshed in a "web of mutual involvement," to use Berliner's expressive phrase.[34] Measuring, counting, and weighing devices tend to be primitive and sparse. Freight is generally not weighed independently by the shipping agent, and sample surveys indicate that it is significantly overreported in weight.[35] Although quality inspection is conducted by an independent organization, its general ineffectiveness is attested to by Soviet authorities. For somewhat different reasons, the transportation system may aid in writing up shipments: its performance is assessed by the volume of traffic it handles. Finally, in the prevailing "sellers' market" customers refrain from complaining about shortages or defective goods, since they are often happy to get anything at all—in any event, they generally prefer not to incur the disfavor of suppliers.[36]

The widespread practice of overreporting may seem strange for a state as authoritarian as the Soviet Union. Grossman gives the following explanation:[37]

> It would seem at first glance that the multiplicity of controlling and auditing agencies . . ., the severity of the punitive measures at their disposal, and the thoroughness of the police system would successfully thwart the commission of such "economic crimes" as the falsification of output data and related illegal acts. Yet even the least acquaintance with Soviet reality leads one to the conclusion that "economic crimes" are extremely prevalent and to the conjecture that for each case that reaches the daylight of publicity there must be many that never do. An important factor is, of course, the inherent advantage that any insider has in concealing irregularities from the outside auditor's view—what in its more extreme form might be called Pooh-Bah's

[34] Berliner describes the basis for this involvement as follows (*Factory and Manager*, pp. 324 f): "Awareness of common interests in plan fulfillment often generates within the enterprise a 'family relationship' in which Party secretary, chief accountant, and other control officials facilitate or overlook the transgressions of an enterprising and successful director and share in the rewards and prestige that come with plan fulfillment. It is the fact that the control officials perceive their own fates as closely interwoven with the success of the enterprise that explains the endurance of the irregular practices of management."

[35] See Ernest Williams, *Freight Transportation in the Soviet Union: A Comparison with the United States*, Occasional Paper 65, New York, NBER, 1959, pp. 11–13; and also Grossman, *Soviet Statistics*, pp. 98 f.

[36] For an extensive discussion of these checks and the ways they are thwarted, see *ibid.*, pp. 84 ff. An example of the willingness of low-priority consumers to accept defective sheet metal is given in *Current Digest*, IX, 48, p. 25.

[37] Grossman, *Soviet Statistics*, p. 91.

Law[38]—aided by the complexities of the very paper work that is intended to entrap the culprit, and abetted by the inspector's corruptibility and his reluctance to stir up a possible hornet's nest.

From this discussion one would gather that the possibilities of simulation diminish, the more closely the product in question is related to areas of high priority and the more precisely it can be measured. Thus, it is doubtful that significant distortion of output occurs in enterprises closely related to defense industries. By the same line of reasoning, one may suppose that the worst examples occur in enterprises producing consumer goods, for checks will be weakest here.

This brief survey of statistical misreporting at the enterprise level may be concluded by noting that underreporting also exists, though not as prevalently as overreporting. The most important cause of underreporting is pilferage or other unauthorized use of products.[39] This phenomenon is, however, not unique to the Soviet Union: output is understated in every country to the extent that there is pilferage. Moreover, it is not clear that pilferage will always cause underreporting. If it takes place before output is recorded, then output will be understated on this score. On the other hand, if it takes place after output is recorded —if, for instance, finished goods are taken out of inventory—then underreporting is not only more difficult but also less necessary. The effect here is, from an accounting point of view, the same as would be caused by overreporting of output; that is to say, fewer goods are available for shipment or for storage in inventory than are entered in the production record. If an enterprise can "lose" unproduced goods in its inventory accounts, it can also "lose" produced but stolen ones.

As one moves beyond the enterprise, less and less is known about possible distortions in statistics. Officials in the processing system are more closely related to the top Soviet leadership than are plant managers, and one would suppose that their activities would be less subject to extensive public criticism. It will be recalled that the processing system has had a dual structure. Each ministry in the economic-administrative organization would seem to have an incentive to inflate the output data reported to it, in order to make its performance look better than it actually is. During the period when the statistical organization was subordinate to the *Gosplan*, a similar incentive operated in that side of the structure. Finally, officials at various territorial levels in both the

---

[38] " . . . as Paymaster-General, I could so cook the accounts that, as Lord High Auditor, I should never discover the fraud" (footnote in original).

[39] For other causes, see *ibid.*, pp. 78 ff.

economic-administrative and (more significantly) the Communist Party organizations are interested in "improving" statistics for their regions.

Although independent tampering with statistics by only one interested party would be risky,[40] cooperative ventures offer more opportunity for success. One can imagine suitable occasions for such activity, but its prevalence and importance are anybody's guess. The few discussions of this matter to be found in the Soviet literature are essentially exhortations to statisticians to be honest and to resist whatever pressures there might be to get involved in "monkeying" with the figures. Speaking in 1955, Starovskii emphasized that the statistical organization was independent of local political authorities, but went on to say that "independence . . . means only that no local organization may force a worker in a [local] statistical administration or in a district or city inspectorate to change a figure if that figure is correct."[41] In 1956, a newspaper article appeared accusing the Central Statistical Administration of collaborating with political authorities in "adjusting" milk production upward by varying percentages in different provinces.[42] Such accusations are very rare, but they seem to testify that joint distortion is at least feasible.[43]

[40] B. P. Martschenko, an émigré Soviet economist, gives an example from personal experience in which he was able to verify that 1939 population data from Ukrainian provinces (*oblasti*) were faithfully reproduced in a compilation issued for internal use by the Ukrainian Statistical Administration, despite the fact that these data showed large deficits in population as a result of collectivization of agriculture. He goes on to say (as quoted in Grossman, *Soviet Statistics*, p. 114): "It must also be noted that the falsification of census data in the course of their processing in the *oblast'* statistical administrations would have been too unwieldy an operation, which would have inevitably become known to many persons in the statistical administrations, and could not have been concealed." These comments are certainly relevant to the matters at issue, but it must be kept in mind that Martschenko's example is drawn from the field of demography, where the pressures for internal distortion may not be as strong as in the case of industrial output. The pressures are, nonetheless, there, as may be seen from the sweeping purge of statistical personnel after the population census of 1937 produced findings distasteful to the Soviet leadership (see *ibid.*, p. 17).

[41] *Vestnik statistiki*, 1955, No. 1, p. 82, as quoted in Grossman, *Soviet Statistics*, p. 103.

[42] V. Surkov, "Counting on 'Incomplete Accounts,' " *Current Digest*, VIII, 14, pp. 37 f (original text in *Izvestia*, April 6, 1956). During my visit to Moscow in the summer of 1956, I submitted a written inquiry to the Central Statistical Administration about articles on inaccurate reporting of data and received the following reply:

"If you are referring to the article published in *Izvestia* on April 6, 1956 (we do not know of any other articles), the author, obviously not sufficiently informed, expressed the opinion that the Central Statistical Administration determined the milk yield on collective farms incorrectly and made corrections for omissions in collective farm accounting. These omissions lay in not including milk from cows attached to the children's institutions on collective farms or milk used to feed shoats on pig farms.

"In regions with a surplus beef production, the milk consumed on the farm is not included in the records. The milk fed to lambs, the milk consumed by the milkmaids, by the people who transport the milk to dairies, and by the collective farmers in whose quarters the cows are temporarily kept—all this milk is often not recorded.

"The USSR Central Statistical Administration has corrected all the collective farm

When we move to the publishing of statistics, we enter a rather different universe. The motive for misreporting at this level is perhaps more properly viewed as political and propagandist than as personal. The veil of secrecy surrounding the activities of the top Soviet leadership, enforced by a rigorous security apparatus, makes it impossible to know what happens to data between final compilation and publication. In particular, there is no way of knowing conclusively whether Soviet authorities keep two sets of books: one containing statistics for internal use only, the other for dissemination to the outside world. However, most Western specialists have concluded, for a variety of reasons, that dual accounts do not exist, in this narrow sense.[44]

The most direct evidence on the question of dual accounts is provided by a statistical annex to the 1941 Plan[45] that was captured during World War II by the Germans and later recaptured by the Americans. This document is labeled "not for publication," and it therefore presumably represents a compilation of data intended for internal use only. When the planned goals in this document are compared with those publicly announced in 1941, no significant discrepancies are found.[46] Although this conclusion applies directly to planned goals for 1941, it should be noted that they are significantly higher in general than published outputs for 1940 (see Tables 1 and 2).[47]

accounting on milk up to 1955. This adjustment amounted to 0.7 per cent of the total milk production in the USSR. Unlike in the U.S.A. and other countries, in the USSR these adjustments are made every year on the basis of a special check.

"At present, the CSA is conducting a routine investigation of the milk yield on collective farms, after which the question of making adjustments on the future data on milk will be discussed.

"The production of grain, meat and other agricultural products is recorded without adjustments."

A similar case involving adjustment of agricultural data was reported by P. Polynsky, "Why are Frauds Shielded in Chernovtsky?" *Current Digest*, IX, 42, pp. 20 f (original text in *Sel'skoe khoziaistvo*, September 12, 1957).

[43] An interesting example of collaboration in statistical misrepresentation, involving officials from the plant level up to Commissar Kaganovich, is recited from personal experience by Victor Kravchenko in *I Chose Freedom*, New York, 1952, pp. 298 ff. Similar cases have been reported in Hungary (see Balassa, *The Hungarian Experience*, pp. 145 and 148).

[44] See Grossman, *Soviet Statistics*, pp. 106 ff.

[45] *Gosudarstvennyi plan razvitiia narodnogo khoziaistva SSSR na 1941 god* [The State Plan for the Development of the USSR National Economy for 1941], Moscow, 1941 (reprinted by the American Council of Learned Societies, 1948).

[46] See Lynn Turgeon, "On the Reliability of Soviet Statistics," *Review of Economics and Statistics*, February 1952, 75–76.

[47] The 1941 Plan seems to have been ambitious, particularly in view of the fact that World War II was in progress elsewhere in Europe, and this supports other evidence that the Soviet Union probably did not expect to get involved in the war (see Chapter 8).

TABLE 1

OUTPUT FOR 1940 AND PLANNED OUTPUT FOR 1941:
SOVIET UNION, 119 INDUSTRIES

	Unit	1940 Output[a]	1941 Planned Output	1941 Planned Output as % of 1940 Output
Pig iron	th.m.t.	14,900	18,000	121
Rolled steel	th.m.t.	13,110	15,830[b]	121
Steel ingots and castings	th.m.t.	18,320	22,450[b]	123
Quality steel	th.m.t.	3,196	3,914	123
Steel sheets (excl. pickled iron)	th.m.t.	1,786	1,752	98
Steel sheets (incl. pickled iron)	th.m.t.	1,822	1,827	100
Steel wire rods	th.m.t.	512	775	151
Steel beams and channels	th.m.t.	428	765	179
Iron and steel pipes	th.m.t.	966	1,100	114
Copper	th.m.t.	160.9	210	131
Nickel	m.t.	8,660	17,200	199
Electric power	bill.kwh	48.3	54.3[b]	112
Electric power plants	mill.kw	11.3	12.4	110
Coal	mill.m.t.	165.9	190.8	115
Coke	mill.m.t.	21.1	23.8	113
Crude petroleum	mill.m.t.	31.1	34.6	111
Natural gas	th.m.t.	2,400	3,435	143
Peat	th.m.t.	33,200	39,615	119
Soda ash	th.m.t.	536	673	126
Phosphoric fertilizer	th.m.t.	1,352	1,980[b]	146
Ground natural phosphate	th.m.t.	381.7	610	160
Synthetic dyes	th.m.t.	33.9	39.5	117
Rosin	th.m.t.	44.1	60.8[b]	138
Paper	th.m.t.	812.4	969.9[b]	119
Paperboard	th.m.t.	150.8	208.3[b]	138
Motor vehicle tires	thousands	3,007	4,000	133
Red bricks	millions	6,723	8,359[b]	124
Fire-clay bricks	th.m.t.	1,731	1,850	107
Quartzite bricks	th.m.t.	546	670	123
Sand-lime, silica, and slag bricks	millions	732	1,083[b]	148
Cement	th.m.t.	5,675	7,998	141
Construction gypsum	th.m.t.	892	1,306[b]	146
Industrial timber hauled	mill.m³	117.9	159.0[b]	135
Lumber	mill.m³	34.8	30.3[b]	87
Roofing iron	th.m.t.	103.4	230.0	222
Asbestos shingles	millions	205.6	253.4[b]	123
Window glass	mill.m²	44.7	62.2[b]	139
Railroad ties	millions	37.1	46.5	125
Rubberoid roofing	th.rolls	1,700	2,556[b]	150
Pergamin subroofing	th.rolls	1,190	2,500	210
Tar-paper roofing	th.rolls	3,900	4,495[b]	115
Railroad rails	th.m.t.	874.8	1,100	126
Sorted asbestos	th.m.t.	147.0	200.0	136
Asphalt	th.m.t.	74.4	150	202
Ginned cotton	th.m.t.	848.6	860.0	101

(continued)

1186953

TABLE 1 (continued)

	Unit	1940 Output[a]	1941 Planned Output	1941 Planned Output as % of 1940 Output
Raw cotton	th.m.t.	2,495	3,010	121
Iron ore	mill.m.t.	29.87	34.03	114
Manganese ore	mill.m.t.	2.6	3.1	121
Automobiles	thousands	5.5	9.0	164
Trucks and buses	thousands	139.9	131.0	94
Diesel and electric locomotives	units	14	16	114
Steam locomotives	units	914	1,300	142
Railroad freight cars	thousands	30.9	60.5[b]	196
Railroad passenger cars	units	1,051	900	86
Tractors (excl. garden)	thousands	31.6	28.0	88
Plows, tractor-drawn	thousands	38.4	35.4	92
Cultivators, tractor-drawn	thousands	32.3	32.5	101
Drills, tractor-drawn	thousands	21.4	33.5	157
Grain combines	thousands	12.8	13.0	102
Haymowers, tractor-drawn	thousands	3.3	3.0	91
Grain-cleaning machines	thousands	4.3	2.3[b]	53
Steam boilers	th.m²	276.3	272[b]	98
Water turbines	th.kw	207.7	280.6	135
Diesel engines	th.hp	248.7	368	148
Other internal combustion engines	th.hp	165	165.3	100
Turbogenerators	th.kw	313.5	644.5	206
Hydroelectric generators	th.kw	154.6	379.3	245
Electric motors (a.c.)	th.kw	1,848	2,622	142
Power transformers	th.kva	3,500	5,120[b]	146
Coal-cutting machines	units	1,256	1,860	148
Machine tools	thousands	58.4	58.1[b]	99
Bench and engine lathes	thousands	11.5	13.8	120
Spinning machines	units	1,109	2,000	180
Looms	units	1,800	3,150	175
Cotton-carding machines	units	1,312	1,970	150
Typesetting machines, linotype	units	145	120	83
Flat-bed printing presses	units	258	260	101
Industrial sewing machines	thousands	20.3	18.0	89
Excavators	units	274	490	179
Scrapers, tractor-driven	units	2,104	2,000	95
Railroad cranes, steam-operated	units	258	145	56
Automatic switchboards	th.lines	37.5	61.5	164
Metallurgical equipment	th.m.t.	23.7	45.0	190
Equipment for oil industry	th.m.t.	15.5	22.0	142
Macaroni	th.m.t.	324	392.1[b]	121
Butter	th.m.t.	226	251[b]	111
Vegetable oil	th.m.t.	798	737	92
Oleomargarine	th.m.t.	121	126.5[b]	105
Cheese	th.m.t.	38.0	44.5[b]	117
Meat	th.m.t.	1,183	1,367[b]	116

(continued)

TABLE 1 (concluded)

	Unit	1940 Output[a]	1941 Planned Output	1941 Planned Output as % of 1940 Output
Sausages	th.m.t.	391.3	395.6[b]	101
Fish catch	th.m.t.	1,404	1,704[b]	121
Soap	th.m.t.	700	748[b]	107
Salt	th.m.t.	4,400	4,780	109
Raw sugar	th.m.t.	2,165	2,745[b]	127
Yeast	th.m.t.	48	77[b]	160
Canned food	mill.cans	1,113	1,263[b]	113
Beer	th.hectoliters	12,130	13,450[b]	111
Cigarettes	billions	100.4	114.2[b]	114
Matches	th.crates	10,000	12,270[b]	123
Vodka	mill.decaliters	92.5	95.7[b]	103
Confectionery	th.m.t.	790	1,098[b]	139
Boots and shoes	mill.pairs	211.0	223.6[b]	106
Rubber footwear	mill.pairs	69.7	82.4[b]	118
Cotton yarn	th.m.t.	650	716[b]	110
Cotton fabrics	mill.m	3,954	4,402[b]	111
Linen fabrics	mill.m	285.2	293.7[b]	103
Silk and rayon fabrics	mill.m	76.6	80.8[b]	105
Woolen and worsted fabrics	mill.m	119.7	128.8[b]	108
Knitted goods	millions	183.0	195.2[b]	107
Hosiery	mill.pairs	485.4	550.9[b]	113
Felt footwear	mill.pairs	17.9	18.3	102
Rubber galoshes	mill.pairs	45.0	55.5[b]	123
Bicycles	thousands	255.0	402.0[b]	158
Electric light bulbs	millions	139.8	142.0[b]	102
Phonographs	thousands	313.7	270.0	86
Radios	thousands	160.5	355.0[b]	221
Clocks and watches	thousands	2,796	3,405	122
Household refrigerators	thousands	3.5	1.5	43

SOURCE: Appendix Table B-2 and *Statistical Abstract of Industrial Output in the Soviet Union, 1913–1955*, New York, NBER, 1956.

[a] On Soviet territory as of end of 1940.

[b] Planned output as given in source adjusted upward to cover acquired Baltic territories. For latter planned output, see *Gosudarstvennyi plan 1941*, pp. 704 ff.

DEFICIENCIES AND DISTORTIONS IN PUBLISHED DATA[48]

Whatever one may conclude about the existence of dual accounts—and the weight of evidence seems to bear against their existence—it is clear that published statistics suffer from lack of reliability because of selectivity, ambiguity, and misrepresentation. For the moment, we shall be concerned primarily with the last two.

[48] This section is based largely on tabular material and notes in *Statistical Abstract of Industrial Output in the Soviet Union, 1913–1955*, New York, NBER, 1956. Examples of defective statistics, in addition to those given here, may be found in Grossman, *Soviet Statistics*, pp. 117 ff.

TABLE 2

FREQUENCY DISTRIBUTION OF PLANNED OUTPUT FOR 1941
AS A PERCENTAGE OF ACTUAL OUTPUT IN 1940:
SOVIET UNION, 119 INDUSTRIES

1941 Planned Output as % of 1940 Output	Number of Industries
Under 85	4
85 to 95	9
95 to 105	15
105 to 115	22
115 to 125	23
125 to 135	5
135 to 145	13
145 to 155	9
155 to 165	6
165 to 175	0
175 to 185	4
185 to 195	1
195 and over	8
Total	119

SOURCE: Table 1.

An important source of ambiguity is failure to clarify the precise coverage of industries. It is sometimes doubtful whether a published datum refers to the sector of an industry under ministerial jurisdiction or to the whole, to large-scale (or state) industry or to the whole, and so on. In some cases there is doubt about territorial coverage. These shortcomings have been remedied in large measure in the recent Soviet statistical abstracts, but some remain, in particular for that stretch of years in which statistics were most heavily suppressed. It is asserted in the Soviet abstracts for both 1936 and 1957 that all data refer to entire industries except where specifically noted to the contrary. Yet examples can be found where all or a substantial portion of small-scale production is not included in early years (e.g., soap, beer, boots and shoes, silk fabrics, and woolen and worsted fabrics), even though no warning is given.

The treatment of the flour industry gives an example of ambiguity in administrative coverage in earlier years. Until the recent appearance of *Industry of the USSR*, output of flour and groats had been published only for the interwar period. In some years output was given for large-scale industry, in later years for all industry except collective farm mills, and in still later years for all industry producing flour from centralized procurements of grain. This amounted to a temporal expansion in the coverage of the industry, not pointed out in the statistical sources, and there was an illusion of substantial growth in output, whereas growth was modest, at least according to the recently published data.

Another case of expanded coverage, not yet clarified, is provided by industrial timber. The data apply to haulage out of the State Forest Reserve, accounting for almost all timber now but for only a fraction in the 1920's. The prerevolutionary counterpart used in Soviet statistics— the Crown Forests—accounted for an even smaller fraction. The changing coverage is not described in usual statistical sources, and the published data therefore exaggerate growth in timber haulage from the pre-revolutionary period to the present.[49]

The effects of territorial expansion during World War II are generally not explicitly revealed in output statistics. Data for 1940 and later years cover the expanded territory, while data for earlier years cover the inter-war territory. Recently, output of some industries has been given for 1913 within the expanded territory, but this does not indicate the gains in 1940 through territorial acquisitions.[50]

Product coverage of industries is less well known than administrative coverage. Uncertainty about stage of fabrication and composition of products applies to standard industrial materials as well as to more highly fabricated products. For instance, it is not known whether the recent data for nonferrous metals refer to only primary metal or both primary and secondary metal, nor is it known at what stage of fabrication output is measured. These are matters of some importance: recent output of copper in the United States is more than doubled by moving from a definition covering only blister copper produced from domestic ore to a definition covering all types of refined copper.[51] In the case of more heterogeneous items (such as ball bearings, machine tools, cameras, and so on), vagueness in definitions is even more serious, particularly since output is often reported in units, actual or conventional.[52] Again, the main deficiency of Soviet statistics is inadequate detail, in this case, of product groups. And, again, the situation has improved recently.

Definitions of industries are not only vague but also subject to change

[49] The data on timber haulage used in our study have been adjusted to provide comparable coverage for all years.

[50] It has been possible to estimate those gains for some industries on the basis of output in the acquired territories in 1937 (see Appendix Table B-3).

[51] *Statistical Abstract of the United States, 1956*, Washington, 1956, p. 750.

[52] Ball-bearing units may vary from one used in bicycles requiring fifty seconds to manufacture and weighing a few grams to one used in railway cars requiring twenty-six hours to manufacture and weighing forty kilograms (see *Planovoe khoziaistvo* [Planned Economy], 1956, No. 5, p. 82).

without notice. Changes of this sort are, of course, often unavoidable—even desirable—and are to be condemned only when they are obscured. Usually a change is signaled by a slight alteration in terminology. It may be the dropping or adding of a qualifying phrase. In the course of our study, we did not find a single instance in which attention was directed by statistical sources to a change in definition. The investigator is left to his own devices in finding out whether there has been a change, what it means, and how it affects comparability of data. Frequently, a shift in definition will become known only through curious inconsistencies in fragmentary information uncovered in the course of research. It may be helpful to expand on this matter by giving a few specific examples.

Up to 1949, the "mineral fertilizer" industry covered soluble superphosphates, nitrates, and potassic compounds. The most important product not included was ground natural phosphate, an unprocessed material that is not readily soluble. Coverage was expanded in 1949 to bring in this product, and output was thereby inflated by about an eighth. Aside from some inconsistencies in data that arose, the only sign of a change at the time was the following alteration in title: up to 1949, the industry had been called "mineral fertilizers (superphosphates, nitrates, and potash)"; since 1949, the parenthetical phrase has been dropped. The nature of the change was confirmed when output series for the components appeared in *Industry of the USSR*. No mention is made of the expansion in coverage over series appearing in earlier sources.

The term "canned food" has covered a variety of products, differing in many instances with the sources giving data. Little is known about the composition of products since the middle 1930's, but a significant relaxation in the meaning of the term took place in the early 1930's, never described in detail in primary statistical sources. Up to that time, "canned food" had been used to mean food packed in hermetically sealed containers; at some point in the early 1930's, it came to mean any kind of preserved food, no matter how packed. Thus, processed foods packed in bulk—as pickles in the the barrel and salt pork—apparently came to be taken in under the name "canned food." In 1934, hermetically sealed products accounted for less than a third of "canned food." Recent information indicates that "canned food" still includes products not hermetically sealed. At the same time, output for the 1930's has been revised substantially downward, which suggests that some of the bulk products—we do not know which ones—have been removed from coverage.

A similar shift in coverage of the "confectionery" industry seemingly took place around the beginning of the Plan period, when cakes and other baked goods were added to the candy already included. During the interwar years, these bakery goods accounted for between 30 and 40 per cent of the output of "confectionery." It seems probable that better grades of bread were also classified as "confectionery" when bread rationing was in effect during the early thirties (there was only one grade of rationed bread). Information for the postwar period shows that bakery goods are still included, but it has never been pointed out that the definition of "confectionery" is considerably broader than for early years.

By tracing through changes in terminology, one notes that the coverage of the "meat" industry has been expanded at least twice. Data for 1930 and later years are given in Soviet sources as applying to "meat and meat products," whereas for earlier years they are given for slaughter weight of meat alone. This expansion in coverage presumably amounted to counting some meat products twice: once at the slaughtering stage and again at the processing stage. A second shift in coverage took place with the publication of *The National Economy of the USSR*; in this source, the industry is called "meat and by-products of Category I," an unexplained expansion in coverage—lard seems to have been added, among other things—that raised output by about a quarter.

Examples could be multiplied, but it is perhaps sufficient to conclude with brief comments on a few other cases. Up to 1928, "soap" included only the common bar soaps used for laundering; after that date, coverage was expanded to include all types of soap. Similarly, the term "leather footwear" originally included only boots and shoes made of leather but later came to include all kinds of footwear—even rebuilt shoes—except those made entirely of felt or rubber. In the case of "vegetable oil," the output for 1928 given in the recent statistical abstracts apparently covers only edible oil, whereas output for later years covers nonedible oil as well. During the pre-Plan period, the "fish catch" included only those fish caught by commercial fishermen; during the Plan period, fish caught in ponds by collective farmers and other local fishermen have also been included, though one may wonder how this is estimated.

In some heterogeneous industries, the output of component products is often aggregated by means of "conventional units." In some cases, Soviet practice differs sharply from Western usage, and the failure of Soviet sources to describe the practice makes it difficult to avoid misinterpretation. For instance, many block-like and brick-like construction materials seem to be counted as "brick," and their output is apparently expressed in some kind of brick equivalents. The output of flat glass is measured in square meters—as in the United States—but only after the different kinds of glass have been converted in an unknown way to conventional units equivalent to window glass with a standard thickness of 2 millimeters. Neither of these procedures is noted or described in primary Soviet sources.

A few specific examples drawn from the technical literature illustrate the complex nature of conventional units. Output of "canned food" is said in statistical sources to be expressed in terms of a conventional can of 400 grams. In fact, the standard unit for hermetically sealed products is a container with a volume of 353.4 cubic centimeters, multiplied by coefficients varying with the product. Thus, beef stew of first and superior grades has a coefficient of 1.13; lamb stew of first grade, 1.2; and lamb stew of superior grade, 1.4. For "canned goods" packed in bulk, the standard unit is a net weight of 400 grams, multiplied by a coefficient varying with density. The rationale for these coefficients is not apparent, unless they are designed to reflect presumed qualitative differences. Similar coefficients are known to be used in the cases of shoes, sausages, lumber, plywood, iron and steel products, producer equipment, agricultural equipment, forest products, and building materials.[53] One Soviet economist, M. A. Tseitlin, states that all but a handful of the output targets listed in the Fourth Five Year Plan were actually expressed in conventional units, involving conversion coefficients of various types, even though they were said to be measured in "physical units." Among the few exceptions were electricity, petroleum, natural gas, and most processed foods.[54]

The stage of fabrication at which output is measured sometimes does not accord with Western practice, and since it is not revealed in primary sources, one may be misled about productive activity. In most countries, the output of cotton fabrics is recorded at the unfinished or "gray goods" stage. This was also the case with Tsarist statistics. During the 1930's, Soviet statistics began recording output at the finished stage, after dyeing and finishing. This change in practice has taken on significance in the postwar period, since substantial quantities of cotton goods have come to be produced in Poland for export to the Soviet Union. It is quite possible that these Polish exports are gray goods later finished in the Soviet Union and hence counted as Soviet output. The same may also

[53] This paragraph is based on S. A. Gorelik, *Statistika* [Statistics], Moscow, 1956, pp. 29 ff; and Grossman, *Soviet Statistics*, pp. 119 f.
[54] *Ibid.*

be true for railway equipment produced in Poland but "finished" (by, say, painting and labeling) in the Soviet Union.

On the other side, there are cases where it is not made clear that output is being measured at primary stages of fabrication. "Granulated sugar" (*sakhar pesok*), for instance, apparently includes all sugars and syrups (converted into "sugar equivalents") at the crudest processing stage. A part is used directly for household consumption, a part is further processed into "refined sugar," and a part is consumed industrially. Similarly, "vegetable oil" includes that consumed directly and that used in making other products (for instance, margarine).

We have already given incidental illustrations of how the ordinary user of Soviet statistics can be badly mistaken about the meaning of terms, because they diverge from customary usage. Two examples may be added: "silk fabrics" is the title used to identify all fabrics made in whole or in part from artificial and synthetic fibers as well as from silk, and "slate" is the title used to identify asbestos shingles.

Misleading language reached its zenith in the postwar years before 1956, a period in which statistics lost all vestiges of being a science and became instead a linguistic art. The practices then followed are illustrated by the case of machine tools. In the postwar announcements of annual percentage increases in output, data were published under no fewer than four different titles for the machine tool industry, varying from one year to the next. A complete series of percentages was not published under any one of these titles. In the general literature, the product was sometimes times referred to as "machine tools" (*stanki*) and sometimes as "metal-cutting machine tools" (*stanki metallorezhushchie*). It appears from the recent Soviet statistical abstracts that the former include forges and presses while the latter do not. Similarly, output was sometimes referred to as "deliveries" or "sales" (*vypusk*) and sometimes as "production" (*produktsiia*). This confused mixture of terms made it impossible to know what was going on in this sector of industry, though careless use of the published figures could lead to an exaggerated picture of performance.

This discussion may be concluded with a few words on the Soviet concept of output itself. According to formal requirements, the product of an enterprise is supposed to be counted as output only when it has passed quality inspection and when it has been delivered to a warehouse or buyer. Goods rejected for failure to meet standards of quality, either by inspectors within a plant or by buyers, are classified as *brak* and are supposed to be excluded from output. But this provision is formally operative only if the defective goods are discovered and reported within the year in which they are produced, a loophole that would seem to encourage bunching shipments of *brak* around the end of a year.[55] In addition, the standards of quality are low in some industries, and *brak* may mean "most defective."[56] Finally, quality inspection leaves much to be desired, as Soviet authorities complain.[57] As Grossman reports: "A safer and clearly very widespread method of writing up output is the inclusion of *brak* in the reported amount of finished product. Direct references in the Soviet press, eyewitness testimony, and the continual complaints about the substandard quality of industrial products bear such ample and conclusive evidence of the prevalence of this practice in Soviet industry, despite severe criminal and administrative sanctions against it, that it is not necessary to dwell on it further at this point."[58] The concrete effects of this practice will be revealed in more detail in the next chapter.

A more specialized problem of interpretation has to do with the measuring of output in machinery industries. As late as 1938, it was common practice in the power equipment industry to count a complex machine as produced whenever a piece of auxiliary equipment was completed. Thus a steam turbine would be reported as produced when its condenser pump, say, was finished. It was said to be normal for two years to pass between the recording of production of final products (such as turbines) and the actual completion; one case was cited in which five years passed.[59] It is, of course, conceivable that the final product would never be produced. There is no way of knowing whether this

---

[55] See *ibid.*, pp. 66 and 70 ff. An apparent recent example of such bunching is given in the article on the Altai Tractor Plant, *Current Digest*, X, 3, p. 27.

[56] In the late 1930's, there were three "standard" grades of textiles and at least three "substandard" grades. It appears that only the worst of the latter qualified as *brak*, since the first two "substandard" grades were offered for sale. For a description of the standards of quality for textiles in those years, see P. Fadeev and D. Zamkovskii, "O kachestve standartov tekstil'nykh tovarov" [On the Worth of the Standards for Textiles], *Voprosy sovetskoi torgovli* [Problems of Soviet Trade], 1936, No. 10, pp. 35–42. The following quotation (p. 38), which has to do with varying "standard" grades, is enlightening: "A consumer who buys three meters of drapery fabric that looks moth-eaten and has all the colors of the rainbow—i.e., is completely useless—receives at best a 7 per cent reduction in price if the fabric is third quality. But if this defect is only in those three meters, then the reduction is only 3 per cent because the fabric is second quality, although it makes absolutely no difference to the consumer who buys that piece whether the defect is in all the material or just in his piece. If the defect is only 2.99 meters long, then the fabric is first quality."

[57] Grossman, *Soviet Statistics*, pp. 87 ff.

[58] *Ibid.*, p. 68. For a careful discussion of the problem of *brak*, see Berliner, *Factory and Manager*, Chapter IX.

[59] I. Nelidov, "Somnitel'nye metody planirovaniia" [Doubtful Planning Methods], *Mashinostroeniia* [Machine Building], September 30, 1938.

practice has continued into the postwar years, but it certainly was important in the interwar period.

INTERNAL EVIDENCE ON RELIABILITY

The evidence suggests that data on physical output are generally less accurate in the Soviet Union than in the West. There can be little doubt that Soviet data are generally exaggerated by a significant amount— precisely how much it is impossible to know. Nevertheless, one must not move from this conclusion to a far broader one, namely, that the data are wholly unreliable and useless. They are not a mere collection of numbers taken out of the air. The internal relations among the statistics demonstrate that they are based on reality, even though they diverge from it. In considering this internal evidence, we shall pass from the least conclusive to the most.

The first thing to be mentioned is that there is a basic consistency among data relating to differing administrative coverages: the larger the coverage, the larger the figures. This is in itself not very meaningful, since the first thing that would be attended to in manipulation of statistics would be this kind of elementary consistency. It is more meaningful for the 1920's than for later years, because two agencies (*VSNKh* and *TsSU*), functioning independently in this regard, collected data for different administrative coverages.

The consistency of data for related products is more significant. For example, in the iron and steel complex the series for iron ore, pig iron, coke, steel ingots, and rolled steel move more or less together, and at the same time diverge in accord with known developments. Since 1928, iron ore production has risen more percentagewise than pig iron production because of deterioration in the quality of ore; pig iron has risen less than steel ingots because of increased use of scrap; and steel ingots have risen more than rolled products because of increased use of castings and forgings. Similarly, output of electric power has grown more rapidly than installed capacity, which is consistent with known trends toward a more even consumption of electricity during the day and over the year. In the textile industry, production has grown more rapidly for cotton than for cotton fabrics, while it has grown less rapidly for wool than for woolen fabrics. Both these divergences are consistent with decreased reliance on imports of cotton, with reduced length of staple, and with increased use of cotton in woolen fabrics. Many more examples of this kind could be given, but these suffice to make the point.

The third line of internal evidence turns about the fact that selectivity and ambiguity are used to conceal whatever it is desired to conceal. Poor performance is habitually masked by silence or evasion. Cases are known of slow-growing and declining industries where no effort has been made to publish data to the contrary; instead, nothing is said at all. In a few cases, like flour milling, data have been ultimately released confirming the worst of Western suspicions. During the postwar years when only annual percentage changes in output were being reported, industries with declines were simply omitted from the list; recently published statistics reveal that some of the declines were substantial (e.g., for many machinery items in 1952). This all merely provides clear evidence that black has not been indiscriminately turned into white in the basic Soviet statistics on physical output.

At the same time the difficulties attributable to the policy of secrecy must not be overlooked. At least until very recently, published Soviet statistics have been carefully selected. To illustrate the selectivity, we may consider frequency distributions of annual relatives of output for three different samples of industries: the first (sample A), as published up to the end of 1955; the second (sample B), as published up to the end of 1956; and the third (sample C), as published up to the end of 1957 (see Table 3). These samples are not strictly comparable in nature. Sample A merely contains all the annual percentage changes in output as announced in reports of plan fulfillment, and the industries covered therefore vary substantially from year to year. Moreover, a number of minor industries and industries with fluctuating product coverage are included. Samples B and C, on the other hand, are composed of industries with essentially continuous output series over the period surveyed. The earlier samples show an upward bias relative to the later ones. The tail of the frequency distributions containing relatives below 100 per cent— i.e., representing industries with annual declines in output—tends to grow increasingly longer as we move from sample A to sample C in each year. In fact, no declines in output are shown in sample A except for 1955. Similarly, the median annual relative—that relative exceeded and fallen short of by half the industries—tends to decline as we move from sample A to sample C. These frequency distributions may be compared with a similar set of distributions for the industries included in the Federal Reserve Board index of U.S. industrial production (see Table 4). The Soviet distributions for sample C accord much more closely in nature with the American distributions than do the Soviet distributions for samples A and B. We note the reduction in bias as more statistics have been revealed. We have no way of knowing whether or how much the bias

TABLE 3

FREQUENCY DISTRIBUTIONS OF ANNUAL RELATIVES OF PHYSICAL OUTPUT FOR
THREE SAMPLES[a] OF INDUSTRIES: SOVIET UNION, 1949–1955

Annual Relatives[b] (per cent)	Number of Industries					
	Sample A	Sample B	Sample C	Sample A	Sample B	Sample C
	1949			1950		
Under 60						
60 to 70						
70 to 80						
80 to 90					1	3
90 to 100		1			1	1
100 to 110	4	4	6	10	10	14
110 to 120	15	11	19	28	21	29
120 to 130	22	21	29	23	24	33
130 to 140	16	12	17	8	7	10
140 to 150	4	6	7	3	3	5
150 to 160	6	3	7	3	2	2
160 to 170	2	3	3	1	1	1
170 to 180	4	3	4	1		
180 to 190	1	1		2	1	1
190 to 200	1	1	2	1	1	1
200 and over	5	3	2			
Total	80	69	96	80	72	100
Median (%)	130	129	128	121	121	121
	1951			1952		
Under 60			2			5
60 to 70			1			1
70 to 80			5		3	4
80 to 90		2	11		1	9
90 to 100		2	13		7	17
100 to 110	10	11	32	28	25	52
110 to 120	35	35	51	24	18	49
120 to 130	15	12	28	15	8	20
130 to 140	9	3	8	4	4	4
140 to 150	3		4	3	2	4
150 to 160			3	2	1	1
160 to 170			2			1
170 to 180	1	2	1			
180 to 190	1		1			1
190 to 200	1	1	1			
200 and over	3	1	10	1		2
Total	78	69	173	77	69	171
Median (%)	118	116	114	115	110	110

(continued)

47

TABLE 3 (concluded)

Annual Relatives[b] (per cent)	Number of Industries					
	Sample A	Sample B	Sample C	Sample A	Sample B	Sample C
	1953			1954		
Under 60			1			2
60 to 70			1			
70 to 80			3		1	3
80 to 90		1	3		1	2
90 to 100		4	14		2	14
100 to 110	22	23	48	27	25	48
110 to 120	37	36	55	37	31	60
120 to 130	13	9	25	11	9	15
130 to 140	5	3	5	5	2	4
140 to 150	5	2	5	3	1	6
150 to 160	2		4	2	1	2
160 to 170				2	2	2
170 to 180	1	1	1	1	1	3
180 to 190				1		
190 to 200				1		2
200 and over	2	2	5	5	1	9
Total	87	81	170	95	77	172
Median (%)	116	114	113	116	113	113
	1955					
Under 60			2			
60 to 70			1			
70 to 80			3			
80 to 90	1	2	11			
90 to 100	2	5	15			
100 to 110	28	23	45			
110 to 120	31	35	55			
120 to 130	18	12	24			
130 to 140	5	2	6			
140 to 150	2	1	6			
150 to 160	1	1	1			
160 to 170	2		2			
170 to 180						
180 to 190	1		1			
190 to 200	3		2			
200 and over	1	1	2			
Total	95	82	176			
Median (%)	115	113	112			

SOURCE: Sample A: *Statistical Abstract of Industrial Output in the Soviet Union*, Supplement, Table 3. Sample B: *ibid.*, Part 1. Sample C: Appendix B.

[a] Sample A refers to output data published up to end of 1955; Sample B, up to end of 1956; and Sample C, up to end of 1957.

[b] Output in specified year as percentage of preceding year.

TABLE 4

FREQUENCY DISTRIBUTIONS OF ANNUAL RELATIVES OF PHYSICAL OUTPUT OF INDUSTRIES IN FEDERAL RESERVE BOARD INDEX OF INDUSTRIAL PRODUCTION: UNITED STATES, 1948–1953

Annual Relatives (per cent)	Number of Industries					
	1948	1949	1950	1951	1952	1953
Under 75	5	17	2	4	7	1
75 to 80	0	9	0	6	0	0
80 to 85	4	18	0	8	6	2
85 to 90	10	21	3	9	18	4
90 to 95	16	38	0	13	17	6
95 to 100	31	28	10	33	46	32
100 to 106	51	32	27	31	53	50
106 to 111	29	17	21	27	22	40
111 to 116	18	4	26	21	9	20
116 to 121	13	3	30	10	2	16
121 to 126	6	0	22	9	3	6
126 and over	10	6	52	22	10	16
Total	193	193	193	193	193	193
Median (%)	103.5	92.4	116.3	103.7	99.5	105.6

SOURCE: Special computation by the Federal Reserve Board.

would be reduced by a full disclosure of data comparable to the practices followed in the United States.

Another aspect of selectivity is suppression of information about industries related to the military effort. Since production in these areas has generally grown faster than the average for all industry, this policy imparts a downward bias to the sample of published output data. In some cases (like nonferrous metals and chemicals), we cannot be sure whether data are suppressed because growth has been fast or because it has been slow. It is even likely that much secrecy is simply due to the traditional Russian love of mystery.

The fourth and most important line of internal evidence on the reliability of Soviet data has to do with the reasonableness of the patterns of growth that emerge from published Soviet data. The sector known as heavy industry is shown to have grown much more rapidly than the sector known as light industry; this certainly accords with general conditions, as every traveler to the Soviet Union can testify. To the person who has studied economic growth in other countries, it is more important to note that there is a general tendency among Soviet industries to grow more slowly percentagewise as they get older and larger, a phenomenon that goes by the name of "retardation in growth"; in this respect, the behavior of the Soviet economy has been quite similar to the

49

behavior of other economies about which a good deal more is known. Along the same lines, the published Soviet data show that the rates of growth of Soviet industries have been closely related to the stages of development from which they started: in general, those industries that were least "advanced" in the prerevolutionary years relative to other countries have grown most rapidly, while those most "advanced" have grown least rapidly. There is also a general consistency in the stage of development of related groups of Soviet industries, as determined by comparisons with various periods of development in the American economy. Finally, there is a basic consistency between transportation and industrial statistics, similar in important respects to the relation holding for the United States in earlier periods of development. There is also a reasonable relation between industrial employment and output. These matters are discussed more concretely later on and need not be elaborated here. The point to be made at this time is that the available Soviet data on physical output present a picture of growth patterns that makes sense.

Some Generalizations About Soviet Data

The evidence bearing on the reliability of Soviet data cannot be summed up in a few words, nor can simple judgments be made. The degree of reliability depends on the purposes for which the data are to be used. In general, absolute magnitudes of physical output are likely to be less accurate than for Western statistics. Similarly, the products to which the data apply are less easily identified. These shortcomings are likely to be less pronounced in industries of high priority, especially if output is subject to rather precise measurement. Thus data on the output of coal are undoubtedly more reliable than those on the output of meat because one has had a higher priority than the other; and data on the output of steel ingots are probably more reliable than those on the output of coal, because one is measured more precisely—and can be checked more precisely—than the other. The shortcomings in absolute magnitudes are most important when levels of output in the Soviet Union are being compared with levels elsewhere. They are somewhat less important when growth trends in Soviet output are being considered, for there is little evidence of a systematic trend in the relative inaccuracy of data, except that data for prerevolutionary and early Soviet years are generally understated in comparison with those for later years. The defects are even less important when percentage movements are being compared among Soviet industries.

We may illustrate with a concrete example. We should allow a wide margin of error in comparing Soviet and American outputs of cotton fabrics: the products are not the same, the units of measurement are not the same, and the Soviet data have an upward bias in addition. The margin of error is probably less significant if the growth of the Soviet cotton fabrics industry is being considered, particularly if growth is being discussed in terms of annual average rates. There is almost certainly an upward bias in the percentage growth over the Soviet period as a whole (because of relative understatement of earlier data), but probably not over some later stretches of years. Finally, the margin of error is likely to be smaller still when comparisons are made between Soviet growth rates for, say, cotton fabrics and steel. Bearing the necessary qualifications in mind and exercising care along the way, we can use Soviet data on physical output to sketch a picture of Soviet industrial growth.

CHAPTER 3

The Product Mix:
Composition, Quality, and Variety

As WE shall measure it, economic growth means expansion in the capacity to produce things, and this cannot be fully revealed in figures. If produced things did not change in nature, there would be only the technical problem of measuring quantities; but growth and change go hand in hand, and the gray area of "qualitative change" cannot be captured in quantitative form.

We are interested in the qualitative changes resulting from greater or lesser productive activity with a given technology. For our purposes, the quality of an item may be taken as improved when more resources are used to produce it, and worsened when fewer are used.[1] The term is, therefore, being used in a very restricted sense, since in ordinary usage it also refers to such things as change in the efficiency with which something is produced, or in its value in use.

Soviet attitudes on production differ from those in the West, and for this reason the pattern of qualitative change has been different. In the background lie two basic factors. First, Soviet industry has been split in two, one sector—heavy and military industry—being systematically favored over the rest. Second, the economic system has an inherent quantitative bias, traceable in part to the working of the system itself and in part to the crusading nature of communism.

These forces work both for and against each other, and the result is mixed as far as the qualitative aspects of growth are concerned. Alec Nove is justified in warning us against sweeping conclusions based on the volume and sharpness of internal complaints about the quality of goods:[2]

> It is generally assumed that poor quality is a characteristic of Soviet production. This assertion has some truth in it, but needs to be carefully qualified. There is evidence that Soviet industry is capable of first-class precision workmanship, and also plenty of evidence to the contrary: of bathroom taps which do not run and textile dyes that do.

[1] Improved quality does not, of course, always result from additional expenditure of resources. With inefficiency not difficult to imagine, a leaky fountain pen could be more costly than a leakproof one. We must suppose that the optimum available technology is, or would be, used in every case being compared.

[2] A. Nove, "The Pace of Soviet Economic Development," *Lloyds Bank Review*, April 1956, pp. 11 ff.

One should beware of concluding that poor quality is an inherently "Soviet" characteristic. It would be wiser to bear in mind that these things are, at least in part, consequences of the sheer pace of Russia's industrial revolution. An industry staffed by half-trained ex-peasants is apt to produce a high proportion of spoiled work, under communism, fascism, feudalism or any other system known to man. With the passage of time, Russia has acquired a fairly large skilled-labour force, but there has not been enough of it to go around, and priority has been given to heavy industry. This, and the inevitable effect of a constant seller's market, has certainly tended to depress the quality of consumers' goods and the standard (as well as the rate) of house building. Even so, this state of affairs cannot be assumed to last indefinitely, and the visitor who finds (as the author of these lines did) that door handles come off in hotels should not conclude that Soviet industry produces defective railway locomotives or machine tools. Door handles have no priority.

It is important not to be misled by the large number of criticisms of defects which appear often enough in the Soviet press. It is easy to catalogue these criticisms and derive from them a picture comforting for the complacent but fundamentally inaccurate. The system as a whole is not chaotic, even though examples of chaos can be properly cited; it does work. The essential fact is that the U.S.S.R. is a vast country of contrasts, which has developed very unevenly, with the good and the bad existing still side by side. One should also remember that inefficiencies in Western countries would be better known if the private affairs of firms were liable to be released to the press. In the U.S.S.R., the authorities use publicity in a carefully selective way. Hence an outburst of criticism directed at some sector is not necessarily proof that it is peculiarly defective, or that its efficiency has declined; the reason may be a decision to launch a campaign to improve it, or possibly even a desire to discredit the minister in charge.

Most of what Nove says should be heeded, but his warning is in a sense too strong. Whatever might be true for the future, Soviet industry in the past has been the model of austerity, and this is relevant in studying its growth. In the emphasis on quantitative growth, the simple has been generally favored over the complex and amount over quality. The result has been an economy with products less varied than in the West, with a product mix more heavily weighted in favor of producer and military goods, and with a quality of goods generally lower.

Many Soviet products in areas like heavy industry and the military sector now equal or excel Western products, demonstrating rapid progress in these fields. But there has not been the across-the-board improvement that has characterized Western industrial growth. The most marked improvements have been in metallurgy, machinery, and munitions; otherwise, growth has been primarily quantitative, consisting in expanded output of standardized commodities.

An anecdote of the second world war[3] portrays this contrast. During an air raid a Western ambassador and his military attaché watched a Soviet anti-aircraft battery manned by young women who maintained a rapid rate of fire on attacking aircraft. The attaché, an artillery officer, was fascinated by the Soviet guns and the efficient way they were being handled. After the raid was over, he took out his pipe for a smoke and broke a dozen matches before getting one to light. Pointing to the matches and the guns, he burst out: "How can people who make and work guns like that make matches like this?"

This contrast needs to be understood, especially in relation to other Soviet developments. We shall see how it conditions responses to stresses in the economic system bringing about unevenly distributed swings in the quality of production. We shall then turn to qualitative trends over the long run, and conclude with a discussion of the product mix in different segments of industry.

Qualitative Changes in the Short Run

The first period of stress faced by the Soviet economy came in the decade following the revolution. Civil war and internal disorder had caused industrial production to fall to around a fifth of its prerevolutionary level by 1920. Although a large segment of industry had already passed over to state ownership, the shaping of a new economic order was to take place while industry was recovering in the period of the New Economic Policy (1921–1928). One characteristic of this formative period was a deterioration in the quality of industrial goods.

This problem was evident at the launching of the five year plans, being widely commented upon by Soviet officials as well as foreign observers. We find William Henry Chamberlin writing as follows in 1929:[4]

There is probably no method of measuring quality as precisely and definitely as one may ascertain quantity in industrial production. But

[3] Related to me by Professor John H. Young.
[4] W. H. Chamberlin, *Soviet Russia*, Boston, 1930, pp. 155 ff.

it is the unanimous testimony of Russian consumers, a testimony which is not contradicted, even by Soviet economic officials and experts with whom I have talked, that the quality of Russian products, especially of wearing apparel and many other articles of immediate consumption, has not reached the pre-war level. Several years ago Leon Trotzky initiated the idea of a commission which should hear complaints regarding the quality of industrial production; its offices were soon flooded with boots that leaked after the first trial, knives that failed to cut, textiles that tore after a short period of wear, etc. Krzhizhanovsky, President of the State Planning Commission, admits that "the quantitative needs of production often compel us to ignore quality." (*Basic Problems of the Control Figures for 1928–1929*, p. 9.) And here is an excerpt from *The Conjuncture of Industry for 1927–1928* (p. 38), a book published under the auspices of the Supreme Economic Council, regarding the quality of production during this period:—

"During the year there were complaints regarding deterioration of quality from the metallurgical industry, because of the increased number of cinders from the coal, and from the railroads, because of the increased quantity of damaged goods in some products of the metallurgical industry. There were also complaints regarding the deterioration of the quality of overshoes, shoes, building material, aniline dyes, some forms of agricultural machinery, etc."

In a report of its findings on consumer goods, the commission referred to by Chamberlin stated, among other things, that galoshes wore only half as long as in 1913, that textiles had similarly depreciated, and that shoes had gotten even worse. In four factories producing cotton textiles, 45 to 63 per cent of gray goods and 24 to 50 per cent of finished goods classified as "standard quality" were found to be defective, or *brak* in the Soviet terminology. The shoes produced in five factories were all characterized by the commission as *brak*. Boxes of matches were found to be 15 per cent short in count, and packages of cigarettes and cheap tobacco (*makhorka*) 20 per cent short in weight.[5]

Conditions in this period are tersely summarized by Professor Calvin Hoover, who wrote in 1931 that "there can be no argument about the miserably poor quality of product of Soviet industry up to the present time. This poor quality is constantly criticized by the Soviet press, and there is an earnest desire to improve it. But partly on account of the

---

[5] I. Z. Kachanov, "O kachestve potrebitel'skikh tovarov" [The Quality of Consumer Goods], *Ekonomicheskoe obozrenie* [Economic Survey], 1929, No. 10, pp. 23, 31, 33, and 39.

necessity for increasing the quantity of production, and partly on account of the shortage of raw material, execrable quality continues to characterize Soviet manufactures."[6]

These conditions persisted and perhaps worsened through the First Five Year Plan, when pressure mounted for accelerated growth. According to Elisha Friedman, "not only was the Plan unrealized with respect to quantity, but far more so with respect to quality of workmanship. This was true not only of finished goods but even of some semi-finished products and raw materials such as coal, coke, ores, and metals."[7] He cites the following examples of poor quality criticized in the Soviet press: raw steel, strip copper, tungsten acid, molybdate of ammonium, calcium carbide, cast-iron taps, insulated electrical wiring, steel castings, copper and bronze fittings, tractors and their component parts, electric light bulbs, footwear, textiles, clothing, glassware, and calculating machines.[8] He says of the tractors:[9]

Because the raw material was poor the finished tractors could not stand up under use. A machine tractor station in Azerbaidzhan received thirty-two tractors from the Stalingrad plant. When they were assembled many defects were revealed. Their rims did not fit; the radiator pipes of thirty tractors leaked at two to seven places. Other difficulties too numerous to mention were found. After running in neutral for a short time the tractors began to backfire because the porcelain of the sparkplugs burst. Similarly the tractors of the Red Putilovetz plant proved inferior in quality. Of a shipment of thirty sent to the Volokolam tractor station one was sent back within four days for an overhauling, and eleven others which could not even start to work were left out in the fields. But the loss from tractors which failed completely was less than from the others which must be stopped every two or three hours for repairs. These criticisms were not confined to the tractor stations. From all over the Soviet Union came sworn complaints of difficulties, such as leaking radiators, poorly cast cylinder heads, loose bearings, broken valve springs, unsatisfactory threading on sparkplugs, etc.

As planning became more realistic and the industrial base expanded, the pressures undermining quality also lessened. There seems to have been

[6] C. B. Hoover, *The Economic Life of Soviet Russia*, New York, 1931, p. 46.
[7] E. M. Friedman, *Russia in Transition*, London, 1933, p. 120.
[8] *Ibid.*, pp. 120 and 282 ff.
[9] *Ibid.*, pp. 283 ff.

a general improvement in quality of goods during the Second Five Year Plan, except in certain areas of consumer goods. An article on textiles appearing in a Soviet trade journal in 1936 states that "only a complete lack of attention to technological processes, a race for quantity, a lack of proper interest in the quality of production, and the existence of regulations that cover up the production of substandard goods have created this vicious circle that has led to a deterioration in the quality of the textiles on the market."[10]

Developments from 1937 to recent years are shrouded in secrecy. The political purges, the mounting military preparedness program, and the retarding industrial growth probably led to a general worsening in quality of production during the short-lived Third Five Year Plan, but the details cannot be known. The growing problem of quality control would seem to be reflected in the issuance by the Presidium of the Supreme Soviet of the ukase of July 10, 1940, stating that "the output of defective or incomplete products that do not meet compulsory standards is a crime against the state equivalent to wrecking," and setting punishments for this crime at five to eight years imprisonment.[11]

Like most economic details, the problem of quality was not commented on widely in the Soviet press during the decade following World War II, but it received increasing attention toward the end of the Fifth Five Year Plan, particularly after Premier Bulganin's report of July 1955 on problems of industrial development.[12] In setting the tone for succeeding discussion, he stated: "It is necessary that those who neglect the quality of production, and thus crudely trample underfoot the interests of the state and the population, be severely punished. Party organizations are called upon to play a great role in the struggle for the quality of production." His references to poor quality included consumer goods, fuels, metallurgy, and machine building.[13]

Bulganin singled out the difficulties in meeting "assortment plans":[14]

---

[10] P. Fadeev and D. Zamkovskii, "O kachestve standartov tekstil'nykh tovarov" [On the Worth of the Standards for Textiles], *Voprosy sovetskoi torgovli* [Problems of Soviet Trade], 1936, No. 10, p. 40. To qualify as *brak*, a cotton fabric had to have more than eight holes and seventeen spots or stains in a bolt of thirty-five to forty meters; a woolen fabric, more than 120 holes and 240 spots or stains (see *ibid.*, p. 37).

[11] *Voprosy sovetskoi torgovli*, 1940, No. 8, p. 3.

[12] N. A. Bulganin, "Concerning Tasks in the Further Advance of Industry, Technical Progress and Improvement of Production Organization" (a speech at the Plenary Session of Communist Party Central Committee, July 4, 1955), *Current Digest of the Soviet Press*, VII, 28, pp. 3–20 and 24 (original text in *Pravda* and *Izvestia*, July 17, 1955). Henceforward this will be cited as: Bulganin, "Tasks."

[13] Bulganin, "Tasks," p. 16.

[14] *Ibid.*

A serious defect in the work of industry is the mistaken practice, which is most harmful to the national economy and which we have not outlived, of the nonfulfillment of the production plan in terms of category quotas.

. . . For example, although the Ministry of Ferrous Metallurgy over-fulfilled the 1954 plan for rolled metal production as a whole by 173,000 tons, it failed to produce 155,000 tons of special large and small rolled steel sections, which are in short supply, 85,000 tons of rolled wire and 25,000 tons of rolled wheels.

Several branches of machine building also do not fulfill the plan for the established categories of goods.

The Ministry of Heavy Machine Building, which overfulfilled the over-all production plan for 1954, failed to fulfill the plan for the production of metallurgical equipment, forging and pressing machines, various types of lifting and transport equipment, diesel engines, and gas generator motors. The Ministry of Machine Tools overfulfilled the plan for 1954 for the total quantity of metal-cutting lathes and forging and pressing machines. However, it has not fulfilled the plan for production of the more important types of heavy machine tools and forging and pressing equipment.

The Ministry of Electrical Equipment overfulfilled last year's over-all production plan. However, the tasks of production of such important types of goods, essential for the national economy, as electric motors exceeding 100 kilowatts, power transformers and generators for steam and hydraulic turbines have been considerably underfulfilled by the ministry.

One can find many similar examples in other fields of industry.

The volume of criticism grew around the end of 1956 and early in 1957, following a year in which difficulties had been encountered in meeting the goals of the new Sixth Five Year Plan, leading finally to abandonment of the plan in the fall of 1957. It may be useful to quote from articles appearing at that time to illustrate that the tendency for quality to deteriorate in times of stress has carried over to recent years.

An editorial, "Constant Attention to Quality of Output," appearing in *Pravda* on December 7, 1956, focused attention on deteriorating quality. It says in part:[15]

. . . Losses from unacceptable production have risen rather than fallen,

[15] *Current Digest*, VIII, 49, p. 24. For more complaints about agricultural equipment, see *ibid.*, p. 26; *ibid.*, IX, 5, p. 27; and *ibid.*, X, 3, pp. 26 f.

and the output of goods of poor quality continues. The quality of the output of a number of tractor and farm machine plants is not good. In the first nine months of 1956 the Ministry of Agriculture's receiving agents were compelled to reject and return to factory assembly shops more than 15 per cent of the machinery intended for shipment to Machine and Tractor Stations and collective farms. The number of defective tractors coming off the lines of the Kharkov and Vladimir Plants has been greater than in 1955. The Stalingrad Tractor Plant has been guilty of especially grave violations of the technical conditions for manufacturing and assembling machines. This enterprise's officials have not organized a struggle against defective output in the machine shops, and as a result many defective parts reach the assembly shops. This has resulted in the rejection as defective of 28 per cent of the DT-54 tractors turned out in the first nine months of 1956. Many machines are being rejected as defective at other plants of the Ministry of Tractor and Farm Machine Building. . . .

Losses from faulty output in Gorky's plants and factories in the first nine months of 1956 amounted to . . . twice as much as the city's enterprises saved in the same period by lowering the cost of production. . . .

. . . A group of machine builders writes *Pravda* that "after spending 1,089 hours machining one part of a surface grinder it had to be melted down again because there were blisters in the castings received from the Vulcan Plant. Many other castings received from this plant also had to be rejected as defective. The Forward Plant delivers castings of even poorer quality. Since the beginning of 1956 our plant has returned about 100 tons of castings to the suppliers as completely useless.". . .

Several weeks later deficiencies were pointed out in production and distribution of spare parts for agricultural machinery. Among other things, it was said that "machinery repairs are being seriously held up by the incomplete assortment [of spare parts]—a lack of such parts as, for instance, drive shafts, piston rings for starting motors, and some others"; that "MTS often receive unsuitable, defective spare parts, made in violation of the technical norms"; and that "parts are still supplied 'in bulk' with the result that MTS receive pistons of one size and piston sleeves of another."[16] A later letter complains about the difficulty of getting tires and tubes.[17]

[16] *Ibid.*, IX, 2, p. 30 (original text of an editorial, "Important Task of Personnel in Industry," in *Pravda*, January 11, 1957).
[17] *Current Digest*, IX, 14, p. 33 (original text of letter from two collective farm chairmen in *Pravda*, April 6, 1957).

Products of ferrous metallurgy and furniture making were also criticized. In the former case, difficulties in meeting plan goals were said to stem in part from the fact that "the steel mills are developing faster than the iron ore industry. The iron content of ore is declining constantly, even though the need for raw material is growing. Many blast furnaces continue to work with damp ore, and their productivity is therefore low."[18] In the case of furniture, the Deputy Minister of Trade is quoted as saying that the products of one factory "not only were poorly made but actually smelled of fish oil." The article says that "sometimes, because the trade personnel are not sufficiently demanding, poor furniture still manages to make its way into the stores." It is said of upholstery cloth that "the fabrics are light in weight, narrow in width and impractical, and their colors are poor."[19]

The quality of leather footwear was appraised in a letter to *Pravda* from a local shoemaker published January 9, 1957, which reads in part as follows:[20]

Every year our industry turns out more footwear. It fulfills the plan as far as quantity goes; however, the quality of the footwear remains low. Every day my work as a shoemaker convinces me of this.

The following factories turn out poor quality footwear: the Kaganovich Plant in Minsk, the Severokhod Plant in Yaroslavl, the Paris Commune Plant in Moscow, and plants in Orel, Shakhty, Yerevan, Tbilisi and many other cities. Very often the products of these plants have to be repaired two or three weeks after they are bought.

Why do shoes wear out so fast? The trouble is that the glue and waxed thread do not hold the soles. The composition inner sole comes off and sticks to the socks, and after a month and a half the leather sole comes off, along with the welt; the nails and the iron and copper screws turn inward and prick the feet; the poor-quality counter lining soon tears and the counter chafes the feet. The tops of the shoes produced at the Shakhty and Tbilisi Plants are especially bad. . . .

Against this volume of complaints about quality in very recent years, we

[18] *Current Digest*, VIII, 50, p. 30 (original text of an article, "Overcome Lag of Ferrous Metallurgy in Dnieper Area," in *Pravda*, December 10, 1956).
[19] *Current Digest*, VIII, 50, p. 33 (original text of an article, "About Comfortable and Beautiful Furniture," in *Izvestia*, December 15, 1956). See also *Current Digest*, IX, 26, p. 16; *ibid.*, IX, 38, p. 24; and *ibid.*, IX, 40, p. 24.
[20] *Ibid.*, IX, 2, p. 31. See *ibid.*, IX, 8, p. 47, for a reply from three officials of a shoe factory published in *Pravda*, February 26, 1957. While admitting the poor quality of footwear, these officials place the blame on inadequate raw materials. See also a letter on children's shoes in *Current Digest*, IX, 26, p. 32 (original text in *Izvestia*, June 29, 1957). On other items of clothing, see *Current Digest*, IX, 35, p. 25, and *ibid.*, IX, 45, p. 29.

must place the accumulating evidence of a trend toward improvement in the quality of consumer goods since the death of Stalin. We see this reflected in eyewitness accounts of qualified observers who have visited the Soviet Union at different times separated by passage of years, in the post-war as well as the interwar period.[21] We may infer the same thing from the increasing diversion of resources to consumer goods: from 1950 through 1955, output of consumer goods apparently grew more rapidly than total industrial output (see Table 59).

In drawing a moral from the instances of quality deterioration described in the Soviet press, we must therefore bear in mind the warnings of Nove and not conclude too much. The focusing of criticism on particular industries—as agricultural machinery, textiles, footwear, furniture—may represent special campaigns to bring about improvements. At the same time this does not explain the bunching of complaints, spread over a wide area of products, that seems to occur when industry is having difficulty fulfilling the quantitative tasks set for it. In times of stress, quality tends, in response to the pressures described in the preceding chapter, to depreciate as the growth rate slows down, making the quantitative record look better than it is. These temporary deteriorations in quality get concentrated in areas of lower priority—particularly consumer goods—but they may spill over into more favored areas if the stress is great enough, as it apparently was in the early Soviet period and during the short-lived Sixth Five Year Plan. Whether such "cyclical" worsening of quality persists over the long run is another story, to which we now turn.

Qualitative Changes in the Long Run[22]

Trends in quality also reflect the basic contrast in priorities. In the favored sectors of industry—primarily within the three "M's": metallurgy,

---

[21] See, e.g., the articles by Elizabeth Swayne in *Printer's Ink*, August 14 and 21, 1959 and *Profit Parade*, July and August, 1959.

[22] The discussion in this section and the following one is based largely on data in the tables and notes of *Statistical Abstract of Industrial Output in the Soviet Union, 1913–1955*, New York, NBER, 1956. Citations will be made only when other sources are used.

Our knowledge of technical conditions has been greatly improved as a result of recent visits to the Soviet Union by U.S. industrial delegations under the cultural exchange programs. Some of the reports that have been issued are: "Russian Metallurgy," *Journal of Metals*, March 1958; *Report on Visit of U.S.A. Plastics Industry Exchange Delegation to USSR, June 2 to June 28, 1958* (Society of the Plastics Industry), New York, n.d.; William E. Vannah, "A Team Reports on Control Inside Russia," *Control Engineering*, November 1958; *Steel in the Soviet Union* (American Iron and Steel Institute), New York, 1959; *A Report on the Visit of an American Delegation to Observe Concrete and Prestressed Concrete Engineering in the USSR* (Portland Cement Association), Chicago, 1959; *A Report on USSR Electric Power Developments, 1958/59* (Edison Electric Institute), New York, 1960; and "Soviet Computing Technology—1959," *Transactions* (Institute of Radio Engineers), March 1960, and *Communications* (Association for Computing Machinery), March 1960.

machinery, and munitions—rapid growth in output has been accompanied by substantial improvement in quality; in the neglected sectors—primarily within the three "C's": consumer goods, construction materials, and chemicals—quality has improved slowly and, in some cases, even depreciated.

Let us recall that, for our purposes, quality is being measured by costliness under the ruling technology and not by usefulness in some other sense. Similarly, we are not concerned at this point with the elements of economic growth that fall customarily under the heading of technological improvements. We are simply trying to isolate those "physical" dimensions of growth in a product that are not captured in the available measures of physical output. Since the item given in statistics as a "product" is usually a mixture of products narrowly defined, qualitative change will involve change in the product mix as well as in the nature of individual products within the mix.

By its very nature, analysis of qualitative change must be descriptive; the results cannot be put in figures, though much of the pertinent evidence may be presented that way. In any case, most of the evidence comes from Soviet sources, and this poses certain problems. As we noted in the preceding chapter, performance in some sectors of industry is shielded from view, and this applies to changes in quality as well as in output. On the one hand, these sectors include declining or very slow-growing industries, where quality is also probably improving very slowly or not at all—possibly even worsening. On the other hand, they also include industries closely related to military production, where, by all visible signs, quality has improved in pace with output.

Again as we have already noted, criticisms of specific industries appearing in the Soviet press may at times be more directly related to campaigns for reform than to worsening conditions. One must be careful to go beyond these sporadic outbursts before drawing conclusions about long-run developments. But this is made difficult by the fact that the qualitative aspects of growth have not been systematically discussed in the Soviet technical literature. The picture of historical changes in quality within a particular industry must be pieced together from widely scattered fragments of information.

Any discussion of qualitative changes, no matter how extensive it may appear to be, is bound to be annoyingly incomplete. Moreover, too much remains unseen to know how representative the fragmentary description actually is. With this repeated warning, we proceed to say what can be said.

The world has witnessed the rapid Soviet progress in the three "M's" and little more need or can be said here. Metals such as steel, aluminum, and tin have been entering increasingly into world trade and have competed successfully with the products of other countries. According to first-hand reports of qualified Western observers, the postwar Soviet iron and steel industry—except possibly for rolling mills—is technically on a comparable footing with the British and American industries,[23] though the products are of somewhat lower quality.[24]

Soviet machinery and equipment, though often copied from Western prototypes and produced on a more standardized basis, have apparently kept pace with technological developments in special areas. This is certainly true of military weapons and equipment, in novel as well as conventional lines, as we know from the fact that fission and fusion bombs have been exploded, powerful rockets launched, satellites orbited, and so on. In warfare itself, the world has observed the high quality of tanks, aircraft, artillery pieces, and rockets. Unfortunately, these "eyewitness" observations cannot be fortified by systematic evidence from open source materials, but there would seem to be no reason to question the Soviet advances in these fields, as far as quality of production is concerned.

Industrial products connected with other favored activities, like education and science, have also probably shown marked improvement over the Soviet period, though extensive documentation is again lacking. Even within the more neglected sector of consumer goods, there has been improvement in durable goods, at least in the sense that new products have been introduced: television, long-playing records, aluminum pots and pans, cameras, watches, and so on. As an example regarding consumer perishables, higher-grade tobaccos have displaced the traditional low-grade *makhorka* absolutely as well as relatively.

In another relatively neglected area, construction materials, there has been a notable improvement in the quality of portland cement—though incidents such as the powdery floors at the recent U.S. exposition in Moscow suggest that there is room for further advance. Output has grown more rapidly for the better grades than for the poorer ones, so that the aggregate output weighted by 1937 Soviet prices rose by 25 per cent more over 1928–37 than aggregate output in simple tonnage. In the

[23] *Steel in the Soviet Union; Economist*, December 3, 1955, pp. 863 ff; *The Russian Iron and Steel Industry*, Special Report No. 57, London, Iron and Steel Institute, 1956; and "The Russian Steel Industry," *Steel Review*, April 1956, pp. 24–48.
[24] *Steel in the Soviet Union*, pp. 191 and 247.

case of roofing materials, asbestos shingles have been replacing roofing paper, the share of the former in output measured in square meters rising from 11 per cent in 1913 to 24 per cent in 1928 and to 32 per cent in 1955. At the same time, roofing iron has declined in importance, offsetting to some extent the shift to asbestos shingles. By 1940, the last year for which data are available, the output of roofing iron had fallen to a quarter of its level in 1913.

These random notes cover only a portion of the cases that might be cited. The imprecise and incomplete nature of the discussion illustrates the handicap an outsider labors under in trying to assess a region of activity shrouded in secrecy. This handicap is further highlighted by the importance attached to travelers' tales—Marco Polo economics—as a source of information on these qualitative matters. We do not yet know enough about the products of Soviet industry to make anything approaching a definitive appraisal of trends in quality.

EXAMPLES OF UNCHANGING OR WORSENING QUALITY

There are a number of industries in which quality of product has failed to improve or has worsened. In part, this has been the kind of development always observed in the early stages of industrialization, as machines replace handicrafts and standardized production begins to serve mass markets. The very word "brummagem," from Birmingham, has been adopted into the English language to stand for shoddy, standardized merchandise. Beyond this, it is characteristic of a centrally directed economic order for the product mix to be simplified and for variety to be de-emphasized in favor of standardized goods. Centralized planning becomes less and less efficient as the number of products multiplies. And, as products are simplified and standardized, some downgrading inevitably occurs. We may observe this in such things as the development of compulsory public education and the governmental postal monopoly in the United States.

But there is also something unique in the Soviet case, as we have emphasized several times: a stress on quantitative performance combined with the favoring of some industrial sectors over others. For industries of high priority the "quantitative bias" may be overshadowed by the obvious gains in quality, as in military weapons and machinery. As one moves down the list of priorities, qualitative improvements are likely to become increasingly secondary until the point is reached at which quality suffers absolutely in favor of quantity. The sacrifice of quality is most pronounced in sectors neglected for reasons of both internal and external policy. These sectors are starved of the more efficient productive techniques and treated as residual claimants for resources.[25]

Coal is an example of a product with relatively high priority—at least until very recently—that has experienced a rather steady deterioration of quality. The sulfur and ash content has been rising, while the calorific content has been falling. Ash content rose gradually from 15.2 per cent in 1940 to 18.6 per cent in 1957.[26] An index of calorific content per ton of coal runs as follows:[27]

1913	100	1940	94
1928	98	1945	85
1932	97	1950	87
1937	95	1955	88

The decline is attributable in large measure to the increasing share of output accounted for by lignite, one of the cheapest forms of coal. Lignite accounted for 4 per cent of output in 1913, 9 per cent in 1928, 8 per cent in 1932, 14 per cent in 1937, and 29 per cent in 1950 and 1955.

There has also been some loss in the quality of Soviet crude petroleum as output has declined in relative importance in the Caucasian fields and risen in the Ural-Volga fields. The sulfur content (which affects actual

[25] We have a recent example of "quantitative bias" with rather far-reaching consequences in the Soviet-type industrialization of Hungary and Poland, which may have some relevance to earlier developments in the Soviet Union as well. The conditions in Hungary are documented in Bela Balassa, *The Hungarian Experience in Economic Planning*, New Haven, 1959, especially pp. 110 ff and 153 ff. In the case of Poland, we find Professor Oscar Lange, a well-known Polish economist, describing some aspects of Polish industrial development through 1956 as follows (see "For a New Economic Program," translated from the Polish in *Zycie Gospodarcze*, July 16, 1956, and reproduced for private circulation by the Center for International Studies, October 1956, pp. 2 and 5): ". . . In industry, production of substandard or unusable goods (rejects) and wastage of materials constitute a serious economic problem. At the beginning, it appeared mainly in the field of consumer goods. The diminishing quality of consumer goods became a serious phenomenon hampering the improvement of living conditions but it did not slow down the production process. At present, production of unusable goods (rejects) has extended to the mechanical industries, production of tools and transport equipment, etc. This threatens to stop the technical processes of production as well as to disrupt the production basis of the national economy. It also undermines the foundations of foreign trade.
". . . It is necessary to stop the race for purely quantitative indices which are attained thanks to low quality and high own costs. This brings about purely fictitious results, the usage of raw materials and of human labour for production of goods which do not produce the intended economic, and often even the intended technical effects (e.g., agricultural machinery improper to any use after a few weeks)."
[26] E. Sokolova, "O strukture toplivnogo balansa SSSR" [Breakdown of Fuel Produced in the USSR], *Voprosy ekonomiki* [Problems of Economics], 1958, No. 5, p. 63.
[27] This index is derived from data given on page 376. Data in *Promyshlennost' SSSR* [Industry of the USSR], Moscow, 1957, pp. 133 and 140, imply no change in calorific content between 1913 and 1955, but the implied content for 1913 is clearly too low (see page 372).

and potential octane ratings of derived fuels) ranges from 0.6 to 6.5 per cent for petroleum from the Ural-Volga fields, as contrasted with 0.01 to 0.4 per cent for petroleum from the Caucasian fields. The share of the Ural-Volga petroleum in total output rose from 6 per cent in 1940 to 29 per cent in 1950 and to 58 per cent in 1955, while the share of Caucasian petroleum fell from 87 per cent in 1940 to 57 per cent in 1950 and to 30 per cent in 1955.[28] The resulting loss in quality—it would be more expensive to produce petroleum with a lower sulfur content—may have been offset in part by an improvement in the geographical distribution of crude petroleum relative to markets for it and its products, but effects of this nature are difficult to assess.

Our remaining examples are generally in areas of lower priority. Phosphoric fertilizers provide the first case. Output is stated to be measured in terms of superphosphate of a given average content of phosphoric acid, and recent sources give a breakdown into superphosphates and ground natural phosphate. Aside from being less soluble than superphosphate, ground natural phosphate can be produced much more cheaply, since it is not processed beyond the grinding of phosphate rock. Ground natural phosphate accounted (in tonnage) for about 15 per cent of all the phosphoric fertilizers produced in 1913, for 10 per cent in 1928, for 45 per cent in 1932, for 30 per cent in 1937, for 17 per cent in 1950, and for 19 per cent in 1955. We note that the quality of phosphoric fertilizers has fluctuated sharply over various spans of years, with a trend toward worsening over the entire Soviet period.[29]

As mentioned in the preceding chapter, the term "bricks" is used in Soviet statistics to cover several things in addition to kilned clay bricks. Apparently, all types of brick-like and block-like building materials are included: bricks proper, silica bricks, sand-lime bricks, slag ("cinder") bricks and blocks, concrete blocks, and so on—possibly even building stone. Very little information is available on the composition of output over long periods, but enough is known about sand-lime and slag bricks to indicate that their share in total output has increased from 4 per cent in 1913 to 14 per cent in 1937 and to 17 per cent in 1955. Since these bricks are less costly (and generally of lower structural quality) than kilned bricks, there has probably been some worsening of the quality of "bricks" as far as this factor is concerned.

[28] M. Brenner, "Problems of Oil in Long-Range Development of USSR National Economy," *Current Digest*, X, 22, p. 5 (original text *Voprosy ekonomiki*, 1958, No. 2, pp. 16–29).

[29] Mineral fertilizers are typically transported and stored in bulk, with further losses in quantity and quality. See, e.g., *Current Digest*, X, 3, p. 29.

Glass presents an interesting example of how quality may be affected by changing the physical unit of measure. Grossman traces the history as follows:[30]

> ... At one time a variety of units was employed, but in the early thirties tonnage became the specified physical dimension in all branches of the glass industry (window glass, bottles, flasks, tumblers). It was chosen for easier production planning (i.e. the construction of input-output ratios, capacity utilization rates, etc.) since both the raw materials for glassmaking and the semifinished product, raw glass, were measured by weight. It was, so to say, material-oriented. But this led the plants to produce the thickest and heaviest sheet glass and glassware, thus greatly contributing to the acute shortage of glass and glassware generally at the time. (The production of thick window glass was also stimulated by technical difficulties in mastering the new continuous sheet glassmaking process). Seen another way, the materials for glassmaking, especially alkali, which were also very scarce, were being used very ineffectively. The crisis finally led to a special resolution of *SNK* [Council of People's Commissars], dated April 2, 1934, which imposed utility-oriented rather than material-oriented units of measure: square meters for window glass, and number of pieces for glassware.

As a result of the second change, glass apparently got thinner and thinner. Flat glass now seems to average 2 millimeters in thickness.[31]

Paradoxically, excessive thickening and thinning of flat glass both amounted to worsening of quality from the point of view of cost, given the optimum continuous sheet process. On the other hand, the supplanting of less expensive "half-white" glass by more expensive "white" glass has improved quality. The share of white glass rose from 23 per cent in 1928 to 67 per cent in 1950.

Because of the shortage of protein in the Soviet diet, continual stress has been placed on expanding the fish catch and improving the quality of fish products. Most of the growth in fish catch has taken place in the postwar period, as a result of wartime acquisitions of rich fishing grounds

---

[30] Gregory Grossman, *Soviet Statistics of Physical Output of Industrial Commodities: Their Compilation and Quality*, Princeton for NBER, 1960, p. 75.

[31] See *Steklo i keramika* [Glass and Ceramics], 1955, No. 3, p. 25. The thinness of flat glass, along with careless handling, accounts for the high breakage rate: 30 to 35 per cent of the flat glass delivered to construction sites seems to be broken on arrival (see Grossman, *Soviet Statistics*, p. 124).

in the Baltic Sea and in the Pacific Ocean off Sakhalin Island. Even so, the heavy subsidies given the industry moved Premier Bulganin to remark that "every fish caught indeed becomes a 'goldfish.' "[32] Moreover, wastage and spoilage now account for around a third of the total catch, compared with about a quarter in 1936.[33]

Soviet authorities grant that progress in improving the quality of fish products leaves much to be desired. Major emphasis has been placed on diminishing the share of salted fish and increasing the shares of fresh, frozen, cured, and canned fish. As can be seen from Table 5, these

TABLE 5
Composition of Soviet Fish Products, Selected Years
(per cent)

	Percentage of Total Output					
	1929	1932	1940	1950	1954	1955
Fresh and frozen fish	22	33	29	27	32	38
Salted fish	70	62	56	62	62	57
Smoked, pickled, cured, and canned fish	8	6	15	11	6	5

Source: *Za sotsialisticheskoe rybnoe khoziaistvo* [For a Socialist Fishing Industry], 1931, No. 6, p. 30; *Socialist Construction in the USSR*, Moscow, 1936, p. 219; *Rybnoe khoziaistvo* [The Fishing Industry], September 1940, p. 17; and *Planovoe khoziaistvo* [Planned Economy], 1956, No. 1, pp. 84 f. Output measured in metric tons.

efforts were successful during the period from 1929 through 1940, though it is doubtful that this represents an improvement over conditions in the pre-Plan period. In any event, the product mix in 1954 and 1955 was similar to the mix in 1932. Salted fish still accounted for considerably more than half of all fish products, and cured and canned fish for less than 6 per cent. The preponderance of salted fish does not mean that Russian tastes run in that direction, as can be seen from the continual efforts to supplant salting by other preservative methods. Salting seems to persist in crude form (*grubye posol'*) because it is less expensive than canning, curing, or refrigerating.

Soap, technically defined, is a fatty acid. In the prerevolutionary period, the fatty acid content of manufactured soap ran about 85 per cent on the average, or about the same as for manufactured soap in the United States. During the First Five Year Plan, fatty acids were increasingly displaced by cheaper "fillers," and the average content dropped to

[32] Bulganin, "Tasks," p. 13.
[33] See *Sovetskaia torgovlia* [Soviet Trade], 1956, No. 7, p. 6. See also the letter to the editor in *Pravda*, February 17, 1957 (translated in *Current Digest*, IX, 7, p. 41).

a low point of about 40 per cent in 1930, rising thereafter to around 50 per cent in 1936. Changes in quality have not been reported during the postwar period, and the silence suggests that the fatty acid content has not been rising. In data on output, the loss in quality is taken into account by recording production in terms of a standard (40 per cent) fatty acid content.

Sugar in the Soviet Union is produced in two forms: as crystals and as lumps. In Soviet statistics, sugar crystals are referred to as "sand" (*pesok*) sugar, and sugar lumps as "refined" (*rafinad*) sugar. "Sand" sugar is essentially a semiprocessed crystallized sugar, whereas "refined" sugar is made by fusing "sand" sugar and cutting it into lumps. During the prerevolutionary period, more than 60 per cent of the "sand" sugar was "refined." This fraction fell to a low point of 14 per cent in 1930, rising thereafter to a peak of 43 per cent in 1937, and falling and rising once again in succeeding years to reach a level of 36 per cent in 1955. Over the entire Soviet period, the quality of sugar has therefore worsened in this respect: less than 40 per cent of the "sand" sugar is now processed into lump form, compared with more than 60 per cent before the revolution.

As we noted in the preceding chapter, in Soviet usage the meaning of "canned food" is much broader than in Tsarist and Western usage, where it is restricted to food packed in hermetically sealed containers. In Soviet statistics the term applies to many types of preserved foods, packed in bulk (e.g., pickles in the barrel) as well as in hermetically sealed containers. Data on the breakdown by hermetically sealed and bulk-packed products are meager, existing only for the Second Five Year Plan. According to figures published at that time, hermetically sealed products accounted for 37 per cent of canned food in 1933, 32 per cent in 1934, 43 per cent in 1935, and 48 per cent in 1936.[34] Since the data on total output of canned food in those years were apparently revised in 1956 to exclude some bulk products, the percentages would now be somewhat higher. In any case, canned food as given in Soviet statistics for 1913 was all hermetically sealed. Hence the product mix was downgraded between 1913 and 1934, from which low point there was a slight improvement up to 1937. To put it another way, according to Soviet data, output of preserved food multiplied about ten times between 1913 and 1937; at the same time, output of hermetically sealed products multiplied only about seven times. Changes in the product

[34] *Socialist Construction*, 1936, p. 219, and *Narodno-khoziaistvennyi plan na 1937 god* [The National Economic Plan for 1937], Moscow, 1937, p. 102.

mix since 1937 are not known well enough to be able to say what has happened to the percentage of hermetically sealed products.

The types of preserved food have changed during the Soviet period. In 1913, 80 per cent of output was accounted for by meat, meat and vegetables, and fish, the remainder being vegetables. Since 1932, 40 per cent or less has been accounted for by the former category, while the variety of other products has apparently expanded to include fruits, evaporated milk, and juices.[35] Tomatoes have typically accounted for a large share, as large or larger than all other vegetables combined.

It should, incidentally, be noted that Soviet food products are still distributed overwhelmingly in bulk, at least as far as the normal household is concerned. Very little progress has been made in packaging, a development that has added substantially to the cost of food processing in the West. The percentages of marketed output bottled or packaged for household use were as follows in 1952: butter, 2.7; vegetable oil, 2; margarine, 30; confectionery, 20; lump sugar, 8; jam, 9.4; salt, 13; beer, 27.5; and macaroni, 3.4. The percentages in 1955 were: butter, 6.4; vegetable oil, 4.5; lump sugar, 12.3; macaroni, 3.2; meat, 2.1; and milk, 9.6. In 1952, more than 80 per cent of the plum jelly was "canned" in 100-liter (26-gallon) barrels, and more than 37 per cent of the other types of jelly in barrels half as large or of equal size. Yeast was put up in packages of 100 grams (3.5 ounces) or more. Lard and other edible fats were not packaged at all, even though they had been packed in boxes and jars before the war.[36]

The leather footwear produced in prerevolutionary Russia was comparable with, and in some cases superior to, Western footwear. The low quality of present day Soviet footwear has already been described. This deterioration in quality has resulted in part from mechanization, but more importantly from troubles in the leather industry that have persisted since collectivization of agriculture in the early 1930's. The output of hard leather fell by 65 per cent between 1928 and 1935,[37] while the output of boots and shoes did not fall at all. In the same period, employment in industries producing leather substitutes multiplied about four times. The output of hard leather had not recovered to its 1928 level by as late as 1955, while the output of boots and shoes had multiplied about 2.7

[35] See *Promyshlennost'*, 1957, p. 399.

[36] F. Dubinin in *Sovetskaia torgovlia*, 1953, No. 7, p. 6; and I. K. Sivolap and A. S. Shatkan, *Pishchevaia promyshlennost' SSSR* [The USSR Food Industry], Moscow, 1957, p. 27.

[37] The quality of tanned leather also worsened in these and succeeding years (see, e.g., Grossman, *Soviet Statistics*, p. 76).

times. By 1940, about 70 per cent of the footwear produced in large-scale industry was made at least in part from leather substitutes; around 10 per cent of all footwear was made out of reclaimed materials, recovered from scraps or wornout shoes. Despite substantial downgrading of standards, between 30 and 40 per cent of the footwear produced in recent years has been substandard.

The cotton textile industry of prerevolutionary Russia was closely related to the British textile industry, because both were based on long-staple Egyptian cotton and because British firms dominated the Russian industry. Use of Egyptian cotton made possible the spinning of fine yarn: in 1913 Russian yarn had an average number of around 52, which is to say that the average length of a gram of yarn was about 52 meters.[38] By way of comparison, the average number has been as high as 51 for British yarn in recent years and around 38 for American yarn (which is spun from a shorter-staple cotton). Hence, prerevolutionary Russian yarn was about as fine on the average as British yarn of recent years, and considerably finer than American yarn.

The fine yarn was utilized to make closely woven cloth, that is, cloth with a high thread count. Thus, in 1913 the average thread count of Russian cotton cloth was apparently around 90.5 threads a square centimeter, or 230 threads a square inch. This is about the same as the thread count for British cloth, which in recent years has averaged between 200 and 250 a square inch. It is considerably higher than the recent counts for American cloth, which have averaged between 150 and 175. Manufacturing cost is higher for high-count than for low-count cloth.

During the Soviet period the quality of cloth has worsened as measured by these two characteristics: fineness of yarn and closeness of weave. No evidence is available on other important characteristics, such as tensile strength of yarn. The known deterioration in quality is shown in Table 6, which presents indexes of average yarn number and average thread count on 1913 as a base. The yarn number declined steadily—the yarn became steadily coarser—during the interwar period, dipped to a low point during World War II, and recovered to approximately the prewar level by 1955, the last year for which the number could be derived. The average yarn number in 1940 and 1955 was around 39, or about the same as for the United States in recent years. Therefore, as far as fineness of yarn is concerned, the Soviet cotton textile industry has moved away from the British standard toward the American one.

[38] The statistics used in this discussion of cotton textiles are explained in Appendix A, technical note 1.

TABLE 6
INDEXES OF SOVIET YARN NUMBER AND THREAD COUNT
FOR COTTON FABRICS, SELECTED YEARS
(1913 = 100)

	Yarn Number	Thread Count
1913	100	100
1928	92	83
1930	92	77
1931	88	76
1932	81	71
1933	77	69
1934	77	73
1940	75	76
1946	63	71
1950	74	76
1951	73	75
1952	75	77
1953	75	78
1954	76	79
1955	76	80

SOURCE: Appendix A, technical note 1.

The thread count reached its low point in 1933, rose thereafter up to World War II, fell during the war, recovered the prewar level about 1950, and rose thereafter to reach a level in 1955 slightly lower than in 1928. At its low point the thread count averaged less than 160 a square inch, and in 1955 it averaged around 185. Hence in this respect, too, the Soviet cotton textile industry has left the British model and approached the American one.

It is of interest that the yarn number has declined more percentagewise than the thread count, so that the weight of a square meter of cloth has increased during the Soviet period. This is merely to say that, as far as weight is concerned, the decline in thread count has been more than offset by the increase in coarseness of yarn. Soviet writers sometimes refer to the increasing density of cloth as evidence of improved quality, whereas in fact it is the consequence of lower quality in the two dimensions usually considered relevant.

Simplification and standardization has accompanied lower quality. In the prerevolutionary period, the Russian textile industry produced about 1,300 types (constructions) of cloth; the number was reduced to 260 in 1929/30. In recent years the number has risen to around 500, but 4 of these apparently account for 54 per cent of total output and 70 for 77 per cent.

In the prerevolutionary period, Russia was the fourth largest producer of silk and synthetic fabrics in the world. The fabrics were predominantly silk and silk mixtures; silk accounted for 93 per cent of the fibers used in weight. In succeeding years rayon became increasingly important: by 1955, rayon accounted for 90 per cent of the fibers used, while silk accounted for only 3 per cent. The remaining 7 per cent was accounted for by other synthetic fibers—mainly kapron, a fiber similar to nylon.[39] Even though Soviet statistics still refer to the industry as "silk fabrics," it now produces essentially rayon fabrics. Whether this should be called a lowering of quality is open to question. From the point of view of fabricating cost, more expensive fabrics have been relatively displaced, and in this sense there has been a loss in quality. But a similar displacement, not so pronounced, has taken place in the United States, for example. On another aspect of quality, Soviet fabrics have become highly standardized: in 1925/26, almost 500 different types of fabric were produced; by 1927/28, the last year for which data are available, the number had been reduced to less than 200.[40]

The quality of woolen and worsted fabrics has certainly deteriorated over the Soviet period, mostly during the early 1930's. This is shown first of all by changes in the product mix. For instance, the fraction of output accounted for by all-wool fabrics fell from 50 per cent in 1930 (which was already well below the average for prerevolutionary Russia) to 14 per cent in 1933. As to the wool itself, cottonized fiber and shoddy came to be increasingly important at the expense of virgin wool. From 1928 through 1931 the share of virgin wool in the weight of fine woolen fabrics fell from 43 to 20 per cent; in coarse woolen fabrics, from 67 to 48 per cent.

A different type of evidence indicates that the lower quality has persisted, though some recovery has been made from the nadir of the mid-1930's. Table 7 shows a percentage breakdown of part-wool and

[39] *Promyshlennost'*, 1957, p. 323, and *Voprosy ekonomiki*, 1956, No. 7, p. 58. There may have been a large increase in the output of silk fabrics around 1952, possibly as a result of a sudden and substantial increase in the imports of raw silk from China. This possible sharp spurt in the production of silk fabrics has proved temporary, and rayon has become once again the dominant raw material of this industry.

[40] *Izvestia tekstil'noi promyshlennosti i torgovli* [News of the Textile Industry and Trade], 1929, No. 2, p. 11.

TABLE 7
COMPOSITION OF SOVIET WOOLEN AND WORSTED FABRICS, SELECTED YEARS
(per cent)

| | | Percentage of Total Output | |
	Worsteds	Fine Woolens	Coarse Woolens
1913[a]	54	20	26
1926[a]	54	25	21
1929[a]	41	34	25
1932	14	47	38
1937	25	37	38
1940	29	39	32
1950[b]	40	38	22
1955[b]	40	43	17

SOURCE: *Statistical Abstract of Industrial Output in the Soviet Union*, Part 4, series 1216.1; *Promyshlennost'*, 1957, p. 330. Output measured in meters.

[a] Large-scale production only.

[b] Ministerial production only. For 1940, the percentages for ministerial output were 30, 43, and 27.

all-wool fabrics into worsteds, fine woolens, and coarse woolens. The share of worsteds fell from 54 per cent in 1913 and 1926 to a low of 14 per cent in 1932, rising thereafter to 29 per cent in 1940 and to 40 per cent in 1955. At the other extreme, the share of coarse woolens rose in the interwar period, though it has fallen in the postwar period apparently below the 1913 level. The share of fine woolens has risen more than the share of coarse woolens, but there is doubt that the distinction between coarse and fine woolens has the same meaning now as in the prerevolutionary period. Almost all fabrics are mixtures of wool and cotton or wool and rayon, though it is difficult to know how important the other fibers have been in recent years. Almost all fabrics were all-wool in 1913; the fraction fell to 50 per cent in 1930, 5 per cent in 1940 and 1950, and 9 per cent in 1955.[41] The average width of fabrics also declined between 1940 and 1955.[42]

Notes on Product Mix

The purpose of this concluding section is to describe the product mix of some industrial sectors and compare it with the typical mix to be found in Western economies, especially the United States. Historical developments will not be so much at issue as the character of Soviet industry in recent years relative to conditions in other countries. Some discussion of

[41] *Za rekonstruktsiiu tekstil'noi promyshlennosti* [For the Reconstruction of the Textile Industry], 1933, No. 12, p. 4; and *Promyshlennost'*, 1957, p. 330.
[42] Grossman, *Soviet Statistics*, p. 121.

this question is needed to provide a background for estimates of comparative levels of industrial production, such as we shall make later for the
Soviet Union and the United States (see Chapter 8).

In general, Soviet industrial products are more simplified and standardized than in the West, even in the more favored sectors of industry.
The Soviet mix of rolled steel products is more limited in variety than the
mix found in most Western countries, and the same is true for most
machinery, as we shall see. In addition, the quality of a number of
narrowly defined products falls short of Western standards. In some
areas, such as military production, Soviet products undoubtedly match or
excel their Western counterparts, but we are unable to comment further
on these for lack of details. Once again we are plagued by paucity of
information, and the examples we cite are simply those about which
something is known.

INDUSTRIAL MATERIALS

We pointed out that lignite now accounts for around 29 per cent of
Soviet coal; in the United States, it accounts for less than 1 per cent.
The quality of Soviet crude petroleum, as indicated by sulfur content and
similar technical standards, is on the average also lower than in the
United States, the petroleum of comparable quality from the Caucasus,
Sakhalin, and the Emba District being outweighed by lower-grade
petroleum from the Ural-Volga region.

Raw steel seems to be up to Western standards in the alloys and
specifications produced, but the range of products is much more limited.
The case is similar for rolled products. From the recurring complaints
about steel castings and about copper and brass products, one would
assume that they are generally of lower quality than in the West. The
established standards for aluminum are, on the other hand, comparable
to those in the West, and there is no evidence to indicate that they are
not generally observed.

We have seen that Soviet glass is very thin, averaging about 2 millimeters in thickness. Plate and other polished glass apparently accounts
for less than 2 per cent of the output in square meters, in conventional
units of 2-millimeter thickness.[43] By contrast, plate and other polished
glass accounted in 1954 for over 60 per cent of the value and approximately
40 per cent of the square footage (unadjusted for differences in thickness)
of all flat glass produced in the United States.[44] Not counting plate

---

[43] The planned percentage for 1956 was 1.7 (*Steklo i keramika*, 1955, No. 3, p. 25).
[44] *Census of United States Manufactures: 1954*, Washington, 1957, Vol. II, Pt. 2, pp.
32A-9 and 32A-12. Laminated glass is excluded from these calculations to avoid double

and other polished glass, the average thickness of window glass in the United States was around 2.7 millimeters in 1954.[45]

Electricity would seem to be homogeneous, but there are important differences between the Soviet and Western products. Throughout the Soviet period, generating capacity has never managed to keep up with the consumption desired at established prices; that is to say, consumption is not rationed by price. Instead, there is a system of priorities governing decisions on whose electricity is to be shut off when consumption threatens to exceed generating capacity. It is not unusual to have the supply of electricity to households and such things as street lighting, even in large cities, cut off without warning. During the middle 1930's, the same thing applied to whole sectors of industry. Another method of rationing is to reduce the current. The allowable variations in frequency and voltage of current are considerably higher on the average than in the United States, but the standards are more rigorous than in the United States in the case of defense industries, where virtually no variations in current are allowed.[46]

MACHINERY

Soviet motor vehicles are highly standardized. About a dozen models of automobiles have been produced in quantity in the Soviet Union. Half of these were introduced in the interwar period and half in the postwar period, almost all being copied from American prototypes. An American automobile company produces more basic models in a year than the Soviet Union has produced to date. Production is even more standardized in the case of trucks, where the two-and-a-half-ton model predominates.[47]

Similarly, it has been Soviet policy to keep a simple structure of basic railroad equipment. Steam locomotives have been the primary source of power, and only six types have been produced in quantity: three for

counting. Square footage of plate glass is not given directly and has been estimated by dividing the value per unit of industrially consumed plate glass (derived from data on p. 32A-12) into total value of shipments of plate glass (given on p. 32A–9).

[45] Derived from data in *ibid.*, p. 32A-9. The thickness of different types of window glass was taken as follows: thin, 1.6 mm.; single strength, 2.31 mm.; double strength, 3.18 mm.; and heavy sheet, 4.5 mm.

[46] This paragraph is based on John Pearce Hardt, "Economics of the Soviet Electric Power Industry" (processed), Research Studies Institute, Air University, Alabama, 1955, pp. 84 ff, 314 ff, and 326 ff. It is interesting to note that the average Soviet load factor was 10 per cent lower than the U.S. factor in 1955 (derived from data in *A Report on USSR Electric Power Developments, 1958-1959*, pp. 74 and 76), indicating less effective use of capacity.

[47] This paragraph is based on *Mashinostroenie* [Machine Building], Moscow, 1947, Vol. II, pp. 264 ff; *Eksportno-importnyi slovar'* [Export-Import Dictionary], Moscow, 1952, Vol. I, pp. 70 ff; and A. A. Kurov, *Avtomobil'* [Motor Vehicles], Moscow, 1938, p. 18.

freight service and three for passenger service. There has, however, been a significant shift in production toward electric and diesel locomotives in the postwar period. Passenger cars are simple and standard.[48]

Agricultural equipment has also been highly standardized. We shall concentrate discussion here on tractors, since considerable information is available on the product mix. During the entire Soviet period, sixteen basic models of regular tractors and one type of garden tractor have been produced. This may be compared with eighteen basic models produced in the United States in 1953 by International Harvester alone. Track-laying crawlers have been favored over wheeled tractors, though both types have been produced at all times. In 1955, crawlers accounted for more than three-quarters of the drawbar capacity of all tractors in use in Soviet agriculture. During the 1920's and early 1930's, there were two básic tractor models produced; during the middle and late 1930's, there were three; and during the 1950's, there were six or seven.[49] The Soviet press has contained frequent complaints that tractors (and other agricultural equipment) are too highly standardized and, as a result, poorly adapted to many agricultural conditions.[50]

Soviet tractors are mainly copies of American models. On this score, it may be useful to quote what Professor Norton T. Dodge has to say in his comprehensive study of the Soviet tractor industry:[51]

Despite the great improvement in the variety of types of tractors produced by the Soviet tractor industry, the models in production still lag behind American models from a technological point of view.

The Soviet Union began with the production of obsolete models, and has not yet completely caught up with developments abroad. Although the Soviet Union made every effort to obtain the latest and best equipment for the factories producing tractors, the tractor models produced were chosen primarily because of their reliability, durability, and proven performance over a period of years. In view of the rough usage to which tractors were subjected under Russian conditions, such considerations were of particular importance. On the other hand, the

[48] *Current Digest*, IX, 39, pp. 24 f.

[49] These data are drawn from Norton T. Dodge, "The Tractor Industry of the USSR" (mimeographed), Washington, Council for Economic and Industry Research, 1955, pp. 23 ff; *Narodnoe khoziaistvo SSSR* [National Economy of the USSR], Moscow, 1956, p. 144; and A. M. Kiriukhin, *Traktory shestoi piatiletki* [Tractors of the Sixth Five Year Plan], Moscow, 1956, p. 36.

[50] See, e.g., the letter from four collective farm chairmen in *Pravda*, February 25, 1957 (translated in *Current Digest*, IX, 8, p. 45).

[51] Dodge, "Tractor Industry," pp. 26 ff.

reliance upon proven foreign models has led to the equipping of Russian agriculture with tractors already rendered obsolete by newer developments abroad.

For example, the Fordson was first produced in this country in 1915, and by the latter half of the 'twenties was already being superseded by newer, more versatile types. In 1928, the year the Russians began to increase Fordson capacity at the Putilov Plant severalfold, Ford shut down his Dearborn plant and ceased production of the Fordson in America.

Production of the International 15/30 began in this country in 1921, and was discontinued at the Milwaukee Plant of International Harvester in 1931, the year mass production of the Russian version of the International began. International Harvester introduced the Farmall in 1923. Ten years later, just as International Harvester was introducing an improved model, production of the Soviet version began at the Krasnyi Putilovets Plant which converted from the production of the Fordson to production of the Universal. Finally, in 1955, a modernized diesel version of the Universal is in the developmental stage. Until the present there has been no change in the basic design.

Caterpillar discontinued production of the 60 model crawler, which had been produced since 1925, in 1930. The Soviet copy was first produced in quantity in 1933, two years after the Caterpillar Diesel had come out. The Soviet version of the Diesel was in production by 1937. Two years earlier, Caterpillar began the production of an improved model, the D-7. Production of the Soviet version was delayed by the war, but in 1946 the first Stalinets-80 was produced. The ancestry of the SKHTZ-NATI and more recent postwar models is more difficult to trace, but all have borrowed heavily on foreign design and technology. The power lift, for example, came into general use in this country in the 'thirties, and the hydraulic lift was introduced in 1940. Production of the hydraulic lift in the Soviet Union did not begin until 1950. Rubber tires were introduced in this country in 1932, and became standard equipment within a few years. No Soviet tractors were equipped with rubber tires, except industrial and towing tractors, until 1950. Only one model, the Universal-4, which is used for cotton pickers, has rubber tires as standard equipment. The MTZ-1 and 2 and the KHTZ may be so equipped, but reports indicate that rubber plants are failing to meet their commitments.

Aluminum alloy sleeve bearings were introduced in this country around 1940. They are still being tested in the Soviet Union. Power steering, oil clutches, automatic hitching, etc., are yet to be incorporated on Soviet tractors. Nevertheless, the Soviets are making rapid improvements in design, and the most archaic models and features will soon be eliminated, according to official pronouncements.

As for machinery other than transportation and agricultural equipment, quality and complexity have undoubtedly improved markedly over the Soviet period. At the same time, it is important to recognize that the general practice is to produce a limited number of standardized models. Models are changed infrequently, and machines are seldom custom-built. The user adapts to the machine, not the machine to the user. Complex machines are often constructed by combining several standardized machines. For example, a so-called "aggregate" machine tool, which is designed for automatic or semi-automatic fabrication of a particular item, is generally made out of standard lathes, milling machines, and so on, put together on a unified mount.

Since Bulganin's speech referred to above, there has been a rather steady campaign to stimulate innovation and modernization in machinery industries. For instance, in an article in *Izvestia*, December 3, 1957, a Soviet professor, A. Rybkin, states in part:[52]

Our country has an enormous stock of metalworking machine tools; the number of machine tools in the Soviet Union surpasses the number in all European countries. However, more than 40% of our machine tools are of simple design. It is quite clear that we must alter this percentage and make more highly productive machine tools instead of simple types, and also make more up-to-date automatic and semi-automatic machine tools. . . .

New bearing materials are necessary because of the great increase in the operating speeds of machinery. Incidentally, this increase has taken place not only in aviation and reaction technology but in many machines used in common industrial processes that operate under high pressure or temperature. Bearings made of the types of steel now employed no longer satisfy growing demands. Consequently it is necessary to make heat-resistant steels or alloys for roller bearings that can provide normal operating conditions for machines operating under high temperatures or pressures.

In his report on industrial organization presented to the Supreme Soviet in May 1957, Khrushchev notes that an automobile plant built in

[52] *Current Digest*, IX, 48, p. 24.

Communist China with Soviet assistance is technically superior to similar plants in the Soviet Union. He then goes on to remark:[53]

> The question arises: Could we, while supplying our Chinese friends with modern equipment, have re-equipped our own auto plants at the same time? We undoubtedly could have, but this was not done because we have the incorrect practice of planning machine-tool output without direct responsibility. As a result, plants produce large quantities of all-purpose, low-output and often obsolete equipment, which is not always needed by industry. Here are the figures. In 1956 our industry produced a total of 121,000 metal-cutting machine tools but less than 22,000 specialized and multiple-unit machine tools, or 18% of the total output. Therefore, with comprehensive planning of the production of equipment and an increase in the output of specialized machine tools, in the course of one year one could re-equip not only the Gorky and Moscow Auto Plants but some other enterprises as well, without failing to meet obligations for deliveries to foreign countries. The equipment removed from the plants as obsolete could be used for repair shops and other auxiliary services in our industry. At the moment, new machine tools are being allocated for this purpose as well as for new production.

CONSUMER GOODS

We noted above that salted fish account for around 60 per cent of Soviet fish products, fresh and frozen fish for 30 to 40 per cent, and cured and canned fish for around 5 per cent. By way of contrast, fish products in the United States (exclusive of wastage, by-products, bait, etc.) were divided as follows over the period 1950–1955: fresh and frozen fish, around 55 per cent; canned fish, around 42 per cent; and cured fish, around 3 per cent. The output of salted fish was negligible.[54]

Almost all Soviet soap is produced in bar or "hard" form. In 1937, hard soap accounted for 94 per cent of output; and in 1954, for 93 per cent. In the United States, the comparable fractions were 56 per cent in 1937 and 20 per cent in 1954.[55] The spectacular growth of detergents in the United States and other Western countries has had no counterpart in the Soviet Union.

---

[53] *Ibid.*, IX, 18, p. 12 (original text in *Pravda* and *Izvestia*, May 8, 1957).

[54] *Statistical Abstract of the United States, 1958*, Washington, 1958, p. 708.

[55] P. Serebrennikov, "O prekrashchenii raskhoda pishchevogo syr'ia na tekhnicheskie tseli" [On Stopping the Use of Edible Raw Materials for Technical Purposes], *Voprosy ekonomiki*, 1956, No. 10, p. 32.

Two final remarks may be made about processed foods. First, the Soviet "sand" sugar is produced in the form of crystals, not as highly processed as the granulated sugar of the West. Second, as we have noted, food processing does not generally extend to the packaging stage in the Soviet Union—not even to the bottling of milk—whereas packaged foods have become the rule in the West, particularly the United States.

In cotton textiles, Soviet fabrics are similar to American ones in average yarn number and thread count, but the variety of goods is much more limited and production is concentrated in lower-grade fabrics. About 150 yarn numbers are now produced in the United States, with 30 to 40 accounting for 95 per cent of output; only 68 yarn numbers are now produced in the Soviet Union, with 15 accounting for 95 per cent of the output. About 2,500 constructions of gray goods are produced regularly in the United States—at least 4,000 from time to time; the number in the Soviet Union is now around 500, with 4 accounting for 54 per cent of the output. Dyeing and finishing of Soviet fabrics fall far below general Western standards, since cheap sulfur dyes are used predominantly. Soviet output of cotton fabrics in linear measure covers narrow-woven as well as broad-woven goods, while American output covers broad-woven goods (those over 12 inches in width) only. The average width of broad-woven fabrics is around 69 centimeters in the Soviet Union and around 100 centimeters in the United States.[56] Both these factors must be kept in mind when comparing output in the two countries, since it is ordinarily expressed in linear, not square, measure.

In the case of silk and synthetic fabrics, rayon is now the dominant fiber in both the Soviet Union and the United States, but there is a difference in its importance in the two countries. In the United States, it accounted for 76 per cent of the combined textile mill consumption of silk, synthetic fibers (nylon, dacron, etc.), and rayon in 1955;[57] in the Soviet Union, for 90 per cent. Synthetic fibers accounted for 23 per cent in the United States, compared with 7 per cent in the Soviet Union; and silk for 1 per cent, compared with 3 per cent. American fabrics are about 20 per cent wider on the average than Soviet fabrics.[58] The variety of Soviet silk and synthetic fabrics is considerably more limited

[56] These remarks are based on data in Appendix A, technical note 1.

[57] *Statistical Abstract of the United States, 1958*, p. 800.

[58] Soviet fabrics vary from 80 to 106 centimeters in width (*Tovarovedenie promyshlennykh tovarov* [Commercial Specifications of Industrial Goods], Moscow, 1954, Vol. II, p. 124) while U.S. fabrics average about 112 centimeters according to data in the *Census of United States Manufactures: 1947.*

than in Western countries, and dyeing and finishing, as in the case of cotton fabrics, is of lower quality.

It is difficult to compare woolen fabrics for the Soviet Union and the United States because of inadequate data on relevant characteristics. American data are no longer compiled for all-wool and part-wool fabrics, but all-wool fabrics accounted for 72 per cent of output in 1929 and for at least 59 per cent in 1935.[59] In the postwar years, blends with synthetic fibers have become more popular, and the fraction has probably fallen. However, it is certainly higher than the 5 to 9 per cent recorded in recent years in the Soviet Union. Soviet blends are predominantly with cotton and rayon; in the United States, with nylon, dacron, and orlon. Up to 1951, only fabrics with 25 per cent or more wool were counted as woolen in American statistics; since 1951, only fabrics with 50 per cent or more. We do not know the comparable standards for the Soviet Union. Coarse woolens have accounted for no more than 14 per cent of output in recent years in the United States,[60] compared with 17 per cent and more in the Soviet Union. Soviet fabrics average around 128 centimeters in width,[61] while American fabrics average around 150 centimeters.

Finally, in the case of consumer durables products tend to correspond with standard, "stripped down" models of the West—they are sometimes direct copies. Mechanization has been slow in some areas. Household sewing machines, for example, are almost all foot-pedal models.

Concluding Remarks

This less than adequate look at the qualitative aspects of Soviet industrial production, hampered by the selective nature of Soviet statistics, can be summarized only in broad terms. In general, industrial products are less complex and varied in the Soviet Union than in the West, and they have improved in quality more slowly. The picture is, however, one of contrasts between the favored sector of the three "M's"—metallurgy, machinery, and munitions—and the neglected sector of the three "C's"— consumer goods, construction materials, and chemicals. In between these extremes lies a number of industries that have experienced mixed qualitative developments. Finally, Soviet industry has been subject to "cyclical swings" in the quality of production, coinciding with swings in the rate of growth of industrial output. When the growth rate slows

[59] *Statistical Abstract of the United States, 1938*, Washington, 1938, p. 784.
[60] *Statistical Abstract of the United States, 1956*, Washington, 1956, p. 816.
[61] Grossman, *Soviet Statistics*, p. 121.

down, quality begins to deteriorate; when it speeds up, quality also tends to improve. The mounting attention being paid in recent years to formerly neglected sectors suggests that this characteristic pattern of qualitative changes, both short- and long-run, may be undergoing transformation. But that is for the future to say.

CHAPTER 4

Growth Trends: A Sample of Industries

THE picture of growth trends in Soviet industry may be brought into focus by looking first at the long-range performance of individual industries. A study of this sort has the obvious shortcoming that the industries included are necessarily the more mature ones in an economy, and hence their recent growth rates may understate the pace of development in some newer, more vigorously growing areas. Reinforcing this bias is the absence of data on rapidly growing industries associated with military production. Counteracting it is the tendency of Soviet statistics to overstate growth over the long run and the absence of data on declining and very slow-growing industries. For instance, only one declining industry (low-grade tobacco) finds its way into our list. We have no way of knowing the quantitative force of these biases, or which may overweigh the other. Despite these and other shortcomings, analysis of trends in individual industries reveals much about the structure of growth and serves as a useful orientation for more refined study, which we shall undertake at a later point.

A sample of seventy industries has been assembled for study (see Table 8), constituting a "basic" sample of the industrial categories for which output data covering the entire Soviet period have been published.[1] The output records of these industries are traced in Chart A-1 (Appendix A), and it can be seen there that almost every industry has displayed variations in short-term growth rates. In addition, output generally declined sharply in the periods immediately following the revolution and during World War II. Long-term growth rates have not been computed as averages of short-term rates for two reasons: first, because all output series have gaps, varying from one to another; and, second, because the breaks in the continuity of growth in the revolutionary and wartime periods make averaging of growth rates hard to justify in a study of growth trends. Growth rates have therefore been calculated from output in the terminal years involved, by means of the compound interest formula.[2]

---

[1] The basic data underlying all statistics in this chapter are given in Appendix B and in technical note 2 of Appendix A. This sample was compiled before the publication of Soviet statistical handbooks in 1957, and it is therefore somewhat smaller than one that could be assembled now.

[2] If we let a represent output in 1913 and $a(1 + r)^{42}$ represent output in 1955, then the link relative of 1955 to 1913 is $(1 + r)^{42}$; the annual relative is $(1 + r)$, the geometric mean or the 42nd root of the link relative; and the average annual rate of growth is r, the annual relative minus unity. The latter is expressed as a percentage by multiplying it by 100.

TABLE 8
GROWTH TRENDS FOR FIXED SAMPLE OF SOVIET INDUSTRIES, 1913–1955

	Average Annual Growth Rate[a] (per cent)		Average Annual Growth Rate[a] (per cent)
Steam turbines	16.8	Sewing machines	4.3
Bicycles	16.4	Construction gypsum	4.2
Motor vehicle tires	16.1	Lumber	4.1
Natural gas	14.6	Red bricks	4.0
Lead	13.7	Rubber footwear	3.8
Power transformers	13.5	Boots and shoes	3.7
Asbestos shingles	12.9	Rails	3.7
Mineral fertilizer	12.5	Butter	3.6
Diesel engines	11.9	Soap	3.5
Electric power	11.2	Window glass	3.5
Zinc	11.1	Railroad freight cars	3.1
Machine tools	10.9	Matches	3.1
Roll roofing	10.1	Looms	3.0
Steam boilers	9.7	Salt	2.6
Canned foods	8.7	Industrial timber	2.5
Macaroni	8.6	Fish catch	2.4
Sulfuric acid	8.6	Crude alcohol	2.4
Peat	8.4	Linen fabrics	2.3
Clocks and watches	8.3	Raw sugar consumption	2.2
Rayon and mixed fabrics	7.5	Vegetable oil	2.2
Synthetic dyes	7.0	Woolen and worsted	
Roofing tiles	6.7	fabrics	2.1
Cement	6.6	Cotton fabrics	2.0
Coal	6.4	Beer	2.0
Sausages	6.3	Meat slaughtering	1.8
Copper	6.1	Railroad passenger cars	1.2
Construction lime	6.1	Starch and syrup	1.1
Steel ingots	5.8	Felt footwear	1.0
Caustic soda	5.7	Silk fabrics	0.4
Coke	5.6	Flour	0.3
Rolled steel	5.5	Steam locomotives	0.2
Paper	5.5	Vodka	−0.0
Cigarettes	5.4	Low-grade tobacco	−0.9
Soda ash	5.4		
Red lead	5.1		
Pig iron	5.0	Median	5.0
Iron ore	5.0	1st quartile	8.5
Crude petroleum	5.0	3rd quartile	2.5

SOURCE: Table B-2.

[a] Calculated from output in terminal years by the compound interest formula. Per capita rates are about 0.9 percentage points lower. Output in 1913 is taken for the interwar territory; in 1955, for the territory of that date.

This procedure amounts to computing an annual percentage rate of growth that, if sustained year after year, would have accumulated to the observed percentage growth over a span of years.[3]

[3] For example, if the output of steel ingots had in fact grown by 5.8 per cent every year from 1913 through 1955, the output in 1955 would have become 10.7 times the output in 1913, the multiple actually recorded in Soviet statistics.

We are interested in knowing not only the trend of growth, but also whether growth has been accelerating or retarding. This may be observed by computing growth rates for subperiods and comparing them. In all computations one must, of course, be careful not to pick periods or subperiods terminating in years whose output is abnormal in relation to the discernible trend; and to do this one must assume that he can distinguish trends from temporary fluctuations. Here is where statistical analysis becomes an art: the difference between a trend and a fluctuation cannot be defined by simple objective rules. And so it also is with the choice of periods for study. Judgments must be made, and they prove right or wrong depending on whether competent observers agree or disagree with them. We have made our judgments, and they will become apparent. Having made them, we try in the concluding section of this chapter to summarize evidence on the general trend of growth rates for individual industries.

Trends over the Soviet Period as a Whole

The growth rates for our sample fall within widely spaced bounds. At the one extreme, output of steam turbines rose at an average annual rate of 16.8 per cent; at the other, output of low-grade tobacco fell at 0.9 per cent. The divergence of these growth rates when applied to a span of forty-two years is shown by noting that between 1913 and 1955 output of low-grade tobacco fell by nearly a third, while output of steam turbines multiplied almost 700 times.

The boundaries of the middle half of growth rates are a better measure of dispersion than the simple range, since the latter depends on possibly unrepresentative extremes. Growth rates for the slowest-growing quarter of industries were lower than 2.5 per cent; for the fastest-growing quarter, higher than 8.5 per cent. This means that output for the middle half of industries multiplied within the range of 2.8 through 31 times during the period 1913–1955.

While output was growing at these rates, population was also increasing. Over the forty-two years in question, population within the relevant territorial limits multiplied 1.4 times, which implies an average growth rate of 0.9 per cent a year.[4] For some purposes it is relevant to adjust growth rates for changes in population, and growth rates for per capita output are about 0.9 percentage points smaller than the rates recorded in Table 8. The per capita rates for the middle half of industries therefore range from 1.6 to 7.6 per cent a year.

---

[4] These growth rates are derived from official Soviet data on population (Table C-3). For comments on their reliability, see note 5 in Chapter 6.

A useful way to illustrate the entire structure of growth rates is by a frequency distribution displaying the number of industries within each class of growth rates (see Chart 2, upper panel). The primary concentration occurs over the range of growth rates from 1 to 7 per cent.[5] The

CHART 2
Frequency Distributions of Growth Rates for Fixed Sample of Soviet Industries, by Number of Industries: 1913–1955

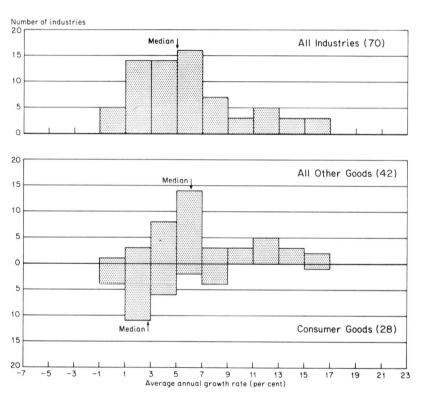

Source: Table 8.

frequencies taper off in both directions from this concentration, with a longer tail in the higher rates.

One reason for this longer right-hand tail is revealed on the lower panel, where the frequency distribution is divided into two parts: one

[5] The differences in the frequencies for each of the three classes distinguished within this range are so small as to be statistically insignificant. Thus, the heaviest concentration (sixteen industries) is at 5 to 7 per cent, but in a larger sample of ninety-six industries the heaviest concentration (twenty-three industries) is at 3 to 5 per cent (see technical note 2, Appendix A).

for industries producing consumer goods and the other for industries producing all other goods—i.e., industrial materials and producer durables. Each of these categories has its own distribution with a primary concentration and a tapering off in both directions.[6] The primary concentration for consumer goods occurs at a significantly lower class (1 to 3 per cent) than for all other goods (5 to 7 per cent); that is to say, the primary concentration for consumer goods overlaps the left-hand tail for all other goods. Industries producing consumer goods have grown at a slower pace than others in two respects: first, they dominate the lower ranges of growth rate; and second, they are distributed over a distinctly lower region of growth.

In looking at the distribution of growth rates in this way, small industries are counted equally with large ones, a disadvantage that can be partly overcome by weighting each industry by some index of its size. This is done in Chart 3, where each industry is represented by its value added in 1928.[7] The resulting distribution of growth rates by value added of industries shows a decidedly more pronounced concentration than the distribution by number of industries, and the concentration occurs at a lower class of growth rates. Put another way, the median annual growth rates for the two types of distributions compare as follows:

Distribution by

	Number of Industries	Value Added of Industries
	(per cent)	
All industries	5.0	2.7
Consumer goods	2.8	2.1
All other goods	6.1	4.9

It might be thought that the structure of growth in the Soviet period is related to the structure during the Tsarist period. Unfortunately, this conjecture cannot be thoroughly tested because the Tsarist statistical record is meager. Long-term growth rates for the two periods can be compared for only twenty-three industries in our fixed sample (see Table 9).

[6] Division into consumer and other goods necessarily involves some rather arbitrary decisions. The twenty-eight industries classified as producing consumer goods are: flour, macaroni, butter, vegetable oil, meat slaughtering, sausages, fish catch, soap, salt, sugar, starch and syrup, canned food, beer, cigarettes, low-grade tobacco, matches, vodka, boots and shoes, rubber footwear, cotton fabrics, linen fabrics, pure silk fabrics, rayon and mixed fabrics, woolen and worsted fabrics, felt footwear, bicycles, household sewing machines, and clocks and watches.

[7] Three of the industries in the fixed sample—clocks and watches, roofing tiles, and sausages—are omitted from this distribution because of inadequate data on value added.

CHART 3
Frequency Distributions of Growth Rates for Fixed Sample of Soviet Industries, by 1928 Value Added: 1913–1955

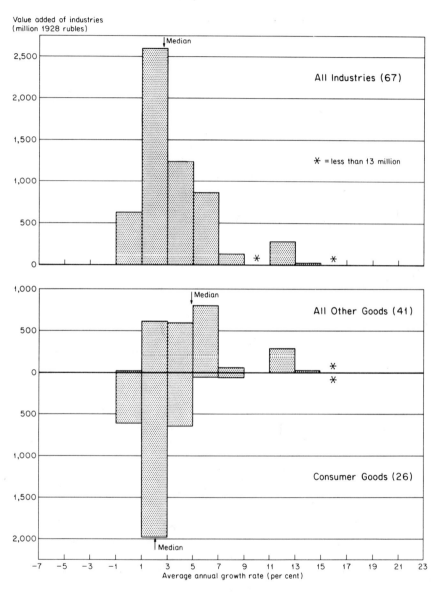

Source: Tables 8 and A-2.

TABLE 9

GROWTH TRENDS FOR TWENTY-THREE INDUSTRIES IN THE TSARIST
AND SOVIET PERIODS

	Average Annual Growth Rate[a] (per cent)		Rank of Growth Rate	
	1870–1913	1913–1955	1870–1913	1913–1955
Steel ingots	15.8	5.8	1	7
Crude petroleum	14.3	5.0	2	14
Caustic soda	13.4[b]	5.7	3	8
Coke	12.4[c]	5.6	4	9
Soda ash	11.8	5.4	5	10
Coal	9.6	6.4	6	5
Macaroni	9.3[d]	8.6	7	3
Sulfuric acid	8.9	8.6	8	4
Cigarettes	7.5	5.4	9	11
Rails	7.3[e]	3.7	10	15
Matches	7.0[d]	3.1	11	16
Pig iron	6.1	5.0	12	12
Iron ore	6.0	5.0	13	13
Raw sugar	5.9	2.2	14	19
Cotton fabrics[f]	5.3	2.0	15	20
Low-grade tobacco	4.8[g]	−0.9	16	23
Copper	4.5	6.1	17	6
Zinc	3.7	11.1	18	2
Salt	3.4	2.6	19	17
Starch and syrup	1.4[d]	1.1	20	21
Crude alcohol	1.1	2.4	21	18
Vodka	0.7	−0.0	22	22
Lead	−0.2	13.7	23	1
Median	6.1	5.0		
1st quartile	3.9	2.4		
2nd quartile	9.5	6.0		

SOURCE: Tables B-1 and B-2.

  [a] See Table 8, note a. For the period 1870–1913, output is taken for Tsarist territory
excluding Finland.

  [b] From 1891.

  [c] From 1890.

  [d] From 1888.

  [e] From 1878.

  [f] For 1870–1913, consumption of ginned cotton.

  [g] From 1881.

The middle half of these twenty-three industries occupies a higher
region of growth rates for the Tsarist period than for the Soviet period:
3.9 through 9.5 per cent a year as compared with 2.4 through 6.0 per
cent. The growth rates are also more uniformly dispersed for the Tsarist
than for the Soviet period (Chart 4, top panel), and there is less difference
between the distributions for consumer goods and all other goods (same
chart, lower panels).

CHART 4
Frequency Distributions of Growth Rates for Twenty-Three Industries, by Number of Industries: Tsarist and Soviet Periods

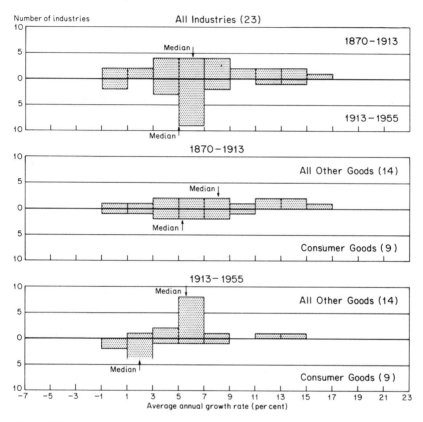

Source: Table 9.

Higher growth rates in the Tsarist period are not systematically related to higher (or lower) growth rates in the Soviet period (see Chart 5). Simple statistical tests show that the slight positive association between ranks of growth rates in the two periods could be attributed to peculiarities of the sample of industries.[8]

This lack of high positive correlation seems curious at first glance, because one would suppose that differential resource endowments would affect growth in the same way in the two periods. The explanation

[8] The coefficient of rank correlation is 0.353, which is barely significant at the 10 per cent level.

CHART 5
Scatter Diagram of Relation Between Ranks of Growth Rates for Tsarist and Soviet Periods, Twenty-Three Industries

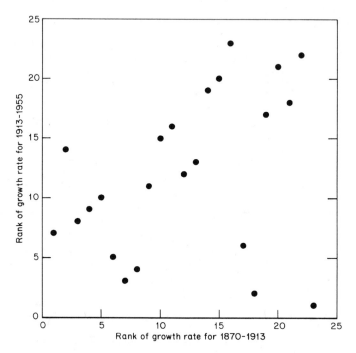

Source: Table 9.

probably lies in several kinds of environmental change. First, foreign trade diminished sharply in importance during the Soviet period, as emphasis was placed on self-sufficiency. Second, the choice pattern of the market place was displaced by the quite different one of the central planning authorities, stressing investment in an effort to "catch up with the West." Third, as a result of the first and second changes, technological progress probably came to be much more unevenly distributed, being concentrated in the favored sectors and largely absent elsewhere.

While the relative speed of growth does not seem to be correlated in the two periods, growth rates tend to be lower, industry by industry, for the Soviet period than for the Tsarist period. Whether this has any bearing on the question of retardation in growth, in view of the turbulent history of the Soviet period, is a matter to be considered later. For the moment, we are concerned only with the facts. The growth rate has risen over the two periods in the case of only four out of twenty-three industries: copper, zinc, crude alcohol, and lead. It is interesting that these four are among seven slowest growing industries in the Tsarist period. For the remaining nineteen industries, the growth rate declined.

These few descriptions about exhaust what can be said from direct comparison of growth rates in the Tsarist and Soviet periods. A more promising line of investigation has to do with the relation between speed of growth during the Soviet period and the "stage of development" from which an industry started. There is more evidence on this question and the findings seem to be significant.

Let us measure the "stage of development" of Russian industries in 1913 by comparing the structure of production in Russia that year with the structure in the United States, a country with a similar resource potential but far more "advanced" industrially at that time relative to its potential. As a rough index of development we may take output in Russia, industry by industry, as a percentage of output in the United States: the higher the percentage, the more advanced the industry is taken to be in comparison with others. This can be done for forty-eight of the seventy industries in our fixed sample.[9] These forty-eight industries may then be ranked in decreasing order on the basis of the output ratios and also on the basis of growth rates (see Table 10). It is apparent from inspection (see Chart 6) that there is a fairly strong inverse relation between "the stage of development" in 1913 and the growth rate for 1913–1955; that is to say, the more advanced the "stage of development," the slower tends to be the growth rate. Statistical measures of rank correlation confirm that this inverse relation is too strong to be attributed solely to chance.[10]

As it stands, this finding should be taken as purely descriptive, with no obvious causal meaning. It says only that the Soviet industries with the most rapid growth have in general been those starting out with the lowest output relative to the United States. Such a pattern of growth could have been the result of planned design as well as of economic

[9] Our measure of "stage of development" has obvious shortcomings in that the Soviet Union and the United States do not have the same differential resource endowments, technological achievements, or priorities. Moreover, as would be expected, a number of problems arise in trying to match Russian and American industries, some of which are discussed in Chapter 8.

[10] The coefficient of rank correlation is -0.685, which is significant at the 0.1 per cent level. It might be thought that this correlation is partly spurious, since output in 1913 appears in both measures being correlated. Spurious correlation seems unlikely, however, because the "stage of development" in 1913 has a strong positive correlation with the "stage of development" in 1928 (see Table 12). The coefficient of rank correlation is 0.832, which is significant at the 0.1 per cent level.

TABLE 10

Relation Between Growth Rate for 1913–1955 and "Stage of Development" in 1913, Forty-Eight Soviet Industries

	Rank According to	
	"Stage of Development," 1913[a]	Growth Rate, 1913–1955
Flour	1	47
Synthetic dyes	2	11
Cigarettes	3	22
Fish catch	4	38
Vegetable oil	5	40
Window glass	6	35
Rubber footwear	7	30
Salt	8	37
Railroad passenger cars	9	45
Sewing machines	10	27
Cotton fabrics	11	42
Raw sugar consumption	12	39
Butter	13	33
Steam locomotives	14	48
Woolen and worsted fabrics	15	41
Caustic soda	16	18
Meat slaughtering	17	44
Crude petroleum	18	26
Rayon and mixed fabrics	19	10
Construction gypsum	20	28
Rails	21	32
Boots and shoes	22	31
Soda ash	23	23
Iron ore	24	25
Construction lime	25	16
Silk fabrics	26	46
Soap	27	34
Rolled steel	28	20
Lumber	29	29
Pig iron	30	24
Steel ingots	31	17
Beer	32	43
Coke	33	19
Cement	34	12
Sausages	35	14
Sulfuric acid	36	9
Railroad freight cars	37	36
Electric power	38	6
Coal	39	13
Paper	40	21
Copper	41	15
Canned food	42	8
Mineral fertilizer	43	5
Bicycles	44	1
Zinc	45	7
Lead	46	4
Motor vehicle tires	47	2
Natural gas	48	3

Source: Tables 8, B-2, and E-1.

[a] Measured by ratio of output in Russia (interwar territory) to output in the United States, both as of 1913. For the United States, a nine-year average centered on 1913 has been used wherever possible. The ranking would not differ significantly if 1913 data were used instead of the centered average.

CHART 6

Scatter Diagram of Relation Between Ranks of Growth
Rate for 1913–1955 and "Stage of Development" in 1913,
Forty-Eight Soviet Industries

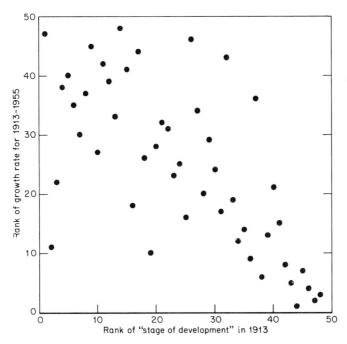

Source: Table 10.

destiny. A closer look at historical details is needed to resolve questions
of this sort.

Trends over the Pre-Plan and Plan Years

The Soviet period in Russia naturally divides itself into two major parts:
the years before the five year plans (the pre-Plan years)[11] and the Plan
years themselves. The point of division is roughly 1928, since the First
Five Year Plan began in October 1928. It should be understood that
this is not a simple division between a market economy, on the one hand,
and a centrally directed economy, on the other. The pre-Plan years

[11] For many purposes, it is also useful to divide the pre-Plan years into the years up to
1921 (War Communism) and the following years (the New Economic Policy). Unfortunately, the output series for our sample of seventy products are not sufficiently
continuous to analyze these periods separately. For a discussion of the difference in
growth, see Chapter 7.

TABLE 11
GROWTH TRENDS FOR FIXED SAMPLE[a] OF SOVIET INDUSTRIES,
1913–1928 AND 1928–1955

	Average Annual Growth Rate[b] (per cent)		Rank of Growth Rate	
	1913–1928	1928–1955	1913–1928	1928–1955
Bicycles	5.4	23.0	12	1
Lead	2.9	20.1	18	2
Motor vehicle tires	10.4	19.4	4	3
Steam turbines	12.8	19.2	2	4
Zinc	−1.8	19.0	58	5
Diesel engines	0.7	18.7	35	6
Mineral fertilizer	4.8	17.1	14	7
Machine tools	1.9	16.3	26	8
Power transformers	10.0	15.5	6	9
Rayon and mixed fabrics	−4.5	14.7	63	10
Asbestos shingles	10.2	14.5	5	11
Electric power	6.5	13.9	8	12
Natural gas	17.0	13.4	1	13
Roll roofing	5.3	12.9	13	14
Canned food	1.9	12.8	28	15
Clocks and watches	2.1	11.9	25	16
Macaroni	3.1	11.8	17	17
Sulfuric acid	3.8	11.2	15	18
Silk fabrics	−16.4	11.3	69	19
Sausages	0.4	10.4	38	20
Copper	−0.2	9.8	46	21
Construction gypsum	−5.2	9.7	67	22
Cement	1.3	9.7	32	23
Construction lime	0.2	9.6	41	24
Iron ore	−2.7	9.5	59	25
Coal	1.3	9.3	31	26
Steel ingots	0.0	9.2	43	27
Steam boilers	10.7	9.1	3	28
Coke	−0.3	9.1	47	29
Rolled steel	−0.4	9.0	49	30
Pig iron	−1.7	9.0	57	31
Caustic soda	0.4	8.7	37	32
Peat	7.9	8.7	7	33
Rails	−3.2	7.7	62	34
Synthetic dyes	6.0	7.6	9	35
Soda ash	2.1	7.2	24	36
Paper	2.5	7.2	21	37
Red bricks	−1.6	7.2	56	38
Crude petroleum	1.5	6.9	30	39
Lumber	0.0	6.7	44	40
Sewing machines	0.3	6.6	39	41
Butter	−1.6	6.6	55	42
Crude alcohol	−4.5	6.5	64	43
Beer	−4.7	5.9	65	44
Railroad passengers cars	−6.5	5.8	68	45
Railroad freight cars	−1.4	5.6	52	46
Looms	−1.4	5.6	53	47
Cigarettes	5.5	5.3	11	48
Rubber footwear	1.8	4.9	29	49

TABLE 11 (concluded)

	Average Annual Growth Rate[b] (per cent)		Rank of Growth Rate	
	1913–1928	1928–1955	1913–1928	1928–1955
Red lead	5.6	4.8	10	50
Industrial timber	−1.5	4.8	54	51
Meat slaughtering	−2.8	4.5	61	52
Fish catch	−1.3	4.5	51	53
Soap	2.4	4.1	23	54
Window glass	2.5	4.0	22	55
Boots and shoes	3.7	3.7	48	56
Raw sugar consumption	−0.3	3.7	16	57
Salt	1.2	3.4	33	58
Starch and syrup	−2.7	3.3	60	59
Matches	2.6	3.3	19	60
Cotton fabrics	0.2	3.0	40	61
Woolen and worsted fabrics	0.7	2.9	34	62
Vodka	−5.0	2.8	66	63
Vegetable oil	1.9	2.4	27	64
Linen fabrics	2.5	2.1	20	65
Felt footwear	−0.2	1.7	45	66
Steam locomotives	0.0	1.2	42	67
Flour	−1.0	1.1	50	68
Low-grade tobacco	0.6	−1.7	36	69
Median	0.7	7.6		
1st quartile	3.0	11.4		
3rd quartile	−1.4	4.5		

SOURCE: Table B-2.

[a] The sample covers sixty-nine industries here because output of roofing tiles around 1928 is not known.

[b] See Table 8, note a.

were characterized by centralized governmental ownership and control of a large segment of industry, though there was also a significant area of (controlled) private enterprise. The comprehensive economic plan, covering all economic activities more or less systematically, is the feature distinguishing the later period.

There is a marked difference in the patterns of industrial growth for the two sets of years (see Table 11 and Charts 7 and 8). More than a third of the industries in our fixed sample, accounting for almost a half of the sample's 1928 value added,[12] showed declines in output over the pre-Plan years, in one case (silk fabrics) by almost 17 per cent a year. The median growth rate is 0.7 per cent a year when based on both number

[12] One industry (roofing tiles) is omitted from all analyses for lack of 1928 output data, and two more (sausages and clocks and watches) are omitted from the analysis involving value added for lack of those data.

CHART 7
Frequency Distributions of Growth Rates for Fixed Sample of Soviet Industries, by Number of Industries: 1913–1928 and 1928–1955

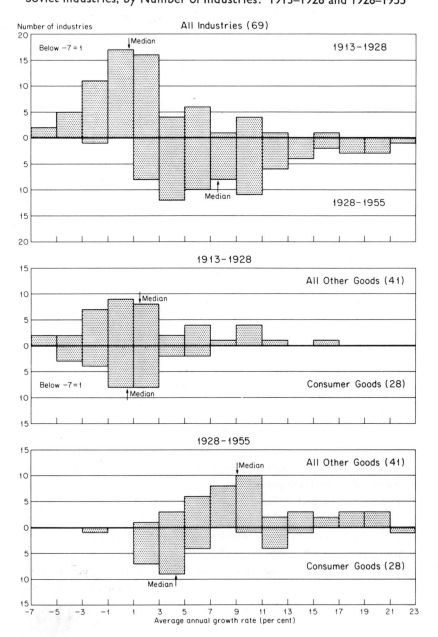

Source: Table 11.

CHART 8
Frequency Distributions of Growth Rates for Fixed Sample of Soviet Industries, by 1928 Value Added: 1913–1928 and 1928–1955

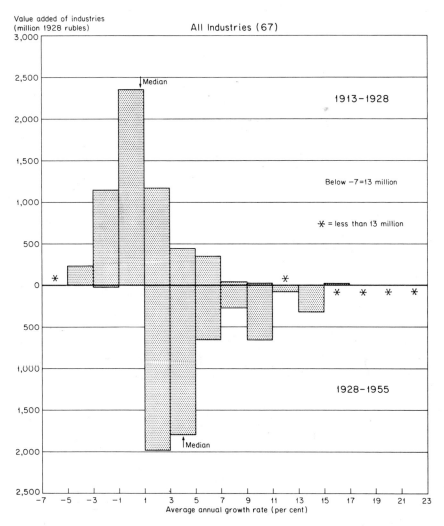

CHART 8 (concluded)

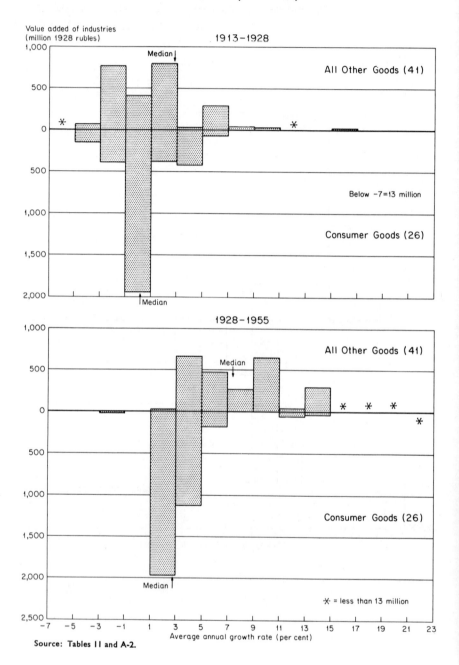

Source: Tables 11 and A-2.

and value added of industries, and it occurs within the primary concentration of growth rates, with a rather smooth tapering off in both directions. There is little difference between the medians for consumer and other goods. Over this period, population increased by 0.5 per cent a year, so that per capita growth rates are about 0.5 percentage points smaller than given.

If generalizations of this sort are warranted at all, it may be said that the pre-Plan years represent a period of almost no growth in the aggregate. This generally poor performance is not surprising for a country experiencing a losing war, a radical economic and social revolution, and violent civil strife over about half the fifteen years under review. Moreover, the remaining half could hardly be counted as normal times in the ordinary sense of the term.

To the extent that our sample of data can be believed and generalized, industrial output rose swiftly in the Plan years—making up, it would seem, for lost time. The median growth rate is 7.6 per cent a year when based on the number of industries and 4.0 per cent when based on the value added of industries. Each frequency distribution of growth rates for the Plan years occupies a higher region of growth than its counterpart for the pre-Plan years. Growth rates for consumer goods are generally much lower than those for all other goods. This, taken together with the similarity in distributions of growth rates for the two categories during the pre-Plan years, makes it clear that the pronounced divergence in growth between consumer and other goods is a phenomenon of the Plan years alone.

The difference in pace and pattern of growth in the two periods is rather sharply revealed in the median annual growth rates derived from the frequency distributions just discussed and summarized below:[13]

Distribution by

	Number of Industries		Value Added of Industries	
	1913–1928	1928–1955	1913–1928	1928–1955
All industries	0.7	7.6	0.7	4.0
Consumer goods	0.4	2.3	0.2	2.7
All other goods	1.5	9.1	0.8	7.4

[13] In assessing the significance of differences in annual growth rates, they should be compared with each other in the form of annual relatives (see footnote 2 above). For example, the annual relatives for consumer and other goods would be 1.004 and 1.015 in the first column and 1.023 and 1.091 in the second. From this formulation, it is apparent that the divergence between the two growth rates is relatively larger in the second than in the first column.

Study of changes in growth rates, industry by industry, conveys the same impression of a markedly faster pace of growth in the Plan than in the pre-Plan years. For sixty-three out of sixty-nine industries, the growth rate rose from one period to the next. The six exceptions are natural gas,

CHART 9

Scatter Diagram of Relation Between Ranks of Growth Rates for
1928–1955 and 1913–1928, Fixed Sample of Soviet Industries

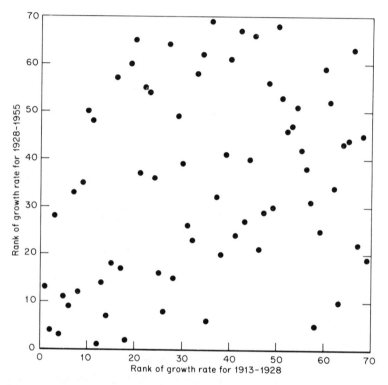

Source: Table II.

steam boilers, cigarettes, red lead, boots and shoes, and linen fabrics. There seems to be little relation between the structures of growth in the two periods (see Chart 9).[14]

When growth rates are adjusted for population changes, the differences between the two periods are somewhat narrowed, since population has grown at the annual rate of 1.1 per cent during the Plan years as compared

[14] The coefficient of rank correlation of growth rates is 0.313, which is significant at slightly less than the 1 per cent level.

with 0.5 per cent during the pre-Plan years. This means, for example, that the middle half (based on number of industries) of growth rates on a per capita basis ranges from about −1.9 to about 2.7 per cent for the pre-Plan years, and about 3.0 to about 11.1 per cent for the Plan years.

CHART 10

Scatter Diagram of Relation Between Ranks of Growth Rate for 1928–1955 and "Stage of Development" in 1928, Forty-Eight Soviet Industries

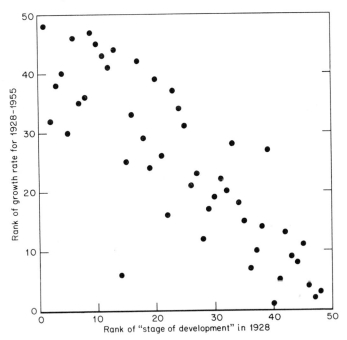

Source: Table 12.

Finally, we may note that there is a strong inverse relation between the rate of growth during the Plan years and the "stage of development" at the beginning of those years (see Table 12 and Chart 10).[15] This relation is even more pronounced than the one already described for the Soviet period as a whole, thereby supporting the conjecture that this relation is at least in part the result of planned design. This seems all the more plausible because the pattern of growth during the Plan years is, as already

[15] The coefficient of rank correlation is −0.803, which is significant at the 0.1 per cent level. Recall that the coefficient of rank correlation between growth rates for 1913–1955 and the "stage of development" in 1913 is −0.685 (see footnote 10 above).

TABLE 12

RELATION BETWEEN GROWTH RATE FOR 1928–1955 AND
"STAGE OF DEVELOPMENT" IN 1928, FORTY-EIGHT SOVIET INDUSTRIES

	Rank According to	
	"Stage of Development," 1928[a]	Growth Rate, 1928–1955
Flour	1	48
Beer	2	32
Fish catch	3	38
Window glass	4	40
Sewing machines	5	30
Vegetable oils	6	46
Cigarettes	7	35
Rubber footwear	8	36
Steam locomotives	9	47
Woolen and worsted fabrics	10	45
Salt	11	43
Boots and shoes	12	41
Cotton fabrics	13	44
Rayon and mixed fabrics	14	6
Synthetic dyes	15	25
Railroad passenger cars	16	33
Raw sugar consumption	17	42
Lumber	18	29
Rails	19	24
Soap	20	39
Soda ash	21	26
Construction lime	22	16
Meat slaughtering	23	37
Railroad freight cars	24	34
Butter	25	31
Rolled steel	26	21
Caustic soda	27	23
Sausages	28	12
Iron ore	29	17
Steel ingots	30	19
Pig iron	31	22
Coke	32	20
Crude petroleum	33	28
Coal	34	18
Cement	35	15
Electric power	36	7
Sulfuric acid	37	10
Construction gypsum	38	14
Paper	39	27
Bicycles	40	1
Mineral fertilizer	41	5
Copper	42	13
Canned food	43	9
Natural gas	44	8
Silk fabrics	45	11
Zinc	46	4
Lead	47	2
Motor vehicle tires	48	3

SOURCE: Tables 11, B-2, and E-1.

[a] Measured by ratio of output in the Soviet Union to output in the United States, both as of 1928. For the United States, a nine-year average centered on 1928 has been used wherever possible. The ranking would not differ significantly if 1928 data were used instead of the centered average.

pointed out, strikingly different from those in earlier periods, both Soviet and Tsarist. That is to say, one could argue without being contradicted by the available evidence that an important reason why growth has been more rapid for relatively less advanced than for relatively more advanced industries is because development has been planned that way.

The turbulence of pre-Plan years has already been mentioned. To complete the record, it must also be noted that the Plan years contained violent disturbances covering at least ten of the twenty-seven years: the collectivization of agriculture, the widespread political purges, and World War II. It is not easy to assess their net effect, since, with the exception of the war, they were basic to the establishment of a system of rigid central control. The war itself had a net depressive effect, though even here there are compensatory factors that should not be overlooked, as we shall discuss later (in Chapter 7). The importance of matters such as these depends on the uses to be made of the various indicators of growth gathered together here. This issue has been commented on in our introductory chapter and will be reviewed again later.

Retardation in Growth

It has been widely observed and well documented that individual industries in an economy tend to slow down in growth as they get older and larger, a phenomenon that goes by the name "retardation in growth."[16] We turn now to see whether this phenomenon also characterizes the Soviet economy.

Some pertinent evidence is summarized in Table 13. For every pair

TABLE 13

MOVEMENTS IN GROWTH RATES FOR INDIVIDUAL SOVIET INDUSTRIES,
VARIOUS PERIODS

| | Number of Industries | | |
	Declines in Growth Rate	Rises in Growth Rate	Total
A. 1870–1913 to 1913–1955	19	4	23
B. 1928–1940 to 1940–1955	60	10	70
C. 1928–1937 to 1950–1955	46	24	70
Both A and B	19	0	23[a]
Both A and C	12	0	23[a]

SOURCE: Tables 9 and B-2.

[a] Industries unaccounted for showed a decline in one pair of periods and a rise in the other.

[16] See Simon Kuznets, *Secular Movements in Production and Prices*, New York, 1930, Chapters I–III, and A. F. Burns, *Production Trends in the United States since 1870*, New York, NBER, 1934, pp. 96 ff.

of periods compared, the number of industries showing a decline in growth rate exceeds by a significant margin those showing a rise. The smallest discrepancy occurs in comparing the periods 1928–1937 and 1950–1955. Interestingly, only consumer goods, the slowest-growing industrial sector, show more rises than declines over that pair of periods (see Table 14).

TABLE 14

MOVEMENTS IN GROWTH RATES FOR FIXED SAMPLE OF SOVIET INDUSTRIES, BY INDUSTRIAL GROUP: 1928–1940 TO 1940–1955 AND 1928–1937 TO 1950–1955

	Declines in Growth Rate	*Number of Industries* Rises in Growth Rate	Total
		1928–1940 to 1940–1955	
Metals	7	0	7
Fuel and energy	6	0	6
Chemicals	9	0	9
Construction materials	10	1	11
Machinery	7	2	9
Consumer goods	21	7	28
Total	60	10	70
		1928–1937 to 1950–1955	
Metals	7	0	7
Fuel and energy	5	1	6
Chemicals	7	2	9
Construction materials	8	3	11
Machinery	6	3	9
Consumer goods	13	15	28
Total	46	24	70

SOURCE: See Table B-2.

For twenty-three industries, there are output data spanning both the Tsarist and Soviet periods. Of these, nineteen showed a retardation in growth both from 1870–1913 to 1913–1955 and from 1928–1940 to 1940–1955; twelve showed a retardation both from 1870–1913 to 1913–1955 and from 1928–1937 to 1950–1955. None of these twenty-three industries showed an acceleration in growth throughout both pairs of periods in either of the two comparisons made.

Concluding Remarks

Analysis of growth trends in samples of industries has revealed certain structural characteristics of Soviet industrial growth, and in doing so has set the stage for more refined analysis. It has also provided some tentative generalizations about the pace of over-all industrial growth. In the next chapter we turn to more complex measures of over-all growth and consider how they may be constructed and what problems are encountered in constructing them.

CHAPTER 5

Aggregative Growth Trends: Measurement

I⊤ HAS become conventional to summarize industrial growth in the form of an index number, which tells how large production is in any year relative to some base year. By reducing all directions of growth down to a single dimension, an index number obviously serves as a synthetic measure that cannot describe much of what has happened. It amounts to the same thing as measuring one's size by combining together height and weight: the resulting measure would reflect the influence of both fatness and tallness, but it would not reveal how fat or how tall one had become. At the same time, the measure of size could be made to depend more or less on fatness or on tallness by varying the way in which the two were combined together—by changing the factors by which each was multiplied before being added together.

The first principle of index number theory is this: no complex process of growth or change can be uniquely described by a single number. There are many ways of making an index number in order to describe a specific case of growth, and no one of these is inherently better than all the others. There are, of course, always better and worse ways of making index numbers intended for specific purposes, but it is a waste of time all the same to search for the one and only perfect measure, irrespective of purpose.

Having said this much, we must hasten to add that we cannot escape relying on index numbers in one form or another. Every seemingly simple datum is, when analyzed, an index number. The only question is how far we go in aggregation and how careful we are in using the aggregates we create.

The Index Number Problem

The "index number problem" has been thoroughly discussed in the technical literature, and it would be presumptuous and out of place to try to duplicate that discussion here.[1] It may prove useful, however, to summarize the most important issues very briefly before moving on to the matters at hand.

---

[1] This section is based on the more technical argument in my article, "On Measuring Economic Growth," *Journal of Political Economy* (February 1957, 51–63), where a selected list of pertinent literature is cited. Practical issues in making production indexes are discussed by Solomon Fabricant in *The Output of Manufacturing Industries, 1899–1937* (New York, NBER, 1940, pp. 325–375), and by C. F. Carter, W. B. Reddaway, and R. Stone in *The Measurement of Production Movements* (London, 1947).

A production index is essentially a synthetic measure that translates diverse growth rates for many different products into the single hypothetical rate that presumably would have obtained if, in fact, all products had grown at the same rate. The index tries to answer the question: How much would a standard basket of goods have grown if all the outputs in that basket had remained in the same ratio to each other instead of changing as they did? For example, we may suppose that in one year there are 100 swords and 200 plowshares produced, and in a second year 300 swords and 400 plowshares. How much has aggregate production of both swords and plowshares grown? An answer can be found if the second basket can somehow be turned into a multiple of the first, and this requires that we imagine what would have happened if the ratio of swords to plowshares had remained at 1 to 2 instead of rising to 3 to 4. The ratio has risen because production of swords has grown more percentagewise than production of plowshares. Some of the swords produced in the second year must be conceptually "beaten" into the plowshares that could have been produced in their place if production of both had grown by the same percentage—which is to say, if the ratio of swords to plowshares had remained at 1 to 2. The question then becomes one of determining the number of plowshares that could be produced in place of each forgone sword, given the productive capacity of the economy. That number is defined by the (marginal) cost of producing a sword relative to the (marginal) cost of producing a plowshare. But for which year are relative (or opportunity) costs to be chosen: the first, the second, or some other? Here enters the "weighting problem."

Opportunity costs of production depend on the product mix, the resource mix, and technological conditions. Although the first two factors may be important, we shall ignore them in this elementary discussion.[2] Opportunity costs will tend to fall for those industries experiencing the most rapid technological progress or benefiting most from increased specialization as the economy grows. A "weighting problem" is likely to arise if these same industries also tend to experience either the most or the least rapid growth in output. Such a relation does tend to exist: the industries with the most rapid technological advance and the greatest economies of scale are also most likely to have the most rapid rates of growth in output. Hence a production index constructed with "late-year" costs as weights will typically show a slower percentage rise in aggregate

[2] These and other complications are taken into account in the article referred to in the preceding note.

output than an index constructed with "early-year" costs as weights. This is illustrated in Table 15 through example *A*.

TABLE 15
CONSTRUCTION OF HYPOTHETICAL PRODUCTION INDEXES

| | Example A | | Example B | |
	Year One	Year Two	Year One	Year Two
Output of swords	100	300	200	550
Output of plowshares	200	400	100	275
Unit cost of swords	$1	$1	$1	$1
Unit cost of plowshares	$1	$2	$1	$2
Aggregate output				
Year-one weights	$300	$700	$300	$825
Year-two weights	$500	$1100	$400	$1100
Production index				
Year-one weights	100	233	100	275
Year-two weights	100	220	100	275

This would seem to end the matter: a production index is likely to be higher or lower depending on the weights used.[3] But there is more to the problem than this. Suppose, for instance, that in our hypothetical example a different basket of goods had been produced in the first year —say, 200 swords instead of 100, and 100 plowshares instead of 200. This would apparently have been possible with the productive capacity in the first year, since a sword costs the same to produce as a plowshare. Suppose further that both swords and plowshares were to grow at the same percentage rate so that there would be no "weighting problem." It would then be possible to produce 550 swords and 275 plowshares in the second year, a basket of goods that is equivalent to the 300 swords and 400 plowshares in example *A*: 125 plowshares have been exchanged for 250 swords, as permitted by the assumed opportunity costs in the second year. We now observe (example *B*) that the production index would be higher than either of the indexes previously calculated. Why? The answer lies in the fact that in both years the good with declining relative costs (swords) accounts for a larger fraction of aggregate output in example *B* than in example *A*. The index number is therefore seen to depend on the actual productive structure in an economy, or, put another way, on the actual baskets of goods produced.

[3] Only the relative weights are pertinent in determining index numbers. If all unit costs in Table 15 were doubled or halved, the production indexes would not be affected.

There is another sense in which the index number depends on the actual baskets of goods produced, and that has to do with radical changes in the directions of growth. To take an extreme example, let us suppose that in year two the production of swords is discontinued altogether and that a new product, butter, comes to be produced instead. How are we to measure the growth in production? We are faced with metamorphosis rather than growth. It is as if we tried to measure how much a caterpillar grows when it turns into a butterfly. If we use year-one weights, we can measure the decrease in production attributable to loss of swords; if we use year-two weights, we can measure the increase attributable to the addition of butter. But the increase and decrease are not directly comparable because butter has been weighted at a "new" cost, which will probably reflect its abnormally high initial cost of production, whereas swords have been weighted at an "old" cost, which may be either higher or lower than the "new" cost would have been (it is lower in our hypothetical example). Although the technical difficulties are less acute, a similar indeterminateness of index numbers exists if the replacement of one good by another is substantial though not complete, or if there are so-called qualitative changes in existing products. The technical problem discussed here is most troublesome in product areas like machinery, where changes in products occur swiftly in response to changing technology and other economic conditions.

There are no fully satisfactory solutions to the problems we have raised. In practice, we pay considerable attention to the narrow weighting problem because we can observe the effect on index numbers of using different available systems of weights. We cannot observe the effects of industrial structure or directions of growth, because we do not know what alternative structures or directions might have existed or exactly how they would have affected the index number. We are, on the other hand, aware of the enormous measurement problems created when there are radical changes in industrial development, as in the case of industrial mobilization in the United States during World War II.[4] But we cannot calculate alternative index numbers for alternative paths of expansion, as we can for alternative weighting systems.

The inability to "measure" effects of alternative paths of expansion should not be taken to mean that this factor has less effect on production indexes than the system of weights one chooses to use. The question of paths of expansion may be crucial when growth rates in two different

[4] See Geoffrey Moore, *Production of Industrial Materials in World Wars I and II*, New York, NBER, Occasional Paper 18, 1944.

economies are being compared. There is no neutral measure of growth in productive capacity with the same meaning for every economy under all conditions. One economy may, for example, be undergoing a radical metamorphosis while the other is essentially growing in size. Or one economy may be placing heavier emphasis than the other on products whose opportunity costs are falling. And so on. In comparing economies, one must somehow standardize the dimensions in which growth is being measured; the way this should be done will depend on the problems at hand. The job requires patience, judgment, and willingness to work with more than one indicator of growth. These issues are of some importance in comparing the industrial growth of the Soviet Union and the United States, and we shall have more to say about them at a later point.

Up to this point, the problems of constructing index numbers have been discussed in terms of idealized variables. There are, of course, great difficulties encountered in moving to their empirical counterparts: statistics on output and costs will, under the best of conditions, fall far short of what might be ideally desired. It does not need repeating here that Soviet statistics, in turn, fall far short of the best of conditions. We have commented in some detail on the deficiencies of data on output, and it may now be added that the deficiencies are even graver in the case of data on prices and costs, in particular because Soviet prices bear a more or less haphazard relation to costs of production. These and other practical considerations will be taken up in the more concrete discussion that follows.

General Description of Our Indexes[5]

In constructing the indexes for this study, we have necessarily been guided by the peculiarities of Soviet industrial growth and the data available for use. We have considered it advisable to construct several different types of indexes (see Tables 16 and 17), rather than to concentrate on only one. These indexes differ in both weighting systems and product coverage, so that the influence of these factors may be at least partially revealed.

There are three primary variants of product coverage, designed to reflect productive activity within industry[5a] at an intermediate stage of fabrication, at the final stages of industrial processing, and over "all" stages of fabrication and processing. These coverages will be referred to as

---

[5] The discussion in this and succeeding sections is supplemented in additional detail by technical note 3 of Appendix A.

[5a] Industry includes manufacturing, mining, logging, fishing, and generating of electricity.

TABLE 16

Indexes of Industrial Production: Soviet Union, Benchmark Years, 1913–1955

	Industrial Materials				Finished Civilian Products			All Civilian Products		
	1913 Weights	1928 Weights	1955 Weights	Moving Weights	1928 Weights	1955 Weights	Moving Weights	1928 Weights	1955 Weights	Moving Weights
Index (1913 = 100)										
1913	100	100	100	100	100	100	100	100	100	100
1928	103	100	99	102	99	92	99	102	107	102
1932	141	131	130	133	126	117	126	144	145	144
1937	249	229	211	233	239	182	239	268	238	268
1940	276	254	232	257	224	173	226	289	231	274
1945	161	148	142	157	92	77	100	167	104	123
1950	364	338	300	331	337	226	295	427	335	397
1955	588	550	463	511	519	353	460	697	488	577
Link Relative (Initial Year of Period = 100)										
1913–1928	103	100	99	102	99	92	99	102	107	102
1928–1932	136	131	131	131	128	127	128	140	136	140
1932–1937	177	175	162	175	189	156	189	186	164	186
1937–1940	111	111	110	110	94	95	94	108	97	102
1940–1945	58	58	61	51	41	44	44	58	45	45
1945–1950	226	229	210	210	367	295	295	256	323	323
1950–1955	162	163	154	154	154	156	156	163	145	145
1928–1955	569	548	468	502	524	382	465	681	457	563

Source: Appendix D. Military products and miscellaneous machinery are excluded. Current territory except 1913, which covers interwar Soviet territory.

TABLE 17

INDEXES OF PRODUCTION FOR INDUSTRIAL GROUPS: SOVIET UNION, BENCHMARK YEARS, 1913–1955

| | Total | | | INTERMEDIATE INDUSTRIAL PRODUCTS | | | | | |
| | | | | Ferrous Metals | | | Nonferrous Metals | | |
	1928 Weights	1955 Weights	Moving Weights	1928 Weights	1955 Weights	Moving Weights	1928 Weights	1955 Weights	Moving Weights
				INDEX (1913 = 100)					
1913	100	100	100	100	100	100	100	100	100
1928	108	95	108	88	87	88	97	99	97
1932	199	161	199	134	136	134	197	217	197
1937	379	257	379	365	'362	365	567	617	567
1940	434	270	417	375	372	375	844	924	847
1945	302	150	232	236	233	235	617	677	621
1950	682	396	612	541	530	534	1,262	1,407	1,290
1955	1,147	610	942	916	900	907	2,267	2,624	2,405
				LINK RELATIVE (INITIAL YEAR OF PERIOD = 100)					
1913–1928	108	95	108	88	87	88	97	99	97
1928–1932	184	170	184	153	157	153	203	220	203
1932–1937	190	160	190	272	267	272	287	285	287
1937–1940	115	105	110	103	103	103	149	150	149
1940–1945	70	56	56	63	63	63	73	73	73
1945–1950	226	263	263	229	228	228	205	208	208
1950–1955	168	154	154	169	170	170	180	187	187
1928–1955	1,058	644	872	1,046	1,040	1,031	2,336	2,665	2,479

TABLE 17 (continued)

INTERMEDIATE INDUSTRIAL PRODUCTS

	Fuel and Electricity			Chemicals			Construction Materials		
	1928 Weights	1955 Weights	Moving Weights	1928 Weights	1955 Weights	Moving Weights	1928 Weights	1955 Weights	Moving Weights
INDEX (1913 = 100)									
1913	100	100	100	100	100	100	100	100	100
1928	150	128	150	146	139	146	88	86	88
1932	323	251	323	270	253	270	142	142	142
1937	667	483	667	571	465	571	193	189	193
1940	854	611	849	584	449	565	188	187	189
1945	711	491	682	247	169	213	89	88	89
1950	1,404	909	1,263	1,007	780	981	268	261	264
1955	2,457	1,435	1,994	1,523	1,127	1,418	411	392	396
LINK RELATIVE (INITIAL YEAR OF PERIOD = 100)									
1913–1928	150	128	150	146	139	146	88	86	88
1928–1932	215	196	215	185	182	185	162	164	162
1932–1937	207	193	207	212	184	212	136	134	139
1937–1940	128	127	127	102	97	99	97	99	98
1940–1945	83	80	80	42	38	38	47	47	47
1945–1950	198	185	185	408	463	463	303	296	296
1950–1955	175	158	158	151	144	144	153	150	150
1928–1955	1,634	1,121	1,329	1,044	810	971	470	455	450

(continued)

TABLE 17 (continued)

CIVILIAN MACHINERY AND EQUIPMENT

	Total			Transportation Equipment			Agricultural Machinery		
	1928 Weights	1955 Weights	Moving Weights	1928 Weights	1955 Weights	Moving Weights	1928 Weights	1955 Weights	Moving Weights
INDEX (1913 = 100)									
1913	100	100	100	100	100	100	100	100	100
1928	143	129	143	90	81	90	251	227	251
1932	426	239	426	385	194	385	510	332	510
1937	1,624	499	1,624	2,155	490	2,155	546	516	546
1940	1,178	338	1,140	1,621	402	1,692	279	207	247
1945	500	79	265	715	102	430	65	30	36
1950	2,886	783	2,637	3,810	773	3,250	1,012	804	959
1955	3,475	889	2,994	4,507	820	3,447	1,382	1,032	1,231
LINK RELATIVE (INITIAL YEAR OF PERIOD = 100)									
1913–1928	143	129	143	90	81	90	251	227	251
1928–1932	299	185	299	430	238	430	203	146	203
1932–1937	381	209	381	560	253	560	107	155	107
1937–1940	73	68	70	75	82	79	51	40	45
1940–1945	42	23	23	44	25	25	23	15	15
1945–1950	577	994	994	533	756	756	1,553	2,648	2,648
1950–1955	120	114	114	118	106	106	136	128	128
1928–1955	2,438	689	2,094	5,030	1,006	3,830	551	455	490

TABLE 17 (concluded)

CONSUMER GOODS

	Total			Food and Allied Products			Textiles and Allied Products			Consumer Durables		
	1928 Weights	1955 Weights	Moving Weights	1928 Weights	1955 Weights	Moving Weights	1928 Weights	1955 Weights	Moving Weights	1928 Weights	1955 Weights	Moving Weights
	INDEX (1913 = 100)											
1913	100	100	100	100	100	100	100	100	100	100	100	100
1928	97	110	97	84	82	84	113	132	113	158	122	158
1932	100	114	100	95	97	95	105	123	105	704	327	704
1937	157	168	157	153	139	153	151	182	151	3,652	672	3,652
1940	171	182	171	162	137	156	174	212	175	2,223	436	2,301
1945	72	78	73	73	72	82	71	83	69	352	52	274
1950	194	196	184	183	148	169	187	217	179	6,152	1,093	5,768
1955	331	316	297	279	227	258	337	333	275	16,704	3,098	16,350
	LINK RELATIVE (INITIAL YEAR OF PERIOD = 100)											
1913–1928	97	110	97	84	82	84	113	132	113	158	122	158
1928–1932	103	103	103	113	118	113	93	93	93	446	268	446
1932–1937	157	148	157	161	143	161	144	148	144	519	206	516
1937–1940	109	108	109	106	99	102	115	117	116	61	65	63
1940–1945	42	43	43	45	53	53	41	39	39	16	12	12
1945–1950	269	252	252	252	205	205	264	261	261	1,747	2,119	2,119
1950–1955	171	161	161	152	154	154	180	154	154	272	283	283
1928–1955	340	287	306	331	277	307	298	252	243	10,574	2,537	10,348

SOURCE: Appendix D. These indexes are components of the index for all civilian industrial products. Current territory except 1913, which covers interwar Soviet territory.

industrial materials, finished civilian products, and all civilian products. The specific products covered (see Tables D-10 and D-11 in Appendix D) and weights used have, of course, been delimited by availability of data.

The index for industrial materials is somewhat misnamed, since it covers both intermediate products (as metals, fuels, construction materials, and so on) and "basic" nondurable consumer goods (as flour, butter, fabrics, and so on). Its construction is patterned after the production index designed by Geoffrey H. Moore in his well-known study of industrial production during wartime in the United States.[6] Since this index covers staple commodities that change in nature only very slowly, its movements are not seriously disturbed by radical changes in the mix of more highly fabricated products.

The index for finished civilian products measures the output of the "final" products of industry, so to speak. It covers transportation and agricultural equipment, construction materials, and both durable and nondurable consumer goods. It does not cover military end items or the more heterogeneous types of machinery. Even with these exceptions, the list of "final" products is by no means exhaustive, and some of the products included (as construction materials) are consumed in part within industry. The coverage it attempts to make is at best only reasonably approximated. Finally, it should be noted that various stages of fabrication are represented, up to the most advanced.

The index for all civilian products is designed to give a comprehensive coverage of industry, including products of all kinds for which reasonably continuous output data and needed weight factors are available. As in the case of the index for finished civilian products, military end items and heterogeneous categories of machinery are not included in the basic indexes. They have, however, been included in derivative indexes that will be explained in a later section.

The weighting systems used are in many fundamental respects the same, but they, too, have been tailored to the needs of the data and the scope of each index. For industrial materials, the output of each product has been weighted by its unit value as of a weight-base year. Each unit value was calculated to exclude, through several estimative procedures, the cost of nonindustrial materials consumed in fabricating the product. This adjustment makes the unit weights approximate the costs of purely industrial activities, though in some cases an unknown degree of double counting remains because some of the products in the index are used

[6] Cited in footnote 4 above.

in producing others. That is to say, the net value weights for some products include values already counted for other products. It was not feasible to eliminate this double counting, which is probably not serious enough to make the resulting index significantly different from what it would have been if more accurate weights had been used. In any case, we followed the procedure originally used by Geoffrey Moore in his production index for industrial materials in the United States.

In order to study the effect of different sets of weights, several weight-base years were used, and unit weights were taken from industry in the United States as well as in the Soviet Union. Three weight bases were used for the Soviet Union: 1913, 1928, and 1955; four were used for the United States: 1914, 1929, 1939, and 1954 (see Table 21). A moving-weight index (see Table 16) was also formed by chaining together four links taken from the indexes with Soviet weights: for 1913–1928, the geometric average of indexes with 1913 and 1928 weights; for 1928–1937, the index with 1928 weights; for 1937–1940, the geometric average of indexes with 1928 and 1955 weights; and for 1940–1955, the index with 1955 weights.

The unit weights used for finished civilian products were derived in the same way as those used for industrial materials. Indexes were constructed with 1928 and 1955 weights, and these were combined into a moving-weight index in the manner already discussed, except that the link for 1913–1928 was taken as the index with 1928 weights. Weights for the United States or for an earlier year were not used because the matching of products in the machinery sector would have been arbitrary.

For all civilian products, we used a composite system of Soviet weights similar to that used in making comprehensive production indexes in Western countries. Outputs of products within industrial groups were combined together by unit weights derived in the manner described above. Outputs of industrial groups, which were as narrowly defined as the needed weights permitted, were then combined by value added for the 1928 weight base, and by employment for the 1955 weight base.[7] A moving-weight index was constructed in the same manner as for finished civilian products.

[7] Output of each product may be expressed in any convenient unit of measure. If output is expressed as an index number (as for a group of products), the unit of measure is the volume of output—perhaps a weighted aggregate—in the comparison-base year. A weight must, of course, be applicable to the unit of measure for the product or group of products that it is attached to, and all weights must be expressed in the same unit of measure (as dollars). This unit of measure, too, may be arbitrarily chosen since only relative weights matter. For example, each weight may be expressed as a percentage of some (any) number.

Details on Weights and Weighting Systems

DERIVATION

Soviet weights are derived from official statistics covering both large- and small-scale industry. They are listed and explained in Tables D-8 and D-9 of Appendix D. For 1928, the basic data have been derived primarily from censuses and annual surveys of industry covering 1926/27, 1927/28, and 1928/29. Since the annual survey for 1927/28 was limited in its industrial coverage and in the types of data published, it was necessary to make adjustments and additional estimates (discussed in Table C-2 of Appendix C) on the basis of statistics for the two adjoining years. Wherever possible, weights were derived as physical output (of a product or group of products) divided into the relevant value of output or value added. For a number of narrowly defined products, we had to compute weights from official price lists, often using medians or averages—wherever possible, weighted averages—of prices for even more narrowly defined products. Some weights were derived quite indirectly, on the basis of information for years rather distant from 1928 and such linking factors as were available. We consider these to be the least bad weights that can be devised but they are far from ideal. They apply to the following products: natural gas, ground natural phosphate, auto-mobiles, locomotives (steam, diesel, and electric), railroad freight cars, street and subway rail cars, paring plows, and phonographs.

The Soviet value weights for 1913 and 1955 are derived almost ex-clusively from official price lists. The prices for 1913 are those devised by Soviet statisticians during the early 1920's to be used in comparing postrevolutionary production with the prerevolutionary level, and as such they have been adjusted to apply to production within the interwar Soviet territory. Except for consumer goods, the prices for 1955 are taken primarily from price handbooks. The prices of consumer goods were derived from several sources and often indirectly. If only a retail price was available, it was reduced by 10 per cent to eliminate trading costs. In the absence of more detailed information, the cost of nonindus-trial materials was estimated in many cases to be the price times the ratio of cost of materials (including scheduled amortization of equipment) to total "cost" as defined in Soviet statistics, total "cost" being wages plus cost of materials. Since price includes profits and—in the case of consumer goods—turnover taxes, a fraction of these items equal to the cost ratio was also eliminated. In some cases (hard leather, soft leather, flour, vegetable oil, canned food, beer, cigarettes, and low-grade tobacco), the

120

cost ratio was taken for 1934, the closest date for which it was available. The special problems connected with the elimination of turnover taxes and profits are discussed in the next section. Aside from the products already mentioned, those with weights most indirectly derived for 1955 are petroleum, all types of mineral fertilizer, starch and syrup, and candy.

The 1955 employment weights used in the index for all cilivian products are based on the percentage distribution of production workers (*promyshlennye rabochie*) among industrial groups, the only such distribution so far published in official Soviet statistics. Production workers are presumably wage earners directly engaged in manufacturing and extractive activities. So-called auxiliary workers, salaried employees, and maintenance and overhead personnel are not counted as production workers. This is obviously a restricted definition of industrial employment, and the percentage distribution may not accord well with one for employment more satisfactorily defined.[8] Unfortunately, as beggars for statistics we cannot choose.

WEIGHTS AND COSTS OF PRODUCTION

As pointed out at the beginning of this chapter, relative weights used in most general-purpose production indexes are supposed to represent relative costs of production. In a highly developed market economy, it is taken for granted that market values—price, unit value added, and so on—approximate relevant costs.[9] This cannot be taken for granted in the Soviet system.

Now that discussion of the subject is no longer forbidden, there has been a growing volume of Soviet literature criticizing the failure of prices to reflect cost of production.[10] Since the critics are influenced by Marxist economic theory—or at least terminology—it is not always clear what they mean by "cost of production." However, there is no doubt from the examples they cite that many Soviet relative prices have no relation whatever to opportunity costs. This is particularly true of prices of consumer goods taken relatively to prices of most other things, because

[8] For 1933 and 1935, percentage distributions of production workers and engaged persons are compared in the notes to Table C-1 in Appendix C.

[9] For a dissenting view, see Joan Robinson, "Mr. Wiles' Rationality: A Comment," *Soviet Studies,* January 1956, pp. 269–273. She argues that prices do not always equal costs in a market economy, and therefore they are no more useful as a measure of cost than in a planned economy. In other words, black is not different from white because both are shades of gray.

[10] For a sample of the Soviet discussion of prices and costs, see *Current Digest of the Soviet Press,* IX, 14 and 34.

turnover taxes—usually at least equal to "costs" of production—apply to the former but not to the latter.[11] It is also true of many relations among prices not directly subject to turnover tax, because of the labyrinth of differential subsidies and taxes established over the years.

In a recent study, Professor Lynn Turgeon concludes that, for a group of sixteen intermediate industrial products, prices more closely approximated "costs" in 1927/28 and 1955 than in any intervening year for which data were available.[12] This much seems to favor our choice of weight bases. However, we must recognize that the Soviet measure of "cost" does not include any imputed return on capital. Nor does it include any subsidies given to, or exclude any special levies made on, the materials consumed by a product in question. Moreover, the "costs" of a product are computed on an average basis for all enterprises producing it, under conditions in which little effort is made to equalize the marginal cost among enterprises, even as cost is defined in the Soviet Union. Finally, Turgeon's study is based on a limited sample of a limited category of products; it does not cover the area of finished goods where discrepancies between cost and price are likely to be the greater.[13]

We have made adjustments to help correct the distortions imposed by excise and turnover taxes. For 1928, we have eliminated excise taxes, which were generally low, from all value data—except for the few possible cases in which the amount of tax may not have been published. For 1955, our procedure for eliminating the costs of nonindustrial materials (see the preceding section) amounts in effect to eliminating a fraction of turnover taxes and profits equal to the ratio of the cost of materials to total "cost" (i.e., combined wages and cost of materials).[14] The remaining turnover tax and profits—a fraction equal to the ratio of wages to total "costs"—is in effect treated as a return on capital and left within the adopted unit value. This procedure is obviously arbitrary, but it seems less bad than the alternatives available.

As a practical matter, the bulk of turnover taxes and profits was eliminated in this way. For a group of twenty-four consumer products, the smallest fraction eliminated was 64 per cent; the median fraction, 88 per

[11] Turnover tax rates have not been systematically published for recent years, but rates for the interwar period have been compiled by N. Jasny in *The Soviet Price System*, Stanford, 1951, pp. 164 ff, and F. Holzman in *Soviet Taxation: The Fiscal and Monetary Problems of a Planned Economy*, Cambridge, Mass., 1955, p. 151.

[12] Lynn Turgeon, "Cost-Price Relationships in Basic Industries during the Planning Era," *Soviet Studies*, October 1957, p. 157.

[13] *Ibid.*, p. 145.

[14] Turnover tax rates are known for salt, soap, and rubber footwear, so that the full amount of tax was eliminated in these cases.

cent.[15] If we might assume that the median turnover tax was about 60 per cent of the wholesale price, the median amount remaining after our adjustment would be about 7 per cent of the wholesale price.

All things considered, we may conclude that the Soviet weights for 1913 and 1928 are reasonable approximations to costs of production, in the latter year because the market still played a substantial role in the Soviet economy. The weights for 1955 are another matter. Within industrial groups composed of closely related industries (as ferrous metals, nonferrous metals, textiles, and so on), they may reflect opportunity costs reasonably well; between industrial groups, they may do so less well. It is even doubtful whether the use of employment as a weight factor for industrial groups improves the situation, not only because employment is merely an estimate of value added (on this, see more below), but also because there is little reason to presume that labor is economically allocated among industries.[16] Whether the weights reflect opportunity costs or not, the only way to find out the effect of a given set on production indexes is to use it and compare the result with those obtained from other sets. We shall present evidence of this sort below.

DIRECT AND IMPUTED WEIGHTS

A production index constructed from ideal data would require infinite detail in both product breakdown and weights. In practice, we have at our disposal only samples of both types of data, which may be more or less representative of the ideal information. Each output series is merely an index or indicator of the behavior of the many subseries included within it. Similarly, the weight attached to each series is a composite of many weights applying to the many subseries taken to be represented by the single indicator. The problem of matching weights and output series is the index number problem in miniature, so to speak. The difficulties here are usually discussed under the question of whether direct or imputed weights are to be used in constructing an index.

[15] The fractions eliminated were as follows (per cent):

Soap	100	Linen fabrics	91	Silk fabrics	80
Salt	100	Candy	90	Knitted goods	78
Rubber footwear	100	Sugar	90	Hosiery	78
Meat	96	Cotton fabrics	89	Canned food	78
Woolen fabrics	93	Vegetable oil	87	Beer	78
Vodka	93	Boots and shoes	87	Hard leather	75
Butter	92	Cigarettes	80	Soft leather	75
Flour	92	Tobacco	80	Matches	64

[16] See P. J. D. Wiles, "Are Adjusted Rubles Rational?" *Soviet Studies*, October 1955, especially pp. 145–148.

It is, of course, clear that the directness of a weight is a matter of degree. We are not in fact faced with a simple choice between direct and imputed weights, but rather with the choice of how the imputation is to be done. And in every case the choice must be made within the framework of available alternatives.

Let us illustrate the issues with a concrete example. We may consider the group of products included within "ferrous metals." Suppose we let this group be represented by three products: iron ore, steel ingots, and rolled steel products. Each of these products contains a large number of identifiable subproducts, and a weighted production index made up from the subproducts, if feasible, would not necessarily behave in the same way as the physical output of the composite indicator. That is to say, a weighted production index of all rolled steel products would not necessarily change percentagewise in the same way as output of all rolled products expressed in metric tons. It then follows that a production index for ferrous metals made up by weighting the three products (iron ore, steel ingots, and rolled steel products) may differ significantly from one made up by weighting all the subproducts. Moreover, there remains the question whether the production index for ferrous metals is to be considered as applying only to the products explicitly covered or also to other miscellaneous products not explicitly covered but generally classified in that category, a question that arises when a weight must be chosen for ferrous metals as a whole in order to construct a production index for all industry. Should the weight be a direct one—i.e., should it be restricted to the products explicitly covered by the production index? Or should it be an imputed one—i.e., should it extend over a group of products considered to be implicitly if not explicitly covered? These same questions could, of course, arise at any level, for "products" as well as "product groups." They are most serious in areas like machinery, which will be discussed separately below.

We have adhered to the rule of using direct weights wherever feasible. Table A-6 in Appendix A outlines the adjustments made in value added for 1928 to bring the weights in the index for all civilian products closer to a direct basis. This procedure amounts to making the production index apply rather strictly to the sector of productive activity actually encompassed by the data used. It applies to "all" industry only if one assumes that the residual of uncovered activity behaved in the aggregate the same as the total covered activity. Particularly in the face of deficient Soviet statistics, we have considered this to be more likely than that the uncovered activity in each separately defined industrial group behaved the same as the covered activity in that group alone. If the latter were considered more likely, the proper procedure would be to impute the full weight for an industrial group to the covered activity within it. We have avoided this kind of imputation wherever possible because it seems reasonable to presume that those products whose output has been published have generally shown a more rapid growth than the related products whose output has not been published—except where the latter have been directly connected with the military effort. Hence, in our opinion, the use of imputed weights introduces an upward bias into indexes of Soviet production.

One notable exception to our rule occurs in our index for all civilian products with 1955 weights. The breakdown of employment was available only for broad industrial groups, and it was impossible to determine the employment applying to our coverage alone. Employment in the printing industry and in other unspecified industries (4.2 per cent of the published total) was not included in our weights, and minor adjustments were made to make the Soviet categories correspond to ours (see Table D-9 in Appendix D). But there remains an unknown degree of imputation of weights to broad industrial groups. The effect on our production index must also remain unknown, though some evidence on the general adequacy of employment weights will be presented below.

We can illustrate the effect of replacing direct with imputed weights in our index for all civilian products with 1928 weights. As imputed weights, we use the total value added for product categories (except miscellaneous machinery) given in detail in Table C-2 of Appendix C and summarized for industrial groups in Table A-6 and the surrounding text of Appendix A. The resulting index compares as follows with the index using direct weights:

	Direct Weights	Imputed Weights	Ratio, Imputed to Direct
1913	100	100	1.00
1928	102	103	1.01
1937	268	284	1.06
1940	289	298	1.03
1955	697	754	1.08

Imputed weights therefore cause the index to rise somewhat more rapidly than direct weights, the greatest divergence applying to the period 1928–1937.[17]

[17] Similar examples of the effects of imputation on production indexes for the United States and the United Kingdom are given in Moore, *Production of Industrial Materials*, pp. 61 ff, and in C. F. Carter and M. Robson, "A Test of the Accuracy of a Production

GROSS AND NET WEIGHTS

The nature and purpose of a production index determine how "gross" or "net" weights should be. It would be misleading to lay down an ironclad rule that "value added" should always be used, because the important issue is what the "value added" is to be computed for. Here, again, the problems are best illustrated by concrete examples.

What weight factor should be applied to the output of steel ingots? This all depends on what that output is taken to represent. In our index for industrial materials, the output of steel ingots is taken to represent all productive activities devoted to making steel ingots that fall within the boundaries of industry, except what is counted elsewhere in the index. Hence the weight should be the price of steel ingots minus the cost (per unit of steel ingots) of nonindustrial ingredients and industrial ingredients treated elsewhere as components of the index. In practice, we have been able to eliminate the former but not the latter.

In the index for all civilian products, on the other hand, the output of steel ingots is taken to represent productive activity only at the last identifiable stage of fabricating ingots, activity at other stages being represented by other output series. In this case, the weight should be the price minus the cost of all ingredients produced elsewhere.[18]

Production indexes attributed to segments of industry will mean different things under these two approaches, and they are quite likely to show substantially different behavior. In the case of intermediate industrial products an index calculated by the method used for industrial materials differs markedly from one calculated by the method used for all civilian products (see Table 18). With 1928 weights, the latter rises much faster than the former between 1913 (or 1928) and 1955; with 1955 weights, much slower. The discrepancies between the two types of indexes cannot be attributed solely to differing weighting systems, since the scope of productive activity covered also differs. If each type of index were assumed to measure accurately what it is designed to measure, the discrepancies would have to be attributed to that difference in scope.

Index," *Journal of the American Statistical Association*, March 1956, 17–23. When elaborate data are available, as in U.S. censuses, refined imputations may be made. See, e.g., the coverage adjustment in Fabricant, *Manufacturing Industries*, pp. 362 ff.

[18] We have found it necessary in some cases to tailor the output series to the available weight instead of the reverse. For example, our series on vegetable oil covers total output including oil consumed in producing oleomargarine. Since we were unable to adjust our 1955 Soviet weights to eliminate double counting of the oil used in margarine, we constructed a new series on vegetable oil excluding the estimated consumption in oleomargarine. Similar adjustments were made for sulfuric acid and raw sugar.

TABLE 18

PRODUCTION OF INTERMEDIATE INDUSTRIAL PRODUCTS AS REPRESENTED
BY TWO DIFFERENT TYPES OF INDEXES: SOVIET UNION, SELECTED YEARS
(1913 = 100)

	1913	1928	1955
1928 weights			
Industrial materials index	100	106	880
All civilian products index	100	108	1,147
1955 weights			
Industrial materials index	100	101	804
All civilian products index	100	95	610

SOURCE: Appendix D.

We would then conclude that productive activity grew less rapidly through an intermediate stage of fabrication than it did through a more advanced stage when calculated in terms of 1928 opportunity costs, but more rapidly when calculated in terms of 1955 opportunity costs. This conclusion must, of course, be conjectural and question-begging since we have no way of determining whether each of the indexes being compared is "correct"—this is, in fact, the basic question we start and end with.

In short, there is no conclusive a priori or experimental test of the correctness of a weighting system. The best we can do is make sure that the method of selecting weights is reasonable for the purpose in view. Results of different approaches may then be compared, but no definitive rationalization of discrepancies is justified.

WEIGHT BASES

A production index may be constructed with a fixed or a moving weight base. The fixed base may be a single year or an average of two or more years. An index constructed with a moving weight base is simply formed by chaining together links, each constructed with a fixed base.

As we stated earlier, it has frequently been observed that, for rapidly growing economies, an industrial production index constructed with an early-year weight base rises significantly more rapidly than one constructed with a late-year weight base. Professor Alexander Gerschenkron has, in particular, called attention to this phenomenon.[19] He gives several

[19] Alexander Gerschenkron, *A Dollar Index of Soviet Machinery Output, 1927–28 to 1937*, RAND Corporation, Santa Monica, 1951, pp. 47–58. See also *Census of U.S. Manufactures, 1954, Indexes of Production*, Washington, 1958, pp. 20 ff, where it is also argued (pp. 24 ff) that this is, at least in part, a stochastic phenomenon, owing to the interdependence of outputs and weights.

examples for indexes of machinery, and we shall cite one. If comparable items of U.S. machinery are weighted in 1899 and 1939 prices, output is shown as multiplying more than fifteen times between 1899 and 1939 with 1899 weights, and less than twice with 1939 weights.[20] This enormous discrepancy reflects more than the effect of weights; it also reflects the inherently arbitrary nature of any measure of machinery production. But it is a striking example of how the combined difficulties in defining products and in choosing appropriate weights may lead to virtually contradictory index numbers when resolved differently.

TABLE 19

EFFECT OF WEIGHT BASE ON PRODUCTION INDEXES FOR
SOVIET INDUSTRY AND INDUSTRIAL GROUPS

	Production in 1955 (1913 = 100)			Ratio		
	1928 Weights (1)	1955 Weights (2)	Moving Weights (3)	(1)/(2)	(1)/(3)	(2)/(3)
Industrial materials[a]	550	463	511	1.19	1.08	0.91
Finished civilian products	519	353	460	1.47	1.13	0.77
All civilian products	697	488	577	1.43	1.21	0.85
Ferrous metals	916	900	907	1.02	1.01	0.99
Nonferrous metals	2,267	2,624	2,405	0.86	0.94	1.09
Fuel and electricity	2,457	1,435	1,994	1.71	1.23	0.72
Chemicals	1,523	1,127	1,418	1.35	1.07	0.79
Construction materials	411	392	396	1.05	1.04	0.99
Transportation equipment	4,507	820	3,447	5.50	1.31	0.24
Agricultural machinery	1,382	1,032	1,231	1.34	1.13	0.84
Food and allied products	279	227	258	1.23	1.08	0.88
Textiles and allied products	337	333	275	1.01	1.23	1.21
Consumer durables	16,704	3,098	16,350	5.39	1.02	0.19

SOURCE: Tables 16 and 17.

[a] With the same product coverage, production indexes based on 1913 and 1928 weights are, respectively, 588 and 513. The ratio of the former to the latter is 1.15.

Some of the differences in production indexes for Soviet industry based on 1928 and 1955 weight bases are summarized in Table 19 and Chart 11. For the entire Soviet period, all but one of the indexes shown (that for nonferrous metals)[21] is higher when based on 1928 weights than when

[20] Gerschenkron, *Soviet Machinery Output*, p. 52. For other, less spectacular examples, see *Census of U.S. Manufactures, 1947, Indexes of Production*, p. 4; *Census of U.S. Manufactures, 1954, Indexes of Production*, p. 20; Carter and Robson, "Accuracy of a Production Index," p. 21; and *A Critique of the United States Income and Product Accounts*, Studies in Income and Wealth 22, Princeton for NBER, 1958, pp. 419 ff.

[21] In this case, it may be that depletion of better-grade ores has more than offset other (relative) cost-reducing factors, such as increased productivity of resources other than mining property.

CHART II
Indexes of Soviet Industrial Production, Grouped by Scope, Benchmark Years, 1913–1955

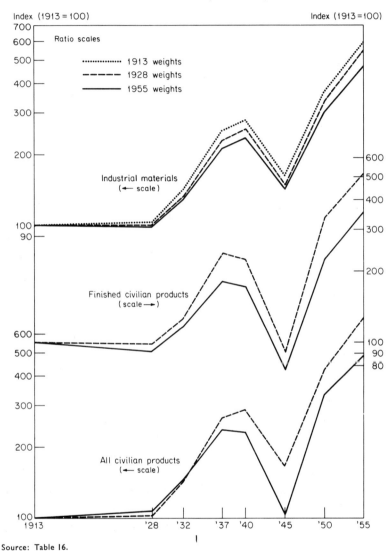

Source: Table 16.

based on 1955 weights. The percentage discrepancies are largest for transportation equipment, consumer durables, fuel and electricity, and chemicals; they are smallest for textiles and allied products, ferrous metals, and construction materials. As to the aggregate indexes, the

129

discrepancy is largest for finished civilian products, next largest for all civilian products, and smallest for industrial materials. To an unknown but probably minor extent, the discrepancies may reflect differences in product coverage, since this varies somewhat in most cases with the weight base (see below).

The indexes based on 1928 and 1955 weights are also compared with moving-weight indexes. While a moving-weight index is a kind of average of fixed-weight components, in one case shown here (textiles and allied products) it is lower than both counterpart fixed-weight indexes. This result—or the reverse, with the moving-weight index higher than both fixed-weight counterparts—can easily occur, depending on how the two fixed-weight indexes behave relative to each other over the links they are taken to represent in the moving-weight index.

ADEQUACY OF EMPLOYMENT WEIGHTS

As we have already noted, the index for all civilian products with 1955 weights has been constructed by weighting industrial groups by employment. The question naturally arises as to how much difference there would have been if value-added weights had been used. Since such weights are not available, we cannot give a direct answer to this question, but we can find out how our index with 1928 weights would be affected if employment weights were substituted for value-added weights.

For these special computations, we derived both direct and imputed 1928 employment weights, corresponding in coverage to the value-added weights already discussed.[22] The index with direct weights is designed to parallel our index with 1928 direct value-added weights, the direct employment weights being applied to the narrowest product categories for which they are available and those product categories being internally weighted by 1928 unit values. The index with imputed weights is designed, on the other hand, to parallel in construction our index with 1955 employment weights, the imputed weights being applied to broad industrial groups internally weighted by 1928 unit values. Two variants of the latter index were prepared, differing in their treatment of weights for transportation equipment, agricultural machinery, and consumer durables. In the first variant, we used the imputed employment weight for each category as derived from detailed 1928 data; in the second, we prorated the total weight for all machinery and metal products to each category by its computed 1928 value of output. The latter procedure

---

[22] The employment weights are set forth and described in Table A-7 and the surrounding text of Appendix A.

was used in our index with 1955 weights because employment was not available for categories of machinery.[23] The second variant, therefore, parallels our method of constructing the index with 1955 weights more closely than the first variant does.

In Table 20, indexes with alternative 1928 employment and value-added weights are compared. The two indexes with direct weights show

TABLE 20

COMPARISON OF PRODUCTION INDEXES FOR SOVIET CIVILIAN INDUSTRIAL PRODUCTS:
1928 VALUE-ADDED AND EMPLOYMENT WEIGHTS,
SELECTED YEARS, 1913–1955
(1913 = 100)

	1913	1928	1940	1955
Value added weights				
Direct	100	102	289	697
Imputed	100	103	298	754
Employment weights				
Direct	100	106	299	703
Imputed, first variant	100	103	278	682
Imputed, second variant	100	106	306	777

SOURCE: See text.

about the same growth over the period 1913–1955. In the case of indexes with imputed weights, the first variant with employment weights rises more slowly than the index with value-added weights, but the second variant rises more rapidly. We may surmise that our index with 1955 employment weights might also rise faster than one using value-added weights, could the latter be constructed. Such an inference is, of course, highly tenuous and cannot be asserted with confidence. In any event, there is no convincing evidence available that an index based on imputed employment weights is likely to diverge significantly, in one direction or the other, from one based on direct value-added weights.

WEIGHTS FROM UNITED STATES INDUSTRY

Production indexes for industrial materials based on U.S. weights are compared in Table 21 with indexes based on Soviet weights. For these comparisons, all indexes have been adjusted to an identical product coverage (forty-nine products), which means that the following five products have been eliminated from the indexes with Soviet weights: oil shale, peat, firewood, plywood, and beer.

[23] See Table D-9 in Appendix D.

TABLE 21

COMPARISON OF PRODUCTION INDEXES FOR SOVIET INDUSTRIAL MATERIALS:
SOVIET AND U.S. WEIGHTS, BENCHMARK YEARS, 1913–1955

	1913	1928	1932	1937	1940	1945	1950	1955
	INDEX (1913 = 100)							
Soviet weights								
1. 1928 weights	100	103	133	240	261	148	359	598
2. 1955 weights	100	102	132	220	238	143	317	501
U.S. weights								
3. 1914 weights	100	107	130	228	246	137	329	536
4. 1929 weights	100	105	131	214	229	126	296	480
5. 1939 weights	100	104	130	224	240	134	315	508
6. 1954 weights	100	104	136	230	246	138	323	519
	RATIO							
3 to 1	1.00	1.03	0.98	0.95	0.94	0.93	0.92	0.90
3 to 2	1.00	1.05	0.99	1.03	1.03	0.96	1.04	1.07
4 to 1	1.00	1.01	0.98	0.89	0.88	0.85	0.83	0.80
4 to 2	1.00	1.03	0.99	0.97	0.97	0.88	0.94	0.96
5 to 1	1.00	1.01	0.98	0.93	0.92	0.90	0.88	0.85
5 to 2	1.00	1.02	0.99	1.02	1.01	0.94	0.99	1.01
6 to 1	1.00	1.00	1.03	0.96	0.94	0.93	0.90	0.87
6 to 2	1.00	1.02	1.03	1.05	1.03	0.97	1.02	1.04

SOURCE: Appendix D. All indexes adjusted to cover the same forty-nine products (see text).

The index with 1914 U.S. weights shows a faster growth over the period 1913–1955 than any other index with U.S. weights. With this exception, however, growth rises uniformly as the weights are moved forward from 1929 to 1955. This behavior does not accord with the general rule already suggested that early-year weights lead to a more rapid growth in indexes than late-year weights. What is the reason for this paradox? One might conjecture that the structure of growth in productivity and output has been significantly different in U.S. and Soviet industry. That is to say, it may be that the products with the greatest decline in opportunity cost in the United States have tended to have the slowest growth in output— and probably the smallest decline in opportunity cost—in the Soviet Union. Such reasoning must remain conjectural until considerably more data are available on the Soviet economy, its growth, and the "rationality" of its price system.[24]

[24] On the last matter, see the interesting discussion by P. J. D. Wiles cited in footnote 16 above. See also Joan Robinson, "Mr. Wiles' Rationality"; D. R. Hodgman, "Measuring Soviet Industrial Expansion: A Reply," *Soviet Studies*, July 1956, 34–45;

The indexes with U.S. weights show production in 1955 as ranging from 480 to 536 per cent of production in 1913. These more or less bracket the 501 per cent shown by the index with 1955 Soviet weights, but even the upper limit falls substantially short of the 598 per cent shown by the index with 1928 Soviet weights.

Details on Product Coverage

FIXED AND VARYING COVERAGE

One important practical problem in constructing production indexes is to provide coverage for the new products continually being introduced into the economy. These new products often grow at a faster percentage rate than many older ones, for reasons discussed in the preceding chapter. Other relevant things being the same, a production index whose product coverage continually expands will tend to show a more rapid rate of growth than one whose coverage is fixed. However, in designing an index with expanding coverage, we necessarily create offsetting behavior.

If new products are to be brought into an index, either late-year weights or a system of moving weights must be used. Early-year weights obviously cannot be used for products not produced in that early year— though the official Soviet index of industrial production has done just that in a way we shall describe later. As we have already noted, a production index based on late-year or moving weights will generally show a slower rate of growth than one with the same product coverage based on early-year weights.

Are we then faced with a dilemma of choosing between two evils? In effect we are not, because a moving-weight index is usually preferred for quite independent reasons. Hence, the only significant issue is whether a fixed or a varying product coverage is to be used. A varying coverage will surely be preferred, provided that the index continues to cover a representative sample of old as well as new industries.

In the case of our indexes for industrial materials, the product coverage is the same for the two variants based on 1928 and 1955 weights, but it is higher for both of these than for the one based on 1913 weights—fifty-four products compared with forty-nine (see Table 22). The five products missing in the latter are hydroelectric power, natural gas, oil shale, magnesite metallurgical powder, and asbestos shingles—all essentially

---

D. Granick, "Are Adjusted Rubles Rational? A Comment," *Soviet Studies*, July 1956, 46–49; and P. J. D. Wiles, "A Rejoinder To All and Sundry," *Soviet Studies*, October 1956, 134–143.

TABLE 22

PRODUCT COVERAGE OF INDEXES OF SOVIET INDUSTRIAL PRODUCTION

| | | Number of Products | | |
	Total	Intermediate Industrial Products	Agricultural and Transportation Equipment	Consumer Goods
Industrial materials				
1913 weights	49	32	0	17
1928 weights	54	37	0	17
1955 weights	54	37	0	17
U.S. weights	50[a]	33	0	17[a]
Finished civilian products				
1928 weights	73	13	27[b]	33
1955 weights	87	16	35[c]	36[d]
All civilian products				
1928 weights	101	43	23	35
1955 weights	119	46	35[c]	38[d]

SOURCE: Table D-10.

[a] The index with 1929 weights does not include beer, and hence covers only sixteen consumer goods and forty-nine products in all.

[b] Includes four series with data missing for one or more benchmark years. For computational convenience, these were not included in the index for all industrial products. They are all of minor importance.

[c] Includes three series with data missing for one or more benchmark years.

[d] Includes two series with data missing for one or more benchmark years.

TABLE 23

EFFECT OF PRODUCT COVERAGE ON PRODUCTION INDEX FOR SOVIET INDUSTRIAL MATERIALS

| | | INDEX, 1913 = 100 | | |
| | *Forty-Nine Products* | | *Fifty-Four Products* | Ratio |
	1913 Weights (1)	1928 Weights (2)	1928 Weights (3)	(3)/(2)
1913	100	100	100	1.00
1928	103	100	100	1.01
1932	141	135	131	0.97
1937	249	222	229	1.03
1940	276	245	254	1.04
1945	161	139	148	1.06
1950	364	318	338	1.06
1955	588	513	550	1.07

SOURCE: Tables D-1 and D-10.

new products in the Soviet Union. If these same products are excluded from the index with 1928 weights, it shows a significantly slower rate of growth over most of the Soviet period than the index with full product coverage (see Table 23). We did not deliberately use the same product coverage for indexes with 1928 and 1955 weights; the available data simply do not permit a meaningful expansion of coverage, probably for the reason to be discussed in the third paragraph below.

In the case of our indexes for finished civilian materials, the one with 1955 weights covers eighty-seven products, while the one with 1928 weights covers only seventy-three. The products included in the former but not in the latter are three types of metallurgical bricks, nine items of agricultural equipment, two items of apparel, and one item of consumer durables. These are virtually all products not produced in quantity in 1928. The index with 1928 weights includes one item of agricultural equipment (combined plows and drills) not included in the index with 1955 weights, because no 1955 price could be found.

Finally, our index for all civilian products with 1955 weights covers 119 products, while the one with 1928 weights covers 101. The products included in the former but not in the latter are those given above plus one type of fuel (oil shale) and three items of transportation and agricultural equipment with incomplete data. Because appropriate prices could not be found, synthetic dyes and ginned cotton were included in the index with 1928 weights but not in the one with 1955 weights.

The differences in coverage just summarized actually understate considerably the extent to which new products and improvements in quality have been incorporated into our indexes. The Soviet practice of expressing output in "conventional units" amounts to adjusting the basic series of physical output to reflect introduction of new products and improvements in quality. Thus, if a new kind of window glass is produced, it is translated into "conventional" square meters on the basis of a coefficient (weight factor) that is designed to reflect its qualitative as well as physical characteristics. Other examples are given in Chapter 2. It is even quite possible, though no specific evidence has been found, that the component items in a heterogeneous series like window glass, paper, cement, canned goods, and so on are weighted together by their prices to form the published series on physical output. There is no doubt in some cases that complicated weight factors are used; the only question is whether they reflect opportunity cost or something else. In any event, many of the "basic" series used in our indexes are undoubtedly weighted subindexes reflecting introduction of new products and improvements in quality.

NARROW AND BROAD SCOPE OF INDEXES

Each of our three types of index represents a different scope of industrial activity, and it is plain from Table 24 and Chart 12 that measured growth

TABLE 24

COMPARISON OF MOVING-WEIGHT INDEXES OF INDUSTRIAL PRODUCTION
WITH DIFFERING SCOPE: SOVIET UNION, BENCHMARK YEARS,
1913–1955

	All Civilian Products (1)	Industrial Materials (2)	Finished Civilian Products (3)	Ratio (1)/(2)	Ratio (1)/(3)
INDEX (1913 = 100)					
1913	100	100	100	1.00	1.00
1928	102	102	99	1.00	1.03
1932	144	133	126	1.08	1.14
1937	268	233	239	1.15	1.12
1940	274	257	226	1.07	1.07
1945	123	157	100	0.78	1.23
1950	397	331	295	1.20	1.35
1955	577	511	460	1.13	1.25
LINK RELATIVE (INITIAL YEAR OF PERIOD = 100)					
1913–1928	102	102	99	1.00	1.03
1928–1932	140	131	128	1.08	1.09
1932–1937	186	175	189	1.06	0.98
1937–1940	102	110	94	0.93	1.09
1940–1945	45	61	44	0.73	1.02
1945–1950	323	210	295	1.54	1.09
1950–1955	145	154	156	0.94	0.93

SOURCE: Table 16.

varies with the scope of the index. Over the period 1913–1955, the index for all civilian products registers a growth 13 per cent faster than the index for industrial materials, and a growth 25 per cent faster than the index for finished civilian products. Over shorter periods, the relations are more complex, in particular because the effects of industrial mobilization and demobilization are reflected differently in the different indexes, for reasons to be explored in the section after next.

The same kind of differential behavior is shown in part by production indexes for U.S. industry (Table 25). Over the period 1913–1955, our index for all products shows a measured growth 19 per cent faster than an index for industrial materials. It is interesting that this divergence is registered in two periods, 1913–1929 and 1939–1947, both of which include a major war. A similar comparison cannot be made with an index for finished products, because such an index is not available for years before 1939. Over the period 1939–1955, the extended Federal Reserve Board index for finished products shows a somewhat more rapid

TABLE 25

Comparison of Moving-Weight Indexes of Industrial Production with Differing Scope: United States, Benchmark Years, 1913–1955

	All Products[a] (1)	Industrial Materials[b] (2)	All Products[a] (3)	Industrial Materials[b] (4)	Finished Products[c] (5)	*Ratio*		
						(1)/(2)	(3)/(4)	(3)/(5)
	index (1913 = 100)		index (1939 = 100)					
1913	100	100				1.00		
1929	188	165				1.14		
1932	100	99				1.01		
1939	188	166	100	100	100	1.13	1.00	1.00
1947	321	269	171	162	182	1.19	1.06	0.94
1950	366	307	195	185	206	1.19	1.05	0.96
1955	473	396	252	238	265	1.19	1.06	0.95
	link relative (initial year of period = 100)							
1913–1929	188	165				1.14		
1929–1932	53	60				0.88		
1932–1939	188	168				1.12		
1939–1947	171	162	171	162	182	1.06	1.06	0.94
1947–1950	114	114	114	114	113	1.00	1.00	1.01
1950–1955	129	129	129	129	129	1.00	1.00	1.00

[a] Table A-32.

[b] 1913–1939, Moore's index as revised by Greenslade and Wallace (R. V. Greenslade and Phyllis A. Wallace, "Industrial Growth in the Soviet Union: Comment," *American Economic Review*, September 1959, p. 689); 1939–1947, an index similar in construction to the link for 1947–1955; 1947–1955, Federal Reserve Board index (*Federal Reserve Bulletin*, December 1959, p. 1469).

[c] 1939–1947, an index similar in construction to the link for 1947–1955; 1947–1955, *ibid.*

rise than the FRB index for all products, the divergence being concentrated, once again, in the period 1939–1947.

In interpreting these comparisons, one must keep in mind that there are some important differences between the Soviet and U.S. counterpart indexes, the most important being that the U.S. index for all products directly covers military products over the years since 1939, while the Soviet index for all civilian products does not. As we shall see below, when the Soviet index is adjusted to reflect estimated output of military products, the long-run divergence of the index for all products from the one for industrial materials becomes remarkably similar for the two countries: 19 per cent for the United States compared with 21 per cent for the Soviet Union over the period 1913–1955.

Another difference is that the Soviet index for industrial materials is based on a fixed sample of products while the U.S. counterpart is not, the product coverage varying over the three links in the index. This

CHART 12
Indexes of Soviet Industrial Production, Grouped by Weighting System, Benchmark Years, 1913–1955

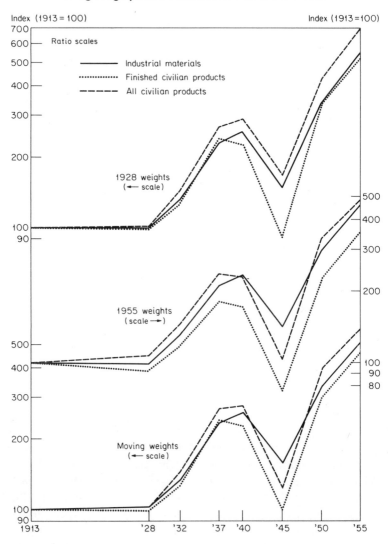

Source: Table 16.

difference is, however, not as important as it might seem since, as we noted earlier, new products and improvements in quality are reflected in the product coverage of our Soviet index by virtue of the Soviet practice of expressing output in conventional units. Moreover, the products in the index account for almost all Soviet materials on which output data have been published for as late as 1955. It is doubtful that many materials of significance in recent times have been omitted.[25]

One should be careful not to leap to the conclusion that any one of our Soviet indexes is inherently a better indicator of Soviet industrial growth than the others. All may either overstate or understate the areas of growth they purport to measure. It is worth noting that, if the basic data on physical output for 1955 were exaggerated by as much as 13 per cent relative to 1913, the index for industrial materials might be more accurate as a measure of over-all industrial growth than the one for all civilian products.

MACHINERY AND EQUIPMENT

Some of the most serious practical difficulties in constructing production indexes arise in the case of durable commodities, particularly capital equipment and military end items. It is virtually impossible to identify meaningful homogeneous categories for some of these items, because so many widely differing varieties are produced, often custom-built, and because basic designs change so swiftly and radically. Whenever such heterogeneous categories of products are included in Western production indexes, they are often represented indirectly by input series—most frequently, man-hours of employment—or by an appropriate value of production deflated by some price index drawn from another sector of industry.

For the United States, the most comprehensive production indexes covering the growth of manufacturing up to World War II are those of Professors Edwin Frickey and Solomon Fabricant.[26] Frickey's index, which covers the period 1860–1914, includes only four items of durable goods, all in the category of transportation equipment: railroad freight cars, railroad passenger cars, automobiles, and vessels. Fabricant's index, which covers the period 1899–1937, also includes only transportation equipment, though in much greater detail: fifty-nine items are included in all, but some cover only short spans of time.[27]

[25] For an apparently contrary view on the comparability of U.S. and Soviet indexes for industrial materials, see Greenslade and Wallace, "Industrial Growth in the Soviet Union." Their argument is commented on in my "Reply," *American Economic Review*, September 1959, especially p. 699.

[26] Edwin Frickey, *Production in the United States, 1860–1914*, Cambridge, Mass., 1947; and Fabricant, *Manufacturing Industries*.

[27] Fabricant also constructed indexes for agricultural implements, phonographs, radios, refrigerators, scales and balances, sewing machines, typewriters, and washing and ironing machines (see Fabricant, *Manufacturing Industries*, pp. 287 ff). All but one (phonographs) begins with 1921 or later, and none is included in the aggregate index for

Fabricant summarized the problems of measurement in the following words:[28]

> The task of measuring the physical output of machinery is complicated by two serious difficulties. In the first place, few of the machinery industries are covered by adequate quantity data on output; and in the second place, the available statistics are ambiguous because the products are not divided into homogeneous subclasses. Inadequacy of data and of subclassification are almost inevitable when the variety of items produced is as wide as it is in the case of machinery, and no classification, no matter how detailed, could be expected to resolve the problem conclusively. The enormous variety of machines illustrates rather pointedly the extent to which our industrial processes are both specialized and mechanized. The continuing improvements in our productive equipment, tools and machines, reflect the drive toward faster, better, cheaper production—a basic factor in our economic progress. In other words, some of the very factors that have made this a machine era also make it impossible for us to measure in a straightforward manner the degree to which the physical volume of output of machines has risen, and the size of the existing stock of mechanical instruments.

The Federal Reserve Board annual index of industrial production in the United States also did not include the more heterogeneous categories of durable goods as it was constructed up to 1940. In that year the coverage of the annual index was expanded to include many of these categories back through 1923, and in 1941 and 1942 it was further expanded to include wartime armaments.[29] Output of these products was measured primarily by man-hours of employed labor adjusted for presumed changes (improvements) in productivity that were estimated by a variety of devices, almost all of which relied on data for other sectors of industry. In the monthly index, the man-hour series accounted for about 33 per cent of the aggregate value of the index in 1935–1939 and for about

---

manufacturing. We have included some of these items, along with others he did not cover, in our index for consumer durables, which is covered by our aggregate index for Soviet industry.

[28] *Ibid.*

[29] *Federal Reserve Bulletin*, August 1940, 753–771; *ibid.*, September 1941, 878–881; and *ibid.*, October 1943, 940–952. It is interesting that the FRB index for manufacturing, as revised in 1940, shows a slower growth over 1923–1939 than Fabricant's index, despite the fact that the former has a broader coverage of machinery than the latter (see *Historical Statistics of the United States, 1789–1945*, Washington, 1949, series J-15 and J-30).

58 per cent in 1943.[30] The resulting index has been criticized, particularly for its measurement of production in wartime.[31]

The FRB index was thoroughly revised in 1953, the reliance on man-hour series being greatly reduced: those used as sole indicators of output in the annual index accounted for 4 per cent of all weights in this revised index and those used along with other information of various types accounted for an additional 13 per cent.[32] Except for a few miscellaneous products of minor importance in other sectors, these series are concentrated in the industrial groups of machinery, transportation equipment, and instruments and related products—which, taken together, also include the bulk of military products. Series in these groups whose output is measured entirely or partially by man-hours account for around 13 per cent of all weights, or more than half the full weight accorded to all series in these groups. In the heterogeneous categories not represented by man-hour series, output is generally broken down in considerable detail: 199 series of farm machinery; 71 series of machine tools; 62 series of commercial refrigeration equipment; 8 series of electric lamps; and so on.[33]

The difficulties in measuring output of heterogeneous machinery may be illustrated by data on machine tools for the United States taken from the *Census of Manufactures* for 1939, 1947, and 1954 (see Table 26). The first problem is to define the boundaries of the industry and to gather comparable data for various years. It is plain even from our simplified presentation that this problem alone is almost without solution, and in this case for a country that publishes voluminous and finely detailed information.

The second problem is to choose an indicator of production. Numbers of tools are not meaningful since by reasonable variations in definition the number can vary enormously: from 190 thousand to 2.4 million in 1947, not taking account of metalworking machinery related to machine tools in their strictest meaning. This should, incidentally, serve as a warning against comparing Soviet and U.S. production of machine tools

[30] Moore, *Production of Industrial Materials*, p. 5, and *Federal Reserve Bulletin*, October 1943, p. 949.

[31] See Moore, *Production of Industrial Materials*, particularly pp. 42 ff. For a defense of the FRB index of wartime production, see Frank R. Garfield, "Measurement of Industrial Production since 1939," *Journal of the American Statistical Association*, December 1944, 439–454.

[32] *Federal Reserve Bulletin*, December 1953, p. 1258. In the monthly index, man-hour series accounted for 45 per cent of the total weights in 1947 (*ibid.*). All further data in this paragraph are taken from *ibid.*, pp. 1239–1291.

[33] The FRB index was further revised as of December 1959, apparently with additional improvement in the handling of man-hour series. The details of this revision are not available at the time of this writing.

TABLE 26

DATA ON PRODUCTION OF METALWORKING MACHINE TOOLS:a UNITED STATES, 1939, 1947, AND 1954

	Physical Output (thousand units)			Value of Output (million dollars)			Percentage of Value Covered by Physical Output		
	1939	1947	1954	1939	1947	1954	1939	1947	1954
Industrial tools									
Boring	1.5	1.4	3.2	14.2	25.8	114.4	100	100	99
Drilling	3.2	21.1	15.2	12.4	33.5	86.1	82	98	99
Gear-cutting	1.7	1.7	2.5	11.2	17.7	48.1	100	100	97
Grinding and polishing	7.6	85.6	53.6	32.4	56.4	154.4	80	78	94
Lathes	27.3	36.2	21.0	49.8	92.9	206.9	95	99	100
Milling	0.3	7.5	11.5	24.2	35.3	121.5	13	100	99
Others[b]	4.1	37.4	16.8	32.6	450.7	780.0	19	14	4
Total, coverage A	c	191.0	123.8	c	712.4	1,511.4	c	40	50
Nonindustrial tools[d]	c	692.6	n.a.	c	30.9	9.3	c		0
Total, coverage B	45.8	883.5	n.a.	176.8	743.2	1,520.7	67	42	49
Power-driven hand tools[e]	n.a.	1,533.8	2,462.3	n.a.	112.2	170.5	n.a.	52	50
Total, coverage C	n.a.	2,417.4	n.a.	n.a.	855.4	1,691.2	n.a.	43	49

Detail and sums may not be consistent because of rounding.

SOURCE: Census of United States Manufactures for 1939, 1947, and 1954.

a Machine tools are defined according to the Standard Industrial Classification as power-driven tools that shape metal by grinding or progressively cutting away chips. They do not include machinery for shaping, pressing, forging, or bending metal, where the shaping action is not dependent on cutting or grinding away chips.

b Includes the following tools: broaching, planing, shaping, centering, cutting-off, keyseating, pipecutting and pipethreading, slotting, other threading and tapping, and otherwise unspecified. Also includes (in value of output) spare parts, rebuilt tools, and attachments and accessories for metalworking tools.

c Most nonindustrial tools are included with industrial tools, distributed by type.

d Tools for home workshops, laboratories, garages, service stations, etc.

e Both electric and pneumatic.

TABLE 27

COMPARISON OF PRODUCTION INDEXES FOR MACHINE TOOLS AND RELATED PRODUCTS: UNITED STATES, 1939, 1947, AND 1954

	Link Relatives (Initial Year = 100)	
Type of Index	1939–1947	1947–1954
Machine tools		
Unweighted number of tools[a]		
Coverage A	417[b]	65
Coverage B	1,929	n.a.
Deflated value of output[a]		
Coverage A	283[b]	149
Coverage B	295	144
Coverage C	n.a.	139
Federal Reserve Board index[c]		
Coverage A	141	n.a.
All metalworking machinery		
Deflated value of output[d]	n.a.	119
Federal Reserve Board index[e]	n.a.	139

[a] Based on data in Table 26. Value deflated by price index for metalworking machinery (*Survey of Current Business*, November 1953, pp. 18 f) extrapolated from 1952 through 1954 by BLS price index for same industrial category (*Statistical Abstract of the United States, 1956*, p. 322). Price index for 1947 is 142.5 per cent of 1939; for 1954, 142.3 per cent of 1947.

[b] For 1939, nonindustrial machine tools are assumed to be of negligible significance in number and value.

[c] *Census of U.S. Manufactures: 1947, Indexes of Production*, p. 21. Index with 1939 and 1947 cross weights.

[d] Coverage C from Table 26, plus value of output of metalworking machinery except machine tools, which was as follows (million dollars): 616.1 for 1939 and 793.9 for 1954. The latter data are taken from the 1954 *Census of Manufactures*. Deflated by price index given in note *a* above.

[e] *Federal Reserve Bulletin*, December 1953, p. 1306, and July 1956, p. 751.

in terms of numbers produced. (The basic Soviet data are given in numbers.) In any event, we note the great discrepancies among a few alternative production indexes presented in Table 27.[34] It is perhaps most interesting that, under the most restricted definition of machine tools (coverage A), the index from number of tools is higher than both the weighted output and deflated value indexes for 1939–1947, but it is lower than the deflated value index for 1947–1954; in fact, the index from numbers shows a decline of 35 per cent in the latter period, while the index from deflated value shows an increase of 49 per cent.

Such difficulties of measurement make any production index for heterogeneous machinery largely arbitrary and generally unreliable, sometimes in direction of movement as well as magnitude. This is

[34] Other illustrations of conflicting indexes of machinery output with varying coverage are given by Gerschenkron, *Soviet Machinery Output*, pp. 34 ff.

particularly true for the Soviet Union, where statistics on output and value do not approach the detail available for the United States. We have, nevertheless, constructed illustrative indexes for miscellaneous machinery, primarily to indicate how much difference there might be in our indexes if these items were included. The series covered by these indexes are shown in Table D-10 of Appendix D; they have been weighted by Soviet prices for 1928 and 1955, as given in Table D-9.[35]

The moving-weight index for machinery and equipment including miscellaneous items rises about 20 per cent more rapidly over the entire Soviet period than the one excluding miscellaneous items; it also rises more rapidly over all subperiods except 1932–1937 and 1945–1950 (see Table 28). For all civilian products, the index including miscellaneous machinery rises about 7 per cent more rapidly over the entire Soviet period than the one excluding it. Most of this discrepancy is introduced during the period 1945–1950, when paradoxically the index for machinery

TABLE 28

MOVING-WEIGHT PRODUCTION INDEXES FOR CIVILIAN INDUSTRIAL PRODUCTS WITH
DIFFERING PRODUCT COVERAGE FOR MACHINERY AND EQUIPMENT:
SOVIET UNION, BENCHMARK YEARS, 1913–1955

	Machinery and Equipment		All Civilian Products	
	Excl. Misc. Machinery	Incl. Misc. Machinery	Excl. Misc. Machinery	Incl. Misc. Machinery
	INDEX (1913 = 100)			
1913	100	100	100	100
1928	143	149	102	103
1932	426	544	144	147
1937	1,624	1,595	268	273
1940	1,140	1,215	274	280
1945	265	380	123	127
1950	2,637	2,900	397	423
1955	2,994	3,627	577	619
	LINK RELATIVE (INITIAL YEAR OF PERIOD = 100)			
1913–1928	142	149	102	103
1928–1932	299	365	140	143
1932–1937	381	293	186	185
1937–1940	70	76	102	103
1940–1945	23	31	45	45
1945–1950	993	763	323	333
1950–1955	114	125	145	146

SOURCE: Tables 16, D-3, and D-4.

[35] To illustrate the problems of measuring output of machinery and equipment, we also constructed twelve different indexes with 1928 weights, varying in coverage and weighting system. These are set forth in Table A-8 and discussed in the surrounding text of Appendix A. We consider here only the moving-weight indexes for machinery and equipment (excluding consumer durables), based in part on 1928 direct value-added weights.

and equipment including miscellaneous items rose less rapidly than the one excluding them. Hence, most of the discrepancy is attributable to the fact that, by including miscellaneous machinery, the increased weight given to the machinery sector during 1945–1950 more than offset the decreased growth of that sector, as far as the net effect on the over-all production index is concerned.

For the period 1928–1937, our indexes for machinery and equipment, when adjusted to cover consumer durables, may be compared with those constructed by two other Western scholars, Alexander Gerschenkron and Donald Hodgman (see Table 29 and Chart 13).[36] Gerschenkron's index is weighted with 1939 prices drawn from U.S. industry, after a painstaking effort to match Soviet and U.S. counterparts in consultation with U.S. manufacturers who had engaged in commercial dealings with the Soviet Union. In Hodgman's index, product groups are weighted by adjusted Soviet wage-bill data for 1934, and individual products within groups are weighted by unit values taken from several U.S. censuses of manufactures. In coverage, these two indexes most closely resemble our index including miscellaneous machinery and consumer durables, although, because of the greater detail in weights, they both utilize a more detailed breakdown of products than ours.

Gerschenkron's index rises less rapidly than Hodgman's, and both rise less rapidly than either of ours based on 1928 Soviet weights, which are also the weights we use for our moving-weight indexes over this period. On the other hand, both Gerschenkron's and Hodgman's indexes rise more rapidly than either of ours based on 1955 Soviet weights. In other words, our indexes based on 1928 and 1955 weights bracket theirs based on more or less "intermediate" weights from the point of view of industrialization, a result we should normally expect. However, the discrepancies are very large for such a short span of time: our highest index for 1937 exceeds Gerschenkron's by 130 per cent and Hodgman's by 94 per cent; our lowest falls short of Gerschenkron's by 25 per cent and Hodgman's by 37 per cent. Under these circumstances, it is hardly meaningful to look for a "correct" production index for machinery.

Similar conclusions emerge from comparisons over a longer period of time with two indexes recently constructed by Demitri Shimkin and Frederick Leedy and by Norman Kaplan and Richard Moorsteen (see Table 29 and Chart 13). The full details underlying these indexes have not yet become available to us, but from the general description they

---

[36] Gerschenkron, *Soviet Machinery Output*, and Donald Hodgman, *Soviet Industrial Production, 1928–1951*, Cambridge, Mass., 1954, pp. 107 and 158 ff.

TABLE 29

Comparison of NBER and Other Western Production Indexes for Civilian Machinery and Equipment: Soviet Union, Benchmark Years, 1928–1955

					NBER			
					Excl. Misc. Mach.		Incl. Misc. Mach.	
	Gerschenkron	Hodgman	Shimkin-Leedy	Kaplan-Moorsteen	1928 Weights	1955 Weights	1928 Weights	1955 Weights
INDEX (1928 = 100)								
1928	100	100	100	100	100	100	100	100
1932	264	258		287	299[a]	185[a]	364[a]	212[a]
1937	525	626	540	601	1,139[a]	386[a]	1,067[a]	436[a]
1940			460	504	826	262	828	326
1945				200	351	61	362	102
1950			1,430	1,470	2,025	607	2,316	779
1955			2,100	2,000	2,438	689	3,021	974
LINK RELATIVE (INITIAL YEAR OF PERIOD = 100)								
1928–1932	264	258		287	299[b]	185[b]	364[b]	212[b]
1932–1937	199	243		210	381[b]	209[b]	293[b]	206[b]
1937–1940			84	84	73	68	78	75
1940–1945				40	42	23	44	31
1945–1950				735	577	994	640	764
1940–1950			313	292	245	232	280	239
1950–1955			147	136	120	114	130	125

SOURCE: Gerschenkron: *Soviet Machinery Output*, p. 25. Includes consumer durables. Hodgman: *Soviet Industrial Production*, p. 107. Includes consumer durables. Kaplan-Moorsteen: Norman M. Kaplan and Richard Moorsteen, "Indexes of Soviet Industrial Output," (mimeographed), II, RAND Corporation, RM-2495, Santa Monica, 1960, p. 237. Shimkin-Leedy: *Ibid.*, as derived from data in Demitri B. Shimkin and Frederick A. Leedy, "Soviet Industrial Growth—Its Cost, Extent and Prospects," *Automotive Industries*, January 1, 1958, p. 7. NBER: Tables D-3 and D-4.

[a] If consumer durables are included to make the indexes comparable with those of Hodgman and Gerschenkron, the values are as follows (see Table A-15): col. 5, 307 and 1205; col. 6, 189 and 394; col. 7, 368 and 1121; and col. 8, 214 and 440.

[b] Including consumer durables (see note *a* above), the values are as follows: col. 5, 307 and 393; col. 6, 189 and 208; col. 7, 368 and 305; and col. 8, 214 and 206.

CHART 13
NBER and Other Western Production Indexes for Civilian Machinery and Equipment: Soviet Union, Benchmark Years, 1928–1955

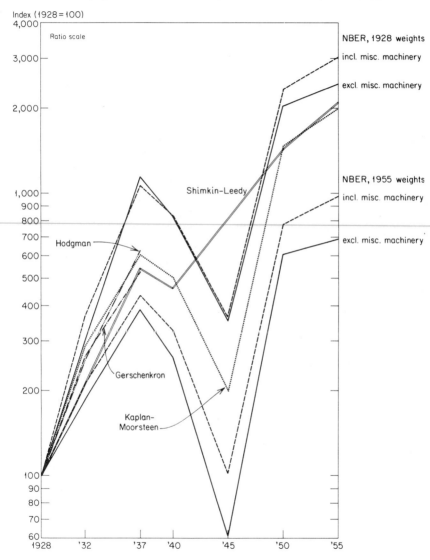

Source: Table 29.

seem to have about the same product coverage as our indexes including miscellaneous machinery, though the breakdown of products seems to be more detailed than ours. The Shimkin-Leedy index is based on 1934 Soviet weights; the Kaplan-Moorsteen index, on 1950 Soviet weights. As would be expected from the fact that their weight bases lie within ours, our indexes bracket theirs over the period as a whole, though not within all subperiods. Two striking cases where this is not so are the periods 1940–1950 and 1950–1955, over which our indexes all rise more slowly than theirs. Moreover, their indexes parallel each other more closely than would probably be predicted from the differences in the weight bases. These irregularities may be due in part to the peculiarities of the Soviet price structure in both 1934 and 1950, as we note in technical note 4 of Appendix A. But a more satisfactory explanation must wait until the details of their two indexes are published.

MILITARY PRODUCTS

The problem of measuring output of military products becomes acute for periods of rapid armament or disarmament surrounding wars. If it were not for war preparations, it would matter little whether munitions were covered or not, since production indexes would not be affected much either way. Hence a dilemma arises because the kind of measurement most needed is the hardest to make.

One can scarcely conceive of industrial production as a continuum running from peacetime through wartime. To restate a question posed earlier: how can we measure how much the caterpillar grows when it turns into a butterfly? In recognition of this problem, the peacetime index of industrial production was suspended in the United Kingdom during World War II; and, though continued in the United States, the resulting attempts to measure output of munitions by labor input have been, as we noted above, widely criticized as misrepresenting actual production.

Geoffrey Moore summed up the matter with reference to American experience:[37]

> Under these circumstances [of a transition from peace to war] it seems best to abandon any attempt to measure total industrial production, for the fact of conversion lends an element of arbitrariness, unreality, and uncertainty to any index that purports to measure the total. There is arbitrariness in the choice of weight factors used to

[37] Moore, *Production of Industrial Materials*, p. 49.

combine discontinuous series; there is unreality in the idea of comparing aggregates that, to a large extent, consist of commodities not common to both peace and war periods; there is uncertainty because widely different results can be obtained by different methods of selecting (a) the weight factors mentioned above, and (b) the series that are to be included. We do not believe these difficulties attach, to nearly the same extent, to an index of industrial materials production. This does not mean that such an index measures total output; but it does measure a part that it is feasible to measure, a part that is of interest *per se*, and a part that does influence the aggregate amount of commodities produced in both peacetime and wartime.

These comments apply to a situation in which data are relatively bountiful. By contrast, data on Soviet mobilization are almost entirely lacking: Grossman speaks revealingly of "the shroud that fell on Soviet economic statistics in the late thirties."[38] That shroud has not yet been lifted as far as military production is concerned, for either the interwar or postwar period. Consequently, few Western scholars have been bold enough to try to estimate military production, and those who have—we show their efforts below—have limited themselves to admittedly rough guesses.

From the strict, scholarly point of view, it would be best to admit the impossibility of accurately measuring military production and restrict indexes to what can be reasonably measured, warning of the limited coverage and permitting anybody to make such adjustments as he wishes. We would have preferred to do this, had it not been for the strong objections raised in authoritative quarters to the effect that inclusion of military production would significantly raise the growth rates we had found for the period 1937–1955, and particularly for 1950–1955.[39] Unfortunately, the objections have not been accompanied by the data needed to do the job, so that we have been forced to make our own estimates without help from the critics. We now present them for what they may be worth (Table 30).

Our estimates are discussed in some detail in technical note 3 of Appendix A, and it will be enough to give a brief summary here. The index for military products is derived from estimated value of output deflated

[38] G. Grossman, "Steel, Planning, and War Preparedness in the USSR," *Explorations in Entrepreneurial History*, Vol. IX, No. 4, p. 231.
[39] See, for example, Allen Dulles's testimony in *Hearings, November 13–20, 1959*, Joint Economic Committee, Congress of the United States, Washington, 1960, pp. 1 ff, especially p. 5; and Greenslade and Wallace, "Industrial Growth in the Soviet Union," especially p. 694.

TABLE 30

PRODUCTION INDEXES ADJUSTED FOR ESTIMATED MILITARY PRODUCTION:
SOVIET UNION, BENCHMARK YEARS, 1913–1955

	Military Products	All Products		Industrial Materials	All Products		Industri Material
		Civilian	Total		Civilian	Total	
	INDEX (1937 = 100)				INDEX (1913 = 100)		
1913		37	35	43	100	100	100
1928		38	36	44	102	102	102
1933	4	57	54	60	152	153	140
1937	100	100	100	100	268	285	233
1940	220	102	112	110	274	318	257
1945	627	46	93	67	123	264	157
1946	92	60	63	76	160	180	178
1950	103	148	138	142	397	393	331
1955	288	215	218	219	577	620	511
	LINK RELATIVE (INITIAL YEAR OF PERIOD = 100)						
1913–1928		102	102	102			
1928–1933		149	149	137			
1933–1937	2,500	176	186	166			
1937–1940	220	102	112	110			
1940–1945	285	45	83	61			
1940–1946	42	59	56	69			
1945–1950	16	323	149	210			
1946–1950	112	247	219	187			
1950–1955	282	145	158	154			

SOURCE: Tables A-10, A-11, and 16. Some data for 1933 are from Appendix D.

by a price index for basic industrial products. The value data are essentially direct estimates through 1948; for later years, they are derived residually, as the difference between earmarked defense expenditures and estimated maintenance and operational costs of the armed forces. The latter were calculated before Khrushchev revealed definite information on the changing size of the armed forces in the postwar period,[40] and hence they are probably too low around 1950 and too high around 1955. Consequently, the index of military production probably shows, on this account, too rapid a rise over the period 1950–1955; covered military production in 1955 may, in fact, be as much as 25 per cent lower than shown.[41] On the other hand, atomic energy is not directly covered by our estimates, and this may be expected to balance against the overstatement of 1955 production of conventional military products.

[40] N. S. Khrushchev, "Report at Supreme Soviet Session," *Pravda*, January 15, 1960 (translated in *Current Digest*, XII, 2, pp. 3 ff).
[41] See the annex to technical note 3 of Appendix A.

When the index for all industrial products is adjusted to include ᴜur estimate of military production, it shows a growth more than 7 per cent faster over 1913–1955 than the index for civilian products only. Interestingly, most of the divergence takes place by 1937, with only a slight divergence since that date. Moreover, the indexes for all products and for industrial materials show a closely parallel movement since 1937, except for the year 1945. On the other hand, the index for all products shows substantially more growth over 1950–1955 than the index for all civilian products, and in this respect our critics have been right.

TABLE 31

Comparison of NBER and Other Western Estimates of Military Production: Soviet Union, Benchmark Years, 1933–1955

	Hodgman[a]	M. G. Clark[b]	Shimkin-Leedy[c]	NBER[d]
1933		39		4
1934			30	
1937	100	100	100	100
1938		127		132
1940	335		128	220
1945	202			627
1950	507		100	103
1955			256	288

[a] Implicit index, derived from data in Hodgman, *Soviet Industrial Production*, pp. 86 ff.

[b] Consumption of steel by the munitions industry for fabrication. (M. Gardner Clark, *The Economics of Soviet Steel*, Cambridge, Mass., 1956. p. 316.) Clark does not offer this as an index of military production, but it has been cited elsewhere as a possible index (see, e.g., Grossman, "Steel, Planning, and War Preparedness").

[c] Shimkin and Leedy, "Soviet Industrial Growth," p. 53. Based on estimated consumption of rolled steel by military end items. Underlying data supplied in dittoed form by author.

[d] Table A-10.

Our estimate of military production is compared in Table 31 with the few available estimates of others. There is a reasonably close correspondence between the Shimkin-Leedy index and ours over the spans 1937–1950 and 1950–1955; over other shorter periods that can be compared, there is little correspondence. The Shimkin-Leedy index is estimated military consumption of rolled steel, derived residually since 1937. Our index hardly agrees at all with the implicit Hodgman index, which he describes as "painfullly rough and ready" and involving "some exceedingly cavalier estimates."[42]

[42] Hodgman, *Soviet Industrial Production*, pp. 88 and 85. We have reconstructed Hodgman's implicit index from the information he gives on how he adjusted his total index to reflect military products.

There are some interesting parallels in the behavior of production indexes for the Soviet Union and the United States when they cover estimated military production. First, as we have already noted, over 1913–1955 the divergence of the index for all products from the one for industrial materials is 19 per cent in the case of the United States and 21 per cent in the case of the Soviet Union (see Tables 25 and 30). Second, an apparently artificial peak occurs in the indexes for all products in both countries in the year of maximum military production during World War II: in 1943 for the United States and in 1945 for the Soviet Union (see Tables 30 and A-32). With reconversion, the U.S. index shows a decline of 28 per cent below this peak by 1946; the Soviet index shows a decline of 32 per cent by the same year, with the bulk of reconversion, according to our estimates, taking place in one year instead of three. Again as we have noted, it is doubtful that the wartime peaks and the consequent declines in these index numbers can be treated as at all commensurate with movements in peacetime indexes, because of the abnormal problems of measuring wartime output already described. The fact that the wartime peaks exaggerate actual expansion of productive capacity is shown by the relative behavior of indexes for all products and for industrial materials: the former shows a rise 58 per cent greater than the latter for the United States over 1939–1943 and 36 per cent greater for the Soviet Union over 1940–1945.

Comparison of Our Production Indexes with Others

THE OFFICIAL SOVIET INDEX

With a rare show of virtual unanimity in the field of Soviet studies, Western scholars have long agreed that the official Soviet index of industrial production grossly exaggerates the industrial growth that has taken place. The reasons for this exaggeration have been widely discussed,[43] and they will be reviewed only very briefly here. Unfortunately, the defects in the Soviet index cannot be carefully examined and precisely defined, because the details underlying it have never been published in such a way that independent scholars might reconstruct it. The only recourse for Western scholars seeking a more adequate index has been to construct their own indexes from such data as have been available. We

---

[43] Some of the Western discussion is cited in footnote 23 of Chapter 2. See also Hodgman, *Soviet Industrial Production*, pp. 1–17; A. Nove, "'1926/27' and All That," *Soviet Studies*, October 1957, 117–130; and F. Seton, "The Tempo of Soviet Industrial Expansion," *Manchester Statistical Society*, January 1957, pp. 4–10. Seton's discussion is a clear and succinct summary of the most relevant issues, and we have patterned our own very brief discussion after his.

shall examine a few of the better-known indexes later and compare them with our own.

The official Soviet index measures "gross industrial production." In principle, gross production of every industrial enterprise is calculated by multiplying the output of every product by its corresponding full transfer price (excluding turnover taxes directly levied on the product) as of a base year. Gross production for all industry is the summed gross production for all enterprises. As new products are introduced or as old ones are modified, new prices "equivalent" to those for the base year are assigned to them, and they are counted in production in the same way as other products.

We cannot flatly predict how the use of gross instead of net weights will, in and of itself, affect the behavior of a production index. Multiple weights will be assigned to some productive activities, particularly the most advanced stages of fabrication. If those activities are growing more rapidly than other underweighted activities, growth of the index will be exaggerated by normal standards. In the Soviet case, the most over-weighted areas—machinery and consumer goods—have grown at countervailing rates. Hence, in the absence of experiments with relevantly constructed index numbers, we have no basis for predicting the likely effect of gross weights from this narrow point of view.

A more significant defect of gross-weighted indexes is that they are sensitive to changes in industrial organization: a drift toward greater specialization in productive processes, characterized by a movement away from vertical integration of activities within a single plant and toward multiplication of independent plants performing specialized operations, is bound to lead to a distorting inflation of gross-weighted production indexes. Any similar changes in the purely administrative structure or statistical reporting system will have the same effect. There is no doubt that sweeping changes of this nature have taken place over the Soviet period, particularly during the First and Second Five Year Plans. It is interesting that V. Starovskii, head of the Central Statistical Administration, complains of the presumed reverse effects on the production index caused by the reorganization of industrial administration in 1957.[44]

[44] V. Starovskii, "Novye zadachi sovetskoi statistiki" [New Tasks of Soviet Statistics], *Kommunist* [The Communist], 1957, No. 14, p. 67: "Under the new industrial administration, individual industrial enterprises will be integrated and concentrated. With the amalgamation of several enterprises, the gross value of output of the new enterprise will be smaller because part of it will be considered intershop turnover, although the physical volume of output will not change. Therefore, it is important to compute indexes of industrial production in such a way as to measure correctly the dynamics of physical

The early weight base used over most of the Soviet period also tends to inflate the index. Through 1950, outputs were weighted with presumed "1926/27" prices. For 1950 on, however, the index has been constructed with a moving weight base: "1952" prices for 1950–1955, and "1955" prices for 1955 and later years.

Perhaps the most serious inflation results from the practice of continuously introducing new products into the index at inflated weights. Since new products tend to grow more rapidly in output than older ones, the over-all rate of industrial growth is seriously exaggerated by this practice. Each new product is supposed to be weighted by the price that it would have had in the weight-base year, had it been produced at that time. During the interwar period, however, the weight actually used was essentially the initial unit cost of production. This weight was inflated on two counts: first, initial costs are generally abnormally high since they include developmental expenses, apply to a pilot rate of production, and do not allow for normally rapid reductions in cost attributable to learning; second, there was a steady and substantial inflation in the price level during this period. The practice of reweighting improved products also opened the way for statistical manipulations by skillful plant managers, who could make a more favorable production record by the simple device of "improving" some of their products and assigning them higher prices.[45]

Although the general price level has tended to fall since 1949, new products are still overweighted because their initial prices are adjusted upward by the same proportion as the decline in the price level since the weight-base year. The distortions in weights on this count are probably less pronounced than during the interwar period, because the weight base is moved forward periodically. Another practice recently adopted

---

output and to exclude the effect of the structure of the enterprises on the total volume of production."

It is by no means clear that Starovskii's presumption of such a downward bias is justified for recent years. In any case, Academician S. G. Strumilin estimates in a recent article (in *Ocherki sotsialisticheskoi ekonomiki SSSR* [Essays on the USSR Socialist Economy], Moscow, 1959, pp. 233–242) that net production in "1926/27" rubles multiplied only about thirteen times over 1928–1955, compared with the twenty-one-fold growth shown by the official index of gross production. For 1956, Strumilin estimates that net production increased by 8.5 per cent; the official index shows 10.7 per cent.

[45] The official Soviet index apparently does not reflect the full inflation in prices. The industrial price level, adjusted to eliminate most turnover taxes, multiplied about eleven times over 1913–1955 and 5.5 times over 1928–1955 (see Table A-17). Hence the deflated official production index for 1955 would read 250 per cent of 1913 and 380 per cent of 1928 (see Table F-2). Both of these values fall below the lower limits of our indexes.

tends, however, to reinforce the distortions. The price weights now used apparently differ according to the region in which the product is produced, whereas formerly a single price was used for each product. For each enterprise, the regional prices are apparently calculated including freight to destination. Hence, production in the more remote, faster-growing regions tends to be overweighted relative to production in the more settled, slower-growing regions.

TABLE 32

COMPARISON OF NBER AND OFFICIAL SOVIET INDEXES OF INDUSTRIAL PRODUCTION: SOVIET UNION, BENCHMARK YEARS, 1913–1955

| | NBER Index[a] | | | | |
	Industrial Materials	Finished Civilian Products	All Civilian Products	All Industrial Products	Official Soviet Index[b]
	INDEX (1913 = 100)				
1913	100	100	100	100	100
1928	102	99	102	102	132
1932	133	126	144	144	267
1937	233	239	268	285	588
1940	257	226	274	318	852
1945	157	100	123	264	782
1950	331	295	397	393	1,476
1955	511	460	577	620	2,729
	LINK RELATIVE (INITIAL YEAR OF PERIOD = 100)				
1913–1928	102	99	102	102	132
1928–1932	131	127	140	140	202
1932–1937	175	189	186	198	220
1937–1940	110	94	102	112	145
1940–1945	61	44	45	83	92
1945–1950	210	295	323	149	189
1950–1955	154	156	145	158	185

[a] Tables 16 and 30. Moving weights.

[b] *Promyshlennost' SSSR* [Industry of the USSR], Moscow, 1957, p. 9.

The official Soviet index is compared with our moving-weight indexes in Table 32 and Chart 14. It shows a much larger percentage increase, or smaller percentage decline, than our index for all industrial products in every subperiod. The same holds true in comparisons with our other indexes, except for the period 1945–1950. The peculiar relative behavior in that subperiod may be attributed to the fact that the official index attempts a direct coverage of armaments production while those of ours just referred to do not. The average annual rates of growth for the official index and our moving-weight index for all industrial products

CHART 14
NBER and Other Indexes of Soviet Industrial Production,
Benchmark Years, 1913–1955

A.   NBER and Official Soviet Indexes, 1913–1955

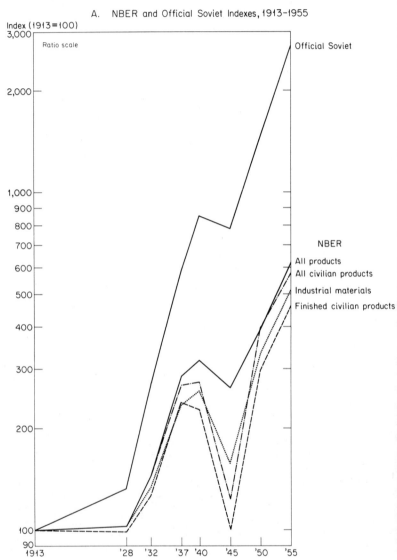

CHART 14 (concluded)

B. NBER and Other Western Indexes, 1928–1955

Index (1928 = 100)

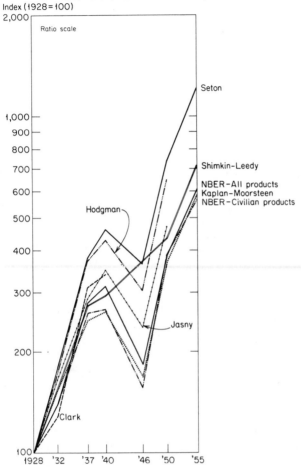

Source: Tables 32 and 33.

are as follows: 1913–1955, 8.2 and 4.4 per cent; 1928–1955, 11.9 and 6.9; 1928–1940, 16.8 and 9.9; 1940–1955, 8.1 and 4.6; 1928–1937, 18.1 and 12.1; and 1950–1955, 13.1 and 9.6.

INDEXES BY WESTERN SCHOLARS

Six production indexes constructed by Western scholars are presented in Table 33. Each of them tends to rise more rapidly over the long run than our moving-weight index for all industrial products, though less rapidly than the official Soviet index (see Table 32 and Chart 14).

TABLE 33

COMPARISON OF NBER AND OTHER WESTERN INDEXES OF INDUSTRIAL PRODUCTION:
SOVIET UNION, BENCHMARK YEARS, 1928–1955

	C. Clark[a]	Jasny[b]	Hodgman[c]	Shimkin-Leedy[d]	Seton[e]	Kaplan-Moorsteen[f]	NBER, All Products[g] Civilian	Total
			INDEX	(1928 = 100)				
1928	100	100	100	100	100	100	100	100
1932	128	165	172		181	154	140	140
1937	310	287	371	274	380	249	261	279
1940	339	350[h]	430	294	462	263	267	312
1946		236	304		365	168	156	183
1950		470[i]	646	434	733	369	387	385
1955				715	1,210	583	563	608
		LINK	RELATIVE	(INITIAL	YEAR	OF	PERIOD = 100)	
1928–1932	128	165	172		181	154	140	140
1932–1937	242	174	216		210	162	186	199
1937–1940	109	122	116	107	122	106	102	112
1940–1946		67	71		79	64	58	59
1946–1950		199	212		201	220	248	210
1950–1955				165	165	158	145	158

[a] Colin Clark, *The Conditions of Economic Progress*, 2d. ed., London, 1951, p. 186.
[b] Naum Jasny, "Indices of Soviet Industrial Production, 1928–1954" (mimeographed), Council f
Economic and Industry Research Report A-46, Washington, 1955, pp. 40 ff.
[c] Hodgman, *Soviet Industrial Production*, p. 89. His adjusted index for large-scale industry.
[d] Shimkin and Leedy, "Soviet Industrial Growth," p. 51. Includes estimated military production
[e] Seton, "Tempo of Soviet Industrial Expansion," p. 30.
[f] Kaplan and Moorsteen, "Indexes of Soviet Industrial Output," p. 235.
[g] Moving-weight index for all industrial products, excluding miscellaneous machinery.
[h] For 1939 territory, 330.
[i] Earlier estimates by Jasny were 427 and 444. With "1926/27 American prices," the estimate is 41
See his "Indices," pp. 40–42.

The indexes have been constructed by widely differing methods.
Colin Clark's index, being one of the earliest, is based on a very small
sample of industries—twelve for the period 1928–1937—weighted together
by his "international units." Naum Jasny's index is based partly on
output series weighted by his Soviet "real 1926/27 prices," and partly on
adjustments of various official Soviet aggregates.[46] Francis Seton's
index is derived from the growth rates for three physical output series
(fuel and hydroelectric power in calories, steel, and electricity) and the
multiple correlation of these growth rates with the growth rate for all
industrial production as calculated for a sample of fourteen Western
countries over three time periods.

[46] For more details on these two indexes, see Naum Jasny, "Indices of Soviet Industrial
Production, 1928–1954" (mimeographed), Council for Economic and Industry Research
Report A-46, Washington, 1955.

The Hodgman, Shimkin-Leedy, and Kaplan-Moorsteen indexes are constructed along conventional lines comparable to those we have followed. The Hodgman index covers large-scale industry in 1928, with the coverage expanding to total industry by around 1933 and thereafter. The product coverage falls off sharply after 1937 because of the limited sample of data available at the time the index was computed. In 1937, 137 products are covered; in 1940, twenty-two; and in 1950, eighteen.[47] He makes some admittedly tenuous adjustments to cover estimated armaments production. As weights he uses 1934 Soviet wage-bill data adjusted to include payroll taxes of various types, except for internal weighting of machinery as described in the earlier section of this chapter on machinery and equipment. Weights are fully imputed throughout all industrial categories to the represented output series, with an additional imputation to the metalworking sector to correct a presumed underweighting by wage-bill data. His index, therefore, differs from ours in a number of respects.

The Shimkin-Leedy index uses a modified version of Hodgman's weights and also includes estimated military production. The product series used seem to cover all industry, rather than large-scale industry. Unfortunately, the details underlying this index have not yet been made fully available, so that we cannot investigate the reasons for its differences from ours, which occur primarily over 1937–1955.

For partly different reasons, we are also unable to rationalize the differences between the Kaplan-Moorsteen index and ours. In this case, the former was published after this study had been completed—the details for the machinery segment have not yet appeared—so that systematic comparisons could not be undertaken. It is a comprehensive index covering civilian products and based on 1950 Soviet weights. A somewhat more informative description is given in the annex to technical note 4 of Appendix A, where their sector indexes are compared with ours. We may note here that their aggregate index rises, over the long run, at a rate between those for our indexes for all civilian products with 1928 and 1955 weights, though Kaplan and Moorsteen seem to feel that the similarity to our index with 1955 weights is less than should be expected on the basis of the closeness of the weight bases.[48]

A large portion of the difference between Hodgman's and our indexes is traceable to his adjustments for presumed undercoverage of the metalworking and armaments sector. We see from Table 34 that his unadjusted

[47] Hodgman, *Soviet Industrial Production*, p. 81.
[48] See Kaplan and Moorsteen, "Indexes of Soviet Industrial Growth," p. 79. This question also is commented on in the annex to technical note 4, Appendix A.

TABLE 34

COMPARISON OF NBER AND HODGMAN INDEXES OF INDUSTRIAL PRODUCTION:
SOVIET UNION, BENCHMARK YEARS, 1928–1950

	Original Hodgman Index		Hodgman-NBER Index[a]		NBER Index[b]		
					All Civilian Products		All Products
	Adjusted[c]	Unadjusted[d]	A	B	A	B	A
INDEX (1928 = 100)							
1928	100	100	100	100	100	100	100
1932	172	163	138	150	140	143	143
1937	371	342	267	283	261	265	279
1940	430	351	289	305	267	272	312
1950	646	527	406	458	387	411	385
LINK RELATIVE (INITIAL YEAR OF PERIOD = 100)							
1928–1932	172	163	138	150	140	143	143
1932–1937	216	211	194	189	186	185	195
1937–1940	116	103	108	108	102	103	112
1940–1950	150	150	141	150	144	151	123

[a] NBER series combined with Hodgman's unadjusted weights (see Table A-15). Miscellaneous machinery excluded from index marked A and included in index marked B.

[b] Moving-weight indexes. Miscellaneous machinery excluded from indexes marked A and included in indexes marked B.

[c] Hodgman, *Soviet Industrial Production*, p. 89. Adjusted for estimated incomplete coverage of the metalworking and armament sector. For adjustments, see *ibid.*, pp. 71–74 and 85–89.

[d] *Ibid.*, pp. 84 and 237. Not adjusted for uncovered metalworking products and armaments.

index for 1950 is almost 20 per cent lower than his adjusted index. In order to trace out additional sources of divergence, we have computed a new index using his wage-bill weights and our output series, without adjusting for presumed undercoverage of the metalworking and armaments sector. This new index, which is comparable in construction with Hodgman's unadjusted index, approaches ours much more closely than Hodgman's original index. The major source of divergence between our indexes and Hodgman's index would therefore seem to be the differing scope of output series. Since our series are designed to cover total output in all years, they show a slower growth in some sectors than his series, which cover only large-scale output in earlier years.[49] More detailed comparisons for industrial sectors, as given in technical note 4 of Appendix A, support this conclusion even more strongly. It should be noted

[49] Adam Kaufman has constructed a production index for industrial materials produced in the large-scale sector, with 1928 weights and the same product coverage as our index of industrial materials. His index shows a rise of 71 per cent over 1927/28–1933, which may be compared with a rise of 78 per cent in Hodgman's "unadjusted" index and 92 per cent in his "adjusted" one (see A. Kaufman, "Small-Scale Industry in the Soviet Union," NBER [in press], Table 17, and Hodgman, *Soviet Industrial Production*, p. 73).

that the new Hodgman-NBER index is lower than Hodgman's original despite the fact that we have substituted our faster-growing machinery sector for his (see Table 29). As a by-product, we have in the new hybrid index another example of the effect of the weighting system on the movement of an index of Soviet industrial production.

Concluding Remarks

We have tried in this chapter to present a fairly detailed account of the problems involved in measuring the aggregate growth of Soviet industrial production and the ways we have met these problems. It will have become clear that any aggregative index one might construct is bound to be less reliable than those for many Western countries because of the peculiar shortcomings of Soviet statistics, the unique organizational structure of the Soviet economy, and the unusual nature of Soviet industrial growth. For this reason we have calculated a variety of production indexes with differing scope and weighting systems, in the belief that the configuration of results is more meaningful than the set of figures presented by one index alone. Fortunately, a reasonable pattern of evidence does emerge, and there is a certain convergence of results allowing us to proceed with the analysis. Nevertheless, we must constantly view the numbers before us as blurred outlines rather than as the sharp figures they appear to be. Many estimates, assumptions, and inferences have had to be made in building the foundation of basic data from which the index numbers have been constructed, and undoubtedly many errors have been made in the process and in subsequent calculations, some discovered and some not. It is in a mood of caution, then, that we move on to the job of interpreting the collected evidence.

CHAPTER 6

Aggregative Growth Trends: Analysis

HAVING made our production indexes, we turn now to analyze what they convey about the course of Soviet industrial growth.[1] In this chapter, we shall provide only a broad sketch, to be filled in more fully in the next one. Should it need repeating, we may say again that the qualifications spelled out in earlier chapters should remain constantly in the background, to dull the edge of deceptively sharp figures.

It is also worth re-emphasizing that broad indexes of production are, under the best of circumstances, only one kind of evidence useful for assessing growth trends. Their usefulness is more limited in the Soviet case than ordinarily because of the questionable reliability of Soviet data, the swift and radical changes that have taken place in the Soviet economy over the last thirty years, and the divergences among growth rates in different sectors. This is to say that the discussion that follows supplements rather than supplants what has come before.

Trends in Production

VARIATIONS IN GROWTH RATES OVER TIME

Average annual growth rates from moving-weight indexes are gathered together for different periods in Table 35. Certain relations hold among these growth rates no matter which production index is used. First, the rate is significantly higher for 1928–1955 than for 1913–1955. This is a trivial observation, since it has been made abundantly clear that there was virtually no growth in over-all production between 1913 and 1928. Second and much less obviously, the growth rate shows a decline between 1928–1940 and 1940–1955 and between 1928–1937 and 1950–1955, both relations suggesting a tendency for growth to retard during the Plan period.

In thinking about trends, one naturally wonders how the Soviet pace of industrial growth compares with the Tsarist pace.[1a] The statistical record for the Tsarist period is, unfortunately, poor, and it is difficult to make any confident judgments on the reliability of such data as have

[1] Recall that industry is taken to include manufacturing, mining, logging, fishing, and generating of electricity.

[1a] For an enlightening discussion of industrial development in the Tsarist period, see Alexander Gerschenkron, "The Rate of Industrial Growth in Russia since 1885," *The Tasks of Economic History*, Supplement VII to *Journal of Economic History*, 1947, pp. 144–174.

ANALYSIS

TABLE 35

AVERAGE ANNUAL GROWTH RATES OF INDUSTRIAL PRODUCTION:
SOVIET UNION, SELECTED PERIODS, 1913–1955
(per cent)

	Industrial Materials	Finished Civilian Products	All Civilian Products	All Products
1913–1955	4.0	3.7	4.3	4.4
1913–1928	0.1	−0.1	0.1	0.1
1928–1955	6.2	5.9	6.6	6.9
1928–1940	8.0	7.1	8.5	9.9
1940–1955	4.7	4.9	5.1	4.6
1928–1937	9.6	10.3	11.2	12.1
1950–1955	9.0	9.3	7.7	9.6

SOURCE: Moving-weight indexes, Table 30. Current territory except 1913, which covers interwar territory. Average annual growth rates calculated from data for terminal years by the compound interest formula.

been recorded. Production indexes have been constructed, perhaps the best known being the one made by Kondratiev in the 1920's.[2] If that index is revised to conform with the present Western methods of constructing production indexes and extended backward from 1885 through 1860, it shows an average annual growth rate of about 5.3 per cent applying to the last half century—and even the last quarter century—of the Tsarist period (see Table 36). A recomputation of the index directly from primary sources by Raymond Goldsmith and Israel Borenstein leads to virtually the same result, while a production index for industrial materials with 1913 weights shows a higher growth rate over 1860–1913 but about the same rate over 1885–1913.

It must be stressed that these indexes for the Tsarist period rest on a weak and unverifiable foundation, in terms of both the sample of industries covered and the reliability of the data.[3] All this is to argue that these indexes cannot be considered as reliable as, say, those for the late nineteenth century in the United States, if only because there was nothing in Tsarist Russia to correspond with the periodic U.S. censuses. With this

[2] *Ekonomicheskii biulleten'* [Economic Bulletin], 1926, No. 2, pp. 17–21; discussed in detail by Ia. P. Gerchuk in *Voprosy koniunktury* [Problems of the Economic Situation], Moscow, 1926, Vol. II, Issue 1, pp. 79–95. This and the other indexes in Table 36 are discussed briefly in technical note 5 of Appendix A.

[3] Our index covers the following numbers of industries: 1860–1880, fourteen; 1880–1885, fifteen; 1885–1888, sixteen; 1888–1895, twenty-one; 1895–1900, twenty-two; 1900–1910, twenty-five; and 1910–1913, twenty-three.

TABLE 36

INDEXES OF INDUSTRIAL PRODUCTION: TSARIST RUSSIA, BENCHMARK YEARS, 1860–1913

	Revised Kondratiev Index	Borenstein-Goldsmith Index	Industrial Materials Index
	INDEX (1913 = 100)		
1860	9.0	8.8	5.7
1865	7.1	7.5	4.3
1870	11	11	6.4
1875	15	14	9.9
1880	19	18	13
1885	23	24	19
1888	25	26	23
1890	29	32	25
1895	40	44	39
1900	59	63	59
1905	61	61	60
1910	84	86	78
1913	100	100	100
	AVERAGE ANNUAL GROWTH RATE (PER CENT)		
1860–1880	3.9	3.6	4.2
1870–1890	5.0	5.5	7.1
1880–1900	5.8	6.5	7.9
1890–1910	5.5	5.1	5.9
1900–1913	4.1	3.6	4.1
1870–1913	5.3	5.3	5.4

SOURCE: Table A-19. Covers current Tsarist territory excluding Finland. For 1913, output of industrial materials (col. 3) in Tsarist territory is 118 per cent of output in interwar Soviet territory. Average annual growth rates calculated from data for terminal years by the compound interest formula.

reservation in mind, we note the average annual growth rate over 1870–1913 was higher than over 1913–1955 and lower than over 1928–1955, though the rate over 1880–1900 is very close to the latter, particularly if territorial gains are eliminated (see Table 38).

INDUSTRIAL STRUCTURE OF GROWTH RATES

Rates of growth have differed substantially among the various sectors of Soviet industry as well as over time (see Table 37 and Chart 15). Dividing the civilian component of industry into ten industrial groups, we find average annual growth rates ranging from 2.3 per cent (food and allied products) to 12.9 per cent (consumer durables) over the entire Soviet period, or from 3.3 per cent (textiles and allied products) to 18.7 per cent (consumer durables) over the Plan period. If these ten groups are further condensed into three major categories, we find the following average

TABLE 37

AVERAGE ANNUAL GROWTH RATES OF INDUSTRIAL PRODUCTION, BY INDUSTRIAL GROUP: SOVIET UNION, SELECTED PERIODS, 1913-1955

(per cent)

	1913–1955	1913–1928	1928–1955	1928–1940	1940–1955	1928–1937	1950–1955
All products	4.4	0.1	6.9	9.9	4.6	12.1	9.6
All civilian products	4.3		6.6	8.5	5.1	11.2	7.7
Intermediate products	5.5	0.5	8.4	11.9	5.6	15.0	9.0
Ferrous metals	5.4	-0.8	9.0	12.8	6.1	17.1	11.2
Nonferrous metals	7.9	-0.2	12.7	19.8	7.2	21.7	13.2
Fuel and electricity	7.4	2.7	10.1	15.5	5.9	18.0	9.6
Chemicals	6.5	2.6	8.8	11.9	6.3	16.4	7.7
Construction materials	3.3	-0.8	5.7	6.6	5.1	9.1	8.5
Civilian machinery and equipment	8.4	2.4	11.9	18.9	6.7	31.0	2.6
Transportation equipment	8.8	-0.7	14.5	27.7	4.9	42.3	1.2
Agricultural machinery	6.2	6.3	6.1	-0.1	11.3	9.0	5.1
Consumer goods	2.6	-0.2	4.2	4.8	3.7	5.5	10.0
Food and allied products	2.3	-1.2	4.3	5.3	3.4	6.9	8.9
Textiles and allied products	2.4	0.8	3.3	3.7	3.1	3.3	9.0
Consumer durables	12.9	3.1	18.7	25.0	14.0	41.8	23.1

SOURCE: Tables 17 and 35. Current territory except 1913, which covers interwar Soviet territory. Average annual growth rates calculated from data in terminal years by the compound interest formula.

165

CHART 15
Indexes of Industrial Production, by Industrial Group:
Soviet Union, Benchmark Years, 1913–1955

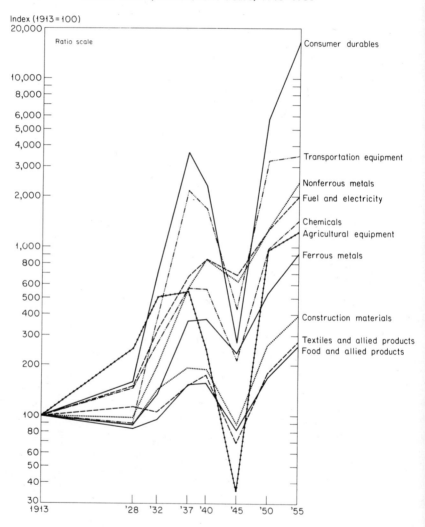

Source: Table 17, moving weights.

annual growth rates for the entire Soviet period and the Plan period, respectively: intermediate industrial products, 5.5 and 8.4 per cent; civilian machinery and equipment, 8.4 and 11.9 per cent; and consumer goods, 2.6 and 4.2 per cent. These data merely confirm what was observed at an earlier point through the study of frequency distributions of growth rates for individual industries.

Although aggregate output increased very little between 1913 and 1928, the growth record varied considerably from one segment of industry to another. At one extreme, the average annual growth rate for agricultural machinery over this period was somewhat higher than it was over the Plan period. Output grew on the average in the cases of agricultural machinery, consumer durables, fuel and electricity, chemicals, and textiles and allied products. It declined in the cases of food and allied products, ferrous metals, construction materials, transportation equipment, and nonferrous metals.

The growth rate declined between 1928–1940 and 1940–1955 in the case of every industrial group except agricultural machinery, which showed an exceptional performance here as well. Similar declines are observed between 1928–1937 and 1950–1955 except for food and textiles, in which cases the growth rate rose. This pattern indicates that the retardation in growth recorded for all industry has been widely diffused through industrial segments.

INDUSTRIAL GROWTH AND TERRITORIAL EXPANSION

During and after World War II, the Soviet Union acquired the Baltic countries, about half of Poland, a part of Rumania, and some other scattered regions. Territory was expanded by about 700 thousand square kilometers (an area larger than France), and population by more than 20 million people as of 1939. The enlarged territory slightly exceeds in area the prerevolutionary territory; on the other hand, the population in 1913 was smaller within the post-1939 territory than within the prerevolutionary territory—159 million as opposed to 166 million.

It is impossible to make an accurate and precise measurement of the industrial gains realized from territorial expansion as of any specific date after 1939. The economic gains were resources that could be employed in a variety of uses, and the specific forms of those resources when acquired merely set temporary limits on their uses. By the nature of the problem, however, about the only way we can measure industrial gains is in terms of acquisitions of existing industrial resources. Ultimate gains will be understated to the extent that acquired areas have since been industrialized more rapidly out of their "own" resources than the rest of the Soviet Union, or overstated to the extent that they have been industrialized less rapidly. We do not have the data needed to shed light on matters of this sort, and it is doubtful that we could say anything very satisfactory under the best of circumstances.

If we keep these qualifications in mind, we may estimate very roughly the industrial gains from territorial expansion. In the first place, we may calculate the relative importance of industrial production in the acquired territories at the time of acquisition. The latest satisfactory date, from the point of view of both normalcy of conditions and availability of data, is 1937. In that year, the production of industrial materials (fifty products) was 6 per cent larger in the expanded territory than in the interwar territory when measured in 1928 prices,[4] and 10 per cent larger when measured in 1955 prices. These figures understate gains for two reasons: first, because they do not fully reflect small-scale production in the acquired territories; and second, because by 1937 those territories had not fully recovered from the Great Depression.

Another approach is to calculate the relative share of industrial production accounted for by the territories lost after the Communist revolution, since, as mentioned above, these areas are in some respects roughly equivalent to those gained during and after World War II. The production of industrial materials (thirty-seven products) in those lost territories was in 1913 about 18 per cent of production within interwar boundaries, when measured in 1913 prices. This figure may also be an understatement in that small-scale production in the lost territories is not fully included.

It is perhaps reasonable to take the geometric average of these three estimates, or 11 per cent, as a rough measure of the increase in industrial production attributable to territorial expansion. On an average annual basis the percentage increase would be as follows: 0.3 per cent for 1913–1955; 0.4 per cent for 1928–1955; and 0.9 per cent for 1928–1940. Growth rates in production adjusted for territorial changes are given in Table 38.

INDUSTRIAL GROWTH AND POPULATION

The discussion of industrial growth in this chapter has been, up to this point, entirely in terms of raw growth rates, unadjusted for growth in population. For some purposes, it is useful to express growth in per

---

[4] This estimate is identical with Naum Jasny's estimate for 1940. See his *The Soviet Economy during the Plan Era*, Stanford, 1951, p. 22. Our estimates are explained in Table D-1, notes *c* and *d*.

TABLE 38

RAGE ANNUAL GROWTH RATES OF INDUSTRIAL PRODUCTION ADJUSTED FOR TERRITORIAL EXPANSION
AND POPULATION GROWTH: SOVIET UNION, SELECTED PERIODS, 1913–1955
(per cent)

	Production Adjusted to Constant Territory[a]				Per Capita Production[b]			
	Industrial Materials	Finished Civilian Products	All Civilian Products	All Products	Industrial Materials	Finished Civilian Products	All Civilian Products	All Products
3–1955	3.7	3.4	4.0	4.1	3.1	2.8	3.4	3.5
3–1928	0.1	−0.1	0.1	0.1	−0.5	−0.7	−0.5	−0.5
3–1955	5.8	5.5	6.2	6.5	5.1	4.9	5.5	5.8
8–1940	7.0	6.1	7.5	8.9	5.5	4.7	6.1	7.4
0–1955	4.7	4.9	5.1	4.6	4.7	4.9	5.1	4.6
8–1937	9.6	10.3	11.2	12.1	8.5	9.2	10.1	11.0
0–1955	9.0	9.3	7.7	9.6	7.2	7.5	5.9	7.8

OURCE: Tables 35 and C-3. For effects of territorial expansion, see text surrounding this table.
Average annual growth in production attributable to territorial expansion is taken as: 0.3 per cent
1913–1955; 0.4 per cent for 1928–1955; and 0.9 per cent for 1928–1940. Average annual growth
s calculated from data for terminal years by the compound interest formula.
Derived from unadjusted production and population. Average annual growth in population is
n as 0.9 per cent for 1913–1955; 0.6 per cent for 1913–1928; 1.0 per cent for 1928–1955; 2.3 per
t for 1928–1940; −0.0 per cent for 1940–1955; 1.0 per cent for 1928–1937; and 1.7 per cent for
0–1955.

capita terms, particularly when one is interested in relating growth in
output to growth in productive capacity.

Population is sometimes, however, a very poor indicator of productive
capacity. At least during the interwar years of the Soviet period, a
sizable fraction of the population was, for all practical purposes, economically unproductive: reducing the labor force in some sectors of the economy—especially agriculture—probably caused no perceptible reduction
in output. This meant, for example, that the great loss of population
through starvation in the 1920's and 1930's probably had the paradoxical
result of increasing the concurrent per capita output: there were fewer
mouths to feed and fewer bodies to clothe, so to speak, without a commensurate reduction in utilized productive capacity. We must also note that
Soviet population statistics are of doubtful reliability for much of the
Soviet period.[5] Under such conditions, there are obvious difficulties in
interpreting the meaning of per capita growth rates.

[5] Full demographic details were last published in connection with the population
census of 1926, though it appears more information than usual will be made public on
the census of 1959. The census of 1937 was declared faulty by Stalin, and most of the

Despite these difficulties, the picture of industrial growth would be incomplete without relating it to population, as is done in Table 38. As would be anticipated, the rates of population growth have varied from period to period during the Soviet era, reflecting, of course, the effects of territorial changes as well as internal demographic conditions. For the periods shown in Table 38, the per capita growth rates are less dispersed than the total growth rates, whether or not the latter are adjusted for territorial coverage. However, retardation is reflected in the per capita growth rates as well as in the total ones.

Trends in Labor Productivity

Growth in productive capacity springs from growth in resources or improved efficiency in their use. In studying the importance of each, the usual procedure is to measure the volume of resources employed, by means of an index combining capital and labor services, and to compare that with the volume of output. Unfortunately, statistics on capital inputs into Soviet industry are in such a poor state that we cannot make this kind of comparison.[6] We must instead be content to compare output and employment of labor.

GROWTH IN INDUSTRIAL EMPLOYMENT

Comprehensive statistics on Soviet industrial employment, wage rates, or hours of work have yet to be published, so that here again we are forced to do the best we can with such partial information as has been made available. Our estimates are presented and discussed in technical note 7 of Appendix A, and we shall describe them only briefly here.

The basic estimates are for persons engaged in industry, expressed in full-time equivalents as measured by the average work-year (in days or

---

leading demographers participating in it were purged; the results were never published, except for a few fragments. A second census was conducted in 1939, and a few aggregative statistics were published. No further figures were published until 1956, when an official estimate for April 1956 was announced. The problems Western scholars have encountered in constructing estimates of population are demonstrated by the fact that Western estimates of population in 1956 had typically run about 10 per cent higher than the figure finally published (see *Statistical Handbook of the USSR*, Harry Schwartz, editor, New York, 1957, p. 16). Our population series (Table C-3) is taken from a working memorandum written by Harold Wool for this study.

[6] Soviet authorities have recently expressed dissatisfaction with the official figures on industrial wealth and have indicated that a full count of inventory will be needed to put the facts in order (see, e.g., V. Starovskii, "Novye zadachi sovetskoi statistiki" [New Tasks of Soviet Statistics], *Kommunist* [The Communist], 1957, No. 14, p. 68). Some results of that count are provided in *Narodnoe khoziaistvo SSSR v 1959 godu* [The USSR National Economy in 1959], Moscow, 1960, pp. 65 ff.

TABLE 39

INDEXES OF INDUSTRIAL EMPLOYMENT, BY INDUSTRIAL GROUP:
SOVIET UNION, BENCHMARK YEARS, 1913–1955
(1913 = 100)

	1913	1928	1933	1937	1940	1950	1955
			MAN-HOURS				
products	100	74	105	151	203	253	284
			PERSONS ENGAGED[a]				
products	100	92	149	210	225	275	333
Ferrous and nonferrous metals	100	66	135	147	142	235	264
Fuel and electricity	100	128	245	258	296	444	540
Fuel	100	127	230	235	272	400	481
Electricity	100	140	485	625	670	1,145	1,475
Chemicals	100	143	399	501	593	631	899
Construction materials[b]	100	76	178	175	204	276	345
Wood materials[b]	100	72	168	180	206	261	269
Mineral materials	100	96	225	152	197	347	502
Machinery and allied products[c]	100	109	408	515	559	721	886
Civilian machinery and equipment	100	129	268	604	412	622	857
Food and allied products	100	75	102	138	145	153	167
Textiles and allied products[d]	100	104	108	139	148	141	181

SOURCE: Table A-24. Note that some industrial groups have a different coverage from that in Table 37.
[a] Full-time equivalents.
[b] Covers paper and matches.
[c] Covers civilian machinery, equipment, and metal products; military products; and consumer durables.
[d] For 1937 and later years, covers furniture.

weeks) in large-scale industry. For all industry, persons engaged have been taken as the sum of workers and employees, members of industrial producer cooperatives, self-employed personnel, and workers in industrial enterprises attached to collective farms. In the virtual absence of data on wages by industrial categories, we are forced to use an unweighted aggregate. Recent evidence suggests that our totals progressively understate the true total after 1933, so that growth in employment since that year is probably significantly understated, perhaps by as much as 15 per cent.[7]

For benchmark years through 1933, persons engaged can be directly estimated for industrial groups as well as for all industry; for later years, the industrial breakdown must be derived indirectly by distributing the aggregate on the basis of published percentage distributions of production workers (*promyshlennye rabochie*). On the basis of evidence for 1933 and 1935, the latter procedure is likely to cause an understatement of persons engaged in producing electricity, machinery and equipment,

[7] See technical note 7 in Appendix A.

and possibly mineral construction materials; it is likely to cause an overstatement in the cases of other industrial categories. Hence, on this count, growth in employment since 1933 may be understated in the former categories and overstated in the latter. The estimates as they stand are given in Table 39.

It is, finally, possible to estimate the annual man-hours of employment in all industry on the basis of rather fragmentary data on average annual days and average daily hours worked by production workers in large-scale industry. Again, the information available is far from ideal, and it is impossible to say how much error there may be in applying it to all persons engaged, or in what direction the error lies. The average annual hours worked, estimated in this way, have fluctuated widely over the Soviet period, falling from 1913 through 1933, rising thereafter almost to the prerevolutionary level by 1950, and falling again through 1955, when they were still higher than in 1928 (see Table A-23 of Appendix A). Hence the total annual man-hours increased less, percentagewise, than total persons engaged over 1913–1955, but more over 1928–1955 (see Table 39).

TABLE 40

INDEXES OF INDUSTRIAL OUTPUT PER UNIT OF LABOR, BY INDUSTRIAL GROUP:
SOVIET UNION, BENCHMARK YEARS, 1913–1955
(1913 = 100)

	1913	1928	1933	1937	1940	1950	19!
			OUTPUT	PER	MAN-HOUR		
All products	100	137	146	188	157	155	21
			OUTPUT	PER	PERSON	ENGAGED[a]	
All products	100	111	103	135	141	143	18
Ferrous and nonferrous metals	100	133	116	254	282	245	37
Fuel and electricity	100	118	150	259	287	284	36
Fuel	100	101	116	178	191	187	23
Electricity	100	184	173	298	371	410	59
Chemicals	100	101	76	130	109	186	18
Construction materials[b]	100	119	81	116	97	101	12
Wood materials[b]	100	121	88	101	90	98	13
Mineral materials	100	109	57	194	127	110	14
Machinery and allied products[c]	100	111	100	274	314	275	36
Civilian machinery and equipment	100	111	249	286	291	449	40
Food and allied products	100	112	91	111	108	110	15
Textiles and allied products[d]	100	109	94	109	118	127	15

SOURCE: Table A-24. Note that some industrial groups have a different coverage from tha Table 37.

[a] Persons engaged in full-time equivalents.

[b] Covers paper and matches.

[c] Covers civilian machinery, equipment, and metal products; military products; and consu durables.

[d] For 1937 and later years, furniture is covered for persons engaged but not for output. This l omission is not likely to be significant.

CHART 16
Indexes of Industrial Output and Employment: Soviet Union, Benchmark Years, 1913–1955

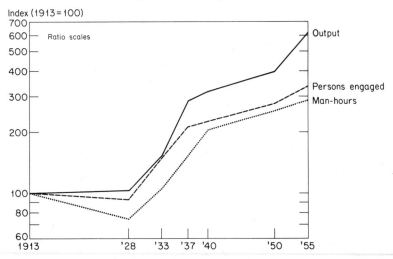

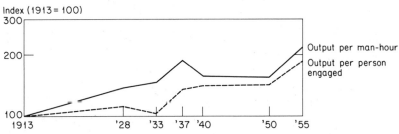

Source: Tables 40 and A-24.

GROWTH IN OUTPUT PER UNIT OF LABOR

Our estimates of movements in Soviet industrial output per unit of labor employed are presented in Tables 40 and 41 and in Charts 16 and 17. According to these estimates, output per man-hour multiplied about 2.2 times between 1913 and 1955 and about 1.6 times between 1928 and 1955, growing at average annual rates of 1.9 and 1.7 per cent; output per person engaged multiplied about 1.9 and 1.7 times, growing at average annual rates of 1.5 and 1.9 per cent. Within shorter spans of years, the two types of measures have differed more markedly from each other, output per man-hour showing a faster growth than output per person engaged in some periods and a slower growth in others. This

173

CHART 17
Indexes of Industrial Output per Person Engaged, by Industrial Group:
Soviet Union, Benchmark Years, 1913–1955

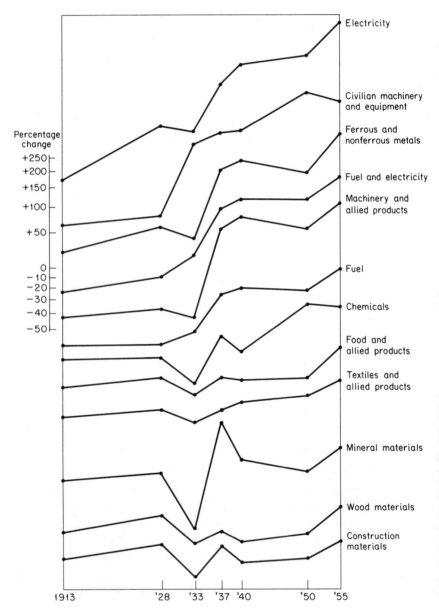

Source: Tabl 40.

174

TABLE 41

AVERAGE ANNUAL GROWTH RATES OF INDUSTRIAL OUTPUT PER UNIT OF LABOR, BY INDUSTRIAL GROUP: SOVIET UNION, BENCHMARK YEARS, 1913–1955

	1913–1955	1913–1928	1928–1955	1928–1940	1940–1955	1928–1937	1950–1955
All products	1.9	2.1	1.7	1.2	2.2	3.6	7.1
			OUTPUT PER MAN-HOUR				
			OUTPUT PER PERSON ENGAGED				
All products	1.5	0.7	1.9	2.0	1.9	2.2	5.4
Ferrous and nonferrous metals	3.2	1.9	3.9	6.5	1.9	7.7	8.8
Fuel and electricity	3.2	1.1	4.3	7.7	1.7	9.1	5.4
Fuel	2.1	0.1	3.2	5.5	1.5	6.5	4.9
Electricity	4.3	4.1	4.4	5.3	3.2	5.5	7.7
Chemicals	1.4	1.1	2.2	0.6	3.4	0.5	-0.5
Construction materials	0.5	1.2	0.1	-1.7	1.6	-0.3	4.0
Wood materials	0.7	1.3	0.4	-2.4	2.7	-2.0	4.0
Mineral materials	0.9	0.6	1.0	1.3	0.8	6.6	3.1
Machinery and allied products	3.1	0.7	4.5	9.1	1.0	10.6	3.5
Civilian machinery and equipment	3.4	0.7	4.9	8.4	2.2	11.1	-2.0
Food and allied products	1.1	0.8	1.2	-0.3	2.5	-0.1	7.2
Textiles and allied products	1.0	0.6	1.2	0.7	1.7	0.0	3.7

SOURCE: Table 40. Average annual growth rates calculated from data for terminal years by the compound interest formula.

follows, of course, from the fluctuations in hours of work for the average worker already commented on.

How much has growth in labor productivity contributed toward growth in output? This question may be answered obliquely by pointing out that, had there been no improvement in output per man-hour (or person engaged), output of all industrial products would have multiplied 46 per cent (or 54 per cent) as much as it did over 1913–1955 and 63 per cent (or 60 per cent) as much over 1928–1955. Hence improved labor productivity may be thought of as accounting for 46 to 54 per cent of the multiplication in output over 1913–1955 and 37 to 40 per cent over 1928–1955, the percentage depending on whether productivity is measured in terms of persons engaged or man-hours.

It is interesting that output per man-hour apparently grew faster over 1913–1928 than over 1928–1955. Despite the fact that industrial output showed no net increase over the pre-Plan years, productive capacity apparently grew at an impressive rate. The growth in output per man-hour over the pre-Plan years was associated with a sharp decline in annual hours of work for the average person engaged in industry, which may have had something to do with the marked improvement in hourly labor productivity. In any event, output per person engaged grew at a much slower average pace than output per man-hour: 0.7 per cent a year compared with 2.2 per cent.

Within the Plan years, labor productivity seems to have accelerated. This seems particularly clear in the case of output per man-hour: the average annual growth rate rose between 1928–1940 and 1940–1955, and between 1928–1937 and 1950–1955. Growth in output per person engaged also accelerated between the latter pair of periods, although it retarded very slightly between the former pair. The difference in behavior of the two measures can be explained by the increase in hours of work in the years surrounding World War II.

The picture for industrial groups is much more mixed. Growth in output per person engaged seems to have retarded over the Plan period in the cases of fuel, mineral construction materials, and machinery and allied products; it seems to have accelerated in the cases of wood construction materials, food and allied products, and textiles and allied products. The trend of growth rates is doubtful in the cases of ferrous and nonferrous metals, electricity, and chemicals.

COMPARISON OF OUR ESTIMATES WITH OTHERS

Few studies of Soviet industrial labor productivity have been made by Western scholars, the two best known probably being those of Hodgman

TABLE 42

COMPARISON OF NBER AND HODGMAN INDEXES OF SOVIET INDUSTRIAL OUTPUT
PER UNIT OF LABOR, BENCHMARK YEARS, 1928–1950

	OUTPUT PER MAN-YEAR			OUTPUT PER MAN-HOUR		
	NBER[a]	Hodgman		NBER[a]	Hodgman	
		Actual[b]	Adjusted[c]		Actual[b]	Adjusted[c]
			INDEX	(1928 = 100)		
928	100	100	100	100	100	100
933	93	103	63	107	113	69
937	122	155	91	137	167	98
940	127	169		115	167	
950	129	201	115	113	183	105
		LINK RELATIVE	(INITIAL	YEAR OF PERIOD = 100)		
928–1933	93	103	63	107	113	69
933–1937	131	150	144	128	148	142
937–1940	104	109		84	100	
940–1950	102	119		98	110	
937–1950	106	130	126	82	110	107

SOURCE: Table 40; Hodgman, *Soviet Industrial Production*, pp. 113 and 117; and as indicated below.
[a] Based on persons engaged. Covers all industry (including military products) except repair shops.
[b] Based on production workers. Output covers large-scale industry in 1928, with the coverage expanding to all industry by around 1933; workers cover almost all industry in all years (see footnote 3 of this chapter).
[c] Hodgman's adjusted production index (see Table 34) divided by our adjusted version of his employment index (see Table 43, columns 2 and 5). Both output and employment cover large-scale industry, with the coverage expanding to all industry by around 1933 (see text).

and Galenson.[8] In addition, there is the very recent estimate by Kaplan and Moorsteen, which is based on a more comprehensive study of Soviet industrial growth.[9] All differ from ours in coverage of output and employment and other important respects, commented on below. The Hodgman and Kaplan-Moorsteen estimates of labor productivity, like ours, are derived from aggregate indexes of output and employment, while Galenson's are based on physical output and employment for a small number of narrowly defined industries, covering only a small segment of industry.[10]

There is very little correspondence between the movements of our indexes of labor productivity and Hodgman's (see Table 42). This is

[8] Donald Hodgman, *Soviet Industrial Production, 1928–1951*, Cambridge, Mass., 1954, pp. 109–122; Walter Galenson, *Labor Productivity in Soviet and American Industry*, New York, 1955.
[9] N. M. Kaplan and R. M. Moorsteen, "Indexes of Soviet Industrial Production" (mimeographed), RAND Corporation, RM-2495, Santa Monica, 1960, pp. 152 ff.
[10] For interwar years beginning with 1928, Galenson's indexes cover the seven industries shown in Table 42; for years beginning with 1932 and generally ending with 1936, they also cover four industries producing durable producer goods (see Galenson, *Labor Productivity*, p. 234).

TABLE 43

COMPARISON OF NBER AND HODGMAN INDEXES OF LABOR INPUTS INTO SOVIET INDUSTRY,
BENCHMARK YEARS, 1928–1950

	MAN-YEARS			MAN-HOURS		
	Hodgman, Production Workers[a]		*NBER, Persons Engaged*[c]	*Hodgman, Production Workers*[a]		*NBER, Persons Engaged*[c]
	Actual	Adjusted[b]		Actual	Adjusted[b]	
		INDEX	(1928 = 100)			
1928	100	100	100	100	100	100
1933	187	304	161	170[d]	277[d]	141
1937	240	407	228	223	379	203
1940	254		244	257		272
1950	322	560	297	354	616	340
		LINK RELATIVE	(INITIAL YEAR OF PERIOD	= 100)		
1928–1933	187	304	161	170	277	141
1933–1937	128	134	142	131	137	144
1937–1940	106		107	115		134
1940–1950	127		122	138		125
1937–1950	134	138	130	159	163	167

SOURCE: Tables A-23 and C-1; Hodgman, *Soviet Industrial Production*, pp. 112 and 116.
[a] Includes repair shops.
[b] Based on series of production workers as given in footnote 13 of this chapter, covering large scale industry in 1928 and all industry thereafter.
[c] Excludes repair shops.
[d] Man-years in 1933 times average annual man-hours in 1932 as given by Hodgman, *Soviet Industrial Production*, p. 116.

due in part to significant differences between the underlying production indexes, commented on at some length elsewhere.[11] It is also due to differences in employment indexes, though these are much less marked despite the fact that Hodgman's index covers only production workers while ours covers all persons engaged (see Table 43). The greatest discrepancy in the movements of the employment indexes occurs over the periods 1928–1933 and 1933–1937 and is explained by the fact that there was a great bulge in employment in repair shops—included in Hodgman's index but excluded from ours—around 1933. In accord with standard custom, it seems doubtful that repair shops should be included in industry.

Two general shortcomings of Hodgman's data deserve further comment. First, military products are covered directly by employment data but only indirectly—and, as Hodgman observes,[12] inadequately—by production data. This seems to make most difference over the period 1940–1950.

[11] See the last section of the preceding chapter and technical note 4 of Appendix A.
[12] Hodgman, *Soviet Industrial Production*, p. 88. See also our discussion surrounding Table 31.

According to our indexes, production of civilian products increased by 44 per cent, production of all products by 23 per cent, persons engaged by 22 per cent, and man-hours by 25 per cent. If the production index for civilian products were used to compute changes in labor productivity, we would find that output per person engaged increased by 18 per cent and output per man-hour by 15 per cent, which are close to the increases of 19 and 10 per cent shown by Hodgman's calculations. If, however, the production index for all products is used, we find that output per person engaged increased by only 2 per cent while output per man-hour decreased by 2 per cent.

Second, the coverage of Hodgman's production index is restricted to large-scale industry in 1928 and gradually expands to encompass all industry around 1933. His employment index, on the other hand, apparently covers all industry in all years, beginning with 1928.[13] If his employment data are adjusted to the same coverage as his output data— as we have done in columns 2 and 5 of Table 43—the movements of his labor productivity indexes are markedly changed, primarily over the

[13] Hodgman uses "industry section" data on production workers in large-scale industry, and these encompass many industries assigned in output statistics for the late 1920's to small-scale industry (see *Socialist Construction in the USSR*, Moscow, 1936, p. 394). While "labor section" data are, for other reasons (see *ibid.*), not strictly comparable in coverage to output data, the definition of large-scale industry was at least consistently applied over those early years. The two sets of data are as follows (average annual number of wage earners in thousands from D. Redding, "USSR Industrial Employment and Its Distribution" (mimeographed), Council for Economic and Industry Research Report No. A-8, Washington, 1955, p. 8):

	1928	*1933*
Large-scale industry		
"Industry section" data	3,699	6,901
"Labor section" data	2,558	4,784
All industry		
"Industry section" data	n.a.	7,900
"Labor section" data	3,865	7,866

To be comparable with his production index, Hodgman's employment data should cover large-scale industry for 1928 and total industry for 1933 onward. In terms of production workers ("industry section" wage earners), the series would run as follows (average annual number in thousands):

1928	2,600
1933	7,900
1937	10,579
1950	14,562

The figure for 1928 has been extrapolated by the "labor section" data given above: the figures for 1937 and 1950 are taken from Barney Schwalberg, *Industrial Employment in the USSR, 1933, 1937, 1950, and 1955*, Bureau of the Census, Series P-95, No. 55, Washington, 1960, p. 51.

period 1928–1933 (see columns 3 and 6 of Table 42). We also note, by comparing these revised indexes with our counterparts, that over this period output per unit of labor showed a much sharper decline within the segment of industry covered by Hodgman than within industry as a whole, from which we can conclude that labor productivity fell in large-scale industry but rose in (at least what was formerly) small-scale industry. The former overbalanced the latter in man-year productivity, but the reverse was true in man-hour productivity, which is probably more significant. More detailed evidence confirming these conclusions will be presented in the next chapter.

Galenson's findings on labor productivity diverge even further from ours than Hodgman's do, as may be seen from Table 44. The primary explanation seems to lie in the small and unrepresentative sample of industries covered by Galenson. Only seven industries were studied for the period 1928–1937, their production workers accounting in the aggregate for 19 per cent of total industrial employment in 1928, 15 per cent in 1933, and 13 per cent in 1937. The coverage is much higher for metals (ranging from 56 to 72 per cent) and fuel (ranging from 52 to 61 per cent); somewhat higher for food and allied products (ranging from 22 to 27 per cent); and much lower for textiles and allied products (ranging from 6 to 9 per cent). Other industrial groups are not covered at all—electricity, chemicals, and construction materials. In general, the covered industries show a more rapid growth in labor productivity than the industrial groups they represent (if we may use our indexes for the latter), and the better represented groups show a more rapid growth than the more poorly represented ones (see Tables 44 and 40). Both factors work to make Galenson's combined index much higher than our aggregate index.

To the extent that they may be directly compared, the Kaplan-Moorsteen indexes of labor productivity behave much more like ours than those of Hodgman and Galenson. As we stated toward the end of the preceding chapter, the Kaplan-Moorsteen indexes appeared too late to make it possible for us to analyze them thoroughly and compare them meaningfully with ours. One comparison that seems justified without extensive adjustments is presented in Table 45, applying to intermediate industrial products—referred to by Kaplan and Moorsteen as "producers' goods other than machinery." Their and our indexes of output per man-year for this sector move in a rather parallel fashion, such differences as there are probably being explainable in terms of the following factors: different weight bases for the production indexes—1950 for theirs and a

TABLE 44

COMPARISON OF NBER AND GALENSON INDEXES OF SOVIET INDUSTRIAL
OUTPUT PER UNIT OF LABOR, BENCHMARK YEARS, 1928–1937[a]
(1928 = 100)

	1928	1933	1937
NBER, all products	100	93	122
Galenson, 7 industries combined			
1928 employment weights	100	120	174
1936 employment weights	100	116	177
NBER, ferrous and nonferrous metals	100	87	191
Galenson, iron ore mining	100	142	319
Galenson, iron and steel	100	106	247
NBER, fuel	100	115	176
Galenson, coal mining	100	135	189
Galenson, crude oil and gas extraction	100	154	200[b]
NBER, food and allied products	100	81	99
Galenson, beet sugar	100	109	157
NBER, textiles and allied products	100	86	100
Galenson, cotton cloth	100	120	142
Galenson, shoes	100	60	88

SOURCE: Table 40; and Galenson, *Labor Productivity*, pp. 234 and 236.

[a] For NBER, derived from output and persons engaged in all industry; for Galenson, from physical output and production workers in the large-scale segment except for the shoe industry, which is fully covered.

Employment covered by Galenson accounts for the following fractions of all persons engaged excluding those in repair shops (Galenson, *Labor Productivity*, pp. 16, 91, 99, 123, 186 f, 214, 216, and 224; and this monograph, Table A-20):

	1928	1933	1937
		(per cent)	
All industries	19.4	15.3	12.9
Ferrous and nonferrous metals	71.9	56.4	57.5
Fuel	61.4	52.2	60.5
Food and allied products	9.4	6.1	6.4
Textiles and allied products	27.3	22.4	26.3

The coverage given here for all industries is smaller for all years than that given by Galenson (p. 242), but we have not been able to reconcile his coverage ratios with the underlying data he cites.

[b] 1938.

moving base for ours; different weighting systems for product groups in the production indexes—estimated wage-bills for theirs and estimated employment for ours; different product coverage in the production indexes—nonferrous metals are excluded from theirs and included in ours, along with other differences in the treatment of individual products; and different concepts of employment—production workers for theirs and persons engaged for ours.

TABLE 45

COMPARISON OF NBER AND KAPLAN-MOORSTEEN INDEXES OF SOVIET OUTPUT PER MAN-YEAR
LABOR FOR INTERMEDIATE INDUSTRIAL PRODUCTS, BENCHMARK YEARS, 1928–1955

| | Output of Intermediate Industrial Products | | Man-Years | | Output per Man-Year | |
	Kaplan-Moorsteen[a]	NBER[b]	Kaplan-Moorsteen, Production Workers	NBER, Persons Engaged	Kaplan-Moorsteen	NBER
1928	100	100	100	100	100	100
1932	192	184	179		108	
1933		198		222		89
1937	311	351	188	229	164	153
1940	334	386	218	260	151	148
1950	467	567	315	363	146	156
1955	748	872	392	423	186	206

SOURCE: Tables 53 and A-20; Kaplan and Moorsteen, "Indexes of Soviet Industrial Output,
pp. 235, 268, and 269.
[a] Based on 1950 Soviet weights.
[b] Based on moving Soviet weights.

There remains, finally, to be considered the official Soviet index of labor productivity (see Table 46). The exact nature of this index is a mystery, apparently even to Soviet economists, though it seems most likely—as the well-known Soviet economist Strumilin has assumed—that it refers to gross output per production worker in large-scale industry.[14] As would be expected from the exaggerated measure of industrial production in the official Soviet index, this index of labor productivity shows a much more rapid growth over the Plan period than ours does.

Concluding Remarks

We have seen that Soviet industrial output multiplied about six times (5.5 times, if territorial gains are eliminated) between 1913 or 1928 and 1955, which is less than the growth over the last forty years of the Tsarist period and more than the growth over the last twenty-five years. Output multiplied about nine times in the case of intermediate industrial products, twenty to thirty times in the case of civilian machinery and equipment, and three times in the case of consumer goods. On a per capita basis, these factors would be about 70 per cent as large for 1913–1955 and 76 per cent as large for 1928–1955.

Over 1913–1955, employment of labor multiplied 2.8 times in terms of man-hours and 3.3 times in terms of man-years; over 1928–1955, the

[14] For some rather convincing comments on the nature of this index, see Schwalberg, *Industrial Employment*, pp. 11 ff.

TABLE 46

COMPARISON OF NBER AND OFFICIAL SOVIET INDEXES OF INDUSTRIAL
OUTPUT PER MAN-YEAR OF LABOR, BENCHMARK YEARS, 1928–1955
(1928 = 100)

| | Output per Man-Year[a] | | Employment | |
	NBER	Official Soviet	NBER[b]	Implied Official Soviet[c]
1928	100	100	100	100
1932		141		231
1933	93		161	
1937	122	258	228	293
1940	127	343	243	317
1950	129	470	297	406
1955	168	679	360	534

SOURCE: Tables 39 and 40; and *Promyshlennost'*, 1957, pp. 25 and 31.
[a] The NBER index refers to output per person engaged; the official Soviet index, apparently to output per production worker in large-scale state and cooperative industry, with varying coverage (see Schwalberg, *Industrial Employment*, pp. 11 ff).
[b] Persons engaged, from Table 39.
[c] Apparently production workers in large-scale industry (see note *a* above). Derived from official Soviet index of large-scale industrial production divided by official Soviet index of output per unit of labor (second column of this table).

comparable factors are 3.8 and 3.6. Employment has therefore accounted for 44 to 56 per cent of the multiplication in output over 1913–1955 and for 60 to 63 per cent over 1928–1955, with improved labor productivity accounting for the remainder. Put another way, output per man-hour (or person engaged) multiplied about 2.2 (or 1.9) times over 1913–1955 and 1.6 (or 1.7) times over 1928–1955.

CHAPTER 7

Some Details of Growth

WE HAVE sketched the bolder outlines of Soviet industrial growth, and we must now take up the task of filling in the more important details. It is inevitable in a large study like this one that details will be slighted and perhaps even distorted, for they are subordinate to the primary objective. This chapter should therefore be looked upon as simply an introduction to the many highly special topics in Soviet industrial development that deserve careful study, much more careful than we can give.

The discussion will proceed chronologically, attention being directed in turn to the pre-Plan period, the prewar Plan period, and finally the postwar period. In each case, we shall try to present the basic characteristics of industrial development over the years in question. Definitive treatment must be left to others.

The Pre-Plan Period

It is difficult to trace out the year-to-year developments in Soviet industry from the revolution to the beginning of the Plan period because data on output are available for only a relatively small sample of industries and most of them refer solely to large-scale production. The latter factor means that production indexes (see Table 47 and Chart 18) probably overstate the rates of both declines and rises in output, though the degree of overstatement must remain unknown. Despite such qualifications, there is little doubt about the general nature of the movements of industrial production during this period.

The year 1913 is widely used, in both Soviet and Western analyses of economic developments in the Soviet Union, to represent prerevolutionary conditions. It is interesting to note, therefore, that industrial output had not reached its prerevolutionary peak in that year: it was significantly higher in each of the three succeeding years, if our indexes are to be believed. During 1917, the year of the revolution, industrial output dropped sharply, by something on the order of 17 per cent. This was, however, a moderate decline compared with what was to follow while the civil war was in progress: during 1918 the decline was on the order of 47 per cent and during 1919, 40 per cent. The bottom was reached in 1920, when industrial output was apparently less than a fifth of the level of 1916, and only a slight recovery was made in 1921. The decline in

184

output was general throughout all segments of industry: over the period 1913–1921, output declined in fifty-one out of fifty-four industries for which data are available.[1] With the end of the civil war and the initiation of the New Economic Policy in 1921, there began a rapid recovery in industrial growth. The

TABLE 47

PRODUCTION INDEXES FOR INDUSTRIAL MATERIALS:
SOVIET UNION, 1913–1928
(1913 = 100)

	1913 Weights	1928 Weights
1913	100	100
1914	110	113
1915	107	109
1916	111	112
1917	92	92
1918	40	43
1919	24	21
1920	22	19
1921	24	21
1922	35	34
1923	43	43
1924	53	52
1925	73	75
1926	91	91
1927	101	98
1928	103	100

SOURCE: Table D-1. Interwar Soviet territory

rise was on the order of 46 per cent during 1922, 23 per cent during 1923 and 1924, 38 per cent during 1925, 25 per cent during 1926, and 11 per cent during 1927. As in the case of the decline, the recovery was general: over the period 1921–1928, output rose in fifty-four out of fifty-five industries for which data are available.[2] Our production indexes indicate

[1] See output series in Table B-2. The three exceptions are corundum and emery, peat, and lignite.
  The decline in output was less pronounced for small-scale industry than for the total, one source estimating that small-scale employment fell no lower than 40 per cent of its prerevolutionary level (V. A. Tikhomirov, "Promyslovaia kooperatsiia na sovremennom etape" [Producer Cooperatives at the Present Stage], *Vestnik promyslovoi kooperatsii* [Bulletin of Producer Cooperatives], 1931, No. 8, p. 3). See the detailed discussion in Adam Kaufman, "Small-Scale Industry in the Soviet Union," NBER (in press), Chapter 4.
[2] See output series in Table B-2. The exception is oil shale.

185

CHART 18
Production Indexes for Industrial Materials:
Soviet Union, 1913–1928

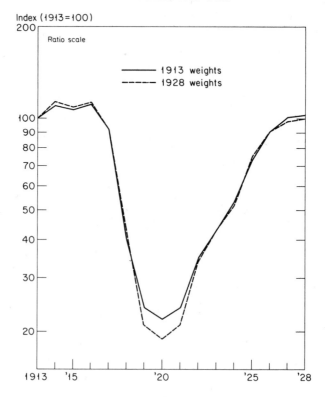

Source: Table 47.

that industrial output had about recovered to its 1913 level by 1927 and 1928, but the indexes do not fully reflect the deterioration in quality of many commodities, particularly consumer goods, discussed earlier in Chapter 3. It is therefore very doubtful that the 1913 level of industrial output had been reached on the eve of the First Five Year Plan; it is virtually certain that the prerevolutionary peak had not been reached.

As would be expected, output showed a net rise in some areas over the entire pre-Plan period and a net decline in others. The following increases were apparently registered (see Table 53): agricultural machinery, 151 per cent; consumer durables, 58 per cent; fuel and electricity, 50 per cent; chemicals, 46 per cent; and textiles and allied products, 13 per cent. On the other side, there were the following declines: food

186

and allied products, 16 per cent; construction materials, 12 per cent; ferrous metals, 12 per cent; transportation equipment, 10 per cent; and nonferrous metals, 3 per cent. Output increased by 43 per cent in the case of machinery and equipment and by 8 per cent in the case of intermediate industrial products, while it decreased by 3 per cent in the case of consumer goods.

Output per man-hour in all industry rose by 37 per cent over the pre-Plan years, and output per person engaged by 11 per cent, the latter reflecting a rise of varying magnitude in every industrial group (see Table 40). The increases in output per person engaged were, in order: ferrous and nonferrous metals, 33 per cent; construction materials, 19 per cent; fuel and electricity, 18 per cent; food and allied products, 12 per cent; machinery and allied products, 11 per cent; textiles and allied products, 9 per cent; and chemicals, 1 per cent. Moreover, the improvement in labor productivity applied to small- as well as large-scale industry (see Table 52). As we noted in the preceding chapter, improved productivity accompanied a substantial reduction in hours of work, at least in large-scale industry.[3]

The First and Second Five Year Plans

DISAPPEARANCE OF SMALL-SCALE INDUSTRY[4]

The boundaries of industry are seldom clear, particularly during the early stages of industrialization. Up to the beginning of the Plan period, a large fraction of Russian industrial output was produced in handicraft shops and similar small establishments, and much of what appears in official statistics to be an increase in output during the succeeding years was essentially a transformation of this small-scale production into factory production. Some of the transformation was, indeed, more statistical than real: the definition of factory, or large-scale, production was expanded to incorporate what was formerly treated as small-scale. The nature of developments during the early part of the Plan period cannot be understood without taking account of the changing role of small-scale industry.

There is no way of knowing exactly what happened to definitions of large-scale industry between 1928 and 1933. The general boundary line between large- and small-scale establishments had been set in the Tsarist period: if sixteen or more persons were employed along with mechanical

[3] See Tables A-21 through A-23 and the surrounding text in Appendix A.
[4] This section is based on the previously cited report by Adam Kaufman.

power, or thirty or more without it, the establishment was considered large-scale.[5] Over time, this general rule was supplanted in some industries by special qualifications adapted to the peculiar conditions of those industries.[6] These were, however, insignificant exceptions compared with those introduced during the early part of the Plan period.

The pressure to show rapid rates of growth led to statistical juggling of various sorts, some tailored to special industries (as flour milling, bread baking, and shoemaking) and others to industry in general. For instance, all state-owned bakeries, whether large or small, came to be counted as large-scale, and most of the village bakeries became state owned. Similarly, all flour mills with at least five grinding units came to be counted as large-scale. A general rule was laid down that all enterprises under the jurisdiction of a Union Republic ministry were to be counted as large-scale, whether they met any other requirements or not. Hence the picture of what actually happened to forms of industrial organization must remain somewhat hazy. Even so, there is little doubt of an appreciable decline in the relative importance of genuinely small-scale industry over this period.

Related to this shift from small- to large-scale production was a definitional expansion of "industry," to bring within its scope a number of activities that had previously been classified elsewhere. These activities included logging, fishing, and various types of food processing carried on in agricultural communities, such as meat slaughtering, processing of dairy products, milling and cracking of grain, and extracting of vegetable oils. These were for the most part small-scale activities that were to be incorporated statistically into "industry," in many cases without any essential change—at least initially—in the form of productive organization.

A brief summary of the statistical record of small-scale industry is presented in Tables 48 through 50. Considerable allowance should be made for possible error of unknown magnitude and direction, since the statistical foundations are weak. During the Tsarist period, virtually no statistics were collected by the central government for this segment of industry, and estimates of the role of small-scale industry are based ultimately on data collected by the local and provincial councils (*zemstva*). It should not be assumed that these data are less reliable than those collected by the Tsarist government; on the contrary, there was generally

---

[5] The Russian word for qualification is *tsenz*. Hence the large-scale establishments meeting the described qualifications have been often characterized, through loose translation, as belonging to the "census industry."

[6] For a summary of changes during the Soviet period before the plans, see A. Yezhov, *Soviet Statistics* (translated from the Russian), Moscow, 1957, pp. 12 ff.

SOME DETAILS OF GROWTH

TABLE 48

PERSONS ENGAGED IN LARGE-SCALE AND SMALL-SCALE INDUSTRY:[a]
SOVIET UNION, SELECTED YEARS, 1913–1933
(full-time equivalents)

| | Thousands | | Per Cent | |
	Large-Scale Industry	Small-Scale Industry	Large-Scale Industry	Small-Scale Industry
1913	2,864	2,942	49	51
1927	2,726	2,098	57	43
1928	2,971	2,408	55	45
1929	3,297	2,232	60	40
1933	8,062	591	93	7

SOURCE: Table C-1 and Kaufman, "Small-Scale Industry," Table A-2.
[a] Including fishing and logging but excluding repair shops.

TABLE 49

PERSONS ENGAGED IN LARGE-SCALE AND SMALL-SCALE SECTORS OF SELECTED INDUSTRIES:
SOVIET UNION, 1927, 1929, AND 1933

| | 1927 | | 1929 | | 1933 | |
	Large-Scale Sector	Small-Scale Sector	Large-Scale Sector	Small-Scale Sector	Large-Scale Sector	Small-Scale Sector
	THOUSANDS					
Metal products	119	188	150	140	413	9
Wood products	23	162	34	160	249	105
Knitted goods	18	48	47	56	156	36
Garment industry	50	278	114	218	403	33
Fur processing	3	31	8	25	41	2
Boots and shoes	27	303	77	240	239	44
Flour and groats	49	118	41	79	59	115
Vegetable oil	12	17	16	18	20	7
Total	301	1,145	487	936	1,580	351
	PER CENT					
Metal products	39	61	52	48	98	2
Wood products	12	88	18	82	70	30
Knitted goods	27	73	46	54	81	19
Garment industry	15	85	34	66	92	8
Fur processing	9	91	24	76	95	5
Boots and shoes	8	92	24	76	84	16
Flour and groats	29	71	34	66	34	66
Vegetable oil	41	59	47	53	74	26
Total	21	79	34	66	82	18

SOURCE: Kaufman, "Small-Scale Industry," Table A-2.

TABLE 50

ESTIMATED PERCENTAGE OF VALUE OF OUTPUT, VALUE ADDED,
AND EMPLOYMENT ACCOUNTED FOR BY SMALL-SCALE INDUSTRY:[a]
SOVIET UNION, SELECTED YEARS, 1913–1933
(per cent)

	Value of Output	Value Added	Employment[b]
1913	34		50
1927	31	30	43
1929	26	26	40
1933	8		7

SOURCE: Table C-2 and Kaufman, "Small-Scale Industry," Table A-3.
[a] Including logging and fishing but excluding repair shops.
[b] Persons engaged in industry expressed in full-time equivalents.

a higher level of statistical competence in these local activities than in the central government.[7] Nevertheless, the statistical investigations raise many problems of comparability of data, uneven and incomplete coverage, and the like.

During the 1920's, while the Soviet authorities were deliberating on methods of directing the economy, an effort was made to gather comprehensive statistics on small-scale production, and also to collate and interpret such statistics as were available for the late Tsarist period. Five censuses of small-scale industry were conducted during the 1920's, the two most comprehensive covering the years 1926/27 and 1928/29. These censuses contain data on value of output, value added, and employment. It is almost certain that these data are understated because it was in the political and economic interests of the small-scale producers to underreport, and the generally poor state of business records in this sector made it impossible to correct the underreporting. Moreover, coverage was incomplete in that many of the small-scale activities not then considered as within industry, but later incorporated, were not surveyed.

The downward bias in data is acknowledged in the following official comment on the census covering 1928/29:[8]

It is necessary to note a certain understatement of the data for the capitalist sector [i.e., establishments hiring at least three employees]. The understatement arises from the tendency of the private entrepreneur to conceal the actual volume of his output, the extent of labor

[7] See, e.g., Bernard Pares, A History of Russia, rev. ed., New York, 1944, p. 402.
[8] Narodnoe khoziaistvo SSSR [The USSR National Economy], Moscow, 1932, p. 647, as quoted in Gregory Grossman, Soviet Statistics of Physical Output of Industrial Commodities: Their Compilation and Quality, Princeton for NBER, 1960, p. 43.

employment, his receipts, etc., which has had a particular impact on the data due to the coincidence of the census period with intensive collectivization [of agriculture] in a number of regions. The under-recording in the private sector is partly compensated by the inclusion of data on home-workers, under the putting-out system, in the private capitalist sector.

While this statement is directed to a very small segment of small-scale industry, it would seem to apply to the entire private sector, which, despite understatement, accounted for 75 per cent of all employment in small-scale industry at this time.[9] The most satisfactory way to picture the disappearance of small-scale industry is through trends in employment. We may look first at persons engaged in industry adjusted to a full-time basis and covering industry (except repair shops) as ultimately defined in the Plan period (see Table 48). We note that between 1913 and 1928, employment fell in the small-scale sector from 2.9 to 2.4 million, while it rose only slightly in the large-scale sector from 2.9 to 3.0 million. Over the next five years, employment declined precipitously in the small-scale sector (from 2.4 to 0.6 million) while rising even more sharply in the large-scale sector (from 3.0 to 8.1 million); hence total employment also rose substantially (from 5.4 to 8.7 million). During the span of five years, the share of employment accounted for by the small-scale sector fell from 43 to 7 per cent. In large part this was, as already mentioned, a statistical mirage: the same thing was merely being called by a different name. But the figures also reflect a radical shift in the structure of industry, as can be seen from the fact that the increase in employment in large-scale industry was 3.3 million greater than the decrease in small-scale industry.

The expanded employment in industry came, of course, from several sources, including additions to the labor force, displaced rural labor, and unemployed and underemployed labor.[10] There had been a considerable

[9] See Kaufman, "Small-Scale Industry," Table 9.
[10] According to one Russian source (I. Berlin and Ia. Mebel', "Strukturnye sdvigi v naselenii i proletariate" [Structural Changes in the Population and the Proletariat], *Voprosy truda* [Labor Questions], 1932, No. 11–12, p. 23), there was a net increase of 6.9 million in hired urban workers over 1927–1931, recruited as follows from the specified sources (millions):

Current urban labor force	
Self-employed	1.2
Unemployed and others	0.8
Urban entrants into labor force	2.1
Rural entrants into labor force	2.8

degree of underemployment in small-scale industry: the average number
of weeks worked was roughly twenty-four in 1926/27, nineteen in 1927/28,
and sixteen in 1928/29.[11] For large-scale industry, the average number
of weeks worked was, by contrast, forty-four in 1927/28.[12] Hence, in
1928 the labor employed in small-scale industry (2.4 million full-time
equivalents) represented a potential employment of roughly 5.6 million,
or a potential addition to employment of 3.2 million, on the basis of the
average work-year then prevalent in large-scale industry.

While the trends in employment give a general view of what happened
to small-scale production, they are somewhat misleading in indicating
changes in the share of real output accounted for by that sector. Labor
was probably less productive in small-scale than in large-scale industry,
and therefore the fraction of labor employed by small-scale industry,
even when corrected to a full-time basis, probably overstates the fraction
of output attributable to it.[13] At the same time, value of output and value
added, the other two measures that are available, tend to understate the
fraction, since sales of small enterprises were probably underreported and
their costs of materials probably overreported for reasons already
mentioned. There is also probably less double counting contained in
value of output for small-scale than for large-scale enterprises, since the
former tended to be more integrated than the latter.

Estimates of all three types are given in Table 50. From this evidence
it seems reasonable to say that the share of industrial production accounted
for by small-scale establishments declined from roughly a third in 1928 to
roughly a twelfth in 1933.

Changes in output over 1928–1933 are given in Table 51 for twenty-
seven products for which small-scale production can be estimated.
Small-scale production declined in every case, while large-scale production declined in only eight cases (red lead, window glass, hard leather,

[11] Total weeks worked (Tikhomirov in *Vestnik promyslovoi kooperatsii*, 1931, No. 8, p. 3,
and *Melkaia promyshlennost' SSSR po dannym vsesoiuznoi perepisi 1929 goda* [Small-Scale
Industry in the USSR According to Data from the All-Union Census of 1929], Moscow,
1932–1933, Vol. I, p. 6) divided by persons engaged (*Statisticheskii spravochnik SSSR za
1928 god* [USSR Statistical Handbook for 1928], Moscow, 1929, p. 487; *Plan*, 1935,
No. 8, p. 12; and *Melkaia promyshlennost'*, p. 6).
[12] Average number of days worked (266 according to *Statisticheskoe obozrenie* [Statistical
Review], 1929, No. 12, pp. 88 f) divided by six.
[13] Small-scale production was most important in industries characterized by a relatively
low net output (value added) per worker. In these industries, it is doubtful that the net
output per worker was significantly higher in large-scale than in small-scale enterprises;
such technological and organizational advantages as the former may have enjoyed were
probably offset by longer hours of work in the latter. Net output per worker was probably
lower for small-scale than for large-scale industry as a whole because employment was more
concentrated in industries of low labor productivity in the former case than in the latter.

OUTPUT OF TWENTY-SEVEN PRODUCTS IN SMALL-SCALE AND LARGE-SCALE INDUSTRY: SOVIET UNION, 1928 AND 1933

Product	Unit	Small-Scale Output			Large-Scale Industry			Total Output		
		1928	1933	Change, 1928–1933	1928	1933	Change, 1928–1933	1928	1933	Change, 1928–1933
Firewood consumed	mill. m³	53	32	−21	26	75	+49	79	107	+28
Red lead	th. m. t.	0.8	0.2	−0.6	4.6	2.6	−2.0	5.4	2.8	−2.6
Red bricks	millions	768	404	−364	1,888	2,959	+1,071	2,656	3,363	+707
Construction gypsum	th. m. t.	108	—	−108	127	446	+319	235	446	+211
Construction lime	th. m. t.	242	—	−242	284	1,394	+1,110	526	1,394	+868
Industrial timber hauled	mill. m³	60.1	—	−60.1	—	98.0	+98.0	60.1	98.0	+37.9
Lumber	mill. m³	6.4	0.5	−5.9	7.6	26.8	+19.2	14.0	27.3	+13.3
Plywood	th. m³	30.4	—	−30.4	164.6	424.3	+259.7	195.0	424.3	+229.3
Window glass	mill. m²	0.7	—	−0.7	33.5	29.8	−3.7	34.2	29.8	−4.4
Hard leather	th. m t.	25.2	0.8	−24.4	63.8	38.9	−24.9	89.0	39.7	−49.3
Soft leather	mill. dcm²	875	50	−825	2,175	2,436	+261	3,050	2,486	−564
Flour	mill. m. t.	16	13	−3	8	7	−1	24	20	−4
Butter	th. m. t.	82.1	34.8	−47.3	—	89.5	+89.5	82.1	124.3	+42.2
Vegetable oil	th. m. t.	338	21	−317	282	300	+18	620	321	−299
Meat	th. m. t.	424	7	−417	254	420	+166	678	427	−251
Fish catch	th. m. t.	840	13	−827	—	1,290	+1,290	840	1,303	+463
Soap (40% fatty acid)	th. m. t.	54	29	−25	306	233	−73	360	262	−98
Starch and syrup	th. m. t.	27	9	−18	69	142	+73	96	151	+55
Canned food	mill. cans	25	—	−25	100	619	+519	125	619	+494
Cigarettes	billions	2.4	—	−2.4	47.1	62.7	+15.6	49.5	62.7	+13.2
Low-grade tobacco	th. m. t.	22.9	—	−22.9	63.0	50.3	−12.7	85.9	50.3	−35.6
Boots and shoes	mill. pairs	79.4	10.8	−68.6	23.6	79.5	+55.9	103.0	90.3	−12.7
Cotton fabrics	mill. m	139	—	−139	2,539	2,732	+193	2,678	2,732	+54
Linen fabrics	mill. m	3.5	—	−3.5	170.9	140.5	−30.4	174.4	140.5	−33.9
Pure silk fabrics	mill. m	0.6	0.1	−0.5	1.3	12.1	+10.8	1.9	12.2	+10.3
Woolen and worsted fabrics	mill. m	34	12	−22	83	74	−9	117	86	−31
Felt footwear	mill. pairs	11.2	1.5	−9.7	4.4	6.1	+1.7	15.6	7.6	−8.0

SOURCE: Table B-2 and Kaufman, "Small-Scale Industry," Tables A-4 and A-5. For the meaning of symbols and abbreviations used, see the general note to Appendix B of this book.
—: Negligible.

flour, soap, low-grade tobacco, linen fabrics, and woolen and worsted fabrics). Declines in the small-scale sector were not fully matched by increases in the large-scale sector in six cases (soft leather, vegetable oil, meat, boots and shoes, cotton fabrics, and felt footwear). In the remaining twelve cases, the declines were more than matched by increases in the large-scale sector, but in all but two cases (canned food and pure silk fabrics) the decline amounted to at least 10 per cent of the increase. These data show that it can be very misleading to measure growth in output over this early part of the Plan period on the basis of large-scale production alone.

TABLE 52

INDEXES OF OUTPUT, EMPLOYMENT, AND OUTPUT PER PERSON
ENGAGED IN LARGE-SCALE AND SMALL-SCALE INDUSTRY:
SOVIET UNION, BENCHMARK YEARS, 1913–1933

	1913	1928	1933
	TOTAL INDUSTRY		
Output of industrial materials[a]	100	100	137
Persons engaged[b]	100	92	149
Output per person engaged	100	109	92
	LARGE-SCALE INDUSTRY		
Output of industrial materials[a]	100	107	183
Persons engaged[b]	100	104	281
Output per person engaged	100	103	65
	SMALL-SCALE INDUSTRY		
Output of industrial materials[a]	100	86	32
Persons engaged[b]	100	82	20
Output per person engaged	100	105	158

SOURCE: Tables 48 and D-1; Kaufman, "Small-Scale Industry," Table A-6.
[a] 1928 weights.
[b] Measured in full-time equivalents.

The movements of production and labor productivity in large- and small-scale industry are represented in Table 52. Output is measured by industrial materials because more comprehensive coverage is not possible on the basis of available data. Small-scale production declined by 14 per cent between 1913 and 1928 and by 73 per cent between 1928 and 1933, while large-scale production was growing over the same periods by 7 and 71 per cent. The movements in labor productivity were in the opposite direction, however: output per person engaged rose by 58 per cent in small-scale industry between 1913 and 1933, but fell by 35 per cent in large-scale industry. It is impossible to determine how much of this was due to shifting of industries from one category to the other and how much to other factors.

GENERAL ECONOMIC DEVELOPMENTS

According to our moving-weight index for all products (Table 53 and
Chart 19), industrial output grew at an average of 12.1 per cent a year

CHART 19

Moving-Weight Indexes of Production, All Industry and
Industrial Groups: Soviet Union, 1928–1940

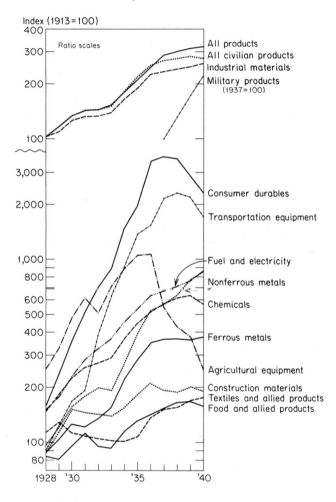

during the period 1928–1937. There was an acceleration in growth from
the earlier to the later years: the average annual rate was 8.8 per cent

TABLE 53

MOVING-WEIGHT INDEXES OF PRODUCTION, ALL INDUSTRY AND INDUSTRIAL GROUPS: SOVIET UNION, 1928–1958

(1913 = 100)

	Industrial Materials	All Products	Total	ALL CIVILIAN PRODUCTS					
				Total	*Intermediate Products*				
					Ferrous Metals	Nonferrous Metals	Fuel and Electricity	Chemicals	Construction Materials
1928	102	102	102	108	88	97	150	146	88
1929	110	116	116	134	104	121	177	184	114
1930	126	134	134	174	126	156	229	226	154
1931	132	143	143	186	121	179	284	256	145
1932	133	144	144	199	134	197	323	270	142
1933	139	153	152	214	155	191	367	289	139
1934	165		182	262	223	266	454	367	154
1935	190		216	313	284	390	532	446	182
1936	226		252	371	350	522	630	513	211
1937	233	285	268	379	365	567	667	571	193
1938	240	298	275	385	368	635	706	616	187
1939	247	311	282	396	361	776	760	634	199
1940	257	318	274	417	375	847	849	565	189
1945	157	264	123	232	235	621	682	213	89
1946	178	180	160	287	262	683	766	326	116
1947	211	219	207	346	295	791	873	468	141
1948	252	276	271	442	371	910	998	619	192
1949	301	343	340	527	456	1,115	1,134	807	226
1950	331	393	397	612	534	1,290	1,263	981	264
1951	373	448	426	689	613	1,521	1,384	1,065	302
1952	397	488	439	734	687	1,779	1,490	1,116	317
1953	430	516	473	775	757	1,951	1,605	1,155	330
1954	466	563	528	859	824	2,118	1,759	1,278	370
1955	511	620	577	942	907	2,405	1,994	1,418	396
1956	547		625		974		2,202	1,561	415
1957	586		686		1,023		2,429	1,682	453
1958	628		715		1,094		2,660	1,804	488

	Machinery and Equipment			Consumer Goods					Civilian and Military Machinery and Equipment	Military Products (1937 = 100)
	Total	Transportation Equipment	Agricultural Machinery	Total	Food and Allied Products	Textiles and Allied Products	Consumer Durables			
1928	143	90	251	97	84	113	158	143	
1929	190	123	328	103	81	129	239		
1930	271	169	481	104	96	112	364		
1931	333	192	619	111	112	108	517		
1932	426	385	510	100	95	105	704		
1933	654	630	704	98	93	102	889	693	4
1934	897	904	887	110	115	101	1,472		
1935	1,274	1,384	1,050	123	131	107	1,950		
1936	1,383	1,546	1,055	144	141	136	3,445		
1937	1,624	2,155	546	157	153	151	3,652	2,597	100
1938	1,626	2,308	426	165	165	155	3,579	2,910	132
1939	1,517	2,190	373	170	166	168		3,209	174
1940	1,140	1,692	247	171	156	175	2,301	3,280	220
1945	265	430	36	73	82	69	274	6,363	627
1946	563	908	78	87	93	84		1,458	92
1947	883	1,350	165	115	115	111		1,564	70
1948	1,425	1,968	389	139	131	136	3,219	2,076	67
1949	2,069	2,700	659	168	164	159	4,512	2,721	67
1950	2,637	3,250	959	184	169	179	5,768	3,639	103
1951	2,248	2,435	1,014	220	197	214	7,420	3,950	175
1952	2,106	2,325	926	230	205	223	8,428	4,839	281
1953	2,312	2,775	900	251	222	240	10,191	4,811	257
1954	2,631	3,095	1,045	280	247	263	13,584	4,916	235
1955	2,994	3,447	1,231	297	258	275	16,350	5,795	288
1956	3,466	3,629	1,637	313	278	284	18,311		
1957	4,086	3,726	2,254	330	287	302	19,488		
1958	3,881	3,991	1,874	353	301	323	21,599		

SOURCE: Tables D-1, D-3, D-4, D-6, A-10, and A-11. Current territory except 1913, which covers interwar Soviet territory.

TABLE 54

AVERAGE ANNUAL GROWTH RATES OF OUTPUT, ALL INDUSTRY AND INDUSTRIAL GROUPS:
SOVIET UNION, FIVE YEAR PLANS
(per cent)

	1928–1932	1932–1937	1937–1940	1940–1945	1945–1950	1950–1955
Industrial materials	6.8	11.8	3.2	−9.4	16.0	9.0
All products	8.8	14.6	3.7	−6.0	8.3	9.6
All civilian products	8.8	13.2	0.7	−14.8	26.4	7.7
Intermediate products	16.5	13.7	3.2	−11.2	21.3	9.0
Ferrous metals	11.0	22.2	1.0	−9.0	17.8	11.2
Nonferrous metals	19.4	23.5	14.2	−6.0	15.8	13.2
Fuel and electricity	21.1	15.7	8.6	−4.3	13.1	9.6
Chemicals	16.6	16.2	−0.4	−17.8	35.8	7.7
Construction materials	12.7	6.3	−0.7	−14.0	24.3	8.5
Machinery and equipment	31.5	30.7	−11.2	−25.5	58.3	2.6
Transportation equipment	44.0	41.1	−8.0	−24.2	49.9	1.2
Agricultural machinery	19.4	1.4	−23.4	−31.9	92.8	5.1
Consumer goods	0.7	9.4	2.9	−15.5	20.3	10.0
Food and allied products	3.1	10.0	0.7	−12.1	15.5	8.9
Textiles and allied products	−1.8	7.6	5.1	−17.0	21.0	9.0
Consumer durables	45.3	39.0	−14.3	−34.8	85.5	23.1
Civilian and military machinery and equipment	37.1a	39.1a	8.1	14.2	−10.6	9.7
Military products	b	123.6a	30.1	23.3	−30.3	22.8

SOURCE: Table 53. Average annual growth rates calculated from data in terminal years by compound interest formula.
a 1933 instead of 1932.
b Output negligible in 1928.

for 1928–1932 and 14.6 per cent for 1932–1937.[14] At the same time, the growth rates for individual industries were much less widely dispersed for the later years than for the earlier ones (see Chart 20).

It should be recalled at this point that there was widespread deterioration in the quality of products during these years, most pronounced in the field of consumer goods and over the period 1928–1932. This means that production indexes tend to exaggerate rises and understate declines in output, and in some cases, as consumer goods, the bias is very substantial. Thus, although our index shows the output of food and allied products as increasing by 13 per cent from 1928 through 1932, it is probable that output, measured in terms of some standard quality, actually declined. Similarly, the decline in output of textiles and allied products was probably greater than the recorded 7 per cent.

[14] For all civilian products, the average annual growth rate was 11.2 per cent for 1928–1937, 8.8 per cent for 1928–1932, and 13.2 per cent for 1932–1937; for industrial materials, 9.6, 6.8, and 11.8 per cent; for finished civilian products, 10.3, 6.6, and 13.6 per cent.

TABLE 55

AVERAGE ANNUAL GROWTH RATES OF OUTPUT PER UNIT OF LABOR,
ALL INDUSTRY AND INDUSTRIAL GROUPS: SOVIET UNION, FIVE YEAR PLANS
(per cent)

	1928–1933	1933–1937	1937–1940	1940–1950	1950–1955
		OUTPUT	PER MAN-HOUR		
products	1.3	6.7	−5.8	−0.1	7.1
		OUTPUT	PER PERSON	ENGAGED	
products	−1.5	7.0	1.4	0.1	5.4
rous and nonferrous metals	−2.7	21.8	3.2	−1.4	8.9
·l and electricity	5.1	14.7	3.5	−0.1	5.4
'uel	2.8	11.2	2.3	−0.2	4.9
:lectricity	−1.2	14.5	7.4	1.0	7.7
emicals	−5.5	14.4	−5.7	5.5	−0.5
nstruction materials	−7.4	9.2	−5.8	0.4	4.1
Vood materials	−6.2	3.6	−3.8	0.9	1.5
Mineral materials	−12.0	35.8	−13.2	−1.4	5.5
¡chinery and allied products	−2.1	28.7	4.6	−1.3	5.9
Civilian machinery and					
equipment	17.5	3.5	0.6	4.4	−2.0
)d and allied products	−4.1	5.1	−0.9	0.2	7.3
xtiles and allied products	−2.9	3.8	2.6	0.8	3.7

SOURCE: Table 40. Note that some industrial groups have a different coverage from that in Table Average growth rates calculated from data for terminal years by the compound interest formula.

The broad structure of growth rates in the two periods 1928–1932 and 1932–1937 is presented in Table 54. Machinery and equipment showed the most rapid growth in both periods, followed by intermediate products and consumer goods. Growth retarded slightly for the first two categories but accelerated sharply for consumer goods between the two periods. Growth retarded in the case of six of the industrial groups listed (consumer durables, transportation equipment, fuel and electricity, agricultural equipment, chemicals, and construction materials) and accelerated in the case of four (ferrous metals, nonferrous metals, food and allied products, and textiles and allied products). The great disparity between growth rates for nondurable consumer goods, on the one side, and for all other goods, on the other, has been commented on many times before; at this stage we need only remark that the disparity was greatest during 1928–1932. Production of military end items began in earnest in the Second Five Year Plan, output expanding about twenty-five times between 1933 and 1937.

Growth in output in the First Five Year Plan was achieved primarily by expanding employment; in the Second, by improving output per person engaged (see Table 55). Roughly speaking, workers were first

CHART 20

Frequency Distributions of Growth Rates of Soviet Industries, Five Year Plans

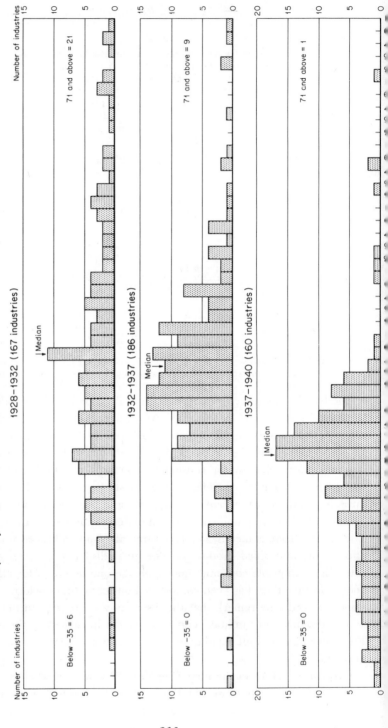

1928–1932 (167 industries)

1932–1937 (186 industries)

1937–1940 (160 industries)

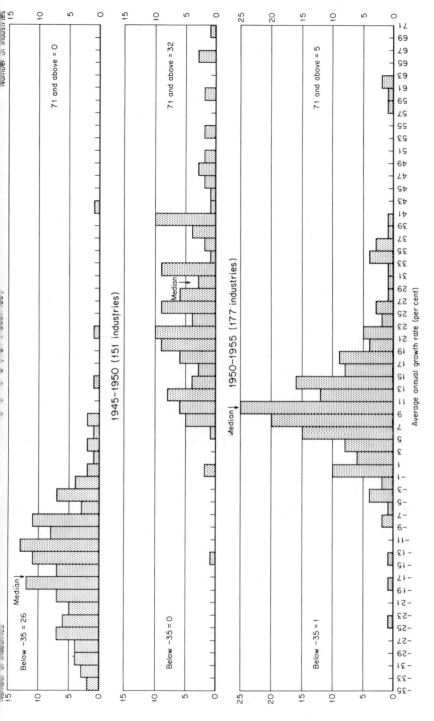

1945-1950 (151 industries)

1950-1955 (177 industries)

Average annual growth rate (per cent)

poured into existing facilities, with a general reduction in output per worker; simultaneously, new facilities were being built and equipped; and, in the succeeding period, new workers were combined with new facilities and equipment to raise both output and output per worker. We observe that output per person engaged fell in eight out of nine industrial groups during 1928–1933 (the exception being civilian machinery and equipment); it rose in all nine groups during 1933–1937.

OUTPUT OF MACHINERY

A few special remarks on the growth of machinery industries seem to be called for because of the great difficulties, already discussed, in devising satisfactory measures of production. In particular, it might be thought that the failure to include some of the more heterogeneous categories of machinery in our production indexes causes an understatement of over-all growth. Before facing that question, we should trace out the broad lines of growth in transportation equipment and agricultural equipment

The output of transportation equipment had fallen by about 10 per cent between 1913–1928. With the growth of the automobile industry, production rose rapidly thereafter and reached its interwar peak in 1938. The average annual rate of growth during 1928–1937 was 42.3 per cent.

By contrast, the output of agricultural equipment had risen by about 150 per cent between 1913 and 1928; and although production continued to rise, the growth rate—9.0 per cent a year during 1928–1937—was much slower than for transportation equipment. Moreover, growth in output was accounted for entirely by tractors: production of agricultural equipment other than tractors shows a cyclical pattern, with a peak in 1930, a trough in 1933, and a second much lower peak in 1937 (see Chart 21). Developments in this industry seem to be rather closely related to agricultural policy, in particular to forced collectivization.

There was a very substantial growth in other segments of the general machinery industry—electrical equipment, mining machinery, machine tools, and so on—but it is impossible to devise satisfactory measures of this growth. The illustrative production indexes we have constructed for this part of the machinery industry show a growth rate roughly the same as for transportation and agricultural equipment taken together. Put another way, inclusion of these heterogeneous machinery items in a general production index does not materially affect the movement of the index over 1928–1937 (see Table 28).

CHART 21
Production of Agricultural Machinery; Soviet Union, 1928–1940

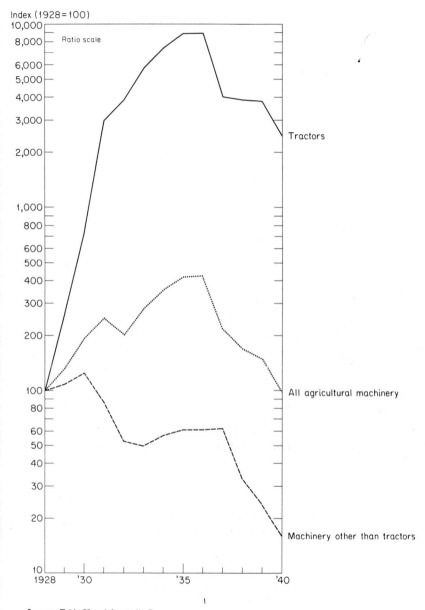

Index (1928=100)

Ratio scale

Tractors

All agricultural machinery

Machinery other than tractors

1928 '30 '35 '40

Source: Table 53 and Appendix D.

203

Growth was also very rapid for consumer durables—bicycles, cameras, light bulbs, phonographs, radios, sewing machines, and motorcycles. The primary explanation here is the extremely low level of production at the beginning of the Plan period.

GROWTH CYCLES

The annual growth rate has a rather interesting cyclical pattern in each of the periods 1928–1932 and 1932–1937, though it is not so pronounced in the latter as in the former (see Table 56). In each period, the peak

TABLE 56

ANNUAL RELATIVES OF PRODUCTION, INDUSTRIAL MATERIALS
AND ALL CIVILIAN PRODUCTS: SOVIET UNION, 1929–1940

	Production as Per Cent of Preceding Year	
	Industrial Materials	All Civilian Products
1929	108	114
1930	115	115
1931	105	107
1932	101	100
1933	104	106
1934	119	120
1935	115	118
1936	119	117
1937	103	106
1938	103	103
1939	103	102
1940	104	97

SOURCE: Table 53.

annual percentage increase in output seems to come in the second year. This finding is supported by behavior in individual industries. If we define a "growth cycle" as existing if the annual growth rate reached a peak in some year other than the terminal years of the period, and if we restrict our attention to industries with annual output data covering the entire period, fifty-seven out of eighty-six industries (or 66 per cent) had a "growth cycle" during 1928–1932, and eighty-six out of 106 industries (or 81 per cent) had one during 1932–1937. Moreover, the second year contained the peak annual growth rate for 69 per cent of the industries with a "growth cycle" during 1928–1932 and for 34 per cent of those with a "growth cycle" during 1932–1937. No other year claimed a larger percentage.[15]

[15] These statistics are calculated from output series in Table B-2.

It is not clear that any mechanical significance should be attached to these "growth cycles" since they are consistent with economic developments unique to each period. For example, the declines in annual growth rates during the period 1928–1932 coincide more or less with intensive collectivization of agriculture. Similarly, the declines in the period 1932–1937 seem to coincide with Stalin's political purges.[16] We shall discuss later whether there is similar evidence of "growth cycles" during the postwar years, for this would have an important bearing on the normalcy of such behavior.

SUCCESS IN MEETING GOALS OF FIVE YEAR PLANS[17]

The output targets set at the beginning of the First and Second Five Year Plans turned out to be rather poor forecasts of events (see Chart 22 and Table 57). For half the products whose targets were listed in physical terms, output reached less than 76 per cent of the target by the terminal year of each plan; the percentage fulfillment would be even lower for the First Plan if we used the maximum instead of the minimum targets. Those products accounting for half the value added (evaluated in 1928 or 1955 rubles) of all listed products in each terminal year had an output that was less than 85 per cent of the target. Finally, the total value added achieved by all listed products was no more than 77 per cent of the "planned" value, both values being expressed in 1928 or 1955 rubles.

Success in meeting planned targets varied from one sector of industry to another, being generally poorest in nonferrous metals, chemicals, construction materials, and consumer goods. Actual value added was within 10 per cent of "planned" value in the cases of fuel and electricity and agricultural machinery in 1932, and of miscellaneous machinery in 1937. It is interesting to note for agricultural machinery that actual value added fell from 98 per cent of "planned" value in 1932 down to 53 per cent in 1937.

---

[16] They may also be related to mobilization for war. At least one Western economist, Gregory Grossman, has argued that 1936 should be included with the following three years to form the period of intensive mobilization ("Steel, Planning, and War Preparedness in the USSR," *Explorations in Entrepreneurial History*, Vol. IX, No. 4, p. 231). This view may be doubted. Although military expenditures did rise substantially in 1936, this was largely due to rising prices following the discontinuance of widespread rationing. If this factor is discounted, expenditures in 1936 seem to fall in line with the rising trend of military expenditures begun in 1934 (see G. F. Grinko, "The Financial Program for 1935," in *Soviet Union 1935*, Moscow and Leningrad, 1935, and *idem*, "Financial Program of the USSR for 1936," in *Second Session of the Central Executive Committee of the USSR*, Moscow, 1936).

[17] Data underlying the discussion in this section are given in technical note 10 of Appendix A.

TABLE 57

FULFILLMENT OF FIVE YEAR PLANS, BY INDUSTRIAL GROUP: SOVIET UNION, 1932, 1937, 1950, AND 195!

	Percentage Fulfilled of Planned Value Added in 1928 Prices				Percentage Fulfilled of Planned Value Added in 1955 Prices			
	1932ᵃ	1937	1950	1955	1932ᵃ	1937	1950	1955
VARIABLE PRODUCT COVERAGEᵇ								
All covered products	74	76	94	99	78	76	94	98
Intermediate products	79	81	104	101	80	80	101	99
Ferrous metals	73	88	107	102	74	87	106	101
Nonferrous metals	60	59	105	81	62	58	103	82
Fuel and electricity	92	88	106	103	95	88	104	104
Chemicals	63	76	96	102	68	78	93	105
Construction materials	73	66	95	90	75	69	93	88
Machinery and equipment	102	77	72	107	110	72	72	110
Transportation equipment	118	79	69	c	119	63	63	c
Agricultural machinery	98	53	98	126	98	84	102	126
Miscellaneous machinery	c	99	77	76	c	111	82	74
Consumer goods	60	62	91	91	65	68	89	93
Food and allied products	57	72	95	86	65	74	90	93
Textiles and allied products	61	56	88	94	67	57	84	94
STANDARD PRODUCT COVERAGEᵈ								
All covered products	77	77	102	100	79	76	99	98
Intermediate products	82	83	104	101	83	80	100	99
Ferrous metals	73	89	106	102	73	88	106	101
Nonferrous metals	60	67	110	80	62	67	111	80
Fuel and electricity	92	86	108	104	95	85	105	104
Chemicals	72	83	89	107	72	83	89	107
Construction materials	78	69	87	88	79	68	87	87
Agricultural machinery	98	53	97	126	98	53	97	126
Consumer goods	61	61	88	90	62	63	90	89
Food and allied products	38	86	105	76	38	86	105	76
Textiles and allied products	65	57	85	94	70	57	86	94

SOURCE: Table A-46.

ᵃ Relates to minimum planned goals for 1932.

ᵇ Largest number of products for which required data are available in each case, as follows:

	Valued in 1928 Prices	Valued in 1955 Prices
1932	37	36
1937	61	64
1950	59	59
1955	34	33

ᶜ Planned output not published.

ᵈ Same sample of eighteen products in each case.

The Third Five Year Plan

GENERAL ECONOMIC DEVELOPMENTS

The course of industrial development changed abruptly during the period 1937–1940: our production indexes all show a sharp retardation in growth rate from the level of earlier periods. If we restrict our attention

CHART 22
Relative Frequency Distributions of Percentages of Planned Output (Five Year Plans) Fulfilled by Value Added: Soviet Union, 1932, 1937, 1950, and 1955

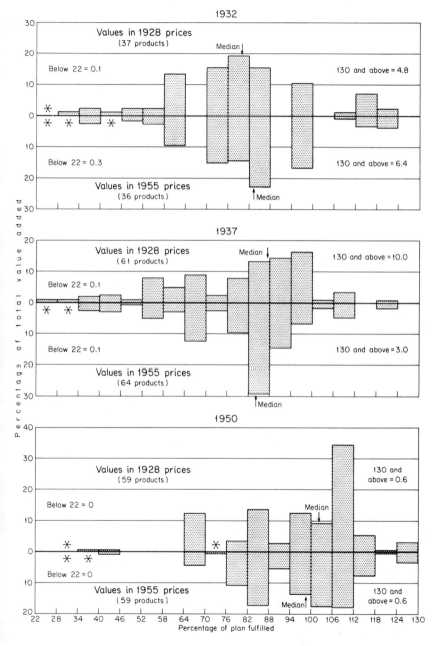

207

CHART 22 (concluded)

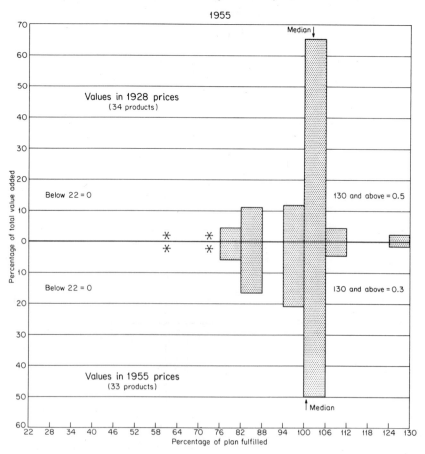

Source: Tables A-45 and D-8.
* Less than 0.5 per cent.

to the indexes based on moving weights, the average annual growth rate fell from 11.8 per cent for 1932–1937 to 3.2 per cent for 1937–1940 in the case of industrial materials, from 13.6 to −2.0 per cent in the case of finished civilian products, from 13.2 to 0.7 per cent in the case of all civilian products, and from 14.6 to 3.7 per cent in the case of all industrial products. These rates do not tell the full story because there was a substantial gain in industrial production attributable to territorial expansion.

In order to interpret the economic development, one must keep in mind the political disturbances of the period. The Great Purge of the Communist Party directed by Stalin reached its zenith in 1937 and 1938, resulting in, among other things, a wholesale turnover of Soviet economic, military, and political leaders.[18] Though it may be impossible to assess the full impact of the purge, there is no doubt that it had an adverse effect on industrial production.

Coupled with the purge was a program of war preparedness, involving substantial diversion of resources from some segments of industry into armaments. Again, for reasons to be elaborated, there is no way to determine how much this mobilization effort had to do with the sharp retardation in growth. Our data on labor productivity (Table 55) do indicate that one apparent effect of disturbances was a significant decline in output per man-hour in industry as a whole. Average annual hours worked increased by about 25 per cent between 1937 and 1940 (see Table A-23), and if this increase applied generally—as seems likely— output per man-hour declined throughout all sectors of industry.

Growth in output retarded sharply in every industrial area, output actually declining in the case of chemicals, construction materials, machinery and equipment, and consumer durables (see Table 54 and Chart 19). The slow rate of growth of the ferrous metals industry was officially blamed for many of these troubles, and trouble in that area was in turn blamed on inadequate development of material inputs such as iron ore, manganese, refractory materials, and lime.[19] In any case, the retardation in growth was so pronounced that aggregate industrial production would have grown very little—if at all—between 1937 and 1940, had it not been for territorial acquisitions. This seems to hold true even after allowance is made for expanding military production, which we now turn to consider.

---

[18] See, e.g., A. F. Khavin, "Razvitie tiazheloi promyshlennosti v tretei piatiletke" [The Development of Heavy Industry in the Third Five Year Plan], *Istoriia SSSR* [History of the USSR], 1959, No. 1, pp. 25 ff. In introducing a detailed discussion of the effects of the purge on industrial personnel, Khavin says the following (p. 25): ". . . In 1936–1939, having wormed their way into J. V. Stalin's confidence, the sworn enemies of the Party and the people Ezhov and Beria—hiding under Stalin's incorrect belief that, as the Soviet Union moved closer to socialism, the class struggle would become more and more intense—started purges of Party and governmental personnel, slandering and annihilating many honest and devoted Party people. Among those purged were many industrial executives.

"The new people put into executive position in industry often did not yet have sufficient experience. In 1937–1938, more than 5,000 new executives were in charge of enterprises, trusts, and chief administrations of heavy industry. Of the 4,000 young specialists who finished technical colleges in the second quarter of 1938, 816 (or more than 20 per cent) were sent directly from college to executive positions in industry. Of the students who were graduated from mining colleges in 1939, fifty-four were appointed chief engineers of mines, and seventy, chief mechanical or electrical engineers. Many workers with no theoretical training were promoted to executive positions."

[19] Khavin in *Istoriia SSSR*, 1959, No. 1, pp. 26 f.

The Soviet armament program was seriously under way by 1933 and 1934, production of conventional weapons already being large by standards of that day.[20] Production rose sharply through 1937, multiplying twenty-five times according to our estimates. Direct employment in military industries had probably reached one million persons by 1937, or about 9 per cent of all persons engaged in industry.[21]

The expansion in military output continued at the pace of about 30 per cent a year over the Third Five Year Plan, output more than doubling and employment about doubling in the course of three years. The additional million persons employed represented about 8.5 per cent of persons engaged in other industries in 1940. We might therefore suppose that, had these resources not been diverted to military production, civilian production would have risen by about 10 or 11 per cent instead of the 2 per cent actually experienced. In that event, output of all products would have grown no more than it did in the face of the armament program. In other words, there is little evidence here that diversion of resources to military production materially affected the over-all rate of industrial growth.

There was, of course, a substantial growth in the size of the armed forces over this period, military personnel rising from something less than 1.5 million in 1937 to something over 4 million in the middle of 1941. This increase of 2.5 million was much larger than the increase of about 900 thousand that took place during the Second Five Year Plan.[22] The accelerated build-up of the armed forces helps to explain why the industrial labor force showed an increase of less than a million persons over 1937–1940 compared with more than 3.5 million over 1933–1937. Persons engaged in industry increased by over 40 per cent in the latter period but by only 7 per cent in the former (see Table A-20).

In any case, Soviet industry had by no means been put on a wartime footing by the end of 1940. The full list of reasons cannot be known, since the happenings of these years are cloaked in mystery, perhaps never to be dispelled. Fewer data on output are available for 1939 than for any other single year in the Plan period, except war years. The political developments of that year were, of course, world shaking. The Hitler-Stalin pact was concluded in August, followed in September by the

[20] See the speeches by Grinko and Tukhachevsky in *Soviet Union 1935*. See also Heinz Guderian, *Panzer Leader*, New York, 1952, p. 141, and John Scott, *Behind the Urals*, Cambridge, Mass., 1942, pp. 106 f.
[21] See note *d* to Table A-20.
[22] These data are taken from the annex to technical note 3 of Appendix A.

German invasion of Poland and the start of World War II. In the wake of German victory in Poland and in accord with the Hitler-Stalin pact, the Soviet Union took possession of the Baltic States and about half of Poland. The war against Finland was launched. From an economic point of view, the gains from territorial acquisitions were substantial, while the drain of the Finnish war was probably very slight. Yet there is every indication from our indexes that industrial output increased by only 4 per cent in 1939 and 2 per cent in 1940—altogether, by less than the gains from territorial expansion. What happened?

One former Soviet official, Victor Kravchenko, has argued that the mobilization effort faltered in 1939:[23]

> The theory that Stalin was merely "playing for time" while feverishly arming against the Nazis was invented much later, to cover up the Kremlin's tragic blunder in trusting Germany. It was such a transparent invention that little was said about it inside Russia during the Russo-German war; only after I emerged into the free world did I hear it seriously advanced and believed. It was a theory that ignored the most significant aspect of the Stalin-Hitler arrangement: the large-scale economic undertakings which drained the USSR of the very products and materials and productive capacity necessary for its own defense preparations.
>
> The simple fact is that the Soviet regime did not use the interval following the Hitler-Stalin pact to arm itself effectively. I was close enough to the defense industries to know that there was a slackening of military effort after the pact. The general feeling, reflecting the mood in the highest official circles, was that we could afford to feel safe thanks to the statesmanship of Stalin. Not until the fall of France did doubts arise on this score; only then was the tempo of military effort stepped up again.

This view seems to be substantiated in an article by A. F. Khavin, a Soviet historian, published in a professional journal in 1959:[24]

> Nevertheless, in the years just before the war, the possibilities of strengthening the defense capacities of the country were far from being fully utilized. This was partly the result of J. V. Stalin's incorrect assessment of the military and political scene on the eve of the war, of

[23] V. Kravchenko, *I Chose Freedom*, New York, 1952, p. 335. See also pp. 362 ff.
[24] Khavin, in *Istoriia SSSR*, 1959, No. 1, pp. 22 f.

his obvious overconfidence in the pact with Germany. Socialist industry had at its disposal productive forces and cadres that enabled it to supply the Red army with the newest equipment. But it was not fully mobilized in time. Old-style tanks and planes were no longer produced, but the mass production of new types of military equipment was slow to be mastered.

Therefore, at the beginning of the war, the Soviet air force had, for instance, as many planes as the enemy force, but they were outmoded and inferior to German planes.

While not addressing himself to the inadequacies of industrial preparation for war, the late Nikolai Voznesensky, former head of the *Gosplan*, commented much earlier on the fact that full mobilization took place only after war had started. He said:[25]

The Patriotic War found Soviet war industry in the process of introducing the production of new equipment, and the mass output of war equipment was not organized as yet. Prior to the Patriotic War, when the menace of Hitlerite Germany against the USSR was being felt more and more, the Soviet government adopted as a precautionary measure the "mobilization plan" with respect to ammunition for the second half of 1941 and 1942, aiming at wartime conversion of industry in the event of a war. The mobilization plan established a program of ammunition production, and defined a program of industrial conversion, especially for the machine-building industry, in the event of an attack by fascist aggressors on the USSR. . . .

In the very first days of the Patriotic War the mobilization plan was transformed into an operational assignment for the expansion of output in the most important—and the most capable of mass production—branch of war industry: the manufacture of ammunition. The machine-building, metallurgical, and chemical industries began an intensive conversion from peacetime to wartime production. The growth of war production was assured by the radical conversion of all industry of the USSR for meeting the needs of the Patriotic War. War industry, basing itself on all the productive capacity of the country, rapidly mastered the production of modern war equipment and changed the technological process of production to the mass continuous output of aircraft, tanks, weapons, and ammunition.

[25] N. A. Voznesensky, *The Economy of the USSR During World War II* (translated from the Russian), Washington, 1948, pp. 46 f, one intervening paragraph omitted.

The ambitious plans for expanding output in 1941, summarized earlier in Tables 1 and 2, also suggest that industrial mobilization was not preoccupying Soviet leaders even as late as 1940. Large increases in output were planned throughout industry, in the sector of consumer goods as well as elsewhere.

It would seem from these lines of evidence that the sharp retardation in growth evident for the period 1937–1940 is not explained by industrial mobilization. The years most needing explanation are 1939 and 1940, when industrial output adjusted to constant territorial coverage seems not to have increased at all despite the fact that the mobilization effort seems to have faltered and even diminished. The Great Purge undoubtedly had more to do with slowing down growth, and even that may not be a full explanation.

Postwar Industrial Developments

EXTENT OF WAR DAMAGE

The Soviet Union suffered very heavy losses during World War II, and this is shown nowhere more graphically than in what happened to population, which according to estimates derived from official data dropped roughly 24 million between 1940 and 1945, whereas in the absence of war it might well have risen by as much as 15 million. The losses in output were also large, industrial production (for example) declining precipitously to an unknown low point around 1943 while large areas of the Soviet Union were being occupied by German troops. In 1945 industrial output stood, according to our indexes, at 83 per cent of its 1940 level, and this is probably an understatement of the decline because of the tendency of indexes to exaggerate wartime production. In 1946, after the sudden and sharp demobilization, output stood at less than 60 per cent of the 1940 level. Industrial and residential property were damaged and destroyed on a large scale. Even with an abundance of statistical detail at our disposal, we could hardly expect to make an adequate and meaningful assessment of the full economic significance of these war losses; faced as we are with only shreds of evidence, we can make only crude guesses. Even then we would have touched on only one—in most respects, a minor—aspect of war losses, namely, "economic" damage.

It is, nevertheless, important that we form some notion of the magnitude of the net economic handicap placed on Soviet industry in resuming its development in the postwar years, so that we may have a better basis for interpreting recent economic performance. One important thing to

213

recognize is that economic aid received during the war and "reparations" collected afterward did mitigate losses significantly.

It has been estimated that Lend-Lease shipments to the Soviet Union averaged about $3 billion annually.[26] The significance of this aid is revealed by noting that Soviet production in 1940 of the fifty items included in our index of industrial materials amounted to only $3.6 billion when valued in U.S. 1939 prices (see Table D-7). The total production of Soviet industry apparently amounted in 1940 to about $8.8 billion.[27] Annual Lend-Lease aid would seem to have been roughly a third of prewar annual Soviet industrial output, about the internal decline in industrial output. To this extent, current losses were being offset.

It is much more difficult to assess the more permanent economic losses in the form of property and manpower. On property we must reason entirely by analogy with the United States, and then in only the crudest way. According to Raymond Goldsmith's estimates, all reproducible tangible assets of the United States as of the end of 1940 were worth about $331 billion when valued at current replacement cost.[28] As a very rough guess, we might suppose that the stock of such assets in the Soviet Union was about a fifth as large as in the United States, which would give an estimate of $65 billion as the replacement value of Soviet reproducible tangible assets in 1940, expressed in current American prices.[29]

[26] Harry Schwartz, *Russia's Soviet Economy*, 2nd ed., New York, 1954, p. 595.

[27] This estimate is reached as value added in dollars in 1928 ($3.6 billion, as given in Table 63) times the production index for all Soviet products (311 per cent of 1928), deflated by the U.S. BLS wholesale price index for other than farm products and foods (89.5 per cent of 1928).

[28] R. W. Goldsmith, D. S. Brady, and H. Mendershausen, *A Study of Saving in the United States*, Vol. III, Princeton, 1956, p. 14.

[29] The official Soviet statement of damages is 679 billion rubles or $128 billion (Voznesensky, *Economy of the USSR*, p. 97). This is said to represent two-thirds of all wealth in territories occupied by the Germans (*ibid.*), and that wealth is implied by other statistics to have been from a third to a half of all wealth in the Soviet Union (*ibid.*, p. 94). Thus the losses are implied to be from a fifth to a third of total wealth. The numerical estimate of losses cannot, therefore, be taken seriously; for even with the obviously high estimates of the fraction of wealth lost, it would imply a total wealth of from $384 to $640 billion. These figures bracket Goldsmith's estimate of $424 billion as the national wealth of the United States in 1940.

Soviet statistics on wealth have recently been officially condemned as inadequate and unreliable by V. Starovskii, present head of the Central Statistical Bureau, in his article, "Novye zadachi sovetskoi statistiki" [New Tasks of Soviet Statistics], *Kommunist* [The Communist], 1957, No. 14, p. 68. As to estimated war damage, Starovskii says: "At the end of World War II the fixed capital of all enterprises in formerly occupied territory was re-assessed. The results of this work, done at various times, did not make it possible to estimate fixed capital in comparable prices. Therefore, the government recognized the necessity of bringing order to this matter."

In recognition of these shortcomings, a comprehensive census of capital was undertaken in 1960, and the results have recently been published in *Narodnoe khoziaistvo SSSR v 1959 godu* [The USSR National Economy in 1959], Moscow, 1960.

We might further suppose, as a very rough guess, that a fifth to a quarter of these assets were destroyed in war.[30] The capital loss would then be, on the basis of these crude assumptions, somewhere between $13 and $16 billion. That is to say, new investment within that range would have been required to restore the stock of tangible reproducible assets to its prewar level. No account is, of course, taken of the retardation in growth of capital that may have occurred as a direct consequence of war.

With those general orders of magnitude in mind, let us now turn to the question of "reparations" and see how they compare with this crude measure of "loss." We have collected together scattered estimates of reparations and aid given by a number of countries to the Soviet Union over 1946–1953; details may be found in technical note 8 of Appendix A. These fragments sum to at least $9 billion in 1938 U.S. prices, or to about $21 billion in current U.S. prices. The latter may be compared with the $12 billion given by the United States to Western Europe under the Marshall Plan.

Our estimate of reparations to the Soviet Union does not include requisitions to support Soviet occupation forces in Europe, confiscations of industrial equipment dismantled before the end of the war, proceeds from the so-called "joint companies" established in the satellite countries of Eastern Europe, labor services of prisoners of war, or benefits from differential trading prices (except in the case of Polish coal). Professor Nicholas Spulber concludes in his authoritative study of postwar economic developments in Eastern Europe that "the over-all contribution of these areas to the Soviet Union of reparations, restitutions, etc., was much more substantial than the value totals would suggest,"[31] further stating[32] that:

The cost of the war participation of Hungary, Romania, and Bulgaria on the Nazi side has placed on them a burden of debt to Russia for a period of not less than 12 years (1944–45–1956). First in the form of reparations, second in the form of joint companies, which grew mostly out of the German assets, and third in the form of the sale and transfer of those assets back to those countries, the Soviet Union has pressed its claims almost inflexibly. It is against this background that

[30] This is suggested by various data given in A. Bergson *et al.*, "Postwar Economic Reconstruction and Development in the U.S.S.R.," *Annals of the American Academy of Political and Social Science*, May 1949, p. 53.
[31] N. Spulber, *The Economics of Communist Eastern Europe*, Cambridge, Mass., 1957, p. 182.
[32] *Ibid.*, pp. 205 f.

we should judge what the Soviet Union claims to have "given" these countries.

In the nature of the case, we cannot make a precise and reliable estimate of the total value of materials and property received by the Soviet Union from other countries during the postwar period. It is quite possible that our estimates of reparations represent no more than half the total. Thus we can imagine a range of $9 to $18 billion in 1938 dollars, which may be compared with our estimate of $13 to $16 billion as the Soviet loss of capital during the war, also expressed in prewar dollars.

The Soviet Union has not, of course, been able to make up for its enormous loss of population—if, indeed, it makes sense to talk about "making up" for such things. Most of these losses occurred among males of working age and, because of lowered birth rates, among the younger age cohorts of both sexes. Economically the result was an immediate reduction in the labor force and a delayed retardation in its rate of growth that was to set in a decade or so after the end of the war—i.e., around 1955. The reduction in the labor force was offset in part by the increased participation of women and by the use of prisoners of war, who were retained and employed on a large scale up to at least 1953.[33] These have been essentially temporizing measures, however; the permanent loss of population has not been economically compensated for, if we assume— as we should—that the lost population would have produced more than enough to maintain itself.

In summary, then, the Soviet Union suffered heavy economic losses in World War II. At the same time, various extraordinary measures resorted to, such as confiscations of foreign materials and property and employment of prisoners of war, considerably mitigated those losses and may very well have fully offset property damage.

RECOVERY OF INDUSTRIAL PRODUCTION, 1945–1950

Output recovered rapidly during the Fourth Five Year Plan (1946 through 1950), apparently reaching its peak prewar level by 1949. Reconversion also occurred rapidly: according to our imperfect measures, output of military products fell by 85 per cent in 1946 and total output by 32 per cent (see Chart 23). These declines are probably exaggerated, however, to the extent that our indexes for 1945 overstate production (see the concluding paragraph of the section on military products in

[33] Schwartz, *Russia's Soviet Economy*, pp. 569 ff.

CHART 23
Moving-Weight Indexes of Production, All Industry and
Industrial Groups: Soviet Union, 1937–1958

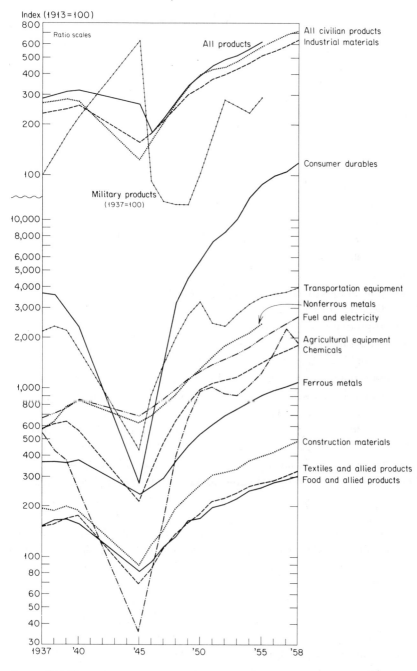

Index (1913=100)

Ratio scales

All civilian products
All products
Industrial materials

Consumer durables

Military products
(1937=100)

Transportation equipment
Nonferrous metals
Fuel and electricity

Agricultural equipment
Chemicals

Ferrous metals

Construction materials

Textiles and allied products
Food and allied products

1937   '40   '45   '50   '55   '58

Source: Table 53.

217

Chapter 5). The shifting of resources was apparently completed before 1948, when military output apparently reached its low point for this period—about 11 per cent of its 1945 level, according to our index—and total output registered a level equal to its previous (exaggerated) 1945 peak. Military output rose sharply again in 1950 with the outbreak of the Korean War, but it reached only about a sixth of its 1945 level. Hence, over 1945–1950, the measured increase in output was larger for civilian products (223 per cent) than for all products (49 per cent) or for industrial materials (111 per cent). By 1950, output was 24 per cent higher than the 1940 level for all products, 29 per cent higher for industrial materials, and 45 per cent higher for civilian products.

Output per unit of labor was roughly the same in 1950 as in 1940, according to our estimates (see Table 40). Such gains as occurred can probably be attributed primarily to technological advances—resulting from wartime experiences, including close contact with the Allies—since it is doubtful that there was a significant increase in industrial capital or improvement in worker's skills between 1940 and 1950. The largest rise in labor productivity came in the machinery and chemicals sectors, with smaller rises for electricity, wood construction materials, and textiles and allied products. Labor productivity apparently declined for metals, fuel, and mineral construction materials.

It would appear that Soviet industry was much more successful in meeting planned goals at the end of the Fourth—and Fifth—Five Year Plan than it had been in the First and Second (see Table 57). Whether this is the result of improved performance or a gradual process of selecting items easiest to plan—only eighteen products in the Fifth Plan appear in all the other plans—is not clear. The estimated 1955 value added of thirty-four planned industries—and value added fulfilled—amounted to less than a sixth of the total value added of industry (see Tables A-43 and A-46).

It is interesting to compare the postwar recovery of industrial output in the Soviet Union with recovery in other countries that suffered considerable war damage. This is done in Table 58 and Chart 24, where industrial growth over recent years is shown for France, Japan, West Germany, and the Soviet Union. Production is measured for the first three countries by their official indexes; for the Soviet Union, by our indexes for industrial materials and for all products. Postwar economic developments have not, of course, been the same in all these countries. In particular, the economic recovery of both Japan and West Germany was held in check by policies of the occupying powers until at least as late as 1948. In any

CHART 24
Indexes of Industrial Production in France, Japan, West Germany, and the Soviet Union, 1938–1958

```
·········· France
—·—·— Japan
············ West Germany
------ Industrial materials ⎫
——— All products        ⎬ Soviet Union
                         ⎭
```

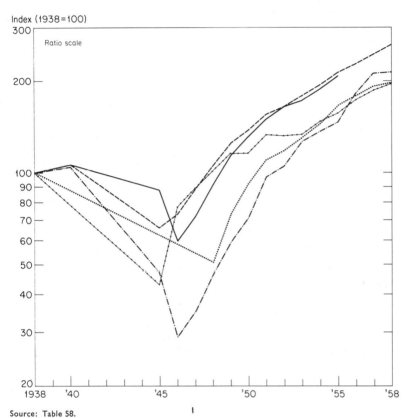

Source: Table 58.

case, it is interesting to note that the over-all course of recovery (and subsequent development) was similar in all these countries, when due allowance is made for different circumstances. France showed a faster growth than the Soviet Union from 1945/46 through 1950, and both Japan and West Germany surpassed this record in a comparable five years of recovery (1948–1953). Growth in all three countries has continued to be rapid by the Soviet standard.

TABLE 58

INDUSTRIAL PRODUCTION IN FRANCE, JAPAN, WEST GERMANY, AND THE SOVIET UNION, 1938–1958

(1953 = 100)

	France	Japan	West Germany	Soviet Union Industrial Materials	Soviet Union All Products
1938	75	79	77	56	58
1940	n.a.	83	n.a.	60	62
1945	32	37	n.a.	37	51
1946	58	23	n.a.	41	35
1947	67	28	n.a.	49	42
1948	76	36	39	59	53
1949	87	47	56	70	66
1950	87	56	71	77	76
1951	100	77	85	87	87
1952	99	83	91	92	95
1953	100	100	100	100	100
1954	110	108	112	108	109
1955	118	116	128	119	120
1956	130	144	138	127	n.a.
1957	140	167	147	136	n.a.
1958	146	168	151	146	n.a.

SOURCE: Table 53 and United Nations, *Statistical Yearbook, 1959*, New York, 1959. Data for years not given in the latter source have been interpolated by indexes in *Statistical Yearbook, 1956* or *1957*.

POSTWAR GROWTH, 1950–1955

During the Fifth Five Year Plan (1951 through 1955), industrial output apparently grew faster than during the First Five Year Plan and slower than during the Second—slower than during both the First and Second taken together (see Table 54). In the case of food and textiles, however, the growth was more rapid than during the First and Second Plans together. Consumer goods outpaced industry as a whole in growth, although, as we shall see, this was in part a result of the rearmament program. Military production continued the expansion begun in 1950—with a dip in 1953 and 1954, following the end of the Korean War and the death of Stalin—and multiplied almost twice as much as all other production.

In fact, industrial developments in the first two years seem to have been dominated by military preparations. Output of civilian machinery and equipment fell by 15 per cent in 1951 and 6 per cent in 1952, while military production was rising very rapidly. In view of behavior in surrounding years, it seems likely that the sudden spurt in the growth of consumer goods in 1951—output increasing by 17 per cent for foods, 20 per cent for textiles, and 29 per cent for consumer durables—was also connected with the re-equipping of troops, whose strength more than doubled between 1948 and 1955.[34]

The end of the Korean hostilities and, particularly, the change of government with Stalin's death clearly left their mark on economic developments. Military production, by our measures, declined by 9 per cent in both 1953 and 1954, though it apparently recovered its 1952 level by 1955. As a counterpart, consumer goods and civilian machinery outpaced all industry in growth over this latter half of the Fifth Plan, the growth rate of consumer goods falling sharply, however, in 1955.

Though there is some evidence of a "growth cycle" during the period of postwar recovery (1945–1950), the picture is more confused for 1950–1955. Out of 170 industries for which the needed output data are available, only eighty-eight (slightly more than half) show a "growth cycle" in the latter period. That is, only about half the industries had a peak rate of growth in some year other than 1951 or 1955. The distribution of peak growth rates for all 170 industries is as follows: 1951, fifty-one; 1952, nineteen; 1953, thirty-four; 1954, thirty-six; and 1955, thirty.[35] These statistics cast further doubt on whether "growth cycles" might be a standard phenomenon of the five year plan.

Output per man-hour apparently grew more rapidly during the Fifth Five Year Plan than during either the Second or the Third (see Table 55). The average annual growth rate for the Fifth Five Year Plan (7.1 per cent) is considerably higher than the rates for both the entire Soviet period (1.9 per cent) and the Plan period (1.7 per cent). In the case of output per person engaged, the growth rate was faster than for the First and Second Plans combined but slower than for the Second Plan alone. For all industrial groups except food and allied products, output per person engaged also grew at a slower rate than for the Second Five Year Plan. For fuel, chemicals, mineral construction materials, and civilian machinery, the growth rate was also slower than for the First and Second Plans combined; for electricity, wood construction materials, food and allied products, and textiles and allied products, it was faster.

[34] See the annex to technical note 3 of Appendix A.
[35] All statistics are derived from the output series in Appendix B.

TABLE 59
ANNUAL RELATIVES OF PRODUCTION, ALL INDUSTRY AND INDUSTRIAL GROUPS:
SOVIET UNION, 1950–1958
(per cent)

	Production as Percentage of Preceding Year								
	1950	1951	1952	1953	1954	1955	1956	1957	195
Industrial materials	110	113	106	108	108	110	107[a]	107[a]	10'
All products	115	114	109	106	109	110			
All civilian products	117	107	103	108	112	109	108[a]	110[a]	10‹
Intermediate products	116	113	107	106	111	110			
Ferrous metals	117	115	112	110	109	110	107	105	10:
Nonferrous metals	116	118	117	110	109	114			
Fuel and electricity	111	110	108	108	110	113	110	110	11(
Chemicals	122	109	105	103	111	111	110	108	10:
Construction materials	117	114	105	104	112	107	105	109	10&
Machinery and equipment	127	85	94	110	114	114	116	118	9!
Transportation equipment	120	75	95	119	112	111	105	103	10:
Agricultural machinery	146	106	91	97	116	118	133	138	8:
Consumer goods	110	120	105	109	112	106	105	105	10:
Food and allied products	103	117	104	108	111	104	108	103	10!
Textiles and allied products	113	120	104	108	110	105	103	106	10:
Consumer durables	128	129	114	121	133	120	112	106	11)
Civilian and military machinery and equipment	134	109	122	99	102	118			
Military products	154	170	161	91	91	123			

SOURCE: Table 53.
[a] Does not cover nonferrous metals and several other products (see Table A-5).

THE YEARS SINCE 1955

The Sixth Five Year Plan began with 1956 and ended less than two years later in the fall of 1957, under circumstances suggesting that its goals were too ambitious.[36] After an interval of a year, a Seven Year Plan

[36] The following statement appeared in a resolution of the Central Committee of the Communist Party issued in December 1956 ("On Completion of Work on Drafting Sixth Five-Year Plan and on Policy of Drawing up Non-Specific Control Figures for 1956–1960 and Economic Plan for 1957," *Current Digest of the Soviet Press*, VIII, 52, 11, original text in *Pravda* and *Izvestia*, December 25, 1956): "In drafting national economic plans, the State Planning Commission, the State Economic Commission and the ministries are not taking sufficient account of practical possibilities for supplying materials and funds for plan assignments, are not providing for sufficient stocks of raw materials, fuel and supplies and are allowing an excessive volume of construction, which creates added strain in carrying out the plan." Abandonment of the Sixth Plan was announced in *Pravda*, September 26, 1957.

was inaugurated to cover 1959 through 1965. On the basis of data published since 1955, we have extended our production indexes for industrial materials and all civilian products through 1958 as given in Table 53.[37] The output of industrial materials increased at an average annual rate of 7.1 per cent over 1955–1958, compared with 9.0 over 1950–1955; the output of all civilian products, at 7.4 per cent, compared with 7.7 per cent. Since the growth of industrial materials seems to have paralleled closely the growth of all products over 1950–1955 (see Table 59), it is

TABLE 60

AVERAGE ANNUAL GROWTH RATES IN PHYSICAL OUTPUT PLANNED FOR 1955–1965
COMPARED WITH THOSE FOR OTHER PERIODS: SOVIET UNION, TWENTY-FOUR INDUSTRIES
(per cent)

	1913–1955	1928–1955	1950–1955	Planned, 1955–1965
Iron ore	5.0	9.8	12.6	8.0
Pig iron	5.0	9.0	11.6	7.3
Steel ingots	5.8	9.2	10.6	6.9
Rolled steel	5.5	9.0	11.1	6.7
Electric power	11.2	13.9	13.3	11.6
Coal	6.4	9.3	8.4	4.1
Crude petroleum	5.0	7.0	13.4	12.7
Natural gas	14.6	13.4	9.3	32.5
Mineral fertilizer	12.5	17.1	11.7	11.2
Paper	5.5	7.2	9.3	6.3
Cement	6.6	9.7	17.1	13.2
Lumber	3.9	6.5	8.8	4.6
Window glass	3.5	4.1	5.4	8.2
Motor vehicles	n.a.	13.6[a]	4.2	6.1
Butter	3.6	6.6	6.6	8.4
Vegetable oil	2.2	2.5	7.4	7.2
Meat slaughtering	2.1	3.3	9.2	11.2
Fish catch	2.4	4.5	9.3	5.5
Raw sugar	2.0	3.7	6.3	10.5
Boots and shoes	3.7	3.7	6.2	6.5
Cotton fabrics	2.0	3.0	8.7	3.9
Silk and rayon fabrics	5.7	14.3	32.3	10.9
Woolen and worsted fabrics	2.1	2.9	10.3	7.1
Hosiery	n.a.	5.2[b]	10.4	4.9
Median	5.0	7.1	9.3	7.2

SOURCE: Table B-2; goals of the Seven Year Plan (taken as midpoints of announced ranges) as given in *Current Digest*, XI, 9, 3 ff. Average annual growth rates calculated from output in terminal years by the compound interest formula.
  [a] 1932–1955.
  [b] 1933–1955.

[37] Because the published record of production has not been complete, we have had to resort to some indirect procedures in extending the industrial materials indexes. They and their possible effects are described in the technical note 3 of Appendix A, in the text surrounding Table A-5.

reasonable to suppose that it has continued to do so in more recent years. Hence growth seems to have slowed down since the end of the Fifth Five Year Plan, more so in the case of all products than in the case of civilian products alone. It is, of course, too early to tell whether this marks a trend or merely a fluctuation.

The official production index shows the same slowing down: an average annual rate of 10.1 per cent for 1955–1958 compared with 13.1 per cent for 1950–1955 (see Table F-2). Moreover, the average annual rate planned for the Seven Year Plan is 8.6 per cent, compared with 11.3 per cent for the Fifth Five Year Plan and 10.5 per cent for the Sixth. The expected retardation holds generally for individual industries reported on (Table 60). By Soviet measures and expectations, the rate of growth in industrial production is retarding.

CHAPTER 8

Industrial Growth:
A Comparison with the United States

THE Soviet record of industrial growth may be placed in perspective by comparing it with the record of other countries. This is not so easy as it might seem, not only because it is difficult to design relevant comparisons, but also because so little is known about the course of industrial development in most countries. The latter factor alone has forced us, with our limited time and resources, to concentrate on comparisons with the United States, a country with relatively abundant historical statistics. The United States is an obvious first choice for comparative study in any case, since it presents a striking contrast in economic system while being similar in size and resource endowment. But while a comparative study reasonably starts with the United States, it should not end there, and we may hope that others will take up where we have left off.

Comparative study may help us in answering two quite different questions. First, we are interested in knowing, for a variety of reasons associated with the current state of world affairs, which country has shown the more rapid industrial growth over recent years, so that we may have some basis for intelligent guesses about relative growth over the very near future. Second, we are interested in knowing which country has been able to generate the more rapid industrial growth under conditions in which "physical" capacities for growth have been roughly equivalent. Our quest here is for a more fundamental test of the growth-generating efficiency of vastly different economic systems under comparable circumstances, a matter of concern for the longer view.

The first question is obviously easier to deal with than the second, because it requires only a description of the "facts" of growth in the two countries over the same span of years. Of course, the facts are in dispute, and the quantitative evidence of growth is more representative and reliable for the United States than for the Soviet Union. But this problem must always be faced, whether the issues at hand are analytical or purely descriptive. The essential point is that, in making comparisons of concurrent growth trends, we are primarily concerned with *what* is or has been happening, not *why*. Our attention is focused on trends likely to be carried forward over an immediate future by their own momentum, in the absence of revolutionary change in conditioning factors.

225

The second question involves a complex problem of analysis that by its very nature defies definitive solution. We try to find historical periods in two countries in which the important determinants of growth are the same in both cases, while the economic systems differ. To do this we need to know, first, what factors affect growth in what degrees and, second, what periods of history in the two countries are comparable. Neither economic theory nor history blesses our task: theory is mute and history mischievous. At best, the periods chosen will be "comparable" only in some rather crude sense. Even so, the exercise is worth doing, as an early step in the successive approximations that mark the path to knowledge.

If industrial economies do go through comparable stages of development in some meaningful sense, setting those American and Soviet periods side by side carries with it an important by-product: it enables us to project Soviet developments into a context with which we are more familiar, and thereby to reason by analogy in directions where direct evidence is lacking. There are also great hazards in reasoning by analogy, but judiciously applied it enriches our knowledge of the likely growth and present status of Soviet industry. Our vision of Soviet industrial growth is clarified by associating it with American developments bracketing the turn of the century, but at the same time the analogy must not be taken too far. The sets of industrial conditions in the two periods abound with anachronisms relative to each other.

Contemporaneous Growth

PRODUCTION

Over the same spans of years, industrial output has generally grown faster in the Soviet Union than in the United States (see Tables 61 and 62 and Chart 25).[1] This seems to be an old story since it was apparently true of the Tsarist era as well: according to our indexes, Russian industry grew slightly faster than American industry over the period 1870–1913, the respective average annual rates being 5.3 and 5.1 per cent. The differential is similar for the Soviet period as a whole: output grew over 1913–1955 at an average annual rate of 4.1 per cent in the Soviet Union, when adjusted to remove territorial gains, compared with 3.8 per cent in the United States. Growth including territorial gains has apparently been faster in the Soviet Union than in the United States for all major sectors of industry except food and allied products (see Table 65). If territorial gains were removed, chemicals and textiles and allied

---

[1] Throughout these comparisons, industry is defined in accord with Soviet usage, including manufacturing, mining, logging, fishing, and generating of electricity.

226

TABLE 61

INDEXES OF INDUSTRIAL OUTPUT, OUTPUT PER UNIT OF LABOR, AND OUTPUT PER CAPITA:
TSARIST RUSSIA, SOVIET UNION, AND UNITED STATES, BENCHMARK YEARS, 1860–1955
(1913 = 100)

Output		Output per Man-Hour Engaged in Industry		Output per Person Engaged in Industry		Output per Head of Population	
Russia or Soviet Union[a]	United States[b]	Soviet Union[c]	United States[d]	Soviet Union[c]	United States[d]	Russia or Soviet Union[e]	United States[f]
10	7					19	22
9	8					16	22
13	12					21	29
17	14					25	30
22	20					31	38
28	23					36	39
38	35					46	54
52	40					59	56
74	51					77	65
72	74					69	86
102	85					89	89
{ 118 / 100 }	100	100	100	100	100	{ 99 / 100 }	100
20	124					20	114
102	172	137	168	111	136	93	140
153	120	146	184	103	129	133	93
285	178	188	205	135	145	238	135
318[g]	214	157	224	141	156	221	159
264[g,h]	344[h]					208[h]	241[h]
393[g]	366	155	272	143	199	298	236
620[g]	473	218	323	186	236	434	280

1860–1913, Table A-19, Borenstein-Goldsmith index with imputed weights; 1913–1955, Table 53,
ing-weight index for all products. 1920 interpolated by indexes for industrial materials in Table 47.
1913, first figure applies to Tsarist territory; second, to interwar territory (see Table D-1, note b).
erwise, current territory.
Table A-32. Current territory.
Table 40.
Table A-36.
From population as given in Table C-3.
From population as given in *Historical Statistics of the United States, Colonial Times to 1957,*
hington, 1960.
Adjusted to exclude territorial gains (estimated as 11 per cent of production beginning with 1940,
xplained in Chapter 6), these figures would be as follows: 1940, 286; 1945, 184; 1950, 354;
1955, 558.
Output is probably exaggerated significantly because of difficulties in measuring output of military
ucts (see Table A-32 and section on military products in Chapter 5).

products would probably be additional exceptions.

Over the Plan period Soviet growth in percentage terms has out-
distanced U.S. growth by a wider margin, making up for a differential
in the other direction for the earlier years. American output grew at

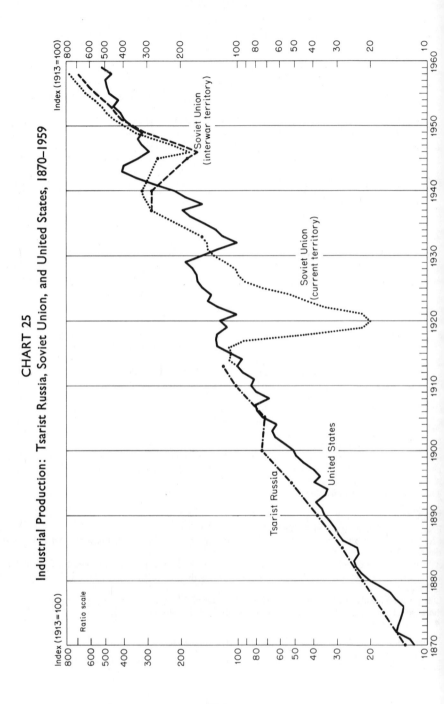

CHART 25

Industrial Production: Tsarist Russia, Soviet Union, and United States, 1870–1959

TABLE 62

ᴇʀᴀɢᴇ Aɴɴᴜᴀʟ Gʀᴏᴡᴛʜ Rᴀᴛᴇs ᴏꜰ Iɴᴅᴜsᴛʀɪᴀʟ Oᴜᴛᴘᴜᴛ, Oᴜᴛᴘᴜᴛ ᴘᴇʀ Uɴɪᴛ ᴏꜰ Lᴀʙᴏʀ, ᴀɴᴅ
Oᴜᴛᴘᴜᴛ ᴘᴇʀ Cᴀᴘɪᴛᴀ: Tsᴀʀɪsᴛ Rᴜssɪᴀ, Sᴏᴠɪᴇᴛ Uɴɪᴏɴ, ᴀɴᴅ Uɴɪᴛᴇᴅ Sᴛᴀᴛᴇs,
Sᴇʟᴇᴄᴛᴇᴅ Cᴏɴᴄᴜʀʀᴇɴᴛ Pᴇʀɪᴏᴅs
(per cent)

	Output		Output per Man-Hour		Output per Person Engaged		Output per Head of Population	
	Russia or Soviet Union	United States	Soviet Union	United States	Soviet Union	United States	Russia or Soviet Union	United States
-1913	5.3	5.1	n.a.	n.a.	n.a.	n.a.	3.7	2.9
-1955	4.1	3.8	1.9	2.8	1.5	2.1	3.5	2.5
-1928	0.1	3.7	2.1	3.5	0.7	2.1	-0.5	2.3
-1955	6.5	3.8	1.7	2.4	1.9	2.1	5.8	2.6
-1940	8.9	1.8	1.2	2.4	2.0	1.1	7.4	1.1
-1955	4.6	5.4	2.2	2.5	1.9	2.8	4.6	3.8
-1937	12.1	1.4	3.6	2.2	2.2	0.8	11.0	-0.9
-1955	9.6	5.3	7.1	3.5	5.4	3.5	7.8	3.5

ᴏᴜʀᴄᴇ: Table 61. For Soviet Union, figures on output adjusted to exclude territorial gains.
ᴀɢᴇ annual growth rates calculated from data for terminal years by the compound interest
ᴜla.

about the same rate over both sets of years—namely, 3.7 or 3.8 per cent
a year—while the Soviet rate rose from 0.1 per cent for the pre-Plan
years to 6.5 per cent for the Plan years, territorial gains excluded. In
turn, relative performance has varied within the Plan period itself.
Over 1928–1940, industrial output grew 8.9 per cent a year in the Soviet
Union, compared with only 1.8 per cent in the United States, reflecting
accelerated activity in the one case and depressed activity in the other.[2]
Over 1940–1955, on the other hand, the average annual growth rate was
higher in the United States than in the Soviet Union: 5.4 per cent
compared with 4.6 per cent.

Moving to the recent postwar years 1950–1955, we find the Soviet
growth rate of 9.6 per cent a year exceeding the American rate of 5.3
per cent by a significant margin. A discrepancy in favor of the Soviet
Union has persisted through 1958, though the Soviet growth rate has
declined to around 7.1 per cent as far as one can see from the published
data (see Table 68, industrial materials). It is too early to say whether

[2] If one starts from the bottom of the Great Depression, competing growth rates may
be found for the United States: 7.0 per cent for 1932–1955 and 9.9 per cent for 1932–1940.
The parallel is not wholly far-fetched, since Soviet growth started with a large reserve of
employable resources in 1928.

the decline is permanent or only temporary, whether this reflects a persistent retardation or a temporary fluctuation. It is also too early to say what is happening to the tempo of American industrial growth, which averaged only 2.2 per cent a year over 1955–1959. In any case, the record for postwar years and for other peacetime years in the Plan period suggests that Soviet industrial growth will continue to be more rapid than U.S. growth over the near future.

We commented in the two preceding chapters on the apparent retardation in Soviet industrial growth, both between the Tsarist and Soviet periods and within the Soviet period. A similar retardation seems to apply to U.S. growth over the two periods of forty-odd years before and after the second decade of the 1900's. However, there are few signs that growth has continued to retard over the more recent long period: the growth rate for 1928–1955 is about the same as for 1913–1928.[3]

PRODUCTION AND POPULATION

The picture of comparative growth in output per head of population is much the same as what we have just sketched for total output (see Chart 26). However, population has grown more slowly in the Soviet Union than in the United States: 1.5 per cent a year over 1870–1913 compared with 2.1 per cent, and 0.9 per cent over 1913–1955 compared with 1.3 per cent. For this reason, the per capita growth rates show a larger discrepancy in favor of the Soviet Union than the total growth rates.

This result points up a defect in making international comparisons of per capita growth rates without taking account of the growth in population by itself. Population growth in the United States, from both internal and external sources, has been directly related to economic progress. This has not been the case in the Soviet Union. In fact, the economic policies of the 1920's and 1930's—and probably the immediate postwar period—directly caused population to grow much more slowly than otherwise, and even to decline temporarily. Of course, the huge wartime losses had the same effect, though they fall into another category. In any case, population has not been a factor limiting growth significantly in the Soviet Union, because a large segment of the population has been "underemployed" in relation to available technology. Hence output

[3] In my earlier report (*Some Observations on Soviet Industrial Growth*, NBER Occasional Paper 55, New York, 1957, p. 625), I argued that there was little evidence of a long-run tendency for U.S. industrial growth to retard. This conclusion now appears to have been too strong, since retardation shows up clearly in *measured* growth. It may still be, of course, that measures for the nineteenth century have an upward bias relative to those for the twentieth, but this would not affect the conclusions drawn here in comparing the Soviet and U.S. growth records since such a bias would not be peculiar to the U.S. measures.

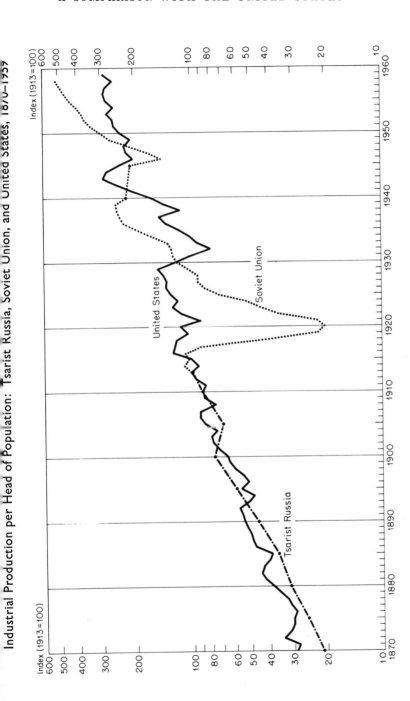

Industrial Production per Head of Population: Tsarist Russia, Soviet Union, and United States, 1870–1959

Source: Tables 47, 53, A-32, and C-3. See note to Chart 25.

231

per capita could increase as a consequence of a slower growth in population. Put the other way around, the growth in per capita output almost certainly would have been slower if the population had grown faster. This would not have applied—at least not with the same force—to the United States.

PRODUCTION AND EMPLOYMENT

Except for the periods 1928–1937 and 1950–1955, industrial labor productivity, as we have been able to measure it, has grown faster in the United States than in the Soviet Union (see Table 62 and Chart 27). In the United States, growth in industrial output has come primarily from improved labor productivity: had there been no improvement in output per man-hour (or person engaged), output would have multiplied 31 (or 42) per cent as much as it did over 1913–1955 and 52 (or 58) per cent as much over 1928–1955. That is, improved labor productivity accounted for 58 to 69 per cent of the multiplication in output over 1913–1955 and for 42 to 48 per cent over 1928–1955, the percentage depending on whether productivity is measured in terms of persons engaged or man-hours. By contrast, improved labor productivity accounted for only 46 to 54 per cent of the multiplication in Soviet output over 1913–1955 and for only 37 to 40 per cent over 1928–1955.

The faster growth in labor productivity on the part of the United States held generally throughout industrial groups (see Table 65). In terms of output per person engaged—the only measure we can make for Soviet industrial groups—Soviet growth over 1913–1955 was faster than U.S. growth over a similar period, 1909–1953, only in the cases of metals (3.2 per cent a year compared with 1.2 per cent) and machinery and allied products (3.1 per cent compared with 2.0 per cent). Soviet growth rates on a man-hour basis were undoubtedly also higher in these sectors than U.S. rates.[4] Over 1928–1955, Soviet growth in output per person engaged was faster than U.S. growth over 1929–1953 in only four industrial groups: the two already mentioned plus fuel and textiles and allied products. In the last two cases, however, Soviet growth was almost certainly slower than U.S. growth on a man-hour basis.[5]

[4] If it were assumed that the average annual hours of work changed in these Soviet industrial groups by the same percentage as for all industry, the Soviet growth rates on a man-hour basis would be higher than the U.S. rates: 3.6 per cent compared with 1.7 per cent in the case of metals, and 3.5 per cent compared with 2.4 per cent in the case of machinery and allied products. The U.S. rates are computed from data in Table A-37.

[5] On the same assumption about Soviet man-hours as given in the preceding footnote, the average annual growth rate for output per man-hour would be 3.0 per cent for the Soviet Union compared with 3.4 per cent for the United States in the case of fuel, and 1.0 per cent compared with 1.9 per cent in the case of textiles and allied products.

CHART 27
Indexes of Output, Employment, and Output per Unit of Labor, by Industrial Group: Soviet Union (1913–1955) and United States (1909–1953)

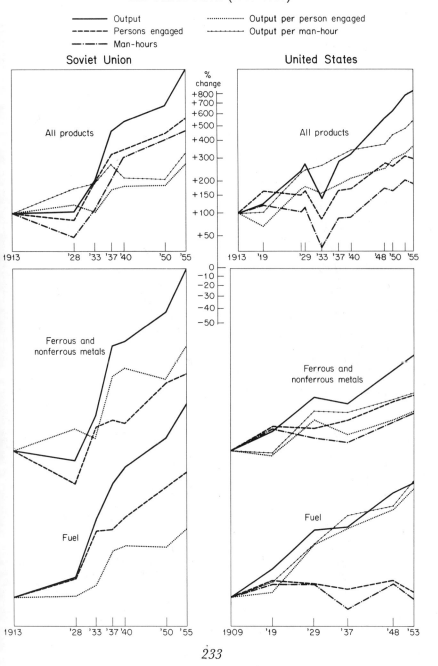

———— Output ·············· Output per person engaged
- - - - - Persons engaged ———·——— Output per man-hour
—·—·— Man-hours

Soviet Union   United States

233

CHART 27 (continued)

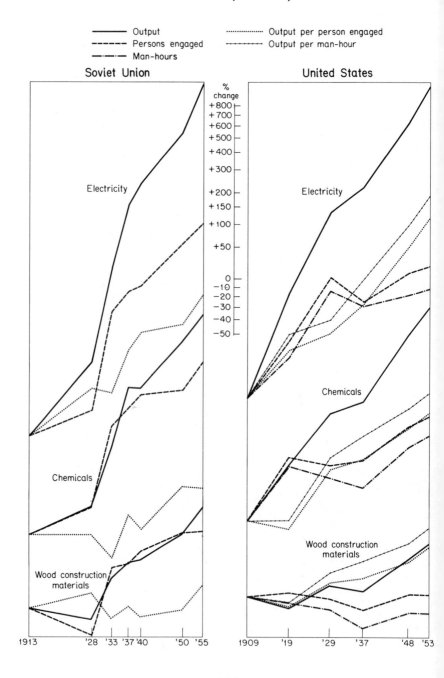

———— Output	·············· Output per person engaged
─ ─ ─ ─ Persons engaged	─·─·─·─ Output per man-hour
─··─··─ Man-hours	

Soviet Union   United States

%
change
+800
+700
+600
+500
+400
+300
+200
+150
+100
+50
0
−10
−20
−30
−40
−50

Electricity

Chemicals

Wood construction
materials

1913   '28 '33 '37 '40   '50 '55

Electricity

Chemicals

Wood construction
materials

1909   '19   '29   '37   '48 '53

234

CHART 27 (concluded)

——— Output   ·········· Output per person engaged
— — — Persons engaged — — — — Output per man-hour
—·—·— Man-hours

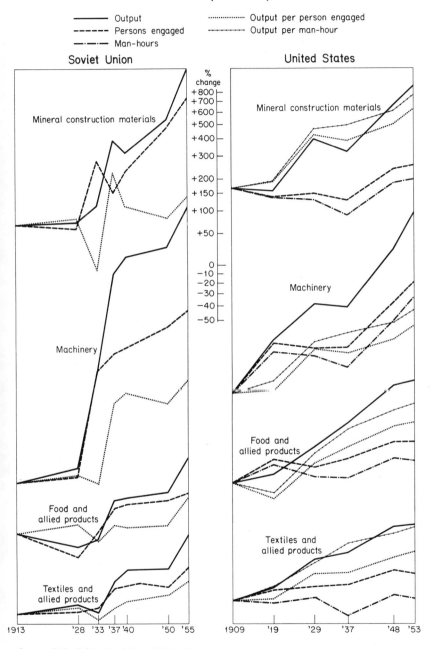

Soviet Union   United States

Source: Tables A-24, A-36, A-37, and Table 40

It is not at all clear whether there is any trend in the growth rate of labor productivity in either of the two countries. If we concentrate on output per man-hour, which seems to be the more meaningful measure, we note (Table 62) that the growth rates for both countries declined between 1913–1928 and 1928–1955, but increased between 1928–1940 and 1940–1955 and between 1928–1937 and 1950–1955. Under these circumstances, the wisest conclusion is that more time and evidence is needed to discover whether there is any long-run drift in these growth rates.[6]

The next and obvious step in a study of growth in labor productivity is to analyze the causes, particularly the role played by the substitution of capital for labor. We are just reaching the stage of knowing something tolerably reliable about the relations among capital inputs, labor inputs, and output during the economic history of the United States. In the recent important work by John W. Kendrick, the ratio of output to capital in U.S. manufacturing and mining is measured as increasing at the average annual rate of 1.0 and 1.3 per cent over 1899–1953, and the ratio of capital to labor at 1.2 per cent.[7] Unfortunately, the poor state of statistics on Soviet capital inputs does not permit equally reliable calculations. A very recent report by Norman Kaplan and Richard Moorsteen reaches the tentative conclusion, based on deficient data, that the stock of Soviet industrial capital grew steadily and considerably faster than output over 1928–1955, though the divergence may have diminished significantly over 1950–1955.[8] In any case, if we were to assume that Soviet capital grew at least as fast as output, the ratio of capital to labor (man-hours) would be found to have grown at an average annual rate of at least 1.9 per cent over 1913–1955, or considerably faster than for the United States over 1899–1953. Put another way, the Soviet Union has apparently had a considerably larger percentage growth in its stock of industrial capital than the United States, but a significantly smaller percentage growth in labor (and capital) productivity.

[6] In a recent paper, I drew the conclusion that U.S. growth in labor productivity had been retarding in recent years (see my "The Structure and Growth of Soviet Industry: A Comparison with the United States," in *Comparisons of the United States and Soviet Economies,* Joint Economic Committee, Congress of the United States, Washington, 1959, pp. 112 and 120, and also in *Journal of Law and Economics,* October 1959, pp. 164 and 174). A more careful reading of the evidence suggests that this conclusion was hasty and incautious. While it is true that both output and labor productivity have grown much more slowly since 1955 than over 1950–1955, this is too limited an experience for such a sweeping conclusion. There appears to be no other evidence of retardation, at least since 1928.

[7] *Productivity Trends in the United States,* Princeton for NBER, 1961, pp. 166 and 148.

[8] "Indexes of Soviet Industrial Output" (mimeographed), RAND Corporation, RM-2495, Santa Monica, 1960, pp. 179 ff and 272.

COMPARATIVE LEVELS OF PRODUCTION, POPULATION,
AND EMPLOYMENT

The comparisons so far have been based on various indexes computed directly for each country, and they can be roughly checked by another, essentially independent set of estimates that at the same time reveals some interesting information of its own. Evaluating the value added of industry in both rubles and dollars for each country, we may estimate Soviet industrial production as a fraction of the U.S. level in 1913, 1928, and 1955. The estimates represent only orders of magnitude; constructed in different ways and with better data, they might vary as much as 10 per cent, possibly more, in either direction. For example, U.S. products are generally of better quality than Russian counterparts, and the differential has tended to widen over the Soviet period, except in special cases of machinery and military products. Yet both U.S. and Soviet products are evaluated at the same prices, thus overstating Soviet production. Similarly, both the output and value of Soviet products tend to be over-stated in official statistics. Other errors of unknown direction are introduced by estimative procedures.[9] Despite such shortcomings, these estimates cannot be dismissed as inherently worse than other summary indexes calculated for the Soviet Union.

According to these estimates (Table 63), Soviet industrial output rose from 11 to 14 per cent of the American level in 1913 up to 20 to 23 per cent in 1955; similarly, output per head of population rose from 7 to 10 per cent up to 17 to 20 per cent. On the other hand, output per person engaged changed little, from 17 to 22 per cent up to 19 to 22 per cent, and output per man-hour from 18 to 24 per cent down to 18 to 21 per cent. In each pair of numbers, the lower one is based on a valuation in ruble prices. These findings are generally consistent with our more direct calculations, which indicated that industrial output and output per

[9] Perhaps the least reliable datum in Table 63 is the estimate of Soviet value added in 1955. This has been taken as the sum of employee compensation, profits, and net "commercial" and unallocated outlays, all of which are rather indirectly derived (see Table F-3). In view of the questionable "rationality" of Soviet pricing and allocative policies, none of these magnitudes can be taken as a reliable measure, by Western standards, of the element of productive activity it seems to represent. This is particularly true of the magnitudes taken to measure the productive contribution of capital (profits and other net outlays), since Soviet authorities avowedly make no effort to compensate capital services on the basis of their alternative costs.

Another possible procedure for 1955 would be to compare only the outlays for employee compensation in U.S. and Soviet industry, which amounts to assuming that employee compensation was the same percentage of value added in both countries. By this procedure (explained in note *d* of Table 63), Soviet value added in 1955 would be derived as 7.8 per cent higher than the figure shown in Table 63, with corresponding changes in other affected data.

TABLE 63

COMPARATIVE LEVELS OF INDUSTRIAL PRODUCTION AND PRODUCTIVITY: SOVIET UNION AND UNITED STATES, 1913, 1928, AND 1955

	Soviet Union			United States			Soviet Union as % of United States		
	1913[a]	1928[b]	1955[c]	1913[a]	1928[b]	1955[c]	1913	1928	1955
Value added of industry									
1. Billion dollars	$1.70	$3.16	$35.3[d]	$12.2	$33.9	$150.7	13.9	9.3	23.4
2. Billion rubles	R3.77	R7.89	R258[d]	R35.7	R126.8	R1,311	10.6	6.2	19.7
Persons engaged in industry									
3. Million full-time equivalents	5.82	5.38	19.4	9.10	11.5	18.2	64.0	46.8	106.6
Man-hours engaged in industry									
4. Billion hours	14.8	11.0	42.1	25.7	26.3	37.8	57.6	41.8	111.4
Population									
5. Million inhabitants	138.0	151.4	197.6	97.2	120.5	165.3	142.0	125.6	119.5
Value added per person engaged									
6. Dollars	$292	$587	$1,820	$1,340	$2,950	$8,280	21.8	19.9	22.0
7. Rubles	R648	R1,470	R13,300	R3,920	R11,000	R72,000	16.5	13.4	18.5
Value added per man-hour engaged									
8. Dollars	$0.115	$0.287	$0.838	$0.475	$1.29	$3.99	24.2	22.2	21.0
9. Rubles	R0.255	R0.717	R6.13	R1.39	R4.82	R34.7	18.3	14.9	17.7
Value added per head of population									
10. Dollars	$12.3	$20.9	$179	$126	$281	$912	9.8	7.4	19.6
11. Rubles	R27.3	R52.1	R1,310	R367	R1,050	R7,930	7.4	5.0	16.5

[a] Dollar values in 1914 U.S. prices; ruble values in 1913 Soviet prices.
[b] Dollar values in 1929 U.S. prices; ruble values in 1928 Soviet prices.
[c] Dollar values in 1954 U.S. prices; ruble values in 1955 prices, excluding most of the applicable turnover taxes.

[d] If employee compensation were taken to be 56 per cent of value added, the fraction applying to U.S. manufacturing in 1955 (see text surrounding Table F-3), value added would be derived as $38.1 billion and 278 billion rubles, or 7.8 per cent higher than shown. Other data would change accordingly.

Notes continue on page 239.

capita grew faster in the Soviet Union than in the United States, while labor productivity grew slower.

At the same time, they imply more rapid growth for Soviet industry than our direct indexes. In the case of value added evaluated in dollars, Soviet growth is indicated as about 60 per cent faster than American growth over 1913–1955; in the case of value added per capita similarly evaluated, about 100 per cent faster. Hence, if we calculate Soviet growth indirectly on the basis of the U.S. production index, Soviet output is indicated as multiplying 7.5 times (6.7 times excluding territorial gains) and per capita output, 5.6 times. By direct calculations, the two multiples are 6.2 (5.6 excluding territorial gains) and 4.3, respectively.

Put alternatively, output is shown as growing at 4.9 per cent a year when calculated indirectly, compared with 4.4 per cent when calculated directly; excluding territorial gains, the two rates are 4.6 and 4.1 per cent. Similarly, growth in per capita output is calculated indirectly as 4.1 per cent a year and directly as 3.5 per cent; growth in output per person engaged, as 1.9 and 1.5 per cent; and growth in output per man-hour, as 2.3 and 1.9 per cent.

The disparity in the results between direct and indirect measures of Soviet industrial growth is somewhat reduced if we make the indirect measure in terms of value added in constant dollars. By this procedure (see the upper part of Table 64), Soviet output is shown as multiplying 7.1 times over 1913–1955 and 6.3 times over 1928–1955, compared with 6.2 and 6.1 times as shown by our production index for all products. Incidentally, the multiplication in U.S. output over both periods is not

---

Notes to Table 63 (continued)
Line
1   *Soviet Union*: Line 2 divided by ruble-dollar ratio with Soviet output weights. For 1913 and 1928, ratio for basic sample of forty-five industries (Table A-30); for 1955, estimated weighted ratio for all industry (Table A-31).
     United States: Table A-42.
2   *Soviet Union*: Table A-43.
     United States: Line 1 multiplied by ruble-dollar ratio with U.S. output weights. For coverage of ratios used, see line 1, Soviet Union.
3   *Soviet Union*: Table A-20.
     United States: Table A-36.
4   *Soviet Union*: Table A-23.
     United States: Table A-36.
5   *Soviet Union*: Table C-3.
     United States: *Statistical Abstract of the United States, 1958*, Washington, 1958, p. 5. Continental United States.
6, 7 Line 1 or 2 divided by line 3.
8, 9 Line 1 or 2 divided by line 4.
10, 11 Line 1 or 2 divided by line 5.

TABLE 64

COMPARATIVE LEVELS OF INDUSTRIAL VALUE ADDED IN CONSTANT DOLLARS:
SOVIET UNION AND UNITED STATES, 1913, 1928, AND 1955
(billion 1954 dollars)

	1913	1928	1955
Deflated value added [a]			
United States	34.9	61.7	150.7
Soviet Union	5.0	5.6	35.3
Gap (U.S. minus S.U.)	29.9	56.1	115.4
Projected value added[b]			
United States	31.9	54.9	150.7
Soviet Union	5.7	5.8	35.3
Gap (U.S. minus S.U.)	26.2	49.1	115.4

[a] Value added in Table 63 deflated by price indexes. For the United States, price index is for manufacturing (1914, 35.0; 1929, 54.8; 1954, 100.0) and is taken as NBER index (D. Creamer, S. P. Dobrovolsky, and I. Borenstein, *Capital in Manufacturing and Mining, Its Formation and Financing*, Princeton for NBER, 1960, p. 261) extrapolated from 1948 by BLS index (*Historical Statistics of the United States, Colonial Times to 1957*, Washington, 1960, Series E-59, p. 118). For the Soviet Union, price index (1914, 34.2; 1929, 56.1; 1954, 100.0) is derived implicitly from value added for forty-five Soviet industries in "current" and constant dollars. Data in "current" dollars are from Table A-26; in constant dollars, from same table as projected by production indexes for Soviet industrial materials with appropriate U.S. weights (see Table 21). Price index is chained for links 1913–1928 and 1928–1955, and each link is taken as the geometric average of the two possible implicit price indexes.
[b] 1955 value added for each country (in 1954 dollars) projected by production index for all industrial products (Table 61).

larger but smaller when measured by the same indirect procedure than when measured by our production index: 4.3 and 2.4 times, compared with 4.7 and 2.8 times.

By way of digression, we should note an important point that emerges from these estimates of value added in constant dollars (Table 64): namely, that the absolute gap between U.S. and Soviet output has steadily grown despite the narrowing in the relative gap. This simply means that the absolute increase in production has been larger in the United States than in the Soviet Union even though the percentage increase has been smaller. By our estimates, the gap in value added measured in 1954 dollars grew by $85 to $90 billion (or by 285 to 340 per cent) between 1913 and 1955 and by $60 to $65 billion (or by 105 to 135 per cent) between 1928 and 1955. In this sense, U.S. growth has exceeded Soviet growth by a wide margin.

Returning to the question of discrepancies between direct and indirect measures of percentage growth, we may observe that differences of the order of magnitude shown by our various estimates for the Soviet Union should not be surprising, given the problems in making accurate and meaningful measures. It is, however, much more difficult to reconcile our figures with the conventional Western estimate—and apparently the latest official Soviet position—that Soviet industrial production was about a third of the U.S. level in 1955.[10] Since, to our knowledge, a full explanation of this widely accepted estimate has never been published, we cannot easily analyze the reasons for the substantial divergence from our estimates. From context, it would seem that the conventional estimate has been derived from inspection of physical output ratios for a list of commodities that can be compared,[11] a method that can be quite misleading for reasons we shall explore later.

For the moment we may point out the implications of this conventional estimate. Taken together with the widely accepted estimate that Russian industrial production, within Soviet boundaries, was 11 to 14 per cent of the U.S. level in 1913,[12] the conventional estimate for 1955 implies that industrial production multiplied 2.4 to 3 times as much in the Soviet Union as in the United States between 1913 and 1955. Since U.S. production multiplied 4.7 times, it would follow that Soviet production multiplied 11 to 14 times, a factor much higher than is shown by any index constructed in the West except that of Seton (see Table 33). It is about twice as high as is shown by our moving-weight index for all products.

The conventional estimate also implies that the 1955 value added of Soviet industry amounted to around $50 billion or, multiplying by a ruble-dollar price ratio of 7.3 (see Table A-31), 370 billion rubles. Since employee compensation seems to have been around 150 billion rubles (see Table F-3), it is implied to be 40 per cent of total value added. In U.S. manufacturing, employee compensation has amounted to around 55 per cent of total value added.[13] It is difficult to believe that labor services in the Soviet Union could be relatively so much less important, or capital services so much more important, than in the United States.

[10] See, e.g., *Soviet Economic Growth: A Comparison with the United States*, Joint Economic Committee, Congress of the United States, Washington, 1957, p. 11. The most recent official Soviet position is that their industrial output was about half the U.S. level in 1958 (see footnote 24 in Chapter 2). Projecting this backward to 1955 by the ratio of the official Soviet to the Federal Reserve Board production index, we find a fraction of 36 per cent for that year.

[11] This procedure is followed by Professor Rolf Wagenführ in his recent article, "Der Wettlauf der Grossmächte," *Frankfurter Allgemeine Zeitung*, July 23, 1960.

[12] Both Khrushchev and Allen Dulles, Director of the Central Intelligence Agency, seem to agree with us that the fraction was within this range (see *Vestnik statistiki* [Statistical Bulletin], 1959, No. 11, p. 17, and *Comparisons of the United States and Soviet Economies, Hearings*, 1960, p. 4).

[13] *Statistical Abstract of the United States, 1958*, p. 774.

The converging lines of evidence now open to us support the view that Soviet industrial production was about a fifth of U.S. production in 1955; they do not support the view that it was a third. Why has the latter seemed so plausible? The answer will become plain as we move to consider the differing structures of industry in these two countries.

SOME STRUCTURAL COMPARISONS

We have already observed that percentage growth in output over contemporaneous periods has been generally faster throughout the different sectors of industry in the Soviet Union than in the United States, while growth in labor productivity has been generally slower (see Table 65 and Chart 27). We may go on to note that the pattern of growth in labor productivity among industrial groups does not seem to be related in the two countries,[14] while the pattern of growth in output does: those industrial groups with relatively faster rates of growth in the one country also tend to have relatively faster rates in the other.[15]

This similarity in growth pattern is largely superficial, however, applying to broad categories of products but not to specific kinds of products within each category. Soviet industrial development, as we pointed out much earlier, has concentrated on quantitative growth of a limited list of products; U.S. development, on proliferation of products and qualitative improvements. For this reason, comparisons of performance by a sample of industries can give a misleading impression of comparative over-all growth, attention being focused on a sector of industry much more important in the Soviet Union than in the United States.

We may see this by examining comparative growth for such a list of commodities (Tables 66 and 67 and Chart 28). Out of forty-seven industries whose performance can be compared over the entire Soviet period,[16] thirty-nine showed a more rapid growth in output in the Soviet

[14] The rank correlation between the two sets of growth rates in labor productivity is only 0.200 for the longer periods compared and 0.333 for the shorter ones, neither of which is significant at the 10 per cent level. The correlation applies to the nine most narrowly defined industrial groups in Table 65, the breakdown of machinery and allied products ignored.

[15] The rank correlation between the two sets of growth rates in output is 0.717 for the longer periods compared and 0.750 for the shorter ones. The first is significant at the 5 per cent level; the second, at the 2 per cent level.

[16] The list of industries—more accurately, commodities—is determined by the availability of data and the feasibility of identifying Soviet and U.S. counterparts. Since Soviet industries are seldom carefully defined in original sources, choice of U.S. counterparts is bound to be somewhat arbitrary, though we have done our best to match what seemed to be the most similar industries. One should also keep in mind that Soviet

(Note 16 continued on page 246)

TABLE 65

AVERAGE ANNUAL GROWTH RATES OF INDUSTRIAL OUTPUT, OUTPUT PER
PERSON ENGAGED, AND OUTPUT PER CAPITA, BY INDUSTRIAL GROUP:
SOVIET UNION AND UNITED STATES, SELECTED CONCURRENT PERIODS
(per cent)

	Soviet Union		United States	
	1913–1955	1928–1955	1909–1953	1929–1953
	OUTPUT			
rous and nonferrous metals	5.6	9.4	2.9	2.0
el and electricity	7.4	10.0	5.5	4.1
Fuel	6.0	8.4	3.5	2.3
Electricity	10.8	16.6	9.8	6.1
emicals	6.9	9.4	6.6	5.1
nstruction materials	3.4	5.9	2.3	2.2
Wood materials	3.1	5.4	1.6	1.9
Mineral materials	4.8	7.4	3.1	2.5
achinery and allied products	8.6	13.0	5.5	4.3
Civilian machinery and equipment	8.8	12.5	6.1	4.6
Metal products	n.a.	n.a.	4.2	3.5
od and allied products	2.3	4.2	3.2	3.2
xtiles and allied products	2.4	3.3	2.3	1.7
	OUTPUT PER PERSON ENGAGED			
rous and nonferrous metals	3.2	3.9	1.2	0.4
el and electricity	3.2	4.3	3.3	4.3
Fuel	2.1	3.2	3.3	2.7
Electricity	4.3	4.4	5.5	5.5
emicals	1.4	2.2	3.3	2.7
nstruction materials	0.5	0.1	2.0	1.6
Wood materials	0.7	0.4	1.5	1.7
Mineral materials	0.9	1.0	3.8	1.2
achinery and allied products	3.1	4.5	2.0	1.1
Civilian machinery and equipment	3.4	4.9	2.1	1.2
Metal products	n.a.	n.a.	1.7	0.8
od and allied products	1.1	1.2	1.9	1.9
xtiles and allied products	1.0	1.2	1.5	1.1
	OUTPUT PER HEAD OF POPULATION			
rous and nonferrous metals	4.7	8.3	1.6	0.8
el and electricity	6.4	8.9	4.1	2.9
Fuel	5.1	7.3	2.2	1.1
Electricity	9.8	15.5	8.4	4.8
emicals	5.9	8.3	5.2	3.9
nstruction materials	2.5	4.9	1.0	1.0
Wood materials	2.2	4.4	0.3	0.7
Mineral materials	3.9	6.3	1.8	1.3
achinery and allied products	7.6	11.9	4.1	3.1
Civilian machinery and equipment	7.8	11.4	4.7	3.4
Metal products	n.a.	n.a.	2.9	2.3
od and allied products	1.4	3.2	1.9	2.0
xtiles and allied products	1.5	2.3	1.0	0.5

SOURCE: Tables A-24, A-37, and C-3. Note that some industrial groups have a different coverage
m that in Tables 37 and 54. For the Soviet Union, figures on output reflect territorial gains. Average
nual growth rates calculated from data for terminal years by the compound interest formula.

TABLE 66

AVERAGE ANNUAL GROWTH RATES COMPARED FOR FORTY-SEVEN INDUSTRIES:
SOVIET UNION AND UNITED STATES, 1913–1955 AND 1928–1955

(per cent)

	AVERAGE ANNUAL GROWTH RATE Soviet Union		AVERAGE ANNUAL GROWTH RATE[a] United States		Ratio of Soviet to U.S. Output[b]		
	1913–1955	1928–1955	1913–1955	1928–1955	1913	1928	1955
Iron ore	5.0	9.5	1.4	2.5	14.6	9.7	67.7
Pig iron	5.0	9.0	1.9	2.7	13.4	8.5	47.2
Steel ingots	5.8	9.2	2.7	3.3	13.3	8.1	42.6
Rolled steel	5.5	9.0	2.7	3.5	14.5	9.0	43.0
Copper	6.1	9.8	0.8	1.6	3.6	1.9	18.1
Lead	13.7	20.1	1.2	1.5	0.3	0.2	37.1
Zinc	11.1	19.0	2.0	3.2	0.8	0.4	20.1
Electric power	11.2	13.9	7.6	7.0	7.0	4.6	27.2
Coal	6.4	9.3	−0.3	−0.8	4.5	4.7	48.1
Coke	5.6	9.1	1.2	1.6	10.5	8.8	63.9
Crude petroleum	5.0	6.9	5.6	4.0	27.0	9.4	20.7
Natural gas	14.6	13.4	6.8	6.9	0.2	0.7	3.4
Soda ash	5.4	7.2	4.4	4.5	20.0	15.0	32.3
Caustic soda	5.7	8.7	6.9	7.0	32.4	10.2	15.9
Sulfuric acid	8.6	11.3	5.2	5.3	7.9	6.1	26.6
Mineral fertilizer	12.5	17.1	5.6	6.7	2.1	24.0	34.9
Synthetic dyes	7.0	7.6	8.9	2.4	136.2	23.4	105.2
Paper	5.5	7.2	2.9	2.7	5.9	4.9	15.9
Motor vehicle tires	16.1	19.4	6.2	2.3	0.4	0.1	9.1
Cement	6.6	9.7	3.0	2.5	9.6	6.1	43.8
Construction gypsum	4.2	9.7	3.4	2.9	22.0	5.1	29.9
Construction lime	6.1	9.6	2.3	3.0	15.6	13.0	74.1
Lumber	4.1	6.7	−0.2	0.7	13.5	16.1	81.9

Rails	3.7	7.7	-1.9	-2.0	17.9	14.5	258.7
Window glass	3.5	4.0	2.0	3.8	57.1	64.5	66.5
Railroad freight cars	3.1	5.6	-3.5	-1.2	5.1	16.6	81.8
Railroad passenger cars	1.2	5.8	-2.0	-3.8	35.5	22.9	180.3
Flour	0.3	1.1	-0.2	-0.1	233.3	206.9	304.8
Butter	3.6	6.6	1.6	-0.5	29.9	11.8	73.8
Vegetable oil	2.2	2.4	3.1	3.1	42.4	50.0	42.4
Meat slaughtering	1.8	4.5	2.2	2.2	27.8	13.2	24.4
Sausages	6.3	10.4	1.6	2.7	10.6	8.2	59.2
Fish catch	2.4	4.5	2.0	2.1	108.8	60.1	125.8
Soap	3.5	4.1	-0.8	-3.3	14.7	16.5	168.3
Salt	2.6	3.4	3.8	4.2	44.8	31.9	27.7
Raw sugar consumption	2.2	3.7	1.7	0.9	35.4	21.4	44.4
Canned food	8.7	12.8	4.5	3.6	2.4	1.7	16.6
Beer	2.0	5.9	0.9	12.1	10.5	79.2	17.4
Cigarettes	5.4	5.3	8.0	5.3	133.7	45.4	48.0
Boots and shoes	3.8	3.7	1.5	1.9	21.0	28.3	47.6
Rubber footwear	3.7	4.9	0.5	-0.6	46.5	35.6	177.6
Cotton fabrics	2.0	3.0	1.4	1.3	37.4	27.3	45.7
Pure silk and nylon fabrics	0.4	11.2	2.5	-0.3	18.7	0.4	7.7
Rayon and mixed fabrics	7.5	14.7	7.7	15.7	23.3	23.3	20.6
Woolen and worsted fabrics	2.1	2.9	-0.3	-0.3	29.2	34.4	80.9
Bicycles	16.4	23.0	3.8	6.5	1.4	3.9	169.6
Sewing machines	4.3	6.6	-0.3	-0.4	35.8	39.7	233.5
Median	5.0	7.7	2.0	2.5	15.6	13.0	44.4

SOURCE: Tables B-2 and E-1.

a Calculated from output in terminal years by the compound interest formula. U.S. output taken as centered nine-year moving average, with minor modifications. Soviet output covers interwar territory for 1913 and postwar territory for 1955.

b Calculated from actual U.S. output in these years, not from centered moving average.

TABLE 67

GROWTH RATES COMPARED FOR FIFTEEN NEW SOVIET INDUSTRIES:
SOVIET UNION (1932–1955) AND UNITED STATES (1928–1955)
(per cent)

	Average Annual Growth Rate[a]		Ratio of Soviet to U.S. Output, 1955[b]
	Soviet Union, 1932–1955	United States, 1928–1955	
Primary aluminum	45.1[c]	12.8[d]	n.a.
Automobiles	11.3[e]	2.9	1.4
Trucks and buses	12.2	3.2	27.0
Tractors	5.4	3.5	43.3
Tractor-drawn plows	2.3	4.1[f]	43.4[f]
Tractor-drawn cultivators	7.5	9.7[f]	59.5[f]
Grain combines	7.1	5.5	75.1
Diesel engines[g]	18.3	15.6[h]	37.7[h]
Electric motors[g]	7.5	6.0[h]	65.4[h]
Margarine	10.7	6.3	66.0
Cheese	9.1	4.0	17.3
Hosiery	5.2[e]	1.6[f]	32.1[f]
Phonographs	12.4	4.9	27.1
Radios	23.2	6.2	24.3
Television sets	111[i]	117.9[j]	6.4
Median	10.7	5.5	34.9

SOURCE: Tables B-2 and E-1.
[a] [b] See same footnotes, Table 66.
[c] 1933–1940, only period for which data are available.
[d] 1928–1940.
[e] 1933 instead of 1928.
[f] 1953 instead of 1955.
[g] Output measured in rated capacity, not in simple units.
[h] 1954 instead of 1955.
[i] 1950–1955.
[j] 1946–1955.

(Continuation of Note 16)
products are often of lower quality—less expensively made—than their U.S. counterparts, and their physical outputs are often relatively overstated. This is particularly true for years after 1913 and, to a lesser degree, 1928, so that the bias mounts over time.

The upward bias in output or quality is likely to be most significant for the following Soviet products: coal, mineral fertilizer, synthetic dyes, paper, lumber, window glass, railroad freight and passenger cars, meat slaughtering, fish catch, canned food, boots and shoes, woolen and worsted fabrics, and sewing machines. In the case of all fabrics, U.S. output in linear measure has been adjusted upward to compensate for the narrower width of Soviet fabrics. Two other adjustments could have been made, but the possibility was not discovered until analysis had gone too far to turn back. One applies to window glass: American output should be adjusted upward by at least 35 per cent to compensate for the lesser thickness of the Soviet product. The other applies to electric power: Soviet output should be adjusted downward to exclude consumption by power stations, which is not counted in American output. The fraction of output represented by such consumption has risen from around 2 per cent in 1913 to around 6 per cent in recent years (see *Promyshlennost' SSSR* [Industry of the USSR], Moscow, 1957, p. 21).

Coverage of U.S. output data is described briefly in Appendix E. Chart A-2 contains graphs of Soviet and U.S. output for the sample of forty-seven industries.

CHART 28
Frequency Distributions of Growth Rates for Forty-Seven Industries:
Soviet Union and United States, 1913–1955 and 1928–1955

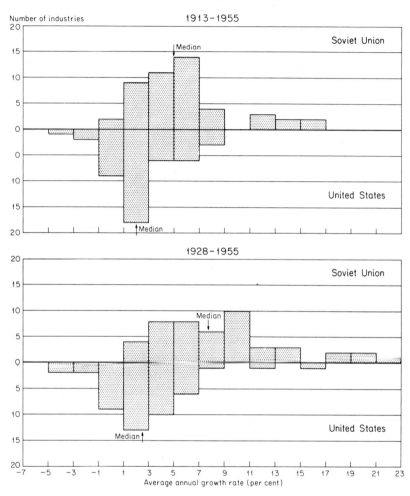

Source: Table 66.

Union than in the United States over 1913–1955, and forty-two showed a more rapid growth over 1928–1955. The median average annual growth rate over 1913–1955 was 5.0 per cent for the Soviet Union compared with 2.0 per cent for the United States; over 1928–1955, 7.7 per cent compared with 2.5 per cent. A similar picture is revealed for fifteen industries that essentially came into being in the Soviet Union during the Plan period: Soviet output grew faster percentagewise in twelve of these industries, and the Soviet median average annual growth rate was 10.7 per cent compared with the U.S. median of 5.5 per cent. From Table 68 we see that the median growth rate for the forty-seven industries is higher than the weighted average rate given by production indexes in the case of the Soviet Union, but lower in the case of the United States. Hence inferences about comparative growth made from

TABLE 68

AVERAGE ANNUAL GROWTH RATES OF INDUSTRIAL OUTPUT CALCULATED IN DIFFERENT WAYS: SOVIET UNION AND UNITED STATES, 1913–1955 AND 1928–1955
(per cent)

	1913–1955		1928–1955	
	Soviet Union[a]	United States	Soviet Union[a]	United States
Production indexes				
All products	4.4	3.8	6.9	3.8
All civilian products	4.3		6.6	
Industrial materials	4.0	3.3	6.2	3.3
Median growth rate for 47 industries[b]	5.0	2.0	7.7	2.5

SOURCE: Tables 25, 35, 62, and A-26. Average annual growth rates calculated from data for terminal years by the compound interest formula.

[a] Includes gains from territorial expansion.

[b] For seventy industries, the median Soviet growth rates are 5.3 per cent for 1913–1955 and 8.0 per cent for 1928–1955 (see Table A-1).

this sample of counterpart industries contain a substantial bias in favor of the Soviet Union. The same point is illustrated somewhat differently by the fact that the ratio of Soviet to U.S. industrial output derived from the sample of industries consistently overstates the ratio derived directly for all industry, and the overstatement increases markedly between 1913 and 1955 (see Table 69). This follows from the fact that the fraction of industrial value added accounted for by this sample of industries has always been higher, over the period in question, in the Soviet Union than in the United States and has declined relatively much more sharply in the latter than in the former (see Table 70).

It is now easy to understand how the ratio of Soviet to U.S. industrial output for recent years could be significantly overestimated: the kinds of products for which direct comparisons can be made constitute a much smaller portion of industry in the United States than in the Soviet Union. Thus, the 1955 Soviet value added (in dollars) of forty-five industries[17]

[17] Two of the sample of forty-seven industries (synthetic dyes and sausages) are not included here because of difficulties in estimating value added for all years.

TABLE 69

COMPARATIVE LEVELS OF VALUE ADDED FOR ALL INDUSTRY AND A SAMPLE OF FORTY-FIVE
INDUSTRIES: SOVIET UNION AND UNITED STATES, 1913, 1928, AND 1955
(per cent)

	Soviet Union as % of United States		
	1913	1928	1955
Value added, all industries			
Dollar prices	13.9	9.3[a]	23.4[a]
Ruble prices	10.6	6.2[a]	19.7[a]
Value added, 45 industries			
Dollar prices	20.8	15.8	40.8[b]
Ruble prices	15.7	10.6	32.7
Median physical output ratio, 47 industries	15.6	13.0	44.4

SOURCE: Tables 63, A-26, and B-2.

[a] The fractions for 1913 projected by the ratio of Soviet to U.S. production indexes for all products (Table 61) give the following (in per cent):

	1928	1955
Dollar prices	8.3	18.2
Ruble prices	6.3	13.9

[b] For forty-seven industries, the median Soviet lag in output behind the United States was thirty-five years in 1955 (see Table 79). Hence U.S. output of these industries in 1920 was about equal to Soviet output in 1955. From a production index for a comparable set of products (Moore's index for industrial materials as given in R. V. Greenslade and P. A. Wallace, "Industrial Growth in the Soviet Union: Comment," *American Economic Review*, September 1959, p. 689), we find that 1955 Soviet output (that is, 1920 U.S. output) was about 41 per cent of 1955 U.S. output, a figure identical with the one calculated directly.

TABLE 70

VALUE ADDED FOR A SAMPLE OF FORTY-FIVE INDUSTRIES AS A PERCENTAGE OF VALUE
ADDED FOR ALL INDUSTRY: SOVIET UNION AND UNITED STATES, 1913, 1928, AND 1955
(per cent)

	1913	1928	1955
Direct calculation[a]			
Soviet Union	67.1	63.1	50.3
United States	45.1	37.0	27.6
Indirect calculation[b]			
Soviet Union	67.1	67.1	55.3
United States	45.1	39.6[c]	27.9

[a] From Tables 63 and A-26. Soviet values in rubles, U.S. in dollars.

[b] Fraction for 1913 projected by ratio of production index for industrial materials (with coverage comparable to the forty-five industries considered here) to production index for all products. Indexes for all products from Table 61; Soviet index for industrial materials from Table 53; U.S. index for industrial materials from Table 25.

[c] 1929.

TABLE 71

SOVIET AND U.S. VALUE ADDED FOR FORTY-FIVE INDUSTRIES COMPARED WITH
U.S. VALUE ADDED FOR ALL INDUSTRIES, BY INDUSTRIAL GROUP, 1955

	United States		Soviet Union, 45 Industries[b]
	All Industries[a]	45 Industries[b]	
	MILLION 1954 DOLLARS		
Ferrous and nonferrous metals	13,972	7,668	3,253
Fuel and electricity	17,864	15,755	4,267
Chemicals	13,084	5,247	828
Construction materials	14,958	3,820	2,839
Machinery and allied products[c]	53,131	333	492
Food and allied products	15,172	5,800	3,775
Textiles and allied products	14,889	2,901	1,473
Printing and publishing	6,628		
Total	149,698	41,524	16,928
	PER CENT OF U.S. TOTAL		
Ferrous and nonferrous metals	9.3	5.1	2.2
Fuel and electricity	11.9	10.5	2.9
Chemicals	8.7	3.5	0.6
Construction materials	10.0	2.6	1.9
Machinery and allied products[c]	35.5	0.2	0.3
Food and allied products	10.1	3.9	2.5
Textiles and allied products	9.9	1.9	1.0
Printing and publishing	4.4		
Total	100.0	27.7	11.3

[a] 1954 census value added for each group projected to 1955 by Federal Reserve Board product index as given in *Statistical Abstract of the United States, 1958*, pp. 718 and 775. Indexes for subgroup (for coverage of industrial groups as used here, see Table A-35) combined by 1957 weight factors given in *Federal Reserve Bulletin*, December 1959, p. 1467. Summed value added differs slightly from figure $150,682 million derived from aggregate value added and production index (see Tables A and 63).
[b] From Table A-26.
[c] Includes consumer durables.

was 41 per cent of the U.S. value added of the same industries (see Table 69), but only 11 per cent of the U.S. value added of all industry (see Table 71). In the case of the Soviet Union, those forty-five industries accounted for around half the value added of all industry; in the case of the United States, for only around a quarter. If we then suppose that Soviet production had come to about 40 per cent of the U.S. level in all other Soviet industries, just as it did in the sample of forty-five industries, then those other industries would have accounted for an additional 11 or 12 per cent of the value added of all U.S. industry. Value added in Soviet industry would then have been about 23 per cent of the U.S. level, or the figure we derived earlier by direct calculation.[18]

Industry is simply more austere in the Soviet Union than in the United States. Many important products now produced in the United States are produced in negligible or relatively small amounts in the Soviet Union. For example, apparel, furniture, paper products, newspapers and periodicals, electronic equipment and parts, and motor vehicles and parts together accounted for more than 17 per cent of U.S. industrial value added in 1954. From casual inspection of the 1954 Census of Manufactures, one can draw up a long list of other products also produced in relatively small volume in the Soviet Union around 1955 but accounting for an additional 13 per cent of U.S. industrial value added.[19]

[18] These same considerations also help to explain why Soviet labor productivity has been overestimated relative to the United States. For example, Walter Galenson estimates that the Soviet output per wage earner immediately before the war was around 40 per cent of the U.S. level (*Labor Productivity in Soviet and American Industry*, New York, 1955, p. 240), a figure more than double our estimate for 1955. If we assume that Galenson's calculations are accurate, the group of industries from which he derives this estimate could not have been equally representative of labor productivity in the two economies. To see this, let us suppose that, in all counterpart industries, Soviet productivity had been 40 per cent of the U.S. level. Then, since the industrial labor forces were of roughly the same size, Soviet production would also have been 40 per cent of the U.S. level. But if our estimates of relative output in 1928 and growth in the two industrial economies in the interwar period are anywhere near correct, Soviet production was less than 25 per cent of the U.S. level just before World War II.

Put another way, the industries included in this comparison then accounted for about a fifth of industrial employment and value added in both the Soviet Union and the United States. Hence U.S. production of this group of products was almost as large as total Soviet industrial production, although only a fifth as many employees were required to produce it.

It is interesting to note that a Soviet economist has recently claimed that Soviet labor productivity was 45 to 49 per cent of the U.S. level in 1954 (A. Kats, "Comparison of Labor Productivity in the Industry of the USSR and the Chief Capitalist Countries," *Current Digest of the Soviet Press*, XI, 32, p. 5; original text in *Sotsialisticheskii trud*, 1959, No. 1, pp. 42–55). This figure is hardly consistent with Galenson's from the Soviet point of view, if we were to grant their persistent claims that labor productivity is growing much faster in the Soviet Union than in the United States. Projecting Kats' figure backward to 1937 by the ratio of the official Soviet index of labor productivity (*Promyshlennost'*, 1957, p. 25) to our U.S. index based on persons engaged (Table A-36), we would find the fraction to be about 30 per cent in 1937.

[19] The list contains the following products: dehydrated fruits and vegetables; packaged seafood; frozen fruits and vegetables; biscuits and crackers; chewing gum; flavoring; miscellaneous food preparations, n.e.c.; cigars; full-fashioned hosiery; hard-surface floor coverings; coated fabric; millwork; synthetic fibers; drugs and medicines; cleaning and polishing preparations (except soap); paints, varnishes, and allied products; toilet preparations; insecticides and fungicides; chemical products, n.e.c.; rubber industries, n.e.c.; leather dress gloves; luggage; handbags and purses; small leather goods; hardware, n.e.c.; plumbing fixtures and fittings; heating and cooking equipment; office and store machines; domestic laundry equipment; laundry and dry cleaning machines; vacuum cleaners; refrigeration machinery; measuring and dispensing pumps; service and household machines, n.e.c.; electrical appliances; engine electrical equipment; storage batteries, primary batteries; X-ray and therapeutic apparatus;

Some, though far from all, differences in structural developments are revealed in the industrial distributions of employment over the years (see Table 72). In both countries, the share of employment in the so-called heavy industries has been increasing at the expense of the share in food processing and textiles and apparel. Machinery and allied products have rather consistently accounted for a larger share in the United States than in the Soviet Union, though some of the discrepancy is made up by the differing importance of consumer goods: in the mid-1950's, they represented about 7 per cent of industrial employment in the United States and about 3 per cent in the Soviet Union.[20] At the same time, the following industrial groups accounted for a larger fraction of employment in Soviet than in U.S. industry: fuel, wood construction materials, mineral construction materials, food and allied products, and textiles and allied products. The following accounted for a smaller fraction: ferrous and nonferrous metals, electricity, chemicals, and machinery and allied products. In general the 1955 Soviet distribution of employment seems to resemble the U.S. distribution more closely for the years 1909 and 1919 than for any other years.

The data compiled here provide some evidence that can shed light on the effects of industrial structure on production indexes for the two countries. It will be recalled from the first section of Chapter 5 that the movements of a production index depend in part on the path of expansion followed by an economy: other relevant things the same, the larger the share of production accounted for by commodities whose relative unit costs are declining over time, the higher is the growth that will be measured by a production index. If we accept unit physical labor cost (the inverse of labor productivity) as an ordinal measure of total unit cost, we may array industries in each country according to reduction in unit cost: the larger the growth in labor productivity, the greater is the reduction in unit cost. Those industries with greater than average growth in productivity may then be taken as having declining relative unit costs,

---

electrical products, n.e.c.; truck trailers; auto trailers; medical equipment and supplies; photographic equipment; jewelry and silverware; musical instruments and parts; toys and sporting goods; office supplies; costume jewelry and notions; plastic products, n.e.c.; brooms and brushes; cork products; fireworks and pyrotechnics; jewelry and instrument cases; lamp shades; miscellaneous manufactured products, n.e.c. (except ordnance).

Total industrial value added was taken as $134.2 billion for 1954 (see Table A-42). All other values were taken from the 1954 census of manufactures.

[20] The U.S. figure is based on the 1957 weights for the Federal Reserve Board index (*Federal Reserve Bulletin*, December 1959, p. 1467) covering automotive products, appliances, television and radio sets, and miscellaneous home goods. The Soviet estimate is taken from Table D-9.

TABLE 63

Comparative Levels of Industrial Production and Productivity: Soviet Union and United States, 1913, 1928, and 1955

	Soviet Union			United States			Soviet Union as % of United States		
	1913[a]	1928[b]	1955[c]	1913[a]	1928[b]	1955[c]	1913	1928	1955
Value added of industry									
1. Billion dollars	$1.70	$2.16	$35.3[d]	$12.2	$33.9	$150.7	13.9	9.3	23.4
2. Billion rubles	R3.77	R7.89	R258[d]	R35.7	R126.8	R1,311	10.6	6.2	19.7
Persons engaged in industry									
3. Million full-time equivalents	5.82	5.38	19.4	9.10	11.5	18.2	64.0	46.8	106.6
Man-hours engaged in industry									
4. Billion hours	14.8	11.0	42.1	25.7	26.3	37.8	57.6	41.8	111.4
Population									
5. Million inhabitants	138.0	151.4	197.6	97.2	120.5	165.3	142.0	125.6	119.5
Value added per person engaged									
6. Dollars	$292	$587	$1,820	$1,340	$2,950	$8,280	21.8	19.9	22.0
7. Rubles	R648	R1,470	R13,300	R3,920	R11,000	R72,000	16.5	13.4	18.5
Value added per man-hour engaged									
8. Dollars	$0.115	$0.237	$0.838	$0.475	$1.29	$3.99	24.2	22.2	21.0
9. Rubles	R0.255	R0.717	R6.13	R1.39	R4.82	R34.7	18.3	14.9	17.7
Value added per head of population									
10. Dollars	$12.3	$20.9	$179	$126	$281	$912	9.8	7.4	19.6
11. Rubles	R27.3	R52.1	R1,310	R367	R1,050	R7,930	7.4	5.0	16.5

[a] Dollar values in 1914 U.S. prices; ruble values in 1913 Soviet prices.
[b] Dollar values in 1929 U.S. prices; ruble values in 1928 Soviet prices.
[c] Dollar values in 1954 U.S. prices; ruble values in 1955 prices, excluding most of the applicable turnover taxes.

[d] If employee compensation were taken to be 56 per cent of value added, the fraction applying to U.S. manufacturing in 1955 (see text surrounding Table F-3), value added would be derived as $38.1 billion and 278 billion rubles, or 7.8 per cent higher than shown. Other data would change accordingly.
Notes continue on page 239.

and the volume of resources' devoted to them—measured by employment—may be determined.[21]

Out of the nine industrial groups into which we have divided all industry (the breakdown of machinery and allied products is, of necessity, ignored), four had greater than average growth in labor productivity over 1913–1955 in the Soviet Union and over 1909–1953 in the United States (compare Tables 62 and 65). They were not the same industrial groups in the two cases, though the same in number. These industrial groups accounted for the following fractions of persons engaged:

United States		Soviet Union	
Year	Per Cent	Year	Per Cent
1909	20.8	1913	24.1
1919	20.4		
1929	21.5	1928	26.4
1937	20.4	1937	41.6
1948	19.3	1950	46.0
1953	17.6	1955	47.0

It therefore appears that the share of employment for industrial groups with greater than average growth in labor productivity has been larger in the Soviet Union than in the United States, no matter what benchmark years are compared.

Similar results obtain for the Soviet period 1928–1955 and the U.S. counterpart 1929–1953. For the Soviet Union, there were five industrial groups with greater than average growth in labor productivity; for the United States, there were three groups. These industries accounted for the following fractions of persons engaged:

United States		Soviet Union	
Year	Per Cent	Year	Per Cent
1929	16.9	1928	28.3
1937	16.2	1937	44.7
1948	14.8	1950	48.9
1953	13.4	1955	50.4

[21] The arrays with cumulated percentages of employment are given in Tables A-39 and A-40. It clearly would have been preferable to use value added instead of employment, but the needed Soviet data do not exist. As may be seen from the data in the cited tables, for industries with the most rapid growth in labor productivity, the percentage share of value added tends to be higher than the percentage share of employment. Moreover, the relevant share of employment in the case of the United States—for which this can be studied—has a growing downward bias over time, apparently because industries with the most rapid growth in productivity experience a more rapid percentage decline in the ratio of unit physical labor cost to total unit cost than other industries do.

We may therefore conclude that industrial groups with relatively declining unit costs over time have accounted for a larger fraction of industrial resources in the Soviet Union than in the United States. On this score, conventional production indexes overstate industrial growth in the Soviet Union relative to the United States. That is to say, if the Soviet path of expansion had more closely paralleled the U.S. path in this respect, the measured growth of Soviet industry would probably have been lower than it is.

To bring the discussion of contemporary structure to a close, we may make a few observations about comparative military production. Some estimates for recent years are brought together in Table 73 covering

TABLE 73

OUTPUT OF CONVENTIONAL MILITARY PRODUCTS: UNITED
STATES AND SOVIET UNION, 1954 AND 1955

VALUE OF CONVENTIONAL MILITARY PRODUCTS[a]

Soviet Union, 1955	
Billion rubles	R42.5
Billion dollars[b]	$8.5
United States, 1954	
Billion rubles[c]	R70.8
Billion dollars	$11.8

VALUE OF MILITARY PRODUCTS AS PERCENTAGE
OF VALUE ADDED OF INDUSTRY

Soviet Union, 1955	
Ruble prices	16%
Dollar prices	26%
United States, 1954	
Ruble prices	6%
Dollar prices	9%

SOVIET VALUE OF MILITARY PRODUCTS AS
PERCENTAGE OF U.S. VALUE

Ruble prices	60%
Dollar prices	72%

SOURCE: Tables A-10, A-31, and A-44.

[a] Excludes atomic energy. However, Soviet value is probably substantially overstated (see annex to technical note 4 of Appendix A). Value applies to items delivered to military authorities and hence excludes double counting. Including atomic energy, the U.S. value is $13.7 billion or 82.2 billion rubles.

[b] Value in rubles divided by ruble-dollar price ratio for machinery (5.0) based on Soviet output weights (see Table A-31).

[c] Value in dollars times ruble-dollar price ratio for machinery (6.0) based on U.S. output weights (see Table A-31).

conventional military products—that is, excluding atomic energy.[22] In using these figures, it should be borne in mind that the Soviet magnitudes may be substantially overstated, in view of some recent evidence summarized in the annex to technical note 4 of Appendix A. Military production is without doubt relatively much more important in Soviet industry than in U.S. industry, the value of military products constituting more than a quarter of industrial value added in the former and less than a tenth in the latter, according to our estimates (all values expressed in dollars).[23] The 1955 Soviet value of military products, as we estimate it, was almost equal to three-quarters of the 1954 U.S. value, both again expressed in dollars.[24] Hence Soviet production relative to the United States in this area far exceeds the average for all industry, a conclusion that holds true for any likely error in the Soviet magnitudes.

Comparable Growth

Once industrialization has gotten under way in a country, the pace of industrial growth at any moment would seem to depend on the resource potential, the state of industrial arts, the prevailing level of industrial output (i.e., the extent to which potential is being utilized), and that catchall, the economic system. The process of economic growth is mysteriously complex and cannot be summarized in these brief comments, but this is not the place to discuss the manifold preconditions and environmental factors essential for sustained economic growth. We take it for granted that industrialization and the accompanying process of growth are a fact in the Soviet Union, just as they were, more incipiently, in Tsarist Russia. We are therefore concerned here only with the more fundamental conditioning factors making that growth faster or slower than it would otherwise be. As far as such things can be quantified, the

[22] Expenditures on the atomic energy program in the United States amounted to $1,895 million in 1954 (*Statistical Abstract of the United States, 1958*, p. 242), or 16 per cent of the value of conventional military products.

[23] Ruble measures are not very meaningful for such comparisons because of the arbitrarily low prices attached to military products in the Soviet Union. Note that the *value* of military products, *not* the value added by industries processing materials into military products, is being compared with the value added for all industry. Hence all stages of industrial processing of military products are being taken into account.

[24] If the overstatement in our estimate of Soviet production of conventional military products is taken to be large enough to offset the missing item of atomic energy, Soviet production is only 62 per cent of the U.S. level including atomic energy (see Table 73, note a).

It is interesting that military production multiplied more than four times in the Soviet Union over 1947–1955 by our estimate (see Table A-10) and over five times in the United States over 1947–1957 (see my "Reply," *American Economic Review*, September 1959, p. 698). The U.S. growth probably started from a lower level relative to the wartime peak, however.

larger the resource potential, the more advanced the technology, and the smaller the output, the more rapid the growth in output will be, given the economic system. None of these factors can be clearly defined, but they can all be represented by certain more or less adequate indicators. Our immediate problem is to find indicators that will allow us to select periods in Soviet and American industrial history that are comparable except with respect to economic system.

What is a good indicator of resource potential? If we may judge from the general practice of comparing economies in per capita terms, it would seem that population is typically used to indicate resource potential. But it is often a poor indicator since populations grow in response to economic development and differently in different economies. Moreover and more importantly, population can grow from immigration as well as from natural increase. As a concrete example for the problem at hand, in the United States the expanding industrial labor force in the latter part of the nineteenth century was recruited in important measure from the economically underutilized population in other countries, including Russia.[25] The expansion in the Soviet Union during the twentieth century came, on the other hand, from the large internal pool of under-utilized population. Hence, compared with the Soviet Union, population understates the resource potential of the nineteenth century United States.

The resource potential of an economy is more adequately described by the volume of all resources at its disposal, including climate and terrain. If this can be precisely and accurately measured, it remains to be done. In the meantime, we are perhaps justified in making the impressionistic judgment that the Soviet Union and the United States have roughly similar resource potentials. Both countries are rich in natural resources, though the specific endowments obviously differ. Against the larger size of the Soviet Union must be offset the substantial climatic and topo-graphical disadvantages—at least in the present state of civilization. Although in total area the Soviet Union is about two and a half times as large as the United States, in inhabitable area it is only about as large. Other relevant things the same—like tastes, technology, population, economic system, and so on—we suppose that the two countries would be able to support roughly equivalent levels of industrial production on the basis of resource endowments.

This leads us to suppose further that, if the state of industrial arts and

[25] Foreign-born persons accounted for about 18 per cent of the net increase in total gainfully occupied population or labor force over 1870–1900 (see Simon Kuznets and Ernest Rubin, *Immigration and the Foreign Born*, NBER Occasional Paper 46, New York, 1954, p. 46).

the aggregate levels of industrial output were the same in the two countries, differences in the rate of growth of industrial output should be attributable to differences in economic systems. Unfortunately, we cannot standardize both the level of output and the state of technology simultaneously in the two countries. To find dates at which output was roughly equivalent, one must go back a number of years in American history. Thus, as we shall see, the level of Russian output in 1913 within the interwar Soviet territory was reached in the United States around 1875. But the state of industrial arts—at least the available body of technology—was less advanced in the United States in 1875 than in the Russia of 1913: the same body of technical knowledge, if not skills, has been available to the two countries at roughly the same dates in history. Therefore, when we standardize the level of output from which growth starts—as we are about to do—any difference that we observe between growth rates in the two countries must be attributed to differences in both technology and economic system. While the effects of each cannot be fully isolated, we can at least say in whose favor the difference in technologies operates and thereby narrow the range of ignorance.

These remarks make the issues seem simpler than they are, because they presuppose that the periods to be compared represent normal times. This is, of course, not so for the Soviet Union, unless we view periodic disasters as a part of normal times there. Since the founding of the Soviet Union, no span of years longer than a decade has been free from major disturbances or recoveries from them. As we have emphasized before, we cannot possibly know which period has had a growth rate similar to what would be expected from a long stretch of normal years, and we must therefore choose several Soviet periods, representing differing circumstances, in making comparisons with American industrial growth.

Subject to the outlined qualifications, a Soviet period would have as its counterpart in the United States a period whose terminal years had the same total industrial output, unadjusted for differences in population, as obtained in the Soviet Union in 1913 and 1955, or whatever years we might wish to choose. If industrial output is measured by weighted aggregates, the Soviet periods 1913–1955 and 1928–1955 are "comparable" with the American period 1875–1914; that is, for both countries industrial output started and ended at roughly the same levels within these periods, insofar as we are justified in making such broad intertemporal and international comparisons.[26] If output is measured by the median

[26] The American dates are derived as follows. Soviet industrial output, calculated in dollar values, was 13.9 per cent of the American level in 1913. Looking back into

performance of a group of individual industries, the Soviet periods are comparable to the American period 1885–1920 (see the annex to this chapter). The dating of these periods implies that it took thirty-five to forty years in the United States to register the same growth as was accomplished over forty-two years in the Soviet Union—or, if the depressed pre-Plan years are ignored, over twenty-seven years.

We must remind ourselves that these periods are comparable only with respect to two of the factors influencing rate of growth: resource potential and prevailing level of industrial output. They are not comparable with respect to the state of the industrial arts. The advantage—a substantial one—is in favor of the Soviet Union, since it has had the technology of the twentieth century at its disposal in working out its industrialization. One can only dream about what difference it would have made to U.S. industrial growth in the nineteenth century if it had proceeded under twentieth century technology.

The choice of comparable stages of development in the industries of the Soviet Union and the United States is, therefore, unavoidably hazy and arbitrary to some degree. We shall summarize here the records of industrial growth in the Soviet Union and the United States over periods of equal length that are comparable in the sense that the beginning year in each case represents roughly the same level of output in the two countries.

We start with the longest period studied for the Soviet Union, 1913–1955. The growth rate over this period—4.1 per cent a year, excluding gains from territorial expansion—is slower than the rate for a comparable U.S. period: 5.1 per cent a year over 1875–1917 or 4.3 per cent over 1885–1927 (see Table 74). On a per capita basis, the Soviet growth rate is higher: 3.5 per cent a year compared with 3.0 per cent. But we must recall the misleading nature of comparisons of per capita rates, in view of the fact that population growth overstates growth in resource potential in the United States compared with the Soviet Union.[27]

American industrial history and smoothing out the cyclical fluctuations in our U.S. production index by means of a nine-year moving average, we find that output in 1875 was also around 14 per cent of the level of 1913. A similar procedure gives the American date 1914 as roughly equivalent, in level of output, to the Soviet date 1955.

[27] If population were taken as a guide to industrial potential, we might identify as comparable "stages of development" those periods in which industrial output per head of population was the same in both countries. This procedure is not only difficult to justify for the reasons just stated, but it is also impossible to apply. The Soviet level of industrial output per capita in 1955 corresponds roughly with the American level in 1887; the Soviet level in 1913 was lower than the American level in 1860, the earliest year for which aggregate industrial output can be calculated. Similar results are found by taking the median dates at which per capita output of a group of industries was the same in both countries.

TABLE 74

AVERAGE ANNUAL GROWTH RATES OF INDUSTRIAL OUTPUT AND OUTPUT PER CAPITA:
SOVIET UNION AND UNITED STATES, SELECTED COMPARABLE PERIODS[a]
(per cent)

| Period for Soviet Union | Output | | Output per Head of Population | | Period for United States |
	Soviet Union[b]	United States	Soviet Union	United States	
1913–1955	4.1	5.1	3.5	3.0	1875–1917
		4.3		2.6	1885–1927
1928–1955	6.5	5.5	5.8	3.4	1875–1902
		4.8		2.9	1885–1912
1928–1940	8.9	6.7	7.4	4.4	1875–1887
		4.6		3.0	1885–1897
		6.5		5.0	1939–1951
1950–1955	9.6	3.2	7.8	1.2	1909–1914
		8.0		5.9	1908–1913

SOURCE: Table 61. Average annual growth rates calculated from data for terminal years by the compound interest formula. For the U.S. periods comparable with 1913–1955 and 1928–1955, a centered nine-year moving average is used for each terminal year.

[a] Periods are comparable for growth in output only, not output per capita. See text.

[b] Excludes territorial gains.

For lack of sufficient data, we cannot compare growth in labor productivity.

If we turn to the Plan period, 1928–1955, we observe that the Soviet growth rate, again adjusted to exclude territorial gains, is higher than for a comparable U.S. period: 6.5 per cent a year compared with 5.5 per cent over 1875–1902 and 4.8 per cent over 1885–1912. The difference in per capita rates is even larger in favor of the Soviet Union. We therefore do not observe comparable U.S. periods, in the limited sense we are using, in which the speed of industrial growth has matched that during the Plan period in the Soviet Union.

For shorter spurts of growth, the Soviet performance also seems to have the edge: the Soviet growth rate over 1928–1940 exceeds the U.S. rates over 1875–1887 and 1885–1897 by a substantial margin. In a sense, this period of Soviet growth may be likened to the twelve years in the United States following the Great Depression; in both cases, growth was beginning again after a decade of depression and stagnation. The Soviet rate is faster in this comparison as well: 8.9 per cent a year compared with 6.5 per cent.

To illustrate a point, we also include a comparison with the Soviet growth rate of 9.6 per cent a year over 1950–1955. If the U.S. period 1909–1914 is chosen for comparison, the U.S. counterpart is 3.2 per cent; if, however, the dates are moved one year back to cover 1908–1913, the counterpart is 8.0 per cent. The point of this is that it proves nothing. The experience of a five-year period, plucked from history, carries no permanent message with it.

A similar picture emerges in comparing growth rates for a group of individual industries. One way of doing this is to proceed industry by industry, studying in each case what has happened to the Soviet lag behind U.S. output as of specific dates for Soviet output. For example, the Soviet output of steel ingots in 1913 had been reached in the United States around 1892; the Soviet output in 1955, around 1926. Hence the Soviet lag was twenty-one years in 1913 and twenty-nine years in 1955. Since the lag increased over this period, it follows that, starting from the same level, U.S. output of steel ingots grew faster, both absolutely and relatively, than Soviet output. Put another way, the same absolute and percentage growth occurred in the United States in thirty-five years as occurred in the Soviet Union in forty-two.

We have studied the behavior of Soviet lags for forty-seven counterpart industries as of a number of benchmark years, and the details are given in the annex to this chapter. The results may be summarized in the form of movements in median lags—that is, those lags exceeded by half the industries and fallen short of by the other half. The median number of years of lag run as follows (for more details, see Table 81):

1913	29
1928	44
1937	36
1950	42
1955	35

We observe that, on the average, Soviet output of this group of industries grew more slowly over 1913–1955, but more rapidly over 1928–1955, than U.S. output over comparable periods. Relative to comparable periods in the United States, Soviet growth was slower over 1913–1928, faster over 1928–1937, slower again over 1937–1950, and faster over 1950–1955. In these comparisons, territorial gains are counted as part of Soviet growth, and in this respect the Soviet Union is favored.

It will be noticed that the Soviet and U.S. periods compared for any one product may differ considerably in length, since what is being compared is the number of years required in each case to accomplish the same

TABLE 75

AVERAGE ANNUAL GROWTH RATES COMPARED FOR FORTY-SEVEN INDUSTRIES: SOVIET UNION AND UNITED STATES, SELECTED COMPARABLE PERIODS

(per cent)

	Soviet Union, 1913–1955 (1)	United States, Comparable Period[a] (2)	United States, 1880–1920 (3)	Soviet Union, 1928–1955 (4)	United States, Comparable Period[a] (5)	United States, 1880–1905 (6)	Soviet Union, 1928–1937 (7)	United States, Comparable Period[a] (8)	Soviet Union, 1950–1955 (9)	United States, Comparable Period[a] (10)
Iron ore	5.0	4.4	5.8	9.5	7.6	7.6	18.3	8.5	12.6	0.4
Pig iron	5.0	5.0	5.9	9.0	7.3	7.5	17.9	8.7	11.7	4.7
Steel ingots	5.8	4.9	9.1	9.2	8.3	11.5	17.2	12.6	10.6	4.8
Rolled steel	5.5	4.7	6.6	9.0	6.5	7.7	15.9	4.7	11.1	3.7
Copper	6.1	8.4	7.6	9.8	10.4	11.0	14.0	13.2	8.8	8.5
Lead	13.7	5.4	4.9	20.1	6.3	5.5	44.0	13.7	18.1	7.2
Zinc	11.1	11.2	7.8	19.0	13.1	8.4	48.0	19.5	14.9	8.4
Electric power	11.2	11.3	34.1	13.9	11.1	47.9	24.6	15.7	13.3	3.5
Coal	6.4	6.6	5.1	9.3	6.4	6.4	14.4	6.9	8.5	6.3
Coke	5.6	5.6	6.9	9.1	7.9	9.2	18.9	18.3	9.5	3.8
Crude petroleum	5.0	7.5	8.1	6.9	8.7	7.5	10.5	10.4	13.3	10.5
Natural gas	14.6	17.7	15.5	13.4	15.4	26.7	24.5	37.2	9.3	9.1
Soda ash	5.4	5.6	10.3	7.2	5.3	13.9	10.4	-17.6	13.9	3.4
Caustic soda	5.7	6.3	n.a.	8.7	6.5	n.a.	12.1	8.9	11.6	8.1
Sulfuric acid	8.6	8.5	n.a.	11.3	9.8	n.a.	23.1	15.5	12.3	6.0
Mineral fertilizer	12.5	9.2	6.4	17.1	10.1	7.3	40.3	18.3	11.7	10.0
Synthetic dyes	7.0	6.9	n.a.	7.6	7.4	n.a.	13.1	15.5	9.6	5.4
Paper	5.5	6.7	5.8	7.2	7.5	7.3	12.7	6.9	9.3	8.6
Motor vehicle tires	16.1	13.8	n.a.	19.4	16.2	n.a.	46.8	21.0	6.6	32.6
Cement	6.6	5.8	10.3	9.7	9.6	12.7	12.8	15.7	17.1	7.3
Construction gypsum	4.2	4.7	9.1	9.7	10.3	11.3	20.0	16.7	10.8	6.4
Construction lime	6.1	n.a.	0.6	9.6	n.a.	0.3	24.4	n.a.	8.4	4.7
Lumber	4.1	3.9	1.5	6.7	4.0	3.2	10.3	4.0	8.8	5.4
Rails	3.7	3.8	2.1	7.7	4.7	4.1	13.1	8.3	10.5	9.8
Window glass	3.5	3.1	3.8	4.0	2.1	4.7	9.8	1.6	5.4	6.7
Railroad freight cars	3.1	6.0	5.3	5.6	10.9	10.0	15.9	23.2	-7.5	3.4
Railroad passenger cars	1.2	-2.5	3.8	5.8	7.5	9.0	10.0	12.2	14.2	2.9

262

	(1)	(2)	(3)	(4)	(5)	(6)	(7)	(8)	(9)	(10)
Flour	0.3	n.a.	1.5	1.1	n.a.	2.3	1.7	n.a.	7.8	n.a.
Butter	3.6	4.6	7.6	6.6	5.6	9.5	9.4	8.4	6.6	4.4
Vegetable oil	2.2	3.9	8.9	2.4	2.8	11.0	−1.5	4.4	7.4	2.8
Meat slaughtering	1.8	3.7	3.1	4.5	5.4	3.6	2.0	6.1	9.1	6.0
Sausages	6.3	5.7	n.a.	10.4	6.6	n.a.	24.1	7.0	9.4	5.2
Fish catch	2.4	2.3	0.7	4.5	1.5	0.7	7.5	0.9	9.3	2.0
Soap	3.5	4.5	4.0	4.1	4.6	4.4	3.6	4.6	5.7	4.2
Salt	2.6	3.3	5.4	3.4	4.1	6.0	3.6	5.2	4.8	4.7
Raw sugar consumption	2.2	3.5	4.3	3.7	4.0	6.6	7.3	4.7	6.3	3.7
Canned food	8.7	8.1	6.2	12.8	10.8	6.0	25.7	11.4	15.9	8.2
Beer	2.0	5.2	1.6	5.9	8.6	5.4	9.7	11.8	7.1	8.0
Cigarettes	5.4	7.3	−2.1	5.3	7.5	9.5	6.8	8.6	9.6	5.6
Boots and shoes	3.7	n.a.	n.a.	3.7	n.a.	n.a.	6.6	n.a.	6.2	2.1
Rubber footwear	3.8	n.a.	n.a.	4.9	n.a.	n.a.	9.9	n.a.	3.5	n.a.
Cotton fabrics	2.0	2.8	3.6	3.0	2.7	2.5	2.8	2.6	8.7	2.6
Pure silk and nylon fabrics	0.4	6.5	7.5	11.2	15.5	8.0	17.3	18.2	32.3	8.2
Rayon and mixed fabrics	7.5	2.8	n.a.	14.7	8.2	n.a.	11.7	11.5	37.3	35.0
Woolen and worsted fabrics	2.1	2.1	1.3	2.9	2.8	1.1	−0.9	5.5	10.2	5.2
Bicycles	16.4	n.a.	n.a.	23.0	n.a.	n.a.	54.5	n.a.	34.7	10.6
Sewing machines	4.3	n.a.	n.a.	6.6	n.a.	n.a.	6.7	n.a.	26.3	n.a.
Medians										
Covered industries[b]	5.0	5.3	5.8	7.7	7.5	7.5	12.8	10.9	9.6	5.5
41 industries[c]	5.4	5.3	n.a.	8.7	7.5	n.a.	13.1	10.9	9.6	5.6
37 industries[d]	5.4	n.a.	5.8	7.2	n.a.	7.5	13.1	10.9	9.6	5.4

SOURCE: Appendixes B and E. Average annual growth rates calculated from output in terminal years by the compound interest formula. In some cases, output series were extended or filled in for a few years by logarithmic extrapolation or interpolation. U.S. output taken as centered nine-year moving average, with minor modifications.

a For each industry, the comparable period is as long as the Soviet period with which it is compared and begins with a year in which U.S. output was at about the same level as for the initial year in the Soviet period, the comparable periods hence differing from one industry to another. They are derived from the lag analysis described in the annex to this chapter.

b For the Soviet Union, forty-seven industries. For the United States, forty-one industries in cols. 2, 5, and 8; thirty-seven in cols. 3 and 6; and forty-four in col. 10.

c The sample of industries in col. 2.

d The sample of industries in col. 3.

TABLE 76

AVERAGE ANNUAL GROWTH RATES FOR THIRTEEN NEW SOVIET INDUSTRIES:
SOVIET UNION AND UNITED STATES, COMPARABLE PERIODS
(per cent)

	Average Annual Growth Rate		Comparable Period of Growth,
	Soviet Union[a]	United States[b]	United States[c]
Primary aluminum	45.1[d]	21.3	1905–1912
Automobiles	11.3[e]	29.4	1903–1925
Trucks and buses	12.2	15.6	1914–1937
Tractors	5.4	6.0	1917–1940
Tractor-drawn plows	2.3	7.3	1923–1946
Tractor-drawn cultivators	7.5	9.1	1929–1955
Grain combines	7.1	10.0	1926–1949
Diesel engines	18.3	18.6	1922–1945
Electric motors	7.5	3.9	1917–1940
Margarine	10.7	5.1	1906–1929
Hosiery	5.2[e]	4.9	1890–1912
Radio receiving sets	23.2	29.6	1921–1944
Television sets	111[f]	278	1946–1951
Median	10.7	10.0	

SOURCE: Appendixes B and E. Average annual growth rate calculated from output in terminal years by the compound interest formula.

[a] 1932–1955, except as noted below.

[b] Growth rates were in general calculated from actual output in beginning year and moving average in ending year. Exceptions are as follows: tractor-drawn plows, tractor-drawn cultivators, and margarine—moving average in beginning year; diesel engines, electric motors, hosiery, and television sets—actual output in ending year. Wherever data were missing for the years used, they were logarithmically interpolated or extrapolated graphically.

[c] A comparable period is taken as twenty-three years beginning with the year in which the level of output first became approximately equal to the Soviet output in 1932, except as noted below.

[d] 1933–1940. Output in 1932 was at an experimental level.

[e] 1933–1955.

[f] 1950–1955.

growth. Similarly, the U.S. periods comparable with any given Soviet period (as 1913–1955) may vary from one industry to another, since the Soviet pattern of output at any particular time has never been precisely duplicated in the United States.

Another method that can be used is to compare growth rates for a group of industries over periods of equal length in the two countries (see Tables 75 through 77 and Chart 29).[28] Here we may proceed as in

[28] The sample of industries compared is the same for both countries in the tables and the upper panel of the chart, but different in the lower panel. In the latter case, the Soviet sample of seventy industries is taken from Table 8; the U.S. sample of sixty-eight industries from A. F. Burns, *Production Trends in the United States since 1870*, New York, NBER, 1934, pp. 309–312, industries numbered 21–91 except 29, 60, and 83.

CHART 29
Frequency Distributions of Growth Rates for Samples of Individual Industries: Soviet Union and United States, Comparable Periods

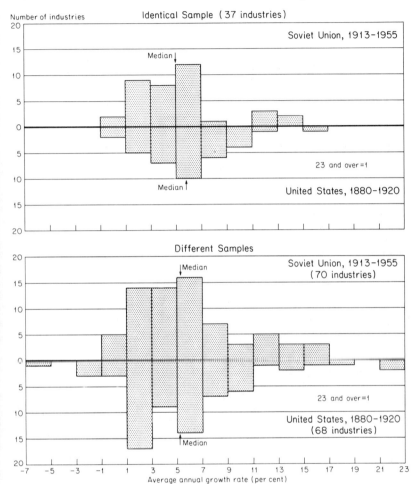

Source: Tables 8 and 75; A. F. Burns, *Production Trends in the United States since 1870*, New York, NBER 1934, pp. 309 ff. See footnote 28 of this chapter.

the study of lags, by choosing a comparable U.S. period for each industry separately, that period being one beginning with a year in which U.S. output was at about the same level as for the initial year of the Soviet period and extending over the same number of years as the Soviet period.

Average annual growth rates are calculated from output in terminal years by the compound interest formula. For six U.S. industries, growth covers 1885–1920.

TABLE 77

AVERAGE ANNUAL GROWTH RATES OF INDUSTRIAL OUTPUT OVER COMPARABLE PERIODS
CALCULATED IN DIFFERENT WAYS: SOVIET UNION AND UNITED STATES
(per cent)

	Soviet Union, 1913– 1955	United States, Comparable Period	Soviet Union, 1928– 1955	United States, Comparable Period
Production index, all products[a]	4.1	5.1	6.5	5.5
Median of growth rates				
41 industries[b]	5.4	5.3	8.2	7.5
37 industries[c]	5.0	5.8	7.2	7.5
Different samples of industries				
for each country[d]	5.3	5.2		

[a] From Table 74, U.S. periods 1875–1917 and 1875–1902. Soviet output excludes territorial gains.

[b] From Table 75. Comparable period applies to each industry separately and hence varies among industries. Soviet output includes territorial gains.

[c] From Table 75, U.S. periods 1880–1920 and 1880–1905. Soviet output includes territorial gains.

[d] From Chart 29, U.S. period 1880–1920. Covers seventy Soviet and sixty-eight U.S. industries. Soviet output includes territorial gains.

Or, for any given Soviet period, we may choose a standard U.S. period for all industries as a basis of comparison. We have done both, in the latter case using the U.S. periods 1880–1920 and 1880–1905 to compare with the Soviet periods 1913–1955 and 1928–1955. In both procedures, Soviet growth, when proper allowance is made for eliminating territorial gains, comes out slower over 1913–1955 than over comparable U.S. periods, but faster over 1928–1955, 1928–1937, and 1950–1955. It is interesting that, for a group of relatively new Soviet industries, Soviet and U.S. growth have been similar over comparable periods (see Table 76).

Concluding Remarks

What can be said about Soviet industrial achievements? In the first place, they have been impressive. In terms of its ability to generate sheer growth in industrial output—the questions of how much the growth has cost, what product mix has evolved, and how the products have been put to use being left aside—the Soviet system of centralized direction has proved itself to be more or less the peer of the market economy, as exemplified by the United States. This much seems beyond dispute even in the face of the questionable reliability of Soviet statistics.

Of course, the character of Soviet industrial growth has not been the same as in Western economies. Enhancement of state power has been the primary objective, the consumer being treated essentially as a residual claimant. Investment goods and munitions have been emphasized at the expense of consumer goods; and other important sectors of the economy— agriculture, construction, and consumer services—have been relatively neglected to help foster industrial expansion. At times, large groups of the population have been sacrificed or made to work in forced labor to promote internal economic policies. Leisure has shown little tendency to grow. This is all well known but deserves repetition to place Soviet industrial achievements in perspective. The character of industrial growth being so different from that in the West, there is a sense in which the two sets of achievements cannot be compared at all.

The last point should be underlined: the pattern of industrial growth observed in the Soviet Union would never be duplicated by a market economy. Sovereign consumers would not choose the paths of growth chosen by Soviet rulers. This raises the awkward question of whether a highly generalized measure of growth has much meaning even as an indicator of expansion in productive capacity available for whatever use it may be put to. As we demonstrated at the beginning of Chapter 5, measures of economic growth, as they are conventionally made in the form of index numbers, depend in fact on the path of growth—on the uses to which productive capacity is put. And, as noted in this chapter, the Soviet path of growth has favored measured growth relative to the United States. If we bowed to the stern dictates of logic, we would be able to compare Soviet and U.S. industrial growth only if both economies served either consumer welfare or state power. But that is ruled out by the very difference in social order whose influence on growth we wish to assess. This dilemma can be mastered only by admitting it—by avoiding the delusion that there is some single-dimensioned, neutral measure of growth, equally meaningful for all types of economies.

The question of economic waste is a related matter and equally difficult to treat. Growth is measured in terms of things "produced," not in terms of things usefully consumed. In a market economy, the two magnitudes are similar but not at all identical: mistakes are made by both entrepreneurs and consumers, rendering some productive activity worthless. The same kinds of mistakes are made in the Soviet Union, probably on a larger scale since centralized planning is involved. In addition, because of the weak position of most buyers, substandard goods often pass for standard quality, goods are damaged and spoiled in transit beyond normal experience in a market economy, and so on. Although Soviet industry does not experience business cycles as they are known in

267

market economies, it is periodically faced with the need to re-allocate resources on a large scale, and the accompanying waste that would appear in the form of temporarily unemployed resources in a market economy will appear, at least in part, in the form of unwanted accumulation of inventories. It is difficult enough to say something sensible about which type of economy has the more waste inherent in it. It is even more difficult to say what all this has to do with problems of measuring growth. Unless wastage has, in some meaningful sense, been growing at different rates in American and Soviet industry, there is nothing to be gained by taking account of this factor as far as comparing growth of industrial output is concerned.

These qualifications serve as warnings against careless comparisons of either the relative size or the relative growth of Soviet and U.S. industry. In particular, broad aggregative measures of industrial output tell us nothing about capacities for specific tasks, such as waging war or promoting consumer welfare. While Soviet industrial output in 1955 may have been, in the aggregate, about a fifth of the American level, production directly available for military purposes was a much larger fraction (almost three-quarters), and production available for consumers a much smaller one. Similarly, growth in the two areas has differed in the same way in the two countries.

It remains to be noted once again that the quantitative achievements of Soviet industry have not been understated by Soviet authorities. The official Soviet index of industrial production embodies a myth that should be dispelled from the popular mind. On this matter, Western scholars speak as one, though they may disagree as to the gravity of the myth. The official Soviet index shows industrial output as multiplying twenty-seven times between 1913 and 1955; the indexes presented here, based on official Soviet data on physical output and unit values and constructed according to conventional Western methods, show output as multiplying five to six times. If our indexes are taken as reasonably accurate, the official index contains a four- to fivefold exaggeration of growth over this period.

Bearing all these qualifications in mind, what may we conclude about the industrial performance of the Soviet Union relative to the United States? First, in level of output, Soviet industry was in 1955 roughly four decades behind the United States; in level of output per head of population, almost seven decades. Second, Soviet growth in output has been somewhat slower over the entire Soviet period, at least through 1955, than U.S. growth over the four decades bracketing the turn of this century, periods that are comparable in the sense that output started at roughly the same level in both cases; on the other hand, Soviet growth in output per head of population has been faster, because of fundamentally different relations in the two countries between population growth and economic growth. Third, Soviet growth in output, both total and per capita, has been faster over the Plan years than U.S. growth over a comparable period. In this and the preceding comparisons, the Soviet Union is favored in that it has had a more advanced technology at its disposal. Fifth, Soviet percentage growth—and Russian percentage growth over the last half century of Tsarist rule—has been faster over concurrent periods than U.S. percentage growth in the cases of total and per capita output, but slower—at least in the Soviet instance—in the case of output per unit of labor. At the same time, absolute growth has been significantly smaller—the gap in absolute industrial production between the two countries has grown steadily. Sixth and finally, industrial output in both countries has experienced a retardation in measured percentage growth between long periods on either side of the second decade of this century. Soviet growth has also retarded within the Soviet and Plan periods, but U.S. growth apparently has not.

Our eyes wander irresistibly toward the future, and we must wonder whether and in what respects Soviet industry might outdistance the industrial sectors of the more dynamic Western economies, such as the United States. Nobody can see a certain answer to that question; it depends on too many imponderables. Growth has not been a mechanical process in either the Soviet Union or the United States. It remains to be seen what strength will be shown by the forces driving growth, so fundamentally different in the two economies.

The first thing to observe is that, even if Soviet industry were to continue indefinitely growing faster, at any time, than U.S. industry, it might never overtake U.S. industry in level of output, though it would get relatively closer and closer. This would be the case if Soviet industry tended to repeat the growth rates experienced earlier in the United States at each successive level of output, with a similar rate of retardation. To catch up in this way does not, of course, imply superior performance. A son will get closer and closer percentagewise to his father in age but will never catch up, despite the fact that every year his percentage increase in age exceeds his father's. The absolute difference in age will never diminish. And, similarly, the absolute difference in industrial production between the United States and the Soviet Union may never vanish—may even continue to increase as it has been—even if percentage growth continues higher in the Soviet Union than in the United States but with similar retardations in both countries.

On the other hand, if the differentials in percentage growth already experienced over concurrent periods were to persist long enough—if the Soviet Union were not to duplicate the growth record of the United States over comparable periods—Soviet output would catch up to the U.S. level at some point in time (see Table 78). For example, if Soviet output in

TABLE 78

YEAR IN WHICH SOVIET AND U.S. INDUSTRIAL OUTPUT WOULD BE
EQUAL UNDER HYPOTHETICAL CONDITIONS

Assumed Average Annual Growth Rate (per cent)		Year of Equality If 1955 Soviet-U.S. Output Ratio Was	
Soviet Union	United States	22%	33%
TOTAL OUTPUT			
4.1	3.8	2515	2355
6.5	3.8	2016	1998
9.6	5.3	1993	1983
7.1	2.2	1985	1979
PER CAPITA OUTPUT			
3.5	2.5	2132	2086
5.8	2.6	2011	1997
7.8	3.5	1997	1986
5.4	0.5	1991	1982

NOTE: The pairs of growth rates apply as follows, from top to bottom: 1913–1955, 1928–1955, 1950–1955, 1955–1958 for the Soviet Union and 1955–1959 for the United States.

1955 is taken as 22 per cent of the U.S. level and the respective growth rates over 1928–1955 are projected indefinitely into the future, total and per capita industrial outputs in the two countries would become equal about a half century from now. Even as the percentage gap steadily closed under these conditions, the absolute gap would continue to increase in favor of the United States for more than thirty years from now.[29] If Soviet output in 1955 were taken as 33 per cent of the U.S. level—the conventional but, in our opinion, less reliable estimate—Soviet industrial output would overtake the U.S. level about four decades from now. Under a variety of similar assumptions, the time required for overtaking could range from two to sixty decades.

[29] At the point of maximum absolute gap, which would be reached around 1992, value added of industry in 1954 dollars would be about $600 billion for the United States and about $340 billion for the Soviet Union.

Finally, it is not out of the question that the Soviet growth rate might retard to, or even below, the U.S. rate before outputs have become equal in the two countries. In this case, Soviet industry would stop catching up and never overtake in level of output.

In a word, many things can happen, none of them inconsistent with what we know about the mysterious subject of economic growth. This should make us pause before making hasty estimates of the comparative future performance of Soviet and U.S. industry.

Annex to Chapter 8

Soviet Lags in Industrial Output Behind the United States

As mentioned in the body of this chapter, one way to assess comparative performance of Soviet and U.S. industry is to make an industry-by-industry study of the behavior of Soviet lags behind the United States in physical output. Such a study is presented here.[30] The rationale underlying it is that most individual industries tend, in the Soviet Union as well as elsewhere, to grow more slowly percentagewise as they get older and larger. Comparison of U.S. and Soviet growth rates over contemporaneous periods may therefore give a misleading impression of relative economic performance to the extent that mature U.S. industries are being compared with youthful Soviet counterparts. Analysis of Soviet lags behind U.S. output provides a simple and direct method of comparing growth over periods in which Soviet and U.S. industries were of equivalent size.

For example, in 1913 the Russian production of steel ingots within the interwar Soviet territory was roughly equal in metric tons to the production achieved in the United States around 1892, or twenty-one years earlier. Hence the lag in 1913 was twenty-one years. The lag had risen to thirty-two years in 1937, falling somewhat from that point to a level of twenty-nine years in 1955 and nineteen years in 1958, when it leapt across the gap caused by the Great Depression. Thus Soviet production of steel ingots was eight years further behind American production in 1955 than it had been in 1913, which is to say that it has taken the Soviet Union forty-two years (1913–1955) to accomplish what the United States had done in thirty-four (1892–1926). On the other hand, in 1958 it was two fewer years behind than in 1913, so that the Soviet Union in this period (1913–1958) accomplished in forty-five years what the United States did in forty-seven years (1892–1939). On a per capita basis, the

[30] The discussion here is essentially an extension and revision of my earlier report, *Some Observations on Soviet Industrial Growth*, NBER Occasional Paper 55, New York, 1957.

lag increased from thirty years in 1913 to forty in 1937, and to forty-nine in both 1955 and 1958. Production per capita was nineteen years further behind in 1955 and 1958 than it had been in 1913; an equal expansion in per capita output had taken place in the United States in twenty-three or twenty-six years, instead of forty-two or forty-five.

Making comparisons of this sort for a number of industries raises the familiar problems of defining each industry in a relevant way and of finding comparable industrial categories for different economies.[31] In general, the industries—it is perhaps more accurate to say "commodities" —chosen for study here are the most narrowly defined categories for which the Soviet Union has published data on physical output covering the entire Soviet period. Relying on narrow concepts of industries makes for obvious difficulties in interpreting differences in growth between economies with differing endowments of resources. These difficulties can be counteracted in part by making comparisons between broadly defined industrial categories. One such comparison is made below between energy-producing industries taken as a whole.[32]

It goes without saying that, even under the best of conditions as far as reliability of data and relevance of counterpart industries are concerned, marked differences are to be expected between the details of industrial growth in the two countries. This industry will grow more rapidly in the United States than in the Soviet Union, while that one will grow more slowly. Where retardation in growth has been so strong in the United States as to cause output of an industry to reach a peak and then decline, there can be the seeming paradox of an increasing Soviet lag despite the fact that Soviet output has come to exceed the U.S. level, as in the case of soap. The two countries have had, in the periods compared, different levels of technological achievement, different economic tastes or objectives, and dissimilar resource endowments. For the purpose at hand, the focus should therefore not be so much on the details of the comparison as on the general outline.

In Tables 79 and 80, the Soviet lag in both total and per capita output is listed for forty-seven industries as of a number of benchmark dates,

---

[31] For comments on some of the difficulties in selecting counterparts, see footnote 16 of this chapter.

[32] Taking energy-producing industries as an example, we find that the petroleum industry has shown a much more rapid development in the United States than in the Soviet Union over comparable periods, while the coal industry has not. The comparatively slower growth of coal output in the United States is essentially the result of an earlier shift to other sources of energy than occurred in the Soviet Union, not of any relatively depressive factors applicable to the energy-producing industry as a whole. It is therefore useful to examine comparative developments in the entire energy-producing industry as well as in its components.

TABLE 79
Lag of Soviet Union Behind United States in Output, Benchmark Dates, Forty-Seven Industries[a]

	Lag (number of years) as of							
	1913	1928	1937	1950	1955	1958	1960 Plan[b]	1965 Plan[c]
Iron ore	28	49	36	35	15	14	d	d
Pig iron	30	48	36	47	39	18	13	10
Steel ingots	21	36	32	38	29	19	17	14
Rolled steel	27	42	35	38	29	18	16	14
Copper	32	47	50	51	51	n.a.	51	n.a.
Lead	94	103	60	62	52	n.a.	49	n.a.
Zinc	46	62	43	50	46	n.a.	46	n.a.
Electric power	13	26	21	24	16	15	13	12
Coal	45	58	49	48	47	44	d	d
Coke	31	46	36	44	30	18	n.a.	n.a.
Crude petroleum	14	26	26	35	34	25	26	19
Natural gas	32	44	52	51	51	34	n.a.	17
Soda ash	23	36	31	36	24	n.a.	22	n.a.
Caustic soda	20	33	25	29	24	n.a.	22	n.a.
Sulfuric acid	20	31	24	30	19	19	n.a.	n.a.[d]
Mineral fertilizer	43	52	27	13	12	13	9	d
Synthetic dyes	10	12	15	14	11	n.a.	n.a.	n.a.
Paper	44	53	46	54	54	54	52	50
Motor vehicle tires	12	24	25	36	39	42	n.a.[d]	n.a.[d]
Cement	19	32	33	42	32	9	d	d
Construction gypsum	13	33	31	42	35	n.a.	n.a.	n.a.
Construction lime	33+	48+	51	11	7	n.a.	n.a.	n.a.[d]
Lumber	62	77	66	67	61	59	62	d
Rails	42	61	57	53	52	n.a.	n.a.[d]	n.a.[d]
Window glass	13	19	0	9	10	6		
Railroad freight cars	33	48	51	62	69	71	72	n.a.
Railroad passenger cars	21	43	46	59	53	57	54	n.a.
Flour	d	d	d	d	d	n.a.	n.a.	n.a.[u]
Butter	21	39	38	37	35	30	31	
Vegetable oil	5	17	26	35	28	19	15	16
Meat slaughtering	36	58	64	66	65	59	46	23
Sausages	39	53	36	41	38[d]	12[d]	n.a.[d]	n.a.[d]
Fish catch	−11	26	4	14	d	d	d	d
Soap	43	50	52	53	52	50	n.a.	n.a.
Salt	17	29	32	37	36	n.a.	n.a.[d]	n.a.[d]
Raw sugar consumption	26	42	35	47	45	35	d	d
Canned food	49	62	45	50	44	44	46	n.a.
Beer	42	58+	66	72	73	n.a.	n.a.	n.a.
Cigarettes	−1	8	11	18	16	17	n.a.	n.a.
Boots and shoes	24+	39+	44	53	44	33	18	14
Rubber footwear	14+	29+	19	d	d	n.a.	n.a.	n.a.
Cotton fabrics	36	40	44	57	48	50	46	49
Pure silk and nylon fabrics[e]	27	62	51	63	67	n.a.	n.a.	n.a.
Rayon and mixed fabrics[e]	16	38	37	21	21	n.a.	n.a.	n.a.
Woolen and worsted fabrics	59	73	83	90	65[d]	56[d]	23[d]	22
Bicycles	14+	29+	38+	15	d	d	d	n.a.
Sewing machines	14+	29+	38+	51+	d	d	d	n.a.
Median[f]	29	44	36	38	35	22	19	12

Notes on page 275.

TABLE 80
LAG OF SOVIET UNION BEHIND UNITED STATES IN PER CAPITA OUTPUT,
BENCHMARK DATES, FORTY-SEVEN INDUSTRIES[a]

	Lag (number of years) as of					
	1913	1928	1937	1955	1958	1960 Plan	1965 Plan
Iron ore	73	88+	52	54	55	51	46
Pig iron	48	84	52	56	57	55	53
Steel ingots	30	46	40	49	49	47	39
Rolled steel	28+	43+	50	52	50	47	39
Copper	52	69	57	65	n.a.	65	n.a.
Lead	105+	120+	109	76	n.a.	75	n.a.
Zinc	53	68	57	59	n.a.	56	n.a.
Electric power	14	27	26	25	20	20	18
Coal	66	80	69	69	64	63	68
Coke	36	53	49	56	57	n.a.	n.a.
Crude petroleum	27	40	34	41	38	39	32
Natural gas	33	45	52	69	49	n.a.	23
Soda ash	27	40	43	45	n.a.	33	n.a.
Caustic soda	19	34	40	35	n.a.	30	n.a.
Sulfuric acid	26	38	32	34	35	n.a.	n.a.
Mineral fertilizer	43+	58+	40	16	17	15	b
Synthetic dyes	14+	12	20	18	n.a.	n.a.	n.a.
Paper	54+	69+	67	71	70	70	71
Motor vehicle tires	13	26	31	42	44	n.a.	n.a.
Cement	30	45	38	47	38	10	b
Construction gypsum	17	43	36	49	n.a.	n.a.	n.a.
Construction lime	33+	48+	57+	75+	n.a.	n.a.	n.a.
Lumber	114+	129+	102	111	113	115	116
Rails	63	78+	77	84	n.a.	n.a.	n.a.
Window glass	34+	44	−2	15	11	b	b
Railroad freight cars	33+	48+	57+	75+	78+	80+	n.a.
Railroad passenger cars	30	48+	57	69	71	66	n.a.
Flour	b	b	b	b	n.a.	n.a.	n.a.
Butter	30	46	50	58	49	49	44
Vegetable oil	16	28	40	44	43	37	38
Meat slaughtering	33+	48+	57+	75+	78+	80+	85+
Sausages	24+	39+	48+	59	54	n.a.	n.a.
Fish catch	33+	48+	57+	19	10	b	b
Soap	34+	49+	58+	76+	79+	n.a.	n.a.
Salt	33+	43	46	58	n.a.	n.a.	n.a.
Raw sugar consumption	43+	58+	66	79	68	60	49
Canned food	43+	58+	62	60	58	56	n.a.
Beer	43+	58+	67+	85+	n.a.	n.a.	n.a.
Cigarettes	0	11	16	23	23	n.a.	n.a.
Boots and shoes	23+	38+	47+	65+	68+	70+	75+
Rubber footwear	14+	29+	38+	56+	n.a.	n.a.	n.a.
Cotton fabrics	43+	58+	67+	85+	88+	87	95+
Pure silk and nylon fabrics[c]	38	58+	64	82	n.a.	n.a.	n.a.
Rayon and mixed fabrics[c]	14+	29+	38+	23	n.a.	n.a.	n.a.
Woolen and worsted fabrics	43+	58+	67+	85+	88+	90+	95+
Bicycles	14+	29+	38+	7	b	b	n.a.
Sewing machines	14+	29+	38+	b	b	b	n.a.
Median[d]	d	d	d	56	52	51	44

Notes on page 275.

including the 1960 and 1965 Plans. More continuous measures may be made as desired from the graphs of output series in Chart A-2. The sample of industries has been dictated by availability of data on physical output, but it does cover a fair number of so-called "basic" industrial materials and consumer "staples." As we have already noted (see Table 70), it is more representative, and increasingly so, of Soviet industry than of U.S. industry, at least since 1913. When U.S. industry of the latter nineteenth century is substituted in this comparison, the differential certainly narrows, though we cannot say by how much. We can say this: the Soviet lags calculated from estimates of aggregate industrial production in the two countries are generally somewhat longer than the median lags calculated from our list of industries; and this suggests that the list comprehends a larger portion of Soviet industrial production than it does of the U.S. production of some thirty to forty years earlier.

Notes for Table 79

SOURCE: Appendixes B and E; announced goals of the Sixth Five Year Plan (*Current Digest*, VIII, 3, pp. 3 ff) and of the Seven Year Plan (*ibid*, XI, 9, pp 3 ff).

a U.S. output taken as centered nine-year moving average, with minor modifications. Soviet output covers interwar territory of the Soviet Union for 1913, 1928, and 1937; postwar territory for other years. A Soviet lead is indicated by a negative sign before the figure. Where U.S. data do not go back far enough to give the full lag, the calculable lag is followed by a plus sign. For basic data, see Chart A-2 and Appendixes B and E.

b Based on original goals of Sixth Five Year Plan, since discontinued.

c Based on goals of Seven Year Plan, taken as midpoints of the given range of "control figures." For lumber, meat slaughtering, butter, and vegetable oil, goals apply to a smaller coverage than for earlier years; they have been adjusted upward by ratio of 1958 outputs on larger and smaller coverage.

d Soviet output exceeds peak U.S. output to date.

e For combined silk, nylon, and rayon fabrics, lags are: twenty-six years for 1955, twenty-one for 1958, and seventeen for 1965 Plan.

f Calculated from data for the following numbers of industries: through 1955, forty-seven; 1958, thirty; 1960 Plan, thirty; and 1965 Plan, twenty-one. For 1913 and 1928, median lag cannot be precisely calculated because of lags of unknown length (lags with plus signs); it has been taken as the approximate midpoint of bounding limits (twenty-six and thirty-one for 1913, and forty-two and forty-seven for 1928). The median lags for the twenty-one industries (twenty in the case of the 1960 Plan) covered for the 1965 Plan are: 1913, twenty-seven; 1928, forty-two; 1937, thirty-six; 1950, forty-two; 1955, thirty-five; 1958, twenty-five; 1960 Plan, sixteen; and 1965 Plan, twelve.

Notes for Table 80

SOURCE: Table C-3 and other sources given in Table 79.

a See notes a, b, and c of Table 79. Soviet population is taken as 212 million in 1960 and 229 million in 1965.

b Soviet output exceeds peak U.S. output to date.

c For combined silk, nylon, and rayon fabrics, lags are: forty-one years for 1955, thirty for 1958, and twenty-eight for the 1965 Plan.

d For 1913, 1928, and 1937, the median lag cannot be calculated because of lags with unknown length (lags with plus signs); the median must exceed thirty-one for 1913, forty-five for 1928, and forty-eight for 1937. Medians cover only thirty-two industries for 1958, twenty for the 1960 Plan, and twenty-one for the 1965 Plan.

TABLE 81

Increase or Decrease (−) in Lag (number of years)

	1913–1928	1928–1937	1937–1950	1950–1955	1913–1955	1928–1955	1955–1965 Plan
Iron ore	21	−13	−1	−20	−13	−34	−15+
Pig iron	18	−12	11	−8	9	−9	−29
Steel ingots	15	−4	6	−9	8	−7	−15
Rolled steel	15	−7	3	−9	2	−13	−15
Copper	15	3	1	0	19	4	n.a.
Lead	9	−43	2	−10	−42	−49	n.a.
Zinc	16	−19	7	−4	0	−16	n.a.
Electric power	13	−5	3	−8	3	−10	−4
Coal	13	−9	−1	−1	2	−11	−47+
Coke	15	−10	8	−14	−1	−16	n.a.
Crude petroleum	12	0	9	−1	20	8	−15
Natural gas	12	8	−1	0	19	7	−34
Soda ash	13	−5	5	−8	1	−12	n.a.
Caustic soda	13	−8	3	−4	4	−9	n.a.
Sulfuric acid	11	−7	6	−11	−1	−12	n.a.
Mineral fertilizer	9	−25	−14	−1	−31	−40	−12+
Synthetic dyes	2	3	−1	−3	1	−1	n.a.
Paper	9	−7	8	0	10	1	−4
Motor vehicle tires	12	1	11	3	27	15	n.a.
Cement	13	1	9	−10	13	0	−32+
Construction gypsum	20	−2	11	−7	22	2	n.a.
Construction lime	15	b	−40	−4	−26+	−41+	n.a.
Lumber	15	−11	1	−6	−1	−16	−61+
Rails	19	−4	−4	−1	10	−9	n.a.
Window glass	6	−19	9	1	−3	−9	−10+
Railroad freight cars	15	3	11	7	36	21	n.a.
Railroad passenger cars	22	3	13	−6	32	10	n.a.
Flour	c	c	c	c	c	c	n.a.
Butter	18	−1	−1	−2	14	−4	−35+
Vegetable oil	12	9	9	−7	23	11	−12
Meat slaughtering	22	6	2	−1	29	1	−42
Sausages	14	−17	5	−3	−1	−15	n.a.
Fish catch	37	−22	10	−14+	c	−26+	c
Soap	7	2	1	−1	9	2	n.a.
Salt	12	3	5	−1	19	7	n.a.
Raw sugar consumption	16	−7	12	−2	19	3	−45+
Canned food	13	−17	5	−6	−5	−18	n.a.
Beer	16+	c	6	1	31	d	n.a.
Cigarettes	9	3	7	−2	17	8	n.a.
Boots and shoes	c	b	9	−9	b	b	−30
Rubber footwear	15	−10+	−19+	c	−14+	−29+	n.a.
Cotton fabrics	4	4	13	−9	12	8	1
Pure silk and nylon fabrics	35	−9	12	4	40	5	e
Rayon and mixed fabrics	22	−1	−16	0	5	−17	e
Woolen and worsted fabrics	14	10	7	−25	6	−8	−43
Bicycles	d	b	−23+	−15+	−14+	−29+	n.a.
Sewing machines	15+	c	13	−51+	−14+	−29+	n.a.
Median[f]	15	−5	6	−4	8	−9	−22

Notes on page 277.

Cyclical fluctuations have been smoothed out of the U.S. output series—essentially through centered nine-year moving averages—so that comparisons would not be made with unusual temporary peaks in U.S. output. On the other hand, Soviet series have not been similarly smoothed because their fluctuations are fundamentally different in nature from our own cycles, and also because sharp discontinuities in the series create serious technical problems. Similarly, no adjustment has been made for gains in Soviet output resulting from territorial expansion during and after World War II; that is, such gains are included in the Soviet data. Therefore, on these scores as well as those mentioned in the preceding paragraph, the lags are computed favorably for the Soviet Union, at least as a general rule.[33]

Bearing in mind the various qualifications that must attend analysis of lags, we note (Table 79) that the median lag in output—that is to say, the lag exceeded in the case of half the industries and fallen short of in the case of the other half—was twenty-nine years in 1913, thirty-six years in 1937, and thirty-five years in 1955. By this measure of average performance, Soviet industrial growth over forty-two years (1913–1955) is seen to correspond roughly with U.S. industrial growth over thirty-six years (1885–1921). Put in terms of changes in lags, the increase in median lag was six years over the period 1913–1955, broken down into an increase of seven years for 1913–1937 and a decrease of one year for 1937–1955. Quite similar conclusions are reached on the basis of median changes in lags (see Table 81). Moreover, we may note that thirty-one out of forty-four industries for which changes and lags can be measured showed an increase for 1913–1955.

[33] Smoothing by a moving average may cause the average to be persistently above actual output when output is rising rapidly and consistently. Hence, in a few cases, lags may have been lengthened for earlier benchmark dates beyond what they would have been under other smoothing devices, though never by more than one or two years. It was considered preferable to adhere to a mechanical rule for smoothing and calculating lags, rather than to try to make minor improvements by *ad hoc* methods.

Notes for Table 81

SOURCE: Table 79.

a See notes a and c to Table 79. Changes in lags that cannot be precisely calculated are footnoted or followed by a plus sign.

b Probable decrease in lag of unknown magnitude.

c Insufficient data to indicate whether lag increased or decreased.

d Probable increase in lag of unknown magnitude.

e For all silk, nylon, and rayon fabrics combined, decrease of nine years in lag.

f Calculated from data for the following numbers of industries: 1913–1928, forty-five; 1928–1937, forty-four; 1937–1950, forty-six; 1950–1955, forty-five; 1913–1955, forty-five; 1928–1955, forty-six; and 1955–1965 Plan, twenty. For 1928–1937, taken as midpoint of bounding limits, −4 and −6.

The picture changes when the analysis is brought forward to 1958 and projected to the future expected by Soviet officials. However, the sample of industries falls sharply—to thirty-two for 1958 and twenty-one for the 1965 Plan—so that comparison with earlier dates is impaired. On the basis of the 1958 sample, the median lag is shown as falling from about thirty years in 1913 to twenty-two years in 1958, a decline of eight years. The basic reason for this sudden sharp decline in lag is that Soviet output in a number of industries came to exceed U.S. production on both sides of the Great Depression. Soviet performance over forty-five years is indicated as equivalent to U.S. performance over fifty-three. On the basis of the even smaller 1965 Plan sample of industries, the median lag is also shown as falling but by only two years between 1913 and 1958— from twenty-seven years to twenty-five years—with an additional "planned" fall of thirteen years between the 1958 and 1965 Plans.

The median lag in per capita output (Table 80) was fifty-six years in 1955, and fifty-two years in 1958. Equally precise calculations cannot be made for other benchmark dates because many per capita lags are so long they cannot be measured—U.S. statistics on physical output do not go back far enough to show output per capita as small as in the Soviet Union. Changes in per capita lags can, however, be measured for thirty-six industries over 1937–1955 and for twenty-nine industries over 1913–1955. The median of these changes is an increase of four years over 1937–1955 (with twenty-six out of the thirty-six industries showing an increase) and of fourteen years over 1913–1955 (with twenty-one out of the twenty-nine industries showing an increase). On the basis of these figures and the median lag of fifty-six years for 1955, the median per capita lag would be estimated as around forty-two years in 1913 and around fifty-two years in 1937. According to our earlier calculations from aggregative data (see footnote 27), the estimate for 1913 considerably understates the lag at that time, so that it is best to avoid pursuing the analysis of per capita lags any further.

The various summary statistics given so far reflect conditions in industries where growth has been deliberately retarded by Soviet authorities as well as in industries where growth has been promoted. The difference in performance between the neglected and favored sectors may be indicated in part by computing separate summary statistics for industries producing consumer goods, on the one hand, and for all other industries, on the other hand. This is done in Table 82, where the last twenty items in Table 79 are taken as consumer goods, and the first twenty-seven items as "other goods." The median lags for consumer goods

TABLE 82

SUMMARY STATISTICS ON SOVIET LAGS BROKEN DOWN BY INDUSTRIES
PRODUCING CONSUMER AND OTHER GOODS
(number of years)

| | Sample of 47 Industries | | | Energy-Producing Industry[b] |
	All	Consumer Goods[a]	Other Goods[a]	
	MEDIAN LAG[c]			
1913	29[d]	31[e]	26	42
1928	44[d]	46[e]	43	56
1937	36	38	36	46
1950	42	44	42	49
1955	35	37	34	48
	CHANGE IN MEDIAN LAG[c]			
1913–1928	+16	+15	+17	+14
1928–1937	−8	−8	−7	−10
1937–1950	+6	+6	+6	+3
1950–1955	−7	−7	−8	−1
1913–1955	+7	+6	+8	+6
1928–1955	−9	−9	−9	−8

SOURCE: Table 79 and technical note 9 of Appendix A.

[a] Consumer goods are taken as the last twenty items in Table 79; other goods, as the remaining twenty-seven.

[b] Excludes firewood. For reasons, see technical note 9 of Appendix A.

[c] For energy-producing industry, lag in aggregate output as measured in thermal units. All changes in median lag agree in direction with median changes in lags that can be calculated from Table 79.

[d] Midpoints of possible bounding limits (twenty-six and thirty-one for 1913, and forty-two and forty-seven for 1928) consistent with lags of imprecise length (lags with plus signs).

[e] Calculated from bounding limits (twenty-four and thirty-eight for 1913, and thirty-nine and fifty-three for 1928) consistent with lags of imprecise length.

are smaller in 1913 and larger in 1937 and 1955 than the median lags for other goods. That is to say, consumer goods have tended to grow more slowly relative to their American counterparts than other goods have. Despite this fact, the medians for nonconsumer goods do not differ significantly from those for all industries taken together.

Another line of evidence on this general issue leads to a similar conclusion. The production of energy may be taken as an indicator of industrial growth, particularly of growth in so-called "basic" industries. One way of estimating the production of energy is to translate the output of coal, petroleum, and so on into their energy content (in, say, British thermal units) and add the energy contents together. This has been done for U.S. and Soviet energy-producing industries to the extent permitted by available data (see Table A-27 and A-28 and Chart A-4). It will be seen (Table 82) that Soviet production of energy has lagged further behind U.S. production than is the case for our sample of forty-seven industries, but between 1913 and 1955 the lag increased by about the same number of years.[34]

We might next raise the question whether Soviet performance relative to the United States resembles Russian performance in the Tsarist

TABLE 83

LAG OF RUSSIA BEHIND UNITED STATES IN OUTPUT,
BENCHMARK DATES BETWEEN 1880 AND 1913, THIRTEEN INDUSTRIES[a]

	Lag (number of years)			Increase or Decrease (—) in Lag		
	1880	1900	1913	1880–1900	1900–1913	1880–1913
Iron ore	36+	21	27	−15+	6	−9+
Pig iron	36	22	29	−14	7	−7
Steel ingots	5	14	20	9	6	15
Copper	25	37	33	12	−4	8
Lead	67	92+	92	25+	−0+	25
Zinc	11	29	35	18	8	24
Coal	36	39	43	3	4	7
Crude petroleum	16	−1	14	−17	15	−2
Rails	22	31	40	9	9	18
Salt	−1	3	16	4	13	17
Raw sugar consumption	10+	24	22	b	−2	b
Cigarettes	−9	−10	−3	−1	7	6
Cotton consumption	32	24	29	−8	5	−3
Median	22	24	29	4	6	8

SOURCE: Appendixes B and E.
[a] Russian output covers Tsarist territory excluding Finland.
[b] Inadequate data to indicate whether lag increased or decreased.

period. Such information as could be gathered on this question is presented in Table 83, where Russian lags are computed for thirteen industries as of three benchmark dates: 1880, 1900, and 1913. As far as this very small sample of industries is concerned, there is a clear tendency for lags to increase. Russian growth in output over thirty-three years of the Tsarist period (1880–1913) is indicated as corresponding roughly

---

[34] If firewood is included as an energy source, the lag in energy production shows a decline over 1913–1955. It is doubtful that much weight should be placed on this last finding, however, since estimates of output of firewood in both the United States and the Soviet Union are necessarily crude and subject to wide margins of error (see the discussion in the text around Tables A-27 and A-28).

with U.S. growth over twenty-six earlier years (1858–1884), but this conclusion is based on too small a sample to be taken literally.[35]

Finally, we may note that Soviet lags have declined substantially over the Plan years taken alone. Since Soviet industry experienced virtually no growth in the aggregate between 1913 and 1928, the median lag in output increased by fifteen years between 1913 and 1928 (see Table 79). Beginning with 1928, the median lag decreased by nine years by 1955 and by twenty-two years by 1958. Soviet output of these industries attained in twenty-seven (or thirty) years a growth that required thirty-six (or fifty-two) years in the United States.

The question remains whether this more rapid growth since 1928 represents the establishment of a new trend, or whether it is in part explained by a process of catching up to an interrupted trend. No firm answer can yet be given to this question, but there is some relevant evidence that can be examined, namely, the performance of Soviet industries that have essentially come into existence during the period 1928–1955. If these new Soviet industries have also gained historical ground on their American counterparts, then there is good support for the belief that a new, more rapid trend of Soviet growth has been established. If not, there is less reason to believe so. The data so far available for fifteen new Soviet industries (Table 84) do not indicate a decline in median lag since 1932, at least through 1958. The Soviet lag has clearly decreased in only three of the fifteen industries: primary aluminum, electric motors, and margarine.

As evidence on the other side, it should be pointed out that Soviet authorities look forward to a much more rapid rate of industrial expansion in the future than has characterized the Soviet period as a whole. The planned goals for 1960, since abandoned, and for 1965 imply considerable ground-gaining on the United States in a large number of industries, in part because of an implied leap across our Great Depression in the case of many products. It remains to be seen to what extent Soviet authorities will be correct in their anticipations.

---

[35] The sample does not seem to be representative of conditions in 1913. We note from the sample of forty-seven industries in Table 79 that the median lag in Russian output within the interwar territory of the Soviet Union is calculated as twenty-nine years. When Russian output is taken within Tsarist territory, the median lag should be smaller, since Tsarist territory was larger than interwar Soviet territory. Contrary to this expectation, the median lag turns out to be the same (see Table 83). Unfortunately, there is no way of telling how this bias might affect the data on changes in median lag over the Tsarist period.

TABLE 84

LAG OF SOVIET UNION BEHIND UNITED STATES IN OUTPUT,
BENCHMARK DATES SINCE 1932, FIFTEEN NEW SOVIET INDUSTRIES

	Lag (number of years) as of						Increase or Decrease (−) in Lag	
	1932	1937	1940	1950	1955	1958	1932– 1955	1932– 1958
Primary aluminum	35	22	16	n.a.	n.a.	n.a.	n.a.	n.a.
Automobiles	30[a]	33	39	41	46	49	16	19
Trucks and buses	18	19	22	29	32	34	14	16
Tractors	15	20	33	32	30	19	15	4
Tractor-drawn plows	9	11	18	22	29	18	20	9
Tractor-drawn cultivators	3	1	11	12	16	14	13	11
Grain combines	6	−5	13	7	12	11	6	5
Diesel engines[b]	10	13	16	8	12	n.a.	2	n.a.
Electric motors[b]	15	19	22	6	9	4	−6	−11
Margarine	26	23	20	9	6	7[c]	−20	−19
Cheese	63+	68+	71+	81	75	n.a.	[d]	n.a.
Hosiery	42+	36	37	47	45	44	[d]	[d]
Phonographs	33+	22	32	40	35	n.a.	[d]	n.a.
Radios	11	14	17	26	26	26	15	15
Television sets	[e]	[e]	[e]	3	7	9	[e]	[e]
Median	17	20	21	24	28	18	14	9

SOURCE: Appendixes B and E.
[a] From 1933.
[b] Output measured in rated capacity, not simple units.
[c] From 1957.
[d] Insufficient data to indicate whether lag increased or decreased.
[e] Output negligible before 1950

CHAPTER 9

Summary

ANY summary of Soviet industrial performance must start with a few words on the difficulties of appraising it. The student of the Soviet economy takes his data from the official Soviet press, and therein lie unusual troubles. Some scholars may find it hard to believe that Soviet statistics are "really" worse than others, because every specialist in no matter what field quickly becomes convinced that no data could be as bad as those he is forced to work with. Why call the kettle black when it is probably no grayer than the pot?

Let us acknowledge at once that all statistics contain faults and errors. Let us also acknowledge that no government or other agency resists the temptation to stretch figures to its own account if it feels it can get away with it. Representative government, competitive scholarship, and free public discourse are the Western institutions that have counteracted error and misrepresentation in statistics, imperfectly to be sure but at least to an important degree.

The peculiar difficulties with Soviet statistics stem, in the first instance, from the system of authoritarian, centralized planning—from what has been called a "command economy." Published statistics come from only one source: the state. There are no independent sources to restrain each other or to be used as checks against each other, except to the extent that related figures published by different state agencies might not be fully coordinated before publication. Moreover, the suppliers of data to the central authorities—the economic and administrative units—have a stake in the figures they report, since their performance is judged on the basis of them. The Soviet statistical authorities do not hide their concern over the misreporting that results from this feature of the economic system.

A second set of difficulties stems from the crusading nature of Soviet communism. Statistics are grist for the propaganda mill. The drive to proselyte prevents Soviet leaders from viewing and dispensing facts in a passive and detached manner.

For both broad reasons, Soviet statistics are selective and of varying reliability and ambiguity. The policy of selectivity has two rather opposing results as far as statistics on physical output are concerned. On the one hand, some areas of poor performance are shielded from view, being underrepresented in published data. On the other hand, some of the

283

more rapidly expanding economic activities associated with the military sector are also not reported on. It is impossible to determine the net bias of the sample of published data—whether there is, on this count, a net over- or understatement of growth.[1]

A few broad generalizations can be made about the reliability of the published statistics. In the first place, absolute output is probably overstated in the case of most industries, particularly for the years within the Plan period, though the degree of overstatement cannot be determined. In the second place, growth in output is also probably overstated relative to a prerevolutionary or an early Soviet base, but not necessarily over other parts of the Soviet period. Over some of the latter years growth may be overstated, over others understated, and over still others more or less accurately reported. This will vary from industry to industry and from one situation to another.

Whatever the faults of data on output of individual industries, they are more reliable than official aggregative measures, such as the official Soviet index of industrial production. Although the details underlying this index have not been made public, Western specialists are generally agreed that, from what they know about the construction and behavior of the index, it heavily exaggerates industrial growth, though apparently decreasingly so in recent years.

There are other factors in addition to the defects in basic statistics that make it difficult to construct meaningful measures of aggregate industrial production. Soviet prices generally do not accurately reflect relative costs of production; the industrial structure has shifted radically over short periods of time and has increasingly favored sectors where growth is most easily achieved; growth rates have differed widely from sector to sector; growth has been interrupted at critical points by major disturbances; and so on. Finally, quantitative growth has not been accompanied by the general improvement in quality that has characterized industrial development in most Western countries.

These considerations make it difficult to summarize Soviet industrial performance in terms of mere numbers. But a summary is useful and necessary, and it cannot be fully qualified at every point without turning it into the voluminous report it is supposed to summarize. In what follows, the necessary qualifications are intended to be implicit throughout, and they should be kept in mind to dull the edge of deceptively sharp figures.

---

[1] These brief comments apply to the condition of economic statistics since 1956. Between 1938 and 1956, statistics on physical output of individual industries were not published at all in the Soviet Union, with a few minor exceptions.

Soviet Industrial Growth

GROWTH IN OUTPUT

Soviet industrial output multiplied more than six times over the period 1913–1955. Performance varied widely among sectors, with output multiplying fifty-eight times in the case of machinery and equipment (including military products), nine times in the case of intermediate industrial products, but only three times in the case of consumer goods. The average annual growth rate was 4.4 per cent for industry as a whole, 10.1 per cent for machinery and equipment, 5.5 per cent for intermediate industrial products, and 2.6 per cent for consumer goods.

Some of this growth is attributable to the territorial expansion that took place during and after World War II. We have estimated that the acquired territories added about 11 per cent to industrial output, and, if we suppose that this relation would also have held true in 1955, the average annual growth rate for all industry over the Soviet period would have to be reduced from 4.4 to 4.1 per cent to eliminate the gains from territorial expansion. The assumptions underlying such an adjustment are, of course, somewhat arbitrary.

The dispersal of growth trends (unadjusted for territorial expansion) may be seen more clearly by examining a finer breakdown of industries. For a sample of seventy industries, growth rates ranged from an average annual decline of 0.9 per cent to an average annual increase of 16.8 per cent; the middle half of these growth rates ranged between increases of 2.5 and 8.5 per cent. The median was 5.3 per cent, which is higher than the weighted average of 4.4 per cent shown by the production index. Industries producing consumer goods dominate a distinct, lower region of growth and are essentially confined to it, while other industries are concentrated about a higher region.

The over-all growth rate is lower for the Soviet period than for the last forty-odd years of the Tsarist period, when the growth rate was 5.3 per cent a year according to our index. Although the latter is based on a weak foundation of data and might have come out differently if better data had been available, one may allow for substantial relative over-statement of Tsarist growth, presuming all the error in that direction, and still conclude that it was faster than growth over the entire Soviet period. As to individual industries, higher growth rates in the one period are not systematically related with either higher or lower growth rates in the other. Here again, the sample is small, covering only twenty-three industries, and conclusions must therefore be tempered.

There has been a rather striking inverse relation between the rapidity of growth in an industry over the Soviet period and its "stage of development" at the beginning of the period. For a sample of forty-eight industries, those whose outputs were the smallest relative to the United States in 1913 have shown a strong tendency to grow the fastest. The tendency is even more pronounced when the Plan period is considered by itself, the stage of development in this case being measured as of 1928 and the growth over 1928–1955. A growth pattern of this sort is to be expected of any country undergoing rapid industrialization, but in the Soviet case the evidence suggests it has been accentuated by planned design, an effort to "overcome and surpass the leading capitalist economies."

Growth has varied widely not only among industries, but also over different spans of time. The early years were marked by disorder, war, and chaos, so that measurable industrial output dropped by 80 per cent between 1913 and 1920. By 1927 or 1928, industrial output had roughly recovered to its 1913 level in quantitative terms, though a general deterioration in the quality of industrial goods over this period meant that the recovery was less complete. Moreover, it was uneven even if no allowance is made for deterioration in quality: the 1913 level of output was not achieved in the case of consumer goods, while it was somewhat exceeded in the case of all other products.

With the institution of the First Five Year Plan at the end of 1928, growth accelerated rapidly and generally except in consumer goods. The acceleration continued through the Second Five Year Plan and extended into consumer goods. Against a background of political purges and partial wartime mobilization, the pace of industrial growth slackened in the succeeding three years of the short-lived Third Five Year Plan, and such growth as took place may be attributed to territorial expansion.

World War II brought with it a sharp decline in output—offset in large part by Lend-Lease shipments—and heavy losses in manpower and capital. Recovery was swift in the Fourth Five Year Plan, being aided by collection of reparations and other economic policies in Eastern Europe, so that the prewar level of industrial output was apparently regained by 1948 or 1949. Rapid growth was maintained through the Fifth Five Year Plan, where our study largely ends. Industrial output about doubled between 1940 and 1955. The annual growth rate has declined somewhat since 1955 to a level slightly above the average for 1928–1955.

Over the Plan period (1928–1955) the average annual rate of growth was 6.9 per cent for all industry (6.5 per cent if territorial gains are excluded), 8.4 per cent for intermediate industrial products, 14.7 per cent for machinery and equipment, and 4.2 per cent for consumer goods. The growth rate has tended to slow down or retard: for all industry, it was 9.9 per cent a year over 1928–1940 (8.9 per cent if territorial gains are excluded) and 4.6 per cent over 1940–1955; or, if the war years are removed from consideration, it was 12.1 per cent a year for 1928–1937, 9.6 per cent for 1950–1955, and 7.1 per cent for 1955–1958. There is a similar retardation in growth for each of the categories of intermediate industrial products, machinery, and consumer goods.

As in other countries, retardation in growth has been general for individual industries, narrowly defined. The available evidence indicates that most industries experienced a slower growth over the Soviet period than over the late Tsarist period, and over the later Soviet years than over the earlier ones. Moreover, most of the industries with retardation in growth from the Tsarist to the Soviet period also had retardation within the latter.

GROWTH IN OUTPUT AND EMPLOYMENT

The growth in industrial output has been accompanied by a rapid expansion of the industrial labor force. The number of persons engaged in Soviet industry, expressed in full-time equivalents, multiplied 3.3 times between 1913 and 1955; the number of man-hours, 2.8 times. Thus 46 to 54 per cent of the growth in output may be attributed to expanded employment and the remaining fraction to increased labor productivity. Put another way, man-hours (or persons engaged) increased at an average annual rate of 2.5 (or 2.9) per cent, while labor productivity increased at an average annual rate of only 1.9 (or 1.5) per cent. The growth in output per person engaged ranged from 0.7 per cent a year for wood construction materials to 4.3 per cent a year for electricity.

Growth in labor productivity, as we have measured it, has fluctuated from period to period, and it is not clear whether there has been any trend toward either retardation or acceleration. Employment in man-hours apparently grew slower than output between 1913 and 1928, 1928 and 1937, and 1950 and 1955; it apparently grew faster between 1937 and 1950, a period of radical structural change in industry. Persons engaged also outpaced output over 1928–1933, another period of radical change, but otherwise grew slower than output. While the growth rate in output per man-hour shows some decline between 1913–1928 and

287

1928–1955 and between 1928–1940 and 1940–1955, it shows a sharp increase between 1928–1937 and 1950–1955.

GROWTH IN OUTPUT AND POPULATION

While industrial employment was multiplying 3.3 times between 1913 and 1955, population multiplied only 1.4 times. Expansion of the industrial labor force was achieved, particularly in the earlier phase of industrialization, by drawing upon a large supply of underutilized labor, attached primarily to agriculture. It follows that growth in industrial output has been more rapid per head of population than per worker: 3.5 per cent a year compared with 1.5 per cent.

Soviet demographic statistics are sketchy and subject to many doubts, so that it is particularly difficult to say anything with confidence about fluctuations in per capita output. According to Soviet data as modified and interpreted by Western scholars, population within Soviet boundaries grew at an average annual rate of 0.6 per cent over 1913–1928, 1.0 per cent over 1928–1937, 6.4 per cent over 1937–1940 (because of territorial expansion), −0.9 per cent over 1940–1950 (because of war and its aftermath), and 1.7 per cent over 1950–1955. Despite a rather erratic relationship between growth in population and industrial output over different spans of years, growth rates have tended to move in the same direction for both total and per capita output. Thus the average annual growth in per capita output rose from −0.5 per cent over 1913–1928 to 5.8 per cent over 1928–1955; within the Plan periods, it fell from 7.4 per cent over 1928–1940 to 4.6 per cent over 1940–1955, or from 11.0 per cent over 1928–1937 to 7.8 per cent over 1950–1955.

Industrial Growth Compared: Soviet Union and United States

CONTEMPORANEOUS GROWTH

Over concurrent periods, industrial output has typically grown faster percentagewise in the Soviet Union than in the United States. This was also true of Russian industry in the late Tsarist period: Russian growth over 1870–1913 was at the average annual rate of 5.3 per cent compared with U.S. growth at 5.1 per cent. The differential was similar over 1913–1955, with growth at 4.1 per cent a year in the Soviet Union, excluding territorial gains, and 3.8 per cent in the United States. At the same time, the absolute growth in industrial production has been much smaller in the Soviet Union than in the United States. Measured in 1954 dollars, the value added of industry rose by about $30 billion in the Soviet Union over this period but by $115 to $120 billion in the United

States. Percentagewise, however, Soviet growth including territorial gains has exceeded U.S. growth in all major sections of industry except for food and allied products. With territorial gains eliminated, Soviet growth was probably also slower—or no faster—than U.S. growth in the cases of chemicals and textiles and allied products.

Over 1913–1928, Soviet output grew at 0.1 per cent a year, with no allowance for deterioration in quality, while U.S. output grew at 3.7 per cent. The differential swung sharply in the other direction over 1928–1955, when growth was at the rate of 6.5 per cent a year in the Soviet Union and 3.8 per cent in the United States. Within the latter period comparative performance showed the same kind of shift: over 1928–1940, the Soviet growth rate was 8.9 per cent a year (territorial gains excluded) compared with the U.S. growth rate of 1.8 per cent; over 1940–1955, on the other hand, the Soviet rate was 4.6 per cent compared with 5.4 per cent. Over 1950–1955, however, the Soviet rate of 9.6 per cent substantially exceeded the U.S. rate of 5.3 per cent. In the few years since 1955, growth has continued to be much faster in the Soviet Union—7.1 per cent a year over 1955–1958—than in the United States—2.2 per cent a year over 1955–1959. It is doubtful, however, that either of these rates has much long-term significance.

Measured percentage growth in output has retarded in both countries between the two periods of forty-odd years before and after the second decade of the twentieth century. Within the more recent long period, measured growth apparently also retarded in the Soviet Union but not in the United States.

Population has generally grown more slowly in Russia and the Soviet Union than in the United States, so that comparative growth in per capita output favors the Soviet Union (or Russia) more than comparative growth in total output. On the other hand, industrial employment has grown more rapidly in the Soviet Union than in the United States: over 1913–1955, man-hours multiplied 2.8 as compared with 1.5 times; persons engaged, 3.3 as compared with 2.0 times. As a consequence, output per unit of labor—and, on the basis of such evidence as is available, output per unit of combined labor and capital—grew faster in the United States than in the Soviet Union over all periods compared except 1928–1937 and 1950–1955. The respective growth rates over 1913–1955 were 2.8 and 1.9 per cent a year. The same generalization applies, at least on a man-hour basis, to all major sectors of industry except metals and machinery and allied products. In the United States, improvement in output per man-hour accounted for 69 per cent of the multiplication in output over 1913–1955; in the Soviet Union, for 54 per cent. The evidence on possible long-term drifts in the growth rate of labor productivity is ambiguous in the case of both countries.

Compared with the United States, a larger fraction of Soviet industrial employment—and, almost certainly, production—has been concentrated in sectors of industry where labor productivity—and probably total resource productivity—has been growing faster than the average. Consequently, measured growth in output is biased upward on this score in the Soviet Union relative to the United States. Had the Soviet path of expansion more nearly represented the U.S. path in this respect, the Soviet production index would have shown a slower rise than it does.

Estimated in current dollars, the value added of Soviet industry rose from about 14 per cent of the U.S. level in 1913 and 9 per cent in 1928 to about 23 per cent in 1955; estimated in current rubles, from about 11 and 6 per cent to about 20 per cent. These estimates for 1955, even when allowance is made for possible error (no less likely upward than downward), are considerably lower than the conventional Western estimate of 33 per cent, which has apparently been based on industry-by-industry comparisons of physical output ratios. Such an estimate will almost certainly exaggerate the comparative level of Soviet output since industry embraces a much smaller range of products in the Soviet Union than in the United States.

While the relative gap in production has been narrowing between the two countries, the absolute gap has been widening. Measured in 1954 dollars, the value added of industry was $25 to $30 billion larger in the United States than in the Soviet Union in 1913, $50 to $55 billion larger in 1928, and $115 billion larger in 1955.

The Soviet value of conventional military products amounted to more than 70 per cent of the U.S. level in 1955 when estimated in current dollars. The value of conventional military products accounted for more than a quarter of the value added of industry in the Soviet Union and for less than a tenth in the United States, all magnitudes again being expressed in dollar terms. It goes without saying that these estimates for the Soviet Union are subject to an even wider range of error than normally (probably upward), since they have been made by roundabout procedures.

Soviet value added per head of population, evaluated in dollars, rose from about 10 per cent of the U.S. level in 1913 and 7 per cent in 1928 to about 18 per cent in 1955. On the other hand, value added per man-hour employed fell from about 24 per cent in 1913 and 22 per cent in 1928 to about 20 per cent in 1955. In all cases the fractions based on evaluations in rubles are smaller but move in the same directions.

COMPARABLE GROWTH

While study of Soviet and U.S. growth over concurrent periods is of interest in its own right and particularly in suggesting the course of events in the immediate future, it does not provide an adequate basis for appraising the growth-generating efficiency of the two economic systems. For this purpose, an attempt must be made to analyze performance over periods in which technological conditions and attained levels of production relative to the resource potential are the same in the two countries. Unfortunately, we cannot standardize both factors simultaneously in historical study: to set the level of production equal—we take the resource potentials as roughly equivalent in the two countries—is to project study back into a period for the United States in which available technology was substantially inferior to that of a "comparable" period for the Soviet Union. Nevertheless, this is the best we can do, and at least we know that the comparison favors the Soviet Union.

On the average and roughly speaking, the aggregate level of industrial production was about the same in the United States of 1875 and the Soviet Union of 1913 or 1928. In the United States, production grew at an average rate of 5.1 per cent a year over 1875–1917 and 5.5 per cent over 1875–1902; in the Soviet Union, at 4.1 per cent over 1913–1955 and 6.5 per cent over 1928–1955, territorial gains excluded. Hence, despite the technological differential in favor of the Soviet Union, U.S. output grew faster over the longer periods compared; on the other hand, it grew slower over the shorter periods, though not perhaps beyond what would be expected in view of the technological differential. Over even shorter periods that leave out the worst years of Soviet performance, growth has also been faster in the Soviet Union than over comparable U.S. periods. For example, the average annual growth rate was 8.9 per cent in the Soviet Union over 1928–1940, compared with 6.7 per cent in the United States over 1875–1887.

In the case of growth in output per head of population, the differential has been more favorable to the Soviet Union, so that Soviet growth exceeds U.S. growth in all comparable periods studied. It is, however, doubtful that this means much from the point of view of comparative economic performance, since population growth has not conditioned—or responded to—industrial growth to the same extent in the Soviet Union as in the United States.

Comparisons of this sort cannot be made for growth in labor productivity, because sufficient data are not available for the earlier periods of

U.S. history. On the basis of evidence for concurrent periods already reviewed, it would seem unlikely that Soviet industry has outperformed U.S. industry of the latter part of the nineteenth century in this respect.

Concluding Remarks

Soviet industrial growth has been impressive. In volume of output alone—no account being taken of human and resource cost, product mix, or the use made of products—Soviet percentage growth has exceeded U.S. growth over contemporary periods, though not over comparable ones. If the U.S. record of growth in industrial output has been impressive in and of itself, without regard for the important consideration of how it has been accomplished, then so has the Soviet record been, in the same limited sense.

At the same time, the Soviet record is neither unprecedented nor inexplicable. As noted, it has been at least matched in the United States under more or less comparable basic conditioning factors, except the economic system; it is being exceeded now by a number of countries in the West, such as Japan, Taiwan, West Germany, and Greece, all of which have experienced a more rapid rate of growth since 1950 than the Soviet Union. Since 1953 it has been roughly matched by France and Italy.

The explanation for the Soviet record lies in the unity of purpose and practice on the part of the rulers—enhancement of state power—and in their selective mobilization of resources—systematic favoring of industry over other sectors and of investment over consumption, including leisure. The cost has been heavy, in terms of resources expended as well as human suffering. The amount of output generated per unit of labor is a fraction of that characterizing industry in the United States, and it has become a progressively smaller fraction despite the fact that industrial capital has apparently grown faster in the Soviet Union than in the United States.

This may all change in the future. We can expect a further gaining on the United States in relative level of industrial output over the years immediately in view, though this need not lead to a reducing of the absolute gap or to an overtaking. There may well be gains in other respects as well. In any case, we cannot know the future from the course of the past. The most we can ask of history is some perspective, some background, against which we can more meaningfully view the unfolding present and interpret the receding past. It is this background that we have tried to sketch here, in a book now at an end.

APPENDIXES

NOTE: In these appendixes the sources are cited by an italicized numbering code followed by the page number. The sources are arranged by that code in the bibliography at the end of the book. In the case of articles, citations are given by an italicized number identifying the periodical or newspaper, followed by the year, issue, and page number.

APPENDIX A

Technical Notes

Technical Note 1 (Chapter 2):
Indicators of the Quality of Cotton Fabrics

FINENESS OF YARN

Cotton yarn is classified by "yarn number," which indicates the length of yarn that weighs a specified amount. Hence the finer the yarn, the higher the yarn number. In the Soviet Union, a metric yarn number is used, specifying the number of meters of yarn weighing one gram. In the United States and the United Kingdom, the yarn number used specifies the number of hanks (each 840 yards long) that weigh a pound. The American or British count is multiplied by 1.6933 in order to translate it into an equivalent Soviet count. According to various Soviet sources, the average yarn number has run as follows in the Soviet Union:

1910	47.1	1939	41.5
1913	52	1940	38.9
1928	48	1946	32.7
1930	47.5	1950	38.5
1931	45.5	1951	39.0
1932	41.6	1952	39.1
1933	39.9	1953	39.2
1934	39.6	1954	39.3
1935	40.9	1955	39.5
1936	43.4		
1937	40.6		

SOURCE: 1910: *96*, 137; 1913, 1939: *331*, 1939, No. 5, 2; 1928: *370*, 1929, No. 12, 36; 1930–1931, 1935–1936: *363*, 1938, No. 1, 77; 1932–1934: *222*, 198; 1937: *339*, 1940, No. 11–12, 14; 1940: *394*, 1947, No. 4; 1946: *394*, 1952, No. 11, 2; 1950–1955: *180*, 338. Alternative data are given as follows: 40 for 1935 in *363*, 1937, No. 2, 67; 39.3 for 1937 in *363*, 1940, No. 7, 59; 32.8 for 1946 in *394*, 1947, No. 4.

Average yarn numbers for the United States and the United Kingdom can be derived from frequency distributions of classes of yarn numbers by weight.[1] For the United States, the average yarn number in metric units was around 39 in 1939 and 37 in 1947; for the United Kingdom,

[1] See, e.g., *609*, 1947, II, 161, 303; *600*, 159; and *648*, 137.

around 51 in 1937 and 48 in 1947. Rostas gives slightly lower figures for both countries for 1937,[2] but his average numbers do not seem to be consistent with the mentioned frequency distributions, at least when yarns made from waste are excluded.

CLOSENESS OF WEAVE

Closeness of weave may be measured by "thread count," which is the number of threads (strands of yarn) contained in both the warp and the woof of a specified area of fabric. An average thread count may be derived by multiplying the average yarn number by the average density of the fabric. For instance, the average yarn number for Russian fabrics was 52 meters per gram in 1913, and the average density was about 174 grams per square meter; hence there were about 9,048 threads (each a meter long) per square meter, or about 90.5 per square centimeter, or about 230 per square inch.

According to various Soviet sources, the average density of cotton fabrics was as follows:

	Grams per Linear Meter	Grams per Square Meter
1913	120.3	174
1927/28	107.4	156
1930	100.2	145
1931	103.3	150
1932	106.6	154
1933	107.1	155
1934	114.0	165
1940	121.9	177
1946	135.5	196
1950	123	178
1951	123	178
1952	123	178
1953	125	181
1954	126	183
1955	127	184

SOURCE: 1913: *567*, Part 1, series 1208.6, col. 1, and series 1205.1, col. 4; 1927/28: *323*, 1929, No. 7–8, 34; 1930–1934: *215*, 206; 1940, 1946: *394*, 1947, No. 4, 7; 1950–1955: *180*, 338. To convert from linear to square meters, average width of fabrics taken as 69 cm (see *410*, 1956, No. 7, 43, and *394*, 1950, No. 7, 9).

[2] *648*, 131.

These data, taken along with those in the preceding section giving average yarn numbers, imply the following thread counts (number of threads per square centimeter):

1913	90.5	1933	62.0	1951	67.6
1928	74.9	1934	66.0	1952	69.6
1930	69.6	1940	69.0	1953	71.0
1931	69.0	1946	64.7	1954	71.9
1932	64.7	1950	68.5	1955	72.7

Average thread counts can be similarly estimated for the United States and the United Kingdom. There are, however, substantial differences in estimates based on alternative measures of the weight of fabrics. Thus, for 1939 the average density of American fabric is about 154 grams per square meter on the basis of the recorded weight of broad woven goods, and about 171 grams per square meter on the basis of the weight of cotton yarns produced; for 1947, the average density is about 181 and 164, respectively.[3] Similarly, for 1937 the average density of British cloth is about 135 grams per square meter on the basis of the weight of yarn consumed, and about 196 on the basis of the weight of yarn produced; for 1947 the average density is about 174 and 242, respectively[4] (data for 1947 converted to square measure on the basis of the average width of cloth in 1937, which may be derived from data in Rostas).[5]

Using these data and the average yarn numbers for the preceding section, we may derive the following estimates of average thread counts for the United States and the United Kingdom (number of threads per square centimeter):

United States		*United Kingdom*	
1939	60 to 67	1937	69 to 100
1947	61 to 67	1947	84 to 116

OTHER CHARACTERISTICS OF QUALITY

The number of constructions of cotton cloth fell from 1,300 in the pre-revolutionary period to 260 in 1929/30, rising to 498 in 1949.[6] In an investigation of 183 enterprises conducted in 1955, it was found that 494

[3] *609*, 1947, II, 161 ff.
[4] *600*, 159 f.
[5] *648*, 130.
[6] *323*, 1929, No. 9, 18, and 1930, No. 3; and *265*, II, 79 ff.

constructions of gray goods were being produced, that 70 of these accounted for 77 per cent and 4 (*mitkal'*, *biaz*, sateen, and gauze) for 54 per cent of total production. It was also found that 68 counts of yarn were produced, that fewer than 300 tons were produced for each of 20 counts and fewer than 50 tons for each of an additional 8 counts, and that 95 per cent of total production was accounted for by 15 counts.[7]

In the United States about 4,000 constructions of gray goods have been produced from time to time and about 2,500 regularly.[8] There are

TABLE A-1

FREQUENCY DISTRIBUTIONS OF GROWTH RATES FOR FIXED AND
TOTAL SAMPLES OF SOVIET INDUSTRIES, 1913–1955 AND 1928–1955

| | NUMBER OF INDUSTRIES | | | | | |
| | *Fixed Sample* | | | *Total Sample* | | |
AVERAGE ANNUAL GROWTH RATE[a] (PER CENT)	Consumer Goods	All Others	Total	Consumer Goods	All Others	Total
			1913–1955			
−1 to 1	4	1	5	4	3	7
1 to 3	11	3	14	12	4	16
3 to 5	6	8	14	9	14	23
5 to 7	2	14	16	4	16	20
7 to 9	4	3	7	4	7	11
9 to 11		3	3		4	4
11 to 13		5	5	1	6	7
13 to 15		3	3		4	4
15 to 17	1	2	3	1	2	3
17 to 19					1	1
Totals	28	42	70	35	61	96
			1928–1955			
−3 to −1	1		1	1		1
−1 to 1					3	3
1 to 3	7	1	8	7	4	11
3 to 5	9	3	12	12	4	16
5 to 7	4	6	10	7	9	16
7 to 9		8	8		16	16
9 to 11	1	10	11	2	12	14
11 to 13	4	2	6	5	5	10
13 to 15	1	3	4	1	9	10
15 to 17		2	2	1	2	3
17 to 19		3	3		4	4
19 to 21		3	3		6	6
21 and over	1		1	1	6	7
Totals	28	31	69	37	80	117

[a] Calculated from output in terminal years by the compound interest formula.

[7] *394*, 1956, No. 1, 6 ff.
[8] *599*, 487–548.

about 150 counts of yarn, 30 to 40 accounting for 95 per cent of output in terms of weight.[9]

Technical Note 2 (Chapter 4):
The Fixed Sample of Seventy Soviet Industries

In Table A-1, the frequency distributions of growth rates over the periods 1913–1955 and 1928–1955 are compared for the fixed sample of industries used in our analysis of growth trends (see Table 8) and for the total sample of industries with the necessary data in Appendix B. The distributions for the fixed and total samples are similar in structure. The major concentrations of industries (modes) tend to occur at lower class intervals for the total than for the fixed sample, but the median growth rates are almost the same. Thus, for 1913–1955, the median growth rates are 5.3 and 5.2 per cent for the fixed and total samples, respectively; for 1928–1955, 8.0 and 8.8 per cent. In brief, the fixed sample seems to be an adequate representation, for the purposes of our analysis, of the total sample at our disposal.

Estimated 1928 value added for sixty-seven of the seventy industries is given in Table A-2. In general, value added applies only to the most advanced stage of fabrication for each relevant item reported separately in Soviet statistics. In the following cases, value added has been estimated for all stages of fabrication within the bounds of industry: soda ash, caustic soda, sulfuric acid, motor vehicle tires, cement, construction gypsum, construction lime, rails, window glass, and rubber footwear. The value added for these sixty-seven industries, estimated in this way, amounts to 73 per cent of the total value added for Soviet industry (excluding repair shops) in 1927/28 (see Table A-43).

Growth trends for the seventy industries are pictured in Chart A-1.

Technical Note 3 (Chapters 5–7):
NBER Indexes of Soviet Industrial Production

GENERAL DESCRIPTION OF METHODS OF CONSTRUCTION

The production indexes constructed in this study are described in some detail in Chapter 5, and these notes are intended merely to fill in minor technical details. The products included in the different indexes are given in Tables D-10 and D-11; the weights, in Tables D-8 and D-9.

In the case of industrial materials and finished civilian products, the production index is constructed for each year by multiplying the output of each product by its unit value (net of the cost of nonindustrial materials

---

[9] *614*, 18, and *609*, 1939, 1947, and 1954.

TABLE A-2

Estimated Value Added for Fixed Sample of Soviet Industries, 1928[a]
(million rubles)

Code		Value Added	Code		Value Added
101	Pig iron	77.4	1101	Steam boilers	4.8
102	Rolled steel	73.7	1103	Steam turbines	0.6
103	Steel ingots	135.7	1105	Diesel engines	3.9
704	Iron ore	27.6	1110	Power transformers	4.0
202	Copper	16.5	1210	Machine tools	2.7
203	Lead	0.9	1214	Looms	1.7
204	Zinc	0.9	1501	Flour	511.5
301	Electric power	274.4	1502	Macaroni	20.8
303.1	Coke	28.0	1503	Butter	61.0
305	Crude petroleum	272.9	1504	Vegetable oil	71.9
306	Natural gas	14.4	1506	Meat	120.7
308	Peat	31.1	1507	Fish catch	194.2
310	Coal	295.5	1508	Soap	44.8
401	Soda ash[b]	15.9	1509	Salt	11.7
402	Caustic soda[b]	7.1	1510	Raw sugar consumption	210.8
404	Sulfuric acid[b]	21.5	1511	Starch and syrup	9.2
405	Mineral fertilizer	2.8	1513	Canned food	12.2
410	Red lead	1.7	1514	Beer	52.2
412	Synthetic dyes	10.7	1515	Cigarettes	61.2
416	Paper	58.0	1516	Low-grade tobacco	14.3
418	Motor vehicle tires[b]	7.1	1517	Matches	20.6
501	Red bricks	64.4	1518	Vodka	74.9
506	Cement[b]	61.0	601	Crude alcohol	34.0
507	Construction gypsum[b]	2.6	1601	Boots and shoes	401.0
508	Construction lime[b]	8.1	1602	Rubber footwear[b]	112.5
509	Industrial timber hauled	577.0	1604	Cotton fabrics	909.6
510	Lumber	136.2	1607	Linen fabrics	102.3
513	Roll roofing	4.4	1609.1	Pure silk fabrics[c]	13.3
516	Asbestos shingles	3.6	1609.2	Rayon and mixed fabrics[c]	29.6
518	Rails[b]	4.4	1611	Woolen and worsted fabrics	217.1
519	Window glass[a]	90.6	1614	Felt footwear	81.2
904	Steam locomotives	17.9	1701	Bicycles	0.9
905	RR freight cars	24.6	1707	Household sewing machines	4.5
906	RR passenger cars	3.6			
				Total, 67 industries	5,787.8

Note: Unless otherwise noted, value added is taken from Table D-9, prorated within groups wherever necessary by value of output computed from data in Tables B-2 and D-8.

[a] Includes 67 of the 70 industries. Clocks and watches, roofing tiles, and sausages are not included for lack of data.

[b] Output in Table B–2 times unit value in Table D–8.

[c] Value added for silk and rayon fabrics prorated by value of output. Outputs from Table B–2; unit value of pure silk fabrics taken as 5 rubles per meter from 1913 prices (2 rubles, as given in *375*, 1933, No. 2) and 1927/28 price index for silk products (251 on 1913 = 100, from *315*, 1928, September, 23 f); unit value of rayon and mixed fabrics from price of cotton fabrics and price ratio of rayon yarn to cotton yarn.

CHART A-I
Physical Output Trends of Fixed Sample of Seventy Soviet Industries

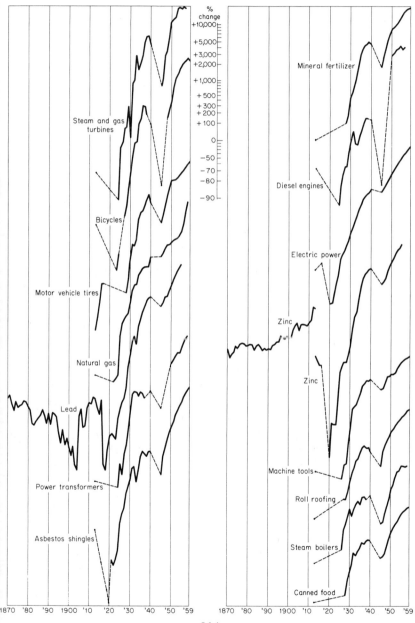

CHART A-I (continued)

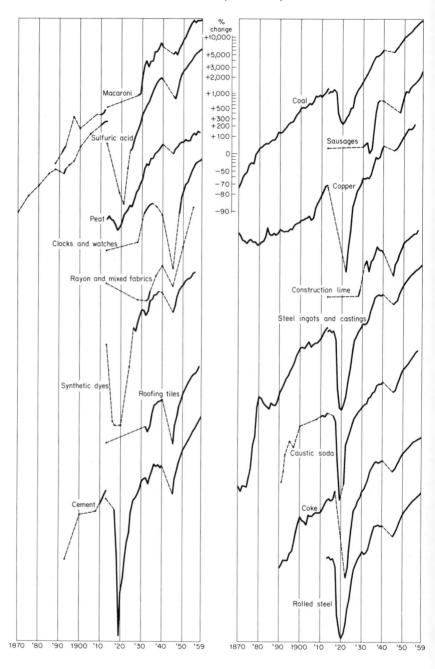

CHART A-I (continued)

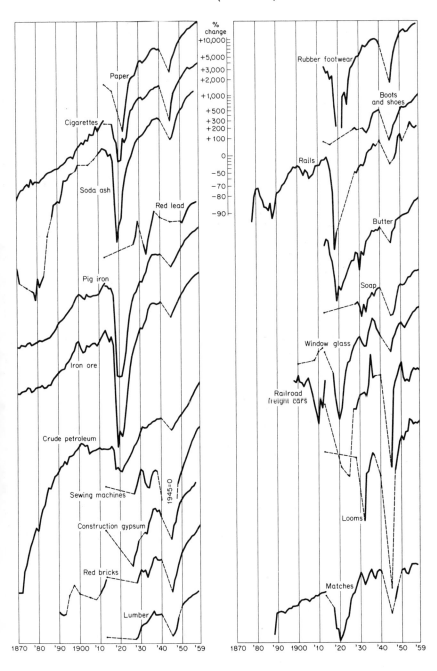

CHART A-1 (concluded)

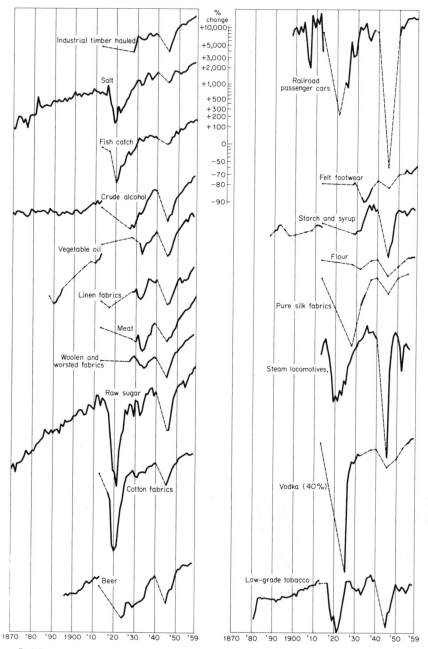

Industrial timber hauled

Salt

Fish catch

Crude alcohol

Vegetable oil

Linen fabrics

Meat

Woolen and worsted fabrics

Raw sugar

Cotton fabrics

Beer

Railroad passenger cars

Felt footwear

Starch and syrup

Flour

Pure silk fabrics

Steam locomotives,

Vodka (40%)

Low-grade tobacco

%
change
+10,000
+5,000
+3,000
+2,000
+1,000
+500
+300
+200
+100
0
-50
-70
-80
-90

1870 '80 '90 1900 '10 '20 '30 '40 '50 '59   1870 '80 '90 1900 '10 '20 '30 '40 '50 '59

Dash line connects nonconsecutive years.
Source: Tables B-1 and B-2. It should be noted that some data are indirectly estimated.

consumed) and by summing the resulting values. The sum for any one year is simply aggregate production in that year valued in the prices (net unit values) of the weight-base year. These aggregate values in constant prices are given in tables in Appendix D. For any one index (as industrial materials, 1928 weights), the aggregate values in constant prices may be converted into index numbers by dividing all values by the value for a chosen base year (as 1913). For example, the index numbers in columns 1–3 and 5–6 of Table 16 are derived from aggregate values in constant prices in Tables D-1 and D-2.

The indexes for all civilian products are constructed in a more complicated manner, with two stages of weighting. To be specific, we may illustrate by the index with 1928 weights. As basic weights we have used value-added data for 1927/28 (for brevity, expressed as 1928) as derived from Soviet censuses and annual surveys of industry for 1926/27, 1927/28, and 1928/29 (see Table C-2 and D-9). Wherever value added is available for individual products, outputs are weighted by value added per unit of output in 1928, in the manner already described. In many cases these value-added data are available only for groups of products, and it is therefore necessary to construct subindexes for these groups (in the form of index numbers with 1928 as unity) on the basis of other weights. The weights used are generally estimates of value added per unit of output in 1928, at least to the extent of excluding the estimated cost of nonindustrial materials consumed in the process of fabrication. The subindexes are incorporated into the over-all index and its components by weighting each (expressed in ratio form) by the value added attributable to it. The indexes, in the form of aggregate values in 1928 prices, are given in Table D-3.

For example, value added is available for the product group consisting of pig iron, rolled steel, and steel ingots and castings, but not for each product separately. An index is constructed for this product group by weighting outputs of each component product by its estimated value added per unit in 1928. As an example, value added for a ton of steel ingots and castings is estimated as the value of a ton of ingots and castings minus the value of a ton of pig iron. The resulting index is translated into index numbers with a 1928 comparison base. Put in ratio form, the index numbers read 1.000 for 1928, 1.498 for 1932, 4.135 for 1937, and so on. This amounts to setting 1928 combined output for the group as the unit of production. The index numbers are, therefore, multiplied by the 1928 value added for the group (286.8 million rubles) to find the aggregate values for the group in 1928 prices.

The index for all civilian products with 1955 weights is constructed in the same manner, except that in this case the basic weights are employment rather than value-added data. This index and its components are given only in the form of index numbers (see Table D-4), since aggregate production expressed in terms of constant employment factors has little economic significance.

ESTIMATES OF MISSING OUTPUT DATA

The output series in Appendix B contain a number of estimates and adjustments made to fill in important gaps in Soviet statistics. In general we have made estimates only where the linkage to known data is reasonably simple and direct. We wish to call attention here to some special estimates that were made to fill in minor gaps in incomplete series so that they might be incorporated into our indexes.

It has not been unusual for Soviet statistical sources to cease publishing output data for a product whose output is rather steadily declining. Thus, for horse-drawn agricultural implements, whose output tended to reach a peak in the late 1920's and early 1930's, output series generally end in the 1930's. Since these implements accounted for most of the production of agricultural equipment in those years, an index excluding them would seriously exaggerate growth of production in this area. We have, therefore, extended these series through the benchmark years, with the general assumption that output reached the zero level by 1940 and later years (for the estimates, see Table B-2). Since these implements are probably still produced in small quantities, our estimates tend to cause some understatement of the growth of production of agricultural equipment between 1937 and 1955.

A similar estimate was made for the output of roofing iron. In 1940, the last year for which output was published, the output of roofing iron was about a quarter of its 1913 level. We have assumed that output fell to zero in 1945 and later benchmark years.

In the case of six series (narrow-gauge railroad cars, street and subway cars, horse-drawn cultivators, combined plows and drills, knitted goods, and hosiery), output for one or more missing benchmark years has been interpolated or extrapolated on the basis of production indexes for related products. These estimates affect indexes for both finished and all civilian products, and they were made differently in each case. In the indexes for finished products, it was assumed that each machinery series moved the same percentagewise over the gap to be filled as the index for all covered machinery items; and that each consumer good moved the same

306

percentagewise as the index for all covered consumer goods. For example, the output of street and subway cars for 1945 was filled in by assuming that it increased by the same percentage from 1940 as the output of all other machinery. In the indexes for all products, the interpolations were made by the product group to which the interpolated series belonged. For example, the 1945 output of street and subway cars was interpolated by the index for covered transportation equipment. Different methods were used in the two types of indexes because the weighting systems—or, put another way, the scopes of productive activity covered—differ in the two cases.

For the illustrative indexes calculated for miscellaneous machinery, estimates of the nature outlined were made for eighteen items with incomplete output series (see Table 28). Interpolations and extrapolations were based on all covered machinery in the case of indexes for finished civilian products, and on all covered miscellaneous machinery in the case of the indexes for all civilian products.

The outlined interpolations and extrapolations were actually made implicitly, by the device of chaining together link indexes for the relevant product groups, each link bridging successive benchmark years and having maximum possible product coverage. Since the estimative procedures differed with the production index involved, implied interpolations and extrapolations for individual products have not been entered into the series in Table B-2.

FRACTION OF INDUSTRIAL ACTIVITY COVERED

For 1927/28, it is possible to make direct estimates of the fraction of value added by industry that is covered by the products in our indexes with 1928 weights. Excluding repair shops, value added by industry in 1927/28 was 7,894 million rubles (see Table A-43). Value added accounted for by covered products in our indexes was 5,879 million rubles for all civilian products excluding miscellaneous machinery (see Table D-3), 5,557 million rubles for industrial materials (see Table D-1), and 4,505 million rubles for finished civilian products excluding miscellaneous machinery (see Table D-2). Hence the fractions of total value added accounted for by covered products in 1927/28 are as follows: 74 per cent for all civilian products, 70 per cent for industrial materials, and 57 per cent for finished civilian products.

It should be understood that the figures referred to as "value added" for industrial materials and finished products are only approximations including an unknown amount of double counting. Unit weights are unit values minus estimated unit costs of nonindustrial materials consumed in the process of fabrication. There is double counting to the extent that some covered products are used in fabricating others, as in the case of coal being used in fabricating steel ingots. It is, of course, more important for industrial materials than for finished products.

INTERPOLATING INDEXES

Our basic production indexes were calculated for benchmark years only (1913, 1928, 1932, 1937, 1940, 1945, 1950, and 1955). Intervening years were covered by special interpolating indexes, with the product coverage varying from year to year but in each case as large as possible.

For industrial materials, annual interpolations were made for the period 1913–1955 (except 1940–1945) in the case of the indexes with 1928 and 1955 weights, and for 1913–1928 in the case of the index with 1913 weights. Interpolations were made in three steps: (1) link relatives were constructed for each adjoining pair of years on the basis of maximum possible product coverage; (2) the links were chained together to span a period terminated by benchmark years (e.g., 1927/28–1932, 1932–1937, etc.); and (3) the interpolating index was adjusted to the corresponding benchmark index by distributing the percentage difference over the intervening years. For ease of computation the difference was distributed linearly; test calculations indicated that logarithmic distribution would not have significantly changed the results. For 1913–1928 an extra step was added because of small product coverage for early years. An index number for 1921/22 was first interpolated between 1913 and 1928 on the basis of twenty-eight products (twenty-four products for the index with 1913 weights), and annual interpolations were then made over 1913–1921/22 and 1921/22–1927/28. The product coverage for adjoining pairs of years is given in Table A-3.

For all civilian products, annual interpolations were made for the period 1928–1955 (except 1940–1945). Each subindex for a product group, as given in Table D-3, was separately interpolated in the manner described above. The number of products covered in adjoining pairs of years are given in Tables A-3 through A-4, except for products assumed to have no output in the relevant years. Coverage for interpolated and benchmark years diverges most in the cases of agricultural equipment, food and allied products, textiles and allied products, and consumer durables. The divergence is significant but less marked for construction materials and transportation equipment in the case of 1955 weights. Elsewhere it is insignificant or nonexistent. In the case of miscellaneous

TABLE A-3

PRODUCT COVERAGE OF INTERPOLATING PRODUCTION INDEXES FOR
INDUSTRIAL MATERIALS AND ALL CIVILIAN PRODUCTS, 1913–1955

| | NUMBER OF PRODUCTS IN INDEX[a] | | |
| | Industrial | All Civilian Products[c] | |
PAIR OF YEARS	Materials[b]	1928 Weights	1955 Weights
1913–1914	14		
1914–1915	14		
1915–1916	14		
1916–1917	13		
1917–1918	18		
1918–1919	18		
1919–1920	18		
1920–1921	22[d]		
1921–1921/22	22[d]		
1921/22–1922/23	27[e]		
1922/23–1923/24	30[f]		
1923/24–1924/25	31[g]		
1924/25–1925/26	31[g]		
1925/26–1926/27	31[g]		
1926/27–1927/28	31[g]		
1927/28–1928/29	49	81	86
1928/29–1929/30	43	82	86
1929/30–1931	43	85	91
1931–1932	43	86	94
1932–1933	53	95	107
1933–1934	53	95	107
1934–1935	53	95	107
1935–1936	53	95	108
1936–1937	53	95	108
1937–1938	43	76	74
1938–1939	41	62	60
1939–1940	42	62	68
1945–1946	42	64	67
1946–1947	41	63	67
1947–1948	41	63	67
1948–1949	42	68	73
1949–1950	42	70	75
1950–1951	46	80	96
1951–1952	46	80	95
1952–1953	46	80	95
1953–1954	46	80	95
1954–1955	47	80	95

[a] Excludes products whose output was, or was assumed to be, zero in the specified pair of years.

[b] Coverage in benchmark index is 54 products in the cases of 1928 and 1955 weights and 49 products in the case of 1913 weights.

[c] Coverage in benchmark index (excluding miscellaneous machinery) is 101 products in the case of 1928 weights and 119 products in the case of 1955 weights. Those products with output assumed to be zero after 1937 (1945 for roofing iron) are 10 in the case of 1928 weights and 11 in the case of 1955 weights.

[d] 20 in the case of 1913 weights.   [f] 25 in the case of 1913 weights.

[e] 23 in the case of 1913 weights.   [g] 26 in the case of 1913 weights.

TABLE A-4

PRODUCT COVERAGE OF INTERPOLATING PRODUCTION INDEXES FOR ALL CIVILIAN PRODUCTS
BY INDUSTRIAL GROUP, 1927/28–1955

| | | | | | | | | | | | NUMBER OF PRODUCTS[a] | | | | | | | | | |
PAIR OF YEARS	Ferrous Metals A	B	Nonferrous Metals A	B	Fuel and Electricity A	B	Chemicals A	B	Construction Materials A	B	Transportation Equipment A	B	Agricultural Machinery A	B	Food and Allied Products A	B	Textiles and Allied Products A	B	Consumer Durables A	B
1927/28–1928/29	5	5	3	3	8	9	12	11	14	17	5	6	10	12	16	16	5	4	3	3
1928/29–1929/30	5	5	3	3	8	9	11	10	13	15	5	6	11	13	16	16	5	4	5	5
1929/30–1931	5	5	3	3	8	9	11	10	13	15	6	7	12	16	16	16	5	4	6	6
1931–1932	5	5	3	3	8	9	12	11	13	15	6	7	12	18	16	16	5	4	6	6
1932–1933	5	5	3	3	8	9	13	12	14	17	6	7	14	19	16	17	9	10	7	8
1933–1934	5	5	3	3	8	9	13	12	14	17	6	7	14	19	16	17	9	10	7	8
1934–1935	5	5	3	3	8	9	13	12	14	17	6	7	14	19	16	17	9	10	7	8
1935–1936	5	5	3	3	8	9	13	12	14	17	6	7	14	20	16	17	9	10	7	8
1936–1937	5	5	3	3	8	9	13	12	14	17	6	7	14	20	16	17	9	10	7	8
1937–1938	5	5	3	3	8	9	11	11	12	12	5	5	11	5	8	9	7	9	6	6
1938–1939	5	5	3	3	8	9	11	11	12	12	5	5	3	5	8	9	7	9	b	b
1939–1940	5	5	3	3	8	9	11	11	12	12	5	5	3	6	8	9	7	9	b	b
1945–1946	5	5	3	3	8	8	12	11	12	11	5	5	4	5	10	12	5	7	c	c
1946–1947	5	5	3	3	8	8	12	11	11	11	5	5	4	5	10	12	5	7	c	c
1947–1948	5	5	3	3	8	8	12	11	11	11	5	5	4	5	10	12	5	7	c	c
1948–1949	5	5	3	3	8	8	12	11	11	11	5	5	4	5	10	12	5	7	5	6
1949–1950	5	5	3	3	8	8	12	11	11	11	5	5	4	5	10	12	5	7	7	8
1950–1951	5	5	3	3	8	8	13	12	13	16	6	7	8	16	12	14	5	7	7	8
1951–1952	5	5	3	3	8	8	13	12	13	15	6	7	8	16	12	14	5	7	7	8
1952–1953	5	5	3	3	8	8	13	12	13	15	6	7	8	16	12	14	5	7	7	8
1953–1954	5	5	3	3	8	8	13	12	13	15	6	7	8	16	12	14	5	7	7	8
1954–1955	5	5	3	3	8	8	13	12	13	15	6	7	8	16	12	14	5	7	7	8

[a] Columns marked A refer to index with 1928 weights; B, to index with 1955 weights. Excludes products whose output was, or was assumed to be, zero in the specified pair of years. Coverage in benchmark indexes is as follows: ferrous metals, 5 and 5; nonferrous metals, 3 and 3; fuel and electricity, 8 and 9; chemicals, 13 and 12; construction materials, 1 and 1 (after 1945); agricultural machinery, 9 and 10 (after 1937).

7 and 8. Output was assumed to be zero for the following products: construction materials, 1 and 1 (after 1945); agricultural machinery, 9 and 10 (after 1937).

b No data available for 1939. Index for 1939 interpolated logarithmically between 1938 and 1940.

machinery, coverage varies so widely from year to year that no effort was made to construct interpolating indexes.

Data for fiscal years (as 1927/28) were not adjusted to a calendar year basis, on the ground that adjustment would be essentially arbitrary. Except where precision is required, fiscal years are generally referred to in the text as calendar years. Since the fiscal year began on October 1, the ending year is used; thus, 1927/28 is generally referred to as 1928.

EXTENSION OF PRODUCTION INDEXES THROUGH 1958

As in the case of years covered by the interpolating indexes, output data are not available for years after 1955 for all products in our benchmark

TABLE A-5

PRODUCT COVERAGE OF PRODUCTION INDEXES FOR INDUSTRIAL MATERIALS
AND ALL CIVILIAN PRODUCTS, BY INDUSTRIAL GROUP,
1955–1958

	Number of Products[a]		
	1955–1956	1956–1957	1957–1958
Industrial materials[b]			
Same products, each pair of years	50	49	46
Same products, all years	41	41	41
All civilian products[c]	100	100	95
Ferrous metals	5	5	5
Nonferrous metals	0	0	0
Fuel and electricity	9	9	9
Chemicals	12	12	10
Construction materials	16	16	14
Transportation equipment	7	7	7
Agricultural machinery	15	15	15
Food and allied products	20	20	20
Textiles and allied products	8	8	8
Consumer durables	8	8	7

[a] Refers to indexes with 1955 weights only. Excludes products whose output was, or was assumed to be, zero in the specified pair of years.

[b] Extrapolating index is based on 54 products (coverage of the benchmark index), with output assumed to remain the same as in the preceding year for those products whose output has not been published (4 in 1956, 5 in 1957, and 8 in 1958). See text.

[c] Extrapolating index is based on 100 products, with output in 1958 assumed to be the same as in 1957 for the 5 products whose 1958 output has not been published. Coverage of the benchmark index is 108 products, excluding those with output assumed to be zero. See Table A-4 for coverage of benchmark indexes for industrial groups.

indexes (see Table A-5). This raises a special problem since the indexes covering the latter years—based solely on 1955 weights—cannot be adjusted to benchmark data, as was done in the case of interpolating indexes. We have tried to meet this problem by making a few adjustments to compensate in part for the missing data.

Data are missing for all three years after 1955 in the case of eight products covered by our benchmark index for all civilian products: copper, zinc, lead, street and subway cars, machines for planting seedlings, cotton pickers, hard leather, and soft leather. In addition, data are missing for 1958 in the case of five other products: soda ash, caustic soda, construction gypsum, construction lime, and phonographs. One may suppose that the primary reason why these data were not published is that growth in output was in some sense abnormally low. Nothing was done to compensate for the data missing for all three years, since it is difficult to know what to do. In the case of those products missing only for 1958, it was assumed that output was the same in that year as in 1957.

The publication record is more uneven in the case of industrial materials. Of the fifty-four products in our benchmark index, four are not reported for 1956, five for 1957, and eight for 1958. Moreover, the list varies from year to year: data are missing for at least one year in the case of thirteen different products. If our index were to be based only on the forty-one products with data available for every year, it would probably exaggerate growth for the sample of fifty-four products, since we may again presume that the missing data represent below average growth. Hence we have followed the expedient of using all fifty-four products and assuming that missing output was equal to output in the preceding year for which it has been published.

Differences in the results of alternative procedures are illustrated in the following table, comparing the index for industrial materials constructed as described with alternative indexes based on maximum product coverage for adjoining pairs of years (Table A-5) and on the same forty-one products for all years:

	Production as % of Preceding Year		
	1956	1957	1958
Constant coverage, 54 products	107.1	107.1	107.2
Variable product coverage	107.4	107.4	107.6
Constant coverage, 41 products	107.8	107.6	108.0

The procedure we have followed results, as expected, in a somewhat lower growth for each year. Whether the lower growth is closer to the truth is another matter, and one that cannot be settled definitively with the data available.

In order to illustrate the difference in results of using alternative weighting systems, three special production indexes were constructed with the following 1928 weights: (a) imputed value added, (b) direct (covered) employment, and (c) imputed employment. The special indexes are given in Table 20 and the uses made of them are discussed in the surrounding text. We shall discuss here the derivation of weights and the methods of constructing the special indexes.

Imputed value-added weights were assigned to the same product categories as direct value-added weights (see Table D-9), the imputed weights being total value added as taken from Table C-2 without an adjustment for product coverage. Rails and roofing iron were not included with construction materials in the special index and hence were not assigned imputed weights. For product categories covered by value-added data but not by output series, value added has been imputed to more inclusive industrial groups as follows: value added for artificial gas to fuel; for pharmaceutical chemicals to chemicals; for china, extraction of minerals, and miscellaneous wood products to construction materials; for primary processing of mixed fibers, hemp and jute, knitted goods, garment industry, and fur products to textiles and allied products. Value added for metal products, printing, and unspecified miscellaneous products was not allocated to specific industrial groups and hence was implicitly imputed to all other industry as a whole.

A second type of adjustment was made. The value added for electricity given in Table C-2 applies only to electricity produced within the jurisdiction of the Commissariat of Electric Power Stations, and the value of this production amounted to only about 45 per cent of the value of total production. Value added for electricity has therefore been raised in accord with this ratio, or by 152 million rubles. Since this amount represents value added for electricity produced within other industrial categories, it should be subtracted from value added for other categories to avoid double weighting. In the absence of more specific information, the amount to be subtracted has been prorated among the other categories on the basis of value added.

Value-added weights, both direct and imputed, are summarized for major industrial categories in Table A-6.

Direct and imputed employment weights—based on Table C-1—were derived and applied in the same manner as their value-added counterparts, with a few minor exceptions. For example, employment

TABLE A-6
Imputed and Direct Value-Added Weights:
Soviet Union, Industrial Groups, 1928

	Million Rubles		Per Cent	
	Imputed[a]	Direct	Imputed[a]	Direct
Ferrous metals	314.8	321.2	4.3	5.4
Nonferrous metals	51.2	18.2[b]	0.7	0.3
Fuel	744.8	651.9[c]	10.3	11.0
Electricity	274.4[d]	274.4[d]	3.8	4.6
Chemicals[e]	317.2	168.5[f]	4.4	2.8
Construction materials	1,150.4	935.8[g]	15.8	15.8
Transportation equipment	89.3	60.8[h]	1.2	1.0
Agricultural machinery[i]	81.9	83.6	1.1	1.4
Miscellaneous machinery	248.1[j]	45.4[k]	3.4	0.8
Food and allied products	1,740.6	1,580.7[l]	24.0	26.7
Textiles and allied products	2,198.7	1,774.9[m]	30.3	30.0
Consumer durables	47.2[j]	8.6[n]	0.7	0.1
Total	7,260.8	5,924.0	100.0	99.9
Unallocated[o]	632.7			
Total incl. unallocated[p]	7,893.5			

Details may not agree with totals because of rounding.

Source: Tables C-2 and D-9.

[a] To compensate for the upward adjustment for electricity, value added for each other industry group has been multiplied by 0.9801. See text.

[b] Excludes unspecified products not covered by our series (34.0 million rubles) as estimated through coverage adjustment (see Table D-9, notes).

[c] Excludes petroleum refining (105.5 million rubles) and artificial gas (2.4 million rubles).

[d] Adjusted upward to cover electricity produced outside Commissariat of Electric Power Stations (152.0 million rubles) as estimated through coverage adjustment.

[e] Includes rubber and paper products.

[f] Excludes pharmaceutical chemicals (19.1 million rubles) and unspecified products not covered by our series (136.0 million rubles) as estimated through coverage adjustment.

[g] Excludes china (33.7 million rubles), extraction of minerals (57.6 million rubles), miscellaneous wood products (159.4 million rubles), and unspecified products not covered by our series (19.8 million rubles) as estimated through coverage adjustment. Includes rails (4.4 million rubles) and roofing iron (28.1 million rubles).

[h] Excludes shipbuilding (30.2 million rubles).

[i] Includes tractors.

[j] Value added for electrical and industrial machinery prorated by computed value of output (see Table D-9).

[k] Excludes metal products not elsewhere covered (398.2 million rubles), and unspecified machinery not covered by our series (247.4 million rubles) as estimated through coverage adjustment.

[l] Excludes unspecified products not covered by our series (195.0 million rubles) as estimated through coverage adjustment.

[m] Excludes primary processing of mixed fibers (13.9 million rubles), hemp and jute (39.9 million rubles), knitted wear (89.4 million rubles), apparel (309.8 million rubles), and unspecified products not covered by our series (15.4 million rubles) as estimated through coverage adjustment.

[n] Excludes unspecified products not covered by our series (39.4 million rubles) as estimated through coverage adjustment.

[o] Includes metal products, printing and publishing, and unspecified miscellaneous products not elsewhere covered.

[p] Excludes railroad repair shops.

data were not available for roofing iron and rails (therefore not included in construction materials) and for felt footwear (therefore not included in textiles and allied products). In addition, imputed employment for the electricity industry was not adjusted to take account of production outside the Commissariat of Electric Power Stations, as was done in the case of imputed value added, because the employment weight factors for 1928 were designed to parallel those for 1955, where no such adjustment was possible. The employment weights for 1928 are summarized for major industrial categories in Table A-7.

To bring the 1928 imputed employment weights into even closer conformity with the 1955 counterparts, an alternative set of weights was computed for machinery and equipment categories, combined employment for machinery, equipment, and metal products being prorated on the basis of computed value of products. These alternative weights are as follows (persons engaged in thousand full-time equivalents):

Transportation equipment	208
Agricultural equipment	338
Miscellaneous machinery	170
Consumer durables	33

These weights were used in constructing the "second variant" of the special index with 1928 imputed employment weights.

MACHINERY AND MILITARY PRODUCTION

As already discussed at length in Chapter 5, index number problems are particularly acute in the area of machinery and allied products. These difficulties are compounded in the case of military items by the absence of detailed Soviet statistics. We present here some alternative production indexes for machinery and military items.

Alternative indexes for civilian machinery and equipment are given in Table A-8 for three different product coverages, in each case calculated by four weighting systems. The component indexes are those given in Table D-4 for transportation equipment, agricultural equipment, miscellaneous machinery, and consumer durables. Each of the indexes is constructed with direct gross-value weights. They are alternatively combined together by direct or imputed value-added or gross-value weights, as indicated in Table A-8.

Of these alternative indexes, those with imputed weights generally rise more rapidly between 1927/28 and 1955 than their counterparts with

TABLE A-7

IMPUTED AND DIRECT EMPLOYMENT WEIGHTS: SOVIET UNION,
INDUSTRIAL GROUPS, 1928

| | PERSONS ENGAGED | | | |
| | Thousand Full-Time Equivalents | | Per Cent | |
	Imputed	Direct	Imputed	Direct
Ferrous metals	245	245	5.0	6.7
Nonferrous metals	36	12[a]	0.7	0.3
Fuel	399	391[b]	8.1	10.8
Electricity	28	63[c]	0.6	1.7
Chemicals[d]	149	70[e]	3.0	1.9
Construction materials	924	626[f]	18.8	17.2
Transportation equipment	110[g]	68[h]	2.2	1.9
Agricultural machinery	62[g]	62	1.3	1.7
Miscellaneous machinery	184[g]	33[i]	3.7	0.9
Food and allied products	820	744[j]	16.7	20.5
Textiles and allied products	1,919	1,315[k]	39.1	36.2
Consumer durables	35[g]	6[l]	0.7	0.2
Total	4,912	3,635	100.0	100.0
Unallocated[m]	467			
Total incl. unallocated[n]	5,379			

Details may not agree with totals because of rounding.

SOURCE: Tables C-1 and D-9.

[a] Excludes unspecified products not covered by our series (24 thous.) as estimated through coverage adjustment (see Table D-9, notes).

[b] Excludes petroleum refining (8 thous.).

[c] Adjusted upward to cover electricity produced outside Ministry of Electric Power Stations (35 thous.) as estimated through coverage adjustment.

[d] Includes rubber and paper products.

[e] Excludes pharmaceutical chemicals and paints and varnishes (34 thous.) and unspecified products not covered by our series (45 thous.) as estimated through coverage adjustment.

[f] Excludes miscellaneous wood products (280 thous.) and unspecified products not covered by our series (18 thous.) as estimated through coverage adjustment.

[g] Total for machine building (391 thous.) prorated by large-scale employment. Additional adjustments as follows: (1) employment for tractors (3 thous.) prorated from land transportation equipment by value of output and transferred to agricultural equipment, and (2) employment for electrical and industrial machinery prorated to miscellaneous machinery and consumer durables by computed value of output (see Table D-9, notes).

[h] Excludes shipbuilding (42 thous.).

[i] Excludes unspecified machinery not covered by our series (151 thous.) as estimated through coverage adjustment.

[j] Excludes unspecified products not covered by our series (76 thous.) as estimated through coverage adjustment.

[k] Excludes primary processing of mixed fibers (4 thous.), hemp and jute (59 thous.), knitted goods (104 thous.), and apparel (437 thous.).

[l] Excludes unspecified products not covered by our series (29 thous.) as estimated through coverage adjustment.

[m] Includes metal products, printing and publishing, and unspecified miscellaneous products not elsewhere included.

[n] Excludes railroad repair shops.

TABLE A-8

PRODUCTION INDEXES FOR MACHINERY AND EQUIPMENT BASED ON 1928 WEIGHTS, WITH VARYING COVERAGE AND METHOD OF CONSTRUCTION: SOVIET UNION, SELECTED YEARS, 1913–1955[a]

(1927/28 = 100)

	1913	1927/28	1937	1940	1945	1950	1955
All civilian machinery and equipment							
Direct value-added weights	66.7	100.0	1,121	852.8	356.4	2,384	3,348
Imputed value-added weights	64.8	100.0	1,179	950.5	371.6	2,648	4,724
Direct gross-value weights	64.9	100.0	1,063	806.5	335.3	2,272	3,208
Imputed gross-value weights	66.6	100.0	1,217	971.6	402.6	2,991	4,616
All civilian machinery and equipment excluding consumer durables							
Direct value-added weights	66.9	100.0	1,067	827.7	362.4	2,316	3,021
Imputed value-added weights	65.0	100.0	1,051	898.7	410.9	2,901	4,063
Direct gross-value weights	65.0	100.0	1,007	779.6	340.3	2,199	2,878
Imputed gross-value weights	67.0	100.0	1,104	926.9	421.2	2,899	4,004
Transportation and agricultural equipment							
Direct value-added weights[b]	70.2	100.0	1,139	826.5	350.9	2,025	2,438
Imputed value-added weights	77.3	100.0	1,358	996.2	428.0	2,409	2,885
Direct gross-value weights	65.1	100.0	946.2	750.1	345.7	2,119	2,518
Imputed gross-value weights	79.1	100.0	1,411	1,038	446.8	2,503	2,748

	Value Added		Gross Value of Output	
	Direct	Imputed	Direct	Imputed
Transportation equipment	60.8	89.1	109.4	220.8
Agricultural equipment	83.6	81.9	175.4	184.1
Miscellaneous machinery	45.4	248.1	86.4	469.1
Consumer durables	8.6	47.2	16.6	90.0

SOURCE: Tables A-6, C-2, D-3, and D-9.

[a] Weights used are as follows (million 1927/28 rubles):

[b] This index is used in our basic index for all industrial products.

direct weights; those with value-added weights, more rapidly than their counterparts with gross-value weights. This relation does not hold over all relevant spans of years, however. In our basic index for all civilian products with 1928 weights, the index for transportation and agricultural equipment based on direct value-added weights is used to represent the machinery and equipment sector (except for consumer durables, which has a separate index). This index rises less rapidly in general than other indexes that might have been chosen. They were not chosen because of the ambiguity of data for heterogeneous categories of machinery.

As to production of military products, the best that can be done is to make informed guesses, based ultimately on official data on military expenditures drawn from published Soviet budgets. From budgetary and related official data, we have first estimated the earmarked expenditures on currently produced military products (Table A-9), and then deflated these figures by price indexes to derive estimated production indexes (Table A-10). The earmarked expenditures probably do not cover atomic energy—treated as "medium machinery" in Soviet statistics —and undoubtedly omit some civilian-type equipment put to military use, just as American statistics on military production do. It would be foolish to pretend that the resulting indexes do more than set rough limits to trends in output. Their main virtue is that they are better than nothing.

For years through 1941 Plan, expenditures on military products may be derived from a reasonably firm base of evidence. The two major sources of ambiguity are, first, lack of evidence on product coverage and, second, the problem of translating some data from "1926/27" rubles to current rubles. As to product coverage, we may infer from the 1941 Plan that production under the commissariats of defense industries was classified wholly under machinery and equipment. Gross production in "1926/27" rubles was planned for 1941 to be 31.9 billion under the defense commissariats and 19.5 billion under the civilian machinery commissariats, for a total of 51.4 billion. Gross production for all machine building and metalworking was planned to be 61.0 billion, or 9.6 billion more.[10] The residual corresponds very closely with the 1940 gross production of metal products and repair shops, the remaining categories within machine building and metalworking (see Table F-1). While this seems to tell us where the production of military products was classified, it does not, of course, tell us what kinds of products were included. We are faced with such questions as whether explosives and ammunition

[10] *490*, 181.

TABLE A-9

SOVIET BUDGETED MILITARY EXPENDITURES,
WITH ESTIMATES BY CATEGORY, 1927/28–1955
(billion rubles)

	Total (1)	Military Products[a] (2)	Pay and Subsistence (3)	All Other[b] (4)	Alternative Estimates	
					Military Products (2a)	All Other (4a)
1927/28	0.76					
1928/29	0.88					
1929/30	1.1					
1931	1.3	0.15	0.70	0.44		
1932	1.3	(0.15)				
1933	1.4	(0.17)				
1934	5.0					
1935	8.2					
1936	14.9					
1937	17.5	10.7	4.0	(2.8)		
1938	23.2	14.6				
1939	39.2	21.4				
1940	56.7	(31.0)	12.3	(13.4)		
1941 Plan	70.9	40.3				
1945	128.2	(44.6)	44.9	(38.5)		
1946	72.6	(6.8)				
1947	66.4	(5.1)				
1948	66.3	(4.9)	32.0	(29.4)	(4.9)	(29.4)
1949	79.2	(13.2)	31.1	(34.9)	(4.9)	(40.2)
1950	82.8	(16.8)	29.1	(36.9)	(8.5)	(45.2)
1951	93.9	(27.9)	29.0	(37.0)	(18.6)	(45.3)
1952	108.6	(42.6)	29.4	(36.6)	(34.3)	(44.9)
1953	105.0	(39.0)	28.8	(37.2)	(30.7)	(45.5)
1954	101.8	(35.7)	28.8	(37.2)	(28.4)	(45.5)
1955	108.1	(42.1)	29.5	(36.5)	(33.8)	(44.8)

NOTE: Figures in parentheses are indirect estimates or residuals.

[a] Earmarked expenditures. Excludes, among other likely things, expenditures on atomic energy and related products.

[b] Probably includes military construction at least through 1931. Construction work appeared elsewhere in the national budget from at least 1937 onward.

SOURCE TO TABLE A-9

Column 1
1927/28–1932:	*420.*
1933:	*464*, 410.
1934–1941 Plan:	*479*, 233.
1945–1947:	*431*, 67.
1948:	*499*, 49.
1949–1955:	*491*, 177.

Column 2

1931:

420. Breakdown of defense expenditures is given as follows:

	Million Current Rubles
Total	1,288
Effectives	697
Transport	207
Buildings	233
War material	153

1932, 1933: Taken as same ratio (0.119) of total expenditures as in 1931.

1937: Estimated gross production in "1926/27" rubles (8.5 billion) multiplied by 1.26 to adjust to current prices, the ratio in the 1941 Plan (see the 1941 Plan below). Gross production in "1926/27" rubles (8.5 billion) derived from 1938 value (see 1938) and statement (*320*, 1959, No. 1, 20 f) that gross production of commissariats of defense industries increased by 36.4% from 1937 to 1938.

1938: Gross production of commissariats of defense industries in "1926/27" rubles (11.6 billion from *501*, 115) multiplied by 1.26 (see 1937).

1939: Estimated gross production in "1926/27" rubles multiplied by 1.26 (see 1937). Gross production in "1926/27" rubles derived from 1938 value (see 1938) and statement (*320*, 1959, No. 1, 21) that gross production of commissariats of defense industries increased by 46.5% from 1938 to 1939. The resulting figure for 1939 (17.0 billion rubles) is almost the same as the planned figure (16.9 billion as given in *501*, 115).

1940: Taken as same ratio (0.546) of total expenditure as in 1939.

1941 Plan: Value of marketed output (*72*, 9). Gross value of output (a slightly different concept, as noted in *467*, 6 f) is given in same source as 31.9 billion rubles in "1926/27" prices.

1945: Residual, official gross production of machinery and equipment (52.8 billion rubles in "1926/27" prices, assumed also to be current prices, as given in Table F-1) minus estimated gross production of civilian items (8.2 billion current rubles as derived in the text).

1946: Derived as follows (billion "1926/27" rubles, assumed to be current rubles also):

	1945	1946
Gross production of industry	128.0	106.9
Civilian products	83.4	100.1
Military products	44.6	6.8

Gross production is taken from Table F-1. For 1945, civilian products are taken as residual; for 1946, they are taken as 120% of 1945, on the basis of *364*, 1/21/47, as cited in *495*, 25.

1947: Planned expenditures (67.0 billion rubles) were stated by the Minister of Finance (*403*, 3/12/47, 7) to represent a reduction of 24% in real terms below expenditures in 1946, despite increases in food prices and salary rates for military personnel. Actual expenditures, lower than planned, therefore represent a reduction of about 25% in real terms. We assume that there was no change in the price of military products and that the 25% reduction in real terms applied here as well as to other items. Our computations imply an average price (and wage-rate) rise of about 24% for items other than military products.

1948: Planned expenditures (66.1 billion rubles) were stated (*403*, 1948, 157) to represent a reduction of 2.5 billion rubles below expenditures in 1947, in "comparable data." We take this to imply a reduction by about 4% in real terms, which would also apply to actual expenditures since they differed little from planned expenditures. We assume again that there was no price change in military products and that the percentage reduction applied there as well as to other items. Our computations imply an average price (and wage-rate) rise of about 4% for items other than military products.

1949:   The official statement accompanying the budget (*403*, 1949, 200) suggests that a significant part of the increase over 1948 was caused by a rise in wholesale prices and railroad tariffs. In the absence of any indications of possible increases in real expenditures, we assume that real expenditures on military products remained the same as in 1948 and inflate for the price increase (169%) by the price index for basic industrial products (excluding petroleum), *432*, 322.

1950–1955:   Residual, total (col. 1) minus sum of pay and subsistence and all other expenditures (cols. 3 and 4). The latter sum is assumed to remain constant at its 1949 value (66.0 billion rubles).

Column 3
1931:   *420*.
1937:   *426*, 18.
1940, 1945:   *429*, 136 f. 1945 assumed same as 1944.
1948–1955:   *491*, 4.

Column 4
1931:   *420*.
1937, 1940, 1945, 1948–1949:   Residual, total (col. 1) minus sum of military products (col. 2) and pay and subsistence (col. 3).
1950–1955:   Sum of pay and subsistence (col. 3) and all other expenditures (col. 4) is assumed to remain constant at the 1949 value (66.0 billion rubles), all other expenditures being taken as residual, sum minus pay and subsistence.

Column 2a
1948:   Same as col. 2.
1949:   Both real expenditures and the price level for military products are assumed to remain the same as in 1948. See text.
1950–1955:   Residual, total (col. 1) minus sum of pay and subsistence (col. 3) and other expenditures (col. 4a). That sum is assumed to remain constant at its 1949 value (74.3 billion rubles).

Column 4a
1948–1949:   Residual, total (col. 1) minus sum of military products (col. 2a) and pay and subsistence (col. 3).
1950–1955:   Sum of pay and subsistence (col. 3) and all other expenditures (col. 4a) is assumed to remain constant at the 1949 value (74.3 billion rubles), all other expenditures being taken as residual, sum minus pay and subsistence.

were included, to say nothing of civilian-type products put to military use.[11]

If we assume that the same relation between current and "1926/27" prices held in 1940 as in the 1941 Plan, we may estimate civilian and military gross production of machinery and equipment as follows (billion rubles):

[11] Jasny argues (*501*, 101) that the production of the defense commissariats included even such items as occupational clothing, but he cites no evidence to support his view.
As we shall discuss more fully in technical note 8 below, conventional military products seem to have been included in machine building and Group "A" until the shift from "1926/27" to "1952" prices, at which time they were apparently transferred to metal products and Group "B."

TABLE A-10

ESTIMATED VALUE, PRICE, AND DEFLATED VALUE INDEXES,
SOVIET MILITARY PRODUCTS
(1937 = 100)

	Value of Output, Current Prices		Price Index		Deflated Value of Output	
	Estimate Aª	Estimate Bᵇ	Estimate Aᶜ	Estimate Bᵈ	Estimate Aᵉ	Estimate Bᶠ
1933ᵍ	2	2	57		4	
1937	100	100	100	100	100	100
1938	136	136	103		132	
1939	200	200	115		174	
1940	290	290	132	117	220	248
1941 Plan	377	377	137		275	
1945	414	414	66	58	627	714
1946	61	61	66	58	92	105
1947	46	46	66	58	70	79
1948	44	44	66	58	67	76
1949	119	44	178	58	67	76
1950	152	78	147	58	103	134
1951	256	172	146	58	175	297
1952	393	319	140	58	281	550
1953	360	285	140	58	257	491
1954	329	264	140	58	235	455
1955	389	314	135	58	288	541

ª From Table A-9, col. 2.

ᵇ From Table A-9, col. 2a.

ᶜ Linked index. 1933–1941, index for basic industrial products except petroleum, *432*, 322 f; 1941–1945, prices of military goods taken as falling by 50% from evidence in *499*, 51–55; 1945–1955, index for basic industrial products except petroleum, *432*, 322, and *576*, 13.

ᵈ Linked index. 1937–1940, index for civilian machinery, *500*, 15; 1940–1945, same as estimate A (see note *c*); 1945–1955, assumed no change in prices of military items.

ᵉ Value A deflated by price index A.

ᶠ Value B deflated by price index B.

ᵍ 1933 is used instead of 1932 because price indexes for years before 1933 are unusually unreliable, in view of widespread rationing.

	1940		1941 Plan	
	"1926/27" Prices	Current Prices	"1926/27" Prices	Current Prices
Civilian items	15.7	17.3	19.5	21.5
Military items	24.6	31.0	31.9	40.3
Total	40.3	48.3	51.4	61.8

The data for the 1941 Plan are taken directly from an official source.[12] For 1940 data in "1926/27" prices, we have the total from official sources (Table F-1); we derive military production as the estimated value in current prices deflated by the price index implicit in the 1941 Plan data; and we take civilian production as the residual. For current prices, the 1940 total is built as the sum of civilian production in "1926/27" prices inflated by the price index implicit in the 1941 Plan data, plus estimated military production (from Table A-9). It is apparent that there is room for error in these calculations.

The 1940 estimate of civilian gross production in current prices is consistent with the values derived from our production indexes with 1928 weights as inflated by available price indexes. If the 1928 gross value of 964 million rubles for machinery and equipment (Table C-2) is extrapolated to 1940 by the indexes in Table A-8, the resulting values in 1928 prices range from 7.2 through 10.0 billion rubles. Inflated by a price index for basic industrial products,[13] the values in 1940 prices range from 16.6 through 23.1 billion rubles; inflated by a price index for civilian machinery,[14] from 12.6 through 17.5 billion. Hence our estimate of 17.3 billion rubles lies toward the bottom of the first range and toward the top of the second. Since it is not clear which price deflator is to be preferred either in principle or in practice, it is not possible to choose one or the other value as the "correct" one.[15]

Direct evidence on the breakdown between military and civilian production ends with the 1941 Plan, and estimates for the postwar years must be made by tenuous roundabout procedures. Inflating our indexes in the manner described above, we derive 1945 civilian production in current rubles as lying within the ranges 8.0 through 10.7 billion rubles and 6.2 through 8.4 billion rubles. Guided by the results for 1940, we choose 8.2 billion rubles as the "best estimate." Supposing the distinction between "1926/27" and current prices had all but vanished by that time, we subtract this figure from 52.8 billion rubles, official gross production of all machine building (Table F-1), to derive an estimate of 44.6 billion rubles for military items. Various bits and pieces of evidence as described in the notes to Table A-9 allow us to extend the estimate for military items through 1948, but the problem of how to treat the price reforms in the next two years seems to make it advisable to carry forth two distinct estimates for later years.

[12] *72*, 9–11. The figures in "1926/27" rubles are gross value of output; those in current rubles, value of marketed output, a slightly different concept. See *467*, 6 f.
[13] *432*, 322. Index excluding petroleum.
[14] *500*, 15.
[15] See the discussion below on deflating expenditures on military products.

In the one case, it is assumed that the output of military items remained constant in 1949 while their prices rose by the average for basic industrial products; in the second case, that neither the output nor the prices of military items changed. A third possibility—that prices of military items rose by more than the average for basic industrial products—is not explored for lack of any basis for a reasonable guess, though it is not clear that this possibility should be ruled out. For succeeding years, expenditures on military products are treated as a residual on the assumption that all other budgeted military expenditures remained constant in the aggregate. Very recent evidence, given in the annex to this technical note, indicates that this assumption is probably unwarranted: other military expenditures were probably lower than we show for 1948 and higher for 1955. The implications of this are discussed in the annex referred to.

The next step is to deflate these estimates of expenditure, and here we face once again the question of the proper price deflator. As a matter of principle, it might be thought that the appropriate deflator would be a price index for machinery, but this may not be so for two reasons. In the first place, prices of military products were arbitrarily set during the war, being cut in half between 1941 and 1943, a period of general inflation. Nothing is known of pricing of military products in the postwar period, though a continued effort to keep prices relatively so low would have required persistent and large subsidies to military industries in the face of a very sharp decline in total subsidies to industry.[16] One is led to conclude that it is highly improbable that prices of military products moved very differently in the postwar period from the general trend.

In the second place, even if prices of military products have moved along with prices of civilian machinery, this does not mean that a conventional price index for machinery is the appropriate deflator for data on expenditures. We face the dual problem of "new" products and the tendency of Soviet managers to evaluate them—even when they are really new—at inflated original cost of production (see the discussion of the official Soviet index of gross production in Chapter 5). It is impossible to know whether these factors are as important for military products as for other types of machinery and equipment, and there is no strong presumption either way.

In the light of these difficulties and the added fact that an extensive price index for machinery has not been published up to the time of this

---

[16] *491*, 143 ff. See also *538*, 259 ff.

writing,[17] we have followed two alternative deflating procedures. First, we have assumed that the price level for military products moved the same as the level for basic industrial products, except between 1941 and 1945, when the former is taken to have fallen by half (see column 3 of Table A-10). This index is used to deflate expenditures on military products estimated under similar assumptions, with the resulting production index shown as estimate A in column 5. Second, we have assumed that the price level for military products moved the same as the level for civilian machinery through 1940, fell by half by 1945, and remained constant thereafter (see column 4). This estimate almost certainly understates the relevant price index by a significant amount. It is used to deflate expenditures estimated under similar assumptions, giving the index shown as estimate B in column 6.

Which production index is more reliable? That cannot be finally answered. In our opinion, estimate A is based on more reasonable assumptions and we accordingly adopt it. But so many roundabout procedures are involved that errors of large magnitude are possible (on which, see the annex to this technical note).

INDEXES ADJUSTED TO COVER MILITARY PRODUCTION

Estimate A may be used to make rough corrections in our production indexes for their failure to cover military products. The relevant adjusted indexes are compared in Table A-11 with their unadjusted counterparts.

In the case of machinery and equipment, the moving-weight index for transportation and agricultural equipment is combined with the index for military products by using 1937 official gross production to weight the two sectors. The index with military products shows a faster growth over the entire Soviet period than its counterpart without military products. Moreover, as one would expect, the former shows a substantial growth between 1937 and 1945 while the latter shows a substantial decline.

In the case of the index for all industry, the adjusted index for machinery and equipment as described above is substituted for the index for transportation and agricultural equipment. It is combined with the remaining component indexes on the basis of the system of moving weights described earlier in this technical note. The index including military products shows a smaller decline over 1937–1945 and a somewhat larger rise over 1913–1955 than its counterpart without military products, again as would be expected.

---

[17] The problems do not all arise from matters of principle. A price index for machinery is no more reliable than a counterpart production index, and for the same reasons.

TABLE A-11

Moving-Weight Indexes of Soviet Industrial Production
Adjusted to Cover Estimated Military Production
(1913 = 100)

| | Machinery and Equipment | | All Products | |
	Civilian (1)	Total (2)	Civilian (3)	Total (4)
1913	100	100	100	100
1928	143	143	102	102
1933	654	693	152	153
1937	1,624	2,597	268	285
1938	1,626	2,910	275	298
1939	1,517	3,209	282	311
1940	1,140	3,280	274	318
1945	265	6,363	123	264
1946	563	1,458	160	180
1947	883	1,564	207	219
1948	1,425	2,076	271	276
1949	2,069	2,721	340	343
1950	2,637	3,639	397	393
1951	2,248	3,950	426	448
1952	2,106	4,839	439	488
1953	2,312	4,811	473	516
1954	2,631	4,916	528	563
1955	2,994	5,795	577	620
1956	3,466		625	
1957	4,086		686	
1958	3,881		715	

Note: All indexes exclude miscellaneous machinery.
Source: Column 1: Table 53.

2: Combined indexes for civilian component (col. 1) and military component (estimate A in Table A-10) weighted by 1937 official gross production (14.2 and 8.5 billion "1926/27" rubles, respectively, as given in Table F-1). The civilian component is slightly overweighted since the weight covers consumer durables, not included in the index. If estimate B had been used for the military component, this index would have differed as follows: 1940, 3,552; 1945, 7,209; 1950, 3,940; and 1955, 8,256.

3: Table 53.

4: Combined indexes for civilian products except machinery and equipment (derived from Tables D-3 and D-4) and for total machinery and equipment (col. 2), appropriately weighted by 1928 value added and 1955 employment. If estimate B had been used for the military component, the index would have differed as follows: 1940, 323; 1945, 252; 1950, 401; and 1955, 666.

ANNEX: MILITARY DATA PUBLISHED IN 1960

In a speech given in January 15, 1960, Nikita Khrushchev revealed for the first time the strength of Soviet armed forces in recent years, together with a hint on current levels of military expenditures in support of troops. This information suggests that the estimates of the latter expenditures in Table A-9 (pay and subsistence plus all other expenditures) are too high for around 1948 and too low for around 1955, since they are based on an assumed constant strength of 4 million (see the cited source) while the actual strength rose from 2.9 to 5.8 million (see Table A-12).

TABLE A-12

SIZE OF SOVIET ARMED FORCES, SELECTED YEARS,
1927–1959
(thousands)

1927	586	1937	1,433	1955	5,763
1931	562	1939	3,000	1956	5,123
1933	600	1941	4,207	1957	3,923
1935	940	1945	11,365	1958	3,623
1936	1,300	1948	2,874	1959	3,623

NOTE: Whether these figures refer to annual averages or strengths as of a specific date is generally not known. Internal security forces are apparently excluded.

SOURCE:

1927, 1937, 1941, 1945,
1948, 1955, and 1959:   Speech of N. Khrushchev on January 15, 1960, as reported in *451*, XII, 2, 9.
1931:   *420.*
1933 and 1935:   Speech of Marshal Tukhachevsky in *228*, 222.
1936:   Marshal Tukhachevsky as quoted in *532*, 1/16/36.
1939:   Telegram of Ambassador Schulenburg to German Foreign Office as reproduced in *530*, 91.
1956:   Strength in 1955 minus reported reduction of 640 thousand (*451*, VII, 45, 26).
1957 and 1958:   Strength in 1956 minus reported reductions of 1,200 and 300 thousand (*451*, X, 1, 3).

In his speech, Khrushchev states that "the proposal to reduce the Soviet Armed Forces [from 3.6 down to 2.4 million] that the government has submitted to the Supreme Soviet for consideration will yield an annual saving of approximately 16,000,000,000 to 17,000,000,000 rubles" (*451*, XII, 2, 13). It is not at all clear what kinds of expenditures are counted within these expected savings. If they are taken as applying solely to the support of troops excluding the production of armaments, and if it is assumed that the savings were calculated on a simple *pro rata* basis, total expenditures in support of troops would be indicated as around 50 billion rubles in 1959, or 13,900 rubles per member of the armed forces. Applying the latter to the strength of the armed forces in 1955 would give an expenditure of 80 billion rubles in support of troops, or 14 billion rubles more than the estimate in Table A-9. Expenditures on military products would be reduced accordingly, or by about a third—from 42 down to 28 billion rubles.

If, as seems unlikely, expenditures on military products were also to be reduced in proportion to the troop cut, the 1955 estimate in Table A-9 for such expenditures would remain substantially correct. Most likely, the correct figure is significantly less than our estimate but not a third less. A reasonable guess might be that our estimate should be reduced by about a fifth. Aside from the fact that we could not do so at such a late point, we thought it unnecessary to revise our index of military production because the upward bias for conventional military products is counterbalanced by the downward bias resulting from the exclusion of atomic energy.

Technical Note 4 (Chapter 5):
Hodgman and Hodgman-NBER Indexes of Soviet Industrial Production

GENERAL DESCRIPTION OF THE HODGMAN INDEX

The Hodgman index has been fully described elsewhere,[18] and we shall not try to do so again. We propose to give only a brief outline of its coverage and method of construction, in sufficient detail to clarify how it differs from our own indexes.

The Hodgman index covers industrial production in so-called large-scale enterprises. For several reasons advanced elsewhere in this book (see Chapter 7), the fraction of total industrial production accounted for by so-called large-scale enterprises rose from less than 70 per cent in 1928 to more than 90 per cent in 1933, and probably to an even higher percentage in succeeding years. Hodgman describes his output series as covering large-scale production, but this is generally the case only for the period 1928–1931, when the share of such production was steadily expanding. For years after 1931, output data published in Soviet sources and used by Hodgman apply with very few exceptions to total production, both small- and large-scale. Hence a substantial part of the growth shown by some of Hodgman's output series, particularly in consumer goods, reflects an accounting in later years of output not covered earlier.

The scope of the productive activity covered by the Hodgman index corresponds with the Soviet definition of industry, except that logging is not directly represented by output data. In the adjusted version of the

[18] See *490* and *558*, 128–142.

index, logging is implicitly included by assigning its weight to other sectors, in a manner to be described below. That is to say, Hodgman makes the implicit assumption that productive activity in logging grew at the same rate as activity in the other covered sectors to which its weight was assigned.[19] For 1928–1937, the index covers 137 products in all, which (according to our definitions of broad categories) may be broken down into thirty intermediate industrial products, forty items of agricultural and transportation equipment, thirty items of miscellaneous machinery, and thirty-seven items of consumer goods (see Table A-13). For 1937–1951, the coverage diminishes to twenty-two products in all because of the paucity of data available on this period when Hodgman did his work.

The basic weights used are wage bills (including payroll taxes) for large-scale industry in 1934. Where such data are available only for a group of products, weighting within the group is based on several types of statistics, typically physical data on employment or labor cost. In the case of machinery, most internal weighting is based on unit values drawn from various censuses of manufactures for the United States.

Imputed weights are used, as opposed to direct or earned weights. The imputation is made in two stages. In the first stage, the full weight of a product group (as chemicals) is assigned to the output series representing that group, whether they fully cover it or not. In the second stage, the full weight of all product groups not considered to be represented by output series is divided between covered machinery, on the one hand, and all other covered products, on the other hand. The resulting indexes are referred to as unadjusted and adjusted, respectively. The percentage weights used in each are shown in Table A-14, where they are given for the major product groups in our indexes.

In using imputed weights, one assumes that the industries not covered by output data showed the same percentage growth as the covered industries to which weights are imputed. This assumption is questionable in the Soviet case, for it seems reasonable to presume that those industries most poorly covered by published output data have generally grown more slowly than related industries covered by output data. This is simply to say that Soviet authorities have not been backward in advertising success, except in areas directly concerned with military production. Assuming unknown growth to be the same as published growth is likely,

---

[19] This procedure of introducing logging by imputing its weight elsewhere is rather curious, since Hodgman states that he did not include an output series for logging in his index "because calculation of an appropriate net value-added weight was considered too risky" (*490*, 57).

in our opinion, to lead to an exaggeration of over-all growth. On this ground, the Hodgman index is open to criticism, particularly the adjusted version, which we shall now examine in more detail.

The adjustment is based on 1934 employment of production workers (large-scale industry) in the covered and uncovered sectors of industry. The covered sector—i.e., those industrial groups represented by output series—accounts for 4.1 million workers, the uncovered for 3.3 million.[20] Hodgman divides the uncovered sector into two parts: uncovered machinery and metalworking (1.3 million workers) and other uncovered industrial groups (2.0 million workers). Employment in all machinery and metalworking industries is 3.088 times employment in the covered portion; for all other industries as a group, the corresponding factor is 1.589.[21] Hodgman therefore multiplies the weight for each of the covered machinery groups in his index by 3.088, and the weight for every other covered industrial group by 1.589. Put another way, this amounts to increasing the percentage weights for machinery categories by 64 per cent, and reducing those for every other industrial group by 15 per cent (see Table A-14).

The inflation of weights for machinery is a questionable procedure, since standard production indexes for the United States, where many more data are available, seldom cover even as large a segment of machinery and metalworking industries as is included in the unadjusted Hodgman index (see the discussion in Chapter 5). Moreover, repair shops account for almost half the expanded coverage (0.6 million workers), and these are almost never counted in industrial production in other countries. Metal products account for almost another quarter (0.3 million workers), and their production grew much more slowly than the production of machinery and probably no faster than the production of industry as a whole (see Table F-1). Finally it seems improbable that the production of ships and various unspecified items of miscellaneous machinery—the other uncovered machinery and metalworking categories—grew as rapidly as the production of machinery reported on in detail.

Outside the machinery and metalworking area, the most important uncovered items, in terms of weight accounted for, fall in the area of construction materials and consumer goods. Logging alone accounts for almost a million workers, or half the employment, in uncovered non-metalworking industries. The procedure of adjustment followed by Hodgman assumes that production of each of the uncovered items grew

[20] *490*, 56.
[21] *490*, 73.

at the same percentage rate as his index for all covered nonmetalworking items. However, his index is 237 per cent of 1928 for covered food and allied products and 229 per cent for covered textiles and retail products (see Table A-15), percentages that are much lower than the corresponding one (308 per cent) for all covered nonmetalworking items,[22] and it seems beyond reasonable doubt that the rate for the uncovered consumer good industries—the most important of which is the garment industry ("needle trades" in Soviet terminology)—would also be lower. In the case of logging, Hodgman's data on large-scale output (in terms of timber removed from forests) show production in 1937 as only 211 per cent of 1929;[23] our own data on total haulage of industrial timber (Table B-2) show production as only 141 per cent. These percentages are also much lower than the corresponding one (269 per cent) for all covered nonmetalworking industries.[24]

In summary, it seems that Hodgman's coverage adjustment (a) does not accord with the practices generally followed in constructing industrial production indexes and (b) probably causes his adjusted index to rise significantly more rapidly than it would if it were constructed with the same product coverage under a system of direct weights, were the necessary data available.[25]

For the period 1937–1951, Hodgman makes a second upward adjustment in his index to offset undercoverage of military production. The adjustment is complicated, involving many assumptions, and it seems best to refer to the original for a full description.[26] The procedure rests on the basic presumption that Hodgman's index correctly measures the production of machinery (excluding armaments) over the period from 1937 to the 1941 Plan, and that the "inflationary bias" in the Soviet measures of gross production of both machinery and armaments over the same period is fully reflected in the percentage divergence of the Soviet index for machinery (excluding armaments) from Hodgman's index for the same category. Hodgman uses this measure of "inflationary bias" to deflate rough estimates of armament production, and then combines the deflated estimates with his index for machinery excluding armaments. He describes the procedure as "painfully rough and ready,"[27] and Seton states that "the resulting inflation of the general index by 13

[22] *490*, 72.
[23] *490*, 58.
[24] *490*, 72.
[25] Seton seems to reach an opposite conclusion, for he argues that the Hodgman index, even as adjusted, probably understates Soviet industrial growth (see *558*, 140).
[26] *490*, 83 ff.
[27] *490*, 88.

per cent for all years after 1937 can only be accepted as an act of faith."[28] Our own comments on problems in measuring military production are given elsewhere (see technical note 3, this Appendix, and Chapters 5 and 7).

COMPUTATION OF THE HODGMAN-NBER INDEX

Our synthetic index was constructed by using Hodgman's weights and our output series, the latter reflecting total as opposed to large-scale production. With a few modifications, we used the same product coverage as Hodgman, except for machinery. The following products were substituted for those used by Hodgman: bituminous coal, anthracite, and lignite, combined by 1928 weights, were substituted for all coal in tons; motor vehicle tires and rubber footwear, combined by 1928 weights, for crude rubber consumption; vegetable oil excluding consumption in oleomargarine for vegetable oil; candy for confectionery; and flour for bread. The following seven products were omitted either because they are not included in our output series or because their output is not adequately measured by existing data: crude petroleum consumed in refining (weight given to crude petroleum); copper ore (weight to non-ferrous metals); plastic pulp and iodine (weight to chemicals); cottonized fiber (weight to cotton fabrics); and knit underwear and outerwear (weight to hosiery).

In general, we used Hodgman's weights in full detail. In the case of some product groups, we weighted internally with 1928 prices instead of using Hodgman's internal weights. Those cases are: pig iron, rolled steel, and steel ingots and castings; copper, lead, and zinc; soda ash, phosphoric fertilizer, sulfuric acid, and synthetic dyes; and lumber and plywood. We also used our moving-weight indexes for agricultural equipment, transportation equipment, miscellaneous machinery, and consumer durables. For an explanation of how these indexes are constructed, see Chapter 5. The basic weights used were those for the unadjusted Hodgman index (see Table A-14). The resulting Hodgman-NBER indexes are presented in Table A-15.

COMPARISON OF HODGMAN, HODGMAN-NBER, AND NBER INDEXES

The product coverages of the Hodgman and NBER indexes are summarized in Table A-13. The coverages are seen to be similar, particularly as between the Hodgman index and the NBER index with 1928 weights. There are, however, some important differences in coverage of machinery not revealed by these summary figures. The larger number of machinery

[28] *558*, 132.

items in the Hodgman index actually reflects greater detail in product breakdown, not broader scope of activity. For example, the Hodgman index includes nine types of machine tools, while the NBER index includes only one series for aggregate machine tools. All in all, there are in the Hodgman index twenty-six items of machinery that are represented

TABLE A-13

PRODUCT COVERAGE OF HODGMAN AND NBER INDEXES OF
SOVIET INDUSTRIAL PRODUCTION

			Number of Products[a]		
	Total	Intermediate Industrial Products	Agricultural and Trans- portation Equipment	Miscellaneous Machinery	Consumer Goods
Hodgman index[b]	137	30	40	30	37
NBER indexes[c]					
1928 weights	130	43	23	29	35
1955 weights	165	46	35	46	38

[a] For the scope of industrial categories, see Table D-10.

[b] Coverage counted from output series in *490*, 205 ff. Applies only to period 1928–1937; for later years, index is based on 22 products (*490*, 194 ff). See text of this technical note for further qualifications.

[c] From Table D-10.

in the NBER index by only seven output series. In this sense, then, the coverage of the Hodgman index is overstated in Table A-13 by nineteen products. It should also be remembered that the coverage shown there applies to the period 1928–1937; for all later years, the total coverage is only twenty-two products.

The Hodgman-NBER index has a slightly different product coverage from those shown. For all years, it covers twenty-nine intermediate industrial products and thirty-four items of consumer goods. The coverage for machinery varies over the periods, since moving-weight indexes were used for each category: through 1937, the coverage is that for the NBER indexes with 1928 weights; from 1937 through 1940, that for NBER indexes with both 1928 and 1955 weights; and from 1940 through 1950, that for NBER indexes with 1955 weights. Hence, total coverage varies from 115 to 144 products.

The weighting systems are put on a comparable basis in Table A-14, which shows for each index the percentage distribution among product groups of the weighted aggregate for 1934. We note that there are marked differences between the implicit 1934 weight structures for the two NBER

TABLE A-14

PERCENTAGE DISTRIBUTION OF 1934 WEIGHTED AGGREGATES FOR NBER
AND HODGMAN PRODUCTION INDEXES AMONG INDUSTRIAL GROUPS[a]

(per cent)

	NBER Indexes		Hodgman Indexes	
	1928 Weights[b]	1955 Weights[c]	Unadjusted[d]	Adjusted[e]
Ferrous metals	7.6	3.9[f]	10.8	9.1
Nonferrous metals	0.5	0.3[f]	1.9	1.6
Fuel	15.3	6.5	14.6	12.3
Electricity	10.7	0.6	2.6	2.2
Chemicals	3.9	4.7	7.7	6.5
Construction materials	15.3	22.0	8.5	7.2
Transportation equipment	5.7	13.5	4.5	7.3
Agricultural machinery	2.7	9.7	3.8	6.2
Miscellaneous machinery	2.8	4.8	9.7	16.0
Food and allied products	20.0	14.3	15.5	13.1
Textiles and allied products	14.7	18.4	19.2	16.2
Consumer durables	0.7	1.4	1.4[g]	2.2[g]
Total	100.0	100.0	100.0	100.0

Details and sums may not agree because of rounding.

[a] For product coverage of industrial groups, see Table D-10.

[b] Calculated from Table D-3. Value for miscellaneous machinery interpolated logarithmically as 303 million rubles.

[c] Calculated from Tables D-4, D-8, and (for electricity only) B-2. For each group, weight for 1955 multiplied by index number for 1934 (1955 = 100), the resulting figure expressed as a percentage of sum of figures for all groups. Index number for miscellaneous machinery interpolated logarithmically as 15.79.

[d] *490*, 215 ff.

[e] *490*, 73 and 215 ff. For each group, unadjusted weight multiplied by coverage adjustment ratio, the resulting figure expressed as a percentage of the sum of figures for all groups. Adjustment ratios are 3.088 for transportation equipment, agricultural equipment, miscellaneous machinery, and consumer durables; 1.589 for all other groups.

[f] 1955 weight for combined ferrous and nonferrous metals (5.7 per cent) apportioned to each group on the basis of computed 1955 aggregate value (31,090 million rubles for ferrous metals and 5,385 million rubles for nonferrous metals). The latter are computed from output in Table B-2 and unit values in Table D-8.

[g] Covers electric light bulbs and articles for home and general use.

indexes, on the one hand, and the actual 1934 structures for the Hodgman indexes, on the other hand. The smallest discrepancies occur for consumer goods; elsewhere, discrepancies are significantly large without a transparent pattern. Such discrepancies reflect in part changes in relative unit costs of production (as measured by the weight factors) from one weight-base year to another,[29] and in part differences in degree of imputation. Electricity is a good example of differences attributable in

[29] It may be doubted that 1934 is a good choice as weight base, since the pricing system was deteriorating seriously at this time. See, e.g., *538*, 258,

large part to imputation: in the NBER index with 1928 weights, the weight covers all producers of electricity; in the Hodgman indexes, and probably in the NBER index with 1955 weights, the weight covers only electric power stations. Machinery categories—particularly miscellaneous machinery—provide other good examples.

A comparison of various indexes, broken down by product groups, is given in Table A-15. For the aggregate, the unadjusted Hodgman index rises more rapidly than the Hodgman-NBER index; the latter, more rapidly than either of the NBER indexes. Using the NBER index with 1928 weights as a basis for comparison, we find that the Hodgman index exceeds it by 29 per cent in 1937 and by 20 per cent in 1950, while the Hodgman-NBER index exceeds it by only 7 and 4 per cent, respectively. Hence the more rapid growth shown by the Hodgman index relative to the NBER index with 1928 weights may be attributed primarily to differences in scope of output series (large-scale as opposed to total production) and only secondarily to differences in weighting structures. Using the NBER index with 1955 weights for comparison, we find that the Hodgman index exceeds it by 47 per cent in 1937 and by 53 per cent in 1950, while the Hodgman-NBER index exceeds it by 22 and 33 per cent. In this case, differences in scope of output series and in weighting structures seem to be about equally important in accounting for the divergence.

For the aggregate excluding miscellaneous machinery, the divergences between the Hodgman-NBER index, on the one hand, and the NBER indexes, on the other, are smaller. The Hodgman-NBER index exceeds the NBER index with 1928 weights by 2 per cent in 1937 and falls short by 3 per cent in 1950; it exceeds the NBER index with 1955 weights by 20 and 29 per cent. Similar comparisons with the Hodgman index have not been made, because a tedious recalculation of the Hodgman machinery index would have been required in order to eliminate the miscellaneous category.

For industrial groups, the Hodgman indexes generally rise more rapidly than the Hodgman-NBER indexes. A slower rise is shown only for machinery and equipment, which is attributable to the fact that machinery groups are internally weighted by Soviet factors in the Hodgman-NBER index and by U.S. factors in the Hodgman index. Machinery aside, the greatest percentage divergences between Hodgman and Hodgman-NBER indexes as of 1937 are for textiles, chemicals, food, and construction materials. Except in the case of chemicals, these divergences are attributable almost wholly to differences in scope of output series, since these are

335

TABLE A-15

<small>Hodgman, Hodgman-NBER, and NBER Production Indexes for Industrial Groups: Soviet Union, Selected Years, 1927/28–1950[a]</small>

(1927/28 = 100)

	1927/28	1932	1934	1937	1940	1950
Aggregate						
Hodgman (unadjusted)	100.0	162.5	213.2	342.2	351.1	527
Hodgman-NBER	100.0	150.3	194.1	283.4	304.7	457
NBER, 1928 weights	100.0	143.6	181.9	265.7	286.3	438
NBER, 1955 weights	100.0	140.6	167.3	232.6	226.9	343
Aggregate excl. misc. machinery						
Hodgman (unadjusted)	n.a.	n.a.	n.a.	n.a.	n.a.	n.a.
Hodgman-NBER	100.0	138.1	180.3	267.3	288.5	405
NBER, 1928 weights	100.0	140.3	178.1	261.3	282.1	417
NBER, 1955 weights	100.0	136.0	161.0	223.2	216.8	314
Ferrous metals						
Hodgman	100.0	150.7	252.3	406.1	n.a.	n.a.
Hodgman-NBER	100.0	155.8	263.2	418.8	431.8	616
NBER, 1928 weights	100.0	153.2	254.8	416.4	428.6	617
NBER, 1955 weights	100.0	156.9	262.1	418.2	430.0	612
Nonferrous metals						
Hodgman	100.0	195.2	322.5	732.9	n.a.	n.a.
Hodgman-NBER	100.0	205.3	311.9	683.0	1,027.4	1,536.
NBER, 1928 weights	100.0	197.3	274.7	583.5	869.2	1,300.
NBER, 1955 weights	100.0	219.7	295.1	626.0	937.0	1,426.
Electricity						
Hodgman	100.0	270.6	420.2	726.9	n.a.	n.a.
Hodgman-NBER	100.0	270.4	419.6	722.4	964.3	1,821.
NBER, 1928 weights	100.0	270.4	419.6	722.4	964.3	1,821.
NBER, 1955 weights	100.0	270.4	419.6	722.4	964.3	1,821.
Fuel						
Hodgman	100.0	196.8	268.8	356.9	n.a.	n.a.
Hodgman-NBER	100.0	194.3	267.4	354.2	446.9	620.
NBER, 1928 weights	100.0	191.5	249.5	347.2	401.1	560.
NBER, 1955 weights	100.0	191.0	266.7	357.3	446.9	642.
Chemicals						
Hodgman	100.0	190.5	284.3	529.6	n.a.	n.a.
Hodgman-NBER	100.0	179.6	256.4	409.3	427.1	647.
NBER, 1928 weights	100.0	184.8	251.6	391.0	400.5	589.
NBER, 1955 weights	100.0	181.7	223.0	334.7	322.9	561.
Construction materials						
Hodgman	100.0	183.3	222.7	309.4	n.a.	n.a.
Hodgman-NBER	100.0	152.4	184.4	257.2	229.0	329.
NBER, 1928 weights	100.0	162.4	175.9	220.3	214.8	306.
NBER, 1955 weights	100.0	164.2	176.3	219.7	217.2	302.

TABLE A-15 (concluded)

	1927/28	1932	1934	1937	1940	1950
:hinery, equip., and consumer durables (incl. misc. mach.)						
̣odgman	100.0	257.8	363.6	625.5	n.a.	n.a.
̣odgman-NBER	100.0	421.3	621.8	920.1	745.1	1,919.9
BER, 1928 weights	100.0	367.5	650.7	1,121.3	852.8	3,236.9
BER, 1955 weights	100.0	214.3	314.1	440.0	327.9	784.0
:hinery, equip., and consumer durables (excl. misc. mach.)						
̣odgman	n.a.	n.a.	n.a.	n.a.	n.a.	n.a.
̣odgman-NBER	100.0	289.2	582.2	992.1	641.7	1,641.1
BER, 1928 weights	100.0	307.0	645.8	1,204.9	859.1	2,129.7
BER, 1955 weights	100.0	189.0	284.1	394.0	266.7	620.0
d and allied products						
̣odgman	100.0	125.0	162.4	237.4	n.a.	n.a.
̣odgman-NBER	100.0	114.0	137.1	186.0	200.2	239.8
BER, 1928 weights	100.0	112.9	136.6	181.4	192.9	217.2
BER, 1955 weights	100.0	119.4	136.4	168.7	167.0	180.0
:iles and allied products						
̣odgman	100.0	135.8	133.7	229.3	n.a.	n.a.
̣odgman-NBER	100:0	102.3	102.3	145.1	179.2	185.0
BER, 1928 weights	100.0	92.6	89.4	133.8	154.3	165.4
BER, 1955 weights	100.0	93.0	87.0	137.9	160.7	164.1

For product coverage of industrial groups, see Table D-10. NBER indexes are calculated from ̣les D-3, D-4, D-8, and (for electricity only) B-2. Hodgman indexes are calculated from data in ̣ 173, 215 ff., 226, 233, and 236 ff. Hodgman-NBER indexes are calculated from Hodgman's ̣hts and NBER output series (Table B-2), as described in text.

areas with important small-scale production in 1928. In the case of chemicals, the divergence results from differences in product coverage and in internal weighting.

The only Hodgman-NBER index that rises more slowly than our NBER index with 1928 weights is the one for machinery, the reason being that the NBER index has 1928 weights while the Hodgman-NBER index has moving weights. None of the Hodgman-NBER indexes rise more slowly than the NBER indexes with 1955 weights.

ANNEX: KAPLAN-MOORSTEEN INDEX OF SOVIET INDUSTRIAL PRODUCTION

An important Western index of Soviet industrial production, constructed by Norman Kaplan and Richard Moorsteen of the RAND Corporation, was published in mid-1960,[30] becoming available to us too late for the careful examination it deserves. Details on the machinery segment, scheduled for later publication, have, in fact, not yet been made available. Therefore, the analysis undertaken here is necessarily, if regretfully, superficial.

[30] 504 and 504a.

The index is of the "comprehensive" type, covering civilian products. Weighting within industrial groups is based on 1950 Soviet prices; among groups, on estimated 1950 Soviet wage bills. It will be recalled that our indexes with comparable coverage have 1928 and 1955 weight bases and that the one with 1955 weights uses employment rather than wage bill to weight industrial groups. In addition, Kaplan and Moorsteen use gross unit values for internal weighting, while we use estimated unit value added wherever possible; their internal weights for consumer goods apply to the retail level including turnover tax, while ours apply to the wholesale level excluding most of the turnover tax; their output series are taken directly from Soviet sources, while some of ours have been adjusted to expand incomplete coverage in earlier years; their classification of industrial groups is somewhat different from ours; and their machinery index is apparently based on a finer breakdown of products than ours and covers "miscellaneous" items, while our basic indexes do not.

These differences make it difficult to choose counterparts from their and our indexes for comparison, but we attempt to do so in Table A-16. Aside from the points already mentioned, it is well to note some specific differences in product coverage. For example, nonferrous metals are covered in our indexes but not in theirs; cigarettes, low-grade tobacco, soap, and starch are included in our "foods and allied products" but in their "consumer non-foods"; and so on. In two cases—chemicals and wood construction materials—we have replaced our basic indexes with the special ones calculated for study of labor productivity. The reason for this is that paper products are classified with chemicals in our basic indexes but with wood materials in the Kaplan-Moorsteen and our special indexes. The main drawback of using our special indexes is that they are based on moving weights.

Bearing these considerations in mind, we may note that the Kaplan-Moorsteen index for all civilian products falls between our counterparts, as would be predicted from the fact that their weight base is also intermediate. They feel, however, that their index differs much more from ours with 1955 weights than should be expected from the closeness of the weight bases,[31] and there are undoubtedly several other reasons to explain the difference. At the same time, the probable effect of the weight bases would be very hard to predict in this case because the Soviet price structure underwent a radical change in 1950 imposed in an effort to correct the serious errors of the equally radical reform of 1949. The resulting price structure, established as it was by emergency

---

[31] *504a*, 79.

TABLE A-16

KAPLAN-MOORSTEEN AND NBER PRODUCTION INDEXES FOR INDUSTRIAL GROUPS:
SOVIET UNION, SELECTED YEARS, 1927/28–1958
(1927/28 = 100)

	1927/28	1932	1937	1940	1945	1950	1955	1958
gregate								
Kaplan-Moorsteen	100	154	249	263	135	369	583	746
NBER incl. misc. machinery								
1928 weights	100	144	266	286	165	439	713	
1955 weights	100	141	233	227	103	343	502	
NBER excl. misc. machinery								
1928 weights	100	140	262	282	163	417	681	
1955 weights	100	136	223	216	97	314	457	567
rous metals								
Kaplan-Moorsteen	100	156	421	433	276	637	1,069	1,291
NBER, 1928 weights	100	153	416	429	270	618	1,046	
NBER, 1955 weights	100	157	418	430	269	612	1,039	1,254
l and electricity								
Kaplan-Moorsteen[a]	100	187	298	357	270	502	848	1,221
NBER, 1928 weights	100	215	444	568	473	934	1,634	
NBER, 1955 weights	100	196	377	477	383	709	1,120	1,494
micals[b]								
Kaplan-Moorsteen	100	258	762	819	368	1,449	2,395	3,105
NBER, moving weights	100		451	450		814	1,132	
od construction materials[b]								
Kaplan-Moorsteen	100	198	254	274	148	348	485	564
NBER, moving weights	100		209	215		296	417	
neral construction materials								
Kaplan-Moorsteen	100	200	385	335	138	532	1,013	1,386
NBER moving weights	100		283	241		368	696	
ilian machinery and equipment								
Kaplan-Moorsteen	100	287	602	505	200	1,471	2,004	2,721
NBER incl. misc. machinery								
1928 weights	100	364	1,067	828	362	2,316	3,021	
1955 weights	100	212	436	326	102	779	974	
NBER excl. misc. machinery								
1928 weights	100	299	1,139	826	351	2,025	2,437	
1955 weights	100	185	386	262	61	607	689	893
d and allied products								
Kaplan-Moorsteen	100	105	157	164	74	150	235	282
NBER, 1928 weights	100	113	181	193	86	217	331	
NBER, 1955 weights	100	118	169	167	88	180	277	323
tiles, allied products, and consumer durables								
Kaplan-Moorsteen	100	114	171	197	74	216	386	468
NBER, 1928 weights	100	94	144	160	63	183	347	
NBER, 1955 weights	100	96	145	164	62	177	294	388

SOURCE: 504a, Table 22; this study, Tables D-3, D-4, and A-24.
Separate indexes for fuel and electricity combined by wage-bill weights in 504a, Table 7.
Paper products included with wood materials, not with chemicals.

measures, was substantially modified over the succeeding five years, and it would therefore not be surprising if production indexes alike in other respects turned out quite differently when based on 1950 and 1955 prices.

In any case, the Kaplan-Moorsteen index rises considerably slower than ours in the case of fuel and electricity; considerably faster in the cases of mineral construction materials and chemicals. The full explanation for these discrepancies would undoubtedly involve all the factors already mentioned, since casual inspection does not suggest a simple reason for the differences. For wood construction materials, the faster growth of the Kaplan-Moorsteen index may result from their weighting timber, lumber, and plywood by gross prices—we used unit value added—and from their using an output series for timber that understates total output in 1928 by about a third, according to our estimates. For the two categories of consumer goods, the differences between their indexes and ours are less pronounced and run in both directions, the explanation for divergences probably lying mainly in the types of weights and output series used. Opinions will vary on whether the counterpart machinery indexes behave as might be expected from the differences in the weight bases—our two indexes with comparable coverage bracket their index. However that may be, further investigation must await publication of the details underlying their index.

Technical Note 5 (Chapter 5): Indexes of Soviet Industrial Prices

Price indexes are a natural by-product of work on production indexes using weights from different years, and we present here such indexes for a few key years and the data on which they are based (Tables A-17 and A-18). The basic prices are supposed to represent only the value per unit attributable to productive activity within the boundaries of industry, derived in general by subtracting the estimated cost of nonindustrial materials consumed in industrial processing. Though these prices are referred to as value added per unit, this is not strictly correct since some double counting of industrial value added is involved (see the discussion in Chapter 5).

Prices generally refer to the wholesale or factory level and exclude excise taxes for 1928. A portion of levied turnover taxes remains in 1955 prices, primarily for consumer goods. In general, we eliminated a fraction equal to the ratio of the cost of materials to the combined cost of materials and labor—in most cases between 80 and 90 per cent.

Our 1928 price indexes for industrial materials on the 1913 base are very close to the official Soviet price indexes for industrial products as a

TABLE A-17
INDEXES OF SOVIET INDUSTRIAL PRICES, 1913, 1928, AND 1955
(per cent)

	1928 as % of 1913		1955 as % of 1928	
	1913 Output Weights	1928 Output Weights	1928 Output Weights	1955 Output Weights
Industrial materials	205.6	198.0	546.0	478.0
Intermediate products	183.0	175.7	494.8	472.0
Metals	175.3	175.8	443.1	466.0
Fuel and electricity	157.6	148.0	530.3	497.9
Chemicals	174.0	159.2	468.8	434.7
Construction materials	268.6	269.6	480.6	458.0
Consumer goods	229.6	224.1	594.1	494.6
Food and allied products	189.9	186.9	727.3	833.6
Textiles and allied products	294.1	271.1	383.9	260.2
Finished industrial products			581.8	370.1
Construction materials			495.9	458.1
Machinery and equipment			990.7	198.9
Transportation equipment			774.4	163.3
Agricultural equipment			1,670.6	372.0
Miscellaneous machinery			295.9	208.8
Consumer goods			576.6	459.4
Food and allied products			804.7	695.6
Textiles and allied products			331.6	255.3
Consumer durables			1,310.8	357.5

SOURCE: Table A-18. Prices exclude most of the applicable turnover taxes (see Chapter 5).

whole. For wholesale prices, the latter are 100 for 1927/28 and 1928/29; for retail prices, 198 for 1927/28 and 203 for 1928/29.[32]

Our indexes relating 1928 and 1955 may be compared with the Bergson-Turgeon-Bernaut indexes for basic industrial products with 1937 output weights.[33] Since prices remained the same, with very few exceptions, from January 1952 to July 1955, the appropriate indexes for comparison would be averages for 1952 and 1956. The relevant Bergson-Turgeon-Bernaut indexes are as follows (1928 = 100):

	1952	1956
Ferrous and nonferrous metals	411	392
Fuel and power	633	573
Chemicals and related products	373	339
Basic industrial products, incl. petroleum	524	489
Basic industrial products, excl. petroleum	525	498

[32] *498*, 784.
[33] *432* and *576*.

TABLE A-18

Basic Data for Indexes of Soviet Industrial Prices (million rubles)

A. VALUE ADDED FOR INDUSTRIAL MATERIALS IN CONSTANT PRICES

	49 PRODUCTS[a]				54 PRODUCTS[b]			
	1913 Value Added		*1928 Value Added*		*1928 Value Added*		*1955 Value Added*	
	1913 Prices	1928 Prices	1913 Prices	1928 Prices	1928 Prices	1955 Prices	1928 Prices	1955 Prices
All materials	2,687.6	5,525.3	2,779.1	5,502.8	5,557.0	30,342.7	30,448.2	145,535.9
Intermediate products	1,385.2	2,535.3	1,499.0	2,633.9	2,688.1	13,299.3	22,376.2	105,612.5
Metals	298.8	523.9	298.9	525.4	525.4	2,327.8	6,013.1	28,020.2
Fuel and electricity	721.4	1,136.7	796.0	1,178.0	1,216.5	6,451.1	8,445.0	42,047.7
Chemicals	111.8	194.5	144.0	229.2	229.2	1,074.5	3,103.8	13,492.6
Construction materials	253.2	680.2	260.1	701.3	717.0	3,445.9	4,814.3	22,052.0
Consumer goods	1,302.4	2,990.0	1,280.1	2,868.9	2,868.9	17,043.4[e]	8,072.0	39,923.4[e]
Food and allied products	806.6	1,532.0	714.3	1,335.0	1,335.0	11,155.3[e]	3,431.1	27,850.0[e]
Textiles and allied products	495.8	1,458.0	565.8	1,533.9	1,533.9	5,888.1[e]	4,640.9	12,073.4[e]

B. VALUE ADDED FOR 70 FINISHED INDUSTRIAL PRODUCTS IN CONSTANT PRICES[d]

	1928 Value Added		*1955 Value Added*	
	1928 Prices	1955 Prices	1928 Prices	1955 Prices
All products	4,369.8	25,424.5	25,749.7	95,287.6
Construction materials	787.9	3,906.8	4,814.1	22,052.0
Machinery and equipment	208.8	2,068.5	8,809.9	17,524.9
Transportation equipment	105.8	819.3	5,322.9	8,694.2
Agricultural equipment	68.7	1,147.7	949.3	3,531.3
Miscellaneous machinery	34.3	101.5	2,537.7	5,299.4
Consumer goods	3,373.1	19,449.2[e]	12,125.7	55,710.7[e]
Food and allied products	1,712.5	13,780.8[e]	5,214.9	36,274.6[e]
Textiles and allied products	1,644.0	5,450.8[e]	5,155.5	13,160.2[e]
Consumer durables	16.6	217.6[e]	1,755.3	6,275.9[e]

NOTE: All unit values are taken from Table D-8; all outputs from Table B-2.

a Products in Table D-10 covered by all production indexes of industrial materials with Soviet weights.

b ... unit value for fish catch is taken as 3,300 rubles (see note b to Table D-8).

c Prices exclude most turnover taxes (see Chapter 5).

d ...

Their indexes for all basic industrial products are seen, when averaged, to lie between ours for all industrial materials with 1928 and 1955 output weights, a result to be expected since their indexes have 1937 weights. Their indexes for product groups do not conform so well to ours for apparent counterparts, as would perhaps also be expected because of inevitable differences in product coverage, judgments on relevant prices, and so on. Their indexes for metals and chemicals are lower than ours and the ones for fuel and power higher. In the latter case, the explanation lies in part in the treatment of turnover taxes, which are included in full in the prices of petroleum products within their index. If those taxes are removed from the 1937 price and it is assumed that they did not change as a percentage of price in later years, the Bergson-Turgeon-Bernaut indexes for fuel and power would be 402 for 1952 and 363 for 1956, both of which are lower than our indexes.

Technical Note 6 (Chapter 6):
Indexes of Industrial Production in Prerevolutionary Russia

None of our discussion of industrial development in prerevolutionary Russia should be taken as definitive, since we have not undertaken an exhaustive study of this period. We have constructed a production index for industrial materials with 1913 weights, but it has many shortcomings and weaknesses, some inherent in the relatively poor statistical record for the period.

The products covered by our index are listed in Table D-11 and the weights are given in Table D-8. Since output data for the prerevolutionary period are essentially the by-product of the factory inspection and tax collection systems, they apply only to large-scale, or factory, production. Output in this sector grew significantly more rapidly than in small-scale enterprises and in hand trades, where the bulk of industrial production took place. Hence an index based on the available data will exaggerate the rate of industrial growth. To a lesser degree, the same is true for indexes covering similar periods of development in Western countries, as the nineteenth century in the United States. We should also note that this exaggeration of growth is not as serious as the exaggeration for the early Soviet period if large-scale production is used to represent total production. In the latter case, the large-scale sector absorbed the small-scale sector within the span of five years (see Chapter 7). During the late nineteenth century the small-scale sector was not being absorbed; it was merely growing more slowly than the large-scale sector.[34]

[34] The development of small-scale industry is discussed in a study by Adam Kaufman,. "Small-Scale Industry in the Soviet Union" (in press).

The small product coverage is perhaps a more serious shortcoming of the prerevolutionary index. Only fourteen products have output data spanning the entire period 1860–1913; nineteen have data spanning the period 1888–1913; and twenty-six—the largest number—have data spanning 1900–1913. In 1913 these twenty-six products accounted for an estimated value added of 2,042 million rubles (Table D-5), while the industrial materials in our index for the Soviet period with 1913 prices accounted for 3,176 million rubles, when adjusted to cover Tsarist territory (Table D-1). Value added in all industry was around 4,400 million if adjusted to Tsarist territory on the basis of data for industrial materials (Table A-43 and D-1). Hence the products covered in our prerevolutionary index accounted in 1913 for about 64 per cent of the value added by industrial materials in our index for the Soviet period and about 46 per cent of the value added of all industry.

For comparative purposes, we show in Table A-19 four indexes of prerevolutionary industrial production (for benchmark years) constructed by other scholars. These indexes differ from ours primarily in weighting systems; product coverage is similar in all indexes shown. In the Kondratiev index as originally constructed, output relatives for each product are weighted by the simple average of attributed percentages of horsepower and employment, and the relatives thus weighted are averaged geometrically.[35] This index covers the period 1885–1913. It has been revised by Raymond Goldsmith to extend it back through 1860 and to transform it to an arithmetically averaged index, in accord with present Western practice. Both versions are shown in Table A-19.

The other two indexes shown there have been constructed by Raymond Goldsmith and Israel Borenstein, using estimated value added in 1887, 1900, and 1908 to weight three separate links that are chained together.[36] Hence these represent efforts to construct moving-weight indexes based on value-added weights. The index has two versions, one using direct weights and the other imputed weights.

It is interesting that the original Kondratiev index most closely parallels ours. Both indexes rise more rapidly over the period shown than any of the other three. Since the primary difference among the indexes is the weighting system, it is somewhat puzzling to find our index with late-year weights rising more rapidly than those with moving weights including earlier weight bases. Perhaps the explanation lies in the Tsarist policy of granting more and more tariff protection to industries

[35] See *311*, 1926, No. 2, 17–21, and *289*, II, issue 1, 79–95.
[36] See *473*, 51 ff.

TABLE A-19

KONDRATIEV, BORENSTEIN-GOLDSMITH, AND INDUSTRIAL MATERIALS INDEXES OF
INDUSTRIAL PRODUCTION: TSARIST RUSSIA, BENCHMARK YEARS, 1860–1913
(1913 = 100)

| | Kondratiev Index | | Borenstein-Goldsmith Index | | Industrial Materials Index |
	Original[a]	Revised[b]	Direct Weights[c]	Imputed Weights[d]	1913 Weights[e]
1860	5.0	9.0	10.1	8.8	5.7
1865	4.0	7.1	9.2	7.5	4.3
1870	6.6	10.8	13.1	10.9	6.4
1875	10.6	14.6	15.7	14.0	9.9
1880	15.4	19.0	20.8	18.4	13.4
1885	20.6	23.2	25.4	23.7	19.2
1888	22.6	24.9	27.9	26.2	22.8
1890	27.3	28.5	33.2	32.0	24.9
1895	39.4	40.0	45.7	44.4	39.1
1900	61.1	59.5	63.6	63.1	59.4
1905	62.0	60.8	62.6	61.3	60.5
1910	83.9	83.7	87.8	86.4	78.2
1913	100.0	100.0	100.0	100.0	100.0

NOTE: Indexes cover current Tsarist territory excluding Finland.

SOURCE: Except industrial materials, *473*, 60 f. Comparison base shifted from 1900.
For description of weighting systems, see text.

[a] Geometric average of weighted output relatives. Extended by Israel Borenstein and Raymond Goldsmith from 1885 through 1860, using Kondratiev's weights and component products.

[b] Arithmetic average of weighted output relatives. Extended as described in note *a* above.

[c] Each product weighted by its value added (see *473*, 52 ff).

[d] Each product weighted by value added of the product group it is taken to represent; weight of unrepresented manufacturing groups imputed to manufacturing as a whole (see *473*).

[e] Products in Table D-11 weighted by net unit values for 1913 in Table D-8. For weighted aggregates, see Table D-5.

that were growing rapidly in this period. It is even more puzzling to find our index corresponding more closely with Kondratiev's geometrically weighted index than with the same one arithmetically weighted. No obvious explanation is at hand for this.

Technical Note 7 (Chapter 6):
Basic Data on Soviet Labor Productivity

The Soviet Union has not yet published a comprehensive set of statistics on industrial employment, wage rates, or hours of work. In this area as in many others, we are forced to reconstruct our own series from such information as has been made available. The reconstructed data are presented in Tables A-20 through A-24.

The basic series is for persons engaged (expressed in full-time equivalents) in enterprises counted statistically within the category of industry.

TABLE A-20

PERSONS ENGAGED IN SOVIET INDUSTRY: INDUSTRIAL GROUPS, BENCHMARK YEARS
(thousand full-time equivalents)

	1913	1928	1933	1937	1940	1950	19
Ferrous and nonferrous metals	425	281	573	626	603	998	1,
Fuel and electricity	335	427	822	864	991	1,489	1,
Fuel	315	399	725	739	857	1,260	1,
Electricity	20	28	97	125	134	229	
Chemicals	70	100	279	351	415	442	
Construction materials[a]	1,304	989	2,318	2,280	2,665	3,601	4,
Wood materials[a]	1,073	768	1,798	1,929	2,210	2,799	2,
Mineral materials	231	221	520	351	455	802	1,
Machinery and allied products	602	663	1,233	3,262	3,550	4,572	5,
Civilian mach. and equip.[b]	303	391	811	1,831[c,d]	1,249[c,d]	1,884[c]	2,5
Metal products[e]	299	272	422	1,431[c,d]	2,301[c,d]	2,688[c]	3,1
Food and allied products	1,072	803	1,094	1,478	1,554	1,637	1,
Textiles and allied products[f]	1,847	1,919	2,000	2,568	2,733	2,602	3,
Total of above	5,655	5,184	8,319	11,429	12,511	15,341	18,
Unallocated[g]	162	195	334	814	589	638	
Total excl. repair shops	5,817	5,379	8,653	12,243	13,100	15,979	19,3
Repair shops	86	86	1,573[h]	283[c]	294[c]	387[c]	3
Grand total	5,903	5,465	10,226	12,526	13,394	16,366	19,6

SOURCE: Table C-1.

[a] Includes paper and matches.

[b] Includes consumer durables.

[c] Sum of machinery and allied products and repair shops apportioned to components by official gross production as estimated in Table F-1. For 1940, repair shops and metal products are apportioned by their 1937 breakdown. For 1937 and 1940, machinery and equipment was adjusted to exclude estimated employment in military production (see note d below).

[d] Conventional military products were apparently included under machinery and equipment up to 1950 and under metal products for 1950 and after (see Appendix F). Using estimated official gross production (Table F-1) to apportion persons engaged in machinery and equipment between civilian and military components, we derive the following (thousands of persons engaged):

	1937	1940
Machinery and equipment	2,925	3,202
Civilian	1,831	1,249
Military	1,094	1,953

Employment in the military component may be treated as insignificant for years before 1937. In accord with this estimated breakdown, we have transferred the military component for 1937 and 1940 from machinery and equipment to metal products.

[e] Includes military products. See note d above.

[f] Includes furniture for 1937 and later years.

[g] Includes printing and publishing and unspecified miscellaneous industries.

[h] Includes 1,302 thousand in the "others" category of machine building and metal products (Table C-1).

TABLE A-21

AVERAGE DAILY HOURS WORKED BY ADULT PRODUCTION WORKERS IN
SOVIET LARGE-SCALE INDUSTRY, BENCHMARK YEARS[a]
(number of hours)

	1913	1928[b]	1933[c]	1936	1940	1950	1956	1959[d]
All large-scale industry	9.9	7.81	6.99	7.03	8.5[e]	8.5[e]	7.96	7.70
Electric power	8.7						7.98	7.14
Coal	10.1	7.32	6.90				7.94	7.03
Petroleum	8.5						7.98	7.94
Ferrous metallurgy	10.1	7.88	6.99				7.98	7.05
Machine building and metal products	9.7	7.91	7.00				7.97	7.81
Chemicals	9.6						7.74	6.91
Paper	10.0						7.97	7.90
Textiles	9.6						7.98	7.96
Cotton	9.39[f]	7.84	7.00					
Leather	10.0						7.99	7.98
Shoes	9.9						8.00	7.98
Food	10.8						8.00	7.99

SOURCE: 1913, 1956, and 1959, *141*, 665; 1928, *222*, 529; 1933, *241*, 192; 1936, *465*, 55.

[a] For all years except 1940 and 1950, actual hours including overtime, according to source. For 1940 and 1950, standard hours roughly adjusted for overtime.

[b] As of March.

[c] As of September 1.

[d] As of the beginning of the year.

[e] Standard eight-hour day (established by the directive of June 28, 1940) with a rough adjustment for overtime. The prevalence of overtime is indicated in *465*, 55.

[f] *222*, 529.

TABLE A-22

AVERAGE ANNUAL DAYS WORKED BY PRODUCTION WORKERS IN SOVIET LARGE-SCALE
INDUSTRY, BENCHMARK YEARS
(number of days)

	1913	1928	1932	1937	1940	1950	1955	1956
worked	257.4	263.0	257.2	260.3	269.8	276.3	273.3	272.1
not worked	107.6	103.0	108.8	104.7	96.2	88.7	91.7	93.9
olidays	88.6	62.3	67.1	66.8	64.0	55.5	55.5	56.9
id vacations	a	14.2	15.1	13.7	13.0	14.9	16.0	16.0
ck leave	5.2	15.3	14.2	17.6	13.9	13.4	13.7	14.6
uthorized absence	2.8	3.6	5.2	4.2	3.6	4.0	5.6	5.4
her absence[b]	11.0	7.6	7.2	2.4	1.7	0.9	0.9	1.0

SOURCE: 1913, *257*, 477 ff; other years, *408*, 1957, No. 2, 91.

[a] Apparently included in holidays.

[b] For example, absence due to mechanical failures.

TABLE A-23

ESTIMATED ANNUAL HOURS WORKED BY PERSONS ENGAGED IN SOVIET INDUSTRY, BENCHMARK YEARS

	Average Annual Hours Worked[a]	Annual Hours Worked (millions)[b]
1913	2,548	14,822
1928	2,054	11,048
1933	1,798[c]	15,558
1937	1,830[d]	22,405
1940	2,293	30,038
1950	2,349	37,535
1955	2,175[e]	42,110

[a] For production workers in large-scale industry. Average daily hours (Table A-21) times average annual days (Table A-22).

[b] Average annual hours for production workers in large-scale industry (preceding column) times full-time equivalent persons engaged in all industry excluding repair shops (Table A-20). Full-time equivalence is measured in our estimates in terms of the average work-year, in days or weeks, of workers and employees in large-scale industry (see Table C-1). Since daily hours were probably lower for large- than for small-scale and for production workers than for other persons engaged, the annual hours estimated here probably understate the actual figures. There is no basis for determining whether there is a trend in relative understatement, either up or down.

[c] Average daily hours in 1933 times average annual days in 1932.

[d] Average daily hours in 1936 times average annual days in 1937.

[e] Average daily hours in 1956 times average annual days in 1955. Since daily hours fell in 1956 (see *529*), average annual hours are understated here to an unknown degree.

TABLE A-24

INDEXES OF EMPLOYMENT AND OUTPUT BY INDUSTRIAL GROUP: SOVIET UNION, BENCHMARK Y»
(1913 = 100)

	1913	1928	1933	1937	1940	1950	195
Ferrous and nonferrous metals							
Output	100	88.1	156.7	374.6	399.7	574.1	98
Persons engaged	100	66.1	134.8	147.3	141.9	234.8	26
Fuel and electricity							
Output	100	150.3	366.9	667.1	847.9	1,261.7	1,99
Persons engaged	100	127.5	245.4	257.9	295.8	444.5	54
Fuel							
Output	100	128.0	266.9	418.2	519.4	746.6	1,14
Persons engaged	100	126.7	230.2	234.6	272.1	400.0	48
Electricity							
Output	100	257.4	841.0	1,859.8	2,483.8	4,690.3	8,75
Persons engaged	100	140.0	485.0	625.0	670.0	1,145.0	1,47
Chemicals							
Output	100	144.0	304.3	649.4	647.5	1,173.4	1,63
Persons engaged	100	142.9	398.6	501.4	592.9	631.4	89

	1913	1928	1933	1937	1940	1950	1955
:ruction materials[a]							
.tput	100	89.9	144.3	202.3	198.7	280.0	424.5
·sons engaged	100	75.8	177.8	174.8	204.4	276.1	345.2
)od materials[a]							
Output	100	86.7	147.6	181.3	186.2	256.2	361.4
Persons engaged	100	71.6	167.6	179.8	206.0	260.9	269.4
neral materials							
Output	100	104.0	129.4	294.8	250.3	382.6	723.7
Persons engaged	100	95.7	225.1	151.9	197.0	347.2	502.2
hinery and allied products[b]							
atput[c]	100	120.8	406.7	1,411.8	1,754.6	1,984.1	3,248.1
·sons engaged	100	108.9	407.8	515.3	558.7	720.8	886.2
vilian machinery and equipment[d]							
Output	100	143.4	666.4	1,727.7	1,200.8	2,791.5	3,472.2
Persons engaged	100	129.0	267.7	604.3	412.2	621.8	857.1
etal products[e]							
Persons engaged	100	91.0	141.1	112.7	116.4	899.0	1,068.6
l and allied products							
Itput	100	84.2	93.0	152.7	156.5	168.7	259.7
:rsons engaged	100	74.9	102.1	137.9	145.0	152.7	167.0
iles and allied products[f]							
utput	100	113.0	102.0	151.2	175.2	178.8	274.5
:rsons engaged	100	103.9	108.3	139.0	148.0	140.9	181.0
ndustrial products[g]							
utput[h]							
Civilian products	100	102.4	152.3	267.5	273.9	396.8	576.9
All products	100	102.4	152.9	284.5	318.3	392.9	619.5
:rsons engaged	100	92.5	148.8	210.5	225.2	274.7	332.8
{an-hours	100	74.5	105.0	151.2	202.7	253.2	284.1

SOURCE: Tables A-20, A-23, and 52 (revised for coverage, as noted below). All output indexes are based on moving weights.

[a] Includes paper and matches.

[b] Includes consumer durables and military products.

[c] Special index combining component indexes for civilian machinery and equipment (this table), military products (estimate A in Table A-10), and metal products. The latter is represented by the index for all civilian products over 1913–1937 and 1945–1955 and by the index for industrial materials over 1937–1945 (both as given in Table 16). This seems to be reasonable in view of the fact that the official Soviet indexes for all industry and for metal products move in a parallel fashion (see Table F-2). Component indexes are weighted together by 1937 official gross production in billion "1926/27" rubles as follows (Table F-1): 14.2 for civilian machinery and equipment, 8.5 for military products, and 2.6 for metal products.

[d] Includes consumer durables but excludes miscellaneous machinery.

[e] Includes military products.

[f] For 1937 and later years, furniture is included for persons engaged but not for output. This latter omission is not likely to be significant.

[g] Excludes repair shops.

[h] Excludes miscellaneous machinery.

Derivation of these figures for major industrial categories is explained in Table C-1. Persons engaged include workers, employees, and self-employed and supervisory personnel. Full time is measured by the average work-year in large-scale industry, expressed in days or weeks. For 1937 and later years, the aggregate of persons engaged has been calculated as the sum of workers, employees, members of industrial producer cooperatives, and workers in industrial enterprises attached to collective farms. Such an aggregate does not include some categories of employees—as "overhead" personnel—normally counted as persons engaged.[37] Members of so-called "industrial collective farms" are also not included. For the same span of years, the aggregate has been distributed among industrial groups on the basis of the percentage distribution of production workers, the only such distribution available. Production workers are wage earners directly engaged in manufacturing or extractive activities, and the ratio of production workers to all persons engaged will vary from one industrial sector to another, as is shown by the statistics for 1933 and 1935 given in the general note to Table C-1. On the basis of the latter statistics, we would conclude that the use of production workers to break down the aggregate probably leads to a significant relative understatement of persons engaged in producing electricity, machinery and equipment, and possibly mineral construction materials, and to a relative overstatement in the cases of other industrial categories. The degree of error cannot be estimated.

After our estimates had been constructed and used in analysis, Barney K. Schwalberg computed another set of data for the Foreign Manpower Research Office of the U.S. Bureau of the Census.[38] The latter data are based on a broader range of source materials than was available at the time our estimates were made and seem to be more reliably constructed than ours. If so, they indicate a significant and growing understatement in our data for 1937 and later years, as is shown by the following comparison:

Thousands of Persons Engaged

	Schwalberg (1)	NBER (2)	(2) ÷ (1) (3)
1933	10,144	10,226	1.008
1937	13,887	12,526	0.902
1950	18,309	16,366	0.894
1955	22,000	19,666	0.848

[37] For a careful description of Soviet labor statistics and the categories of industrial labor, see *551*.

[38] See *551*.

Both sets of figures as given here include repair shops in all years and exclude private artisans in 1933. We have not substituted Schwalberg's figures for ours because that would have required massive recalculations at too late a date. The apparent trend in understatement in our figures should be kept in mind in interpreting our findings on labor productivity.

Soviet statistics on hours of work are limited to production workers in large-scale industry. Moreover, average annual hours must be computed from separate data on average daily hours and average annual days worked, the latter not being available in an industrial breakdown. Total annual hours worked by persons engaged in industry are calculated by applying these average annual hours to all persons engaged. Average daily hours are probably lower for production workers than for other persons engaged, and for large-scale industry than for small-scale industry. Average annual days worked are not likely to differ significantly among these categories, since full-time employment has generally been defined in terms of average annual days or weeks for wage earners in large-scale industry. As a result of the probable differences in daily hours, average annual hours for production workers in large-scale industry, calculated in the manner described, probably understate those for all persons engaged in total industry. Hence, our figures for total annual hours worked are understated. There is no solid evidence to determine whether the relative understatement is larger for some years than for others. Although small-scale industry was relatively more important in earlier than in more recent years, the effects of this trend on average daily hours may have been offset by the growing relative importance of "non-production" workers and employees.

It should be noted that the coverage of the industrial categories used for persons engaged differs in some cases from the coverage of similar categories for which our basic production indexes have been computed. Those differences are indicated in Table A-20 and A-24, and the affected production indexes in the latter table have been adjusted accordingly. In addition, a special production index has been constructed for machinery and allied products, as explained in that table.

Technical Note 8 (Chapter 7):
Economic Aid and Reparations Received by the Soviet Union
After World War II

The data given in Table A-25 include the postwar economic aid from the Allies (primarily the United States) and the direct reparations collected from enemy countries, generally as reported by the Soviet

ECONOMIC AID AND REPARATION PAYMENTS TO THE SOVIET UNION, 1946–1953
(million dollars)

	Reparation Dollars ("1938 dollars")	Current Dollars
Lend-Lease and UNRRA	333	450
East Germany	6,195	15,488
Hungary	205	512
Rumania	493	986
Poland	1,231	2,462
Finland	438	866
Italy	100	200
Manchuria	100	200
Total	9,095	21,164

SOURCE:

Lend-Lease and UNRRA: Materials in Lend-Lease pipeline at end of war: $250 million; UNRRA aid: $200 million (*554*, 597). We assume these are in 1945 dollars; they have been deflated to 1938 dollars by BLS wholesale price index (*649*, 1956, 320).

East Germany: *590*, 15, where cited as estimates by Leon Herman. From an official Soviet statement (*364*, 5/16/50), collections through 1950 were 3,650 million "1938 dollars," with 210 million to be collected annually (continued through 1953). Implied total from official statement: 4,280 million "1938 dollars," or 2,000 million less than our figure. See also *531*.

Hungary: *590*, 15, gives 160 million "1938 dollars" and 400 million current dollars. We have added Soviet requisitions of so-called Hungarian debts to Germany amounting to 45 million "1938 dollars" (*437*, 111, and *565*, 172). The latter translated into current dollars by conversion factor of 2.5 implied by reparations data.

Rumania: In "1938 dollars," *565*, 172 and 175. Translated into current dollars by conversion factor of 2 (see text). *590*, 15, gives smaller estimates, apparently excluding so-called restitutions: 226 million "1938 dollars" and 570 million current dollars.

Poland: Estimate consists of two parts: (a) reparations for industrial plant and equipment acquired by Poland in territories taken from Germany and (b) benefits from special prices accorded to the Soviet Union for Polish coal. Reparations were to be a quarter of acquired plant and equipment (*565*, 29), which Molotov presumably valued at 6 billion "1938 dollars" (according to *524*, 158). An official Polish source (*549a*, 8/24/45) gives the figure 500 million "1938 dollars." Our estimate (875 million "1938 dollars") is a simple average of these two. Translated into 1,750 million current dollars by conversion factor of 2 (see text).

Polish coal was apparently sold to the Soviet Union at an eighth to a tenth of the world price over the period 1946–1953 (*437*, 152, and *522*, I, 219). Average world price was about $12 a ton over 1946–1949 (*437*, 152) and about $18 over 1950–1953 (*580*, 1953, 231). About 6.5 million tons were delivered each year over the entire period (*522*, I, 219). We therefore estimate benefits of 712 million current dollars. Translated into 356 million "1938 dollars" by conversion factor of 2 (see text). For a higher estimate, see *457*, 464.

Finland: *421*, *509*, and *521*. Estimated from following components: (a) reparations of 227 million "1938 dollars" or 445 million current dollars (*421*, 336); (b) transport services of 7 million current dollars, translated into 3.5 million "1938 dollars" by conversion factor of 2 (see text); (c) transferred German assets valued at 7 million "1938 dollars," translated into 14 million current dollars by conversion factor of 2; and (d) assets in territory ceded by Finland to Soviet Union valued at 400 million current dollars, translated into 200 million "1938 dollars" by conversion factor of 2.

Italy: In "1938 dollars," *571*, "Treaty of Peace with Italy," Article 24. Primarily Italian assets in Balkan countries. Translated into current dollars by conversion factor of 2 (see text).

Manchuria: In "1938 dollars," official Soviet statement as quoted in *554*, 106. Translated into current dollars by conversion factor of 2 (see text). Mr. Edwin Pauley, U.S. Representative to the Reparations Commission, estimated reparations at 2 billion 1938 dollars (quoted in *554*), or 20 times the official Soviet figure that we have used.

Union. They do not include Soviet proceeds from so-called joint companies established in European satellite countries, discriminatory trading prices (except for Polish coal), transit privileges, levies for support of occupation troops and administration, the forced labor of prisoners of war and internees, and other indirect exactions. They also do not include the value of machinery and equipment in occupied territories dismantled by Soviet occupation forces before the end of the war (on the dismantling policy in Eastern Europe, see *565*, 184).

Reparations to the Soviet Union were presumably calculated in terms of 1938 "world prices," raised by 10 to 15 per cent and translated into U.S. dollars on the basis of the 1938 gold content of the dollar; but there is no doubt that prices were discounted substantially in favor of the Soviet Union. For example, in 1946 the value of Hungary's reparations deliveries in current dollars (calculated at the official exchange rate) was about four times the value in "1938 dollars" (*549a*, 8/24/45, 170), whereas in 1946 the BLS wholesale price index for the United States was only 1.5 times its 1938 level (*649*, 1956, 320). This suggests that, at least in the case of Hungary, the reparations in "1938 dollars" may be less than 40 per cent of their value in actual 1938 dollars.

Mr. Lauri Kivinen, former chairman of the Finnish Delegation for Reparations Industries, comments on the "1938 dollars" as follows (*509*, 13):

> Indeed, in talking of the dollars in which the war reparations were calculated Finns used the name "war reparation dollars," thus wishing to illustrate the fact that they had nothing in common with the monetary unit of the United States. Each item of the agreement had its own "war reparation dollar rate," expressed in Finnish marks, depending on the price fixed in the autumn of 1944. An "exchange ratio" of one "war reparation dollar = 5,000 Finnmarks was no rarity (the official exchange rate of the U.S. dollar in 1945–48 was $1.00 = 136 Finnmarks, and in 1949–52 it was $1.00 = 231 Finnmarks).

A careful and thorough study of Finnish reparations gives them in "1938 dollars" as $226.5 million[39] and in current dollars as $444.7 million (*421*, 336), the latter being the sum of payments in current U.S. prices over the period 1946–1952.[40] These data imply a ratio of about

---

[39] The same source points out that, if commodities had been priced in accord with the reparations agreement, the value would have been $269.3 million in adjusted "1938 dollars" (*421*, 330).

[40] In 1952 U.S. prices, the value would be $546 million (*421*, 336); in 1955 U.S. prices, $826 million (*510*, 14, and *649*, 1956, 962).

two postwar dollars to one "1938 dollar." The evidence already cited here suggests that this conversion factor is too low for other countries with less control over reparations programs. For lack of more definitive estimates, we have, however, used this conversion factor whenever estimates of reparations were lacking for specific countries in either "1938 dollars" or current dollars. In converting from "1938 dollars," current dollars are probably understated by using this factor; in converting from current dollars, "1938 dollars" are probably overstated, though not sufficiently to offset their understatement of actual 1938 dollars.

The estimates in Table A-25 have been pieced together from fragmentary information and are obviously only crude approximations to the values they seem to measure. There can be little doubt that the net effect is understatement in terms of both 1938 U.S. and current U.S. prices. In the absence of more detailed and accurate statistics, there is no way of determining the degree of understatement.

Technical Note 9 (Chapter 8):
Basic Data for Comparisons Between the United States and the Soviet Union

We discuss here some characteristics of the basic data underlying various comparisons made in the text between U.S. and Soviet industry. This note is divided into four sections, dealing with data on (1) individual industries; (2) production of energy; (3) ruble-dollar price ratios; and (4) aggregative output, employment, and value added.

DATA ON INDIVIDUAL INDUSTRIES

In Chapter 8 and its annex, U.S. and Soviet growth trends are analyzed for two samples of industries, a basic sample consisting of forty-seven industries long established in both economies and a supplementary sample consisting of thirteen industries relatively new in the Soviet Union. Physical output for these counterparts is presented graphically in Charts A-2 and A-3, which are based on Tables B-1, B-2, and E-1.

A detailed breakdown of estimated value added for the basic sample is given in Table A-26, covering 1913, 1928, and 1955 for both countries. For each year and each country, value added is estimated in both rubles and dollars, the dollar values applying to U.S. prices of an adjoining year. Synthetic dyes and sausages, though included in the basic sample, are not covered in this table because necessary data could not be reconstructed for all years. The estimates of value added are used in weighting frequency distributions of growth rates and in calculating

Physical Output Trends of Basic Sample of Forty-Seven Industries:
Soviet Union and United States

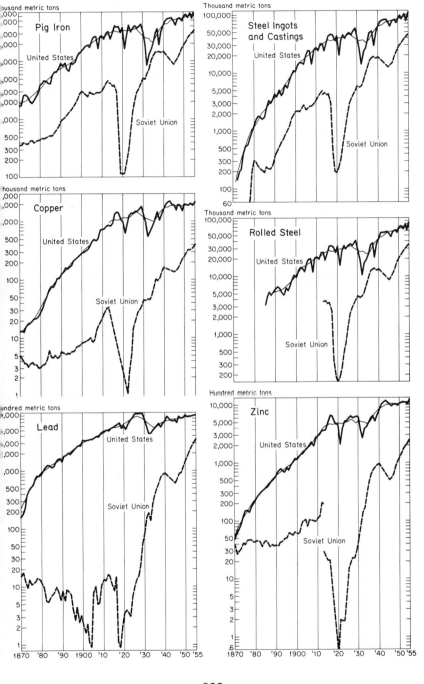

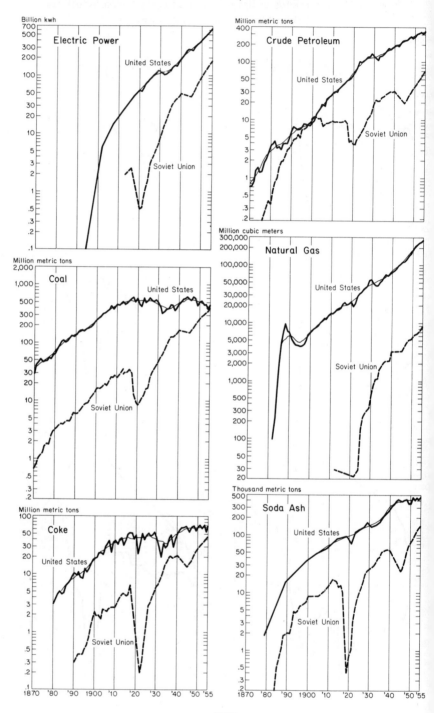

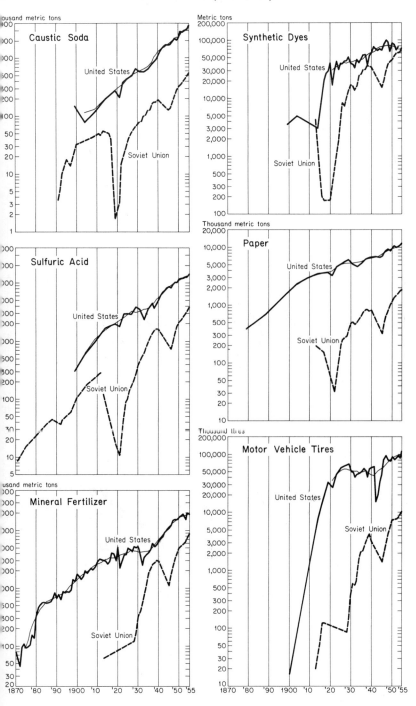

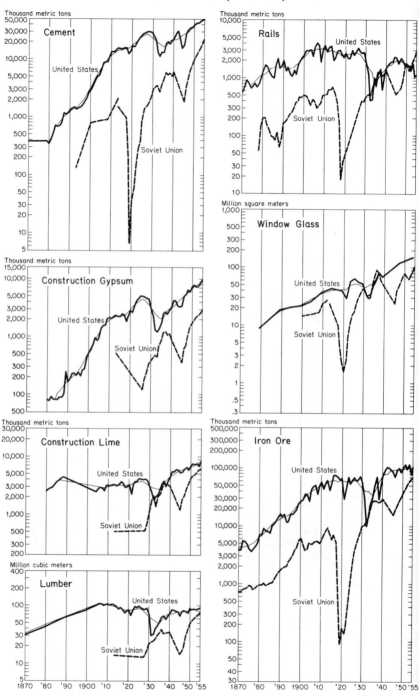

Thousand metric tons — Cement
United States
Soviet Union

Thousand metric tons — Rails
United States
Soviet Union

Thousand metric tons — Construction Gypsum
United States
Soviet Union

Million square meters — Window Glass
United States
Soviet Union

Thousand metric tons — Construction Lime
United States
Soviet Union

Thousand metric tons — Iron Ore
United States
Soviet Union

Million cubic meters — Lumber
United States
Soviet Union

CHART A-2 (continued)

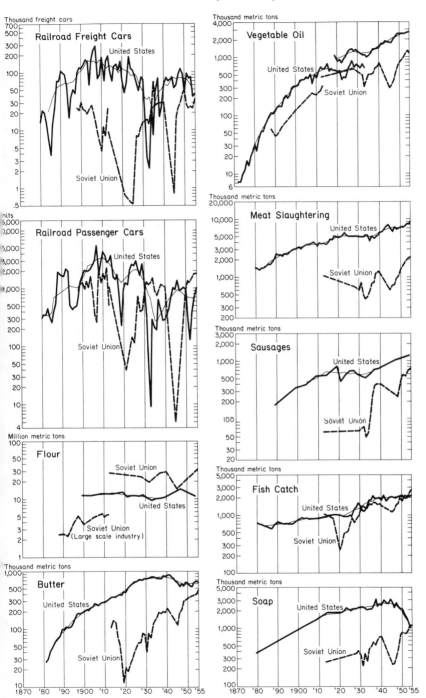

359

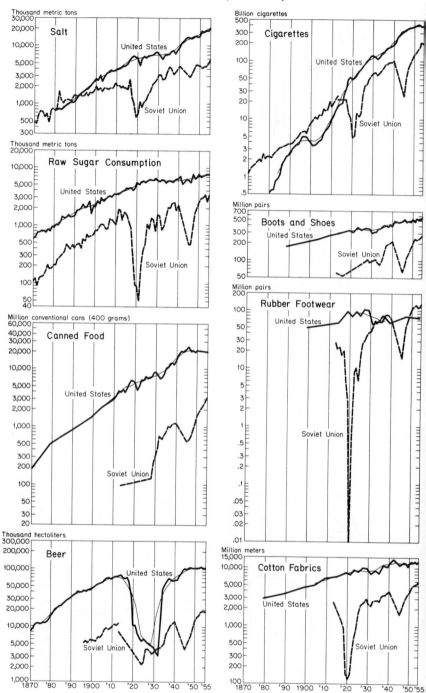

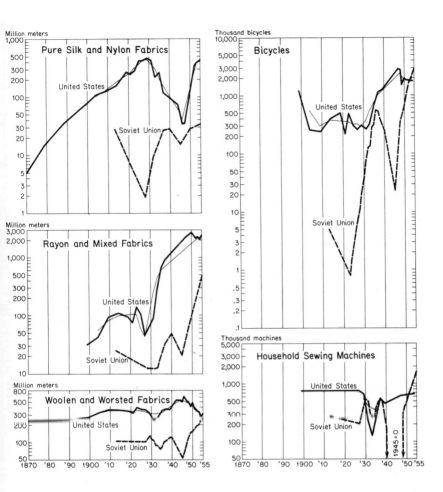

Source: Tables B-1, B-2, and E-1.
Ratio scales.
Thin line represents nine-year moving average for the U.S.

ESTIMATED VALUE ADDED CALCULATED IN RUBLES AND DOLLARS
FOR BASIC SAMPLE OF FORTY-FIVE INDUSTRIES:[a]

| | SOVIET UNION | | | | | |
| | 1913 Value Added | | 1928 Value Added | | 1955 Value Added | |
CODE	1913 Rubles (1)	1914 Dollars (2)	1928 Rubles (3)	1929 Dollars (4)	1955 Rubles[b] (5)	1954 Dollars (6)
Total, 45 industries	2,534	1,144	5,033[c]	1,990[c]	129,739	16,928
Intermediate industrial products	945.2	326.5	1,965	639.1	87,705	11,188
Metals	190.7	88.4	332.6	140.5	21,741	3,253
704 Iron ore		12.8	27.6	14.5	1,670	395.
101 Pig iron		9.4		12.2	2,599	393.
103 Steel ingots and castings	171.6		286.8		14,441	2,272
102 Rolled steel		58.1		108.4		
202 Copper	18.4	7.8	16.5	4.9	1,242	111.
203 Lead	0.20	0.07	0.87	0.20	1,348	43.
204 Zinc	0.48	0.18	0.87	0.29	441.4	38.
Fuel and electricity	495.4	103.7	885.2	221.8	44,552	4,267
301 Electric power	89.8	36.9	274.4	79.0	13,316	1,505
302–4 Coal	182.5	27.8	295.5	50.5	23,298	1,009
303.1 Coke	26.4	3.4	28.0	7.7	3,314	228.
305 Crude petroleum	195.5	35.5	272.9	82.8	3,681	1,508
306 Natural gas	1.2	0.11	14.4	1.8	943.0	16.
Chemicals	84.8	23.7	179.6	66.5	11,269	828.
401 Soda ash	11.3	2.2	15.9	7.5	395.2	52.
402 Caustic soda	6.5	1.4	7.1	1.7	464.8	13.
404 Sulfuric acid	6.4	3.2	17.6	4.3	556.6	93.
405 Mineral fertilizer	3.0	0.93	5.6	17.6	1,931	86.
416 Paper	56.6	14.4	126.3	34.7	3,539	426.
418 Motor vehicle tires	1.0	1.6	7.1	0.73	4,382	156.
Construction materials	174.3	110.7	567.1	210.3	10,143	2,839
506 Cement	27.8	8.2	61.0	16.1	2,608	366.
507 Construction gypsum	3.5	0.82	2.6	0.28	287.0	9.

(continued)

GENERAL NOTE: Unless otherwise noted, each estimate is intended to represent value added at all stages of fabrication within the bounds of industry, as defined in this study, through the final stage represented by the product specified in the stub. Also unless otherwise noted, value of output or value added means unit value or unit value added (Table D-8) times output (Table B-2 or E-1, as appropriate). Estimates in the table made solely by this procedure are not further explained in the special notes below, except for column 3.

In the notes for columns 8, 10, and 12, items identified as census data are taken from official U.S. censuses of mines and quarries, manufactures, or electric utilities, as appropriate.

[a] The basic sample contains forty-seven industries, but synthetic dyes and sausages are not included here because of difficulties in estimating value added for all years.

[b] Prices exclude most of the applicable turnover taxes (see Chapter 5).

[c] The dollar figure excludes beer while the ruble figure does not. Ruble figures excluding beer are: 4,981, 2,988, and 1,300 for the Soviet Union; and 46,973, 11,430, and 4,274 for the United States.

[d] Reliable data are not available for beer in this year, because of prohibition.

UNITED STATES AND SOVIET UNION, 1913, 1928, AND 1955
(millions)

	UNITED STATES				
1913 Value Added		*1928 Value Added*		*1955 Value Added*	
1913 Rubles (7)	1914 Dollars (8)	1928 Rubles (9)	1929 Dollars (10)	1955 Rubles[b] (11)	1954 Dollars (12)
16,115	5,496	47,039[c]	12,565[c]	397,139	41,524
11,655	3,774	35,378	8,931	317,784	32,490
1,911	856.0	5,301	2,056	54,548	7,668
}1,281	87.4	284.5	149.9	2,466	584.3
	70.5	}3,532	144.2	5,503	832.0
	}436.2		}1,335	33,875	5,329
506.9	216.1	887.1	266.0	6,877	615.6
64.5	23.3	362.5	83.1	3,632	116.3
58.5	22.5	235.1	77.9	2,195	190.5
6,991	1,372	17,577	4,017	165,314	15,755
1,283	526.6	5,914	1,702	66,216	5,526
4,065	619.9	6,314	1,080	48,396	2,095
251.9	32.4	319.3	88.1	5,184	357.8
724.1	131.6	2,912	883.4	17,783	7,286
666.7	61.3	2,118	263.9	27,735	490.3
1,529	778.4	8,731	1,481	82,255	5,247
56.5	10.8	106.1	49.7	1,224	162.0
20.1	4.2	69.9	16.6	2,921	82.9
81.4	40.1	287.6	71.0	2,095	351.7
145.6	45.0	233.7	73.6	5,539	248.8
962.6	245.3	2,572	705.8	22,216	2,675
263.2	433.0	5,462	564.7	40,260	1,727
1,224	767.5	3,768	1,376	15,668	3,820
289.9	85.8	1,003	264.7	5,954	836.0
15.9	3.7	51.2	5.6	959.2	32.2

(continued)

SOURCE TO TABLE A-26

Column 1

Iron ore, pig iron, steel ingots and castings, and rolled steel: Value of output of steel ingots and castings plus value added by rolled steel, the sum (358.0 million rubles) times 1927/28 ratio (0.4792) of value added for all component products (Table D-9) to same kind of sum. 1913 unit value added for rolled steel (27.5 rubles per m. ton) is taken to be the same fraction (0.4119) of unit value for steel ingots and castings as in 1927/28.

Electric power: Value of output times 1927/28 ratio (0.6385) of value added to value of output, as both are given in Table C-2. Unit value (0.0725 rubles) taken as average of cost per kwh in Moscow (0.067 rubles) and Leningrad (0.0781 rubles), arbitrarily raised by 10 per cent to reflect distributional costs. Basic data from *38*.

Coal: Value of output times 1927/28 ratio for coal and coke (0.8003) of value added to value of output, as both are given in Table C-2.

Coke: Value added in coke ovens. Unit value added (6.0 rubles per m. ton) is taken to be the same fraction (0.7755) of unit value for bituminous coal as in 1927/28.

Copper, lead, and zinc: Value of output (33.5, 0.36, and 0.88 million rubles) times 1927/28 ratio (0.5506) of value added (col. 3) to value of output.

| | | SOVIET UNION | | | | |
| | | *1913 Value Added* | | *1928 Value Added* | | *1955 Value Added* |
CODE		1913 Rubles (1)	1914 Dollars (2)	1928 Rubles (3)	1929 Dollars (4)	1955 Rublesᵇ (5)	1954 Dollar (6)
508	Construction lime	4.0	2.2	8.1	4.6	620.5	80.4
510	Lumber	112.0	83.3	400.4	159.8	5,821	2,187
518	Rails	3.8	4.7	4.4	6.5	207.5	107.
519	Window glass	23.2	11.5	90.6	23.0	598.8	88.
Transportation equipment		16.5	10.4	28.2	10.5	970.1	255.
905	Railroad freight cars	7.2	4.4	24.6	8.2	720.3	121.
906	Railroad passenger cars	9.3	6.0	3.6	2.3	249.8	133.
Consumer goods		1,572	806.6	3,040ᶜ	1,341ᶜ	41,063	5,485
Food and allied products		805.2	631.7	1,352ᶜ	971.6ᶜ	28,051	3,775
1501	Flour	365.4	341.6	511.5	438.8	5,696	756.4
1503	Butter	17.8	8.2	61.0	11.8	902.9	80.
1504	Vegetable oil	37.9	11.6	71.9	42.5	1,869	136.0
1506	Meat slaughtering	62.9	34.0	120.7	36.3	934.9	178.6
1507	Fish catch	134.4	116.7	194.2	227.1	9,032	889.6
1508	Soap	11.2	5.7	44.8	20.8	464.3	859.6
1509	Salt	10.0	4.5	11.7	8.2	1,140	32.
1510	Raw sugar consumption	112.3	43.0	210.8	45.7	2,821	172.7
1513	Canned food	3.1	2.6	12.2	6.3	1,608	149.9
1514	Beer	34.7	27.2	52.2	d	1,404	187.
1515	Cigarettes	15.5	36.6	61.2	134.1	2,180	332.6
Textiles and allied products		763.4	168.8	1,683	357.7	11,580	1,473
1601	Boots and shoes	269.4	40.3	401.0	127.6	2,937	516.6
1602	Rubber footwear	65.9	13.9	112.5	24.2	607.1	190.0
1604	Cotton fabrics	309.8	58.2	909.5	122.2	4,842	455.8
1609.1	Pure silk and nylon fabrics	35.4	18.6	13.3	8.5	1,209	78.8
1609.2	Rayon fabrics			29.6			
1611	Woolen and worsted fabrics	82.9	37.8	217.1	75.2	1,985	232.
Consumer durables		3.7	6.1	5.4	11.5	1,432	236.7
1701	Bicycles	0.32	0.04	0.91	0.22	864.9	57.9
1707	Sewing machines	3.4	6.1	4.5	11.3	566.6	178.8

Crude petroleum: Value of output (239.1 million rubles) times 1927/28 ratio (0.8176) of value added to value of output.

Natural gas: Unit value added (0.0426 rubles per m³) is taken to be the same fraction (0.0020) of value added per m. ton of crude petroleum as in 1955.

Caustic soda: Value added at last stage of fabrication. Unit value added (118 rubles per m. ton) is taken to be difference between unit values of caustic soda and soda ash. Former (189 rubles per m. ton) is taken to be same fraction (2.6712) of latter as in 1927/28.

Sulfuric acid: Value of output not used in fertilizer.

Rails: Value added in rolling rails.

Railroad freight and passenger cars: Value of output (12.6 and 16.1 million rubles) times 1927/28 ratio (0.5737) of value added (col. 3) to value of output. 1913 price taken from *28*; for passenger cars, average of class II and class III.

Soap: Value of output (33.3 million rubles) times 1927/28 ratio (0.3363) of value added (col. 3) to value of output. 1913 price taken from *28*; assumed to apply to 80% fatty acid content.

oncluded)

		UNITED STATES			
1913 Value Added		*1928 Value Added*		*1955 Value Added*	
1913 Rubles (7)	1914 Dollars (8)	1928 Rubles (9)	1929 Dollars (10)	1955 Rubles[b] (11)	1954 Dollars (12)
25.6	14.1	62.3	35.0	837.3	108.5
830.2	617.6	2,481	990.3	7,105	2,669
21.3	26.2	30.3	44.5	80.2	41.6
40.6	20.1	140.4	35.6	731.8	132.5
167.7	103.3	164.3	59.8	1,019	222.3
141.5	86.4	148.6	49.6	880.2	148.0
26.2	16.9	15.7	10.2	138.6	74.3
4,291	1,618	11,496[c]	3,575[c]	78,337	8,812
1,544	997.2	4,340[c]	2,074[c]	51,525	5,800
156.6	146.4	247.2	212.1	1,869	248.2
59.6	27.6	517.8	100.0	1,223	108.5
89.5	27.4	143.9	85.1	4,410	320.8
225.9	122.0	913.7	275.1	3,833	732.1
123.6	107.3	323.2	378.0	7,177	706.9
76.3	39.1	272.0	126.0	275.9	510.8
22.3	10.1	36.7	25.8	4,120	115.9
316.9	121.3	983.7	213.1	6,352	388.8
131.4	109.6	701.1	362.9	9,675	902.2
329.8	259.0	65.9	d	8,050	1,073
11.6	27.4	134.9	295.7	4,540	692.7
2,715	601.6	7,122	1,467	26,059	2,901
1,280	191.4	1,417	450.9	6,174	1,086
141.7	29.9	316.1	68.1	341.9	107.0
827.9	155.6	3,328	447.1	10,602	998.1
181.1	95.0	1,430	282.2	6,486	442.8
284.2	129.7	630.9	218.5	2,455	287.0
33.0	19.7	34.5	34.3	752.5	110.7
23.5	2.7	23.2	5.7	509.8	34.1
9.5	17.0	11.3	28.6	242.7	76.6

Boots and shoes: Value of output. Price per pair taken as average for men's boots (6.50 rubles), women's shoes (3.00 rubles), and men's civilian shoes (3.98 rubles); from *28*.

Rubber footwear: Value of output. Price from *28*.

Bicycles: Value of output (0.63 million rubles) times 1927/28 ratio (0.5170) of value added (col. 3) to value of output. 1913 price from *28*.

Sewing machines: Value added. Unit value added derived as 1927/28 unit value added (from col. 2 and Table B-2) times price ratio for bicycles (0.7858), 1913 to 1927/28.

Column 2: Col. 8 times 1913 ratio of Soviet to U.S. output. Ratio for steel ingots and castings is used for combined iron and steel products.

Column 3

All items except those noted below: Value added taken from Table D-9, prorated within groups wherever necessary by value of output.

Soda ash, mineral fertilizer, paper, motor vehicle tires, cement, construction gypsum, construction lime, lumber, window glass, and rubber footwear: Values computed from Tables B-2 and D-8.

Caustic soda: Value added in last stage of fabrication computed from Tables B-2 and D-8. Unit value added is taken as difference between unit values of caustic soda and soda ash.

Rails: Value added in rolling rails computed from Tables B-2 and D-8.

Column 4: Col. 10 times 1928 ratio of Soviet to U.S. output. Ratio for steel ingots and castings is used for combined ingots and rolled products.

Column 5

Iron ore: Value of output (2,098 million rubles) times 1954 U.S. ratio (0.7962) of census value added to census value of shipments.

Pig iron: Value of output (11,488 million rubles) times 1954 U.S. ratio (0.2262) of census value added to census value of shipments for blast furnaces.

Steel ingots and castings and rolled steel: Value of output of steel ingots and castings (22,635 million rubles) times 1954 U.S. ratio (0.6380) of census value added for steel works and rolling mills to computed value of output of steel ingots and castings ($6,301 million).

Copper, lead, and zinc: Value of output (2,243, 2,367, and 774.9 million rubles) times 1927/28 ratio (0.5506) of value added to value of output (see col. 1 notes).

Electric power: Value of output (23,321 million rubles) minus cost of fuel and materials. Latter estimated from computed total cost (15,965 million rubles) and percentage distribution of costs by type (*180*, 170).

Coal: Value of output (29,111 million rubles) times 1927/28 ratio for coal and coke (0.8003) of value added to value of output (see col. 1 notes).

Caustic soda: Value added in last stage of fabrication. Unit value added is taken as difference between unit values of soda ash and caustic soda.

Sulfuric acid: Value of output not used in fertilizers.

Rails: Value added in rolling rails.

Railroad freight and passenger cars: Value of output (1,256 and 435.4 million rubles) times 1927/28 ratio (0.5737) of value added (col. 2) to value of output.

Fish catch: Unit value taken as 3,300 rubles (see note b to Table D-8).

Soap: Value of output (1,381 million rubles) times 1927/28 ratio (0.3363) of value added (col. 3) to value of output.

Bicycles: Value of output (1,673 million rubles) times 1927/28 ratio (0.5170) of value added (col. 3) to value of output.

Sewing machines: Value of output (1,096 million rubles) times 1927/28 ratio (0.5170) of value added (col. 3) to value of output.

Column 6: Col. 12 times 1955 ratio of Soviet to U.S. output. Ratio for steel ingots and castings is used for combined ingots and rolled products.

Column 7: Col. 1 times 1913 ratio of U.S. to Soviet output. Ratio for steel ingots and castings is used for combined iron and steel products.

Column 8

Iron ore: 1914 value of shipments ($71.9 million, *626*) times 1919 ratio (0.8129) of census value added to census value of products, times ratio of 1913 to 1914 output.

Pig iron: 1914 census value added for blast-furnace products ($53.1 million) times ratio of 1913 to 1914 output.

Steel ingots and castings and rolled steel: 1914 census value added for steel-mill products ($327.8 million) times ratio of 1913 to 1914 output of steel ingots and castings.

Copper: Value of output times 1919 ratio (0.8613) of census value added in ore mining and primary smelting to census value of products in primary smelting.

Lead and zinc: Value of output times 1919 ratio (0.5571) of census value added for combined lead and zinc mining and primary smelting to census value of products in primary smelting.

Electric power: Value of output times 1912 ratio for commercial central electric stations (0.7313) of census value added to census gross income. 1913 output interpolated logarithmically between 1912 and 1917. Value added taken as gross income minus purchased fuel, power, supplies, and materials.

Coal: Value of output times 1919 ratio (0.8290) of census value added to census value of products.

Coke: 1914 census value added ($24.2 million) times ratio of 1913 to 1914 output. Census value added for entire coke industry (not including gas-house coke) prorated by census value of products.

Petroleum and natural gas: Value of output times 1919 ratio for petroleum natural gas, and natural gasoline (0.6637) of census value added to census value of products.

Soda ash: 1914 value of output.

Caustic soda: 1914 output times difference between 1914 unit values of caustic soda and soda ash (*618*).

Mineral fertilizer: 1914 census value added ($45.2 million) times ratio of 1913 to 1914 output.

Paper, motor vehicle tires, and window glass: 1914 value of output.

Rails: Output times difference between 1914 unit value of rails and steel ingots (*618*).

Railroad freight and passenger cars: 1914 census value added ($45.8 and $20.9 million) times ratio of 1913 to 1914 output. Census value added for combined cars prorated by detailed census value of products for steam-railroad cars.

Flour: 1914 value added.

Soap, boots and shoes, and rubber footwear: 1914 census value added.

Cotton, silk and synthetic, and woolen and worsted fabrics: 1914 value added.

Bicycles: 1914 census value added for bicycles and motorcycles prorated by census value of products.

Sewing machines: 1914 census value added.

Column 9: Col. 3 times 1928 ratio of U.S. to Soviet output. Ratio for steel ingots and castings used for combined ingots and rolled products.

Column 10

Iron ore: 1929 value added ($176.0 million) times ratio of 1928 to 1929 output.

Pig iron: 1929 value added for blast-furnace products ($161.1 million) times ratio of 1928 to 1929 output.

Steel ingots and castings and rolled steel: 1929 value added for steel-mill products ($1,462 million) times ratio of 1928 to 1929 output of steel ingots and castings.

Copper, lead, and zinc: 1929 census value added for ore mining and smelting and refining ($298.3, $82.8, and $77.9 million) times ratio of 1928 to 1929 output. Census value added in secondary smelting and refining prorated by detailed census value of products for secondary ingots and pigs.

Electric power: Value of output times 1927 ratio for commercial central electric stations (0.7701) of census value added to census gross income. Value added taken as gross income minus purchased fuel, power, supplies, and materials.

Coal: 1929 census value added ($1,141 million) times ratio of 1928 to 1929 output.

Coke: 1929 census value added ($134.8 million) times ratio of 1928 to 1929 output. Census value added for entire coke industry (not including gas-house coke) prorated by census value of products.

Petroleum and natural gas: Value of output times 1939 ratio for petroleum, natural gas, and natural gasoline (0.7790) of census value added to census value of shipments.

Soda ash: 1929 value of output.

Caustic soda: 1929 output times difference between 1929 unit values of caustic soda and soda ash (*618*).

Mineral fertilizer: 1929 value added ($72.7 million) times ratio of 1928 to 1929 output.

Paper, motor vehicle tires, and window glass: 1929 value of output.

Rails: Output times difference between 1929 unit values of rails and steel ingots (*618*).

Railroad freight and passenger cars: 1929 census value added ($88.8 and $15.5 million) times ratio of 1928 to 1929 output. Census value added for combined cars prorated by detailed census value of products for steam-railroad cars.

Flour: 1929 value added.

Soap: 1929 census value added ($129.8 million) times ratio of 1928 to 1929 output.
Boots and shoes and rubber footwear: 1929 census value added.
Cotton, silk and synthetic, and woolen and worsted fabrics: 1929 value added.
Bicycles: 1929 census value added for bicycles and motorcycles prorated by census value of products.
Sewing machines: 1929 census value added.

Column 11: Col. 5 times 1955 ratio of U.S. to Soviet output. Ratio for steel ingots and castings is used for combined ingots and rolled products.

Column 12

Iron ore: 1954 value added ($435.7 million) times ratio of 1955 to 1954 output.
Pig iron: 1954 value added for blast furnaces ($620.2 million) times ratio of 1955 to 1954 output.
Steel ingots and castings and rolled steel: 1954 value added for steel works and rolling mills ($4,020 million) times ratio of 1955 to 1954 output of steel ingots and castings.
Copper: 1954 census value added for ore mining and smelting and refining ($548.7 million) times ratio of 1955 to 1954 output. Census value added for secondary smelting and refining prorated by detailed census costs of metals consumed.
Lead and zinc: 1954 census value added for ore mining and smelting and refining ($114.5 and $160.3 million) times ratio of 1955 to 1954 output. Census value added for combined lead and zinc ore mining prorated by value of each in terms of recoverable content of ores (*638*). Census value added for secondary smelting and refining prorated by detailed census costs of metals consumed.
Electric power: 1954 value added ($4,816 million, see Table A-42) times ratio of 1955 to 1954 output.)
Coke: 1954 census value added ($357.8 million) times ratio of 1955 to 1954 output. Census value added for all coke-oven products prorated by census value of products.
Crude petroleum and natural gas: 1954 census value added ($6,789 and $459.0 million) times ratio of 1955 to 1954 output. Census value added in oil- and gas-field contract services divided between petroleum and natural gas by relative census value added.
Caustic soda: Output times difference between 1954 unit values of caustic soda and soda ash. Former is taken as census value of total shipments divided by census quantity of total shipments.
Mineral fertilizer: 1954 census value added times ratio of 1955 to 1954 output.
Rails: Output times difference between 1954 unit values of rails and carbon steel ingots. Both unit values are taken as value of total shipments divided by quantity of total shipments.
Railroad freight and passenger cars: 1954 census value added ($135.4 and $44.2 million) times ratio of 1955 to 1954 output. Census value added for railroad and street cars prorated by census value of shipments.
Soap: 1954 census value added.
Boots and shoes: 1954 census value added for footwear (except rubber) and house slippers ($985.8 million) times ratio of 1955 to 1954 output.
Rubber footwear: 1954 census value added.
Bicycles: 1954 census value added for bicycles and motorcycles prorated by census value of shipments.
Sewing machines: 1954 census value added.

ruble-dollar ratios.

The basic sample of industries accounted for the following percentages of value added for all industry (Tables A-26, A-42, and A-43):

	1913	*1928*	*1955*
Soviet Union	67	63	50
United States	45	37	28

CHART A-3
Physical Output Trends of Fifteen New Soviet Industries:
Soviet Union and United States

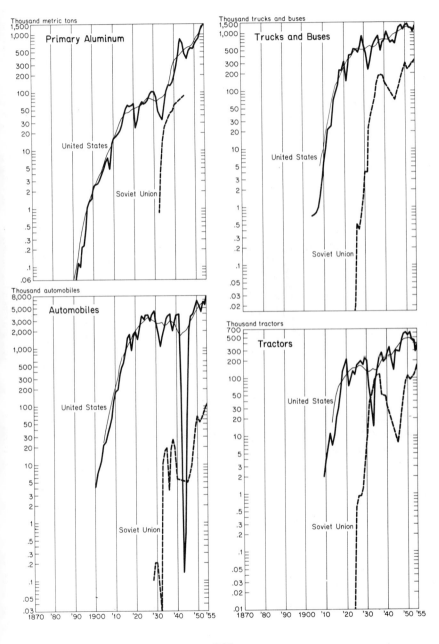

CHART A-3 (continued)

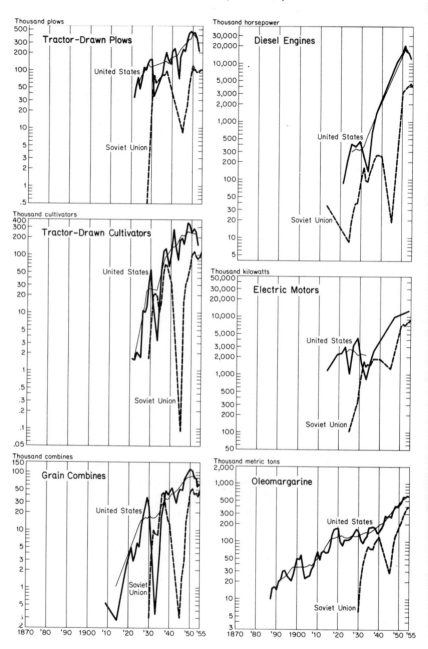

CHART A-3 (concluded)

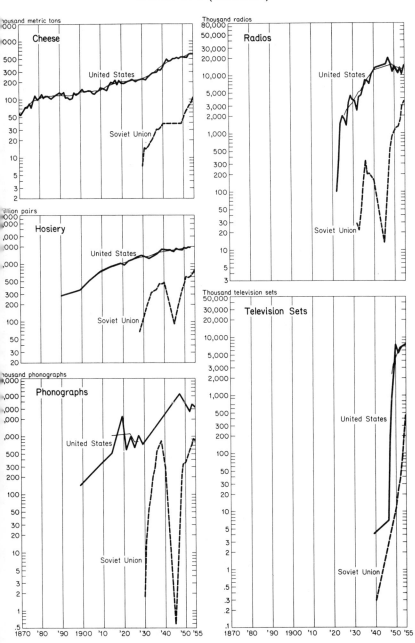

Source: Tables B-1, B-2, and E-1.
Ratio scales.
Thin line represents nine-year moving average for the U.S.

PRODUCTION OF ENERGY

Basic data on production of energy are given in the Tables A-27 and A-28, which are self-explanatory, and Chart A-4. It might have been preferable, for the purposes of our analysis, to have used consumption rather than production in the two countries, but sufficient data were not available on net imports of fuel into the Soviet Union for many of the years involved. Between 1913 and 1938, the Soviet Union shifted from being a net importer of fuel to being a net exporter, so that growth in production overstates growth in consumption. In the postwar period, the Soviet Union probably once again became a net importer, so that growth in production probably understates growth in consumption over some of these years. For the United States, the long-run trend has been for net imports to become increasingly large relative to production in terms of thermal content. Net imports were negligible before 1910 and had risen to around 3 per cent of production in 1955. Hence growth of production understates growth in consumption over that period, but only slightly.

We constructed our own estimates of coal in thermal units instead of using data published in recent Soviet sources, because the latter cannot be reconciled with other data on physical output and thermal content as given in earlier as well as more recent sources. Thus we find the total thermal content of coal for 1913 given as 641.6 billion b.t.u. (161.7 billion calories) on page 133 of *Promyshlennost' SSSR* (*180*), while the thermal content of Donbas coal alone is implied as 696.4 billion b.t.u. (175.5 billion calories) by its output of 25.3 million metric tons (given on page 142 of the same source) and its thermal content of 6,860 calories per ton (given in standard Soviet sources, such as the book by Savinskii cited in Table A-28).

The short table below compares the b.t.u. content per metric ton of coal as we have calculated it with the content implied by data in *Promyshlennost' SSSR* (*180*, 133 and 140) (million b.t.u.):

	Our Data (1)	Promyshlennost' (2)	Ratio (2)/(1)
1913	26.5	22.0	0.83
1940	24.8	23.5	0.95
1945	22.6	21.4	0.95
1950	23.2	21.9	0.94
1955	23.4	22.1	0.94

The official Soviet figures are lower than ours for all years in which comparisons can be made, but the ratio of the official figure to ours is

PRODUCTION OF ENERGY IN THE UNITED STATES, 1860–1955
(trillion b.t.u.)

	Coal, Petroleum, and Natural Gas (1)	Total Excluding Firewood (2)	Total (3)		Coal, Petroleum, and Natural Gas (1)	Total Excluding Firewood (2)	Total (3)
1860	379	480		1908	12,295	12,771	
1861	436	539		1909	13,587	14,100	
1862	468	575		1910	14,836	15,375	
1863	564	674		1911	14,763	15,328	
1864	620	732		1912	15,833	16,418	
1865	628	744	3,585	1913	16,927	17,536	
1866	769	887		1914	15,559	16,195	
1867	811	931		1915	16,163	16,822	18,594
1868	869	993		1916	17,944	18,625	
1869	873	1,001		1917	19,787	20,487	
1870	884	1,012		1918	20,529	21,230	
1871	1,243	1,374		1919	17,441	18,159	
1872	1,365	1,498		1920	20,602	21,340	
1873	1,545	1,679		1921	16,646	17,266	
1874	1,421	1,558		1922	16,506	17,149	
1875	1,404	1,543	4,492	1923	22,494	23,179	
1876	1,431	1,572		1924	20,274	20,922	
1877	1,642	1,783		1925	20,903	21,571	23,020
1878	1,590	1,733		1926	23,049	23,777	
1879	1,876	2,019		1927	22,379	23,155	
1880	2,002	2,146		1928	21,949	22,803	
1881	2,385	2,531		1929	23,796	24,612	
1882	2,865	3,012		1930	21,308	22,060	
1883	3,145	3,294		1931	18,275	18,943	
1884	3,285	3,434		1932	15,607	16,320	
1885	3,091	3,242	5,975	1933	16,924	17,635	
1886	3,279	3,432		1934	18,038	18,736	
1887	3,812	3,967		1935	18,921	19,727	21,086
1888	4,386	4,542		1936	21,598	22,410	
1889	4,135	4,292		1937	22,997	23,868	
1890	4,619	4,780		1938	19,814	20,680	
1891	4,888	5,052		1939	21,653	22,491	
1892	5,121	5,289		1940	24,089	24,969	
1893	5,176	5,350		1941	26,060	26,994	
1894	4,873	5,055		1942	28,124	29,260	
1895	5,467	5,657	7,937	1943	29,407	30,711	
1896	5,491	5,692		1944	31,572	32,916	
1897	5,715	5,928		1945	30,681	32,123	33,340
1898	6,228	6,456		1946	29,916	31,322	
1899	7,171	7,409		1947	33,672	35,098	
1900	7,643	7,893		1948	34,409	35,890	
1901	8,316	8,580		1949	29,067	30,606	
1902	8,685	8,974		1950	32,849	34,422	
1903	10,205	10,526		1951	36,047	37,606	
1904	10,171	10,525		1952	35,249	36,830	
1905	11,386	11,772	13,550	1953	35,554	37,076	
1906	11,946	12,360		1954	33,916	35,365	
1907	13,917	14,358		1955	37,453	38,900	

Notes on page 374.

CHART A-4
Physical Output Trends of Energy:
Soviet Union and United States

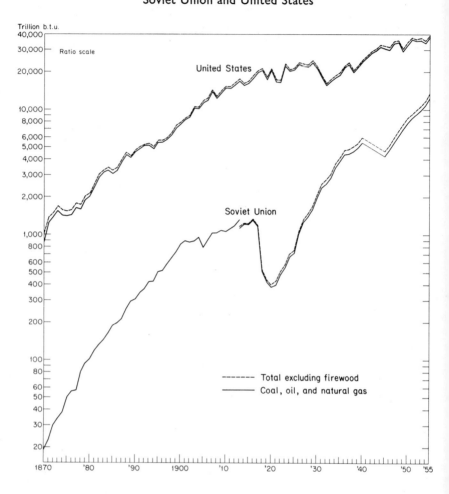

Source: Tables A-27 and A-28.

Notes to Table A-27

Column 1

1860–1898: Data taken from *626*, 142 ff. Converted into b.t.u. at heat unit values given in *649*, 1958, 528.

1899–1951: *613*, 22 and 62 f. Total mineral fuels (G 163a) minus imports of petroleum (G 169a).

1952–1955: *649*, 1958, 528.

Column 2

1860–1898: Col. 1 plus water power. Water power extrapolated from 1899 (see below) by series on water power in *643*, 378.

1899–1951: *613*, 22 and 62 f. Grand total energy (G 160a) minus imports of petroleum (G 169a).

1952–1955: *649*, 1958, 528.

Column 3

All years: Col. 2 plus firewood. Average annual consumption of firewood for decades (*641*, 26) centered and converted into b.t.u. at standard heat unit value as in col. 1 above.

374

TABLE A-28

PRODUCTION OF ENERGY IN RUSSIA AND THE SOVIET UNION, 1860–1955
(trillion b.t.u.)

	Coal and Petroleum[a] (1)		Coal and Petroleum[a] (1)		Coal, Petroleum, and Natural Gas[b] (1)	Total Excluding Firewood[b] (2)	Total[b] (3)
1860	8	1900	840	1913	1,138	1,160	1,684
1861	10	1901	897	1914	1,209	1,234	
1862	9	1902	876	1915	1,205	1,227	
1863	10	1903	886	1916	1,306	1,327	
1864	11	1904	952	1917	1,174	1,192	
1865	10	1905	795	1918	510	524	
1866	12	1906	900	1919	424	440	
1867	12	1907	1,032	1920	382	400	
1868	13	1908	1,033	1921	399	425	
1869	17	1909	1,079	1922	481	508	
1870	19	1910	1,056	1923	542	573	
1871	23	1911	1,117	1924	666	702	
1872	30	1912	1,193	1925	715	750	
1873	34	1913	1,321	1926	1,009	1,054	
1874	38			1927	1,256	1,323	
1875	50			1928	1,392	1,468	1,882
1876	56			1929	1,592	1,689	
1877	57			1930	1,986	2,099	
1878	80			1931	2,386	2,554	
1879	93			1932	2,548	2,753	3,319
1880	101			1933	2,849	3,049	
1881	119			1934	3,423	3,700	
1882	133			1935	3,853	4,157	
1883	145			1936	4,372	4,730	
1884	163			1937	4,434	4,812	5,435
1885	189			1938	4,621	5,044	
1886	197			1939	4,931	5,384	
1887	214			1940	5,480	5,995	6,839
1888	257						
1889	295			1945	4,286	4,656	5,353
1890	309			1946	4,749	5,188	
1891	345			1947	5,406	5,905	
1892	370			1948	6,146	6,724	
1893	421			1949	6,970	7,596	
1894	427			1950	7,784	8,468	9,196
1895	509			1951	8,470	9,171	
1896	518			1952	9,130	9,811	
1897	585			1953	9,831	10,585	
1898	657			1954	10,751	11,569	
1899	726			1955	12,316	13,357	13,996

[a] Tsarist territory excluding Finland.
[b] Current Soviet territory (for prerevolutionary years, interwar territory).

NOTES TO TABLE A-28

For each fuel, output as given in Tables B-1 and B-2 multiplied by b.t.u. content. Content is given for benchmark years in the table below; for intervening years, content was interpolated (except in the case of hydroelectric power for years after 1937, for which content was derived from *180*, 181); for 1860–1913, content for 1913 was used. Gaps caused by missing output data were interpolated on the basis of computed output in b.t.u.'s.

Notes continue on page 376.

significantly lower for 1913 than for other years. Since our figures have all been derived by a consistent procedure, we can only conclude that the cited Soviet source significantly understates the thermal content of coal in 1913. This conclusion is supported by the fact that a technical Soviet source on the economics of the fuel industry published in 1957 gives data implying a thermal content of 26.4 million b.t.u. per metric ton of coal in 1913, a figure virtually identical with ours.[41]

Firewood presents a rather different problem. Data on Soviet output for the interwar years vary enormously from one source to another. The variation may be attributed in part to differences in coverage, but that cannot be the entire explanation. Here, again, there seems to be little doubt that output for early years has been significantly understated in recent statistical abstracts, due allowance being given for possible legitimate differences in coverage, never adequately described. Thus, on page 249 of *Promyshlennost' SSSR*,[42] output is given as 33.4 and 25.7 million cubic meters for 1913 and 1928, respectively. These figures are only about 10 per cent of total consumption of firewood (including peasant use) given in other sources, some published much earlier.[43] They are

[41] *7*, 12.
[42] See also *114*, 57.
[43] *173*, 17, and *363*, 1929, No. 5, 327 ff.

Notes to Table A-28 (continued)

B.T.U. Contents per Unit of Soviet Fuels,[a] Benchmark Years
(million b.t.u.)

Fuel	Unit	1913	1928	1932	1937	1940	1945	1950	19
Coal	m. ton	26.488	25.857	25.712	25.113	24.795	22.640	23.153	23.
Anthracite	m. ton	27.06	27.06	27.06	27.06	27.06	27.06	27.06	27.
Bituminous	m. ton	26.90	26.83	26.77	26.70	26.54	26.20	26.27	26.
Lignite	m. ton	15.83	15.40	15.40	15.16	15.20	15.30	15.18	15.
Crude petroleum	m. ton	39.68	39.68	39.68	39.68	39.68	39.68	39.68	39.
Natural gas[b]	thous. m³	40.906	40.906	40.906	40.906	40.906	40.906	40.906	40.
Peat	m. ton	12.499	12.499	12.499	12.499	12.499	12.499	12.499	12.
Oil shale	m. ton	9.067	9.067	9.067	9.067	9.067	9.067	9.067	9.
Hydroelectric power	thous. kwh	29.443	22.776	21.138	17.332	16.582	15.999	15.055	13.
Firewood	m³	5.241	5.241	5.241	5.241	5.241	5.241	5.241	5.

[a] B.t.u. contents of equivalent fuels in the United States are (same units as table): anthracite, 27.998; bituminous coal, 28.880; petroleum, 41.71; natural gas, 37.947; and firewood, 5.36. For source, see Table A-27.

[b] 1 kg. of natural gas equals 1.1 m³ (see series 306, Table B-2).

Source: Caloric content of each fuel (given in *195*, 281) multiplied by no. of b.t.u. per calorie (3.968). In the case of coal, derived from regional breakdown of output (*272*, 42 ff) by using coefficients of thermal content of different kinds of coal in different regions (given in *195*, 281). In the case of hydroelectric power, derived from no. of grams of conventional fuel per kwh (given in *180*, 181). For firewood, 1 conventional ton of fuel (7,000 calories) equals 5.3 m³ (see series 309, Table B-2).

also significantly smaller than the corresponding figures of 68.0 and 50.5 million cubic meters published in a recent Soviet technical source.[44]

The implied thermal content per cubic meter of firewood is, on the other hand, much higher in the recent Soviet abstracts than in other Soviet sources. According to the former, there are 7.3 thousand b.t.u. per cubic meter;[45] according to the latter, 5.2 thousand.[46] A partial explanation of this difference may be that the former sources give output on a dried basis, while the latter do not. Even if this were the case, the difference in output data could not be fully reconciled.

Our interwar data on total thermal content of firewood have been taken directly from Ioffe (79, 148). His figures are slightly more than double those in recent Soviet abstracts, but still no more than a third of those on total consumption cited above.

The data on production of firewood in the United States are also highly unreliable and almost certainly not comparable with the Soviet data. It will be noted from the appended tables that production of energy excluding firewood was about the same in the Soviet Union in 1913 as in the United States in 1870, while production including firewood was only about 40 per cent as large. It seems most improbable that firewood was relatively so much less important as a source of industrial energy in prerevolutionary Russia than it was in the United States of 1870.

RUBLE-DOLLAR PRICE RATIOS

Ruble-dollar price ratios can be calculated from two sets of data in our study: production indexes for Soviet industrial materials weighted in both Soviet and U.S. prices (summarized for a standardized product coverage in Table A-29) and estimated Soviet and U.S. value added in both dollars and rubles for the basic sample of forty-five industries (Table A-26). Ruble-dollar ratios derived from the first set of data apply only to Soviet baskets of goods, while those derived from the second apply to U.S. baskets as well. The resulting average ruble-dollar ratios are summarized in Table A-30.

When the two sets of ratios are compared for Soviet baskets of goods, it will be noted that there are some significant differences, particularly for 1955 and the categories of construction materials and consumer goods. These differences are attributable to different product coverages and procedures for estimating value added. In the case of industrial materials, product coverage and value-added weights were designed for the purpose

[44] 7, 12.
[45] 180, 133 and 249.
[46] 7, 12, and 363, 1936, No. 1, 61.

of constructing a production index, not for calculating ruble-dollar ratios. Much more care was given to the latter objective in matching counterparts and estimating unit value added in the case of the basic sample of forty-five industries. Both product samples account for about the same total value added in each year.[47] Hence the ruble-dollar ratios calculated from the latter data are probably more meaningful than those calculated from the former.

TABLE A-29

Estimated Value Added Calculated in Rubles and Dollars for Soviet Industrial Materials: Industrial Groups, 1913, 1928, and 1955
(millions)

	1913 Value Added[a]		1928 Value Added[b]		1955 Value Added[c]	
	1913 Rubles	1914 Dollars	1928 Rubles	1929 Dollars	1955 Rubles	1954 Dollars
All industrial materials	2,426.4	1,190.8	4,981.7	1,991.5	136,279	16,449
Intermediate products	1,124.0	364.6	2,165.2	640.9	96,355	12,296
Metals	298.8	100.4	525.4	120.7	28,020	3,965
Fuel and electricity	467.2	95.6	719.4	216.7	35,634	3,802
Chemicals	111.8	41.0	229.2	67.0	14,658	1,139
Construction materials	246.2	127.6	691.3	236.6	21,520	3,391
Consumer goods	1,302.4	826.1	2,816.5	1,350.6	40,045	4,153
Food and allied products	806.6	660.1	1,282.6	987.3	27,972	2,929
Textiles and allied products	495.8	166.0	1,533.9	363.4	12,073	1,224

Source: Tables D-10 and D-8. The 1955 unit value for fish catch is taken as 3,300 rubles (see note *b* to Table D-8).

[a] Forty-six products.

[b] Forty-nine products.

[c] Fifty products. Ruble prices exclude most of the applicable turnover taxes (see Chapter 5).

A major weakness of both sets of data, from the point of view of comprehensiveness, is failure to cover machinery and equipment. Ruble-dollar price ratios for machinery and equipment were apparently generally higher in 1913 and 1928 than the average for other products,[48] but few useful measures of them are available. Since machinery and equipment accounted for only about 5 per cent of persons engaged in Soviet industry in 1913 and about 7 per cent in 1928 (see Table A-39), the average ruble-dollar ratio for all industry based on the Soviet basket of goods would probably be little affected by including that category. This is not so likely to be the case for the ratio based on the U.S. basket,

[47] The fractions of value added of all industry accounted for by the forty-five industries are given in the first section of this technical note.

[48] See *500*, 127 ff.

TABLE A-30

ESTIMATED RUBLE-DOLLAR RATIOS FOR UNIT VALUE ADDED, BY INDUSTRIAL GROUP:
U.S. AND SOVIET OUTPUT WEIGHTS, 1913, 1928, AND 1955

| | SOVIET OUTPUT WEIGHTS | | | | | | U.S. OUTPUT WEIGHTS | | |
| | Industrial Materials[a] | | | Basic Sample, 45 Industries[b] | | | Basic Sample, 45 Industries[b] | | |
	1913[c]	1928[d]	1955[e]	1913[c]	1928[d]	1955[e]	1913[c]	1928[d]	1955[e]
All covered products	2.04	2.50	8.28	2.22	2.50	7.66	2.93	3.74	9.56
Intermediate industrial products	3.08	3.38	7.84	2.90	3.07	7.84	3.09	3.96	9.78
Metals	2.98	4.35	7.07	2.16	2.37	6.68	2.23	2.58	7.11
Fuel and electricity	4.89	3.32	9.37	4.78	3.99	10.44	5.10	4.38	10.49
Chemicals	2.73	3.42	12.87	3.58	2.70	13.60	1.96	5.90	15.68
Construction materials	1.93	2.92	6.35	1.57	2.70	3.57	1.65	2.73	4.10
Railroad cars	n.a.	n.a.	n.a.	1.59	2.69	3.80	1.62	2.75	4.58
Consumer goods	1.58	2.09	9.64	1.95	2.23	7.49	2.65	3.20	8.89
Food and allied products	1.24	1.30	9.55	1.27	1.34	7.43	1.55	2.06	8.88
Textiles and allied products	4.58	4.22	9.86	6.94	4.70	7.86	4.51	4.86	8.98
Bicycles and sewing machines	n.a.	n.a.	n.a.	0.61	0.47	6.05	1.68	1.01	6.80

n.a.: not applicable.
[a] From Table A-29.
[b] From Table A-26.
[c] Ratio, 1913 rubles to 1914 dollars.
[d] Ratio, 1928 rubles to 1929 dollars. Excludes beer.
[e] Ratio, 1955 rubles to 1954 dollars. Ruble prices exclude most of the applicable turnover taxes (see Chapter 5).

since machinery and equipment accounted for about 12 and 20 per cent of persons engaged and value added in U.S. industry in those two years (see Table A-38). Hence we can say that for 1913 and 1928 the ratios for "all covered products" in Table A-30 understate the appropriate ratios for all industry, more in the case of those based on U.S. output weights than in the case of those based on Soviet output weights.

TABLE A-31

SUMMARY OF RUBLE-DOLLAR PRICE RATIOS FOR INDUSTRY IN 1955:
U.S. AND SOVIET OUTPUT WEIGHTS[a]

	Soviet Output Weights	U.S. Output Weights
All industry	7.3[b]	8.7[c]
Intermediate products and consumer nondurables	7.7[d]	9.7[d]
Machinery and equipment	4.8[e]	6.0[f]

[a] Ruble prices exclude most of the applicable turnover taxes (see Chapter 5).

[b] The two components weighted by relative persons engaged in 1955 (Table A-39). The ruble-dollar ratio for intermediate products and consumer nondurables is taken as applying to all products except machinery and equipment.

[c] The two components weighted by relative value added in 1953 (Table A-38), as described above. The same result obtains if persons engaged are used as weights.

[d] From Table A-26, excluding transportation equipment and consumer durables. Ruble-dollar ratios are for unit value added.

[e] The figure for machinery and equipment is taken to bear the same ratio to the figure for intermediate products and consumer nondurables in the case of Soviet output weights as in the case of U.S. output weights.

[f] *423*, 47. This value is the mean of adjusted sample price ratios weighted within groups by imputed U.S. value of shipments and among groups by imputed U.S. value added. The mean of unadjusted ratios, similarly weighted, is 6.9 (*423*, 31).

The situation is different for 1955. Abraham Becker has computed an average ruble-dollar ratio based on a large sample of machinery using the U.S. basket of goods,[49] and it lies between 6:1 and 7:1, both of which are significantly lower than our average ratio of almost 10:1 for other products, the bulk of applicable turnover taxes excluded (see Table A-31). We have assumed that the same relative differences would apply to ratios based on the Soviet basket of goods, and have accordingly estimated such a ratio for machinery. We have then proceeded to calculate average ratios for all industry by weighting the ratios for machinery and for other products by their respective shares of persons engaged in the case of the

[49] *423*.

Soviet Union and value added in the case of the United States. Use of persons engaged in the latter case makes no significant difference. The averages thus estimated are given in Table A-31 for all industry and the two components.

It goes without saying that calculations of this type are based on a number of arbitrary decisions as to the comparability of products and prices in the two countries. The difficulties are particularly acute in the case of heterogeneous and unique products, such as are found in the machinery category. Matching of all products has generally been based on physical likeness, without adjustment for relevant qualitative differences. As we point out in Chapter 3, Soviet goods are generally inferior in quality to their U.S. counterparts. Also, prices on official lists tend, for a variety of reasons discussed in the text, to be lower than the effective prices at which products get entered into Soviet accounts of gross production. In these respects, the ruble-dollar ratios for 1955 given here understate the appropriate values.

It is interesting to observe that ruble-dollar price ratios are systematically lower when based on Soviet output weights than when based on U.S. output weights. There are only two exceptions in Table A-30: chemicals and textiles in 1913. This means there is a weighted negative correlation between Soviet-U.S. ratios for price and output. Put in economic terms, those items whose production in the Soviet Union is smallest relative to the United States tend to have the highest prices relative to the United States. This implies a similar relation between relative scarcities and relative prices in the two countries.

AGGREGATIVE OUTPUT, EMPLOYMENT, AND VALUE DATA

Indexes of Industrial Production in the United States

For the purposes of this study, we have constructed an index of industrial production for the United States extending from 1860 through 1959 (Table A-32). From 1899 onward, the index covers manufacturing, mining, and electric and gas utilities; for earlier years, manufacturing and mining only. The new Federal Reserve Board index, revised as of December 1959,[50] is used from 1929 onward. For earlier years, component indexes (Table A-33) were combined by a system of moving income-originating weights (Table A-34). Links were constructed for each decade with a one-year overlap (1869–1879, 1879–1889, etc)., each weight for a link being the arithmetic average of weights in the terminal

[50] *620*, December 1959, 1469.

TABLE A-32

INDEX OF INDUSTRIAL PRODUCTION: UNITED STATES,
1860–1959
(1913 = 100)

Year	Index	Year	Index	Year	Index	Year	Index	Year	Index
1860	7.48	1880	20.3	1900	50.6	1920	124.0	1940	213.9
1861	7.49	1881	22.3	1901	56.7	1921	100.1	1941	275.5[a]
1862	6.94	1882	23.9	1902	63.2˙	1922	125.9	1942	340.3[a]
1863	7.88	1883	24.4	1903	65.4	1923	144.4	1943	405.2[a]
1864	8.35	1884	23.1	1904	62.3	1924	137.7	1944	398.7[a]
1865	8.00	1885	23.2	1905	73.6	1925	153.0	1945	343.6[a]
1866	9.84	1886	27.9	1906	78.9	1926	163.1	1946	291.7
1867	10.3	1887	29.5	1907	80.6	1927	164.5	1947	320.9
1868	10.8	1888	30.6	1908	68.0	1928	171.8	1948	333.9
1869	11.6	1889	32.6	1909	80.2	1929	188.3	1949	317.7
1870	11.7	1890	35.0	1910	85.3	1930	155.6	1950	366.3
1871	12.3	1891	36.0	1911	82.2	1931	129.7	1951	398.7
1872	14.6	1892	38.8	1912	93.7	1932	100.5	1952	411.7
1873	14.4	1893	34.7	1913	100	1933	119.9	1953	447.3
1874	13.9	1894	33.7	1914	94.1	1934	129.7	1954	421.4
1875	13.5	1895	39.7	1915	109.3	1935	149.1	1955	473.2
1876	13.4	1896	36.9	1916	129.6	1936	178.3	1956	489.4
1877	14.6	1897	39.7	1917	129.7	1937	194.5	1957	492.7
1878	15.5	1898	44.7	1918	128.8	1938	152.3	1958	457.0
1879	17.5	1899	49.2	1919	113.2	1939	188.0	1959	517.3

NOTE: These index numbers are derived from others (with varying base years) that are generally given with as few as two places. Our numbers being essentially ratios of the underlying data, we have recorded them here to an extra place so that the underlying data, or other ratios, might be faithfully reproduced. In the body of our analysis, they are rounded to one less place.

SOURCE: See Tables A-33 and A-34.

[a] The figures for these years are probably too high because of the methods used to estimate war production (see our discussion in Chapters 5 and 7 and *640*). The FRB is re-examining these years and has made a preliminary estimate (*620*, December 1959, 1469) that their current index overstates industrial production in 1943 by about 6 per cent. Accordingly, our index number would be reduced from 405 down to 382.

Other estimates are even lower. If Moore's index for industrial materials (*640*, 33) is combined with the new FRB index for electric and gas utilities (*620*, October 1956, 1063) by 1939 income-originating weights (*653*, 130), the following index numbers are derived: 1940, 216; 1941, 252; 1942, 255; and 1943, 257.

years. That is, a modified Edgeworth weighting formula was used.[51] The links were then chained together.

The new FRB index extends back to 1919, but we preferred to use NBER indexes for part of this period because they are derived directly from census data, while the FRB components for manufacturing and mining have been only partially adjusted to census benchmarks for the

[51] See *618*, 358 ff. The only exception was the first link, 1860–1869, in which only 1869 weights were used because of the unsatisfactory coverage of the 1860 census.

TABLE A-33

COMPONENT INDEXES USED FOR INDEX OF INDUSTRIAL PRODUCTION
IN THE UNITED STATES

Sector	Period	Index
Manufacturing	1860–1899	Frickey, *622*, 54
	1899–1929	Fabricant, *618*, 44.
Mining	1860–1880	Persons, *642*, 170.
	1880–1899	Leong, *632*, 28.
	1899–1929	Barger and Schurr, *603*, 14.
Electric and gas utilities	1899–1929	Weighted index, Gould, *625*, 131. Gaps were filled in as follows: for all gas, 1900 interpolated linearly; for electricity, 1903–1906 and 1908–1911 interpolated logarithmically, and 1899–1901 extrapolated logarithmically on the basis of output of electricity in kilowatt hours in 1880 and 1902 (see our Table E-1). Resulting figures combined by implicit weights for 1902–1907 and 1907–1912 links in Gould's total weighted index.
Manufacturing, mining, and electric and gas utilities	1929–1959	*626b* and *626c*.

TABLE A-34

INCOME-ORIGINATING WEIGHTS USED FOR INDEX OF INDUSTRIAL
PRODUCTION IN THE UNITED STATES
(million dollars)

	Manufacturing	Mining	Electric and Gas Utilities
1869	780	80	
1879	1,110	140	
1889	2,360	210	
1899	3,170	390	40
1909	5,550	730	170
1919	16,200	1,800	424
1929	21,888	2,048	1,631

SOURCE: *Manufacturing*, 1869–1909: Extrapolated by value added in manufacturing. From 1899 onward, taken from *618*, 638; for earlier years, from *609*, 1920.

1919: *629*, 163.

1929: *653*, 130.

Mining, 1869–1909: Extrapolated by value of minerals, as given in *626*, 141, and *606*, 66.

1919, 1929: Same as for manufacturing.

Electric and gas utilities, 1899, 1909: Extrapolated by sum of gross revenue for electricity and value of products for gas (*626*, 159, and *625*, 155). Revenue for 1909 is linearly interpolated between 1907 and 1917; for 1899, linearly extrapolated on the basis of 1902–1907.

1919: *629*, 660.

1929: *653*, 130.

relevant years.[52] The differences in the two sets of indexes are as follows:[53]

	1929 as % of 1919	1939 as % of 1929
Manufacturing		
FRB	153	98
NBER (Fabricant)	164	103
Mining		
FRB	151	99
NBER (Barger-Schurr)	166	94

If we had used the FRB index from 1919 onward instead of from 1929 onward, our index of industrial production would have read 434 for 1955 and 419 for 1958 (on 1913 = 100) instead of 473 and 457, or about 8 per cent lower. This is accounted for by the slower growth of the FRB index over 1919–1929 than of the combined NBER indexes.

Production indexes for industrial groups (see Table A-37) have been compiled from indexes with narrower coverage used in John W. Kendrick's book *Productivity Trends in the United States (628)*. Kendrick's indexes apply to the narrowest industrial categories listed in Table A-35, being constructed with moving weights on the basis of a modified Edgeworth index-number formula. They have been combined into broader categories, comparable with those used for Soviet industry, by using 1929 value-added weights, also listed in the cited table.

Employment and Labor Productivity

Our data on industrial employment in the United States are also drawn from the Kendrick study and are summarized in Tables A-35, A-36, and A-37. Data on persons engaged (in full-time equivalents) and man-hours are unweighted aggregates. Both cover wage earners, salaried employees, proprietors, and estimated unpaid family workers. Industrial coverage has been adjusted to be as comparable as possible to our data for the Soviet Union. The percentage distributions of value added and persons engaged in Tables A-38 and A-40 are computed for a special purpose and exclude some sectors of industry, as specified there.

The data for the Soviet Union in Table A-39 are based on data discussed in technical note 7 of this appendix. As in the case for the United

[52] *620*, December 1953, 1249 f. The new FRB index uses the NBER (Gould) index for electric and gas utilities through 1929.
[53] *626*, 141 and 179; *613*, 66.

TABLE A-35

VALUE ADDED, PERSONS ENGAGED, AND MAN-HOURS OF PERSONS
ENGAGED: UNITED STATES, INDUSTRIAL GROUPS, 1929

	Value Added (million dollars)	Persons Engaged (thousands)	Man-Hours (millions)
Ferrous and nonferrous metals			
Metal mining	1,184	124	314
Primary metal products	2,436	698	1,663
Fuel and electricity			
Fuel			
Anthracite mining	328	151	282
Bituminous mining	808	474	925
Crude petroleum and gas	1,075	218	513
Petroleum and coal products	781	124	330
Electricity			
Electric utilities	1,705	311	756
Chemicals			
Chemicals and allied products	1,727	350	824
Rubber products	538	172	401
Construction materials			
Wood materials			
Lumber and products except furniture	1,397	738	1,726
Paper and allied products	817	279	737
Mineral materials			
Nonmetallic mining and quarrying	961	90	279
Stone, clay, glass products	1,136	394	880
Machinery and allied products			
Machinery and equipment			
Machinery (except electrical)	3,069	927	2,373
Electrical machinery	1,386	422	1,039
Transportation equipment	2,356	651	1,453
Metal products			
Instruments and misc. manufacturing	769	274	609
Fabricated metal products	1,927	661	1,516
Food and allied products			
Food and kindred products	3,121	862	2,079
Beverages	193	44	100
Tobacco manufacturers	817	128	291
Textiles and allied products			
Textile mill products	2,227	1,199	2,930
Apparel and related products	1,678	702	1,470
Furniture	532	225	548
Leather and leather products	757	354	816
Total of above	33,725[a]	10,572[a]	24,854[a]
Printing and publishing	2,234[a]	581[a]	1,346[a]
Unallocated manufacturing	693[a]	785[b]	1,159[b]
Logging and fishing, n.e.c.	553[c]	236[d]	600[e]
Grand total	37,205	12,174	27,959

SOURCE: Except as noted, data compiled by Kendrick for *628*. Kendrick's industrial groups are classified in the stub according to our categories.

Notes continue on page 386.

TABLE A-36
OUTPUT AND EMPLOYMENT IN U.S. INDUSTRY:
SELECTED YEARS, 1899–1955

	Amount[a]		Index (1929 = 100)		
	Persons Engaged (thousands)	Man-Hours (millions)	Output[b]	Persons Engaged	Man-Hours
1899	6,198	16,614	26.1	50.9	59.4
1909	9,013	23,379	42.6	74.0	83.6
1913	9,099	25,738	53.1	74.7	92.1
1919	12,086	28,779	60.1	99.3	102.9
1928	11,469	26,316	91.2	94.2	94.1
1929	12,174	27,959	100.0	100.0	100.0
1933	8,461	16,737	63.7	69.5	59.9
1937	12,207	24,421	103.3	100.3	87.3
1940	12,475	24,587	113.6	102.5	87.9
1948	17,082	35,734	177.3	140.3	127.8
1950	16,711	34,703	194.5	137.3	124.1
1953	18,952	39,312	237.5	155.7	140.6
1955	18,226	37,758	251.3	149.7	135.0

[a] Derived from data used in *628*. Covers mining, manufacturing, electric utilities, and agricultural services, forestry, and fisheries. While agricultural services and a part of forestry lie outside the scope of industry as defined in this study, employment was relatively small and could not be estimated independently. Data for electric utilities were extrapolated from 1953 to 1955 by persons engaged in electric and gas utilities, Department of Commerce national income series.

[b] From Table A-32.

States, the percentage distributions in Tables A-39 and A-41 exclude some specified sectors of industry.

Value Added by Industry

Estimates of value added by U.S. and Soviet industry, comparably defined, are given in Tables A-42 and A-43 for key years. Derivation of those estimates is fully explained in notes to the tables. Data on value added by industrial groups are presented in several other tables, where sources are also described.

Notes to Table A-35 (continued.)

[a] Census data with minor adjustments. These data, except printing and publishing and unallocated manufacturing, are used in calculations for industrial groups (see Tables A-37 and A-38).

[b] Difference for manufacturing between data from the Department of Commerce national income series (adjusted to include unpaid family workers) and data from the Census of Manufacturers.

[c] From Table A-42.

[d] Persons engaged in agricultural services, forestry, and fisheries from Department of Commerce national income series.

[e] Employees (127 million) and proprietors (109 million) times average hours (2,434 and 2,677, respectively) as estimated by Kendrick.

TABLE A-37

INDEXES OF OUTPUT AND EMPLOYMENT, BY INDUSTRIAL GROUP:
UNITED STATES, BENCHMARK YEARS, 1899–1953
(1929 = 100)

	1899	1909	1919	1929	1937	1948	1953
ɔus and nonferrous metals							
ɹtput	27.5	51.1	65.6	100.0	92.3	140.8	169.2
rsons engaged	55.1	75.5	102.8	100.0	110.7	140.0	151.8
an-hours	61.0	84.3	110.8	100.0	93.8	121.4	134.1
ɹtput per person engaged	55.1	75.5	102.8	100.0	110.7	140.0	151.8
ɹtput per man-hour	45.1	60.6	59.2	100.0	98.4	116.0	126.2
and electricity							
ɹtput	16.4	30.8	52.4	100.0	116.1	217.2	294.3
rsons engaged	39.0	68.6	89.4	100.0	92.6	104.3	95.3
an-hours	41.2	68.6	84.7	100.0	74.7	98.2	86.9
ɹtput per person engaged	42.1	44.9	58.6	100.0	125.4	208.2	308.8
ɹtput per man-hour	39.8	44.9	61.9	100.0	155.4	221.2	338.7
ɪel							
Output	24.7	42.9	61.7	100.0	103.9	161.6	182.1
Persons engaged	48.7	83.7	103.8	100.0	92.3	103.8	89.5
Man-hours	52.4	84.3	100.0	100.0	72.5	99.4	81.9
Output per person engaged	50.7	51.3	59.4	100.0	112.6	155.7	203.5
Output per man-hour	47.1	50.9	61.7	100.0	143.3	162.6	222.3
ectricity							
Output	2.0	9.7	36.0	100.0	137.5	314.8	491.0
Persons engaged	8.8	22.0	44.8	100.0	96.3	106.3	116.0
Man-hours	10.7	26.1	43.5	100.0	83.2	95.7	103.1
Output per person engaged	22.8	44.0	80.3	100.0	142.8	296.1	423.3
Ouṭput per man hour	18.6	37.1	82.7	100.0	165.3	328.9	476.2
nicals							
ɹtput	15.2	25.7	52.0	100.0	116.0	272.3	381.7
rsons engaged	33.1	49.2	110.5	100.0	101.9	162.1	185.8
an-hours	39.1	57.4	115.8	100.0	88.1	146.6	169.0
ɹtput per person engaged	45.9	52.2	47.1	100.0	113.8	168.0	205.4
ɹtput per man-hour	38.9	44.8	44.9	100.0	131.7	185.7	225.9
ıtruction materials							
ɹtput	46.1	70.7	64.0	100.0	89.2	146.3	181.8
rsons engaged	73.8	104.0	99.2	100.0	88.5	115.5	117.6
an-hours	84.5	116.4	106.7	100.0	80.1	104.0	105.5
ɹtput per person engaged	62.5	68.0	64.5	100.0	100.8	126.7	154.6
ɹtput per man-hour	54.6	60.7	60.0	100.0	111.4	140.7	172.3
ood materials							
Output	64.0	86.5	74.8	100.0	92.2	139.2	168.2
Persons engaged	75.0	103.0	100.9	100.0	87.0	106.0	105.8
Man-hours	88.3	117.1	108.3	100.0	79.0	95.7	94.8
Output per person engaged	85.3	84.0	74.1	100.0	106.0	131.3	159.0
Output per man-hour	72.5	73.9	69.1	100.0	116.7	145.5	177.4

(continued)

TABLE A-37 (concluded)

	1899	1909	1919	1929	1937	1948	1953
Mineral materials							
Output	27.2	53.9	52.6	100.0	86.0	153.7	196.1
Persons engaged	71.1	106.0	95.7	100.0	91.7	135.3	142.4
Man-hours	76.6	115.0	103.2	100.0	82.4	121.7	128.2
Output per person engaged	38.3	50.8	55.0	100.0	93.8	113.6	137.7
Output per man-hour	35.5	46.9	51.0	100.0	104.4	126.3	153.0
Machinery and allied products							
Output	18.5	32.5	63.4	100.0	96.2	200.6	310.5
Persons engaged	37.5	56.7	106.4	100.0	100.7	177.0	230.7
Man-hours	43.7	62.5	105.7	100.0	86.7	156.1	209.3
Output per person engaged	49.3	57.3	59.6	100.0	95.5	113.3	134.6
Output per man-hour	42.3	52.0	60.0	100.0	111.0	128.5	148.4
Machinery and equipment							
Output	16.8	27.5	63.6	100.0	95.7	204.6	333.1
Persons engaged	33.9	48.6	109.7	100.0	101.8	185.0	242.8
Man-hours	54.2	84.3	104.6	100.0	89.6	148.5	194.7
Output per person engaged	49.6	56.6	58.0	100.0	94.0	110.6	137.2
Output per man-hour	42.9	51.9	59.9	100.0	111.9	128.4	154.4
Metal products							
Output	23.1	45.1	62.8	100.0	97.3	190.7	253.5
Persons engaged	45.1	73.9	99.4	100.0	98.3	159.9	204.9
Man-hours	54.2	84.3	104.6	100.0	89.6	148.5	194.7
Output per person engaged	51.2	61.0	63.2	100.0	99.0	119.3	123.7
Output per man-hour	42.6	53.5	60.0	100.0	108.6	128.4	130.2
Food and allied products							
Output	42.6	62.8	70.3	100.0	133.9	215.9	231.5
Persons engaged	58.0	81.4	110.5	100.0	110.8	137.2	138.2
Man-hours	68.3	92.1	115.7	100.0	98.5	124.2	123.3
Output per person engaged	73.4	77.1	63.6	100.0	120.8	157.4	167.5
Output per man-hour	62.4	68.2	60.8	100.0	135.9	172.4	187.4
Textiles and allied products							
Output	40.4	59.5	69.5	100.0	103.6	151.4	156.6
Persons engaged	59.6	83.5	95.7	100.0	101.7	122.1	117.7
Man-hours	71.7	96.7	94.0	100.0	80.5	104.0	100.3
Output per person engaged	67.8	71.3	72.6	100.0	101.9	125.0	133.
Output per man-hour	56.3	61.5	73.9	100.0	128.7	145.6	156.

SOURCE: Special computations from data in *628*. See Table A-35 for coverage of industrial grou
and for data necessary to reconstruct absolute figures for persons engaged and man-hours.

TABLE A-38

PERCENTAGE DISTRIBUTION OF VALUE ADDED AND PERSONS ENGAGED BY INDUSTRIAL GROUP:
UNITED STATES, BENCHMARK YEARS
(per cent)

	1899	1909	1919	1929	1937	1948	1953
			VALUE ADDED				
ous and nonferrous metals	16.0	12.8	11.2	10.7	11.8	9.6	10.7
and electricity	7.0	9.3	11.6	14.0	15.5	13.7	11.1
ıel	6.3	7.3	9.0	8.9	9.6	10.8	7.9
ectricity	0.7	2.0	2.6	5.1	5.9	2.9	3.2
micals	4.7	5.0	6.5	6.7	7.1	8.0	8.6
struction materials	17.1	17.3	12.2	12.7	11.0	11.4	11.0
ood materials	10.2	9.8	7.2	6.5	5.7	6.6	6.1
ineral materials	6.9	7.5	5.0	6.2	5.3	4.8	4.9
hinery and allied products	18.9	20.1	27.7	28.2	26.4	29.6	36.6
achinery and equipment	11.9	12.0	20.6	20.2	19.1	21.5	27.3
etal products	7.0	8.1	7.1	8.0	7.3	8.1	9.3
d and allied products	17.5	16.6	12.4	12.3	14.9	13.5	11.4
tiles and allied products	18.8	18.9	18.4	15.4	13.3	14.2	10.6
ıls	100.0	100.0	100.0	100.0	100.0	100.0	100.0
			PERSONS ENGAGED				
ous and nonferrous metals	8.4	7.9	7.9	7.8	8.6	7.8	7.6
and electricity	9.2	11.1	10.7	12.0	11.2	9.0	7.5
ıel	8.7	10.2	9.4	9.1	8.4	6.8	5.3
ectricity	0.5	0.9	1.3	2.9	2.8	2.2	2.2
micals	3.2	3.2	5.4	4.9	5.0	5.8	5.9
struction materials	20.5	19.8	13.9	14.2	12.6	11.8	10.8
ood materials	14.1	13.3	9.6	9.6	8.4	7.3	6.6
ineral materials	6.4	6.5	4.3	4.6	4.2	4.5	4.2
hinery and allied products	20.3	21.1	29.2	27.8	28.0	35.3	41.5
achinery and equipment	12.5	12.4	20.5	19.0	19.3	25.1	29.8
etal products	7.8	8.7	8.7	8.8	8.7	10.2	11.7
d and allied products	11.1	10.7	10.7	9.8	10.8	9.7	8.8
tiles and allied products	27.3	26.2	22.2	23.5	23.8	20.6	17.9
ıls	100.0	100.0	100.0	100.0	100.0	100.0	100.0

ums and detail may not agree because of rounding.
ɔURCE: See Tables A-35 and A-37. Printing and publishing, unallocated manufacturing, and
·ing and fishing (n.e.c.) are excluded.

TABLE A-39

PERCENTAGE DISTRIBUTION OF VALUE ADDED AND PERSONS ENGAGED
BY INDUSTRIAL GROUP: SOVIET UNION, BENCHMARK YEARS
(per cent)

	Value Added 1928	*Persons Engaged*						
		1913	1928	1933	1937	1940	1950	1!
Ferrous and nonferrous metals	4.9	7.5	5.4	6.9	5.5	4.8	6.5	
Fuel and electricity	11.5	5.9	8.2	9.9	7.6	7.9	9.7	
Fuel	9.9	5.6	7.7	8.7	6.5	6.8	8.2	
Electricity	1.6	0.4	0.5	1.2	1.1	1.1	1.5	
Chemicals	4.2	1.2	1.9	3.4	3.1	3.3	2.9	
Construction materials	15.3	23.1	19.0	27.9	19.9	21.3	23.5	2
Wood materials[a]	11.5	19.0	14.8	21.6	16.9	17.7	18.2	1
Mineral materials	3.8	4.1	4.3	6.3	3.1	3.6	5.2	
Machinery and allied products[b]	11.4	10.6	12.8	14.8	28.5	28.4	29.8	3
Civilian machinery and equip.	6.2	5.4	7.5	9.7	16.0	10.0	12.3	1
Metal products	5.2	5.3	5.2	5.1	12.5	18.4	17.5	1
Food and allied products	23.2	19.0	15.5	13.2	12.9	12.4	10.7	
Textiles and allied products[c]	29.3	32.7	37.0	24.0	22.5	21.8	17.0	1
Total	100.0	100.0	100.0	100.0	100.0	100.0	100.0	10

Sums and details may not agree because of rounding.

SOURCE: Value added, Table C-2; persons engaged, Table A-18. Excludes repair shops unallocated industries.

[a] Includes paper and matches.
[b] Includes consumer durables and military products.
[c] Includes furniture for 1937 and later years.

Estimated U.S. Military Production in 1954

Data on production of conventional military end products in the United States are not published in comprehensive or easily accessible form. Summary series are published for the value of production and procurements, but these figures are likely to differ significantly from production alone, as may be seen in Table A-44. We present there such estimates of the value of output and value added for conventional military end products as we have been able to reconstruct from basic statistics in the 1954 census of manufactures. In the case of aircraft and ships and boats, statistics are available in adequate detail, but there is a problem in how to treat intermediate products since a final bill of goods is not specified. In the case of that large group of products covered by the category "ordnance and accessories," the only published figures are value added for the entire category and selected statistics for small arms. We have estimated the value of final ordnance products from value added and the relation between value added and value of output in related industries.

TABLE A-40

CUMULATED PERCENTAGE OF VALUE ADDED AND PERSONS ENGAGED ACCOUNTED FOR BY INDUSTRIAL GROUPS ARRAYED BY GROWTH IN LABOR PRODUCTIVITY OVER SELECTED PERIODS: UNITED STATES, BENCHMARK YEARS

(per cent)

CUMULATED PERCENTAGES

INDUSTRIAL GROUPS ARRAYED BY GROWTH IN OUTPUT PER MAN-HOUR	1909 VA	1909 PE	1919 VA	1919 PE	1929 VA	1929 PE	1937 VA	1937 PE	1948 VA	1948 PE	1953 VA	1953 PE
(1909–1953)												
1	2.0	0.9	2.6	1.3	5.1	2.9	5.9	2.8	2.9	2.2	3.2	2.2
2	7.0	4.1	9.1	6.7	11.8	7.8	13.0	7.8	10.9	7.8	11.8	8.1
3	14.3	14.3	18.1	16.1	20.7	16.9	22.6	16.2	21.7	14.8	19.7	13.4
4	21.8	20.8	25.1	20.4	26.9	21.5	27.9	20.4	26.5	19.3	24.6	17.6
5	41.9	41.9	50.8	49.6	55.1	49.3	54.3	48.4	56.1	54.6	61.2	59.1
6	58.5	52.6	63.2	60.3	67.4	59.1	69.2	59.2	69.6	64.3	72.6	67.9
7	77.4	78.8	81.6	82.5	82.8	82.6	82.5	83.0	83.8	84.9	83.2	85.8
8	87.2	92.1	88.8	92.1	89.3	92.2	88.2	91.4	90.4	92.2	89.3	92.4
9	100.0	100.0	100.0	100.0	100.0	100.0	100.0	100.0	100.0	100.0	100.0	100.0
(1929–1953)												
1					5.1	2.9	5.9	2.8	2.9	2.2	3.2	2.2
2					11.8	7.8	13.0	7.8	10.9	8.0	11.8	8.1
3					20.7	16.9	22.6	16.2	21.7	14.8	19.7	13.4
4					33.0	26.7	37.5	27.0	35.2	24.5	31.1	22.2
5					39.5	36.3	43.2	35.4	41.8	31.8	37.2	28.8
6					54.9	59.8	56.5	59.2	56.0	52.4	47.8	46.7
7					61.1	64.4	61.8	63.4	60.8	56.9	52.7	50.9
8					89.3	92.2	88.2	91.4	90.4	92.2	89.3	92.4
9					100.0	100.0	100.0	100.0	100.0	100.0	100.0	100.0

SOURCE: Table A-37 and A-38.
VA: value added.
PE: persons engaged.

TABLE A-41

CUMULATED PERCENTAGE OF VALUE ADDED AND PERSONS ENGAGED ACCOUNTED FOR BY INDUSTRIAL GROUPS ARRAYED BY GROWTH IN LABOR PRODUCTIVITY OVER SELECTED PERIODS: SOVIET UNION, BENCHMARK YEARS

(per cent)

INDUSTRIAL GROUPS ARRAYED BY GROWTH IN OUTPUT PER PERSON ENGAGED[a]	Value Added, 1928		CUMULATED PERCENTAGE Persons Engaged[b]						
	Unadjusted[b]	Adjusted[c]	1913	1928	1933	1937	1940	1950	1955
(1913–1955)									
1	1.6	4.6	0.4	0.5	1.2	1.1	1.1	1.5	1.6
2	6.5	10.3	7.9	5.9	8.1	6.6	5.9	8.0	7.6
3	17.9	13.6	18.5	18.7	22.9	35.1	34.3	37.8	38.8
4	27.8	24.6	24.1	26.4	31.6	41.6	41.1	46.0	47.0
5	32.0	27.4	25.3	28.3	35.0	44.7	44.4	48.9	50.4
6	55.2	54.1	44.3	43.8	48.2	57.6	56.8	59.6	60.1
7	84.5	84.1	77.0	80.8	72.2	80.1	78.6	76.6	78.1
8	88.3	86.3	81.1	85.1	78.5	83.2	82.2	81.8	84.4
9	99.8	99.9	100.1	99.9	100.1	100.1	99.9	100.0	100.0
(1928–1955)									
1	11.4	3.3		12.8	14.8	28.5	28.4	29.8	31.2
2	13.0	7.9		13.3	16.0	29.6	29.4	31.3	32.8
3	17.9	13.6		18.7	22.9	35.1	34.3	37.8	38.8
4	27.8	24.6		26.4	31.6	41.6	41.1	46.0	47.0
5	32.0	27.4		28.3	35.0	44.7	44.4	48.9	50.4
6	61.3	57.4		65.3	59.0	67.2	66.2	65.9	68.4
7	84.5	84.1		80.8	72.2	80.1	78.6	76.6	78.1
8	88.3	86.3		85.1	78.5	83.2	82.2	81.8	84.4
9	99.8	99.9		99.9	100.1	100.1	99.9	100.0	100.0

a Table 40.
b Table A-39.
c Table A-6, direct weights.

TABLE A-42

Estimated Value Added in U.S. Industry, 1913, 1928, and 1955
(million dollars)

	1914	1929	1954
Manufacturing	9,386	30,591	116,913
Mining	1,086	4,356	11,546
Logging, n.e.c.	282	432	547
Fishing	111	121	356
Electric power	589	1,705	4,816
Total	11,459	37,205	134,178
	1913 in 1914 Prices	1928 in 1929 Prices	1955 in 1954 Prices
Total	12,181	33,931	150,682

Source

Manufacturing, 1914, 1929, 1954: *626*, series J-10, as continued.

Mining, 1914: Value of mineral products (*626*, series G-1) times average ratio (0.5146) of census value added to value of mineral products for 1909 and 1919. Census value added taken as census value of products minus cost of supplies and materials, fuel and power, and contract work (*649*, 1926, 702).

1929: Estimates of Kendrick (sum of components in Table A-35).

1954: *649*, 1958, 720.

Logging, n.e.c., 1914: Cost of materials for the industrial category, lumber and timber products (*597*, 126).

1929: Cost of materials for the industrial category, forest products, basic industries (*649*, 1932, 740).

1954: Value of stumpage cut in the industrial category, lumber and timber basic products (*609*, 1954, 24A–20).

Fishing, 1914: Fish catch (Table E-1) times unit value (Table D-8).

1929: Fish catch (Table E-1) times 1930 unit value to fishermen (*649*, 1958, 703).

1954: Value of fish catch to fishermen (*649*, 1958, 703).

Electric power, 1914: Output (logarithmically interpolated in Table E-1) times unit value (Table D-8) times 1912 ratio for commercial central electric stations (0.7313) of value added to gross income (see notes to col. 8, Table A-26).

1929: Output (Table E-1) times unit value (Table D-8) times 1927 ratio for commercial central electric stations (0.7701) of value added to gross income (see notes to col. 10, Table A-26).

1954: Value added for electric utilities times ratio (1.155) of total output in kilowatt hours to output of utilities (*649*, 1956, 529). Value added taken as revenue (*649*, 1956, 532) minus operating expenses excluding maintenance (*650*, xxii, and *651*, xvi). For publicly owned utilities, covered operating expenses including depreciation were divided by 0.6, ratio of covered revenues to total revenues for publicly owned utilities as estimated by source, and maintenance was taken

393

TABLE A-43

Estimated Value Added in Soviet
Industry,[a] 1913, 1927/28, and 1955
(million rubles)

1913	3,774
1927/28	7,894
1955	258,000

[a] Excludes repair shops.

Source

1913: Gross value of output (9,245 million rubles as estimated in *506*) multiplied by 1928/29 ratio (0.4082) of value added to gross value (Table C-2). A very similar figure for 1913 value added (3,750 million rubles) is derived by projecting 1927/28 value added backward by the production index excluding miscellaneous machinery (Table D-3) and deflating the result by the price index for industrial materials with 1913 weights (Table A-17).
1927/28: From Table C-2.
1955: Net production excluding turnover taxes, from Table F-3.

TABLE A-44

Estimated Value of Military Production: United States, 1954
(million dollars)

	Value[a]	Value Added[b]
Conventional military products		
Production[c]		
Aircraft	6,811	5,867
Ships and boats	465	297
Ordnance and accessories	4,500	2,040
Total	11,776	8,204
Production and procurements[d]		
Aircraft	8,334	
Missiles	504	
Ships	1,090	
Other	6,030	
Total	15,958	
Atomic energy[d]	1,895	

Notes to Table A-42 (continued)

as the same ratio (0.1456) of total operating expenses as for privately owned utilities.

Total, 1914, 1929, 1954: Sum of components.
1913, 1928, 1955: Value added in 1914, 1929, and 1954, respectively, times appropriate annual relative of industrial production (Table A-32).

Notes to Table A-44

ᵃ Represents value of final products only, that is, those products to be delivered to military users. Value of intermediate products produced and consumed within industry is excluded. Value of output is measured on a product basis, as opposed to an establishment basis, and generally by value of work done, as opposed to value of shipments.

ᵇ Except for ordnance and accessories, value added is adjusted to a product basis. At the narrowest industrial level for which such data are available, value added on an establishment basis was multipled by the ratio for corresponding gross value of data on a product basis to date on an establishment basis. Adjusted value added was then apportioned to appropriate subindustries on the basis of gross value on a product basis. For details, see notes to each item.

ᶜ Data from *609*, 1954.

ᵈ Data from *649*, 242.

NOTES ON DATA RELATING TO PRODUCTION (TABLE A-44)

Aircraft

Value of output: Sum for the following industries (figures in parentheses refer to SIC code): military-type aircraft (3721111); modifications, conversions, and overhaul of military aircraft (3721411); other aeronautical services on military aircraft, including guided missile production in aircraft plants and research and development (3721511); military aircraft engine parts (3722211); and other aeronautical services on military aircraft engines, including research and development (3722311). For engine parts, value of shipments; for all others, value of work done. The remaining products classified in the aircraft industry (372) are essentially parts and components for those already enumerated, and we have assumed that the former's value is reflected in the latter's. This treatment leads to some understatement of the value of final products, since some parts and components are purchased by military users as spare parts. We have treated engine parts (3722211) as purchased spare parts and counted their value accordingly.

Value added: Value added adjusted to a product basis (see note b) for aircraft and primary services (3721), aircraft engines (3722), aircraft propellers (3723), and aircraft equipment n.e.c. (37290) apportioned by the share of military products in total value of work done (or shipments) within each industry. For this purpose, value of shipments of military components and parts was, of course, counted within each industry. For aircraft propellers, apportionment was based on the military share for complete propellers (3723011); for aircraft equipment n.e.c., on the military share for aircraft (3721111).

Ships and boats

Value of output: Value of work in military shipbuilding and repairing (37311, 37312, and 37313) and military boat repairing (3732211), plus value of shipments in military boatbuilding (3732111).

Value added: Value added adjusted to a product basis (see note b) for shipbuilding and repairing (3731) and boatbuilding and repairing (3732) apportioned by the share of military products in total value of work done (or shipments) within each industry.

Ordnance and accessories

Value of output: Not published. Estimated as value added divided by 0.45, the approximate average ratio for such similar industries as internal combustion engines (3519), tractors (3521), farm machinery (3522), and construction and mining machinery (3531).

Value added: Summed value added on an establishment basis for private and governmental production. Adjustment to a product basis could not be done for lack of data. Excludes nonmilitary small arms (19512), whose value added was estimated from value of shipments and 1947 ratio for small arms (1951) of value added to value of shipments. Includes other nonmilitary products classified within this industry.

Technical Note 10 (Chapter 7):
Basic Data on Fulfillment of Five Year Plans

This note presents the data underlying the analysis of the fulfillment of output goals in the five year plans. The physical output goals included in this analysis are given in Table A-45; the estimated value added corresponding to these goals and to actual outputs is given in Table A-46, expressed in both 1928 and 1955 rubles. In calculating value added, each output, planned and actual, has been multiplied by the relevant price net of the cost of nonindustrial materials, as that price is given in Table D-8. Estimated value added is shown for the full sample in each plan—that is, every product with an output goal that is also represented in our output series in Appendix B—and for the sample of eighteen products that is common to all plans (see Table A-47).

TABLE A-45

PHYSICAL OUTPUT GOALS OF SOVIET PRODUCTS AS GIVEN IN
FIVE YEAR PLANS, 1932, 1937, 1950, AND 1955

	Unit[a]	1932[b] Minimum	1932[b] Maximum	1937	1950[c]	1955[c]
Ferrous metals						
Pig iron	th.m.t.	8,000	10,000	18,000	19,500	(34,000)
Rolled steel	th.m.t.	6,300	8,000	14,000	17,800	(34,000)
Steel ingots	th.m.t.	8,300	10,400	19,000	25,400	(44,000)
Iron ore	mill.m.t.	14.8	19.4	36.9	40.0	
Manganese ore	mill.m.t.	0.96		2.7		
Nonferrous metals						
Aluminum	th.m.t.			80		
Copper	th.m.t.	64.5	84.7	155.0	[215]	[470]
Lead	th.m.t.			120	[156]	[390]
Zinc	th.m.t.	38.0	77.4	100	[125]	[310]
Fuel and electricity						
Electric power	bill.kwh	17	22	38.0	82.0	(164)
Coal	mill.m.t.	68.0	75.0	152.5	250.0	(373.4)
Coke	mill.m.t.			23.7	30.0	
Crude petroleum	mill.m.t.	19.0	21.7	45.0	35.4	(70.0)
Natural gas	mill.m³			2,750	8,400	(10,370)
Oil shale	th.m.t.			2,600		(10,800)
Peat	mill.m.t.	10.4	12.3	25.0	44.3	(46.0)
Firewood	mill.m³			107.1		
Chemicals						
Soda ash	th.m.t.			750.0	800	(1,378)
Caustic soda	th.m.t.				390.0	(580)
Sulfuric acid	th.m.t.	1,270	1,450	2,080		
Mineral fertilizer	th.m.t.				5,100	(9,400)
Phosphoric fertilizer	th.m.t.	1,950	2,550	2,550		
Ground natur. phosphate	th.m.t.			2,900	400.0	
Synthetic dyes	th.m.t.			37.7	43.0	
Paper	th.m.t.	650	750	1,000	1,340	(1,740)
Motor vehicle tires	thous.			3,000		
Rubber footwear	mill.pairs	60	75	120	88.6	
Construction materials						
Red brick	mill.	7,700	9,300	8,000	[10,500]	[20,000]
Fire-clay bricks	th.m.t.			2,300	2,780	
Quartzite bricks	th.m.t.			800	980	
Cement	th.m.t.	6,000	7,000	7,500	10,500	(22,400)
Industrial timber	mill.m³	116.6		174.4	(187)	(250)
Lumber	mill.m³	32.8	42.5	43.0	39.0	
Plywood	th.m³			735.0	810	
Roll roofing	mill.m²				[190]	[386]
Roofing iron	th.m.t.	575				
Asbestos shingles	mill.				410	(1,420)
Window glass	mill.m²	79	101	227	80	

(continued)

		Unit[a]	1932[b] Minimum	1932[b] Maximum	1937	1950[c]	1955
	Transportation equip.						
901	Automobiles	thous.			60.0	65.6	
902	Trucks and buses	thous.			140.0	434.4	
903	Diesel and elec. locom.	units			290	520	
904	Steam locomotives	units	700	825	2,900	2,200	
905	Railroad freight cars	thous.	12.6				
906	Railroad passenger cars	units			3,500	2,600	
	Agricultural mach.						
1001	Tractors	thous.	50	55	96.0	112.0	(13
1002	Tractor-drawn plows	thous.				111.0	
1007	Tractor-drawn cultivators	thous.				82.3	
1009	Tractor-drawn drills	thous.				83.3	
1025	Tractor-drawn threshers	thous.				18.3	
1016	Grain combines	thous.			25		
	Miscellaneous mach.						
1101	Steam boilers	th.m²			385	540	(96
1102	Water turbines	th.kw				1,022	(2,45
1103	Steam and gas turbines	th.kw			1,400	2,906	(5,47
1210	Machine tools	thous.			40.0	74.0	
1214	Looms	units				25,000	
	Food and allied products						
1501	Flour	mill.m.t.				19	
1503	Butter	th.m.t.			180	275	(57
1504	Vegetable oil	th.m.t.	850	1,100		880	(1,45
1504.1	Oleomargarine	th.m.t.			120	250	
1505	Cheese	th.m.t.			37		
1506	Meat	th.m.t.			1,250	1,300	(2,76
1507	Fish catch	th.m.t.			1,900	2,200	(2,77
1508	Soap (40%)	th.m.t.			1,300	870	
1509	Salt	th.m.t.	3,240	3,250			
1510	Raw sugar	th.m.t.	2,200	2,600	2,800	2,400	(4,49
1513	Canned food	mill.cans	500	650	2,400		(3,20
1519	Beer	th.hectol.	2,829		7,500	15,000	
1515	Cigarettes	bill.	75		140		
1516	Low-grade tobacco	th.crates	4,200	4,900	6,000		
1517	Matches	th.crates	10,700	12,200	13,000	9,900	
601	Crude alcohol	th.hectol.			7,500	10,080	
	Textiles and allied products						
1601	Boots and shoes	mill.pairs	70	80	205	240	(31
1603	Cotton yarn	th.m.t.	570	620		685	
1604	Cotton fabrics	mill.m	4,360	4,700	6,250	4,686	(6,27
1607	Linen fabrics	mill.m	424	492	591	420.0	
1611	Woolen and worsted fabrics	mill.m	192.0	270.0	270	159.4	(23
1613	Hosiery	mill.pairs			1,000	580.0	
	Consumer durables						
1701	Bicycles	thous.			700		
1703	Electric light bulbs	mill.			180		
1704	Phonographs	thous.			1,500		
1705	Radios	thous.			700		

SOURCE: 1932, *165*; 1937, *175*; 1950, *55*; 1955, *29*.

[a] For abbreviations, see general note at the beginning of Appendix B.

[b] Where only one goal is given, it is shown in the middle of the two columns.

[c] Parentheses indicate the figure is derived from a base output and a given percentage incre brackets, that the figure is derived from an estimated base output in the same way.

ACTUAL AND PLANNED (FIVE YEAR PLAN) VALUE ADDED OF SOVIET PRODUCTS, 1932, 1937, 1950, AND 1955

BILLION 1928 RUBLES

		1932 Actual	1932 Planned Min.	1932 Planned Max.	1937 Actual	1937 Planned	1950 Actual	1950 Planned	1955 Actual	1955 Planned
All covered products	A	8.9	12.1	14.2	20.2	26.7	33.4	35.4	40.9	41.1
	B	7.0	9.0	10.5	12.9	16.7	22.1	21.8	37.2	31.1
Intermediate products	A	5.9	7.5	8.9	13.1	16.2	21.8	21.0	34.4	34.2
	B	5.2	6.3	7.4	10.4	12.5	19.0	18.3	32.6	32.3
Ferrous metals	A	1.0	1.4	1.8	2.8	3.2	4.2	3.9	6.6	6.5
	B	1.0	1.3	1.6	2.6	3.0	3.9	3.7	6.6	6.5
Nonferrous metals	A	0.1	0.1	0.1	0.3	0.4	0.4	0.4	0.8	0.9
	B	0.1	0.1	0.1	0.2	0.2	0.3	0.3	0.5	0.7
Fuel and electricity	A	2.5	2.7	3.3	6.3	7.2	12.2	11.5	21.2	20.5
	B	2.5	2.7	3.3	5.3	6.2	11.6	10.7	20.6	19.9
Chemicals	A	0.4	0.6	0.7	1.0	1.3	1.1	1.2	1.4	1.4
	B	0.2	0.3	0.3	0.4	0.4	0.5	0.6	0.8	0.8
Construction materials	A	2.0	2.7	3.0	2.7	4.1	3.9	4.1	4.3	4.8
	B	1.5	1.9	2.0	1.8	2.7	2.6	3.0	3.9	4.5
Machinery	A	0.4	0.4	0.4	3.0	3.9	5.3	7.4	1.2	1.1
	B	0.3	0.3	0.3	0.3	0.5	0.6	0.6	0.9	0.7
Transportation equipment	A	0.2	0.1	0.2	2.5	3.2	4.4	6.3	n.i.	n.i.
	B	n.i.	n.i.	n.i.	n.i.	n.i.	n.i.	n.i.	n.i.	n.i.
Agricultural machinery	A	n.i.	n.i.	n.i.	0.5	0.7	0.7	0.7	0.9	0.7
	B	0.3	0.3	0.3	0.3	0.5	0.6	0.6	0.9	0.7
Miscellaneous machinery	A	n.i.	n.i.	n.i.	0.2	0.5	0.6	0.4	0.3	0.4
	B	n.i.	n.i.	n.i.	n.i.	n.i.	n.i.	n.i.	n.i.	n.i.
Consumer goods	A	2.6	4.2	4.8	4.1	6.7	6.3	6.9	5.3	5.8
	B	1.5	2.4	2.8	2.2	3.6	2.5	2.9	3.7	4.1
Food and allied products	A	0.4	0.8	0.9	1.8	2.5	2.7	2.8	2.2	2.5
	B	0.2	0.4	0.5	0.4	0.5	0.5	0.4	0.6	0.8
Textiles and allied products	A	2.1	3.5	3.9	2.0	3.5	3.6	4.1	3.1	3.3
	B	1.3	2.0	2.3	1.8	3.1	2.1	2.4	3.1	3.3
Consumer durables	A	n.i.	n.i.	n.i.	0.3	0.6	n.i.	n.i.	n.i.	n.i.
	B	n.i.	n.i.	n.i.	n.i.	n.i.	n.i.	n.i.	n.i.	n.i.

(continued)

		1932 Actual	1932 Planned Min.	1932 Planned Max.	1937 Actual	1937 Planned	1950 Actual	1950 Planned	1955 Actual	1955 Planned
					BILLION 1955 RUBLES					
All covered products	A	35.9	46.3	53.4	88.1	116.5	126.4	134.1	159.8	163.6
	B	28.6	36.3	41.4	50.3	65.9	82.0	82.7	130.7	132.8
Intermediate products	A	26.2	32.8	37.8	56.1	70.1	83.7	83.2	121.6	123.1
	B	23.2	28.1	31.9	42.3	52.9	71.7	71.5	115.8	116.9
Ferrous metals	A	4.7	6.3	7.9	12.5	14.4	18.1	17.1	28.7	28.3
	B	4.3	5.8	7.3	11.5	13.1	16.9	15.9	28.7	28.3
Nonferrous metals	A	0.3	0.5	0.7	1.4	2.5	2.9	2.8	5.4	6.6
	B	0.3	0.5	0.7	0.8	1.2	1.9	1.7	3.0	3.9
Fuel and electricity	A	8.7	9.1	10.6	23.3	26.4	37.9	36.5	59.2	56.9
	B	8.7	9.1	10.6	17.3	20.4	35.2	33.3	57.8	55.4
Chemicals	A	1.4	2.0	2.4	3.8	4.8	3.4	3.6	4.6	4.3
	B	0.9	1.2	1.4	1.6	1.9	2.3	2.5	3.5	3.3
Construction materials	A	11.2	14.8	16.2	15.2	22.1	21.5	23.2	23.8	27.1
	B	9.1	11.4	11.8	11.1	16.2	15.5	18.0	22.7	26.2
Machinery	A	2.1	1.9	2.1	6.8	9.4	10.5	14.5	3.3	3.0
	B	0.8	0.8	0.9	0.8	1.5	1.7	1.8	2.6	2.1
Transportation equipment	A	1.3	1.1	1.2	4.1	6.5	6.3	10.0	n.i.	n.i.
	B	n.i.	n.i.	n.i.	n.i.	n.i.	n.i.	n.i.	n.i.	n.i.
Agricultural machinery	A	0.8	0.8	0.9	1.7	2.1	2.5	2.5	2.6	2.1
	B	0.8	0.8	0.9	0.8	1.5	1.7	1.8	2.6	2.1
Miscellaneous machinery	A	n.i.	n.i.	n.i.	1.0	0.9	1.6	2.0	0.7	0.9
	B	n.i.	n.i.	n.i.	n.i.	n.i.	n.i.	n.i.	n.i.	n.i.
Consumer goods	A	7.6	11.6	13.5	25.2	37.0	32.2	36.4	34.9	37.5
	B	4.6	7.4	8.7	7.2	11.5	8.5	9.5	12.3	13.9
Food and allied products	A	3.6	5.6	6.4	18.2	24.6	25.0	27.8	25.4	27.3
	B	0.7	1.8	2.1	2.0	2.3	2.1	2.0	2.8	3.7
Textiles and allied products	A	4.0	6.0	7.1	6.3	11.0	7.3	8.6	9.5	10.1
	B	3.9	5.6	6.6	5.2	9.2	6.4	7.5	9.5	10.1
Consumer durables	A	n.i.	n.i.	n.i.	0.7	1.3	n.i.	n.i.	n.i.	n.i.
	B	n.i.	n.i.	n.i.	n.i.	n.i.	n.i.	n.i.	n.i.	n.i.

SOURCE: Table A-45, B-2, and D-8.
n.i.: Not included.

400

TABLE A-47
List of Soviet Products Covered in Study of Plan Fulfillment, 1932, 1937, 1950, and 1955

| | VARIABLE PRODUCT COVERAGE | | | | | | | | Standard |
| | Valued in 1928 Prices | | | | Valued in 1955 Prices | | | | Product |
	1932	1937	1950	1955	1932	1937	1950	1955	Coverage
overed products	37	61	59	34	36	64	59	33	18
ermediate products	21	31	28	21	21	32	28	20	13
errous metals	5	5	4	3	5	5	4	3	3
101	X	X	X	X	X	X	X	X	X
102	X	X	X	X	X	X	X	X	X
103	X	X	X	X	X	X	X	X	X
704	X	X	X		X	X	X		
706	X	X			X	X			
Nonferrous metals	2	4	3	3	2	4	3	3	2
201		X				X			
202	X	X	X	X	X	X	X	X	X
203		X	X	X		X	X	X	
204	X	X	X	X	X	X	X	X	X
uel and electricity	4	8	6	6	4	8	6	6	4
301	X	X	X	X	X	X	X	X	X
302, 303, 304	X	X	X	X	X	X	X	X	X
303.1		X	X			X	X		
305	X	X	X	X	X	X	X	X	X
306		X	X	X		X	X	X	
307		X		X		X		X	
308	X	X	X	X	X	X	X	X	X
309		X				X			
Chemicals	4	8	7	4	4	7	5	3	1
401		X	X	X		X	X	X	
402			X	X			X	X	
404	X	X			X	X			
405			X	X					
405.1	X	X			X	X			
406		X	X			X	X		
412		X	X						
416	X	X	X	X	X	X	X	X	X
418		X				X			
1602	X	X	X		X	X	X		
Construction materials	6	6	8	5	6	8	10	5	3
501	X	X	X	X	X	X	X	X	X
502						X	X		
504						X	X		
506	X	X	X	X	X	X	X	X	X
509	X	X	X	X	X	X	X	X	X
510	X	X	X		X	X	X		
511		X	X			X	X		
513			X	X			X	X	
514	X				X				
516			X	X			X	X	
519	X	X	X		X	X	X		

(continued)

401

TABLE A-47 (concluded)

	VARIABLE PRODUCT COVERAGE								Standard Product Coverage
	Valued in 1928 Prices				Valued in 1955 Prices				
	1932	1937	1950	1955	1932	1937	1950	1955	
Machinery	3	9	15	4	3	10	15	4	1
Transportation equipment	2	5	5	0	2	5	5	0	0
901		X	X			X	X		
902		X	X			X	X		
903		X	X			X	X		
904	X	X	X		X	X	X		
905	X				X				
906		X	X			X	X		
Agricultural machinery	1	1	5	1	1	2	5	1	1
1001	X	X	X	X	X	X	X	X	X
1002			X				X		
1007			X				X		
1009			X				X		
1016						X			
1025			X				X		
Miscellaneous machinery	0	3	5	3	0	3	5	3	0
1101		X	X	X		X	X	X	
1102			X	X			X	X	
1103		X	X	X		X	X	X	
1210		X	X			X	X		
1214			X				X		
Consumer goods	13	21	16	9	12	22	16	9	4
Food and allied products	8	13	11	6	8	13	11	6	1
1501		X				X			
1503		X	X	X		X	X	X	
1504	X		X	X	X		X	X	
1504.1		X	X			X	X		
1505		X				X			
1506		X	X	X		X	X	X	
1507		X	X	X		X	X	X	
1508		X	X			X	X		
1509	X				X				
1510	X	X	X	X	X	X	X	X	X
1513	X	X		X	X	X		X	
1514	X	X	X		X	X	X		
1515	X	X			X	X			
1516	X	X			X	X			
1517	X	X	X		X	X	X		
601		X	X			X	X		
Textiles and allied products	5	4	5	3	4	5	5	3	3
1601	X	X	X	X	X	X	X	X	X
1603	X		X						
1604	X	X	X	X	X	X	X	X	X
1607	X	X	X		X	X	X		
1611	X	X	X	X	X	X	X	X	X
1613						X	X		
Consumer durables	0	4	0	0	0	4	0	0	0
1701		X				X			
1703		X				X			
1704		X				X			
1705		X				X			

NOTE: An X means the product is included in the indicated category in Table A-46. Products corresponding to the number code are given in the list of output series at the beginning of Appendix. Standard product coverage applies to all years.

APPENDIX B

Output Series

General Note

Appendix B contains Russian and Soviet output series from 1860 through 1959. Output figures for 1913 refer in Table B-1 to Tsarist territory excluding Finland, but in Table B-2 to interwar Soviet territory. The output of individual products in 1937 on interwar and postwar Soviet territory is given in Table B-3. Additional statistical information and notes may be found in *Statistical Abstract of Industrial Output in the Soviet Union, 1913–1955*, Parts 1–5 and Supplement, NBER, New York, 1956 and 1957.

A dash (—) means that there was no production or that it was negligibly small. A blank space means that no definite information was found. Estimates and adjustments of other types are indicated by square brackets. A single asterisk (*) indicates that the figure refers to the calendar year in which the fiscal year given in the stub ended. A double asterisk (**) indicates that the figure refers to the fiscal year ending in the calendar year given in the stub. A dagger (†) indicates that the figure is from a source published after our analysis was completed and hence is not used in our study.

ABBREVIATIONS

bill.	= billion	kwh	= kilowatt hour
conven.	= conventional	m	= meter
dcm.	= decimeter	m²	= square meter
dcm²	= square decimeter	m³	= cubic meter
hectol.	= hectoliter	m.t.	= metric ton
hp	= horsepower	mill.	= million
kg	= kilogram	sq.	= square
kva	= kilovolt ampere	th. or thous.	= thousand
kw	= kilowatt		

List of Output Series

I   INTERMEDIATE INDUSTRIAL PRODUCTS

A. Ferrous Metals

101	Pig iron	*chugun*
102	Rolled steel	*prokat*
103	Steel ingots and castings	*stal', stal'nye slitki*

B. Nonferrous Metals

201	Primary aluminum	*aliuminii pervichnyi*
202	Copper	*med', chernovaia med'*
203	Lead	*svinets*
204	Zinc	*tsink*

C. Fuel and Energy

301	Electric power	*elektro-energiia*
301.1	Hydroelectric power	*gidroelektricheskaia energiia*
302	Anthracite	*antratsit*
303	Bituminous coal	*kamennyi ugol'*
303.1	Coke	*koks*
304	Lignite	*buryi ugol'*
305	Crude petroleum	*neft'*
306	Natural gas	*gaz prirodnyi*
307	Oil shale	*goriuchie slantsy*
308	Peat	*torf*
309	Firewood (consumption)	*drova (potreblenie)*
310	Coal (total)	*ugol'*

D. Chemicals

401	Soda ash	*kal'tsinirovannaia soda*
402	Caustic soda	*kausticheskaia soda*
404	Sulfuric acid	*sernaia kislota*
404.1	Sulfuric acid (not used in phosphoric fertilizer)	
405	Mineral fertilizer	*mineral'nye udobreniia*
405.1	Phosphoric fertilizer (18.7% P_2O_5)	*fosfornye udobreniia, superfosfat*
405.2	Ammonium sulfate	*sul'fat ammoniia, sernokislyi ammonii, azotnye udobreniia (v perechete na sul'fat ammoniia)*
405.3	Potash fertilizer (41.6% K_2O)	*kaliinye udobreniia*
406	Ground natural phosphate	*fosforitnaia muka*
410	Red lead	*surik, svintsovyi surik*
411	Zinc oxide	*tsinkovye belila, okis' tsinka*
412	Synthetic dyes	*sinteticheskie krasiteli, iskusstvennye krasitel'nye veshchestva*
416	Paper	*bumaga*

417	Paperboard	*karton*
418	Motor vehicle tires	*avtopokryshki*
419	Rayon and other synthetic fibers	*iskusstvennoe volokno*
420	White lead	*svintsovye belila*

E. Construction Materials

501	Red bricks	*kirpich, stroitel'nyi kirpich*
502	Fire-clay bricks	*shamot, shamotnyi kirpich*
503	Magnesite bricks	*magnezitovyi kirpich, magnezit*
504	Quartzite bricks	*dinas, kvartsitovyi kirpich*
505	Sand-lime, silica, and slag bricks	*kirpich silikatnyi i shlakovyi*
506	Cement	*tsement*
507	Construction gypsum	*stroitel'nyi gips, alebastr*
508	Construction lime	*stroitel'naia izvest'*
509	Industrial timber hauled	*vyvozka delovoi drevesiny*
510	Lumber	*pilomaterialy*
511	Plywood	*fanera*
512	Magnesite metallurgical powder	*metallurgicheskii poroshok*
513	Roll roofing	*miagkaia krovlia*
514	Roofing iron	*krovel'noe zhelezo*
515	Roofing tiles	*cherepitsa*
516	Asbestos shingles	*shifer, shifer krovel'nyi*
518	Rails	*rel'sy*
519	Window glass	*steklo okonnoo*

F. Materials of Agricultural Origin

601	Crude alcohol (100%)	*spirt-syrets*
602	Ginned cotton	*khlopok-volokno*
602.1	Ginned cotton consumption	*potreblenie khlopka-volokna*
603	Raw cotton	*khlopok-syrets*
604	Hard leather	*zhestkaia kozha*
605	Soft leather	*miagkaia kozha*
606	Raw silk	*shelk-syrets*
607	Unwashed wool	*surovaia sherst'*

G. Metallic Minerals

704	Iron ore	*zheleznaia ruda*
706	Manganese ore	*margantsevaia ruda*

II PRODUCER DURABLES

A. Transportation Equipment

901	Automobiles	*legkovye avtomobili*
902	Trucks and buses	*gruzovye avtomobili i avtobusy*
903	Diesel and electric locomotives	*teplovozy i elektrovozy*
904	Steam locomotives, main-line (units)	*parovozy magistral'nye, shiroko-koleinye*
904.1	Steam locomotives, main-line (conven. units)	*parovozy magistral'nye, shiroko-koleinye*
905	Railroad freight cars	*vagony tovarnye*
906	Railroad passenger cars	*vagony passazhirskie*
907	Railroad cars, narrow-gauge and factory use	*vagony uzkokoleinye*
908	Street and subway cars	*tramvainye vagony i metro-vagony*

B. Agricultural Machinery

1001	Tractors (excl. garden)—units	*traktory (bez sadovo-ogorodnykh)*
1001.1	Tractors (excl. garden)—capacity	*traktory (bez sadovo-ogorodnykh)*
1002	Tractor-drawn plows (not paring plows)	*plugi traktornye (bez lushchil'-nikov)*
1003	Tractor-drawn paring plows	*lushchil'niki traktornye*
1004	Horse-drawn plows	*plugi konnye*
1005	Tractor-drawn harrows	*borony traktornye*
1006	Horse-drawn harrows	*borony konnye*
1007	Tractor-drawn cultivators	*kul'tivatory traktornye*
1008	Horse-drawn cultivators	*kul'tivatory konnye*
1009	Tractor-drawn drills	*seialki traktornye*
1010	Horse-drawn drills	*seialki konnye*
1011	Combined plows and drills	*bukkera*
1013	Tractor-drawn potato planters	*traktornye kartofelesazhalki*
1014	Machines for planting seedlings	*rassadoposadochnye mashiny*
1016	Grain combines	*kombainy zernovye*
1017	All other combines	*prochie kombainy*
1018	Windrowers	*vindrouery, zhatki riadkovye dlia razdel'noe uborki*
1019	Horse-drawn reapers	*zhatki konnye*
1020	Cotton pickers	*khlopkouborochnye mashiny*
1021	Tractor-drawn haymowers	*senokosilki traktornye, kosilki trak-tornye*

1022	Horse-drawn haymowers	*senokosilki konnye*
1023	Tractor-drawn rakers	*grabli traktornye*
1024	Horse-drawn rakers	*grabli konnye*
1025	Tractor-driven threshers	*molotilki traktornye*
1026	Horse-driven threshers	*molotilki konnye*
1027	Grain-cleaning machines	*zernoochistitel'nye mashiny*
1028	Horse-drawn winnowers	*veialki konnye*
1029	Horse drivings	*privody konnye*
1030	Chaff and silo cutters	*solomorezki i silosorezki*

C. Prime Movers and Electrical Machinery

1101	Steam boilers	*parovye kotly*
1102	Water turbines	*vodianye turbiny*
1103	Steam and gas turbines	*parovye i gazovye turbiny*
1104	Locomobiles	*lokomobili*
1105	Diesel engines	*dizeli*
1106	Other internal combustion engines	*prochie dvigateli vnutrennego sgoraniia, prochie neftianye dvigateli*
1107	Turbogenerators	*turbogeneratory*
1108	Hydroelectric generators	*gidrogeneratory*
1109	Electric motors, A.C.	*elekromotory peremennogo toka*
1110	Power transformers	*silovye transformatory*

D. Mining and Industrial Machinery

1201	Coal-mining combines	*ugol'nye kombainy*
1202	Coal-cutting machines	*vrubovye mashiny*
1203	Electric mining locomotives	*elektrovozy rudnichnye*
1204	Ore-loading machines	*porodopogruzochnye mashiny*
1205	Deep-shaft pumps	*nasosy glubinnye*
1206	Turbodrills	*turbobury*
1210	Machine tools	*stanki metallorezhushchie*
1210.1	Bench and engine lathes	*tokarnye stanki*
1211	Electric furnaces	*elektropechi*
1212	Spinning machines	*priadil'nye mashiny, vatera*
1213	Winding machines	*motal'nye mashiny*
1214	Looms	*tkatskie stanki*
1215	Cotton-carding machines	*grebnechesal'nye mashiny, chesal'nye mashiny dlia khlopka*

1216	Knitting machines	*viazal'nye mashiny*
1217	Leather-spreading machines	*zatiazhnye mashiny, kozhevennye*
1218	Leather-dressing machines	*mezdril'nye mashiny, kozhevennye*
1219	Typesetting machines, linotype	*nabornye mashiny, linotipy*
1220	Flat-bed printing presses	*ploskopechatnye mashiny*
1221	Industrial sewing machines	*promyshlennye shveinye mashiny*
1222	Metal-pressing machine tools	*kuznechno-pressovye mashiny*
1222.1	Presses	*pressy*

E. Construction and Road Building Machinery

1301	Excavators	*ekskavatory*
1302	Trench excavators	*kanavokopateli*
1303	Stone crushers	*kamnedrobilki*
1304	Road graders (not self-propelled)	*greidery*
1305	Self-propelled road graders	*avtogreidery*
1306	Concrete mixers	*betonomeshalki*
1307	Tractor-driven scrapers	*skrepery traktornye*
1308	Bulldozers	*bul'dozery*
1309	Railroad cranes, steam-operated	*zheleznodorozhnye parovye krany*
1310	Self-propelled cranes (not RR cranes)	*avtomobil'nye krany*
1311	Overhead traveling cranes	*mostovye krany*
1312	Tower cranes	*bashennye krany*
1313	Electric elevators	*elektricheskie elevatory, lifty, pod'emniki*

F. Other Producer Durables

1401	Telephones	*telefonnye apparaty*
1402	Hand-operated switchboards	*ruchnye telefonnye stantsii, ruchnye kommutatory*
1403	Automatic exchange switchboards	*avtomaticheskie telefonnye stantsii*
1405	Calculating machines	*schetnye mashiny, arifmometry*
1406	Typewriters	*pishushchie mashiny*

III CONSUMER GOODS

A. Food and Allied Products

1501	Flour	*muka*
1502	Macaroni	*makaronnye izdeliia*
1503	Butter	*maslo zhivotnoe*

1504	Vegetable oil	*maslo rastitel'noe*
1504.1	Oleomargarine	*margarin*
1504.2	Vegetable oil minus oleomargarine	
1505	Cheese	*syr*
1506	Meat slaughtering	*miaso*
1506.1	Sausages	*kolbasnye izdeliia*
1507	Fish catch	*ulov ryby*
1508	Soap (40% fatty acid)	*mylo*
1509	Salt	*sol'*
1510	Raw sugar consumption	*sakhar-pesok, potreblenie*
1510.1	Refined sugar	*sakhar-rafinad*
1510.2	Raw sugar minus refined sugar and sugar in candy	
1511	Starch and syrup	*krakhmal i patoka*
1512	Yeast	*drozhzhi*
1513	Canned food	*konservy*
1513.1	Canned meat	*miasnye konservy*
1513.2	Canned fish	*rybnye konservy*
1513.3	Canned milk	*molochnye konservy*
1513.4	Canned vegetables and fruit	*ovoshchnye i fruktovye konservy*
1514	Beer	*pivo*
1515	Cigarettes	*papirosy*
1516	Low-grade tobacco	*makhorka*
1517	Matches	*spichki*
1518	Vodka (40% alcohol)	*vodka*
1519	Candy	*konfety*

B. Textiles and Allied Products

1601	Boots and shoes	*obuv' kozhanaia*
1602	Rubber footwear	*rezinovaia obuv'*
1603	Cotton yarn	*khlopchatobumazhnaia priazha*
1604	Cotton fabrics	*khlopchatobumazhnye tkani*
1605	Cotton thread	*khlopchatobumazhnye nitki*
1606	Linen yarn	*l'nianaia priazha*
1607	Linen fabrics	*l'nianye tkani*
1609	Silk and rayon fabrics	*tkani shelkovye i iz iskusstvennogo shelka*
1609.1	Pure silk fabrics	*tkani iz chistogo shelka*
1609.2	Rayon and mixed fabrics	*tkani iz iskusstvennogo shelka*
1610	Woolen yarn	*sherstianaia priazha*

1611	Woolen and worsted fabrics	*sherstianye i polusherstianye tkani*
1612	Knitted goods	*trikotazhnye izdeliia*
1613	Hosiery	*chulochno-nosochnye izdeliia*
1614	Felt footwear	*valianaia obuv'*

C. Consumer Durables

1701	Bicycles	*velosipedy*
1702	Cameras	*fotograficheskie apparaty*
1703	Electric light bulbs	*elektricheskie lampy*
1704	Phonographs	*patefony, grammofony*
1705	Radios	*radiopriemniki*
1706	Television sets	*televizory*
1707	Household sewing machines	*shveinye mashiny bytovye*
1708	Clocks and watches	*chasy vsekh vidov*
1709	Motorcycles	*mototsikly*

	103 Steel (th.m.t.)	202 Copper (th.m.t.)	203 Lead (th.m.t.)	204 Zinc (th.m.t.)	305 Crude Petroleum (mill.m.t.)
1860	1.6	5.20	1.09	1.84	—
1861	1.9	4.93	0.81	2.54	—
1862	2.0	4.75	0.88	2.58	—
1863	2.0	4.82	1.17	2.47	0.01
1864	3.5	4.51	1.35	2.94	0.01
1865	3.9	4.15	1.63	3.09	0.01
1866	4.3	4.42	1.71	3.14	0.01
1867	6.3	4.24	1.74	2.95	0.02
1868	9.6	4.39	1.64	3.25	0.03
1869	7.6	4.26	1.07	3.63	0.04
1870	8.8	5.05	1.65	3.78	0.03
1871	7.2	4.52	1.77	2.73	0.03
1872	9.2	3.72	1.22	3.03	0.03
1873	8.9	3.66	0.94	3.38	0.07
1874	8.6	3.27	1.34	4.13	0.09
1875	12.9	3.65	1.08	3.99	0.13
1876	17.9	3.87	1.17	4.62	0.19
1877	44.3	3.50	1.20	4.73	0.25
1878	64.2	3.52	1.40	4.65	0.33
1879	210.0	3.12	1.36	4.32	0.40
1880	307.3	3.20	1.15	4.39	0.35
1881	293.3	3.46	0.99	4.55	0.66
1882	247.7	3.59	0.57	4.47	0.83
1883	221.9	4.36	0.54	3.67	0.99
1884	207.0	6.22	0.63	4.32	1.48
1885	192.9	4.72	0.71	4.59	1.91
1886	241.8	4.57	0.78	4.20	1.90
1887	225.5	4.99	0.99	3.62	2.36
1888	222.3	4.60	0.80	3.87	3.01
1889	258.7	4.80	0.58	3.69	3.28
1890	378.4	5.73	0.84	3.77	3.78
1891	433.5	5.46	0.56	3.68	4.53
1892	515.0	5.32	0.88	4.37	4.69
1893	630.8	5.46	0.84	4.50	5.53
1894	703.0	5.41	0.74	5.01	4.92
1895	879	5.85	0.41	5.03	6.75
1896	1,022	5.83	0.26	6.26	6.79
1897	1,225	6.94	0.45	5.88	7.27
1898	1,619	7.29	0.24	5.66	8.33
1899	1,897	7.53	0.32	6.33	8.96
1900	2,216	8.26	0.22	5.96	10.38
1901	2,228	8.47	0.16	6.10	11.56
1902	2,184	8.82	0.23	8.27	11.08
1903	2,434	9.23	0.11	9.89	10.41
1904	2,766	9.84	0.09	10.61	10.89
1905	2,266	8.51	0.78	7.91	7.56
1906	2,496	9.35	1.01	10.09	8.17
1907	2,671	13.29	0.50	10.12	8.66
1908	2,698	16.23	0.52	9.96	8.74
1909	2,940	18.44	1.06	9.61	9.30
1910	3,314	22.69	1.31	10.84	9.63
1911	3,949	26.44	1.24	12.21	9.18
1912	4,503	32.66	1.62	20.32	9.29
1913	4,918	33.10	1.53	19.36	9.23

(continued)

	310 Coal (mill.m.t.)	401 Soda Ash (th.m.t.)	404 Sulfuric Acid (th.m.t.)	405.1 Phosphoric Fertilizer (th.m.t.)	411 Zinc Oxide (th.m.t.)
1860	0.30	[—]	5.1	[—]	[—]
1861	0.38	[—]			
1862	0.35	[—]			
1863	0.36	[—]			
1864	0.40	[—]			
1865	0.38	0.35	6.5	[—]	[—]
1866	0.45				
1867	0.44				
1868	0.45				
1869	0.60	1.28			
1870	0.69	1.32	7.9	[—]	[—]
1871	0.83	0.77			
1872	1.09				
1873	1.17				
1874	1.29				
1875	1.70	[0.63]	[15.5]	[—]	[—]
1876	1.82				
1877	1.79	0.56			
1878	2.52	0.54			
1879	2.92	0.40			
1880	3.29	0.89	23.0	[—]	
1881	3.49	0.67			
1882	3.78	0.81			
1883	3.98	1.00			
1884	3.93				
1885	4.27	5.00	36.72	[—]	
1886	4.58				
1887	4.53	11.1			
1888	5.19	18.0	43.54	0.86	1.01
1889	6.21	18.6			
1890	6.01	20.1	[40.0]	1.36	[0.90]
1891	6.23	19.6			0.84
1892	6.95	27.7	36.5	1.07	0.23
1893	7.61	46.1	44.3	6.94	0.25
1894	8.76	45.9			
1895	9.10	47.8	[52.0]	[18.7]	
1896	9.38	58.6			
1897	11.20	61.1	59.8		0.29
1898	12.31				
1899	13.97	69.8			
1900	16.16	86.2	105.7	48.1	
1901	16.53				
1902	16.47				
1903	17.86				
1904	19.61				
1905	18.67	86.9	[177.7]	[80.5]	
1906	21.73				
1907	26.00				
1908	25.91	109.1			
1909	26.82				
1910	25.43	132.2	249.7	112.9	2.85
1911	28.42	148.2	275.3	123.3	3.74
1912	31.13	164.2	283.7	150.1	3.78
1913	36.05	160.0	[292.2]	115.0	

(continued)

	420 White Lead (th.m.t.)	501 Red Bricks (large-scale) (millions)	506 Cement (th.m.t.)	518 Rails (th.m.t.)	519 Window Glass (mill.m²)
1860	[—]				
1861					
1862					
1863					
1864					
1865	[—]				
1866					
1867					
1868					
1869					
1870	[—]				
1871					
1872					
1873					
1874					
1875	[—]				
1876					
1877					
1878				55.3	
1879				147.1	
1880				201.4	
1881				206.6	
1882				153.3	
1883				128.7	
1884				98.3	
1885				95.5	
1886				87.0	
1887				114.0	
1888	3.10			63.0	
1889				88.4	
1890	[3.05]	833		166.1	
1891		764		172.0	
1892	3.01	744		193.2	
1893	3.58	760	137	230.8	
1894				250.0	
1895	[5.77]	[1,617]		302.2	
1896				366.6	
1897	7.95	2,474		398.8	
1898				468.4	
1899				464.0	
1900	8.32	1,768	803	496.1	14.3
1901				481.5	
1902				419.5	
1903				337.9	
1904				420.1	
1905	[10.07]	[1,531]	[865]	383.1	[15.8]
1906				299.5	
1907				330.9	
1908	11.15	1,388	902	361.2	16.8
1909				500.0	
1910	12.15	1,763	1,210	505.2	23.8
1911	11.25	2,114	1,484	507.9	25.3
1912	11.08	2,341	1,757	623.9	27.2
1913	18.00	[3,090]	2,131	640.9	

(continued)

	601 Crude Alcohol (100%) (th.hectol.)	602.1 Ginned Cotton Consumption (th.m.t.)	1501 Flour (large-scale) (mill.m.t.)	1504 Vegetable Oil (large-scale) (th.m.t.)	1509 Salt (th.m.t.)
1860	[3,507]**	46.5			429.7
1861	[3,507]**	43.3			431.8
1862	[3,507]**	13.9			749.2
1863	3,507**	17.7			506.6
1864	3,848**	26.8			363.0
1865	3,143**	26.0			501.9
1866	2,861**	48.3			646.6
1867	3,859**	54.0			724.5
1868	3,206**	41.9			602.8
1869	3,696**	52.5			651.6
1870	3,851**	45.9			475.3
1871	3,442**	68.2			456.7
1872	4,043**	59.0			650.5
1873	4,056**	57.8			755.5
1874	3,864**	76.4			725.5
1875	3,870**	85.4			585.4
1876	3,398**	77.1			683.7
1877	3,258**	72.6			474.3
1878	3,422**	117.6			781.7
1879	4,383**	105.6			817.9
1880	4,024**	94.1			779.3
1881	3,810**	148.6			831.1
1882	4,007**	127.0			1,667
1883	3,973**	146.6			1,138
1884	4,134**	120.8			1,024
1885	4,137**	124.0			1,133
1886	3,865**	137.4			1,197
1887	3,673**	184.4			1,157
1888	4,349**	136.9	2.43	60.3	1,113
1889	4,033**	170.8			1,394
1890	3,868**	136.4	2.47	44.6	1,390
1891	3,853**	151.6	2.37	47.1	1,351
1892	3,364**	163.7	2.33	54.6	1,459
1893	3,405**	186.7	2.66	63.3	1,351
1894	3,793**	190.3			1,354
1895	3,711**	201.4	[3.89]	[81.4]	1,540
1896	3,931**	224.2			1,347
1897	3,801**	224.5	5.12		1,562
1898	3,655**	233.3			1,505
1899	3,602**	264.2			1,681
1900	4,130**	262.2	3.71	126.7	1,968
1901	4,253**	264.1			1,706
1902	3,853**	285.5			1,847
1903	3,609**	294.8			1,659
1904	4,049**	298.8			1,908
1905	4,190**	273.3	[4.86]	[195.2]	1,844
1906	4,526**	296.1			1,790
1907	4,855**	319.3			1,872
1908	5,226**	346.5		236.5	1,847
1909	5,601**	348.5	5.55		2,243
1910	5,237**	361.8	4.86	226.6	2,051
1911	6,067**	350.5	5.35	252.1	2,011
1912	5,474**	420.9	5.39	262.3	1,858
1913	6,063**	424.2		325.0	1,981

(continued)

	1510 Raw Sugar Consumption (th.m.t.)	1511 Starch and Syrup (th.m.t.)	1514 Beer (th.hectol.)	1515 Cigarettes (billions)	1516 Low-Grade Tobacco (th. 20-kg. crates)	1610 Woolen Yarn (th.m.t.)
1860	57.3**			0.34		
1861	57.3**			0.36		
1862	47.5**			0.41		
1863	35.9**			0.50		
1864	53.0**			0.52		
1865	72.9**			0.51		
1866	55.2**			0.66		
1867	104.5**			0.71		
1868	122.7**			0.81		
1869	82.8**			1.07		
1870	105.4**			1.14		
1871	122.7**			1.40		
1872	89.6**			1.57		
1873	122.1**			1.64		
1874	128.3**			1.86		
1875	132.0**			2.02		
1876	155.7**			1.84		
1877	207.5**			2.50		
1878	173.7**			2.02		
1879	181.8**			2.24		
1880	205.5**			2.24		
1881	203.1**			2.19	964.9	
1882	261.1**			[2.43]	1,305	
1883	287.3**			[2.66]	2,188	
1884	308.9**			[2.90]	2,237	
1885	343.3**			3.13	2,112	
1886	475.7**			3.25	2,182	
1887	425.1**			3.34	2,184	
1888	389.0**	88		3.47	2,135	
1889	465.1**			3.69	2,111	
1890	403.1**	106		3.74	2,093	
1891	466.4**	110		3.82	2,125	
1892	485.7**	131		4.25	1,878	
1893	399.5**	133		4.58	2,095	17.9
1894	578.5**			4.98	2,062	
1895	528.6**	[110]		5.70	2,326	[28.5]
1896	679.5**		5,364	5.93	2,277	
1897	634.6**	87.4	5,657	6.09	2,257	
1898	654.4**		5,374	5.71	2,304	
1899	682.7**		5,913	7.70	2,340	
1900	794.1**	89.4	5,872	8.62	2,484	54.9
1901	806.6**		5,744	9.67	2,623	
1902	959.4**		5,706	10.76	2,372	
1903	1,053**		6,682	9.94	2,956	
1904	1,041**		6,674	11.82	3,089	
1905	854**	[100]	7,291	11.77	2,984	[64.9]
1906	872**		8,796	15.05	3,225	
1907	1,279**		9,300	14.36	3,098	
1908	1,257**	106.6	8,760	14.60	3,537	70.2
1909	1,129**		9,253	20.39	3,626	
1910	1,033**	130.6	10,198	16.73	3,698	73.8
1911	1,882**	131.4	10,990	19.84	3,699	75.4
1912	1,848**	130.7	10,666	22.53	4,262	82.0
1913	1,235**	125	11,612	25.89	4,390	110.2

SOURCES TO TABLE B-1

103 *Steel*

1860–1877	*92*, 47.
1878–1885	*70*, xv.
1886–1910	*196* (1892), 29; (1893–1894), lxxxi; (1904), xxvi; (1909), xxii; (1910), i.
1911–1913	*155*, 217. Given as combined output of iron and steel, but iron is assumed to be insignificant.

202 *Copper*

1860–1880	*263*, I, issue 2, sec. iv, appendix, vii.
1881–1882	*253* (1890), 150.
1883–1910	*196* (1892), 12, i; (1893–1910), i.
1911–1913	*197*, 72 f.

203 *Lead*

1860–1880	*263*, I, issue 2, sec. iv, appendix, vi.
1881–1882	*91*, 28.
1883–1890	*253* (1890), 148; (1896), 200.
1891–1910	*196* (1892), i; (1893–1910), i.
1911–1913	*197*, 94 f.

204 *Zinc*

1860–1880	*263*, I, issue 2, sec. iv, appendix, xii.
1881–1882, 1891–1910	*196* (1887), xix; (1892), i; (1893–1910), i.
1883–1890	*253* (1890), 148; (1896), 200.
1911–1913	*197*, 96 f.

305 *Crude petroleum*

1860–1913	*180*, 153. Rounded.

310 *Coal*

1860–1875	*253* (1890), 151.
1876–1910	*196* (1887), xxi; (1892), 43; (1893–1910), i.
1911–1913	*197*, 156 f.

401 *Soda ash*

1860–1865, 1869–1871, 1877–1883, 1885, 1887–1897, 1899–1900	*122*, II, 676. For 1865, 1871, 1877–1883, 1885, and 1888, approximate data.
1875	Interpolated between 1871 and 1877.
1905, 1908, 1910–1913	*61*, 205. Output of 3 main factories only (Donsoda, Berezniki, and Slaviansk).

404 *Sulfuric acid*

1860, 1870, 1880, 1885, 1888, 1893, 1897, 1900	*122*, II, 564.
1865, 1875, 1890, 1895, 1905	Interpolated.
1892	*258* (1892), sec. ii, 212.
1910–1912	*48*, issue v, 2.
1913	Same percentage increase in output assumed between 1912 and 1913 as between 1911 and 1912.

405.1 *Phosphoric fertilizer*

1860, 1865, 1870, 1875, 1880, 1885	Assumed to be zero.
1888, 1890, 1892–1893	*258* (1888), sec. iii, 22; (1890), sec. ii, 378; (1892), sec. ii, 214; (1893), sec. ii, 108.
1895	Interpolated between 1893 and 1900.
1900	*27*, I, table 22, 192 f.
1910–1912	*48*, issue v, 32.
1913	*16*, 27.

411 *Zinc oxide*

1860, 1865, 1870, 1875	Assumed to be zero.
1888, 1891–1893, 1897	*258* (1888), sec. iii, 23; (1891), sec. ii, 193; (1892), sec. ii, 215; (1893), sec. ii, 109; (1897), sec. iii, 179.
1890	Interpolated between 1888 and 1891.
1910–1912	*48*, issue v, 10.

420 *White lead*

1860, 1865, 1870, 1875	Assumed to be zero.
1888, 1892–1893, 1897	*258* (1888), sec. iii, 23; (1892), sec. ii, 215; (1893), sec. ii, 109; (1897), sec. iii, 179.
1890 1895, 1905	Interpolated.
1900, 1908	*27*, I, table 22, 188 f; II, table 19, 186 f.
1910–1912	*48*, issue v, 10.
1913	*193*, 241.

501 *Red bricks*

1890–1893, 1897	*258* (1890), sec. ii, 270; (1891), sec. ii, 206; (1892), sec. ii, 229; (1893), sec. ii, 124; (1897), sec. ii, 112.
1895, 1905	Interpolated.
1900, 1908	*27*, I, table 10, 120 f; II, table 10, 122 f.
1910–1912	*48*, issue iv, 16.
1913	Taken as 144% of output in interwar territory (2,144 mill., *104*, 437), the ratio for 1912 (*27*, II, table 5, 30 f).

506 *Cement*

1893	*258* (1893), sec. ii, 124.
1900, 1908	*27*, I, table 10, 120 f; II, table 10, 122 f.
1905	Interpolated between 1900 and 1908
1910–1912	*48*, issue iv, 6.
1913	Taken as 141% of output in interwar territory (Table B-2), the ratio for 1912 (*27*, II, table 5, 30 f).

518 *Rails*

1878–1882	*196* (1887), xxxxvii.
1883–1910	*64*, annex, 18.
1911–1912	*90*, 23.
1913	Sum of railroad rails (*142*, 303) and mining rails (total length of latter's production in Russian Empire is given as 109% of production in Soviet territory, which is 47.9 th. m. tons, *244*, 231).

519 *Window glass*

1900, 1908	*27*, I, table 10, 118 f; II, table 10, 118 f.
1905	Interpolated between 1900 and 1908.
1910–1912	*48*, issue iv, 36 f.

601 *Crude alcohol* (*100%*)

1859/60–1861/62	Assumed to be same as in 1862/63.
1862/63–1888/89	*45* (issue VIII), 386 f; (issue XVII), 580; (issue XXIII), 465. For 1862/63–1868/69, raised by 14%, Poland's share in production in these years (issue VIII, 386).
1889/90–1912/13	*252* (1900), 44; (1909), 24; (1914), 67.

602.1 *Ginned cotton consumption*

1860–1889   *271*, 307.

1890–1913   *95*, 461 ,455.

1501 *Flour*

1888, 1890–1893, 1897   *258* (1888), sec. iii, 51 f; (1890), sec. iii, 404 f; (1891), sec. iii, 222 ff; (1892), sec. ii, 248 ff; (1893), sec. ii, 147 f; (1897), sec. ii, 30 ff.

1895, 1905   Interpolated

1900, 1908   *27*, I, table 26, 214 ff; II, table 21, 214 ff.

1910–1912   *48*, issue i, 2 ff.

1504 *Vegetable oil*

1888, 1890–1893   *258* (1888), sec. iii, 53 f; (1890), sec. iii, 406 ff; (1891), sec. ii, 224 ff; (1892), sec. ii, 250 ff; (1893), sec. ii, 149 ff.

1895, 1905   Interpolated.

1900, 1908   *27*, I, table 26, 218 f; II, table 21, 220 f.

1910–1912   *48*, issue i, 24 ff.

1913   Taken as 123% of output in interwar territory (264 th. m. tons, *301*, 11 ff, 38), the ratio for 1912 (*27*, II, table 9, 5 f, 114).

1509 *Salt*

1860–1880   *263*, I, issue 2, sec. iv, appendix, xiii. Sum of rock, lake, and evaporated salt. For 1861, 1876, and 1878, this sum does not agree with given totals.

1881–1908   *196* (1892), 60; (1894–1909), i.

1909–1910   *155*, 327.

1911–1913   *197*, 132 f. Excludes salt in brine.

1510 *Raw sugar consumption*

1859/60–1861/62   *30*, 13. Raised by 12.9%, Poland's share in total production in 1867/68 (*45*, issue II, 487).

1862/63–1903/04   *45* (issue II), 487; (issue III), 352 f; (issue IV), 451 ff; (issue VI), 331 ff; (issue XVII), 701; (issue XXIII), 517; (1902), 681; (1906/07), 397.

1904/05–1912/13   *252* (1909), 130; (1914), 2.

1511 *Starch and syrup*

1888, 1890–1893, 1897   *258* (1888), sec. iii, 55; (1890), sec. iii, 408 f; (1891), sec. ii, 227; (1892), sec. ii, 253; (1893), sec. ii, 152 f; (1897), sec. ii, 38 ff. Includes potato flour, except for 1897.

1895, 1905   Interpolated.

1900, 1908   *27*, I, table 26, 220 f; II, table 21, 224 f.

1910–1912   *48*, issue i, 32 ff.

1913   Taken as 108.6% of output in interwar territory (Table B-2), the ratio for 1912 (*27*, II, table 9, 116).

1514 *Beer*

1896–1913   *252* (1900), 180; (1909), 117; (1914), 149.

1515   *Cigarettes*

1860–1880 — *263*, II, issue 4, sec. v, 31. For 1860–1871, raised by 19%, Poland's share of total production in 1871 (*263*).

1881, 1885–1913 — *45* (issue XIII), 486 f; (issue XVII), 766 f; (issue XVIII), 778 f; (1900), 684 f; (1902), 693, sum of first- and second-grade cigarettes; (1906/07), 406, sum of first- and second-grade cigarettes; (1909), 615; (1910), 720 ff; (1914), 632 f.

1882–1884 — Interpolated.

1516   *Low-grade tobacco*

1881–1882 — *157*, appendix, 29. Converted into crates.

1883–1889 — *45* (issue XXIII), 534. Converted into crates.

1890–1913 — *252* (1900), 434; (1900), 242; (1914), 32. Converted into crates.

1610   *Woolen yarn*

1893 — *258* (1893), sec. ii, 86.

1895, 1905 — Interpolated.

1900, 1908 — *27*, I, table 39, 272 f; II, table 30, 260 f.

1910–1912 — *48*, issue X, 2 ff.

1913 — Taken to be 236.9% of output in interwar territory (Table B-2), the ratio for 1912 (*27*, II, table 12, 136 ff).

419

TABLE B-2

Oᴜᴛᴘᴜᴛ Sᴇʀɪᴇs: Sᴏᴠɪᴇᴛ Uɴɪᴏɴ, 1913–1959

	101 Pig Iron (th.m.t.)	102 Rolled Steel (th.m.t.)	103 Steel Ingots and Castings (th.m.t.)	201 Primary Aluminum (th.m.t.)	202 Copper (th.m.t.)
1913	4,216	3,660	4,231		31.1
1914	4,137	3,791	4,466		
1915	3,764	3,394	4,120		
1916	3,804	3,509	4,276		
1917	2,964	2,542	3,080		
1918	596.9	359	402		
1919	116.5	180	199		
1920	115.8	148	194		
1921	117.3	178	220		
1921/22	179.9	260	318		1.08
1922/23	313.8	476	615		2.62
1923/24	669.6	693	993		5.09
1924/25	1,309	1,397	1,868		14.3
1925/26	2,203	2,261	2,911		20.4
1926/27	2,961	2,757	3,592		27.0
1927/28	3,282	3,433	4,251		30.0
1928/29	4,021	3,930	4,854		35.5
1929/30	4,964	4,561	5,761		44.5
1931	4,871	4,287	5,620		44.3
1932	6,161	4,428	5,927	0.86	45.0
1933	7,110	5,065	6,889	4.43	44.3
1934	10,430	7,034	9,693	14.4	53.3
1935	12,490	9,446	12,590	25.1	76.0
1936	14,400	12,450	16,400		100.8
1937	14,490	12,970	17,730	37.7	97.5
1938	14,650	13,260	18,060	43.8	103.2
1939	14,520	12,730	17,560	47.0	[142]
1940	14,900	13,110	18,320	59.9	160.9
1945	8,803	8,485	12,250	86.3	[135]
1946	9,862	9,578	13,350		[143]
1947	11,220	11,060	14,530		[156]
1948	13,740	14,220	18,640		[187]
1949	16,390	18,000	23,290		[224]
1950	19,170	20,890	27,330		[247]
1951	21,910	24,030	31,350		[282]
1952	25,070	26,810	34,490		[324]
1953	27,410	29,390	38,130		[321]
1954	29,970	32,070	41,430		[337]
1955	33,310	35,340	45,270		[377]
1956	35,800	37,800	48,700		
1957	37,000	40,200	51,200		
1958	39,600	42,900	54,900		
1959	43,000	47,000	59,900		

(continued)

TABLE B-2 (continued)

	203 Lead (th.m.t.)	204 Zinc (th.m.t.)	301 Electric Power (bill.kwh)	301.1 Hydroelectric Power (bill.kwh)	302 Anthracite (mill.m.t.)
1913	1.52	2.95	1.94	0.03	4.78
1914	1.08	2.41			5.12
1915	0.85	2.04			5.08
1916	1.46	2.02	2.58	0.04	6.24
1917	0.11				5.92
1918	0.09				2.09
1919	0.19				1.49
1920	0.35	0.05	0.50		1.37
1921	0.39	0.20	0.52	0.01	1.50
1921/22	0.34	[0.19]	0.78*	0.01	2.22
1922/23	0.31	0.19	1.15*	0.02	2.33
1923/24	0.69	0.52	1.56*	0.03	3.52
1924/25	1.02	1.49	2.93*	0.04	3.34
1925/26	1.34	1.89	3.51*	0.05	5.36
1926/27	1.52	2.27	4.20*	0.26	6.92
1927/28	2.34	2.25	5.01*	0.43	8.00
1928/29	5.49	3.01	6.22*	0.46	9.67
1929/30	8.63	4.33	8.37*	0.55	12.14
1931	15.5	8.95	10.69	0.59	16.01
1932	18.7	13.7	13.54	0.81	18.14
1933	13.7	16.6	16.36	1.25	20.73
1934	27.2	27.2	21.01	2.38	22.25
1935	36.4	46.5	26.29	3.68	24.81
1936	48.7	63.3	32.84	4.01	28.15
1937	62.3	76.5	36.17	4.18	28.01
1938	77.8	83.1	39.37	5.08	31.06
1939	85.1	[91]	43.20	4.71	33.88
1940	[89.4]	[95]	48.31	5.11	36.40
1945	[60]	[50]	43.26	4.84	17.61
1946	[71]	[54]	48.57	6.05	22.48
1947	[90]	[63]	56.49	7.28	27.00
1948	[92]	[85]	66.34	9.37	32.06
1949	[116]	[106]	78.26	11.51	38.44
1950	[144]	[123]	91.23	12.69	41.77
1951	[179]	[142]	104.0	13.72	44.70
1952	[210]	[176]	119.1	14.91	46.74
1953	[256]	[199]	134.3	19.20	49.20
1954	[289]	[213]	150.7	18.56	52.91
1955	[331]	[246]	170.2	23.17	60.76
1956			191.7	29.0	67.2
1957			209.7	39.4	72.5
1958			233.4	46.5	78.1
1959			264		[81.0]

(continued)

TABLE B-2 (continued)

	303 Bituminous Coal (mill.m.t.)	303.1 Coke (mill.m.t.)	304 Lignite (mill.m.t.)	305 Crude Petroleum (mill.m.t.)	306 Natural Gas (mill.m³)
1913	23.21	4.4	1.13	9.23	29
1914	25.63	4.6	1.15	9.18	
1915	24.96	4.2	1.40	9.44	
1916	26.24	4.4	1.99	9.97	
1917	23.04	6.4	2.35	8.80	
1918	9.46		1.55	4.15	
1919	6.25		1.71	4.45	
1920	5.36		2.02	3.85	
1921	6.00		2.02	3.78	
1921/22	7.10	0.2*	2.01	4.66	[22]
1922/23	8.19	0.3	2.18	5.28	25
1923/24	11.07	0.6	1.74	6.06	28
1924/25	11.56	1.4	1.62	7.06	140
1925/26	17.99	2.8	2.42	8.32	228
1926/27	22.54	3.4	2.82	10.29	271
1927/28	24.45	4.2	3.06	11.63	304
1928/29	26.92	5.0	3.48	13.68	331
1929/30	31.15	6.2*	4.49	18.45	520
1931	34.73	6.8	6.01	22.39	847
1932	39.33	8.4	6.89	21.41	1,049
1933	46.74	10.2	8.87	21.49	1,066
1934	60.53	14.2	11.38	24.22	1,533
1935	70.53	16.7	14.30	25.22	1,791
1936	81.11	19.9	17.57	27.43	2,053
1937	81.87	20.0	18.09	28.50	2,179
1938	83.67	19.6	18.54	30.19	2,200
1939	91.08	20.2	21.25	30.26	[2,200]
1940	103.6	21.1	25.95	31.12	3,219
1945	81.82	13.6	49.91	19.44	3,278
1946	91.82	15.4	49.77	21.75	3,750
1947	105.3	17.5	51.00	26.02	4,590
1948	117.9	20.9	58.23	29.25	5,070
1949	130.7	24.3	66.41	33.44	5,240
1950	143.5	27.7	75.86	37.88	5,761
1951	157.8	30.7	79.46	42.25	6,222
1952	168.3	33.7	85.87	47.31	6,346
1953	175.1	36.9	96.11	52.78	6,866
1954	190.8	40.3	103.4	59.28	7,484
1955	215.9	43.6	114.6	70.79	8,981
1956	236.8	46.6	125.2	83.80	12,070
1957	256.0	48.6	135.0	98.3	18,580
1958	274.9	50.9	142.8	113.2	29,080
1959	[278.6]	53.4	[146.9]	129.5	

(continued)

TABLE B-2 (continued)

	307 Oil Shale (th.m.t.)	308 Peat (mill.m.t.)	309 Firewood (consump.) (mill.m.t.)	401 Soda Ash (th.m.t.)	402 Caustic Soda (th.m.t.)
1913	[—]	1.69	100	160	55.1
1914		1.90		156.8	
1915		1.68		127.0	
1916		1.62		136.0	50.2
1917		1.36		102.0	40.7
1918		1.09		18.9	7.9
1919	4.5	1.23		4.0	1.7
1920	29.8	1.39		7.8	
1921	19.0	2.02		9.9	3.2
1921/22	17.3	2.16*	[90]	30.7*	15.0
1922/23	29.8	2.43*		54.8*	20.1
1923/24	11.7	2.86*	86	78.1*	26.2
1924/25	1.1	2.72*		98.1*	35.7
1925/26	1.9	3.55*		120.6*	43.6
1926/27	9.4	4.91*	[95]	164.6*	51.4
1927/28	0.6	5.32*	79	217.3	58.6
1928/29	9.4	6.91*	[71]	238.7	65.4
1929/30	27.2*	8.08*	[98]	263.1	71.5
1931	150	12.36	[102]	275.8	78.0
1932	318	14.79	108	287.8	80.8
1933	174	13.85	107	329.7	101.4
1934	206	18.25	[111]	398.0	104.3
1935	417	18.5	[116]	422.1	125.9
1936	468	22.5	128	503.4	128.2
1937	515	24.0	[119]	528.2	163.7
1938	562	26.5	[125]	542.7	176.6
1939		29.9	[136]	564.7	177.5
1940	1,683	33.2	[161]	536.1	190.4
1945	1,387	22.4	[133]	235.3	128.2
1946		27.3	[135]	257.0	139.7
1947		30.6	[138]	338.6	178.2
1948		34.4	[140]	489.4	223.5
1949		36.0	[143]	643.2	283.3
1950	4,716	36.0	[139]	748.6	324.8
1951		39.8	[137]	823.7	351.9
1952		37.2	[137]	999.1	390.4
1953		38.6	[124]	1,194	448.1
1954		45.0	123	1,312	498.1
1955	10,793	50.8	122	1,437	563.4
1956	11,600	44.8	120	1,545	631.0
1957	12,400	54.9	123	1,618	[662.6]
1958	13,200	52.8	124		
1959	13,700				

(continued)

TABLE B-2 (continued)

	404 Sulfuric Acid (th.m.t.)	404.1 Sulfuric Acid (not used in phosph. fertil.) (th.m.t.)	405 Mineral Fertilizer (th.m.t.)	405.1 Phosphoric Fertilizer (18.7% P_2O_5) (th.m.t.)	405.2 Ammonium Sulfate (th.m.t.)
1913	121	105	60.9	47.1	13.8
1914					
1915					
1916				[13.1]	
1917				[9.3]	
1918				[21.6]	
1919	17	13		[12.4]	
1920				[6.8]	
1921	11	10		[4.0]	
1921/22				[5.6]	
1922/23	45	42		[8.2]	
1923/24	89	82		[19.9]	
1924/25	100	87		[38.6]	
1925/26	145	124		[62.2]	
1926/27	176	151		[72.6]	
1927/28	211	173	122.7	111.5	11.2
1928/29	265	216	161.7	145.1	16.6
1929/30	396	293	322.3	302.9	19.4
1931	464	341	388.9	361.4	27.5
1932	552	389	536.2	478.7	55.6
1933	627	442	701.7	545.0	110.9
1934	782	547	1,114	691.9	226.0
1935	994	611	1,792	1,126	374.5
1936	1,197	770	2,216	1,257	552.8
1937	1,369	868	2,590	1,473	761.6
1938	1,544	1,001	2,782	1,596	828.1
1939	1,625	1,068	2,980	1,638	958.8
1940	1,587	1,127	2,856	1,352	971.7
1945	781	702	1,109	233.6	744.7
1946	725	534	1,659	560.9	894.1
1947	996	724	2,280	798.8	1,124
1948	1,479	999	3,230	1,411	1,353
1949	1,845	1,189	4,210	1,930	1,686
1950	2,125	1,326	5,009	2,351	1,908
1951	2,372	1,531	5,371	2,472	2,079
1952	2,662	1,759	5,795	2,655	2,236
1953	2,919	1,927	6,323	2,919	2,356
1954	3,292	2,153	7,293	3,350	2,649
1955	3,798	2,495	8,716	3,834	2,984
1956	4,323	2,847	9,860	[4,340]	[3,370]
1957	4,569	2,985	10,550	[4,660]	[3,620]
1958	4,804	3,124	11,210	[4,940]	[3,830]
1959	5,100	3,360	11,700	[5,130]	[3,990]

(continued)

TABLE B-2 (continued)

	405.3 Potash Fertilizer (41.6% K$_2$O) (th.m.t.)	406 Ground Natural Phosphate (th.m.t.)	410 Red Lead (th.m.t.)	411 Zinc Oxide (th.m.t.)	412 Synthetic Dyes (th.m.t.)
1913	—	7.9	2.4		4.29
1914					
1915					
1916					0.20
1917					0.17
1918					
1919					
1920					0.17
1921					
1921/22					0.56
1922/23		4.9			
1923/24		4.2			1.80
1924/25		6.1			
1925/26		6.5			8.29
1926/27		9.3	[4.0]	[5.6]	7.37
1927/28	—	12.7	[5.4]	[7.1]	10.25
1928/29	—	46.5	[10]	[11.0]	13.30
1929/30	—	181.3			16.79
1931	—	312.1			16.26
1932	1.9	384.6	4.0	6.75	13.54
1933	45.8	332.0	2.75	6.25	16.00
1934	196.0	284.3	4.74	8.06	24.02
1935	291.6	530.9	6.93	12.1	25.34
1936	406.6	623.0	[10]	[10.0]	30.30
1937	355.8	649.9	[15]	[23.0]	30.96
1938	357.9	631.5			35.30
1939	383.2	582.2			
1940	532.3	381.7	11.9	21.6	33.87
1945	130.7	10.1	9.9	13.0	15.14
1946	203.5	50.6			19.53
1947	357.1	75.6			28.12
1948	465.7	238.0			37.97
1949	594.1	375.3			42.52
1950	750.4	483.2	10.2	35.7	46.53
1951	820.4	553.6	9.5	34.6	53.46
1952	904.7	598.8	11.5	43.1	58.60
1953	1,048	645.1	14.8	50.8	59.47
1954	1,295	766.4	17.3	61.9	63.34
1955	1,898	924.0	19.2	65.1	73.67
1956	[2,150]	[1,050]	20.5	72.1	77.00
1957	[2,300]	[1,120]	21.0	81.4	
1958	[2,440]	[1,190]	21.5	91.3	
1959	[2,540]	[1,240]			

(continued)

TABLE B-2 (continued)

	416 Paper (th.m.t.)	417 Paperboard (th.m.t.)	418 Motor Vehicle Tires (thous.)	419 Rayon and Other Synthetic Fibers (th.m.t.)	501 Red Bricks (millions)
1913	197.0	20.0	19.2	0.15	[3,377]
1914			31.5		
1915			56.0		
1916	154.6†		120.5		
1917			120.4		
1918					
1919					
1920					
1921					
1921/22	31.7	2.5			
1922/23	61.0	10.4			
1923/24	107.8	18.5			
1924/25	211.0	23.5			
1925/26	254.0	33.0			
1926/27	268.0	44.5			
1927/28	284.5	47.1	85	0.2	2,656
1928/29	384.9	62.5	148		3,548
1929/30	495.3	77.0	368		4,413
1931	505.2	62.0	573		[4,254]
1932	471.2	73.0	553	2.8	4,367
1933	506.1	79.0	679		3,363
1934	565.8	91.5	1,547		4,383
1935	640.8	107.8	2,084		5,245
1936	763.5	133.2	2,209		7,191
1937	831.6	144.2	2,698	8.6	7,471
1938	832.8	149.2	3,595		6,732
1939	799.8	159.0	4,221		6,700
1940	812.4	150.8	3,007	11.1	6,723
1945	321.1	55.9	1,370	1.1	1,868
1946	516.7	97.7	1,988		2,971
1947	647.5	140.7	2,954		3,663
1948	778.6	180.5	4,072		5,392
1949	995.4	232.1	5,680		7,036
1950	1,193	291.8	7,401	24.2	8,792
1951	1,342	333.9	7,519	35.4†	11,010
1952	1,461	383.7	7,599	49.2†	12,560
1953	1,612	442.5	8,114	62.3†	14,050
1954	1,769	499.3	9.281	78.8	15,541
1955	1,863	543.0	10.190	110.5	17,340
1956	1,993	587.7	11,334	128.9	18,000
1957	2,126	656.6	12,784	148.7	20,600
1958	2,237	719.9	14,395	166.6	[23,300]
1959	2,300		15,500	179	[26,600]

(continued)

TABLE B-2 (continued)

	502 Fire-Clay Bricks (th.m.t.)	503 Magnesite Bricks (th.m.t.)	504 Quartzite Bricks (th.m.t.)	505 Sand-Lime, Silica, and Slag Bricks (millions)	506 Cement (th.m.t.)
1913	572	8.0	—	[123]	1,520
1914					
1915					
1916					
1917					963.2
1918					183.5
1919					6.6
1920					36
1921					63.9
1921/22					141.6
1922/23		1.4			271
1923/24		5.5			392
1924/25		10.7			872
1925/26	350	12.1	87.2		1,403
1926/27	402	14.9	100.2		1,574
1927/28	465	20.3	96.5	134	1,850
1928/29	603	27.5	115.0	207	2,232
1929/30	637	35.6	156.5	337	3,006
1931	718			[426]	3,336
1932	793	41	178	533	3,478
1933	936	47.0	203	459	2,709
1934	1,345	62.0	334	589	3,536
1935	1,350	[82.0]	488	714	4,488
1936	1,671	[103.0]	620	1,154	5,872
1937	1,780	96	594	1,195	5,454
1938				854	5,688
1939				894	5,197
1940	1,731	104	546	732	5,675
1945	1,453	139	522	158	1,845
1946				268	3,373
1947				396	4,718
1948				713	6,455
1949				1,101	8,147
1950	2,631	233	734	1,387	10,190
1951	2,832	292	739	1,794	12,070
1952	3,104	361	795	2,298	13,910
1953	3,324	427	840	2,739	15,960
1954	3,564	503	831	3,223	18,990
1955	3,878	608	728	3,484	22,480
1956	4,024	748	655	3,521	24,900
1957	4,202	785	623	4,072	28,900
1958	4,334	848	620	[4,700]	33,300
1959				[5,400]	38,800

(continued)

TABLE B-2 (continued)

	507 Construction Gypsum (th.m.t.)	508 Construction Lime (th.m.t.)	509 Industrial Timber Hauled (mill.m³)	510 Lumber (mill.m³)	511 Plywood (thous.m³)
1913	[520]	[510]	75.0	[14]	130
1914					
1915					
1916					
1917					
1918					
1919					
1920					
1921					
1921/22					
1922/23					
1923/24					
1924/25					
1925/26	123				
1926/27	183			[13]*	[143]
1927/28	235	526	60.1	[14]*	[195]
1928/29	[342]	[698]	81.1	[17]*	[257]
1929/30			115.2	21.9*	
1931		[1,814]	104.1	23.8	
1932	475	[2,107]	99.4	24.4	423
1933	446	[1,394]	98.0	27.3	424.3
1934	688	[2,077]	99.7	30.6	497
1935	856	[2,280]	117.0	34.0	554
1936	1,195	[2,906]	128.1	39.8	636.6
1937	1,212	3,750	114.2	33.8	672.3
1938	1,087	3,285	114.7		
1939	1,132	3,247	126.1	34.4	
1940	892	3,006	117.9	34.8	732
1945	357	1,172	61.6	14.7	192
1946	596	1,824	80.3	16.2	242
1947	684	2,149	99.0	19.4	
1948	1,048	2,721	132.7	30.1	
1949	1,460	3,412	151.3		
1950	1,721	4,154	161.0	49.5	657
1951	1,958	4,660	184.5	56.0	767
1952	2,211	4,923	184.6	60.5	883
1953	2,390	5,314	179.9	66.4	946
1954	2,539	5,810	205.8	69.0	1,024
1955	2,870	6,205	212.1	75.6	1,049
1956	3,000	6,388	222.1	76.6	1,121
1957	3,504	7,248	237.9	81.6	1,156
1958			252	87	1,229
1959					

(continued)

TABLE B-2 (continued)

	512 Magnesite Metallurgical Powder (th.m.t.)	513 Roll Roofing (mill.m²)	514 Roofing Iron (th.m.t.)	515 Roofing Tiles (millions)	516 Asbestos Shingles (millions)
1913	21.0	8.8	406.2	30.4	9
1914			391.3		
1915			297.8		
1916			167.4		2.5
1917			105.7		
1918			71.9		
1919			48.3		0.82
1920			18.0		0.49
1921			[26.4]		2.71
1921/22			34.8		2.17
1922/23	4.9		75.2		2.75
1923/24	8.1		111.6		3.92
1924/25	20.0		178.0		11.9
1925/26	27.7		283.5		16.6
1926/27	29.4	19.3	334.3		21.6
1927/28	34.8	19.2	369.3		38.5
1928/29	48.6	25.4	396.1		51.3
1929/30	69	39.8	315.3		65.9
1931		55.3	157.3		105.0
1932	72	66.0	98.4	59.0	111.8
1933	86	89.4	102.9	47.9	61.4
1934	101	95.4	124.8	60.3	100.2
1935	[123]	122.2	142.2	101.7	169.4
1936	[153]	152.2	178.8	137.9	209.7
1937	186	161.4	179.0	142.1	107.0
1938		148.6	151.5	159.1	170.3
1939		149.4		162.6	200.8
1940	208	127.1	[103.4]	173.3	205.6
1945	196	71.2	[—]	29.6	83.6
1946		125.8		63.1	169.5
1947		166.3		90.9	243.0
1948		199.7		135.6	329.0
1949		237.7		168.6	450.5
1950	313	285.5	[—]	222.5	546.4
1951	403	316.9		268.1	695.4
1952	450	360.0		319.1	878.4
1953	511	405.4		376.6	1,074
1954	572	445.9		428.8	1,262
1955	667	503.5	[—]	472.1	1,488
1956	757	536.0	[—]	498.4	1,809
1957	934	580.9	[—]	557.4	2,153
1958	913	647.5	[—]	662.5	2,393
1959		690	[—]		2,605

(continued)

429

TABLE B-2 (continued)

	518 Rails (th.m.t.)	519 Window Glass (mill.m²)	601 Crude Alcohol (100%) (th.hectol.)	602 Ginned Cotton (th.m.t.)	603 Raw Cotton (th.m.t.)
1913	636.4	23.7	4,670	223.0	740
1914	703.8				
1915	557.6				
1916	407.4				
1917	171.3	10.1			
1918	17.7	4.4			
1919	35.4	2.3			
1920		1.6			
1921		2.5			
1921/22		5.8*			20*
1922/23		10.8*			
1923/24		14.9*			346*
1924/25		16.3			544*
1925/26		22.9*			540*
1926/27		29.4*	[1,950]		718*
1927/28	390.4	34.2*	2,330	207.9	821*
1928/29	383.1	40.3	2,100†	237.9	864*
1929/30	461.8	43.1	2,790†	257.4	1,113*
1931	515.1	33.4	3,890†	337.7	1,290
1932	495.1	29.5	3,650	395.3	1,271
1933	593.9	29.8	3,883	378.5	1,315
1934	860.1	50.1	4,723	419.7	1,176
1935	952.9	69.8	6,074	437.2	1,712
1936	1,260	87.9	6,972	596.2	2,390
1937	[1,180]	79.3	7,670	716.7	2,582
1938	1,098	59.6	9,320†	893.0	2,690
1939		51.3	9,450†		2,790
1940	1,360	44.7	8,990	848.6	2,495
1945	[530]	23.3	2,650	312.2	1,290
1946		39.9	3,365		1,700
1947	650	47.8	3,670		2,100
1948	880	59.0	5,510		[2,500]
1949	1,580	71.5	6,890	821.0	[3,235]
1950	1,751	76.9	7,300	952.7	3,750
1951	1,300	67.7	8,100	1,265	3,937
1952		62.0	8,910	1,360	3,975
1953		76.0	10,520	1,320†	4,050
1954	2,300	86.4	11,360		4,425
1955	2,882	99.8	12,780	1,488	4,087
1956	2,408	112.2	12,880	1,348	
1957	2,247	120.9	15,720	1,430	
1958	2,419	132.9	16,340	1,460	
1959		140			

(continued)

TABLE B-2 (continued)

	604 Hard Leather (th.m.t.)	605 Soft Leather (mill.dcm²)	606 Raw Silk (m.t.)	607 Unwashed Wool (th.m.t.)	704 Iron Ore (mill.m.t.)
1913	[23.0]	[1,150]	380	[178]	9.21
1914					7.66
1915					5.94
1916				178	7.25
1917					5.33
1918					0.59
1919					0.09
1920					0.17
1921					0.14
1921/22			2.4	132	0.19
1922/23				108	0.41
1923/24			56	114	0.94
1924/25				130	2.22
1925/26			126	148	3.43
1926/27			241	159	4.81
1927/28	[89.0]	[3,050]	397	177.6	6.13
1928/29			618	178.8	8.00
1929/30			762	138.9	10.66
1931			810	98.3	10.59
1932	52.9	3,414	837	69	12.09
1933	39.7	2,486	774	62	14.45
1934	32.9	2,485	901	65	21.51
1935	31.2	2,733	1,210	79	26.85
1936	42.0	3,374	1,510	96	27.83
1937	59.0	4,283	1,624	106	27.77
1938	62.0	4,506		133	26.59
1939	69.5	4,892		[162]	26.92
1940	70.3	4,925	1,816	[153]	29.87
1945	21.8	1,810	989		15.86
1946					19.33
1947					23.34
1948					27.99
1949					32.57
1950	60.2	4,120	1,855	177	39.65
1951				189	44.93
1952				216	52.58
1953			2,083†	230	59.65
1954				226	64.35
1955	84.8	5,676	2,172	251	71.86
1956	[89.8]		2,142		78.1
1957			2,259		84.3
1958			2,196		88.8
1959					94.4

(continued)

TABLE B-2 (continued)

	706 Manganese Ore (mill.m.t.)	901 Automobiles (thous.)	902 Trucks and Buses (thous.)	903 Diesel and Electric Locomotives (units)	904 Steam Locomotives (units)
1913	1.25	[—]	[—]	[—]	477
1914	0.91				762
1915	0.54				883
1916	0.47				616
1917	0.39				409
1918	0.13				200
1919	0.07				74
1920	0.13				90
1921	0.01				78
1921/22	0.06				115
1922/23	0.22				96
1923/24	0.43		0.01		169
1924/25	0.68		0.02		148
1925/26	1.03		0.50		302
1926/27	0.84		[0.41]		359
1927/28	0.70*	0.1	0.67	—	479
1928/29	1.41*	0.2	1.5	—	575
1929/30	1.39	0.2	4.0	—	625
1931	0.88	—	4.0	2	810
1932	0.83	0.03	23.9	4	827
1933	1.02	10.3	39.4	18	930
1934	1.82	17.1	55.3	27	1,165
1935	2.39	19.0	77.7	38	1,518
1936	3.00	3.7	132.8	59	1,153
1937	2.75	18.2	181.7	36	1,172
1938	2.27	27.0	184.1	36	1,216
1939	2.25	19.6	182.1	23	1,011
1940	2.56	5.5	139.9	14	914
1945	1.47	5.0	69.7		8
1946	1.73	6.3	95.9	1	243
1947	2.04	9.6	123.4	41	674
1948	2.26	20.2	176.9	107	1,032
1949	2.90	45.7	230.3	210	1,187
1950	3.38	64.6	298.3	227	985
1951	4.12	53.6	235.1	189	665
1952	4.40	59.7	248.2	185	254
1953	4.64	77.4	276.8	248	668
1954	4.59	94.7	309.2	278	758
1955	4.74	107.8	337.5	328	654
1956	4.94	97.8	366.8	377	490
1957	5.15	113.6	381.8	670	—
1958	5.37	122.2	389.2	1,055	—
1959		124.5	370.5	1,437	—

(continued)

TABLE B-2 (continued)

	904.1 Steam Locomotives (conven. units)	905 RR Freight Cars (thous.)	906 RR Passenger Cars (units)	907 RR Cars, Narrow-Gauge (units)	908 Street and Subway Cars (units)
1913	265	9.7	1,065		270
1914					
1915					
1916					
1917					
1918					
1919					
1920					
1921		0.78	39		
1921/22					
1922/23					
1923/24		0.57	144		
1924/25		0.54	114		
1925/26			298		
1926/27		7.95	726		
1927/28	478	7.87	387	256	414
1928/29	602	11.3	414	750	
1929/30	631	13.9	817	1,538	
1931	810	14.4	1,295	2,262	
1932	828	15.2	1,141	2,959	1,076
1933	941	13.0	1,274	3,488	
1934	1,257	20.7	1,495	4,556	
1935	1,796	69.6	887	5,125	
1936	1,566	27.5	725	10,700	
1937	1,582	29.8	912	7,100	376
1938	1,620		1,167		
1939	1,348				
1940	1,220	30.9	1,051		258
1945	10	0.8	5		
1946	312	17.3			
1947	861	23.8			
1948	1,300	30.5			
1949	1,488	43.5			
1950	1,249	50.8	912		436
1951	886	28.4	1,327		369
1952	344	24.4	1,229		409
1953	903	25.1	1,483		421
1954	1,035	23.9	1,751		502
1955	943	34.4	1,772		425
1956		40.2	1,799		760
1957		38.3	1,856		911
1958		40.3	1,782		929
1959		38.6	1,800		

(continued)

TABLE B-2 (continued)

	1001 Tractors (excl. garden) (thous.)	1001.1 Tractors (excl. garden) (th.hp)	1002 Plows, Tractor-Drawn (thous.)	1003 Paring Plows, Tractor-Drawn (thous.)	1004 Plows, Horse-Drawn (thous.)
1913	—		[—]	[—]	671.1
1914					
1915					
1916					133.4
1917					49.9
1918					12.8
1919					23.0
1920					89.3
1921					100.5
1921/22					159.3
1922/23	—				206.5
1923/24	0.01				173.5
1924/25	0.60	6			582.8
1925/26	0.90	9			945.0
1926/27	0.91	9			1,037
1927/28	1.27	27	0.51	0.39	1,173
1928/29	3.28	54	3.6	2.10	1,746
1929/30	9.10	137	19.8	5.19	2,222
1931	37.87	527	82.1	12.0	389.7
1932	48.93	762	61.1	6.71	56.2
1933	73.73	1,199	67.2	2.18	110.9
1934	93.97	1,772	74.6	5.08	126.3
1935	112.6	2,333	83.0	7.53	104.3
1936	112.9	2,598	82.3		
1937	50.98	998	96.4	35.8	[104]
1938	49.20	1,401	72.8		
1939	48.10	1,332			
1940	31.65	993	38.4	12.8	[—]
1945	7.73	221	8.5	—	[—]
1946	13.30	426	14.8		
1947	27.80	975	23.9		
1948	56.90	1,989	53.5		
1949	88.20	2,907	82.9		
1950	108.8	3,614	121.9	76.4	[—]
1951	91.83	3,065	107.7	74.0	
1952	98.65	3,243	94.5	31.5	
1953	111.3	3,639	95.2	23.7	
1954	135.4	4,152	101.0	29.9	
1955	163.4	4,827	103.2	29.0	[—]
1956	183.5		123.5	16.5	[—]
1957	203.8		127.8	18.5	[—]
1958	219.7		164.0	26.9	[—]
1959	213.5		155		[—]

(continued)

TABLE B-2 (continued)

	1005 Harrows, Tractor-Drawn (thous.)	1006 Harrows, Horse-Drawn (thous.)	1007 Cultivators, Tractor-Drawn (thous.)	1008 Cultivators, Horse-Drawn (thous.)	1009 Drills, Tractor-Drawn (thous.)
1913	[—]	97.4	[—]		[—]
1914					
1915					
1916		25.4			
1917		6.5			
1918		0.1			
1919		1.0			
1920		2.6			
1921		6.2			
1921/22		15.4			
1922/23		26.8			
1923/24		125.8			
1924/25		174.5			
1925/26		310.2			
1926/27		355.4			
1927/28	—	590.0	[—]	50.2	0.6
1928/29	—	672.3	1.6	45.5	
1929/30	25.52	813.7	[—]	79.0	
1931	44.14	226.2	[19.7]	33.2	
1932	15.90	58.4	21.3	8.0	28.4
1933	10.70	29.6	19.5	13.6	
1934	4.95	58.9	[10.2]	38.0	
1935	3.97	61.7	14.4	57.0	
1936			50.2		
1937	8.5	[62]	68.1	[57.0]	62.9
1938			64.8		
1939					
1940	3.8	[—]	32.3	[—]	21.4
1945	—	[—]	0.09	[—]	1.6
1946			15.9		6.7
1947			31.8		19.4
1948			41.7		41.0
1949			59.2		64.0
1950	10.1	[—]	98.9	[—]	118.4
1951	8.0		116.1		136.5
1952	7.7		94.3		130.1
1953	7.1		87.5		95.3
1954	7.6		93.8		95.3
1955	9.7	[—]	112.6	[—]	123.3
1956	10.1	[—]	149.6	[—]	199.4
1957	11.4	[—]	208.1	[—]	278.1
1958	14.0	[—]	177.2	[—]	218.3
1959		[—]	121.5	[—]	136.5

(continued)

TABLE B-2 (continued)

	1010 Drills, Horse-Drawn (thous.)	1011 Combined Plows and Drills (thous.)	1013 Potato Planters, Tractor-Drawn (thous.)	1014 Machines for Planting Seedlings (units)	1016 Grain Combines (thous.)
1913	67.8		[—]	[—]	[—]
1914					
1915					
1916	13.7				
1917					
1918					
1919					
1920	9.9				
1921	5.0				
1921/22	8.5				
1922/23	10.7				
1923/24	9.7				
1924/25	30.0				
1925/26	62.0				
1926/27	58.1				
1927/28	57.2	30.17	—	—	—
1928/29	99.0	30.27	—		—
1929/30	149.4	18.35	—		0.3
1931	43.1	4.42	—		3.5
1932	19.8	3.75	0.24	520	10.0
1933	19.2	5.86	0.17		8.6
1934	27.1	0.29	—		8.2
1935	33.5	—	—		20.2
1936					42.6
1937	[34]	[—]	4.1	396	43.9
1938					22.9
1939					14.8
1940	[—]	[—]	3.6	150	12.8
1945	[—]	[—]	—	1	0.3
1946					1.5
1947					2.8
1948					14.5
1949					29.2
1950	[—]	[—]	2.5	535	46.3
1951			6.0	551	53.3
1952			7.3	1,000	42.2
1953			4.8	1,277	43.1
1954			23.7	7,254	38.6
1955	[—]	[—]	24.2	5,930	48.0
1956	[—]	[—]	6.6		81.1
1957	[—]	[—]	9.3		131.5
1958	[—]	[—]	5.0		65
1959	[—]	[—]			

(continued)

TABLE B-2 (continued)

	1017 All Other Combines (thous.)	1018 Windrowers (thous.)	1019 Reapers, Horse-Drawn (thous.)	1020 Cotton Pickers (thous.)	1021 Haymowers, Tractor- Drawn (thous.)
1913	[—]	[—]	98.7	[—]	[—]
1914					
1915					
1916			22.2		
1917			7.6		
1918			0.6		
1919			1.0		
1920			2.3		
1921			5.5		
1921/22			5.5		
1922/23			11.7		
1923/24			13.4		
1924/25			55.8		
1925/26			106.6		
1926/27			132.2		
1927/28	—	—	190.4	—	[—]
1928/29		—		—	—
1929/30		—		—	—
1931		0.95		0.94	14.21
1932	—	2.37	25.4	2.20	15.58
1933		1.84	43.1	1.12	2.53
1934		2.04	78.2	0.43	2.03
1935		0.50	87.4	0.08	5.95
1936					
1937	—	—	[87]		1.30
1938					
1939					
1940	—	—	[—]	—	3.30
1945	—	[—]	[—]	—	—
1946					
1947					
1948					
1949					
1950	2.96	0.5	[—]	4.74	41.2
1951	2.84			9.84	87.3
1952	2.92			4.00	104.5
1953	4.49	0.7†		3.60	57.7
1954	25.64	0.7		3.39	22.0
1955	33.28	2.4	[—]	0.56	22.6
1956	53.42	81.2	[—]	0.89	27.2
1957	94.2	144.6	[—]		46.4
1958	51.4	94.8	[—]		73.5
1959			[—]		83.8

(continued)

437

TABLE B-2 (continued)

	1022 Haymowers, Horse-Drawn (thous.)	1023 Rakers, Tractor-Drawn (thous.)	1024 Rakers, Horse-Drawn (thous.)	1025 Threshers, Tractor-Driven (thous.)	1026 Threshers, Horse-Driven (thous.)
1913	12.20	[—]		[—]	35.1
1914					
1915					
1916					
1917					15.2
1918					0.1
1919					0.1
1920					1.2
1921	4.07				1.7
1921/22	5.00				19.7
1922/23					25.9
1923/24					13.6
1924/25					35.6
1925/26	18.78				56.5
1926/27	40.7				66.8
1927/28	57.1	—	—	4.46	86.7
1928/29	78.4		1.08	5.43	96.7
1929/30	134.7		19.18	12.39	
1931	80.1		55.63	19.74	
1932	39.4	—	24.36	18.90	—
1933	60.3		45.64	13.61	0.02
1934	62.2		45.30	13.72	4.20
1935	70.0		51.57	12.86	6.50
1936				9.6	
1937	[70]	—	[52]	6.6	[6.50]
1938					
1939					
1940	[—]	0.9	[—]	2.2	[—]
1945	[—]	—	[—]	0.8	[—]
1946					
1947					
1948					
1949					
1950	[—]	5.8	[—]	15.5	[—]
1951		13.8		7.1	
1952		17.4		4.1	
1953		21.3		3.7	
1954		25.1		5.3	
1955	[—]	25.6	[—]	3.8	[—]
1956	[—]	11.0	[—]	3.4	[—]
1957	[—]	3.1	[—]	6.5	[—]
1958	[—]	11.1	[—]	10.1	[—]
1959	[—]		[—]		[—]

(continued)

TABLE B-2 (continued)

	1027 Grain- Cleaning Machines (thous.)	1028 Winnowers, Horse-Drawn (thous.)	1029 Horse Drivings (thous.)	1030 Chaff and Silo Cutters (thous.)	1101 Steam Boilers (thous. m²)
1913	[—]	45.0	36.30	[—]	19.1
1914					
1915					
1916		9.8			
1917		3.2			
1918		0.5			
1919		0.8			
1920		3.3			
1921		2.0	0.48		
1921/22		9.8	2.15		
1922/23		11.6	14.2		
1923/24		23.8	14.0		
1924/25		58.8	30.3		
1925/26		98.2	44.3		32.8
1926/27		140.9	55.0		71.4
1927/28	—	168.6	61.0	14.7	87.9
1928/29	—				126.4
1929/30	—				166.1
1931	—				125.3
1932	0.01	[—]	[50]	15.9	163.3
1933	0.03				200.3
1934					226.0
1935	0.20				197.3
1936	0.50				265.4
1937	1.0	[—]	[50]	1.0	208.2
1938	3.8				240.0
1939					
1940	4.3	[—]	[—]	1.6	276.3
1945	—	[—]	[—]	0.5	90.3
1946					95.0
1947					135.1
1948					179.4
1949					247.5
1950	6.4	[—]	[—]	20.4	358.7
1951	6.3			26.3	423.5
1952	6.6			20.0	572.6
1953	6.7			14.0	709.7
1954	8.2			25.0	745.4
1955	10.1	[—]	[—]	47.0	[925]
1956	10.0	[—]	[—]	33.6	[910]
1957	10.0	[—]	[—]	33.8	[875]
1958	12.1	[—]	[—]	32.4	[905]
1959	15.7	[—]	[—]		

(continued)

TABLE B-2 (continued)

	1102 Water Turbines (th.kw)	1103 Steam and Gas Turbines (th.kw)	1104 Locomobiles (th.hp)	1105 Diesel Engines (th.hp)	1106 Other Internal Combustion Engines (th.hp)
1913	—	5.9		35.1	
1914					
1915					
1916					
1917					
1918					
1919					
1920					
1921					
1921/22					
1922/23					
1923/24		2.0		8.4	
1924/25	4.7	16.3		18.0	
1925/26	3.9	20.0		28.2	
1926/27	9.7	34.0		38.4	
1927/28	12.0	35.7	14.6	38.9	58.8
1928/29	19.7	82.0	16.8	69.2	84.0
1929/30	31.9	24.1	27.3	103.4	154.9
1931	42.4	207.7	40.6	157.8	136.0
1932	59.5	239.0	35.5	95.8	116.5
1933	52.9	634.5	26.9	92.4	133.1
1934	74.6	363.8	21.3	131.4	202.1
1935	56.8	473.9	51.0	158.0	243.4
1936	72.7	622.9	65.5	212.2	262.3
1937	88.3	1,068	70.8	259.7	[260]
1938	52.5†	1,135†	84.3	261.8	
1939	144.8†	1,377†			
1940	207.7	972		248.7	[165]
1945	40.6	189		18.7	
1946	196.7†	245			
1947	323.9†	618			
1948	336.3†	724			
1949	339.9†	1,242			
1950	314.9	2,381		3,226	
1951	478.2	2,663		3,575	
1952	571.5	2,873		3,997	
1953	718.9	4,036		4,351	
1954	1,262	4,202		4,585	
1955	1,492	4,069		4,005	
1956	1,581	4,268		4,403	
1957	1,308	4,062			
1958					
1959					

(continued)

TABLE B-2 (continued)

	1107 Turbo- generators (th.kw)	1108 Hydroelectric Generators (th.kw)	1109 Electric Motors (A.C.) (th.kw)	1110 Power Transformers (th.kva)	1201 Coal-Mining Combines (units)
1913		[—]		96.3	[—]
1914					
1915					
1916					
1917					
1918					
1919					
1920					
1921					
1921/22					
1922/23					
1923/24				76.5	
1924/25	10.3		104.4	196.0	
1925/26	16.3			127.4	
1926/27	51.8			291.7	
1927/28	75.0	—	258.6	403.2	—
1928/29	136.5	—	321.7	791.1	[—]
1929/30	186.0	—	632.6	1,525	[—]
1931	518.0	18	1,101	3,182	[—]
1932	826.0	259	1,658	3,426	—
1933	385.0	202	1,385	3,330	2
1934	335.0	131	1,485	2,874	2
1935	425.5	47	1,451	3,461	10
1936		[47]	1,653	3,203	
1937	514.0	47.1	1,833	2,743	—
1938	374.0				
1939					
1940	313.5	154.6	1,848	3,500	22
1945	185.5	79.6	1,240	1,800	5
1946					
1947					
1948					
1949					
1950	676.5	257.8	6,780	10,200	344
1951	1,425	497.9	7,355	11,700	353
1952	1,824	686.0	7,096	13,900	320
1953	2,677	790.4	7,747	15,700	403
1954	2,536	1,280	8,207	15,600	483
1955	3,113	1,413	8,819	19,600	731
1956	3,807	1,377	9,782	23,700	793
1957	4,100	1,500	11,700	26,900	910
1958			13,706	30,500	1,118
1959					

(continued)

441

TABLE B-2 (continued)

	1202 Coal-Cutting Machines (units)	1203 Electric Mining Locomotives (units)	1204 Ore-Loading Machines (units)	1205 Deep-Shaft Pumps (thous.)	1206 Turbodrills (units)
1913	[—]	[—]			
1914					
1915					
1916					
1917					
1918					
1919					
1920					
1921					
1921/22					
1922/23					
1923/24					
1924/25					
1925/26					
1926/27					
1927/28	—	—			
1928/29	59	—			
1929/30	124	—			
1931	291	—			
1932	298	87			
1933	372	245			
1934	488	161			
1935	524	220			
1936	421	169			
1937	572	301		20.9	
1938	1,100				
1939					
1940	1,256	511	194	31.9	90
1945	1,833	651	11	39.8	244
1946					
1947					
1948					
1949					
1950	900	2,305	986	65.7	978
1951	771	2,083	952	78.3	1,370
1952	666	2,007	1,182	91.1	2,296
1953	751	1,809	1,155	92.8	2,724
1954	376	2,031	1,621	88.4	2,895
1955	405	1,816	1,792	79.7	2,589
1956	463	2,147	2,304	79.9	2,772
1957	875	2,744	2,255	86.2	3,489
1958	973	3,417	2,536	88.0	4,164
1959					

(continued)

TABLE B-2 (continued)

	1210 Machine Tools (thous.)	1210.1 Bench and Engine Lathes (thous.)	1211 Electric Furnaces (units)	1212 Spinning Machines (units)	1213 Winding Machines (units)
1913	1.5		—		[—]
1914					
1915					
1916					
1917					
1918					
1919					
1920					
1921					
1921/22					
1922/23					
1923/24					
1924/25					
1925/26	1.1				
1926/27	1.9				
1927/28	2.0	0.83	2	66	—
1928/29	4.3	1.5			
1929/30	8.0	3.3			
1931	18.2	7.1			
1932	19.7	7.1	370	39	89
1933	21.0	7.8		330	
1934	25.4	9.1		488	
1935	33.9	6.8		646	
1936	44.4	8.3		690	
1937	48.5	15.2	465	884	50
1938	55.3				
1939	55.0				
1940	58.4	11.5	237	1,109	27
1945	38.4	13.1	1,345	11	—
1946	40.3				
1947	50.4				
1948	64.5				
1949	64.9				
1950	70.6	24.1	1,924	1,958	169
1951	71.2	23.1	2,006	1,614	207
1952	74.6	23.9	2,325	1,771	284
1953	91.8	27.3	2,707	1,729	261
1954	102.4	29.5	2,612	1,889	253
1955	117.1	31.3	2,719	2,040	235
1956	124.0			1,666	258
1957	131.0	33.4		1,877	218
1958	138.6	34.1		1,065	122
1959	146				

(continued)

TABLE B-2 (continued)

	1214 Looms (units)	1215 Cotton-Carding Machines (units)	1216 Knitting Machines (units)	1217 Leather-Spreading Machines (units)	1218 Leather-Dressing Machines (units)
1913	4,600			[—]	[—]
1914					
1915					
1916					
1917					
1918					
1919					
1920					
1921					
1921/22					
1922/23					
1923/24					
1924/25					
1925/26					
1926/27					
1927/28	3,700		1,809	—	—
1928/29					
1929/30					
1931					
1932	300		1,806	[—]	—
1933	1,928	181	2,555		
1934	2,118	428	2,761		
1935	3,254	837			
1936	4,461				
1937	4,095	1,210		108	56
1938					
1939					
1940	1,800	1,312		—	—
1945	20	2		—	—
1946					
1947	2,240				
1948	3,990				
1949	6,900				
1950	8,700	2,228		200	78
1951	7,200	2,664		310	106
1952	10,000	2,119		—	75
1953	10,200	2,167		10	61
1954	17,300	2,436		100	86
1955	16,000	1,800		222	98
1956	14,000	1,400		160	162
1957	14,500	1,165		200	197
1958	14,400	1,126		181	163
1959	15,900				

(continued)

TABLE B-2 (continued)

	1219 Typesetting Machines, Linotype (units)	1220 Flat-Bed Printing Presses (units)	1221 Industrial Sewing Machines (thous.)	1222 Metal- Pressing Mach. Tools (thous.)	1222.1 Presses (units)
1913	[—]	[—]	[—]		
1914					
1915					
1916					
1917					
1918					
1919					
1920					
1921					
1921/22					
1922/23					
1923/24					
1924/25					
1925/26					
1926/27					586
1927/28	—	—	—		1,194
1928/29	—	—	—		
1929/30	—	—	—		
1931	—	—	2.5		
1932	2	—	8.8	1.1	797
1933	29	80	16.1		384
1934	79	66	16.6		697
1935			17.6		
1936					
1937	300	300	23.6	3.1	2,111
1938					
1939					
1940	145	258	20.3	4.7†	4,061
1945	50	42	3.3		2,466
1946					
1947					
1948					
1949					
1950	355	821	34.0	7.7†	4,562
1951	376	885	34.9		3,508
1952	227	971	35.6		4,100
1953	216	1,140	45.2	11.2†	6,169
1954	328	923	49.0		8,323
1955	457	767	43.3	17.1†	12,071
1956	579	1,009	58.3	19.6	
1957	681	1,092	72.9	22.8	
1958	858	1,114	89.2	25.0	
1959				28.5	

(continued)

TABLE B-2 (continued)

	1301 Excavators (units)	1302 Trench Excavators (units)	1303 Stone Crushers (units)	1304 Road Graders (units)	1305 Self-Propelled Road Graders (units)
1913	[—]				[—]
1914					
1915					
1916					
1917					
1918					
1919					
1920					
1921					
1921/22					
1922/23					
1923/24					
1924/25					
1925/26					
1926/27					
1927/28	—	39	63	97	—
1928/29	—	105	392	342	
1929/30	—	416	793	769	
1931	2	489	1,309	1,428	
1932	85	444	1,642	1,165	—
1933	116	397	1,351	1,693	
1934	290	255	1,196	1,267	
1935	458	199		749	
1936	573		673		
1937	522	[200]	[670]	660	—
1938	492				
1939	310				
1940	274				—
1945	10				—
1946	76				
1947	630				
1948	1,832				
1949	2,754				
1950	3,540				20
1951	3,755				40
1952	3,701				44
1953	4,156				219
1954	4,865				607
1955	5,250				1,014
1956	6,784			1,810	1,646
1957	9,535				2,064
1958	10,159				2,662
1959	10,200				2,800

(continued)

TABLE B-2 (continued)

	1306 Concrete Mixers (units)	1307 Scrapers, Tractor- Driven (units)	1308 Bulldozers (units)	1309 RR Cranes, Steam (units)	1310 Self-Propelled Cranes (units)
1913		[—]	[—]	[—]	[—]
1914					
1915					
1916					
1917					
1918					
1919					
1920					
1921					
1921/22					
1922/23					
1923/24					
1924/25					
1925/26					
1926/27					
1927/28	25	—	—	—	[—]
1928/29	372			1	
1929/30	720			—	
1931	1,633			12	
1932	1,104	—	—	122	—
1933	492			151	
1934	433			83	
1935				112	
1936					
1937	1,211	2,400	136	418	137
1938					
1939					
1940	1,584	2,104	118	258	139
1945	466	34	1	37	17
1946					
1947					
1948					
1949					
1950	4,373	2,089	3,788	478	4,152
1951	5,194	3,392	3,516	603	3,555
1952	5,220	3,386	4,475	635	3,321
1953	5,623	4,144	5,794	696	4,808
1954	6,485	3,067	6,669	715	4,926
1955	7,503	2,025	7,511	641	5,505
1956		1,991	9,520	344	5,590
1957		2,500	10,429	321	6,270
1958		2,664	10,963	400	6,944
1959					

(continued)

TABLE B-2 (continued)

	1311 Overhead Traveling Cranes (units)	1312 Tower Cranes (units)	1313 Electric Elevators (units)	1401 Telephones (thous.)	1402 Hand-Operated Switchboards (th. lines)
1913		[—]		[52.0]	
1914					
1915					
1916					
1917					
1918					
1919					
1920					
1921					
1921/22					
1922/23					
1923/24				13.3	
1924/25				21.7	
1925/26				57.1	
1926/27				98.6	
1927/28	61	[—]	155	58.5	24.5
1928/29	139		166	84.3	48.1
1929/30	193		219	117.0	91.2
1931	342		245	249.0	163.9
1932	625	—	389	234.5	190.3
1933	708		373	232.9	151.3
1934	330		256	241.0	135.2
1935	373		252	258.3	212.6
1936				274.5	[239.2]
1937	375	3	722	252.6	[239]
1938					
1939					
1940		57	513		
1945		3	44		
1946					
1947					
1948					
1949					
1950		1,199	466		
1951		1,962	859		
1952		2,324	932		
1953		2,648	1,411		
1954		3,119	1,613		
1955		3,241	1,957		
1956		2,845	2,829		
1957		3,470	3,340		
1958		2,611	4,126		
1959					

(continued)

TABLE B-2 (continued)

	1403 Automatic Switchboards (th. lines)	1405 Calculating Machines (thous.)	1406 Typewriters (thous.)	1501 Flour (mill.m.t.)	1502 Macaroni (th.m.t.)	1503 Butter (th.m.t.)
1913				28	30	104
1914						136.6
1915						128.7
1916						73.7
1917						56.6
1918						28.0
1919						11.5
1920						21.0
1921						18.2
1921/22						25.2
1922/23						29.5
1923/24						[39.6]
1924/25						[49.6]
1925/26						[56.7]
1926/27		2.4				[58.9]
1927/28	22.0	5.2	—	24	47	82.1
1928/29	30.1	8.0	—		50	77.8
1929/30	40.2	12.8	—		99	41.0
1931	83.8	30.1	0.14		160	82.8
1932	84.1	41.4	1.44	[20]	185	71.4
1933	50.0	54.5	4.02		149	124.3
1934	69.8	64.6	8.12		181	138.0
1935	136.0	59.8	9.69		185	159
1936	96.0	58.0	17.09		262	189
1937	86.8		20.82	28	264	185
1938					306	199
1939					388	191
1940	37.5			29	324	226
1945	2.7			15	243	117
1946					270	186
1947					238	218
1948					311	292
1949					364	317
1950	132.0			22	440	336
1951	166.1				496	355
1952	139.3				617	371
1953	140.5			27†	740	382
1954	206.5				850	389
1955	201.0			32	958	463
1956	245.2			32	862	557
1957	260.2			33	957	635
1958	310.0			33	950	659
1959					961	712

(continued)

TABLE B-2 (continued)

	1504 Vegetable Oil (th.m.t.)	1504.1 Oleomargarine (th.m.t.)	1504.2 Vegetable Oil Minus Oleomargarine (th.m.t.)	1505 Cheese (th.m.t.)	1506 Meat Slaughtering (th.m.t.)
1913	471	—	471		1,042
1914					
1915					
1916					
1917					
1918					
1919					
1920					
1921					
1921/22					
1922/23					
1923/24					
1924/25					
1925/26					
1926/27					
1927/28	620	—	620		678
1928/29		[—]			
1929/30		6.3		7.1	609
1931		20.6		14.5	794
1932	490	38.3	451.7	14.3	483
1933	321	51.8		15.6	427
1934	422	69.2		18.2	461
1935	492	81.8		20.4	586
1936	503	75.0		25.3	773
1937	539	74.0	465	31.0	812
1938	643	93†		30.5	1,140
1939	693	107†		33.2	1,291
1940	798	121	677	38.0	1,183
1945	292	28	264		613
1946	326	39†			733
1947	403	85†			753
1948	549	126†			939
1949	722	149†		38.0	1,062
1950	819	192	627	48.0	1,438
1951	919	219†		58.0	1,570
1952	999	272		67.0	1,782
1953	1,160	337		78.0	1,989
1954	1,280	391		87.0	2,188
1955	1,168	399	769	106.0	2,226
1956	1,525	437	1,088		2,371
1957	1,685	449	1,236		2,798
1958	1,446	396	1,050		[3,011]
1959					[3,759]

(continued)

TABLE B-2 (continued)

	1506.1 Sausages (th.m.t.)	1507 Fish Catch (th.m.t.)	1508 Soap (40% fatty acid) (th.m.t.)	1509 Salt (th.m.t.)	1510 Raw Sugar Consumption (th.m.t.)
1913	60.0	1,018	[254]	1,959	1,347
1914				1,860	1,705
1915				1,738	1,504
1916				2,610	1,186
1917		893		1,283	912
1918				1,040	342
1919				586.1	95
1920		257		663.7	89
1921		298		1,103	51
1921/22		483*		855.4	210
1922/23		499*		1,066	378
1923/24		535*		1,175	457
1924/25		721*		1,442	1,064
1925/26		897*		1,625	873
1926/27		747*		2,144	1,333
1927/28		840*	[360*]	2,336	1,283
1928/29		956*	[390*]	2,670	823
1929/30	64.2	1,283*	[325*]	3,158	1,507
1931	70.3	1,441	[219]	3,182*	1,486
1932	75.3	1,333	357	2,636	828
1933	49.1	1,303	262	2,734	995
1934	58.4	1,547	426	3,545	1,404
1935	112.0	1,520	479	4,350	2,032
1936	244.4	1.631	557	[4,166]	1,998
1937	368.6	1,609	495	3,200	2,421
1938	305.0	1,542	606†	3,500†	2,520
1939		1,566	676†	3,800†	1,826
1940	391.3	1,404	700	4,400	2,165
1945		1,125	229	2,900	465
1946		1,208	233	3,100†	466
1947		1,534	298	3,900†	981
1948	245.6	1,575	432	4,700†	1,666
1949	351.2	1,953	735	4,600†	2,042
1950	491.7	1,755	816	4,500	2,523
1951	575.3	2,142	779	4,100†	2,979
1952	553.8	2,107	795	4,400†	3,067
1953	642.4	2,195	882	4,500†	3,434
1954	713.1	2,505	1,067	4,800†	2,611
1955	770.2	2,737	1,077	5,700	3,419
1956	824.0	2,849	1,266	6,000	4,354
1957	900	2,761	1,341	6,100	4,491
1958	1,000	2,931	1,360	6,200	5,434
1959	1,200	3,000	1,400		6,000

(continued)

TABLE B-2 (continued)

	1510.1 Refined Sugar (th.m.t.)	1510.2 Raw Sugar Minus Refined Sugar and Sugar in Candy (th.m.t.)	1511 Starch and Syrup (th.m.t.)	1512 Yeast (th.m.t.)	1513 Canned Food (mill. 400-gram cans)
1913	828	483	145	9.35	95
1914	937				
1915	859				
1916	841				
1917	251				
1918	61				
1919	18				
1920	17				
1921	8				
1921/22	50				
1922/23	130				
1923/24	302			8.29	
1924/25	449			14.1	
1925/26	412			18.7	
1926/27	575			21.1	
1927/28	656	575	[96]	19.3	125
1928/29	523		[93]	18.2	240
1929/30	216		[104]*	19.5*	320
1931	241		[106]*	21.1	420
1932	438	242	107	24.3	692
1933	349		151	24.1	619
1934	487		194	27.7	722
1935	719		249	35.3	808
1936	1,060		292	47.6	1,002
1937	1,032	1,135	247	[48]	982
1938	1,137		306†		1,104
1939	935		233†		1,148
1940	628	1,354	247	[48]	1,113
1945	54	362	36		558
1946	100		57†		583
1947	169		71†		669
1948	293		128†		868
1949	481		214†		1,162
1950	701	1,527	242	48	1,535
1951	859		236†	[59]	1,848
1952	1,017		223†	[68]	2,064
1953	1,252		240†	[75]	2,358
1954	1,275		191†	[86]	2,741
1955	1,285	1,833	233	[95]	3,217
1956	1,591	2,394	254		3,601
1957	1,538	2,594	263		3,795
1958	1,766	3,283	243		4,055
1959					4,300

(continued)

TABLE B-2 (continued)

	1513.1 Canned Meat (mill. cans)	1513.2 Canned Fish (mill. cans)	1513.3 Canned Milk (mill. cans)	1513.4 Canned Vegetables and Fruit (mill. cans)	1514 Beer (th. hectol.)
1913	67.6	9.6	—	17.9	8,064
1914					
1915					
1916					
1917					
1918					
1919					
1920					
1921					
1921/22					
1922/23					
1923/24					2,276
1924/25					2,513
1925/26					4,084
1926/27					4,141
1927/28	8.0	42.4	—	74.6	3,907
1928/29					3,400
1929/30					[3,700]
1931					3,920
1932	129.3	161.2	3.1	398.6	4,210
1933					4,315
1934					4,568
1935					5,186
1936					7,436
1937	65.1	123.3	52.8	740.8	8,960
1938					10,310†
1939					10,740†
1940	108.1	120.3	70.4	814.0	12,130
1945					4,050
1946					5,690†
1947					6,840†
1948					7,075
1949					9,835
1950	291.1	200.2	81.5	961.8	13,080
1951					15,170
1952					16,080
1953	359.0†	403.4†	183.5†	1,407†	18,330
1954					18,890
1955	467.3	604.6	238.6	1,907	18,470
1956	516.4	689.0	276.8	2,119	18,070
1957	545.5	636.4	326.8	2,287	19,650
1958					19,900
1959					

(continued)

453

TABLE B-2 (continued)

	1515 Cigarettes (billions)	1516 Low-Grade Tobacco (th. 20-kg. crates)	1517 Matches (th. crates)	1518 Vodka (40% alcohol) (mill. decaliters)	1519 Candy (th.m.t.)
1913	22.1	3,934	3,757	118.9	72.6
1914					
1915					
1916					
1917	22.0	4,078	2,279		
1918	12.7	1,423	1,019		
1919	10.2	936	1,008		
1920	4.85	1,069	632		
1921	5.15	596	782		
1921/22	12.6	663	976		
1922/23	10.8	977	1,425		
1923/24	13.0	1,548	1,640		
1924/25	26.3	2,525	3,276	0.7	
1925/26	37.3	4,235	3,950	24.3	
1926/27	40.7	4,250	4,170	39.6	[64.2]
1927/28	49.5	4,293	5,532	55.5	[103]
1928/29	57.7*	3,299	6,844	52.7	[142]
1929/30	61.7*	3,167	9,157	61.3	174.0
1931	64.8	2,980	7,675	74.7	333.5
1932	57.9	3,274	5,642	72.0	296.6
1933	62.7	2,513	6,876		222.5
1934	67.8	2,918	9,080		334.1
1935	78.6	3,750	10,730		[363]
1936	85.9	5,021	8,194		[458]
1937	89.2	5,343	7,163	89.7	508.5
1938	95.9	5,600†	9,516		[537]
1939	97.6†	4,300†	10,240		[500]
1940	100.4	4,600	10,000	92.5	366.0
1945	25	700	1,864	44.3	98.0
1946	50.8†	1,200			[157]
1947	74.3†	1,300†	3,300		[203]
1948	92	2,000†	5,300		[333]
1949	108	2,600†			[445]
1950	125	3,800	10,200	62.8	590
1951	141	3,200†	10,800		[651]
1952	158	2,900†	9,100		[682]
1953	183	3,500†	8,900	95.4†	[702]
1954	207	3,200†	11,300		[679]
1955	198	2,700	13,300	116.9	602
1956	203	3,200	13,500	122.9	739
1957	215	3,900	13,600	140.2	718
1958	232	3,800	13,000	145.3	[760]
1959	243				[820]

(continued)

TABLE B-2 (continued)

	1601 Boots and Shoes (mill. pairs)	1602 Rubber Footwear (mill. pairs)	1603 Cotton Yarn (th.m.t.)	1604 Cotton Fabrics (mill. meters)	1605 Cotton Thread (mill. reels)
1913	60.0	27.9	271.0	2,582	417
1914		[22.3]			
1915		[23.6]			
1916	54.0	[17.5]			
1917		[20.0]	210.7	[1,205]	
1918		[5.98]	117.6	[932]	
1919		[2.67]	19.3	[153]	
1920		[0.01]	15.1	[120]	
1921		[0.64]	21.8	151	
1921/22		[8.74]	71.5*	347*	
1922/23		[10.3]	87.4*	642*	
1922/24		6.3	116.2*	923*	
1924/25		[16.1]	196.9*	1,678*	
1925/26		[26.0]	252.1*	2,273*	
1926/27	[95]	29.6	283.6*	[2,480]	
1927/28	[103]	36.3	324.0	2,678	473
1928/29	[95]	42.1	353.8*	2,996	
1929/30		42.4	287.4*	2,351	
1931		53.9	313,8	2,242	
1932	103.0	64.7	355.1	2,694	699
1933	90.3	62.2	367.3	2,732	
1934	85.4	65.0	387.7	2,733	
1935	103.6	76.4	384.0	2,640	
1936	143.2	82.0	480.0	3,270	
1937	182.9	84.6	532.9	3,448	892
1938	192.9	85.5	[528.9]	3,460	
1939	205.7	80.3	[561.5]	3,763	
1940	211.0	69.7	650	3,954	1,212
1945	63.1	15.1	303	1,617	555
1946	81.2	30.8		1,901	
1947	112.8	51.3		2,541	
1948	134.0	71.1		3,150	
1949	163.6	91.8		3,601	
1950	203.4	110.4	663	3,899	1,013
1951	239.7	122.5		4,768	
1952	237.7	123.2		5,044	
1953	239.4	111.8	899†	5,285	1,558†
1954	257.8	115.8		5,590	
1955	274.5	131.4	1,038	5,905	1,929
1956	287.0	145.0	977	5,457	1,950
1957	317.3	150.7	1,016	5,588	1,948
1958	355.8	158.7	1,063	5,789	1,862
1959	389				

(continued)

TABLE B-2   (continued)

	1606 Linen Yarn (th.m.t.)	1607 Linen Fabrics (mill. meters)	1609 Silk and Rayon Fabrics (mill. meters)	1609.1 Pure Silk Fabrics (mill. meters)	1609.2 Rayon and Mixed Fabrics (mill. meters)
1913	53.3	120.0	[52]	[28]	[24.0]
1914					
1915					
1916					
1917	52.0	97.0†			
1918	27.9				
1919	15.2				
1920	10.3				
1921	8.38				
1921/22					
1922/23	34.4				
1923/24	45.2				
1924/25	47.6				
1925/26	67.8				
1926/27	67.4		[9.2]		
1927/28	61.6	174.4*	[14]	[1.9]	[12.1]
1928/29	70.4	176.8	[18]		
1929/30	78.2*	196.3	17.8		
1931	57.0	141.5	19.5		
1932	54.5	133.6	21.5	9.5	[12.0]
1933	57.6	140.5	26.0	12.2	13.8
1934	66.8	162.1	31.4	14.3	17.1
1935	83.0	215.6	38.2		
1936		295.2	51.7		
1937	97.5	285.2	58.9	[26.1]	[32.8]
1938		269.8	58.8		
1939		257.7	70.4		
1940	109.0	285.5	76.6	[28.1]	[48.5]
1945	40.2	106.5	36.2	[15.3]	[20.9]
1946		112.6	48.7		
1947		141.4	65.4		
1948		184.1	81.7		
1949		225.5	105.0		
1950	99.0	282.2	129.7	[28.8]	[100.9]
1951		313.5	174.3		
1952		256.5	224.6		
1953	95.6†	288.9	400.4		
1954		287.4	517.0		
1955	105.4	305.4	525.8	[33.7]	[492.1]
1956	137.0	383.2	752.0		
1957	147.2	424.2	804.9		
1958	169.2	481.2	844.8		
1959					

(continued)

TABLE B-2 (continued)

	1610 Woolen Yarn (th.m.t.)	1611 Woolen and Worsted Fabrics (mill. meters)	1612 Knitted Goods (mill. pieces)	1613 Hosiery (mill. pairs)	1614 Felt Footwear (mill. pairs)
1913	46.5	[105.0]			[16]
1914					
1915					
1916					
1917					
1918	24.9				
1919	9.9				
1920	7.6				
1921	6.8				
1921/22	13.7*				
1922/23	15.7				
1923/24	20.5				
1924/25	29.3				
1925/26	35.8				
1926/27	43.8	[103]			
1927/28	49.5	[117]	8.3	67.7*	15.6
1928/29	57.3	[129]			16.6
1929/30	71.0*	114.5*			
1931	73.0	107.9			
1932	71.0	88.7	39.0	208.0	9.4
1933	67.5	86.1	53.3	250.9	7.6
1934	61.0	77.9	76.1	322.9	7.9
1935	65.5	84.0	89.2	340.7	9.1
1936	73.0	101.5	121.8	358.7	11.2
1937	76.6	108.3	156.0	408.6	13.4
1938		113.2	168.9	451.1	
1939		122.4	170.7	457.4	
1940	82.6	119.7	183.0	485.4	17.9
1945	39.9	53.8	50.0	91.0	13.3
1946		70.9	76.4	133.9	
1947		95.0	100.2	196.7	
1948		123.7	127.2	282.0	
1949		148.6	163.7	375.1	
1950	101.6	155.2	197.5	472.7	22.4
1951		175.6	257.2	597.8	
1952		190.5	298.4	584.9	
1953	137.2†	208.7	340.7	611.9	23.8†
1954		243.2	402.6	674.8	27.2
1955	167.5	252.3	431.6	772.2	24.5
1956	179.5	268.5	433.9	803.2	24.2
1957	187.9	283.8	464.9	844.7	26.4
1958	201.2	302.6	495.2	887.2	28.5
1959			541	926	31

(continued)

TABLE B-2 (continued)

	1701 Bicycles (thous.)	1702 Cameras (thous.)	1703 Electric Light Bulbs (millions)	1704 Phonographs (thous.)	1705 Radios (thous.)
1913	4.9	[—]	2.85	—	[—]
1914			2.56		
1915					
1916			4.58		
1917					
1918					
1919					
1920			0.26		
1921			1.11		
1921/22			2.02		
1922/23	0.8		3.82		
1923/24	1.5		6.51		
1024/25			10.7		
1925/26			14.4		
1926/27	6.9		14.4		
1927/28	10.8	—	13.7	—	[—]
1928/29	21.0	—	19.1	—	
1929/30	35.4	3.0	33.2	1.7	
1931	80.9	23.0	44.0	15.7	
1932	125.6	29.6	54.7	57.7	29.0
1933	132.4	115.3	69.5	99.3	22.2
1934	274.5	168.6	83.6	204.8	48.0
1935	324.2	150.7	101.0	284.7	128.1
1936	557.5	268.0	113.2	575.5	334.1
1937	540.7	353.2	116.6	675.1	200.0
1938	385.6	207.5	[134.0]	843.5	202.4
1939					
1940	255.0	355.2	139.8	313.7	160.5
1945	23.8	0.01	52.9	0.6	13.8
1946					
1947					
1948	344.0	157.4		208.3	532
1949	496.0	166.9	167.0	339.6	878
1950	649.3	260.3	212.9	366.8	1,071
1951	1,157	357.2	256.0	454.6	1,233
1952	1,650	459.1	278.6	558.4	1,295
1953	1,903	499.1	297.6	702.5	1,640
1954	2,384	767.9	318.7	920.2	2,894
1955	2,884	1,023	356.8	847.5	3,530
1956	3,120	1,195	409.5	388.1	3,772
1957	3,318	1,322	467.6	191.1	3,551
1958	3,651	1,472	530.1		3,901
1959	3,300	1,600			4,000

(continued)

TABLE B-2 (concluded)

	1706 Television Sets (thous.)	1707 Household Sewing Machines (thous.)	1708 Clocks and Watches (thous.)	1709 Motorcycles (thous.)
1913	—	271.8	700	0.1
1914				
1915				
1916				
1917				
1918				
1919				
1920				
1921				
1921/22				
1922/23				
1923/24				
1924/25				
1925/26				
1926/27		202.1		
1927/28	—	285.6	950	—
1928/29		425.2		—
1929/30		538.5		—
1931		500.8	2,990	0.02
1932	—	318.8	3,557	0.11
1933		265.8	4,093	0.12
1934	—	260.9	4,371	0.37
1935		402.8	4,497	1.20
1936		490.0		6.7
1937	—	510.1	4,028	13.1
1938		502.5		
1939				
1940	0.3	175.2	2,796	6.8
1945	—	—	336	4.7
1946				
1947				
1948		307.0	3,070	
1949		411.0	5,960	91.9
1950	11.9	501.7	7,566	123.1
1951	25.3	668.0	9,645	125.1
1952	37.4	804.5	10,490	104.4
1953	84.1	993.2	12,840	143.3
1954	254.3	1,281	16,400	205.9
1955	494.7	1,611	19,710	244.5
1956	596.2	1,914	22,600	297.0
1957	707.8	2,267	23,500	336.5
1958	979.3	2,686	24,800	400.1
1959	1,300	2,900	26,200	500

Sources to Table B-2

101 Pig iron

1913–1932	*222*, 133. For 1913 and 1927/28–1932, also *138*, 62.
1933–1956	*180*, 106, 427.
1957–1959	*364*, 1/27/58; 1/16/59; 1/22/60.

102 Rolled steel

1913	*32*, 30. A later source (*141*, 62) gives 3.5 mill. m. tons.
1914–1926/27	Data in *222*, 133 ff, adjusted upward to include pipes and forgings from ingots. For details, see *567*, Part 2, series 108.1.
1927/28–1956	*180*, 106, 427.
1957–1959	*364*, 1/27/58; 1/16/59; 1/22/60.

103 Steel ingots and castings

1913–1955	*180*, 106.
1956–1958	*141*, 158 f.
1959	*364*, 1/22/60.

201 Primary aluminum

1932–1934	*221*, 190.
1935	Based on 1934 output and announced annual relative (174.3%, *148*, 117).
1937	*267*, 204.
1938	*223*, 62.
1939	Based on 1938 output and percentage increase for first half of 1939 over first half of 1938 (107.3%, *318*, 9/21/39).
1940	Based on 1937 output and percentage increase between 1937 and 1940 (159%, *321*, 2/21/41).
1945	Based on 1940 output and percentage increase between 1940 and 1945 (144%, *321*, 4/2/46).

202 Copper

1913, 1921/22–1933	*221*, 190.
1934	*399*, 1936, No. 3, 4. Also, *146*, 128.
1935–1936	*149*, 70. For 1936, preliminary.
1937	Based on 1938 output and announced annual relative (105.8%, *399*, 1939, No. 9, 3).
1938	*223*, 62.
1939	Based on 1937 output and percentage increase between 1937 and 1939 (146%, *318*, 5/23/40).
1940	Based on 1937 output and percentage increase between 1937 and 1940 (165%, *321*, 2/21/41).
1945–1954	Based on 1955 output and announced annual relatives for 1946–1952 and 1954–1955 (106%, 109%, 120%, 120%, 110%, 114%, 115%, 105%, and 112%, *364*, 1/21/47; 1/18/48; 1/20/49; 1/18/50; 1/26/51; 1/29/52; 1/23/53; 1/21/55; 1/30/56). Annual relative for 1953 (99%) was based on annual relatives for 1951–1952 and 1954–1955 and on percentage increase between 1950 and 1955 (153%, *364*, 4/25/56). Annual relatives for 1954–1955 are for refined copper.

1955   Based on 1955 production in Kazakhstan (estimated at 166 th. m. tons) and the percentage of total output of copper produced in Kazakhstan (44%, *325*, 12/18/55). Kazakh production in 1955 was estimated as follows: 1955 output is stated to be 179% of 1950 output (*325*, 12/18/55); 1950 output is stated to be 100.5% of output planned for 1950 (*325*, 12/16/51), which is stated to be 2.6 times 1940 output (*325*, 1/28/49); 1940 output is stated to be 7 times 1913 output (*363*, 1952, No. 3); 1913 output is given as 5.07 th. m. tons (*65*, 586).

203 *Lead*

1913–1921	*197*, 94 f. For 1913, also *221*, 190.
1921/22–1932	*221*, 190.
1933–1935	*399*, 1936, No. 3, 7.
1936	Based on 1935 output and announced annual relative (133.6%, *399*, 1937, No. 2, 119).
1937	Based on 1932 output and percentage increase between 1932 and 1937 (233%, *318*, 3/4/39).
1938–1939	Based on 1937 output and announced annual relatives for 1938–1939 (124.8% and 109.4%, *399*, 1939, No. 9, 3; *318*, 6/24/39).
1940	Assumed to be 105% of 1939 output.
1945	Assumed to be 120% of 1943 output (estimated at 49.9 th. m. tons from statement in *293*, 24, that output in eastern regions of USSR in 1943 was 59 times output in entire USSR in 1915 and from assumption that there was no output outside eastern regions in 1943).
1946–1955	Based on 1945 output and announced annual relatives for 1946–1954 (119%, 126%, 102%, 126%, 124%, 125%, 117%, 122%, and 113%, *364*, 1/21/47; 1/18/48; 1/20/49; 1/10/50; 1/26/51; 1/29/52; 1/23/53; 1/31/54; 1/21/55). Annual relative for 1955 (114.1%) was based on annual relatives for 1951–1954 and on increase between 1950 and 1955 (2.3 times, *364*, 4/25/56).

204 *Zinc*

1913–1916, 1920–1921, 1922/23–1924/25	*197*, 96 f. For 1913 and 1922/23–1924/25, also *221*, 190.
1921/22	Interpolated on the basis of lead (series 203).
1925/26–1933	*221*, 190.
1934–1935	*399*, 1936, No. 3, 11.
1936	Based on 1935 output and announced annual relative (136.9%, *399*, 1937, No. 2, 119).
1937	Output in 1937 is stated (*399*, 1938, No. 9) to be 85% of planned output in Second Five Year Plan (90 th. m. tons in *294*, 138).
1938	Output in 1938 is stated (*336*, 12/16/45) to be 5 times output in 1933.
1939–1940	Extrapolated on the basis of lead (series 203).
1945	Assumed to be 130% of 1943 output (estimated at 38.4 th. m. tons from statement in *293*, 24, that output in eastern regions of USSR in 1943

was 18.8 times output in entire USSR in 1915 and from assumption that there was no output outside eastern regions in 1943).

1946–1955

Based on 1945 output and announced annual relatives for 1946–1954 (108%, 116%, 136%, 124%, 117%, 115%, 124%, 113%, and 107%, *364*, 1/21/47; 1/18/48; 1/20/49; 1/18/50; 1/26/51; 1/29/52; 1/23/53; 1/31/54; 1/21/55). Annual relative for 1955 (116%) was based on annual relatives for 1951–1954 and on increase between 1950 and 1955 (2 times, *364*, 4/25/56).

301   Electric power

1913, 1916, 1921–1955	*180*, 171.
1920	*296*, 33.
1956–1958	*141*, 158 f.
1959	*364*, 1/22/60.

301.1   Hydroelectric power

1913, 1916, 1921–1956	*180*, 171, 427. A later source (*141*, 158 f) gives 0.04 bill. kwh for 1913.
1957–1958	*141*, 158 f.

302   Anthracite

1913–1921	*197*, 156 ff. For 1913, also *222*, 100 f.
1921/22–1929/30	*222*, 100 f.
1931–1955	*180*, 144.
1956–1958	*141*, 204.
1959	Based on 1959 output of all coal (506.5 mill. m. tons, *364*, 1/22/60) and percentage breakdown of coal in 1958.

303   Bituminous coal

1913, 1921/22–1955	*180*, 144.
1914–1921	*197*, 156 ff.
1956–1958	*141*, 204.
1959	Derived in same way as anthracite (series 302).

303.1   Coke

1913–1917, 1921/22–1925/26	*285*, 257. For 1913, also *138*, 55.
1926/27	*185*, 423.
1927/28–1928/29	*74*, 290. For 1927/28, also *138*, 55.
1930–1934	*222*, 19, 153. For 1932, also *138*, 55.
1935–1955	*180*, 115.
1956	*138*, 60.
1957–1959	*364*, 1/27/58; 1/16/59; 1/22/60.

304   Lignite

1913, 1921/22–1933	*222*, 100 f. For 1927/28–1933, also *138*, 67.
1914–1921	*197*, 156 ff.
1934–1955	*180*, 144.
1956–1958	*141*, 204.
1959	Derived in same way as anthracite (series 302).

305   Crude petroleum

1913–1956	*180*, 153, 427.
1957, 1959	*364*, 1/27/58; 1/22/60.
1958	*141*, 62.

306 *Natural gas*

1913, 1922/23–1923/24	Output in m. tons (*66*, 240) times 1,100, the average ratio for 1927/28 and 1937 of m³ to m. tons implied by data in *222*, 113; *267*, 202; and *180*, 156.
1921/22	Extrapolated from 1922/23 on the basis of crude petroleum (series 305).
1924/25–1926/27, 1928/29–1931, 1933–1934	Output in m. tons (*222*, 113) times 1,100, as for 1913.
1927/28, 1932, 1937, 1940, 1945, 1950, 1955	*180*, 156.
1935–1936	Output in m. tons (combined output of petroleum and natural gas minus output of petroleum, *267* 202) times 1,100, as for 1913.
1938	Output in m. tons (combined output of petroleum and natural gas in *223*, 51, minus adjusted output of petroleum in *357*, 1939, No. 3, 8) times 1,100, as for 1913.
1939	Assumed to be same as in 1938.
1946–1949	Based on 1945 output and announced annual relatives for 1946–1949 (114%, 122%, 110%, and 103%, *364*, 1/21/47; 1/18/48; 1/20/49; 1/18/50). Difference (2 percentage points) between link relatives for 1945–1950 and chained annual relatives distributed linearly.
1951–1952	Based on 1950 output and announced annual relatives for 1951–1952 (108% and 102%, *364*, 1/29/52; 1/23/53).
1953–1954	Based on 1955 output and announced annual relatives for 1953–1954 (109% and 120%, *364*, 1/21/55; 1/30/56).
1956–1958	*141*, 158 f.

307 *Oil shale*

1913	Assumed no production
1919–1924/25	*197*, 2 f.
1925/26–1926/27	*66*, 248.
1927/28	*200*, 49.
1928/29	*79*, 155.
1930–1934	*132*, vol. 24, 51 ff.
1935–1937	*172*, 100.
1938	*318*, 6/9/39.
1940, 1945, 1950, 1955–1956	*180*, 166, 427.
1957–1959	*364*, 1/27/58; 1/16/59; 1/22/60.

308 *Peat*

1913–1934	*222*, 130. For 1913 and 1928, also *138*, 70. A later source (*141*, 158 f) gives 13.5 mill. m. tons for 1932.
1935–1955	*180*, 165.
1956–1958	*141*, 158 f.

309 *Firewood (consumption)*

1913, 1927/28, 1932–1933, 1936	Consumption in conventional tons of fuel (*79*, 148) multiplied by 5.3, the ratio of m³ to conventional tons implied by data in *7*, 12, and *363*, 1936, No. 1, 6.

1921/22, 1926/27, 1928/29–1931, 1934–1935	Based on consumption data of limited coverage (*172*, 90 f) and the ratio of that series to the series in *79*, 148, for the years covered in the preceding note. Converted into m³ as for 1913.

1923/24 — *363*, 1925, No. 3, 105 f. Sum of consumption by urban population and for industrial uses. Converted from sazhens³ at 1 sazhen³ = 9.7127 m³.

1937–1940, 1945–1953 — Based on consumption of coal (detailed NBER estimates of regional distribution of coal output in calorific value) and ratio of firewood to coal consumption for 1937 (*363*, 1946, No. 2, 101), 1938, 1940, 1950, and 1953 (derived from *363*, 1955, No. 3, 40). For years in between, ratio interpolated. Converted into m³ as for 1913.

1954–1955 — *180*, 248.
1956–1958 — *141*, 251.

401 *Soda ash*

1913, 1927/28–1940, 1945–1956 — *180*, 194, 427.
1914–1917, 1920–1927 — *61*, 205 ff. Sum of production of 3 soda ash plants (Donsoda, Slavsoda, and Berezniki).
1918–1919 — *249*, 306.
1957 — *364*, 1/27/58.

402 *Caustic soda*

1913, 1927/28–1940, 1945–1955 — *180*, 194.
1916–1919, 1921 — *417*, 1931, No. 1, 58.
1921/22–1923/24 — *15*, 62.
1924/25–1926/27 — *329*, 1931, No. 1, 21.
1956 — *138*, 60.
1957 — Assumed same percentage increase as for soda ash (series 401).

404 *Sulfuric acid*

1913, 1927/28–1940, 1945–1956 — *180*, 196, 428.
1919 — *418*, 1947, No. 11, 1077.
1921 — *488*, 70.
1922/23 — *66*, 54.
1923/24 — *285*, 262. Oleum included.
1924/25 — *329*, 1931, No. 1, 21.
1925/26 — *15*, 71.
1926/27 — *17*, 1st ed., vol. 59, 588.
1957–1958 — *141*, 158 f.
1959 — *364*, 1/22/60.

404.1 *Sulfuric acid (not used in phosphoric fertilizer)*

1913, 1919, 1921, 1922/23–1940, 1945–1959 — Total output of sulfuric acid (series 404) minus amount of sulfuric acid used in phosphoric fertilizer (series 405.1), calculated as 340 kg. of sulfuric acid per ton of phosphoric fertilizer, from *417*, 1939, No. 3, 11.

405 *Mineral fertilizer*

1913, 1927/28–1940, 1945–1959 — Sum of phosphoric fertilizer, ammonium sulfate, and potash fertilizer (series 405.1, 405.2, and 405.3).

405.1   *Phosphoric fertilizer* (18.7% P$_2$O$_5$)

1913, 1927/28–1940, 1945–1955	*180*, 192.
1916	Recomputed from data (15 to 20 th. m. tons, *417*, 1932, No. 10, 8) considered to be in 14% P$_2$O$_5$.
1917–1920	Recomputed from data considered to be in 14% P$_2$O$_5$ (*261*, 244).
1921–1922	Recomputed from data considered to be in 14% P$_2$O$_5$ (*137*, 8).
1922/23–1926/27	Recomputed from data considered to be in 14% P$_2$O$_5$ (*260*, vol. 24, 470).
1956–1959	Based on total mineral fertilizer including ground natural phosphate (10.9, 11.7, 12.4, and 12.9 mill. m. tons, *180*, 427; *364*, 1/27/58; 1/16/59; 1/22/60) and percentage share of phosphoric fertilizer for 1955.

405.2   *Ammonium sulfate*

1913, 1927/28–1940, 1945–1955	*180*, 192. Given as nitrogenous fertilizer expressed in terms of ammonium sulfate.
1956–1959	Derived in same way as phosphoric fertilizer (series 405.1).

405.3   *Potash fertilizer* (41.6% K$_2$O)

1913, 1927/28–1940, 1945–1955	*180*, 192.
1956–1959	Derived in same way as phosphoric fertilizer (series 405.1).

406   *Ground natural phosphate*

1913, 1927/28–1940, 1945–1955	*180*, 192. Given as 19% P$_2$O$_5$.
1922/23–1926/27	*260*, vol. 24, 470.
1956–1959	Derived in same way as phosphoric fertilizer (series 405.1).

410   *Red lead*

1913	*27*, table 8, 15 f. For large-scale industry in 1912.
1926/27–1928/29	Output of large-scale industry (3.56, 4.63, and 8.86 th. m. tons, *222*, 178) divided by its estimated percentage share of total output (*567*, Part 4, Table B).
1932–1935	*222*, 178. Sum of lead monoxide (*glet*) and lead oxide (*surik*).
1936	Planned output (*148*, 136) assumed fulfilled.
1937	Planned output (*149*, 90) assumed fulfilled.
1940, 1945, 1950–1955	*180*, 198.
1956–1958	*141*, 226.

411   *Zinc oxide*

1926/27–1928/29	Output of large-scale industry (4.97, 6.11, and 9.59 th. m. tons, *185*, 424; *222*, 179) divided by its estimated percentage share of total output (*567*, Part 4, Table B).
1932–1935	*222*, 179.
1936	Planned output (*148*, 136) assumed fulfilled.
1937	Planned output (*149*, 90) assumed fulfilled.
1940, 1945, 1950–1955	*180*, 198.
1956–1958	*141*, 226.

412   *Synthetic dyes*

1913	*16*, 35.
1916–1917, 1920	*303*, 1934, No. 8, 458.
1921/22	*193*, xlvi. State-owned industry only.

1923/24

Based on 1927/28 output and percentage that 1923/24 output was of 1927/28 output (17.5%, *368*, 1939, No. 6, 289).

1925/26–1926/27

185, 424. State-owned industry only.

1927/28–1935

222, 177.

1936

363, 1937, No. 8, 190.

1937

Based on 1923/24 output and its percentage of 1937 output (17.2%, *368*, 1939, No. 6, 289).

1938

18, 819.

1940, 1945, 1950–1956

180, 197, 428.

1946–1949

Based on 1945 output and announced annual relatives for 1946–1949 (129%, 144%, 135%, and 112%, *364*, 1/21/47; 1/18/48; 1/20/49; 1/18/50).

416 *Paper*

1913

221, 234.

1917, 1958

141, 256.

1921/22–1923/24

308, 1927, No. 11–12, 711.

1924/25

215, 193

1925/26–1940, 1945–1956

180, 268, 429.

1957, 1959

364, 1/27/58; 1/22/60.

417 *Paperboard*

1913

221, 234.

1921/22–1923/24

308, 1927, No. 11–12, 711.

1924/25–1940, 1945–1955

180, 268. A later source (*141*, 256) gives 545.2 th. m. tons for 1955.

1956–1958

141, 256.

418 *Motor vehicle tires*

1913

222, 179.

1914–1917

324, 1937, No. 11, 57.

1927/28–1940, 1945–1955

180, 199.

1956–1958

141, 228.

1959

364, 1/22/60.

419 *Rayon and other synthetic fibers*

1913

17, 1st ed., vol. 62, 247, 263 ff.

1927/28, 1932, 1937, 1940, 1945, 1950, 1955

180, 323.

1951–1954, 1956–1958

141, 227.

1959

364, 1/22/60.

501 *Red bricks*

1913

Total bricks (estimated at 3.5 bill. from data in *215*, 227, adjusted for size, see notes to series 705.1 in *567*, Part 3) minus sand-lime, silica, and slag bricks (series 505).

1927/28–1940, 1945–1955

Total bricks (*180*, 291) minus sand-lime, silica, and slag bricks (series 505).

1956–1958

Total bricks (*141*, 264) minus sand-lime, silica, and slag bricks (series 505).

1959

Total bricks (*364*, 1/22/60) minus sand-lime, silica, and slag bricks (series 505).

502 *Fire-clay bricks*

1913

363, 1938, No. 12, 38.

1925/26–1926/27

185, 294.

1927/28–1928/29	*139*, 223.
1929/30	*162*, 12.
1931	*17*, 1st ed., vol. 61, 810.
1932, 1937, 1940, 1950–1955	*180*, 297.
1933–1934	*222*, 183.
1935–1936	*149*, 94 f. For 1936, preliminary.
1956–1958	*141*, 266.

503   *Magnesite bricks*

1913, 1925/26, 1928/29	*363*, 1938, No. 12, 38.
1922/23–1924/25	*66*, 542.
1926/27–1927/28	*186*, 102. For 1926/27, does not include production of magnesite by metallurgical enterprises, which appears to be negligible.
1929/30, 1934	*162*, 12.
1932, 1937, 1940, 1945, 1950–1955	*180*, 297.
1933	*222*, 183.
1935–1936	Estimated from shares of refractory materials (see notes to series 715.6 in *567*, Part 3).
1956–1958	*141*, 266.

504   *Quartzite bricks*

1913	*363*, 1938, No. 12, 38.
1925/27–1926/27	*185*, 294.
1927/28–1928/29	*139*, 223.
1929/30	*162*, 12.
1932, 1937, 1940, 1945, 1950–1955	*180*, 297.
1933–1934	*215*, 227
1935–1936	*149*, 94 f. For 1936, preliminary.
1956–1958	*141*, 266.

505   *Sand-lime, silica, and slag bricks*

1913	Original data (87.3 mill., *27*, table 5, 30 f) adjusted upward for incomplete coverage (see *567*, Part 3, series 708.6).
1927/28–1929/30	*363*, 1931, No. 8, 144.
1931	Total bricks (4,680 mill., *180*, 291) times ratio of sand-lime, silica, and slag bricks to total bricks interpolated between 1928/29 and 1932 (derived as 0.091 from *180*, 291).
1932–1937, 1939–1940, 1945–1955	*180*, 291.
1938	*190*, 56 f.
1956–1957	*141*, 264.
1958–1959	Based on total bricks (*141*, 264; *364*, 1/22/60) and percentage share of sand-lime, silica, and slag bricks in 1955.

506   *Cement*

1913	*223*, 67. Also, *138*, 79.
1917–1919, 1921–1922	*84*, 244.
1920, 1923–1926, 1956	*180*, 277, 429.
1926/27	*249*, 304 f.
1927/28–1931	*215*, 183.
1932–1940, 1945–1955	*138*, 79.
1957–1959	*364*, 1/27/58; 1/16/59; 1/22/60.

507   *Construction gypsum*

1913

Taken as 85% of output in Russian Empire (610 th. m. tons, midpoint of range, *192*, 206 ff), the ratio for 1912 (*192*, 206 ff).

1925/26–1926/27   *66*, 187.
1927/28, 1937–1940, 1945–1955   *180*, 282.
1928/29   *393*, 1930, No. 2, 105. Output given for enterprises said to account for 90% of total output.
1932   *87*, 84.
1933   *221*, 214.
1934   *148*, 424.
1935–1936   *149*, 92 f. For 1936, preliminary.
1956–1957   *141*, 262.

508   *Construction lime*

1913

Based on total lime (630 th. m. tons, converted from poods, *17*, 1st ed., vol. 27, 536 f) and ratio of construction lime to total lime in 1927/28 (calculated as 0.081 from this series and *393*, 1937, No. 11, 25).

1927/28, 1937–1940, 1945–1955   *180*, 282.
1928/29

Based on total lime (estimated at 866 th. m. tons from *393*, 1930, No. 2, 105) and ratio of construction lime to total lime interpolated between 1927/28 and 1937 (calculated from this series and *267*, 205).

1931

Based on total lime (2,272 th. m. tons, *356*, 1933, No. 3, 80) and ratio used in 1928/29.

1932–1934

Based on total lime (2,650, 1,966, and 2,636 th. m. tons, *215*, 227, 180–182) and ratio used in 1928/29.

1935–1936

Based on total output of lime (2,906 and 3,721 th. m. tons, *149*, 92 f) and ratio used in 1928/29.

1956–1957   *141*, 262.

509   *Industrial timber hauled*

1913   *13*, 57 ff, as quoted in *514*, 155.
1927/28–1929/30   *202*, 170, as quoted in *514*, 155.
1931–1940, 1945–1954   *138*, 78.
1955   *180*, 249.
1956–1958   *141*, 164 f.

510   *Lumber*

1913, 1926/27–1928/29

Output of large-scale industry (11.9, 12.3, 13.6, and 16.6 mill. m³, *220*, 126) divided by its estimated percentage share of total output (*567*, Part 4, Tables A and B).

1930–1931   *220*, 126.
1932–1935   *222*, 190.
1936   *79*, 183.
1937   *363*, 1939, No. 2, 99.
1939   *13*, 162, 192, as quoted in *516*, 118.
1940   *342*, 1947, No. 10, 10.
1945, 1950–1955   *180*, 248.
1946–1948

Based on 1945 output and announced annual relatives for 1946–1948 (110%, 120%, and 155%, *364*, 1/21/47; *340*, 1948, No. 2, 50, as quoted in *516*, 118; *342*, 1949, No. 1, 1).

1956–1958   *141*, 164 f.

511   *Plywood*

1913	*187*, 114 ff, as quoted in *516*, 122. Also, *222*, 190.
1926/27–1928/29	Output of large-scale industry (137.4, 185.4, and 246.9 th. m³, *220*, 126) divided by its estimated percentage share of total output (*567*, Part 4, Table B).
1932–1935	*222*, 190. For 1935, preliminary.
1936	*341*, 1937, No. 5, 3.
1937	*13*, 122, 155, as quoted in *516*, 122.
1940, 1945, 1950–1955	*180*, 248.
1946	Based on 1945 output and announced annual relative (125.9%, *340*, 1947, No. 1, 53).
1956–1958	*141*, 164 f.

512   *Magnesite metallurgical powder*

1913, 1925/26–1928/29	*363*, 1938, No. 12, 38.
1922/23–1924/25	*66*, 542.
1929/30, 1934	*162*, 12.
1932, 1937, 1940, 1945, 1950–1955	*180*, 297.
1933	Total refractory materials (1,272 th. m. tons in *222*, 183) minus fire-clay, magnesite, and quartzite bricks (series 502, 503, and 504).
1935–1936	Estimated from shares of refractory materials (see notes to series 715.6 in *567*, Part 3).
1956–1958	*141*, 266.

513   *Roll roofing*

1913	*138*, 58.
1927	*369*, 12/5/53, as quoted in *454*, 119.
1927/28–1940, 1945–1955	*180*, 299. A later source (*141*, 164 f) gives 503.7 mill. m² for 1955.
1956–1958	*141*, 164 f.
1959	*364*, 1/22/60.

514   *Roofing iron*

1913–1920, 1921/22–1934	*222*, 133 ff.
1921	Interpolated linearly between 1920 and 1921/22.
1935–1936	*382*, 1937, No. 3, 70.
1937	*363*, 1938, No. 11, 87.
1938	*210*, 47.
1940	Based on estimated output of roofing and pickled iron and estimated share of roofing iron. Output of pickled iron is stated (*12*, 33) to account for 1.5% of total output of rolled steel in 1940. Share of roofing iron (74.1%) was obtained by a linear interpolation between 1938 percentage (71.6%) and 1941 planned percentage figure (75.4%).
1945, 1950, 1955–1959	Assumed no production.

515   *Roofing tiles*

1913, 1932–1940, 1945–1955	*180*, 299.
1956–1958	*141*, 266.

516   *Asbestos shingles*

1913, 1935–1940, 1945–1955	*180*, 299.
1916, 1919	*192*, 216.
1920–1921	*135*, 310.

1921/22–1925/26	*393*, 1930, No. 2, 94.
1926/27	*187*, 105.
1927/28–1934	*356*, 1935, No. 21, 14.
1956–1958	*141*, 164 f.
1959	*364*, 1/22/60.

518 *Rails*

1913–1919	*244*, 231. Sum of mining and railroad rails.
1927/28–1934	*222*, 135. Sum of mining and railroad rails.
1935–1936	*382*, 1937, No. 3, 70. Sum of mining and railroad rails.
1937	Interpolated linearly between 1936 and 1938.
1938	*210*, 59, 61. Sum of mining rails and first and second quality railroad rails.
1940, 1950, 1955	*180*, 110.
1945	Extrapolated from 1940 on the basis of the index of construction materials (Table D-4).
1947–1949	Based on 1950 output and announced annual relatives for railroad rails for 1947–1949 (134%, 180%, and 111%, *364*, 1/18/48; 1/20/49; 1/18/50).
1951, 1954	*580*, 1955, B-34 and C-21.
1952	Based on 1951 output and announced annual relative for railroad rails for 1952 (153%, *364*, 1/23/53).
1956–1958	*141*, 190.

519 *Window glass*

1913, 1928	*138*, 58.
1917–1920	Converted from data in tons (*261*, 244 f).
1921–1927	Converted from data in tons (*137*, 6 f).
1928–1940, 1945–1955	*180*, 312.
1956–1958	*141*, 164 f.
1959	*364*, 1/22/60.

601 *Crude alcohol* (100%)

1913, 1927/28, 1932, 1937, 1940, 1945, 1950, 1955	*180*, 372.
1926/27	Output of large-scale industry (derived as 1,876 th. hectoliters from *185*, 510, taking 1 vedro as 12.3 liters) divided by its estimated percentage share of total output (*567*, Part 4, Table B).
1928/29–1931, 1938–1939, 1956–1958	*141*, 319.
1933–1935	*222*, 23.
1936	*149*, 102 f. Preliminary.
1946	Based on 1945 output and announced annual relative (127%, *364*, 1/21/47).
1947–1949, 1951–1954	Based on 1950 output and announced annual relatives for 1948–1954 (150%, 125%, 106%, 111%, 110%, 118%, and 108%, *364*, 1/20/49; 1/18/50; 1/26/51; 1/29/52; 1/23/53; 1/31/54; 1/21/55). A later source (*141*, 319) gives absolute figures very close to the estimates derived here.

602 *Ginned cotton*

1913, 1927/28, 1932, 1937, 1940, 1945, 1950, 1955	*180*, 324.

1928/29–1931, 1933–1934	*215*, 202. Cotton ginned at state farms excluded in 1931.
1935–1936	*149*, 98 f. For 1936, preliminary.
1938	*363*, 1940, No. 9, 81.
1949, 1951–1952	Based on 1950 output and announced annual relatives for 1950–1952 (116%, 133%, and 107%, *364*, 1/26/51; 1/29/52; 1/23/53).
1953, 1956–1958	*141*, 272 f.

603 Raw cotton

1913, 1922	*178*, 59.
1924–1926	*261*, 186.
1927	*249*, 207.
1928–1934	*204*, 192.
1935	*222*, 345.
1936	*363*, 1937, No. 8, 196.
1937	*87*, 94.
1938	*219*, 68.
1939–1940	*98*, 402.
1945, 1950	*108*, 79.
1946–1947	Based on 1945 output and annual relatives for 1946–1947 (134% and 121%, *3*, 30).
1948	Output in 1948 is stated (*3*, 30) to have reached its prewar level.
1949	Based on 1949 output of ginned cotton (series 602) and ratio of output of raw cotton to ginned cotton in 1950.
1951–1955	Based on 1950 -output and index (1950 = 100, 1951 = 105, 1952 = 106, 1953 = 108, 1954 = 108, 1955 = 109, *138*, 98).

604 Hard leather

1913, 1927/28	Output of large-scale industry (18.1 and 63.8 th. m. tons, *27*, table 11, 124; *69*, 72) divided by its estimated percentage share of total output (*567*, Part 4, Tables A and B).
1932–1937	*69*, 72, 74.
1938–1939	*518*, 66.
1940, 1945, 1950, 1955	*180*, 357.
1956	Based on 1956 output in RSFSR (58.3 th. m. tons, *136*, 100) and percentage share of RSFSR output in total output in 1955 (64.9%, *136*, 100).

605 Soft leather

1913	Based on 1923/24 output of large-scale industry (*82*, 39) and ratio of 1913 to 1923/24 output for hard leather (*27*, table 11, 124, and *82*, 39).
1927/28	Output of large-scale industry (2,175 mill. dcm², *69*, 72) divided by its estimated percentage share of total output (*567*, Part 4, Table B).
1932–1937	*69*, 72, 74.
1938–1939	*518*, 66. Sum of Russian and chrome leather.
1940, 1945, 1950, 1955	*180*, 356.

606 Raw silk

1913, 1923/24	*17*, 1st ed., vol. 62, 248.
1921/22	*193*, 594. Output of the Silk Trust only.

1925/26–1926/27	*185*, 358.
1927/28–1934	*215*, 205. For 1934, preliminary.
1935–1936	*79*, 194.
1937, 1940, 1945, 1950, 1955	*180*, 323.
1953, 1956–1958	*141*, 272 f.

607 *Unwashed wool*

1913	Assumed to be same as in 1916.
1916, 1931–1936	*151*, 76.
1922–1930	*152*, 151.
1937	*267*, 82.
1938	*219*, 73.
1939–1940	Based on number of sheep and goats (80.9 and 76.7 mill., *138*, 128) and assumption that each sheep gives 2 kg of wool.
1950–1952, 1954–1955	Based on 1953 output and index (1950 = 100, 1951 = 107, 1952 = 122, 1953 = 130, 1954 = 128, 1955 = 142, *138*, 101).
1953	*19*, 131.

704 *Iron ore*

1913, 1927/28–1940, 1945–1955	*180*, 115.
1914–1924/25	*197*, 24 f. For 1913, also *138*, 55.
1925/26–1926/27	*200*, 2 f.
1956	*138*, 60.
1957	*141*, 62.
1958–1959	*364*, 1/16/59; 1/22/60.

706 *Manganese ore*

1913–1924/26	*197*, 52 f.
1925/26–1926/27	*200*, 4 f.
1928–1929, 1931–1934	*222*, 153.
1930, 1939–1940, 1945–1955	*180*, 115.
1935–1936	*149*, 68 f. For 1936, preliminary.
1937	*267*, 203
1938	*363*, 1939, No. 8, 155.
1956–1958	*141*, 193.

901 *Automobiles*

1913	Assumed no production.
1927/28–1940, 1945–1955	*180*, 223.
1956–1958	*141*, 162 f.
1959	*364*, 1/22/60.

902 *Trucks and buses*

1913	Assumed no production.
1923/24–1925/26	*407*, 1927, No. 10, 19.
1926/27	Based on less comprehensive series in *315* and ratio of this series to that one for 1927/28.
1927/28	*222*, 165. A more recent source (*141*, 162 f) gives 0.79 th.
1928/29–1940, 1945–1955	*180*, 223, 428. Total motor vehicles minus automobiles.
1956–1958	*141*, 162 f.
1959	*364*, 1/22/60.

903 *Diesel and electric locomotives*

1913	Assumed no production.

| 1927/28–1940, 1945–1956 | *180*, 220, 422. Sum of electric and diesel locomotives. |
| 1957–1959 | *364*, 1/27/58; 1/16/59. |

904   *Steam locomotives (main-line)—units*

1913, 1927/28–1940, 1945–1955	*180*, 220.
1914–1921	*407*, 1922, No. 2, 71; No. 4–8, 72.
1921/22–1923/24	*182*, 194, xlii.
1924/25	*183*, 149.
1925/26–1926/27	*312*, 1926, No. 12, 74; 1930, No. 2, 119.
1956	*138*, 61.
1957–1959	Production was discontinued after 1956.

904.1   *Steam locomotives (main-line)—conventional units*

| 1913, 1927/28–1940, 1945–1955 | *180*, 220. |

905   *Railroad freight cars*

1913, 1937, 1940	*138*, 56.
1921	*245*, 121.
1923/24	*246*, 116.
1924/25	*183*, 149.
1926/27	*17*, 1st ed., vol. 6, 513.
1927/28–1935	*222*, 163 f.
1936	*149*, 80 f. Preliminary.
1945–1955	*180*, 222.
1956	*138*, 62.
1957–1959	*364*, 1/27/58; 1/16/59; 1/22/60.

906   *Railroad passenger cars*

1913, 1940	*138*, 56.
1921	*407*, 1922, No. 10–12, 73.
1923/24	*52*, 220.
1924/25	*183*, 149.
1925/26	*77*, 89. Electric cars excluded.
1926/27	*17*, 1st ed., vol. 6, 513.
1927/28–1935	*222*, 164.
1936	*149*, 80. Preliminary.
1937	*267*, 207.
1938	*346*, 7/15/39. Electric cars excluded.
1945, 1950–1956	*180*, 220, 428.
1957, 1959	*364*, 1/27/58; 1/22/60.
1958	*141*, 162 f.

907   *Railroad cars, narrow-gauge and for factory use*

1927/28–1934	All railroad freight cars minus main-line cars (both in *222*, 163).
1935	All freight cars (*149*, 80 f) minus main-line cars (*222*, 163).
1936	All freight cars (*32*, 29) minus main-line cars (*149*, 80 f).
1937	All freight cars (*79*, 169) minus main-line cars (*267*, 207).

908   *Street and subway cars*

| 1913, 1927/28, 1932, 1937, 1940, 1950–1955 | *180*, 220. |
| 1956–1958 | *141*, 240 f. |

1001   *Tractors (excl. garden tractors)—units*

1913	*260*, vol. 23, 800 f.
1922/23–1923/24	*249*, 304.
1924/25–1925/26, 1936, 1938–1939, 1946–1949	*138*, 75.
1926/27	*312*, 1929, No. 1, 190.
1927/28–1935	*222*, 160. Sum of wheel tractors and caterpillar tractors.
1937, 1940, 1945, 1950–1955	*180*, 228 f.
1956–1958	*141*, 162 f.
1959	*364*, 1/22/60.

1001.1   *Tractors (excl. garden tractors)—capacity*

1924/25–1925/26, 1927/28–1940, 1945–1955	*138*, 76.
1926/27	*180*, 226.

1002   *Tractor-drawn plows (excl. paring plows)*

1913	Assumed no production.
1927/28–1935	*222*, 161.
1936	*149*, 78 f. Preliminary.
1937, 1940, 1950	*138*, 57.
1938	*223*, 64.
1945	Based on 1946 output and announced annual relative (175%, *364*, 1/21/47).
1946	Planned output for 1947 (40 th., *364*, 2/28/47) is stated to be 270% of 1946 output (*364*, 3/1/47).
1947–1949	Based on 1950 output and announced annual relatives for 1948–1950 (224%, 155%, and 147%, *364*, 1/20/49; 1/18/50; 1/26/51).
1951–1955	*180*, 230 f.
1956–1958	*141*, 162 f.
1959	*364*, 1/22/60.

1003   *Tractor-drawn paring plows*

1913	Assumed no production.
1927/28–1935	*222*, 161. For 1935, preliminary.
1937, 1940, 1945, 1950–1955	*180*, 230 f.
1956–1958	*141*, 244.

1004   *Horse-drawn plows*

1913	*203*, 674 f.
1916	*407*, 1922, No. 2, 71.
1917	*84*, 244.
1918–1926/27	*249*, 304.
1927/28–1935	*222*, 161.
1937	Assumed to be same as in 1937.
1940, 1945, 1950, 1955–1959	Assumed no production.

1005   *Tractor-drawn harrows*

1913	Assumed no production.
1927/28–1935	*222*, 161. Sum of disk-type and lever-smoothing tractor-drawn harrows (the latter assumed negligible in 1933–1935).
1937, 1940, 1945, 1950–1955	*180*, 230 f.
1956–1958	*141*, 244.

1006   *Horse-drawn harrows*

1913	*203*, 674 f.

1916	*407*, 1922, No. 2, 71.
1917	*84*, 244.
1918–1927/28	*249*, 304.
1928/29–1935	*222*, 161.
1937	Assumed to be same as in 1935.
1940, 1945, 1950, 1955–1959	Assumed no production.

1007 *Tractor-drawn cultivators*

1913, 1927/28, 1929/30	Assumed no production.
1928/29, 1933, 1938	*223*, 64.
1931, 1934	Based on data for cultivators for all-round plowing (16.5 and 8.5 th., *222*, 161) and ratio for 1933 of these data to tractor-drawn cultivators.
1932, 1937, 1940, 1950	*138*, 57.
1935–1936	*149*, 74 f. For 1936, preliminary.
1945	Based on 1946 output and announced annual relative (1,700%, *364*, 1/21/57).
1946	Planned output for 1947 (37 th., *364*, 2/28/47) is stated to be 233% of 1946 output (*364*, 3/1/47).
1947–1949	Based on 1950 output and announced annual relatives for 1948–1950 (131%, 142%, and 167%, *364*, 1/20/49; 1/18/50; 1/26/51).
1951–1955	*180*, 230 f.
1956–1958	*141*, 162 f.
1959	*364*, 1/22/60.

1008 *Horse-drawn cultivators*

1927/28–1935	*222*, 161. Sum of horse-drawn cultivators for all-round plowing and for interplowing (the latter being obtained as the difference between all interplowing cultivators and tractor-drawn ones).
1937	Assumed to be same as in 1935.
1940, 1945, 1950, 1955–1959	Assumed no production.

1009 *Tractor-drawn drills*

1913	Assumed no production.
1927/28, 1932, 1937, 1940, 1950	*138*, 57.
1945	Based on 1946 output and announced annual relative (429%, *364*, 1/21/47).
1946	Planned output for 1947 (30 th., *364*, 2/28/47) is stated to be 445% of 1946 output (*364*, 3/1/47).
1947–1949	Based on 1950 output and announced annual relatives for 1948–1950 (211%, 156%, and 185%, *364*, 1/20/49; 1/18/50; 1/26/51).
1951–1955	*180*, 230 f.
1956–1958	*141*, 162 f.
1959	*364*, 1/22/60.

1010 *Horse-drawn drills*

1913	*203*, 674.
1916	*407*, 1922, No. 2, 71.
1920–1926/27	*249*, 304.
1927/28–1935	*222*, 161.
1937	Assumed to be same as in 1935.
1940, 1945, 1950, 1955–1959	Assumed no production.

1011 *Combined plows and drills*

1927/28–1935	*222*, 161. Sum of tractor-drawn and horse-drawn.

475

| 1937, 1940, 1945, 1950, 1955–1959 | Assumed no production since none reported for 1935 or in 1941 Plan. |

1013   *Tractor-drawn potato planters*

1913	Assumed no production.
1927/28–1935	*222*, 162.
1937, 1940, 1945, 1950, 1955	*180*, 230 f.
1956–1958	*141*, 244.

1014   *Machines for planting seedlings*

| 1913 | Assumed no production. |
| 1927/28, 1932, 1937, 1940, 1945, 1950–1955 | *180*, 230 f. |

1016   *Grain combines*

1913	Assumed no production.
1927/28–1940, 1945–1955	*180*, 232.
1956–1958	*141*, 162 f.

1017   *All other combines*

1913	Assumed no production.
1927/28, 1932, 1937, 1940, 1945, 1950–1955	*180*, 230 f. Sum of corn, flax, potato, beet, and silo-harvesting combines.
1956	*138*, 62. Sum of corn, beet, and silo-harvesting combines.
1957–1958	*364*, 1/27/58; 1/16/59.

1018   *Windrowers*

1913, 1945	Assumed no production.
1927/28–1935	*222*, 162. For 1935, preliminary.
1937, 1940, 1950, 1954–1955	*138*, 57.
1953, 1956–1958	*141*, 162 f.

1019   *Horse-drawn reapers*

1913	*203*, 676 f.
1916	*407*, 1922, No. 10/12, 67.
1917–1921	*84*, 244.
1921/22	*193*, 162.
1922/23–1927/28	*312*, 1929, No. 1, 188 ff. For 1922/23–1923/24, large-scale state industry.
1932–1935	*222*, 162. Data are for large-scale industry, but output of small-scale industry assumed negligible.
1937	Assumed to be same as in 1935.
1940, 1945, 1950, 1955–1959	Assumed no production.

1020   *Cotton pickers*

1913	Assumed no production.
1927/28–1935	*222*, 162. For 1935, preliminary.
1937, 1940, 1956	*138*, 57.
1945, 1950–1955	*180*, 230 f.

1021   *Tractor-drawn haymowers*

1913, 1927/28	Assumed no production.
1928/29–1935	*222*, 162. For 1935, preliminary.
1937, 1940, 1945, 1950–1956	*180*, 230 f, 428.
1957–1958	*141*, 244.
1959	*364*, 1/22/60.

1022 *Horse-drawn haymowers*
1913	*203*, 674.
1921–1921/22	*193*, 162 f.
1925/26	*315*.
1926/27–1935	*222*, 162.
1937	Assumed to be same as in 1935.
1940, 1945, 1950, 1955–1959	Assumed no production.

1023 *Tractor-drawn rakers*
1913	Assumed no production.
1927/28, 1932, 1937, 1940, 1945, 1950–1955	*180*, 230 f.
1956–1958	*141*, 244.

1024 *Horse-drawn rakers*
1927/28–1935	*222*, 162. For 1935, preliminary.
1937	Assumed to be same as in 1935.
1940, 1945, 1950, 1955–1959	Assumed no production.

1025 *Tractor-driven threshers*
1913	Assumed no production.
1927/28–1931, 1933–1935	*222*, 162. Sum of tractor-driven grain, corn, and rice threshers. For 1935, output of rice threshers assumed negligible.
1932, 1937, 1940, 1945, 1950–1958	*180*, 230 f.
1936	*363*, 1937, No. 8, 188.
1956–1958	*141*, 244.

1026 *Horse-driven threshers*
1913	*203*, 676 f, 691.
1917–1923/24	*84*, 244.
1924/25–1928/29	*312*, 1929, No. 1, 190; 1929, No. 12, 144.
1932–1935	*222*, 162. Data are for large-scale industry, but output of small-scale industry assumed negligible.
1937	Assumed to be same as in 1935.
1940, 1945, 1950, 1955–1959	Assumed no production.

1027 *Grain-cleaning machines*
1913, 1927/28–1931	Assumed no production.
1932, 1937, 1940, 1945,. 1950–1956	*180*, 230 f, 428.
1933, 1935–1936, 1938	*363*, 1939, No. 8, 160; 1937, No. 3, 231. For 1938, preliminary.
1957–1958	*141*, 244.
1959	*364*, 1/22/60.

1028 *Horse-drawn windrowers*
1913	*203*, 676 f.
1916	*407*, 1922, No. 2, 71.
1917–1921	*84*, 244.
1921/22–1927/28	*312*, 1929, No. 1, 188 ff.
1932, 1937, 1940, 1945, 1950, 1955–1959	Assumed no production.

1029 *Horse drivings*
1913	*203*, 676 f.
1921	*245*, 121.
1921/22	*193*, 158.

1922/23–1923/24	*182*, 196.
1924/25	*183*, 151.
1925/26–1926/27	*185*, 243.
1927/28	*186*, 124.
1932, 1937	Assumed as rough average of output over 1925/26–1927/28.
1940, 1945, 1950, 1955–1959	Assumed no production.

1030   *Chaff and silo cutters*

1913	Assumed no production.
1927/28, 1932, 1937, 1940, 1945, 1950–1955	*180*, 230 f.
1956–1958	*141*, 244.

1101   *Steam boilers (capacity)*

1913, 1932, 1937	*138*, 56.
1925/26	*183*, 103.
1926/27	*312*, 1930, No. 2, 119.
1927/28–1931, 1933–1935	*222*, 154. For 1935, preliminary.
1936	*32*, 26.
1938	*223*, 64.
1940, 1945–1954	*180*, 218 f, 214 f.
1955–1958	Capacity in tons of steam per hour (*141*, 160 f) times 1954 ratio for capacity of m² to tons of steam per hour (*180*, 214 f).

1102   *Water turbines (capacity)*

1913, 1927/28–1934	*222*, 20, 154. For 1932, also *138*, 56. For 1928–1931 and 1934, a more recent source (*141*, 239) gives 8.4, 11.6, 28.5, 42.8, and 72.9 th. kw.
1924/25–1926/27	*407*, 1927, No. 10, 12. Converted from horse power at 1 hp = 0.746 kw.
1935	*149*, 70. A more recent source (*141*, 239) gives 52.9 th. kw.
1936	*32*, 26. A more recent source (*141*, 239) gives 74.1 th. kw.
1937, 1940	*138*, 56.
1938–1939, 1946–1949, 1957	*141*, 239.
1945, 1950–1956	*180*, 217, 428.

1103   *Steam and gas turbines (capacity)*

1913, 1927/28–1934	*222*, 154. For 1913, 1927/28, and 1932, also *138*, 56.
1923/24, 1925/26	*407*, 1927 No. 10, 11
1924/25	*346*, 1/21/39.
1926/27	*312*, 1930, No. 2, 119.
1935	*149*, 70.
1936	*32*, 26.
1937, 1940	*138*, 56.
1938–1939, 1956–1957	*141*, 238 f. All turbines are given as 6,631 th. kw for 1958 in *141*, 160 f, and 7.6 mill. kw for 1959 in *364*, 1/22/60.
1945–1955	*180*, 216.

1104   *Locomobiles (capacity)*

1927/28–1935	*222*, 154. For 1935, preliminary.
1936	*149*, 70 f. Preliminary.
1937	*267*, 206.
1938	*223*, 64.

1105   *Diesel engines (capacity)*

1913, 1927/28–1935	*222*, 20, 154. For 1913, 1927/28, and 1932, also *138*, 56. For 1935, preliminary.
1923/24–1925/26	*407*, 1927, No. 10, 12.
1926/27	*312*, 1930, No. 2, 119.
1936	*363*, 1937, No. 8, 188.
1937, 1940, 1945, 1950–1955	*180*, 214 f.
1938	*223*, 64.
1956	*138*, 61.

1106   *Other internal combustion engines (capacity)*

1927/28–1934	*222*, 154.
1935–1936	*149*, 70 f. For 1936, preliminary.
1937	Assumed to be same as in 1936.
1940	Assumed to be same as 1941 planned output (*72*, 29).

1107   *Turbogenerators (capacity)*

1924/25, 1938	*346*, 1/21/39.
1925/26	*315*.
1926/27	*312*, 1929, No. 2, 159.
1927/28–1935	*222*, 155. For 1927/28 and 1932, also *138*, 56. For 1935, preliminary.
1937, 1940, 1956	*138*, 56.
1945, 1950–1955	*180*, 214 f.
1957	*364*, 1/27/58. All generators are given as 5,186 th. kw for 1958 in *141*, 160 f, and 6.5 mill. kw for 1959 in *364*, 1/22/60.

1108   *Hydroelectric generators (capacity)*

1913	Assumed no production.
1927/28–1933	*221*, 44. For 1932, also *138*, 56.
1934–1935	*215*, 69.
1936	Assumed to be same as in 1935.
1937, 1940, 1945, 1950–1955	*180*, 214 f.
1956	*138*, 61.
1957	*364*, 1/27/58

1109   *Electric motors—A.C. (capacity)*

1924/25	*346*, 1/21/39. Assumed to be "normal" motors only although not explicitly stated.
1927/28–1933	*222*, 45. For 1927/28 and 1932, also *138*, 56.
1934	*215*, 70.
1935–1936	*149*, 70 f. For 1936, preliminary.
1937, 1940	*138*, 56.
1945, 1950–1955	*180*, 214 f.
1956–1958	*141*, 160 f.

1110   *Power transformers (capacity)*

1913, 1927/28–1935	*222*, 20, 155. For 1935, preliminary.
1923/24–1924/25	*184*, 150.
1925/26	*185*, 258.
1926/27	*312*, 1929, No. 2, 159.
1936	*149*, 70 f. Preliminary.
1937	*267*, 35, 206.
1940, 1945, 1950–1955	*180*, 214 f.
1956–1958	*141*, 160 f.

1201   *Coal-mining combines*

1913, 1928/29–1931	Assumed no production.

1927/28, 1932–1935   *215*, 72.
1937, 1940   *138*, 56.
1945, 1950–1955   *180*, 212 f.
1956–1958   *141*, 158 f.

1202   *Coal-cutting machines*
1913   Assumed no production.
1927/28–1935   *222*, 155.
1936   *149*, 74 f. Preliminary.
1937, 1940, 1945, 1950–1955   *180*, 212 f.
1938   *223*, 155.
1956–1958   *141*, 235.

1203   *Electric mining locomotives*
1913   Assumed no production.
1927/28–1935   *222*, 155. For 1935, preliminary.
1936   *149*, 80 f. Preliminary.
1937, 1940, 1945, 1950–1955   *180*, 212 f.
1956–1958   *141*, 235.

1204   *Ore-loading machines*
1940, 1945, 1950–1955   *180*, 212 f. A more recent source (*141*, 235) gives 1,965 for 1955.
1956–1958   *141*, 235.

1205   *Deep-shaft pumps*
1937, 1940, 1945, 1950–1955   *180*, 212 f.
1956–1958   *141*, 235.

1206   *Turbodrills*
1940, 1945, 1950–1955   *180*, 212 f.
1956–1958   *141*, 235.

1210   *Machine tools*
1913   *32*, 26.
1925/26–1926/27   *185*, 208.
1927/28–1940, 1945–1955   *180*, 207.
1956–1958   *141*, 158 f.
1959   *364*, 1/22/60.

1210.1   *Bench and engine lathes*
1927/28–1934   *222*, 156.
1935–1936   *149*, 72 f. For 1936, preliminary.
1937, 1940, 1945, 1950–1955   *180*, 208 f.
1957–1958   *141*, 233.

1211   *Electric furnaces*
1913, 1927/28, 1932, 1937, 1940, 1945, 1950–1955   *180*, 214 f.

1212   *Spinning machines*
1927/28, 1932, 1937, 1940   *138*, 57.
1933–1935   *215*, 73.
1936   *149*, 74 f. Preliminary.
1945, 1950–1955   *180*, 234 f.
1956–1958   *141*, 164 f.

1213   *Winding machines*
1913   Assumed no production.

1927/28, 1932, 1937, 1940, 1945, 1950–1955	*180*, 234 f.
1956–1958	*141*, 246.

1214 *Looms*

1913, 1927/28, 1940, 1950, 1954–1955	*138*, 57.
1932–1934	*215*, 73. For 1932, also *138*, 57.
1935–1936	*149*, 74 f. For 1936, preliminary.
1937	*267*, 207.
1945	*180*, 234 f.
1947–1949	Based on 1950 output and announced annual relatives for 1948–1950 (178%, 173%, and 126%, *364*, 1/20/49; 1/18/50; 1/26/51).
1951–1953	Based on 1954 output and announced annual relatives for 1952–1954 (139%, 102%, and 169%, *364*, 1/23/53; 1/31/54; 1/21/55).
1956–1958	*141*, 164 f.
1959	*364*, 1/22/60.

1215 *Cotton-carding machines*

1933–1935	*215*, 73.
1937	*267*, 35, 207.
1940, 1945, 1950–1955	*180*, 234 f.
1956	*31*, 74.
1957–1958	*141*, 246.

1216 *Knitting machines*

1927/28	*186*, 122.
1932–1934	*215*, 73.

1217 *Leather-spreading machines*

1913, 1932	Assumed no production.
1927/28, 1937, 1940, 1945, 1950–1955	*180*, 234 f.
1956–1958	*141*, 246.

1218 *Leather-dressing machines*

1913	Assumed no production.
1927/28, 1932, 1937, 1940, 1945, 1950–1955	*180*, 234 f.
1956–1958	*141*, 246.

1219 *Typesetting machines (linotype)*

1913	Assumed no production.
1927/28–1934	*215*, 73.
1937, 1940, 1945, 1950–1955	*180*, 234 f.
1956–1958	*141*, 246.

1220 *Flat-bed printing presses*

1913	Assumed no production.
1927/28–1934	*215*, 173.
1937, 1940, 1945, 1950–1955	*180*, 234 f.
1956–1958	*141*, 246.

1221 *Industrial sewing machines*

1913	Assumed no production.
1927/28–1935	*222*, 168. For 1935, preliminary.

| 1937, 1940, 1945, 1950–1955 | *180*, 234 f. For 1950, 1953, and 1955, a more recent source (*141*, 246) gives 35.9, 48.5, and 49.4 th. |
| 1956–1958 | *141*, 246. |

1222 *Metal-pressing machine tools*

| 1932, 1937, 1940, 1950, 1953, 1955–1958 | *141*, 235. |
| 1959 | *364*, 1/22/60. |

1222.1 *Presses*

1926/27–1927/28	*186*, 122.
1932, 1937, 1940, 1945, 1950–1955	*180*, 211.
1933–1934	*222*, 157.

1301 *Excavators*

1913	Assumed no production.
1927/28–1933	*221*, 59. For 1932, also *138*, 58.
1934, 1938–1939, 1945–1955	*180*, 236.
1935	*149*, 76 f.
1936	*363*, 1937, No. 8, 188.
1937	*267*, 35, 207. Also *138*, 58.
1940	*138*, 58.
1956–1958	*141*, 164 f.
1959	*364*, 1/22/60.

1302 *Trench excavators*

| 1927/28–1935 | *222*, 166. For 1935, preliminary. |
| 1937 | Assumed to be same as in 1935. |

1303 *Stone crushers*

1927/28–1934	*222*, 166.
1936	*149*, 76 f. Preliminary.
1937	Assumed to be same as in 1935.

1304 *Road graders (except self-propelled)*

1927/28–1935	*222*, 166. For 1935, preliminary.
1937	*267*, 41.
1956	*31*, 73.

1305 *Self-propelled road graders*

1913	Assumed no production.
1927/28, 1932, 1937, 1940, 1945, 1950–1955	*180*, 234 f. For 1950, a more recent source (*141*, 164 f) gives 33.
1956–1958	*141*, 164 f.
1959	*364*, 1/22/60.

1306 *Concrete mixers*

| 1927/28–1934 | *222*, 166. |
| 1937, 1940, 1945, 1950–1955 | *180*, 234 f. |

1307 *Tractor-driven scrapers*

1913	Assumed no production.
1927/28, 1932, 1937, 1940	*138*, 58.
1945, 1950–1955	*180*, 234 f.
1956–1958	*141*, 164 f.

1308 *Bulldozers*

| 1913 | Assumed no production. |

1927/28, 1932, 1937, 1940	*138*, 58.
1945, 1950–1955	*180*, 234 f.
1956–1958	*141*, 164 f.

1309 *Steam-operated railroad cranes*

1913	Assumed no production.
1927/28–1934	*222*, 166.
1935	*215*, 80. Preliminary.
1937	*267*, 41.
1940, 1945, 1950–1955	*180*, 237.
1956–1958	*141*, 248.

1310 *Self-propelled cranes (except railroad cranes)*

1913, 1927/28	Assumed no production.
1932, 1937, 1940, 1945, 1950–1955	*180*, 237.
1956–1958	*141*, 164 f.

1311 *Overhead traveling cranes*

1927/28–1934	*222*, 166. Sum of electric and hand-operated overhead traveling cranes.
1935	*215*, 80. Preliminary. Sum of electric and hand-operated overhead traveling cranes
1937	*267*, 41.

1312 *Tower cranes*

1913, 1927/28	Assumed no production.
1932, 1937, 1940, 1945, 1950–1955	*180*, 237. For 1953 and 1955, a more recent source (*141*, 248) gives 2,747 and 3,329.
1956–1958	*141*, 248.

1313 *Electric elevators*

1927/28–1934	*222*, 166. Sum of freight and passenger electric hoisting cranes.
1935	*215*, 80. Preliminary. Sum of freight and passenger electric hoisting cranes.
1937, 1940, 1945, 1950–1955	*180*, 237. For 1955, a more recent source (*141*, 248) gives 1,973.
1956 1960	*141*, 248.

1401 *Telephones*

1913	Estimate of hand-operated telephones for 1912, built up from data for geographical regions in *48*. Data are given in both physical and value terms for part of output and in only value terms for part, in which case physical output was estimated from value per unit for the former.
1923/24–1924/25	*315*. Hand-operated telephones only, assuming that production of automatic telephones was negligible before 1927/28.
1925/26–1926/27	*185*, 258. Hand-operated telephones only.
1927/28–1935	*222*, 165. Sum of hand-operated and automatic telephones. For 1935, preliminary.
1936	*149*, 84 f. Preliminary.
1937	*267*, 206.

1402 *Hand-operated switchboards*

1927/28–1935	*222*, 165. For 1935, preliminary.
1936	Estimated on the basis of the number of outlets (339.4 th., *149*, 84 f).

483

1937   Assumed to be same as in 1936.

1403   *Automatic switchboards*

1927/28–1931, 1933–1935   *222*, 165. Sum of large and small automatic switchboards. For 1935, preliminary.

1932, 1940, 1945, 1950–1955   *180*, 214 f.
1936   *149*, 84 f. Preliminary.
1937   *267*, 206.
1956–1958   *141*, 236 f.

1405   *Calculating machines*

1926/27   *186*, 122.
1927/28–1935   *222*, 168. For 1935, preliminary.
1936   *149*, 86 f. Preliminary.

1406   *Typewriters*

1927/28–1933   *222*, 168.
1934–1937   *79*, 177.

1501   *Flour*

1913, 1927/28, 1937, 1940, 1945,   *180*, 372.
   1950, 1955
1932   Assumed.
1953, 1956–1958   *141*, 302 f.

1502   *Macaroni*

1913, 1927/28–1940, 1945–1955   *180*, 403.
1956   Based on 1957 output and announced annual relative (111%, *364*, 1/27/58).
1957–1958   *364*, 1/27/58; 1/16/59; 1/22/60.

1503   *Butter*

1913, 1935–1936, 1938–1940,   *138*, 90.
   1945–1954
1914–1922/23   *124*, 20.
1923/24   Interpolated linearly between 1922/23 and 1924/25.

1924/25–1926/27   Estimated from incomplete data on share of cooperatives in marketing of butter (*352*, 1927, No. 20–21, 12 ff.)

1927/28–1934   *222*, 217. Also, *138*, 90.
1937   *267*, 210. Also, *138*, 90.
1955   *180*, 386.
1956–1958   *141*, 168 f. Plan fulfillment announcements (*364*, 1/27/58; 1/16/59) gave 621 and 647 th. m. tons for 1957 and 1958.

1959   *364*, 1/22/60.

1504   *Vegetable oil*

1913, 1932, 1937, 1940, 1956   *138*, 59, 65.
1927/28   *166*, 191. Total output of vegetable oil.
1933–1936, 1938–1939, 1945–1955   *180*, 392.
1957–1958   *141*, 65.
1959   *364*, 1/22/60.

1504.1   *Oleomargarine*

1913, 1927/28, 1937, 1940, 1945,   *180*, 372
   1950, 1955

1928/29	Assumed no production.
1930–1934	*222*, 222.
1935–1936	*149*, 104 f. For 1936, preliminary.
1938–1939, 1946–1949, 1951	*300*, 170.
1952–1954	Based on 1955 output and announced annual relatives for 1953–1955 (124%, 116%, and 102%, *317*, 1/31/54; *364*, 1/21/55; 1/30/56).
1956–1958	*141*, 302 f.

1504.2 *Vegetable oil minus oleomargarine*

1913, 1927/28, 1932, 1937, 1940, 1945, 1950, 1955–1958	Vegetable oil (series 1504) minus oleomargarine (series 1504.1).

1505 *Cheese*

1930–1934	*222*, 217.
1935–1936	*149*, 102 f. For 1936, preliminary.
1937	*299*, 12.
1938–1939	*353*, 1940, No. 2–3, 6.
1940	Based on 1950 output and percentage increase between 1940 and 1950 (128%, *410*, 1951, No. 4, 10).
1949, 1951–1955	Based on 1950 output and announced annual relatives for 1950–1955 (129%, 120%, 115%, 116%, 112%, and 122%, *364*, 1/26/51; 1/29/52; 1/23/53; 1/31/54; 1/21/55; 1/30/56).
1950	Planned output for 1954 (97 th. m. tons, *364*, 10/30/53) is stated (*ibid.*) to be twice 1950 output.

1506 *Meat slaughtering*

1913, 1927/28, 1929/30–1931	*180*, 378.
1932, 1937	*363*, 1939, No. 5, 161.
1933, 1938	*223*, 77. For 1938, preliminary.
1934	*414*, 2/14/35.
1935–1936	*149*, 102 f. For 1936, preliminary.
1939–1940	Total meat incl. by-products (*180*, 378) times 1938 ratio (78.8%) of meat excl. by-products (1938 above) to meat incl. them (*180*, 378).
1945–1950	Total meat incl. by-products (*180*, 378) minus 1950 share of by-products in total (7.6%, *180*, 378).
1951–1955	Total meat incl. by-products (*180*, 378) minus interpolated share of by-products in total (7.6% in 1950 to 11.8% in 1955, *180*, 378).
1956–1957	Total meat incl. by-products minus by-products (*141*, 306 f).
1958–1959	Total meat incl. by-products (*141*, 168 f, and *364*, 1/22/60) minus 1957 share of by-products in total (10.5%, *141*, 306 f).

1506.1 *Sausages*

1913, 1938	*89*, 112.
1929/30–1931	*348*, 1932, No. 11, 22.
1932–1934	*222*, 215.
1935–1936	*149*, 104 f. For 1936, preliminary.
1937	*363*, 1939, No. 5, 161.
1940, 1950, 1955	*180*, 380.
1948–1949, 1951	Based on 1950 output and announced annual relatives for 1949–1951 (143%, 140%, and 117%, *364*, 1/18/50; 1/26/51; 1/29/52).

485

1952–1954, 1956	Based on 1955 output and announced annual relatives for 1953–1956 (116%, 111%, 108%, and 107%, *364*, 1/31/54; 1/21/55; 1/30/56; *180*, 429).
1957	Based on 1958 output and announced annual relative for 1958 (106%, *364*, 1/16/59).
1958–1959	*364*, 1/16/59; 1/22/60.

1507   *Fish catch*

1913	*17*, 1st ed., vol. 50, 26. Also, *138*, 89.
1917, 1920–1927, 1955	*180*, 381.
1928, 1935–1936, 1938–1940, 1945–1954	*138*, 39.
1929–1931, 1933–1934	*215*, 216. Also, *138*, 89.
1932, 1937	*321*, 3/28/46. Also, *138*, 89.
1956–1958	*141*, 168 f.
1959	*364*, 1/22/60.

1508   *Soap (40% fatty acid)*

1913	Output of large-scale industry (200.6 th. m. tons, *301*, 13) divided by its 1926/27 percentage share of total output (*567*, Part 4, Table A). The original official figure of 128 th. m. tons, not used here since it is apparently not expressed in 40% fatty acid content, has recently been raised to 168 th. m. tons (*141*, 168).
1928–1929	Output of state and cooperative industry (derived as 307 and 348 th. m. tons from 1930 output and percentage increases of hard household soap in *222*, 229) divided by its estimated percentage share of total output (*567*, Part 4, Table B).
1930–1931	Based on 1932 output and annual relatives for 1931–1932 derived from output of hard household soap adjusted to 40% fatty acid from data for state industry (*347*, 1934, No. 12, 48 ff).
1932, 1937	*87*, 86. Also *138*, 59.
1933	*146*, 146.
1934	*148*, 430.
1935–1936	*149*, 102. For 1936, preliminary.
1938–1939	*300*, 178
1940, 1950, 1954	*138*, 59.
1945, 1955	*180*, 372.
1946–1949	Based on 1950 output and announced annual relatives for 1947–1950 (128%, 145%, 170%; and 111%, *364*, 1/18/48; 1/20/49; 1/18/50, 1/26/51).
1951–1953	Based on 1954 output and announced annual relatives for 1952–1954 (102%, 111%, and 121%, *364*, 1/23/53; 1/31/54; 1/21/55). A later source (*141*, 168 f) gives 878 th. m. tons for 1953.
1956–1958	*141*, 168 f.
1959	*364*, 1/22/60.

1509   *Salt*

1913–1924/25	*197*, 132 f.
1925/26–1926/27	*199*, 904.
1927/28–1935	*222*, 174.

1936	Based on output subject to planning in 1936 (4,007 th. m. tons, *149*, 104 f) and ratio for 1935 of total output to output subject to planning (latter 4,184 th. m. tons, *149*, 104 f).
1937, 1940, 1945, 1950, 1955	*180*, 372.
1938–1939, 1946–1949, 1951–1952, 1954	*300*, 176.
1953, 1956–1958	*141*, 302 f.

1510   *Raw sugar consumption*

1913–1926/27, 1940	*180*, 373.
1927/28–1928/29, 1936, 1938–1939, 1945–1955	*138*, 91.
1930–1931, 1933–1935	*222*, 220, 226. Also, *138*, 91.
1932	*362*, 1936, No. 2, 50.
1937	*176*, 296.
1956	*140*, 65.
1957, 1959	*364*, 1/27/58; 1/22/60.
1958	*141*, 65.

1510.1   *Refined sugar*

1913–1940, 1945–1955	*180*, 373.
1956–1958	*141*, 304.

1510.2   *Raw sugar minus refined sugar and sugar in candy*

1913, 1927/28, 1932, 1937, 1940, 1945, 1950, 1955	Raw sugar (series 1510) minus refined sugar (series 1510.1) and 50% of candy (series 1519).

1511   *Starch and syrup*

1913, 1937, 1940, 1945, 1950, 1955	*180*, 372.
1927/28–1928/29	Output of large-scale industry (69.1 and 68.6 th. m. tons, *222*, 227) divided by its estimated percentage share of total output (*567*, Part 4 Table B).
1930–1934	*222*, 227. Sum of starch and syrup. For 1930/1931, original data cover enterprises that produced 93% of starch and 94% of syrup in 1932 and have been adjusted upward accordingly.
1935–1936	*149*, 104 f. For 1936, preliminary.
1938–1939, 1946–1949, 1951–1952, 1954	*300*, 179.
1953, 1956–1958	*141*, 302 f.

1512   *Yeast*

1913, 1925/26	*184*, 396.
1923/24–1924/25	*183*, 635.
1926/27	*185*, 515.
1927/28	*361*, 1929, No. 11–12, 596.
1928/29–1934	*222*, 228.
1935–1936	*149*, 104 f. For 1936, preliminary.
1937	Assumed to be same as in 1936.
1940	Assumed to be same as in 1950.
1950	Planned output for 1955 (95 th. m. tons, *364*, 10/30/53) is stated (*ibid.*) to be twice output in 1950.
1951–1953	Based on 1950 output and annual relatives for the RSFSR for 1951–1953 (124%, 116%, and 110%, *321*, 2/7/52; 1/30/53; *364*, 2/9/54).

| 1954–1955 | Planned outputs (*364*, 10/30/53) assumed fulfilled. |

1513 *Canned food*

1913	*138*, 59.
1927/28–1940, 1945–1956	*180*, 398, 430.
1957–1958	*141*, 168 f.
1959	*364*, 1/22/60.

1513.1 *Canned meat*

1913, 1932, 1937, 1940, 1950, 1955	*180*, 399.
1927/28	Based on total output of canned food (series 1513) and percentage breakdown calculated from *166*, 274.
1953, 1956–1957	*141*, 315.

1513.2 *Canned fish*

| 1913, 1927/28, 1932, 1937, 1940, 1950, 1953, 1955–1957 | Same sources as for canned meat (series 1513.1). |

1513.3 *Canned milk*

| 1913, 1927/28, 1932, 1937, 1940, 1950, 1953, 1955–1957 | Same sources as for canned meat (series 1513.1). |

1513.4 *Canned vegetables and fruit*

| 1913, 1927/28, 1932, 1937, 1940, 1950, 1953, 1955–1957 | Same sources as for canned meat (series 1513.1). |

1514 *Beer*

1913	*222*, 228.
1923/24–1924/25	*183*, 401. Converted from vedros at 1 vedro = 12.3 liters.
1925/26–1926/27	*185*, 517,
1927/28	*186*, 565.
1928/29	*388*, 1930, No. 1, 40.
1930	Output of state industry (3,383 th. hectoliters for 1930, *222*, 228) plus estimated output of cooperative and private industries (obtained from rough linear extrapolation of data in *186*, 565, with output negligible in 1931).
1931, 1933–1934	*222*, 228.
1932, 1937, 1940, 1945, 1950, 1955	*180*, 372.
1935–1936	*149*, 104 f.
1938–1939, 1946–1947	*300*, 174.
1948–1949, 1951–1954	Based on 1950 output and announced annual relatives for 1949–1954 (139%, 133%, 116%, 106%, 114%, and 103%, *364*, 1/18/50; 1/26/51; 1/29/52; 1/23/53; 1/31/54; 1/21/55).
1956–1958	*141*, 302 f.

1515 *Cigarettes*

1913, 1929–1934	*222*, 220.
1917–1925/26	*261*, 246.
1926/27	*249*, 311.
1927/28, 1937, 1940, 1945, 1955–1956	*180*, 372, 430.
1935	*148*, 177.
1936	*149*, 105. Preliminary.

1938	*223*, 77. Preliminary.
1939, 1946–1947	*300*, 177.
1948–1949, 1951–1954	Based on 1950 output and announced annual relatives for 1949–1954 (117%, 116%, 113%, 112%, 116%, and 113%, *364*, 1/18/50; 1/26/51; 1/29/52; 1/23/53; 1/31/54; 1/21/55).
1950	Planned output for 1954 (200 bill., *364*, 10/30/53) is stated (*ibid.*) to be 160% of 1950 output.
1957–1959	*364*, 1/27/58; 1/16/59; 1/22/60.

1516 *Low-grade tobacco*

1913	*222*, 228.
1917–1922/23	*261*, 246. Large-scale industry only, but output of small-scale industry seems to have been negligible.
1923/24–1924/25	*183*, 527.
1925/26	*184*, 358.
1926/27–1927/28	*185*, 523.
1928/29–1931	*361*, 1929, No. 11–12, 596; 1932, No. 1–2, 13.
1932, 1937	*363*, 1939, No. 5, 161.
1933	*362*, 1935, No. 2–3, 95.
1934–1935	*148*, 431.
1936	*149*, 104 f. Preliminary.
1938–1939, 1946–1949, 1951–1952, 1954	*300*, 177.
1940, 1945, 1950, 1955	*180*, 372.
1953, 1956–1958	*141*, 302 f.

1517 *Matches*

1913, 1931	*215*, 187.
1917	*261*, 246.
1918–1919, 1921	*249*, 306 f.
1920, 1921/22–1929/30, 1932–1939, 1945	*342*, 1946, No. 6–7, 13, 15.
1940, 1950–1955	*180*, 267.
1956–1958	*141*, 254.

1518 *Vodka (40% alcohol)*

1913, 1927/28, 1932, 1937, 1940, 1945, 1950, 1955	*180*, 372.
1924/25–1926/27	*185*, 511.
1928/29	*312*, 1929, No. 12, 193.
1930–1931	*361*, 1932, No. 1–2, 13. For 1931, preliminary.
1953, 1956–1958	*141*, 302 f.

1519 *Candy*

1913	Confectionery (109 th. m. tons, *138*, 59) times share of candy in confectionery (66%, *27*, III, 118 f).
1926/27–1928/29	Output of large-scale industry (38.5, 66.8, and 101.0 th. m. tons, *388*, 1928, No. 5, 36 f; 1930, No. 1, 40) divided by its estimated percentage share of total output (*567*, Part 4, Table B).
1930–1931	Confectionery (271 and 518 th. m. tons, *180*, 401) times share for smaller industrial coverage of candy in confectionery in 1934 (64%, *222*, 228).
1932, 1937, 1940, 1950, 1955	*180*, 402.
1933–1934	*222*, 228.

489

1935–1936	Confectionery (606.4 th. m. tons for 1935, *149*, 104 f; derived as 810.1 th. m. tons for 1936 by adjusting downward data in *383*, 1937, No. 1, 37) times interpolated share of candy in confectionery (64% in 1934, *222*, 228, to 57.9% in 1937, *22*, 402).
1938–1939	Interpolated between 1937 and 1940.
1945	Confectionery (212 th. m. tons, *180*, 401) times 1940 share of candy in total (46.4%, *180*, 402).
1946–1949	Interpolated between 1945 and 1950.
1951–1954	Interpolated between 1950 and 1955. A later source (*141*, 317) gives 748 th. m. tons for 1953.
1956–1957	*141*, 317.
1958–1959	Confectionery (1,673 and 1,800 th. m. tons, *141*, 302 f, and *364*, 1/22/60) times 1957 share of candy in confectionery (45.6%, *141*, 317).

1601 *Boots and shoes*

1913, 1933–1940, 1945–1955	*138*, 87. A later source (*141*, 166 f) gives 238.1 mill. pairs for 1953 and 271.2 mill. pairs for 1955.
1916	*69*, 58.
1926/27–1928/29	Output of large-scale industry (15.2, 23.6, and 38.9 mill. pairs, *69*, 69 ff) divided by its estimated percentage share of total output (*567*, Part 4, Table B).
1932	*118*, 92. It is not clear whether this includes rebuilt shoes. A later source (*141*, 166 f) gives 86.9 mill. pairs.
1956–1958	*141*, 166 f.
1959	*364*, 1/22/60.

1602 *Rubber footwear*

1913	*215*, 176.
1914–1917	Taken as 115% of output of rubber galoshes (19.4, 20.5, 15.2, and 17.4 mill. pairs, *49*, 214; *261*, 244), the ratio for 1913.
1918–1922/23	Taken as 102% of output of rubber galoshes (5.86, 2.62, 0.01, 0.63, 8.57, and 10.1 mill. pairs, *261*, 244), the ratio for 1923/24.
1923/24	*324*, 1937, No. 11, 69.
1924/25–1925/26	Taken as 102.5% and 103% of output of rubber galoshes (15.7 and 25.3 mill. pairs, *261*, 244), which are linear interpolations of ratios for 1923/24 and 1927/28.
1926/27	*185*, 25. Given for galoshes, but implied output for 1913 in this source coincides with 1913 output of rubber footwear.
1927/28–1928/29, 1931–1934	*222*, 179. For 1927/28 and 1932, also *138*, 59.
1929/30, 1935, 1938–1939, 1945–1955	*180*, 199. A later source (*141*, 166 f) gives 110.8, 113.1, and 134.6 mill. pairs for 1950, 1953, and 1955.
1936	*149*, 92.
1937	*267*, 205.
1940	*138*, 59.
1956–1958	*141*, 228.

1603 *Cotton yarn*

1913, 1935–1936	*79*, 191.
1917	*261*, 246 f.

1918 1922	*249*, 308 f.
1923–1927, 1929	*137*, 8.
1927/28, 1940, 1945, 1950, 1955	*180*, 323.
1930–1934	*215*, 206.
1937	*87*, 85.
1938	Output in 1939 is stated (*176*, 282) to be 32.6 th. m. tons more than in 1938.
1939	Taken as 111.4% of ministerial output 504 th. m. tons, *363*, 1940, No. 9, 88), the ratio planned for 1941 (*72*, 71).
1953, 1956–1958	*141*, 272 f.

1604   *Cotton fabrics*

1913, 1927/28–1932, 1937–1940, 1946–1954	*138*, 83.
1917	*261*, 246. Estimate.
1918–1920	*249*, 308 f. Estimates.
1921–1926	*137*, 8.
1926/27	Output of large-scale industry (2,370 mill. meters, *249*, 308) divided by its estimated percentage share of total output (*567*, Part 4, Table B).
1933–1936	*79*, 192.
1945, 1955	*180*, 323.
1956–1958	*141*, 164 f.

1605   *Cotton thread*

1913, 1927/28, 1932, 1937, 1940, 1945, 1950, 1955	*180*, 323.
1953, 1956–1958	*141*, 272 f.

1606   *Linen yarn*

1913	*269*, 192.
1917	*261*, 246.
1918–1920, 1922/23–1926/27	*249*, 308.
1921, 1930–1931	*137*, 8.
1927/28, 1937, 1940, 1945, 1950, 1955	*180*, 323.
1928/29	*370*, 1929, No. 23–24, 128.
1932–1935	*215*, 227. For 1935, preliminary.
1953, 1956–1958	*141*, 272 f.

1607   *Linen fabrics*

1913	*17*, 1st ed., vol. 37, 525. Also, *138*, 58.
1917, 1956–1958	*141*, 274.
1928	*138*, 58.
1928/29–1931, 1934–1940, 1945–1955	*180*, 328.
1932	*363*, 1939, No. 5, 161.
1933	*215*, 73.

1609   *Silk and rayon fabrics*

1913, 1926/27–1928/29	Output of large-scale industry (40, 6.47, 9.6, and 13.0 mill. meters, *333*, 1953, No. 18, 20; *249*, 308 f; *215*, 210) divided by its estimated percentage share of total output (*567*, Part 4, Tables A and B).
1929/30–1933	*215*, 210. Also, *138*, 86.
1934–1936, 1938–1940, 1945–1954	*138*, 86. A later source (*141*, 65) gives 77.3 mill. meters for 1940.

1937	*87*, 85. Also, *138*, 86.
1955	*180*, 323.
1956–1958	*141*, 166 f.

1609.1 *Pure silk fabrics*

1913 — Silk and rayon fabrics (series 1609) times share of pure silk in total (54%, *17*, 1st ed., vol. 62, 247; *375*, 1933, No. 3–4, 55).

1927/28 — Apparent consumption of raw silk (estimated at 121 tons from series 606 and net imports in *283*, 190 f, 522 f) times 1913 ratio of silk fabrics to consumption of raw silk (estimated at 1,806 tons from *ibid.*).

1932–1934 — *215*, 210. Sum of silk, pile fabrics, piece goods, and silk for sieves.

1937 — Apparent consumption of raw silk in 1937 (estimated at 1,687 tons from series 606 and net imports in *409*, 1937, No. 12, 29) times 1913 ratio (see 1927/28 above).

1940, 1945, 1950, 1955 — Raw silk (series 606) times 1913 ratio (see 1927/28 above).

1609.2 *Rayon and mixed fabrics*

1913, 1927/28, 1932, 1937, 1945, 1950, 1955 — Summed rayon fabrics and mixed fabrics. Rayon fabrics derived as rayon (series 419) times 1940 ratio of rayon fabrics to rayon. Mixed fabrics derived as silk and rayon fabrics (series 1609) minus summed pure silk fabrics (series 1609.1) and rayon fabrics.

1933–1934 — Summed rayon fabrics (*215*, 210) and mixed fabrics (derived as residual as above).

1940 — Summed rayon fabrics and mixed fabrics (derived as residual as above). Rayon fabrics derived from silk and rayon fabrics (series 1609) times share of rayon fabrics in total (31.4%, *394*, 1946, Nos. 7–8, 8).

1610 *Woolen yarn*

1913, 1930–1931	*269*, 199.
1918–1926/27	*249*, 308.
1927/28, 1937, 1940, 1945, 1950, 1955	*180*, 323.
1928/29, 1936	*79*, 191.
1932–1935	*215*, 209. For 1935, preliminary.
1953, 1956–1958	*141*, 272 f.

1611 *Woolen and worsted fabrics*

1913, 1926/27–1928/29 — Output of large-scale industry (103.1, 85.2, 93.2, and 100.6 mill. meters, *363*, 1939, No. 8, 155; *249*, 308 f; and *79*, 194) divided by its estimated percentage share of total industry (*567*, Part 4, Tables A and B).

1930–1931, 1935–1940, 1945–1954	*138*, 85.
1932–1934	*215*, 209.
1955	*180*, 323.
1956–1958	*141*, 166 f.

1612 *Knitted goods*

1927/28, 1937, 1940 — *138*, 58. Sum of knitted outer garments and underwear.

1932–1934	Sum of knitted outer garments (*215*, 210) and underwear (*222*, 204).
1935–1936, 1938–1939, 1945–1955	*180*, 343. Sum of knitted outer garments and underwear.
1956	*140*, 64.
1957–1959	*364*, 1/27/58; 1/16/59; 1/22/60. Sum of knitted outer garments and underwear.

1613   *Hosiery*

1928, 1937, 1940	*138*, 58.
1932	*363*, 1939, No. 5, 161.
1933–1934	*222*, 204.
1935–1936, 1938–1939, 1945–1955	*180*, 343.
1956–1958	*141*, 166 f.
1959	*364*, 1/22/60.

1614   *Felt footwear*

1913	Assumed to be same as 1927/28.
1927/28	Sum of state and cooperative industry (4.4 mill. pairs, *376*, 1930, No. 5–6, 13) and estimated *kustar'* industry (taken to be same as in 1928/29).
1928/29	*376*, 1930, No. 5–6, 13. Sum of state (2.6 mill.), cooperative (2.8 mill.), and *kustar'* industry (11.2 mill.).
1932, 1937, 1940, 1945, 1950, 1954–1955	*138*, 59.
1933–1934	*222*, 205.
1935–1936	*363*, 1937, No. 3, 235. For 1936, preliminary.
1953, 1956–1958	*141*, 166 f.
1959	*364*, 1/22/60.

1701   *Bicycles*

1913, 1932, 1937, 1940, 1950	*138*, 59.
1922/23	*51*, 186.
1923/24	*52*, 222.
1926/27	*315*.
1927/28–1931, 1933–1934	*222*, 165. For 1927/28, also *138*, 59.
1935–1936	*149*, 88 f. For 1936, preliminary.
1938	*363*, 1939, No. 8, 182. Preliminary.
1945, 1951–1955	*180*, 362.
1948–1949	Based on 1950 output and announced annual relatives for 1949–1950 (144% and 131%, *364*, 1/18/50; 1/26/51).
1956	*140*, 65.
1957–1958	*141*, 168 f.
1959	*364*, 1/22/60.

1702   *Cameras*

1913	Assumed no production.
1927/28–1935	*222*, 168.
1936	*149*, 88 f. Preliminary.
1937, 1940, 1950	*138*, 59.
1938	*363*, 1939, No. 8, 182. Preliminary.
1945, 1951–1955	*180*, 362.
1948–1949	Based on 1950 output and announced annual relatives for 1949–1950 (106% and 156%, *364*, 1/18/50; 1/26/51).
1956–1958	*141*, 168 f.

1959   *364*, 1/22/60.

1703 *Electric light bulbs*

1913, 1916, 1921	*193*, 175, xlvi.
1914, 1920	*192*, 93.
1921/22–1926/27	*312*, 1929, No. 1, 189.
1927/28, 1932, 1937, 1940, 1945, 1950–1955	*180*, 214 f.
1928/29–1931, 1933–1935	*222*, 167. For 1935, preliminary.
1936	*149*, 72 f. Preliminary.
1938	Electric light bulbs up to 150 watts (*363*, 1939, No. 8, 182) times ratio of all bulbs to bulbs up to 150 watts interpolated between 1933 (*ibid.*) and 1941 Plan (*72*, 170).
1949	Based on 1950 output and announced annual relative (128%, *364*, 1/26/51).
1956–1958	*141*, 236 f.

1704 *Phonographs*

1913, 1937, 1940, 1950	*138*, 59.
1927/28–1935	*222*, 168.
1936	*149*, 88 f. Preliminary.
1938	*363*, 1939, No. 8, 182. Preliminary.
1945, 1951–1955	*180*, 363.
1948–1949	Based on 1950 output and announced annual relatives for 1949–1950 (163% and 108%, *364*, 1/18/50; 1/26/51).
1956	*140*, 65.
1957	*141*, 301.

1705 *Radios*

1913, 1927/28	Assumed no production.
1932, 1937	*138*, 59. Given as radio and television sets, but it is assumed that no television sets were produced during these years.
1933–1936	*79*, 176.
1938	*363*, 1939, No. 8, 182. Preliminary.
1940, 1945, 1950–1955	*180*, 363. A later source (*141*, 300) gives 3,549 th. for 1955.
1948–1949	Based on 1950 output and announced annual relatives for 1949–1950 (165% and 122%, *364*, 1/18/50; 1/26/51).
1956–1958	*141*, 300.
1959	*364*, 1/22/60.

1706 *Television sets*

1913, 1927/28, 1932, 1934, 1937	Assumed no production.
1940, 1945, 1950–1955	*180*, 363.
1956–1958	*141*, 300.
1959	*364*, 1/22/60.

1707 *Household sewing machines*

1913, 1937, 1940, 1945, 1950–1955	*180*, 362.
1926/27	*186*, 122.
1927/28–1935	*222*, 168. For 1927/28 and 1932, also *138*, 59.
1936	*149*, 88 f. Preliminary.
1938	*363*, 1939, No. 8, 182. Preliminary.
1948–1949	Based on 1950 output and announced annual relatives for 1949–1950 (134% and 122%, *364*, 1/18/50; 1/26/51).

| 1956–1958 | *141*, 168 f. |
| 1959 | *364*, 1/22/60. |

1708   *Clocks and watches*

1913	*138*, 59.
1927/28, 1932, 1937, 1940, 1945, 1950–1956	*180*, 362, 429.
1931, 1933–1935	*222*, 168. Clocks and watches minus electric clocks. For 1935, preliminary.
1948–1949	Based on 1950 output and announced annual relatives for 1949–1950 (194% and 127%, *364*, 1/18/50; 1/26/51).
1957, 1959	*364*, 1/27/58; 1/22/60.
1958	*141*, 166 f.

1709   *Motorcycles*

1913, 1937, 1940, 1950	*138*, 59.
1927/28–1931	*222*, 165. For 1927/28, also *138*, 59.
1932–1935	*215*, 83. For 1932, also *138*, 59.
1936	*149*, 88 f. Preliminary.
1945, 1951–1956	*180*, 362, 429.
1949	Based on 1950 output and announced annual relative (134%, *364*, 1/26/51).
1957–1958	*141*, 168 f.
1959	*364*, 1/22/60.

TABLE B-3

OUTPUT OF INDIVIDUAL PRODUCTS IN 1937: INTERWAR AND POSTWAR SOVIET TERRITORY

| | | | Output | |
Code	Product	Unit	Interwar Territory	Postwar Territory
101	Pig iron	th. m.t.	14,490	14,490
102	Rolled steel	th. m.t.	12,970	12,990
103	Steel ingots and castings	th. m.t.	17,730	17,730
201	Primary aluminum	th. m.t.	37.7	37.7
202	Copper	th. m.t.	97.5	97.5
203	Lead	th. m.t.	62.3	62.3
204	Zinc	th. m.t.	76.5	76.5
301	Electric power	bill. kwh	36.2	37.0
301.1	Hydroelectric power	bill. kwh	4.18	4.18
302	Anthracite	mill. m.t.	28.01	28.01
303	Bituminous coal	mill. m.t.	81.87	83.87
303.1	Coke	mill. m.t.	20.0	20.0
304	Lignite	mill. m.t.	18.09	18.09
305	Crude petroleum	mill. m.t.	28.5	28.97
306	Natural gas	mill. m³	2,179	3,000
307	Oil shale	th. m.t.	515	1,637
308	Peat	mill. m.t.	24.0	24.5
401	Soda ash	th. m.t.	528.2	528.2
404	Sulfuric acid	th. m.t.	1,369	1,369
405	Mineral fertilizer	th. m.t.	2,590.1	2,979.1
405.1	Phosphoric fertilizer	th. m.t.	1,427.7	1,625.7
405.2	Ammonium sulfate	th. m.t.	761.6	761.6
405.3	Potash fertilizer	th. m.t.	355.8	591.8

(continued)

TABLE B-3 (concluded)

Code	Product	Unit	Output Interwar Territory	Output Postwar Territory
406	Ground natural phosphate	th. m.t.	649.9	660.0
410	Red lead	th. m.t.	15.0	15.5
412	Synthetic dyes	th. m.t.	309.6	309.6
416	Paper	th. m.t.	831.6	886.8
417	Paperboard	th. m.t.	144.2	148.8
418	Motor vehicle tires	thous.	2,698	2,698
501	Bricks	mill.	7,471	7,845
502	Fire-clay bricks	th. m.t.	1,780	1,780
505	Sand-lime, silica, and slag bricks	mill.	1,195	1,220
506	Cement	th. m.t.	5,454	5,761
507	Construction gypsum	th. m.t.	1,212	1,284
508	Construction lime	th. m.t.	3,750	3,840
510	Lumber	mill. m³	33.8	37.9
511	Plywood	thous. m³	672.3	752.0
513	Roll roofing	mill. m²	161.4	165.9
516	Asbestos shingles	mill.	187.0	193.6
519	Window glass	mill. m²	79.3	81.5
601	Crude alcohol	thous. hectol.	7,670	7,820
604	Hard leather	th. m.t.	59	67
605	Soft leather	mill. dcm²	4,283	4,840
704	Iron ore	th. m.t.	27,770	27,770
1501	Flour	mill. m.t.	28.0	31.1
1503	Butter	th. m.t.	185.2	240
1504	Vegetable oil	th. m.t.	539	539
1505	Cheese	th. m.t.	31.0	31.3
1506	Meat slaughtering	th. m.t.	812	1,074
1507	Fish catch	th. m.t.	1,609	2,169
1508	Soap	th. m.t.	495	500
1509	Salt	th. m.t.	3,200	3,200
1510	Raw sugar consumption	th. m.t.	2,421	2,587
1510.1	Refined sugar	th. m.t.	1,032	1,032
1513	Canned food	mill. cans	982	1,002
1514	Beer	th. hectol.	8,960	9,700
1515	Cigarettes	billions	89.2	92.5
1516	Low-grade tobacco	th. 20-kg. crates	5,343	5,343
1517	Matches	th. crates	7,163	7,503
1601	Boots and shoes	mill. pairs	182.9	184
1602	Rubber footwear	mill. pairs	84.6	87.7
1603	Cotton yarn	th. m.t.	532.9	543.4
1604	Cotton fabrics	mill m.	3,448	3,488
1607	Linen fabrics	mill. m.	285.2	289
1609	Silk and rayon fabrics	mill. m.	58.9	62.7
1611	Woolen and worsted fabrics	mill. m.	108.3	115.1
1613	Hosiery	mill. pairs	408.6	417.5
1701	Bicycles	thous.	540.7	588.3
1705	Radios	thous.	200	277

SOURCE: Derived from Table B-2 and 567. In certain additional cases, output in acquired territories was assumed negligible. Output in acquired territories is generally understated since small-scale production is not fully accounted for.

APPENDIX C

Employment, Value, and Population Data

TABLE C-1

ᴚsONS ENGAGED IN INDUSTRY, BY INDUSTRIES: SOVIET UNION, BENCHMARK YEARS, 1913–1955
(thousand full-time equivalents)

Industry	1913	1927/28	1933	1937	1940	1950	1955
I. Ferrous and nonferrous mining and metallurgy	425	281	573	626	603	998	1,121
Large-scale	425	281	573				
Small-scale	—	—	—				
A. Extraction of iron ore	49	27	45				
Large-scale	49	27	45				
Small-scale	—	—	—				
B. Extraction of manganese ore	7	6	8				
Large-scale	7	6	8				
Small-scale	—	—	—				
C. Ferrous metallurgy	242	212	365				
Large-scale	242	212	365				
Small-scale	—	—	—				
D. Nonferrous mining and metallurgy	127	36	155				
Large-scale	127	36	155				
Small-scale	—	—	—				
I. Fuel	315	399	725	739	857	1,260	1,514
Large-scale	314	397	725				
Small-scale	1[a]	2	—				
A. Coal and coke	208	283	494				
Large-scale	208	283	494				
Small-scale	—	—	—				
B. Crude petroleum	47	41	31				
Large-scale	47	41	31				
Small-scale	—	—	—				
C. Petroleum refining	7	8	54				
Large-scale	7	8	54[b]				
Small-scale	—	—	—				
D. Peat	52	67	146				
Large-scale	52	65	146[c]				
Small-scale	—	2	—				
I. Electric power stations	20	28	97	125	134	229	295
Large-scale	20	28	95				
Small-scale	—	—	2				
ᴠ. Chemicals (incl. rubber)	70	100	279	351	415	442	629
Large-scale	56	76	264				
Small-scale	14	24[d]	15				
A. Basic chemicals	13	18	54				
Large-scale	13	18	54				
Small-scale	—	—	- -				

(continued)

TABLE C-1 (continued)

Industry	1913	1927/28	1933	1937	1940	1950	195
B. Paints and varnishes	n.a.	n.a.	10				
Large-scale	n.a.	5	9				
Small-scale	n.a.	n.a.	1				
C. Pharmaceutical chemicals	n.a.	n.a.	72				
Large-scale	n.a.	5	71				
Small-scale	n.a.	n.a.	1				
D. Rubber and asbestos	17	31	54				
Large-scale	17	31	54				
Small-scale	—	—	—				
E. All other chemicals	40	17	89				
Large-scale	26[d]	17[e]	76				
Small-scale	14	—	13				
V. Machine building and metal products	602	663	1,504	3,262	3,550	4,572	5,7●
Large-scale	391	446	1,488				
Small-scale	211	217	16				
A. Machine building	303	391	811	2,925[f]	3,202[f]	1,884[f]	2,5●
Large-scale	250	336	804				
Small-scale	53[g]	55	7				
1. Land transportation equipment (incl. tractors)	n.a.	n.a.	355				
Large-scale	n.a.	55	348				
Small-scale	n.a.	n.a.	7				
2. Shipbuilding	n.a.	n.a.	106				
Large-scale	n.a.	42	106				
Small-scale	n.a.	n.a.	—				
3. Agricultural machinery (excl. tractors)	n.a.	n.a.	110				
Large-scale	n.a.	51	110				
Small-scale	n.a.	n.a.	—				
4. Electrical and industrial machinery	n.a.	n.a.	240				
Large-scale	n.a.	188	240				
Small-scale	n.a.	n.a.	—				
B. Metal products	299	272	422	337[f]	384[f]	2,688[f]	3,1●
Large-scale	141	110	413				
Small-scale	158[g]	162	9				
VI. Wood products, paper, and logging	1,073	768	1,798	1,929	2,210	2,799	2,8●
Large-scale	176	180	1,687				
Small-scale	897	588	111				
A. Plywood and lumber	89	92	252				
Large-scale	89	92	247				
Small-scale	—	—	5				

(continued)

TABLE C-1 (continued)

Industry	1913	1927/28	1933	1937	1940	1950	1955
B. Miscellaneous wood products	498	280	354				
Large-scale	27	29	249[h]				
Small-scale	471	251[i]	105				
C. Matches	23	17	19				
Large-scale	23	17	19				
Small-scale	—	—	—				
D. Pulp and paper	50	49	53				
Large-scale	37	43	53				
Small-scale	13[j]	6	—				
E. Logging	413	331	1,120				
Large-scale	—	—	1,119				
Small-scale	413[k]	331	1				
II. Construction materials	231	221	520	351	455	802	1,160
Large-scale	168	162	495				
Small-scale	63	59	25				
A. Cement industry	n.a.	22	33				
Large-scale	19	22	33				
Small-scale	n.a.	—	—				
B. Bricks and other construction materials	n.a.	83	161				
Large-scale	87	47	145				
Small-scale	n.a.	36	16				
C. Glass	n.a.	71	83				
Large-scale	59	71	83				
Small-scale	n.a.	—	—				
D. Others	n.a.	45	243				
Large-scale	3	22	294[l]				
Small-scale	n.a.	23	9				
II. Printing	79	115	123	150	134	147	157
Large-scale	70	76	115				
Small-scale	9	39	8				
A. Printing and publishing	n.a.	71	n.a.				
Large-scale	49	64	n.a.				
Small-scale	n.a.	7	n.a.				
B. Stationery and art equipment	n.a.	44	n.a.				
Large-scale	21	12	n.a.				
Small-scale	n.a.	32	n.a.				
X. Textiles and allied products	1,847	1,919	2,000	2,568	2,733	2,602	3,343
Large-scale	773	968	1,800				
Small-scale	1,074	951	200				
A. Cotton ginning	n.a.	5	16				
Large-scale	11	5	16				
Small-scale	n.a.	—	—				

(continued)

TABLE C-1 (continued)

Industry	1913	1927/28	1933	1937	1940	1950	195!
B. Primary processing of fibers	n.a.	4	73				
Large-scale	n.a.[m]	4	73				
Small-scale	n.a.	—	—				
C. Cotton fabrics	n.a.	610	516				
Large-scale	501	547	515				
Small-scale	n.a.	63	1				
D. Linen fabrics	n.a.	95	72				
Large-scale	71	93	72				
Small-scale	n.a.	2	—				
E. Woolen fabrics	n.a.	182	126				
Large-scale	91	77	97				
Small-scale	n.a.	105[n]	29				
F. Silk fabrics	n.a.	34	25				
Large-scale	35	18	25				
Small-scale	n.a.	16	—				
G. Hemp and jute products	n.a.	59	86				
Large-scale	17	25	56				
Small-scale	n.a.	34[o]	30				
H. Knitted goods	n.a.	104	192				
Large-scale	6	31	156				
Small-scale	n.a.	73	36				
I. Garment industry	n.a.	410	436				
Large-scale	6	79[n]	403				
Small-scale	n.a.	331	33				
J. Leather industry	n.a.	93	48				
Large-scale	17	45	47				
Small-scale	n.a.	48	1				
K. Fur industry	n.a.	27	43				
Large-scale	4	5	41				
Small-scale	n.a.	22	2				
L. Boots and shoes, production and repair	n.a.	296	283				
Large-scale	14	39	239				
Small-scale	n.a.	257	44				
M. Others			84				
Large-scale			60				
Small-scale			24				
X. Food and allied products	1,072	803	1,094	1,478	1,554	1,637	1,7!
Large-scale	448	322	905				
Small-scale	624	481	189				
A. Flour and groats	n.a.	167	174				
Large-scale	50	42	59				
Small-scale	n.a.	125[p]	115				

(continued)

TABLE C-1 (continued)

Industry	1913	1927/28	1933	1937	1940	1950	1955
B. Sugar	148	60	91				
Large-scale	148	60	91				
Small-scale	—	—	—				
C. Confectionery	n.a.	42	64				
Large-scale	26	22	58				
Small-scale	n.a.	20	6				
D. Vegetable oil	n.a.	34	27				
Large-scale	13	14	20				
Small-scale	n.a.	20	7				
E. Starch and syrup	n.a.	5	15				
Large-scale	9	3	14				
Small-scale	n.a.	2	1				
F. Alcohol, wine, yeast, and vodka	25	39	76				
Large-scale	25	39	76[q]				
Small-scale	—	—	—				
G. Beer and malt	12	15					
Large-scale	12	15					
Small-scale	—	—	—				
H. Tobacco and makhorka	32	29	21				
Large-scale	32	29	21				
Small-scale	—	—	—				
I. Salt	20	7	9				
Large-scale	20	7	9				
Small-scale	—	—	—				
J. Grease, tallow, and soap	n.a.	14	27				
Large-scale	11	11	24				
Small-scale	n.a.	3	3				
K. Fishing	277	229	180				
Large-scale	—	30	179				
Small-scale	277[r]	199[r]	1				
L. Others	n.a.	162	410				
Large-scale	102	50	354				
Small-scale	n.a.	112[s]	56				
I. All others	83	80	211	664	455	491	669
Large-scale	23	33	186				
Small-scale	60[t]	47	25				
A. China and pottery	n.a.	39	37				
Large-scale	21	25	31				
Small-scale	n.a.	14	6				
B. Others	n.a.	41	174				
Large-scale	2[u]	8[v]	155				
Small-scale	n.a.	33[w]	19				

(continued)

TABLE C-1 (concluded)

Industry	1913	1927/28	1933	1937	1940	1950	1955
Total excl. repair shops	5,817	5,379	8,653	12,243	13,100	15,979	19,36
Large-scale	2,864	2,971	8,062				
Small-scale	2,953	2,408	591				
XII. Repair shops	86	86	1,573	283^r	294^r	387^r	305
Large-scale	86	86	1,303				
Small-scale	—	—	270				
A. District railroad repair shops	86	86	271				
Large-scale	86^x	86^x	271				
Small-scale	—	—	—				
B. Other repair shops	n.a.	n.a.	1,302				
Large-scale	n.a.	n.a.	1,032^y				
Small-scale	n.a.	n.a.	270^y				
Total incl. repair shops	5,903	5,465	10,226	12,526	13,394	16,366	19,66
Large-scale	2,950	3,057	9,365				
Small-scale	2,953	2,408	861				

—: negligible.

a Includes all mining products.

b Includes all kinds of fuel processing.

c Includes oil shale.

d Includes paints, varnishes, and pharmaceutical chemicals.

e Includes tar (4.4 th.), chemical wood processing (1.2 th.), and others (11.7 th.).

f Sum of machine building, metal products, and repair shops apportioned to components by official gross production as estimated in Table F-1. For 1940, repair shops and metal products are apportioned by their 1937 breakdown. Conventional military products were apparently included under machine building up to 1950 and under metal products for 1950 and after; atomic energy may be included under machine building. See Appendix F.

g Total small-scale for machine building and metal products apportioned to components by small-scale employment in 1927/28.

h Includes furniture and prefabricated houses.

i Includes carts and sleds.

j Paper products.

k Employment in 1927/28 extrapolated by haulage of industrial timber (Table B-2). Data underestimated because seasonal workers hired with their own horses are not included.

Includes extraction of minerals (125 th.) and others (109 th.).

m Distributed among individual fibers.

n Includes felt and felt products.

o Includes mixed fibers.

p Derived from total no. of weeks worked in 1927/28 and the percentage share of total weeks worked accounted for by flour milling and grain cracking in 1928/29 (129, 189). This was divided by average annual no. of weeks worked in large-scale flour industry (45.4).

q Includes beer and malt.

r Employment in 1926/27 (203.7 th., 216, 126) extrapolated by fish catch (Table B-2).

s Includes bakeries (49.3 th.), dairy products (31.5 th.), and others (31.3 th.).

t School supplies and other products.

u Artificial gas.

[v] Includes water supply (7.4 th,) and artificial gas (0.9 th.).
[w] Includes processing of materials of animal origin (10.6 th.).
[x] No. of workers is taken to be half the 1932 level (*222*, 3 ff) and salaried personnel the same fraction of workers as for machine building in 1913 (see Table C-1a below).
[y] Given in Soviet sources as "others" under machine building and metal products. The large-scale component is known to include maintenance repair shops, and we have assumed the entire category applies to repair shops of various kinds.

SOURCES AND DERIVATION OF TABLE C-1

(Note: Exceptions to these general explanations are separately footnoted above.)

1913

Total industry: Sum of large- and small-scale industry.
Large-scale industry: For "census" industry, sum of no. of workers (*145*, 398 ff, or *222*, 3 ff) and of salaried personnel, the latter derived by dividing no. of workers by ratio of workers to salaried personnel. The ratios used are given in Table C-1a below, which is derived from data in the 1918 industrial census on employment in 1913 in "census" enterprises that still existed in 1918 (*201*, 180 f). When data were lacking for particular industries the avg. ratio for all covered industries was used.

TABLE C-1a

RATIO OF WORKERS TO SALARIED PERSONNEL IN LARGE-SCALE INDUSTRY, BY INDUSTRIAL GROUP, 1913

Extraction and processing of minerals	15.4
Mining and metallurgy	16.3
Metal products	10.8
Machine building	10.0
Wood products	8.5
Chemical industry	7.5
Food industry	8.1
Products of animal origin	5.4
Leather and fur industry	14.7
Cotton industry	23.0
Woolen industry	16.9
Silk industry	24.4
Linen industry	20.0
Hemp industry	25.8
Mixed fibers	14.5
Garment industry	15.2
Paper industry	15.5
Printing industry	10.1
Scientific, school, and art equipment	7.3
Water supply and gas industry	4.5
All industries above	14.6

Small-scale industry: Estimates of no. of persons engaged in "noncensus" industry in 1913 on interwar Soviet territory made by a special committee of the Central Statistical Administration (*10*, pt. II, 91 ff). These estimates were reduced to full-time equivalents by multiplying them by ratio of no. of weeks worked in 1913 (see Table C-1b below) to full-time work year for "census" industry (assumed to be 48 weeks). When data were lacking for particular industries, the avg. no. of weeks worked for all covered industries was used to compute the ratio. The data in Table C-1b were derived from *10*, 196.

APPENDIX C

TABLE C-1b

AVERAGE NUMBER OF WEEKS WORKED PER YEAR IN SMALL-SCALE INDUSTRY,
BY INDUSTRIAL GROUP, 1913

Extraction and processing of minerals	19.2
Metal products	31.2
Machine and machine tool building	26.8
Wood products	27.6
Chemical industry	16.8
Products of animal origin	27.2
Leather and fur industry	29.2
Cotton industry	24.0
Woolen industry	20.8
Silk industry	38.8
Linen industry	25.2
Hemp industry	22.8
Mixed fibers	27.2
Garment industry	30.4
Paper products	32.4
Scientific, school, and art equipment	31.6
All industries above	27.0

1927/28

Total industry: Sum of large- and small-scale industry.
Large-scale industry: Sum of no. of workers (derived from no. of workers in 1928/29 and percentage increase between 1927/28 and 1928/29, *388*, 1929, No. 12, 88 ff) and no. of salaried personnel as of Jan. 1, 1928 (*390*, 1928, No. 8, 12 ff).
Small-scale industry: Total no. of weeks worked in small-scale industry (*407*, 1931, No. 8) apportioned among industries according to the percentage distribution for 1928/29 (*129*, 118 ff). For each industry, the total no. of weeks worked was divided by the avg. no. of weeks worked per worker in the corresponding large-scale industry. The latter averages are derived from the no. of days worked in each large-scale industry (*388*, 1929, No. 12, 88 ff) divided by 6 times the avg. annual no. of workers in the corresponding large-scale industry.

1933

Total industry: Sum of large- and small-scale industry.
Large-scale industry: Avg. annual no. of workers (*362*, 1935, No. 7, 41 ff) times ratio of total no. of persons engaged to no. of workers (derived from labor statistics for 1933, *268*, 62 ff).
Small-scale industry: Taken from 1933 census (*362*, 1935, No. 7, 41 ff). Does not include "unorganized" *kustari* and artisans, which are given elsewhere (*362*, 1936, No. 1, 14 ff) as 295,000 in the city and 115,000 in the country. The value of their output is given (*362*, 1935, No. 8, 9) as less than 100 million rubles.

1937

Total industry: The total no. of persons engaged in all industry is the sum of (1) the avg. annual no. of production employees (10,112 th., *140*, 50); (2) members of industrial producer coops (estimated at 1,500 th. from *206*, 40); and (3) workers in collective farm enterprises, estimated at 914 th. from no. of workers in such enterprises in the RSFSR in 1935 (645 th., *362*, 1936, No. 20, 10) divided by ratio of no. of collective farms in RSFSR to no. in USSR in 1937 (derived as 706 from *136*, 125, and *140*, 100). These figures for collective farm workers are apparently not in full-time equivalents and have not been adjusted. The total thus derived was broken down by industries according to the percentage distribution of production workers in industry (*140*, 49).

1940

Total industry: The total no. of persons engaged in all industry is the sum of (1) the avg. annual no. of production employees (10,967 th., *140*, 48); (2) members of industrial producer coops, estimated at 1,628 th. from members of all producer coops in 1940

506

(1,832 th., *321*, 10/17/40) times ratio of members in industrial coops to all members in 1955 (0.888 from data in *136*, 44, and *140*, 205); and (3) workers in enterprises belonging to collective farms (assumed to be 800 th., the same as in 1950). The total thus derived was broken down by industries according to the percentage distribution of production workers in industry (*140*, 49).

1950

Total industry: The total no. of persons engaged in all industry is the sum of (1) the avg. annual no. of production employees (14,144 th., *140*, 205); (2) members of industrial producer coops, estimated at 1,422 th. from the members of producer coops in the RSFSR in 1950 (1,008 th., *136*, 267) times the ratio of producer coop members in the USSR to those in the RSFSR in 1955 (derived as 1.41 from *138*, 44, and *140*, 267); and (3) workers in enterprises belonging to collective farms, estimated at 800 th. from no. of such enterprises (around 400 th. in 1949, *138*, 42) and the assumption that each enterprise had an avg. of 2 full-time workers. The total thus derived was broken down by industries according to the percentage distribution of production workers in industry (*140*, 49).

1955

Total industry: The total no. of persons engaged in all industry is the sum of (1) the avg. annual no. of production employees (17,367 th., *140*, 205, including a small no. of workers in nonfunded auxiliary enterprise directly attached to ministries); (2) members of industrial producer coops (1,600 th., *180*, 23); and (3) workers in enterprises belonging to collective farms, estimated at 700 th. from the no. of such enterprises (350 th., *140*, 48) and the assumption that each enterprise had an avg. of 2 full-time workers. The total thus derived was broken down by industries according to the percentage distribution of production workers in industry (*140*, 49).

GENERAL NOTE

The data on persons engaged in industry in 1937, 1940, 1950, and 1955 suffer from two main shortcomings. First, the total employment figures given in Soviet sources do not cover industrial overhead services, some categories of nonproduction employees, members of so-called "industrial collective farms," and industrial activities classified elsewhere (such as oil prospecting). Lack of information makes it impossible to estimate, even approximately, the overhead and maintenance personnel; but some information is available on the other categories of employment. Domestic help and day workers, who are not included in the total no. of persons engaged in industry, are given in Table C-1c below (*269*, 10 f):

TABLE C-1c
DOMESTIC HELP AND DAY WORKERS

	Thousands	Per Cent of Total Employment
1928	809.0	7.0
1929	706.0	5.8
1930	399.0	2.7
1931	352.0	1.9
1932	341.5	1.5
1933	292.4	1.3
1934	288.8	1.2
1935	300.0	1.2

It may be assumed that at least a third of these workers were employed in industry. Employment in forestry improvement, excluded from industrial employment, was 2.5% of total employment in 1932, 2.45% in 1937 (*223*, 138), and 2.45% in 1940 (*72*, 543, 512). Employment in oil prospecting, also excluded, was 0.6% of total employment in 1940 (*72*, 512 ff).

The second shortcoming of employment data for 1937 onward is that the percentage breakdown by industry (*140*, 49) applies only to so-called "production" workers. Hence

APPENDIX C

the ratio of production workers to salaried personnel is implicitly taken to be the same in all industries, which is not so. Employment in industries with a larger than average proportion of nonproduction personnel to production workers (such as machine building and electric power stations) is thereby understated. Employment in others with a smaller than average proportion (such as the fuel industry) is overstated. Table C-1d below shows the differences in percentage distributions of production workers and persons engaged by industry in 1933 and 1935 (data taken from *138*, 49; *259*, 71 ff; and Table C-1, this appendix).

TABLE C-1d

PERCENTAGE DISTRIBUTION OF LABOR FORCE, 1933 AND 1935

	Production Workers (1)		Persons Engaged (2)		Col. 1 as % of Col. 2 (3)	
	1933	1935	1933	1935	1933	1935
Ferrous and nonferrous metallurgy	5.6	7.1	5.6	7.0	100	101
Fuel	7.2	7.9	7.1	7.6	101	104
Electric power	0.8	0.8	0.9	0.9	89	89
Chemicals (incl. paper)	2.8	3.4	2.7	3.5	104	97
Machine building and metal products	25.8	25.3	27.4	26.6	94	95
Wood, paper, and logging	18.0	20.1	17.6	19.4	102	104
Construction materials	4.0	4.9	5.1	4.8	78	102
Printing	1.1	1.2	1.2	1.3	92	92
Textiles and allied products	19.8	17.3	19.5	16.3	102	106
Food and allied products	11.8	10.2	10.8	10.7	109	95
Others	3.1	1.7	2.1	1.8	148	94

The relations between the two distributions (col. 3) are similar in both years except in the cases of chemicals, mineral construction materials, food and allied products, and "other industries." These inconsistencies may be explained by incomparabilities in the industrial classifications for the two sets of data for 1933. The data on production workers are taken from a source published in 1956 (*138*), while those on engaged persons are taken from sources published in the 1930's. It seems probable that the scope of some industrial categories (like "other industries") was redefined between 1933 and 1956.

For further comments on the reliability of our data on persons engaged, see Appendix A, technical note 7.

(million current rubles)

EMPLOYMENT, VALUE, AND POPULATION DATA

Industry	Turnover 1926/27	Turnover 1927/28	Turnover 1928/29	Value of Output 1926/27	Value of Output 1927/28	Value of Output 1928/29	Value Added 1926/27	Value Added 1927/28	Value Added 1928/29
I. Electric power stations				158.9	191.7	237.3	101.5	122.4	151.5
Large-scale	—	—		158.9	191.7	236.5	101.5	122.4	151.0
Small-scale			0.8	—	—	0.8	—	—	0.5
II. Fuel				1,025.5	1,186.9	1,315.7	682.8	759.9	844.0
Large-scale	—	0.9	1.4	1,025.5	1,186.0	1,314.3	682.8	759.2	842.8
Small-scale				—	0.9	1.4	—	0.7	1.2
A. Coal and coke				354.4	416.7	455.1	287.3	333.5	364.2
Large-scale	—			354.4	416.7	455.1	287.3	333.5	364.2
Small-scale				—	—	—	—	—	—
B. Petroleum				615.0	713.9	787.4	347.0	392.8	436.1
Large-scale	—			615.0	713.9	787.4	347.0	392.8	436.1
Small-scale				—	—	—	—	—	—
1. Crude petroleum and natural gas extraction				304.2	336.0	375.4	260.2	287.3	321.1
Large-scale	—			304.2	336.0	375.4	260.2	287.3	321.1
Small-scale				—	—	—	—	—	—
2. Petroleum refining				310.8	377.9	412.0	86.8	105.5	115.0
Large-scale	—			310.8	377.9	412.0	86.8	105.5	115.0
Small-scale				—	—	—	—	—	—
C. Peat				51.4	52.0	67.8	46.0	31.1	40.7
Large-scale	—	0.9	1.4	51.4	51.1	66.4[a]	46.0	30.4	39.5[b]
Small-scale				—	0.9	1.4	—	0.7	1.2
D. Artificial gas				4.6	4.3	5.4	2.6	2.4	3.0
Large-scale	—			4.6	4.3	5.4	2.6	2.4	3.0
Small-scale				—	—	—	—	—	—
III. Ferrous mining and metallurgy				677.1	720.3	845.3	300.9	321.2	382.0
Large-scale	—			677.1	720.3	845.3	300.9	321.2	382.0
Small-scale				—	—	—	—	—	—

(continued)

TABLE C-2 (continued)

Industry	Turnover 1926/27	1927/28	1928/29	Value of Output 1926/27	1927/28	1928/29	Value Added 1926/27	1927/28	1928/29
A. Mining of ferrous ores	—	—		38.3	44.0	65.7	29.9	34.4	51.4
Large-scale				38.3	44.0	65.7	29.9	34.4	51.4
Small-scale				—	—	—	—	—	—
1. Iron ore	—	—		30.7	35.4	46.6	23.9	27.6	36.3
Large-scale				30.7	35.4	46.6	23.9	27.6	36.3
Small-scale				—	—	—	—	—	—
2. Manganese ore	—	—		7.6	8.7	19.0	6.0	6.8	15.0
Large-scale				7.6	8.7	19.0	6.0	6.8	15.0
Small-scale				—	—	—	—	—	—
B. Ferrous metallurgy	—	—		638.9	676.2	779.6	271.0	286.8	330.6
Large-scale				638.9	676.2	779.6	271.0	286.8	330.6
Small-scale				—	—	—	—	—	—
IV. Nonferrous mining and metallurgy									
Large-scale	—			80.6	95.0	79.0	46.6	52.2	34.5
				80.6	94.8	78.6	46.6	52.1	34.3
Small-scale		0.2	0.4		0.2	0.4		0.1	0.2
A. Mining of nonferrous ores									
Large-scale	—			41.6	51.4	14.7	32.5	36.5	11.3
				41.6	51.2	14.3[c]	32.5	36.4	11.1[c]
Small-scale		0.2	0.4		0.2	0.4		0.1	0.2
B. Nonferrous metallurgy	—	—		39.0	43.6	64.3	14.1	15.7	23.2
Large-scale				39.0	43.6	64.3	14.1	15.7	23.2
Small-scale		—		—	—	—	—	—	—
V. Machine building and metal products				1,593.5	1,696.1	2,233.0	786.9	874.2	1,148.1
Large-scale	247.5	284.7	313.1	1,368.7	1,431.3	1,936.3	665.8	736.0	997.1
Small-scale				224.8	264.8	296.7	121.1	133.2	151.0
A. Machine building				945.2	963.9	1,424.2	462.0	476.0	702.7
Large-scale	20.8	48.1	73.9	924.9	917.1	1,352.3	450.9	449.5	661.7
Small-scale				20.3	46.8	71.9	11.1	26.5	41.0
1. Land transportation equip. (incl. tractors)				206.2	142.3[d]	246.9	92.7	64.0[d]	111.1

Small-scale	7.0	3.8	0.5	11.7	6.3	0.7	12.2	6.6	0.7
3. Agricultural machinery (excl. tractors)	117.4	80.5[d]	58.9	256.8	177.3[d]	133.2			
Large-scale	102.1	72.5	58.5	231.0	163.8	132.4			
Small-scale	15.3	8.0	0.4	25.8	13.5	0.8	26.6	14.0	0.9
4. Electrical and industrial machinery	427.3	301.3	273.0	789.7	559.1	506.0			
Large-scale	408.6	286.6	262.8	755.4	532.0	487.2			
Small-scale	18.7	14.7	10.2	34.3	27.1	18.8	35.0	27.6	19.2
B. Metal products	445.5	398.2	324.8	808.8	732.2	648.2			
Large-scale	335.5[e]	286.4	214.8	584.0[e]	514.2	443.8			
Small-scale	110.0	111.8	110.0	224.8	218.0	204.4	239.2	236.6	226.7
VI. Extraction of minerals for chemical, construction, glass and china industries	57.3	37.5	26.6	79.7	52.3	37.0			
Large-scale	44.7	28.8	21.7	62.3	40.2	30.3			
Small-scale	12.6	8.7	4.9	17.4	12.1	6.7	17.6	12.2	6.8
VII. Chemicals	172.6	132.6	116.2	408.5	310.9	271.4			
Large-scale	154.8	118.0	105.4	370.8	281.1	250.4			
Small-scale	17.8	14.6	10.8	37.7	29.8	21.0	38.0	30.1	21.2
A. Basic chemicals	52.1	43.1	39.7	103.5	85.6	78.6			
Large-scale	51.7	42.8	39.4	102.4	84.7	78.0			
Small-scale	0.4	0.3	0.3	1.1	0.9	0.6	1.1	0.9	0.6
B. Paints and varnishes	27.7	23.5	19.7	72.3	60.8	49.9			
Large-scale	24.6	20.8	17.5	63.1	53.5	44.8			
Small-scale	3.1	2.7	2.2	9.2	7.3	5.1	9.2	7.2	5.1
C. Pharmaceutical chemicals	26.4	19.1	16.6	69.2	50.0	43.6			
Large-scale	25.7	18.5	16.2	67.3	48.5	42.6			
Small-scale	0.7	0.6	0.4	1.9	1.5	1.0	1.9	1.5	1.0
D. All other chemicals	66.6	46.9	40.4	163.6	114.7	99.2			
Large-scale	52.9[f]	35.9	32.4	138.1[f]	94.5	85.0			
Small-scale	13.7	11.0	8.0	25.5	20.2	14.2	25.7	20.4	14.4
VIII. Construction materials	152.4	122.7	110.8	246.4	199.5	181.3			
Large-scale	113.9	92.5	89.8	190.8	155.6	150.6			
Small-scale	38.5	30.2	21.0	55.6	43.9	30.7	55.8	44.1	31.0

(continued)

TABLE C-2 (continued)

Industry	Turnover 1926/27	1927/28	1928/29	Value of Output 1926/27	1927/28	1928/29	Value Added 1926/27	1927/28	1928/29
A. Cement				63.1	67.4	79.6	31.8	33.9	40.1
Large-scale				62.2	66.0	77.7	31.3	33.2	39.1
Small-scale	0.9	1.4	1.9	0.9	1.4	1.9	0.5	0.7	1.0
B. Bricks and other construction materials				118.2	132.1	167.0	79.0	88.8	112.4
Large-scale				88.3	89.6	113.2	58.4	59.3	74.9
Small-scale	30.1	42.7	54.0	29.9	42.5	53.8	20.6	29.5	37.5
IX. Glass and china industries				160.7	171.0	210.1	105.5	112.2	137.0
Large-scale				158.3	167.2	205.0	104.3	110.2	135.6
Small-scale	2.4	3.8	5.1	2.4	3.8	5.1	1.2	2.0	2.6
A. Glass				115.8	121.1	151.3	75.2	78.5	98.0
Large-scale				113.5	117.5	146.5	74.0	76.6	95.5
Small-scale	2.3	3.6	4.9	2.3	3.6	4.8	1.2	1.9	2.5
B. China				44.9	49.9	58.7	30.3	33.7	39.6
Large-scale				44.8	49.7	58.4	30.3	33.6	39.5
Small-scale	0.1	0.2	0.3	0.1	0.2	0.3	0.06	0.1	0.1
X. Extraction of all other minerals (incl. asbestos, excl. salt)				28.9	32.7	42.0	17.8	20.1	25.8
Large-scale				28.3	31.7	40.7	17.5	19.6	25.1
Small-scale	0.6	1.0	1.3	0.6	1.0	1.3	0.3	0.5	0.7
A. Asbestos				6.9	7.8	9.3	4.7	5.3	6.4
Large-scale				6.9	7.8	9.3	4.7	5.3	6.4
Small-scale	0.01	0.02	0.03	0.01	0.02	0.03	0.01	0.01	0.01
B. All other mineral products				22.1	24.8	32.6	13.1	14.8	19.3
Large-scale				21.5	23.9	31.4	12.8	14.3	18.7
Small-scale	0.6	0.9	1.3	0.6	0.9	1.2	0.3	0.5	0.6
XI. Rubber products				148.7	184.0	225.9	83.1	102.6	126.0

Small-scale	201.0	232.6	257.1	183.6	219.4	248.5	110.9	124.3	133.9
A. Plywood and lumber				369.9	402.0	484.5	134.0	144.9	173.5
Large-scale	16.0	16.5	16.5	356.0	386.6	468.1	126.4	137.3	166.3
Small-scale				13.9	15.4	16.4	7.6	7.6	7.2
B. Miscellaneous wood products				261.2	319.3	372.6	137.1	159.4	178.6
Large-scale	185.0	216.1	240.6	91.5	115.3	140.5	33.8	42.6	51.9
Small-scale				169.7	204.0	232.1	103.3	116.8	126.7
C. Matches				30.3	34.4	45.2	18.1	20.6	27.0
Large-scale	—	—	—	30.3	34.4	45.2	18.1	20.6	27.0
Small-scale				—	—	—	—	—	—
XIII. Logging	765.0	721.8	814.0	765.0	721.8	814.0	612.0	577.0	651.0
Large-scale				—	—	—	—	—	—
Small-scale				765.0[g]	721.8[h]	814.0[g]	612.0[i]	577.0[i]	651.0[i]
XIV. Pulp and paper				181.6	192.5	256.2	84.0	88.4	117.7
Large-scale	13.6	14.0	14.0	169.7	179.6	242.6	78.9	83.3	112.7
Small-scale				11.9	12.9	13.6	5.1	5.1	5.0
XV. Textiles and allied products				3,798.2	4,193.5	4,893.5	1,397.9	1,532.6	1,778.2
Large-scale	392.7	479.3	551.3	3,465.8	3,789.8	4,431.0	1,250.6	1,367.1	1,599.6
Small-scale				332.4	403.7	462.5	147.3	165.5	178.6
A. Cotton industry				2,541.3	2,775.5	3,148.9	855.3	930.4	1,047.7
Large-scale	87.4	115.0	139.0	2,474.5	2,687.4	3,042.1	838.4	908.3	1,021.1
Small-scale				66.8	88.1	106.8	16.9	22.1	26.6
1. Cotton ginning				186.9	212.0	267.2	18.3	20.9	26.4
Large-scale	1.1	1.8	2.5	185.8	210.5	265.3	18.2	20.6	25.9
Small-scale				1.1	1.5	1.9	0.1	0.3	0.5
2. Cotton textiles				2,354.4	2,563.5	2,881.6	837.0	909.5	1,021.3
Large-scale	86.3	113.1	136.5	2,288.7	2,476.9	2,776.8	820.2	887.7	995.2
Small-scale				65.7	86.6	104.8	16.8	21.8	26.1
B. Flax and mixed fibers				254.9	249.6	305.4	117.6	116.2	141.5
Large-scale	7.6	9.6	11.4	248.2	241.1	295.4	115.1	113.3	138.4
Small-scale				6.7	8.5	10.0	2.5	2.9	3.1

(continued)

TABLE C-2 (continued)

Industry	Turnover			Value of Output			Value Added		
	1926/27	1927/28	1928/29	1926/27	1927/28	1928/29	1926/27	1927/28	1928/29
1. Primary processing of mixed fibers				32.4	34.7	48.8	13.1	13.9	19.4
Large-scale	2.3	4.7	7.0	30.2	30.6	43.0	12.1	12.3	17.3
Small-scale				2.2	4.1	5.8	1.0	1.6	2.1
2. Processing of flax				222.4	214.8	256.5	104.5	102.3	122.1
Large-scale	5.2	4.9	4.4	218.0	210.5	252.4	103.0	101.0	121.1
Small-scale				4.4	4.3	4.1	1.5	1.3	1.0
C. Wool industry				538.0	595.6	698.0	199.7	217.1	250.2
Large-scale	75.6	103.7	128.7	464.1	496.9	577.7	185.0	198.5	228.2
Small-scale				73.9	98.7	120.3	14.7	18.6	22.0
1. Wool washing				16.6	16.8	28.0	1.7	1.7	2.9
Large-scale	0.4	0.6	0.7	16.2	16.3	27.3	1.7	1.7	2.8
Small-scale				0.4	0.5	0.7	0.04	0.08	0.1
2. Wool products				521.4	578.7	670.1	197.9	215.3	247.1
Large-scale	75.1	103.2	128.0	447.9	480.6	550.4	183.3	196.8	225.3
Small-scale				73.5	98.1	119.7	14.6	18.5	21.8
D. Silk industry				96.0	132.8	191.9	31.7	42.9	60.6
Large-scale	25.0	36.3	46.5	77.0	102.0	150.2	23.1	30.6	45.0
Small-scale				19.0	30.8	41.7	8.6	12.3	15.6
E. Hemp and jute products				86.7	99.4	116.7	34.8	39.9	46.8
Large-scale	19.2	23.5	27.1	69.9	78.3	91.9	29.4	33.0	38.7
Small-scale				16.8	21.1	24.8	5.4	6.9	8.1
F. Knitted goods				161.0	210.0	280.4	70.2	89.4	116.8
Large-scale	81.1	91.0	98.0	105.4	150.5	218.7	42.1	60.2	87.4
Small-scale				55.6	59.5	61.7	28.1	29.2	29.4
G. Felt products				120.4	130.4	152.2	88.6	97.0	114.7
Large-scale	96.8	100.2	100.6	26.8[j]	33.5	54.9[j]	17.5[j]	23.4	40.8[j]
Small-scale				93.6	96.9	97.3	71.1	73.6	73.9
XVI. Garment industry				794.5	896.0	1,119.3	243.8	274.9	338.1

514

	(1)	(2)	(3)	(4)	(5)	(6)	(7)	(8)	(9)
(continued)					355.5	301.3	201.5	235.0	213.0
A. Leather, natural and artificial				601.6	581.2	617.3	159.2	152.9	160.2
Large-scale				392.8	414.5	497.7	95.6	100.8	121.1
Small-scale	213.4	170.1	121.7	208.8	166.7	119.6	63.6	52.1	39.1
B. Fur products				87.2	129.7	169.8	25.1	34.9	44.1
Large-scale				25.9	50.5	75.1	7.4	14.4	21.5
Small-scale	67.1	86.3	102.9	61.3	79.2	94.7	17.7	20.5	22.6
C. Boots and shoes, production and repair				634.3	645.0	762.5	249.0	247.9	281.0
Large-scale				139.3	205.4	391.9	45.8	67.5	128.9
Small-scale	532.5	472.9	398.7	495.0	439.6	370.6	203.2	180.4	152.1
XVIII. Grease, tallow, soap, and perfume				171.2	218.4	246.5	58.1	73.5	82.5
Large-scale				145.8	197.4	230.5	49.3	66.7	77.9
Small-scale	25.9	21.3	16.0	25.4	21.0	16.0	8.8	6.8	4.6
XIX. Food and allied products (excl. fishing)				4,649.4	5,447.2	6,088.6	1,279.8	1,487.4	1,657.9
Large-scale				2,560.5	3,069.2	3,494.7	840.7	991.3	1,120.2
Small-scale	2,102.4	2,388.4	2,601.0	2,088.9	2,378.0	2,593.9	439.1	496.1	537.7
A. Flour milling and grain cracking				2,299.3	2,608.0	2,809.0	451.4	511.5	549.6
Large-scale				870.8	973.6	1,018.8	194.3	217.2	227.3
Small-scale	1,428.5[k]	1,634.4[k]	1,790.2[k]	1,428.5	1,634.4	1,790.2[l]	257.1	294.3	322.3[m]
B. Beet sugar				443.0	604.5	605.2	154.5	210.8	211.1
Large-scale				443.0	604.5	605.2	154.5	210.8	211.1
Small-scale	—	—	—	—	—	—	—	—	—
C. Confectionery				156.3	217.2	311.4	52.6	73.0	104.6
Large-scale				99.1	149.2	234.6	33.2	50.0	78.6
Small-scale	58.1	69.1	77.9	57.2	68.0	76.8	19.4	23.0	26.0
D. Vegetable oil				201.1	245.6	296.2	59.0	71.9	86.5
Large-scale				129.6	173.1	224.9	37.5	50.2	65.2
Small-scale	71.6	72.5	71.3	71.5	72.5	71.3	21.5	21.7	21.3
E. Starch and syrup				30.8	28.0	46.2	9.8	9.2	15.1
Large-scale				26.5	20.6	36.0	8.3	6.4	11.2
Small-scale	4.3	7.4	10.2	4.3	7.4	10.2	1.5	2.8	3.9

(continued)

515

TABLE C-2 (concluded)

Industry	Turnover 1926/27	Turnover 1927/28	Turnover 1928/29	Value of Output 1926/27	Value of Output 1927/28	Value of Output 1928/29	Value Added 1926/27	Value Added 1927/28	Value Added 1928/29
F. Wine, yeast, and vodka	5.7	7.1	8.3						
Large-scale				362.7	362.7	372.1	165.0	164.8	168.7
Small-scale				357.9	356.6	364.8	163.5	162.9	166.6
				4.8	6.1	7.3	1.5	1.9	2.1
G. Beer and malt	0.5	0.7	0.8						
Large-scale				104.2	97.1	95.4	65.4	60.9	59.8
Small-scale				103.7	96.5	94.7	65.3	60.7	59.6
				0.5	0.6	0.7	0.1	0.2	0.2
H. Tobacco and makhorka	1.9	2.4	2.8						
Large-scale				169.7	177.6	186.5	72.1	75.5	80.1
Small-scale				168.1	175.5	184.1	71.6	74.9	79.4
				1.6	2.1	2.4	0.5	0.6	0.7
I. Salt	—	—	—						
Large-scale				17.1	16.4	19.8	12.3	11.7	14.2
Small-scale				17.1	16.4	19.8	12.3	11.7	14.2
				—	—	—	—	—	—
J. Others	531.9	594.8	639.5						
Large-scale				865.2	1,090.2	1,347.0	237.6	297.9	368.1
Small-scale				344.7	503.3	711.8	100.2	146.3	207.0
				520.5	586.9	635.2	137.4	151.6	161.1
XX. Fishing	209.2[k]	211.0[k]	236.5[k]	209.2[n]	242.8[h]	276.3[o]	167.4[i]	194.2[i]	221.0[i]
Large-scale				—	31.8[p]	36.2[p]	—	25.4[o]	29.0[p]
Small-scale				209.2	211.0[p]	240.1[p]	167.4	168.8[o]	192.0[p]
XXI. Printing, publishing, stationery, etc.	53.3	60.3	65.4						
Large-scale				265.8	294.5	377.9	143.2	158.8	204.5
Small-scale				216.6	237.9	315.7	112.8	124.6	167.6
				49.2	56.6	62.2	30.4	34.2	36.9
A. Printing and publishing	24.5	18.2	11.3						
Large-scale				211.7	220.5	265.2	109.0	112.7	134.2
Small-scale				190.0	204.2	254.8	95.5	102.7	128.1
				21.7	16.3	10.4	13.5	10.0	6.1
B. Stationery and art equipment	28.8	42.1	54.1						
Large-scale				54.1	74.1	112.7	34.2	46.1	70.4
Small-scale				26.6	33.8	60.9	17.3	21.9	39.6
				27.5	40.3	51.8	16.9	24.2	30.8
XXII. All others	151.1	172.0	222.2				82.6	88.5	105.7

Total excl. repair shops	5,543.4	5,883.3	6,229.8	17,334.1	19,330.6	22,669.2	7,170.1	7,893.5	9,252.7
Large-scale				11,994.7	13,650.1	16,626.4	4,998.8	5,662.0	6,872.3
Small-scale				5,339.4	5,680.5	6,042.8	2,171.3	2,231.5	2,380.4
XXIII. District railroad repair shops				150.0	180.0	219.0	73.2	88.2	107.1
Large-scale				150.0[q]	180.0[q]	219.0[q]	73.2[r]	88.2[r]	107.1[r]
Small-scale				—	—	—	—	—	—
Total incl. repair shops	5,543.4	5,883.3	6,229.8	17,484.1	19,510.6	22,888.2	7,243.3	7,981.7	9,359.8
Large-scale				12,144.7	13,830.1	16,845.4	5,072.0	5,750.2	6,979.4
Small-scale				5,339.4	5,680.5	6,042.8	2,171.3	2,231.5	2,380.4

—: negligible

a 1927/28 value of output extrapolated by output (Table B-2).

b Value of output times 1927/28 ratio of value added to value of output.

c Includes lead, tin, and silver ore. Not comparable with 1927/28 data.

d Value of output for tractors was 6.8 mill. rubles (Tables B-2 and D-8); value added, 3.1 mill. rubles on the assumption that the ratio of value added to value of output was the same as for all land transportation equipment.

e Includes machine-made metal products for mass consumption, other ferrous products, type foundry products, and nonferrous metal products.

f Includes tar, chemical wood processing, and other chemical products.

g Marketed output in current prices (104, 422). Because of its close ties with agriculture, logging is put into small-scale industry.

h Output times price (Tables B-2 and D-8).

i Assumed to be 80% of value of output, the approximate ratio for most extractive industries.

j Derived from data for the garment and other apparel industry.

k Assumed to be same as value of output.

l Total including flour milling (363, 1929, No. 9, 281) minus total excluding flour milling (129, 118).

m Value of output in 1928/29 (assumed to be same as turnover) times ratio of value added to turnover in 1924/25 (both given in 248, 249).

n Output (Table B-2) times price (280 rubles/m. ton, from output and value of output in 1926/27 prices for 1927/28 in 166, 10).

o Output (Table B-2) times price (assumed to be same as for 1927/28 in Table D-8).

p Total apportioned on the basis of employment in 1927/28 (see Table C-1).

q Value of output for machine building, metal products, and repair shops minus value of output for machine building and metal products, both in "1926/27" rubles (467, 340 f). Data for 1927 used for 1926/27.

r Value of output times ratio of value added to value of output in machine building.

517

APPENDIX C

Sources and Derivation of Table C-2

(Note: Exceptions to these general explanations are separately footnoted above.)

Turnover (valovoi oborot) is the value of all goods produced and work done on a shop basis. That is, value is calculated at the transfer of goods from one shop within an enterprise to another.

Value of output (valovaia produktsiia) is the value of goods produced and work done on an enterprise basis, but including some intershop transfers in a few industries (e.g., textiles, ferrous metals, and meat packing).

Value added (uslovnaia chistaia produktsiia) is value of output minus the value of materials, fuel, and electricity consumed in the process of fabrication. As defined here, value added includes amortization and taxes.

Turnover (small-scale industry)

1926/27: Derived primarily from *249*, 482 ff. Additional breakdown taken from *137*, 88 ff, and estimated from the percentage distribution within an industry averaged for 1924/25 (*248*, 245 ff) and 1928/29 (*129*, 11 f, 117 ff). When no data were available for 1924/25, the 1928/29 distribution was used.

1927/28: Avg. turnover for 1926/27 and 1928/29 times ratio for total small-scale value of output (1.0156) of 1927/28 (*363*, 1929, No. 9, 281) to avg. for 1926/27 and 1928/29.

1928/29: Derived primarily from *129*, 11 f. Additional breakdown derived from data in *129*, 118 ff.

Value of Output (large-scale industry)

1926/27: Derived from *47*, table 3, 84 ff.

1927/28: Derived from *249*, 324 ff.

1928/29: Taken from *388*, 1929, No. 12, 88 ff.

Value of Output (small-scale industry)

1926/27: Turnover times avg. ratio of value of output to turnover for 1924/25 (both in *248*, 245 ff) and for 1928/29.

1927/28: Avg. value of output for 1926/27 and 1928/29 times ratio for total small-scale value of output (1.0156) of 1927/28 (*363*, 1929, No. 9, 281) to avg. for 1926/27 and 1928/29.

1928/29: Taken from *129*, 14 ff.

Value Added (large-scale industry)

1926/27: Large-scale value of output minus cost of basic and auxiliary materials and fuel consumed (*47*, table 3, 84 ff).

1927/28: Large-scale value of output times 1926/27 ratio for large-scale industry of value added to value of output.

1928/29: Large-scale value of output times 1926/27 ratio for large-scale industry of value added to value of output.

Value Added (small-scale industry)

1926/27: Turnover times avg. ratio of value added to turnover for 1924/25 (both in *248*, 245 ff) and for 1928/29 (both in *129*, 14 ff). When no ratio could be computed for 1924/25, the 1928/29 ratio was used.

1927/28: Avg. value added for 1926/27 and 1928/29 times ratio for total small-scale value of output (1.0156) of 1927/28 (*363*, 1929, No. 9, 281) to avg. for 1926/27 for 1928/29.

1928/29: Value of output minus cost of materials and fuel consumed (*129*, 118 ff) times ratio of turnover in basic source (*129*, 14 ff) to turnover in the other source (*129*, 118 ff), the latter adjustment being required because of differences in coverage.

TABLE C-3

ESTIMATED POPULATION: RUSSIA AND SOVIET UNION, SELECTED YEARS, 1858–1958[a]
(million persons)

Year	Value	Year	Value
1858	72.8	1928	151.4
1860	74	1929	153.9
1865	80	1930	155.8
1870	86	1931	157.4
1875	92	1932	158.2
1880	99	1933	158.7
1885	106	1934	159.6
1890	113	1935	160.7
1895	122	1936	162.4
1897	125.6	1937	165.2
1900	132		
1905	144	1938	168.6
1910	157	1939	172.1
1913[a]	164.2	1940	198.9
1913[a]	138.0	1945	175.3[b]
1914	140.8		
1915	142.2	1946	174.9
1916	142.2	1947	175.0
1917	142.2	1948	176.1
		1949	178.5
1918	140.8	1950	181.5
1919	139.2		
1920	136.7	1951	184.7
1921	135.4	1952	187.9
1922	135.2	1953	191.0
		1954	194.2
1923	136.1	1955	197.6
1924	138.6		
1925	141.8	1956	201.0
1926	145.3	1957	204.0
1927	148.6	1958	207.2

[a] Current territory. For 1913, first figure applies to Tsarist territory, the second to Soviet interwar territory. The former is estimated as the latter times the ratio for Jan. 1, 1914, of population in the two territories.

[b] Annual change for 1945–1946 is assumed to be double the change for the first half of 1946 as estimated by Harold Wool (592).

SOURCE:

1858	286, 8.
1860, 1865, 1870, 1875, 1880, 1885, 1890, 1895	Interpolated logarithmically between 1858 and 1897.
1897	156, I, iii.
1900, 1905, 1910	Interpolated logarithmically between 1897 and 1913.
1913–1955	592. Population as of July 1.
1956–1958	Population as of July 1. Logarithmic interpolation between official estimate of 200.2 mill. as of April 1956 (138, 17) and census enumeration of 208.8 as of January 15, 1959 (141, 7).

APPENDIX D

Production Indexes and Weights

General Note

THE indexes given in Appendix D are, in general, expressed as values in constant prices. The exception is the index for all civilian industrial products in Table D-4, which is given in the form of index numbers since it is weighted by employment in 1955.

The series included in these indexes are given in Tables D-10 and D-11; weights, in Tables D-8 and D-9. The weighting systems used are described in Chapter 5 and Appendix A, technical note 3.

TABLE D-1
Indexes for Industrial Materials: Soviet Union, 1913–1955
(million constant rubles)

	1913 Prices[a]			1928 Prices[a]			1955 Prices[a]		
	Total	Intermediate Industrial Products	Consumer Goods	Total	Intermediate Industrial Products	Consumer Goods	Total	Intermediate Industrial Products	Consumer Goods
1913	2,687.6[b]	1,385.1[b]	1,302.5[b]	5,535.9	2,545.9	2,990.0	33,225.7	13,136.4	20,089.3
1914	2,948			6,239			38,093		
1915	2,869			6,061			37,459		
1919	2,972			6,193			40,060		
1617	2,477			5,111			33,149		
1918	1,064			2,373			14,463		
1919	649			1,153			7,984		
1920	583			1,052			7,582		
1921	634			1,175			8,971		
1921/22	927			1,865			14,114		
1922/23	1,144			2,360			15,782		
1923/24	1,412			2,878			18,191		
1924/25	1,957			4,133			24,826		
1925/26	2,437			5,037			30,760		
1926/27	2,714			5,405			31,149		
1927/28	2,779.1	1,498.9	1,280.2	5,556.9	2,688.0	2,868.9	32,862.5	13,299.1	19,563.4
1928/29				6,039			35,219		
1929/30				6,884			41,957		
1931				7,183			44,134		
1932	3,781.0	2,562.8	1,218.2	7,264.0	3,876.3	3,387.7	43,144.7	22,896.3	20,248.4

Year									
1933				7,583			44,180		
1934				9,006			52,467		
1935				10,366			59,112		
1936				12,325			68,774		
1937	4,897.3	6,683.1	1,785.8	12,689.5[c]	4,086.1[c]	8,603.4[c]	41,593.5[d]	28,498.0[d]	70,091.5[d]
1938				13,073			71,987		
1939				13,395			74,452		
1940	5,496.1	7,428.0	1,931.9	14,059.4	4,457.4	9,602.0	47,653.6	29,542.1	77,195.7
1945	3,455.5	4,324.2	868.7	8,179.5	1,998.3	6,181.2	31,275.1	16,044.8	47,319.9
1946				9,510			53,849		
1947				11,351			63,810		
1948				13,834			75,296		
1949				16,533			90,224		
1950	7,745.4	9,773.6	2,028.2	18,698.7	4,815.4	13,883.3	67,536.3	31,991.4	99,527.7
1951				21,092			112,047		
1952				22,758			119,274		
1953				25,326			129,089		
1954				27,517			139,787		
1955	12,582.5	15,807.8	3,225.3	30,448.0	8,072.0	22,376.0	105,612.7	48,134.4	153,747.1

a The product coverage is the same for the indexes based on 1928 and 1955 prices, but slightly smaller for the index based on 1913 prices (see Table D-10). Weights are given in Table D-3.

b The values on Tsarist territory for 1913, for a smaller product coverage, are 2,806.2, 1,594.1, and 1,212.1 mill. rubles for all industrial materials, intermediate industrial products, and consumer goods, respectively. The following series are not covered: 308, 309, 405.2, 405.3, 406, 510, 513, 604, 605, 1506, 1507, and 1614. The corresponding values on Soviet territory are: 2,374.4, 1,309.4, and 1,065.0 mill. rubles, respectively.

c The values on post-World War II territory for 1937, for a slightly smaller product coverage, are 12,552.6, 8,176.4, and 4,376.2 mill. rubles for all industrial materials, intermediate industrial products and consumer goods, respectively. The following series are not covered: 309, 512, 1511, and 1614. The corresponding values on pre-World War II territory for 1937 are 11,857.6, 7,866.9, and 3,990.7 mill. rubles, respectively.

d The values on post-World War II territory for 1937, for a slightly smaller product coverage (see note c above), are 71,172.6, 38,806.6, and 32,366.0 mill. rubles for all industrial materials, intermediate industrial products, and consumer goods, respectively. The corresponding values on pre-World War II territory for 1937 are 64,916.4, 37,416.5, and 27,499.9 mill. rubles, respectively.

TABLE D-2

INDEXES FOR FINISHED CIVILIAN INDUSTRIAL PRODUCTS, BY GROUPS: SOVIET UNION, BENCHMARK YEARS, 1913–1955[a]

(million constant rubles)

| | ALL FINISHED CIVILIAN PRODUCTS | | | | | | MACHINERY AND EQUIPMENT | | | | | |
| | Including Miscellaneous Machinery | | Excluding Miscellaneous Machinery | | Construction Materials | | Total Including Miscellaneous Machinery | | Total Excluding Miscellaneous Machinery | | Consumer Durables | |
	1928 Prices	1955 Prices	1928 Prices	1955 Prices	1928 Prices	1955 Prices	1928 Prices	1955 Prices	1928 Prices	1955 Prices	1928 Prices	1955 Prices
1913	4,608	31,173	4,555	31,006	846.3	4,411.7	245.3	1,769.3	191.4	1,602.5	10.5	311.7
1927/28	4,594	28,825	4,505	28,613	837.5	4,242.4	373.1	2,270.6	284.8	2,058.9	16.6	380.6
1932	6,241	37,316	5,745	36,224	1,312.8	6,704.0	1,314.9	4,914.7	818.8	3,823.1	74.0	1,018.5
1937	11,641	58,590	10,884	56,474	2,168.3	10,817.6	3,693.6	10,099.7	2,936.6	7,983.8	383.8	2,093.7
1940	10,925	55,817	10,199	53,657	2,064.5	10,476.5	2,844.1	7,578.5	2,117.2	5,417.9	233.6	1,359.3
1945	4,525	24,888	4,181	23,771	836.4	4,262.4	1,237.4	2,378.7	892.8	1,261.5	37.0	160.8
1950	18,070	75,797	15,364	70,242	3,006.1	14,781.1	7,926.5	18,091.0	5,221.2	12,536.2	646.5	3,408.0
1955	27,639	117,774	23,632	109,370	5,180.1	24,775.8	10,308.8	22,637.1	6,301.8	14,232.8	1,755.3	9,657.3

| | CONSUMER GOODS | | | | | |
| | Total | | Food and Allied Products | | Textiles and Allied Products | |
	1928 Prices	1955 Prices	1928 Prices	1955 Prices	1928 Prices	1955 Prices
1913	3,516.8	24,992.0	1,938.0	19,723.9	1,568.3	4,956.4
1927/28	3,383.1	22,311.8	1,722.5	16,361.0	1,644.0	5,570.2
1932	3,613.6	25,696.9	1,945.8	19,260.9	1,593.8	5,417.5
1937	5,779.3	37,672.7	3,079.0	27,191.7	2,316.5	8,387.3
1940	6,016.9	37,762.5	3,152.0	26,753.6	2,631.3	9,649.6
1945	2,451.5	18,247.0	1,355.0	14,282.6	1,059.5	3,803.6
1950	7,137.0	42,924.6	3,599.8	29,110.2	2,890.7	10,406.4
1955	12,149.9	70,361.2	5,239.1	44,631.7	5,155.5	16,072.2

[a] Product coverage differs for the indexes based on 1928 and 1955 prices (see Table D-10). Weights are given in Table D-8.

524

INDEX FOR ALL CIVILIAN INDUSTRIAL PRODUCTS, 1928 WEIGHTS, BY GROUPS: SOVIET UNION, 1913, 1928–1955[a] (million constant rubles, 1928 prices)

| | All Industrial Products | | Intermediate Industrial Products | | | | | |
	Including Miscellaneous Machinery	Excluding Miscellaneous Machinery	Total	Ferrous Metals	Nonferrous Metals	Fuel and Electricity	Chemicals	Construction Materials
1913	5,768.0	5,742.3	2,186.0	366.7	18.7	616.2	155.5	1,068.9
1927/28	5,924.0	5,878.6	2,370.0	321.2	18.2	926.3	168.5	935.8
1928/29		6,681	2,927	381	23	1,091	213	1,219
1929/30		7,667	3,809	462	29	1,411	261	1,646
1931		8,239	4,073	444	33	1,750	296	1,550
1932	8,508.5	8,249.0	4,350.2	492.1	36.9	1,990.3	311.4	1,519.5
1933		8,745	4,685	568	36	2,261	334	1,486
1934		10,471	5,736	818	50	2,798	424	1,646
1935		12,389	6,852	1,041	73	3,278	515	1,945
1936		14,484	8,111	1,283	98	3,882	593	2,255
1937	15,742.1	15,361.0	8,274.9	1,337.5	106.2	4,110.5	658.9	2,061.8
1938		16,061	8,570	1,346	117	4,387	721	1,999
1939		16,532	9,037	1,316	144	4,732	750	2,095
1940	16,960.9	16,583.3	9,481.7	1,376.6	158.2	5,262.1	674.8	2,009.9
1945	9,774.6	9,593.4	6,593.4	866.6	115.7	4,380.1	284.6	946.3
1946		11,439.5	7,680	964	125	4,917	402	1,272
1947		13,933	9,058	1,089	143	5,694	561	1,571
1948		17,442	11,000	1,371	169	6,581	741	2,138
1949		21,190	13,009	1,690	206	7,598	960	2,555
1950	26,002.1	24,530.4	14,903.0	1,983.8	236.7	8,652.0	1,162.5	2,868.0
1951		27,003	16,788	2,277	275	9,693	1,261	3,282
1952		29,314	18,456	2,549	323	10,802	1,340	3,442
1953		32,439	20,158	2,809	347	11,967	1,422	3,613
1954		36,335	22,385	3,055	374	13,316	1,578	4,062
1955	42,247.5	40,033.5	25,077.3	3,358.3	425.1	15,139.4	1,758.7	4,395.8

(continued)

	Machinery and Equipment					Consumer Goods			
	Total Incl. Miscellaneous Machinery	Total Excl. Miscellaneous Machinery	Transport. Equipment	Agricult. Machinery	Miscellaneous Machinery	Total	Food and Allied Products	Textiles and Allied Products	Consumer Durables
1913	127.0	101.3	67.9	33.4	25.7	3,455.0	1,878.4	1,571.2	5.4
1927/28	189.8	144.4	60.8	83.6	45.4	3,364.2	1,580.7	1,774.9	8.6
1928/29		193	83	110		3,561	1,521	2,027	13
1929/30		275	114	161		3,583	1,803	1,760	20
1931		337	130	207		3,829	2,104	1,697	28
1932	690.9	431.4	261.3	170.1	259.5	3,467.4	1,784.4	1,644.3	38.3
1933		663	427	235		3,398	1,747	1,603	48
1934		909	613	296		3,826	2,160	1,587	79
1935		1,291	939	351		4,247	2,461	1,681	105
1936		1,401	1,049	352		4,972	2,649	2,137	186
1937	2,025.8	1,644.7	1,462.7	182.0	381.1	5,441.3	2,867.6	2,375.0	198.8
1938		1,707	1,557	150		5,784	3,174	2,404	206[b]
1939		1,633	1,490	143		5,862	3,081	2,624	157[b]
1940	1,571.0	1,193.4	1,100.4	93.0	377.6	5,908.2	3,049.1	2,738.1	121.0
1945	687.9	506.7	485.0	21.7	181.2	2,493.3	1,363.7	1,110.4	19.2
1946		757	717	39		3,003	1,615	1,351	37[b]
1947		1,041	959	82		3,834	1,972	1,791	71[b]
1948		1,592	1,422	170		4,850	2,498	2,215	137[b]
1949		2,363	1,998	265		5,918	3,062	2,592	264
1950	4,395.2	2,923.5	2,585.8	337.7	1,471.7	6,703.9	3,433.0	2,936.0	334.9
1951		2,310	2,020	290		7,905	3,926	3,567	412
1952		2,404	2,105	299		8,454	4,189	3,802	463
1953		2,759	2,436	323		9,522	4,433	4,525	564
1954		3,147	2,761	386		10,803	4,903	5,122	778
1955	5,733.8	3,519.8	3,058.9	460.9	2,214.0	11,436.4	5,239.6	5,287.4	909.4

a For product coverage, see Table D-10; for weights, Table D-9.
b Interpolated logarithmically.

	All Industrial Products			Intermediate Industrial Products				
	Including Miscellaneous Machinery	Excluding Miscellaneous Machinery	Total	Ferrous Metals	Nonferrous Metals	Fuel and Electricity	Chemicals	Construction Materials
1913	100	100	100	100	100	100	100	100
1927/28	107.0	106.8	94.7	86.6	98.6	128.1	139.0	86.2
1928/29		125	120	104	127	149	172	113
1929/30		141	157	124	166	183	198	153
1931		136	141	120	196	223	231	144
1932	150.4	145.2	161.1	135.9	216.6	250.5	252.5	141.5
1933		148	165	157	202	287	260	139
1934		172	192	227	291	354	310	152
1935		211	227	286	418	406	376	178
1936		233	264	350	559	473	423	206
1937	248.9	238.4	257.3	362.2	617.2	483.5	465.5	189.4
1938		241	260	366	698	506	500	185
1939		245	273	358	848	548	508	196
1940	242.8	231.5	269.9	372.4	923.9	610.6	448.9	187.2
1945	110.3	103.9	150.4	232.8	677.3	490.6	168.7	88.1
1946		135	186	260	745	551	259	115
1947		175	224	293	863	628	372	140
1948		229	286	368	993	718	492	190
1949		287	341	452	1,216	816	641	224
1950	367.4	335.4	395.6	530.2	1,406.8	908.6	780.2	261.1
1951		360	446	608	1,659	996	846	299
1952		371	475	682	1,941	1,072	887	314
1953		400	502	751	2,128	1,155	918	327
1954		446	556	817	2,311	1,266	1,016	366
1955	537.4	487.7	609.7	900.1	2,624.1	1,435.3	1,126.7	392.4
1956		529		967		1,585	1,241	411
1957		580		1,015		1,748	1,337	448
1958		605		1,086		1,914	1,434	483

(continued)

TABLE D-4 (concluded)

	Machinery and Equipment					Consumer Goods			
	Total Incl. Miscellaneous Machinery	Total Excl. Miscellaneous Machinery	Transport. Equipment	Agricult. Machinery	Miscellaneous Machinery	Total	Food and Allied Products	Textiles and Allied Products	Consumer Durables
1913	100	100	100	100	100	100	100	100	100
1927/28	129.0	129.0	81.5	227.0	129.2	110.1	82.1	132.2	122.1
1928/29		168	104	303		120	84	147	203
1929/30		227	132	421		111	93	121	297
1931		231	163	371		112	103	113	350
1932	273.5	239.1	194.1	332.1	682.0	113.8	97.2	122.9	326.8
1933		283	230	389	778	107	92	114	376
1934		362	312	463		117	112	115	449
1935		548	527	585		126	120	123	516
1936		502	405	698		154	138	156	656
1937	561.9	498.5	490.4	515.9	1,314.0	168.3	138.5	182.3	671.7
1938		481	529	377		175	146	190	618[b]
1939		438	498	306		184	151	204	519[b]
1940	421.0	338.3	402.3	206.8	1,402.2	181.1	137.1	212.5	436.1
1945	131.7	78.8	102.3	30.3	760.7	77.9	72.0	83.1	51.6
1946		167	216	65		93	82	102	119[b]
1947		262	321	138		122	101	135	273[b]
1948		423	468	326		148	115	165	610[b]
1949		614	642	552		179	144	193	855
1950	1,004.4	782.8	772.9	803.9	3,635.4	196.0	147.8	216.9	1,093.4
1951		667	579	850		234	173	259	1,406
1952		625	553	776		244	180	270	1,597
1953		686	660	754		267	195	291	1,931
1954		781	736	876		298	217	319	2,574
1955	1,256.2	888.8	819.7	1,031.9	5,618.0	316.4	227.5	333.1	3,098.3
1956		1,029	863	1,372		334	245	344	3,470
1957		1,213	886	1,889		352	253	366	3,693
1958		1,152	949	1,571		376	265	391	4,093

TABLE D-5

INDEX FOR INDUSTRIAL MATERIALS: RUSSIA,
BENCHMARK YEARS, 1860–1913[a]
(million constant rubles, 1913 prices)

1860	116.4
1865	86.9
1870	130.8
1875	203.0
1880	273.2
1885	391.6
1888	466.5
1890	509.0
1895	797.8
1900	1,212.4
1905	1,234.5
1910	1,597.7
1913	2,041.8

[a] For product coverage, see Table D-11; for weights, Table D-8.

TABLE D-6

INDEXES FOR INDUSTRIAL MATERIALS: SOVIET UNION, 1955–1958[a]
(million constant rubles, 1955 prices)

	50 Products	49 Products	46 Products	41 Products	54 Products[b]
1955	146,659	145,904	144,601	137,085	153,747
1956	157,556	156,757		147,739	164,643
1957		168,373	166,853	158,934	176,260
1958			179,608	171,654	189,015

[a] See Appendix A, technical note 3, for description of the indexes.
[b] Output assumed to remain the same as in preceding year for those products whose output has not been published (4 for 1956, 5 for 1957, and 8 for 1958).

TABLE D-7

INDEXES FOR INDUSTRIAL MATERIALS, U.S. Weights: SOVIET UNION,
BENCHMARK YEARS, 1913–1955[a]
(million constant dollars)

	1914 Prices	1929 Prices	1939 Prices	1954 Prices
1913	1,192.1	1,904.7	1,518.0	3,216.3
1927/28	1,256.3	1,991.5	1,556.7	3,296.2
1932	1,527.3	2,489.3	1,944.6	4,298.9
1937	2,680.5	4,077.2	3,354.6	7,309.2
1940	2,901.8	4,368.6	3,602.1	7,834.0
1945	1,609.6	2,394.1	1,993.9	4,356.7
1950	3,876.4	5,641.6	4,706.5	10,272.0
1955	6,308.2	9,146.4	7,581.6	16,449.3

[a] For product coverage, are Table D-10; for weights, Table D-8. Product coverage is the same for all indexes except the one with 1929 weights, which excludes beer.

529

TABLE D-8

Unit Value Weights Used in All Indexes of Industrial Production

Code		Type of Weight[a]	Soviet Union (rubles)			United States (dollars)			
			1913 (1)	1927/28 (2)	1955 (3)	1914 (4)	1929 (5)	1939 (6)	1954 (7)
I. Intermediate Industrial Products									
A. Ferrous metals									
101	Pig iron	va/m.ton		52.5	316				
102	Rolled steel	va/m.ton		47.7	198				
103	Steel ingots and castings	v/m.ton	62.4	115.8	500	21.48	25.49	33.47	78.66
103	Steel ingots and castings	va/m.ton		70.9	246				
B. Nonferrous metals									
202	Copper	v/m.ton	1075.7	995	5,950	293	388	229	650
203	Lead	v/m.ton	238.7	675	7,150	86	139	110	302
204	Zinc	v/m.ton	297.3	700	3,150	112	146	115	238
C. Fuel and electricity									
301	Electric power	v/kwh		0.0858	0.137				
301.1	Hydroelectric power	v/kwh		0.0486	0.082				
302	Anthracite	v/m.ton	9.6	10.8	98	0.02600	0.02045	0.01717	0.01398
303	Bituminous coal	v/m.ton	7.7	9.8	77	2.284	5.758	4.007	9.395
303.1	Coke	va/m.ton		7.6	76	1.286	1.963	2.034	4.971
304	Lignite	v/m.ton	3.05	6.9	57				
305	Crude petroleum	v/m.ton	25.9	28.7	52	1.118	1.706	1.280	2.702
306	Natural gas	v/m³		0.058	0.105	5.80	9.14	7.36	19.88
307	Oil shale	v/m.ton		5.7	39.7	0.00561	0.00763	0.00763	0.00356
308	Peat	v/m.ton	4.9	8.8	34				
309	Firewood	v/m³	2.46	5.7	34.9				
310	Coal (total)	v/m.ton	6.10						
D. Chemicals									
401	Soda ash	v/m.ton	70.8	73	275	12.7	29.7	23.1	36.4
402	Caustic soda	v/m.ton		195	1,100				

530

Code	Item	Unit							
	phoric fertilizer	v/m.ton	30.5	101.9	183	11.2	14.5	11.3	22.7
405.1	Phosphoric fertilizer	v/m.ton	116.6	39.9	135	59.19	48.79	30.50	42.21
405.2	Ammonium sulfate	v/m.ton	134.9	100	340	21.80	20.34	16.47	13.89
405.3	Potash fertilizer	v/m.ton	11.3	62.4	210	3.459	3.442	3.220	6.172
406	Ground natural phosphate	v/m.ton	294.3	12	42	130	193	187	256
410	Red lead	v/m.ton	348	830	7,300				
411	Zinc oxide	v/m.ton		850	2,800				
412	Synthetic dyes	v/m.ton		2,500					
416	Paper	v/m.ton	287.5	444	1,900	70.00	116.3	93.02	228.7
417	Paperboard	v/m.ton	202.7	275	1,780	38.25	56.44	44.89	123.6
418	Motor vehicle tires	v/tire	50.9	83	430	13.20	8.22	7.44	15.39
420	White lead	v/m.ton	312.9						
E.	**Construction materials**								
501	Bricks, red	v/thous.	19.4	38	205	6.12	10.65	11.67	28.22
502	Bricks, fire-clay	v/m.ton			179				
503	Bricks, magnesite	v/m.ton			355				
504	Bricks, quartzite	w/m.ton			227				
505	Bricks, sand-lime, silica, and slag	v/thous.	69.3	38	160	6.13	10.80	10.41	24.74
506	Cement	v/m.ton	18.3	33	116	5.411	8.695	8.637	16.29
507	Construction gypsum	v/m.ton	6.7	11	100	1.55	1.22	1.52	3.355
508	Construction lime	v/m.ton	7.9	15.4	100	4.326	8.643	7.787	12.96
509	Industrial timber hauled	v/m³	8	12	78				
510	Lumber	v/m³	53.8	28.6	155	5.95	11.42	9.31	28.93
	Lumber	va/m³			77				
511	Plywood	v/m³		131.9	900				
	Plywood	va/m³			822				
512	Magnesite metallurgical powder	v/m.ton		286.7	122	12.43	8.795	8.115	5.399
513	Roll roofing	v/m²	0.19	0.355	1.035	0.0633	0.0974	0.0770	0.139
514	Roofing iron	v/m.ton		192	1,248				
	Roofing iron	va/m.ton		76	748				
515	Roofing tiles	v/th.tiles		147	563	1.02	2.54	1.98	3.75
516	Asbestos shingles	v/th.pieces		127	377				
518	Rails	v/m.ton	6	11.2	572				
	Rails	va/m.ton			72				

(continued)

TABLE D-8 (continued)

Code		Type of Weight[a]	Soviet Union (rubles)			United States (dollars)			
			1913 (1)	1927/28 (2)	1955 (3)	1914 (4)	1929 (5)	1939 (6)	1954 (7)
E. Construction materials (continued)									
519	Window glass	v/m²	0.98	2.65	6.0	0.469	0.694	0.551	0.932
F. Materials of agricultural origin									
601	Alcohol, crude	va/hectoliter	5.9	15.1	110	4.20	7.27	3.91	7.29
602.1	Cotton, ginned (consumption)	va/m.ton	1,040						
604	Leather, hard	va/m.ton	463	750	8,900	506	593	383	511
605	Leather, soft	va/th.dcm²	16.9	27	300	17.0	19.8	16.4	32.9
G. Metallic minerals									
704	Iron ore	v/m.ton		5.5	29.2				
706	Manganese ore	v/m.ton		13.1	70				
II. Producer Durables									
A. Transportation equipment									
901	Automobiles	v/unit		10,800	12,100				
902	Trucks and buses	v/unit		11,258	14,150				
903	Diesel and electric locomotives	v/unit		235,000	1,040,000				
904	Steam locomotives (main-line)	v/unit		100,100	890,000				
905	Railroad freight cars	v/unit		5,450	36,500				
906	Railroad passenger cars	v/unit		16,400	245,700				
907	Railroad cars, narrow-gauge	v/unit		1,700	10,500				
908	Street and subway cars	v/unit		7,800	146,900				
B. Agricultural machinery									
1001	Tractors	v/unit		5,352	16,000				
1002	Plows, tractor-drawn	v/unit		135	2,225				
1003	Paring plows, tractor-drawn	v/unit		190	3,075				
1004	Plows, horse-drawn	v/unit		21.5	350				
1005	Harrows, tractor-drawn	v/unit		92.7	2,300				
1006	Harrows, horse-drawn	v/unit		20.9	350				
1007	Cultivators, tractor-drawn	v/unit		105	1,700				

Code		Unit		
1009	Drills, tractor-drawn	v/unit	243.3	2,000
1010	Drills, horse-drawn	v/unit	150	1,000
1011	Combined plows and drills	v/unit	65	
1013	Potato planters, tractor-drawn	v/unit		4,400
1014	Machines for planting seedlings	v/unit		7,350
1016	Combines, grain	v/unit		20,500
1017	Combines, all other	v/unit		14,400
1018	Windrowers	v/unit		4,200
1019	Reapers, horse-drawn	v/unit	163.3	840
1020	Cotton pickers	v/unit		22,700
1021	Haymowers, tractor-drawn	v/unit	166	5,050
1022	Haymowers, horse-drawn	v/unit	127.5	530
1023	Rakers, tractor-drawn	v/unit		2,680
1024	Rakers, horse-drawn	v/unit	74	695
1025	Threshers, tractor-driven	v/unit	2,272	6,055
1026	Threshers, horse-driven	v/unit	245	650
1027	Grain-cleaning machines	v/unit		4,925
1028	Winnowers, horse-drawn	v/unit	245	700
1029	Horse drivings	v/unit	130	950
1030	Chaff and silo cutters	v/unit		1,455
	C. Prime movers and electrical machinery			
1101	Steam boilers—capacity	v/m²	103.4	181.4
1102	Water turbines—capacity	v/kw	46.9	120
1103	Steam and gas turbines	v/kw	34.3	87
1104	Locomotives	v/hp	151.1	680
1105	Diesel engines	v/hp	192.5	357
1106	Other internal combustion engines	v/hp	176.4	245
1107	Turbogenerators	v/kw	24.3	40
1108	Hydroelectric generators	v/kw	66	108
1109	Electric motors—AC	v/kw	101.3	109
1110	Power transformers	v/kva	18.8	11.2
	D. Mining and industrial machinery			
1201	Coal-mining combines	v/unit		56,200

(continued)

TABLE D-8 (continued)

Code		Type of Weight[a]	Soviet Union (rubles)			United States (dollars)			
			1913 (1)	1927/28 (2)	1955 (3)	1914 (4)	1929 (5)	1939 (6)	1954 (7)
	D. Mining and industrial machinery (continued)								
1202	Coal-cutting machines	v/unit			32,100				
1203	Electric mining locomotives	v/unit			22,500				
1204	Ore-loading machines	v/unit			59,700				
1205	Deep-shaft pumps	v/unit			465				
1206	Turbodrills	v/unit			13,000				
1210	Machine tools	v/unit		2,549	17,600				
1211	Electric furnaces	v/unit			10,300				
1212	Spinning machines	v/unit		12,000	35,600				
1213	Winding machines	v/unit			26,800				
1214	Looms	v/unit		900	7,400				
1215	Cotton-carding machines	v/unit		5,900	11,400				
1216	Knitting machines	v/unit		1,100	5,800				
1217	Leather-spreading machines	v/unit			15,900				
1218	Leather-dressing machines	v/unit			16,200				
1219	Typesetting machines, linotype	v/unit		10,700	31,000				
1220	Flat-bed printing presses	v/unit		8,500	70,000				
1221	Industrial sewing machines	v/unit		132	890				
1222.1	Presses	v/unit		400	3,100				
	E. Construction and road building machinery								
1301	Excavators	v/unit		129,400	97,500				
1302	Trench excavators	v/unit		18,200	12,000				
1303	Stone crushers	v/unit		20,600	24,000				
1304	Road graders (ex. self-propelled)	v/unit		5,900	8,000				
1305	Road graders, self-propelled	v/unit			60,000				
1306	Concrete mixers	v/unit		3,500	3,400				
1307	Scrapers, tractor-driven	v/unit			27,300				

534

Code	Item	Unit							
1308		v/unit			6,000				
1309	Railroad cranes, steam	v/unit			126,000				
1310	Self-propelled cranes	v/unit			48,000				
1311	Overhead traveling cranes	v/unit			95,100				
1312	Tower cranes	v/unit			55,000				
1313	Electric elevators	v/unit			5,300				
	F. Other producer durables								
1401	Telephones	v/unit		34	107.5				
1402	Switchboards, hand-operated	v/unit		29	29				
1403	Switchborads, automatic	v/unit		35	195				
1405	Calculating machines	v/unit		400	1,400				
1406	Typewriters	v/unit		500					
	III. Consumer Goods								
	A. Food and allied products								
1501	Flour	va/m.ton	13.05	21.3	178	12.1	17.9	14.4	22.3
1502	Macaroni	va/m.ton		256	1,800				
1503	Butter	va/m.ton	171	429	1,950	79.4	143	82.5	173
1504	Vegetable oil	va/m.ton	80.4	120	1,600	43.4	68.6	51.8	116.4
1504.1	Oleomargarine	va/m.ton		909	2,600				
1504.2	Vegetable oil minus oleomargarine	va/m.ton		120	1,600				
1506	Meat slaughtering	va/m.ton	60.4	103	420	32.6	53.6	46.7	80.2
1507	Fish catch	v/m.ton	132	289	6,300[b]	114.7	270.4	142.1	325.0
1508	Soap (40%)	v/m.ton		370	1,282				
1509	Salt	v/m.ton		7.2	34.2[c]	2.307	3.526	2.912	5.627
1510	Raw sugar consumption	va/m.ton	5.0	184	825	31.9	35.6	28.9	50.5
1510.1	Refined sugar	va/m.ton	83.4	246	2,025				
1510.2	Raw sugar minus refined sugar and sugar in candy	va/m.ton		184	825				
1511	Starch and syrup	va/m.ton		104	627				
1513	Canned food	va/can	0.033	0.0564	0.50	21.7	39.7	36.3	57.1
1514	Beer	va/hectoliter	4.3	13.4	76	0.0272	0.0504	0.0310	0.0466
1515	Cigarettes	va/thous.	0.7	1.3	11	3.38	2.71	5.61	10.13
1516	Low-grade tobacco	va/20-kg. crate	1.6	3.5	43	6.28	5.78	6.06	16.1

(continued)

535

TABLE D-8 (concluded)

Code		Type of Weight[a]	Soviet Union (rubles)			United States (dollars)			
			1913 (1)	1927/28 (2)	1955 (3)	1914 (4)	1929 (5)	1939 (6)	1954 (7)
A.	Food and allied products (continued)								
1517	Matches	va/crate		6.2	27				
1518	Vodka (40%)	va/hectoliter		14	250				
1519	Candy	va/m.ton		962	2,386				
B.	Textiles and allied products								
1601	Boots and shoes	va/pair		2.1	10.7				
1602	Rubber footwear	v/pair		3.1	33				
	Rubber footwear	va/pair		1.18	4.62				
1604	Cotton fabrics	va/meter	0.12	0.347	0.82	0.0221	0.0457	0.0337	0.0772
1607	Linen fabrics	va/meter	0.23	0.662	1.0	0.0750	0.1983	0.1478	0.3520
1609	Silk and rayon fabrics	va/meter	0.68	3.0	2.3	0.254	0.398	0.0767	0.1428
1610	Woolen yarn	va/m.ton	2595.6						
1611	Woolen and worsted fabrics	va/meter	0.79	1.855	6.8	0.3604	0.6673	0.4974	0.9199
1612	Knitted goods	va/piece			4.6				
1613	Hosiery	va/pair			1.2				
1614	Felt footwear	va/pair	0.62	5.2	63	1.10	1.70	1.03	5.04
C.	Consumer durables								
1701	Bicycles	v/unit		162.5	580				
1702	Cameras	v/unit		45	720				
1703	Electric light bulbs	v/unit		0.45	1.25				
1704	Phonographs	v/unit		247	340				
1705	Radios	v/unit		122	300				
1707	Household sewing machines	v/unit		30.3	680				
1708	Clocks and watches	v/unit			171.6				
1709	Motorcycles	v/unit		1,600	4,000				

536

a Where more than one weight is given, the unit value added was used in the indexes for all civilian products in the following cases: steel ingots and castings (Tables D-3 and D-4), lumber, plywood, roofing iron, and rails (Table D-4). For 1913, it was used in the prerevolutionary index (Table D-5) in the case of rails; for 1928 and 1955, in the index for civilian finished products (Table D-2) in the case of rubber footwear. A complete list of weights used in the indexes for all civilian products is given in Table D-9.

b By error this price was not adjusted to exclude estimated turnover tax. The fact that this price was obviously too high was called to our attention by Naum Jasny in his review of the final draft. Unfortunately, it was then too late to undertake the massive recalculations required to correct the error. Fortunately, fish catch has grown at about the same percentage pace as all foods and as all industrial materials, so that its overweighting does not materially affect the indexes in which it is involved. The price was corrected to 3,300 rubles in our computations of price indexes (see Table A-18) and of value added and ruble-dollar ratios used in comparisons between the Soviet Union and the United States (see Tables A-26 and A-29). The adjusted price of 3,300 rubles was derived as follows: average retail price of 12,600 rubles (see source notes to this table) times ratio of commercial fish products excluding spoilage to fish catch (taken as 0.56, average over 1940 and 1959 from 300, 44), times 1955 ratio of all retail sales excluding turnover taxes to those including them (0.52 from retail sales of 501.9 bill. rubles as given in 226, 40, and turnover taxes of 242.4 bill. rubles as given in 141a, 799), times 0.9 to eliminate retailing mark-up. The amount of turnover taxes eliminated may, of course, be too large or too small, depending on how the rate for fish products compares with the average for all products.

c By error the unit value of 200 rubles including turnover tax was used in the index for industrial materials. This error was not discovered until it was too late to make the necessary recalculations. It is not too serious as is shown by general correspondence of all indexes for industrial materials.

dcm	= decimeter
hp	= horsepower
kg.	= kilogram
kva	= kilovolt-ampere
kw	= kilowatt
kwh	= kilowatt-hour
m²	= square meter
m³	= cubic meter
m.ton	= metric ton
thous. or th.	= thousand
sq.	= square
v	= value
va	= value added

SOURCE AND DESCRIPTION OF WEIGHTS IN TABLE D-8

Note: Unless otherwise stated, aggregate values were converted into unit values or vice versa on the basis of output as given in Appendixes B and E.

Derivation of 1913 Soviet Weights (col. 1)

103	Steel ingots and castings	Price of rails (68.4 rubles/m. ton, *243*, 644) times 1927/28 price ratio of steel to rails (see series 103 and 518, col. 2).
202	Copper	*243*, 644. Price.
203	Lead	*259*, v. Price.
204	Zinc	*259*, v. Price.
302	Anthracite	*234*, 7 f. Median of 1914 prices for 15 kinds in the Donbas.
303	Bituminous coal	*234*, 6 ff. Median of 1914 prices for 17 kinds in the Donbas.
304	Lignite	*28*, 7. Price.
305	Crude petroleum	*259*, 78. Avg. price for 2 kinds in Baku.
308	Peat	*28*, 7. Price.
309	Firewood	*28*, 17. Price.
310	Coal (total)	Value (*10*, 91). Output is sum of series 302, 303, and 304.
401	Soda ash	*259*, 98.
404	Sulfuric acid	*28*, 18. Price.
405.1	Phosphoric fertilizer	*28*, 21. Price converted from 13% P_2O_5 basis to 18.7% basis.
405.2	Ammonium sulfate	*259*, v. Price.
405.3	Potash fertilizer	*259*, v. Price.
406	Ground natural phosphate	1927/28 unit value (col. 2) divided by price index for mining industry (1913 = 100, 1928 = 106, *312*, 1929, No. 6, 179).
410	Red lead	*243*, 652. Avg. of monthly prices.
411	Zinc oxide	*243*, 646. Price.
416	Paper	*28*, 38. Avg. price for 36 kinds.
417	Paperboard	*28*, 38. Avg. price for 10 kinds.
418	Motor vehicle tires	1927/28 unit value (col. 2) divided by price index for rubber industry (1913 = 100, 1928 = 163, *312*, 1929, No. 6, 179).
419	White lead	*243*, 646. Price.
501	Red bricks	*28*, 6. Price.
505	Sand-lime, silica, and slag bricks	*28*, 6. Price.
506	Cement	*28*, 6. Avg. of prices for Portland and Roman cement.
507	Construction gypsum	*28*, 6. Price.
508	Construction lime	*28*, 6. Price.
510	Lumber	*28*, 44. Avg. of 12 prices for logs.
511	Plywood	1927/28 unit value (col. 2) divided by price index for wood products industry (1913 = 100, 1928 = 245, *312*, 1929, No. 6, 179).
513	Roll roofing	*234*, 11. Price per 3 sazhen² converted at 1 sazhen = 2.134 meters.
518	Rails	Price (68.4 rubles/ton, *243*, 644) minus unit value of steel (see series 103).
519	Window glass	1927/28 unit value (col. 2) divided by price index for glass industry (1913 = 100, 1928 = 271, *312*, 1929, No. 6, 179).

601 Crude alcohol · · · · · · · · · · Price (14 rubles/hectoliter, converted from data for 40% alcohol in vedros, *259*) times 1927/28 ratio of unit value added (col. 2) to unit value (35.57 rubles/hectoliter, converted from data for 40% alcohol in vedros, *166*, 294).

602.1 Ginned cotton consumption · · · Value added of cotton industry on Soviet territory (*201*, 192 f). Consumption is 325 th. m. tons, *363*, 1940, No. 9, 78.

604 Hard leather · · · · · · · · · · · Price (1,759 rubles/m. ton, derived by dividing 1927/28 price, median of 28 prices in *400*, 597 f, by price index for leather, 1913 = 100, 1927/28 = 162, *312*, 1929, No. 6, 179) times 1927/28 ratio of unit value added (col. 2) to price.

605 Soft leather · · · · · · · · · · · Price (64.4 rubles/th. dcm², derived by dividing 1927/28 price, median of 22 prices in *400*, 598, by price index for leather, 1913 = 100, 1927/28 = 162, *312*, 1929, No. 6, 179) times 1927/28 ratio of unit value added (col. 2) to price.

1501 Flour · · · · · · · · · · · · · · Avg. unit value added of wheat and rye flour. Avg. price of wheat flour (*28*, 23 f) minus avg. price of wheat (*28*, 45). Avg. price of rye flour (*28*, 23 f) minus avg. price of rye (*28*, 45).

1503 Butter · · · · · · · · · · · · · · Price (*28*, 23) minus price of milk in butter (1,029 rubles/m. ton, derived from price of milk, *363*, 1925, No. 11, 33, and no. of kg. of milk in 1 kg. of butter, derived as 21 from *37*, vol. 3, 1290).

1504 Vegetable oil · · · · · · · · · · Price of sunflower seed oil (*28*, 23) times 1927/28 ratio of unit value added (col. 2) to price (described in col. 2).

1506 Meat slaughtering · · · · · · · · Avg. of prices for beef and pork (*28*, 45) minus price of product marketed by agriculture (*363*, 1925, No. 11, 333).

1507 Fish catch · · · · · · · · · · · · *363*, 1925, No. 11, 340. Price.

1509 Salt · · · · · · · · · · · · · · · Value (*10*).

1510 Raw sugar consumption · · · · · Price (*247*, 71) times ratio of value added to gross value in food industry (*201*, 194).

1513 Canned food · · · · · · · · · · · Price (0.149 rubles/can, derived by dividing 1927/28 avg. price weighted by product composition, *166*, 74, by price index for food industry, 1913 = 100, 1927/28 = 169, *312*, 1929, No. 6, 179) times 1927/28 ratio of unit value added (col. 2) to price.

1514 Beer · · · · · · · · · · · · · · · Price (6.8 rubles/hectoliter, derived by dividing 1927/28 price, *166*, 294, by price index for beer industry, 1913 = 100, 1927/28 = 313, *312*, 1929, No. 6, 179) times 1927/28 ratio of unit value added (col. 2) to price.

1515 Cigarettes · · · · · · · · · · · · Price (1.50 rubles/th., derived by dividing 1927/28 price, *166*, 294, by price index for tobacco industry, 1913 = 100, 1927/28 = 190, *312*, 1929, No. 6, 179) times 1927/28 ratio of unit value added (col. 2) to price.

1516 Low-grade tobacco · · · · · · · · Price (5.10 rubles/crate, derived by dividing 1927/28 price, *166*, 294, by price index for makhorka industry, 1913 = 100, 1927/28 = 223,

312, 1929, No. 6, 179) times 1927/28 ratio of
unit value added (col. 2) to price.

1604 Cotton fabrics

Avg. price for 6 kinds (*28*, 28 f) times ratio of
value added to gross value in cotton industry
(*201*, 195).

1607 Linen fabrics

Avg. price for 15 kinds (*28*, 34 f) times ratio of
value added to gross value in linen industry
(*201*, 196).

1609 Silk and rayon fabrics

Price (*375*, 1933, Mar.–Apr.) times ratio of
value added to gross value in silk industry
(*201*, 195).

1610 Woolen yarn

Value of sales divided by volume of sales for 3
kinds (*243*, 243).

1611 Woolen and worsted fabrics

Avg. price for 9 kinds (*28*, 31 f) times ratio of
value added to gross value in woolen industry
(*201*, 195).

1614 Felt footwear

Avg. price for 2 kinds (*28*, 37) minus price of felt
used in shoes (1.59 rubles/pair, derived from
price of felt, *28*, 31, and amount of felt used in
one pair of shoes, avg. of 4¼ lbs., *28*, 31).

Derivation of 1927/28 Soviet Weights (col. 2)

101 Pig iron

Weighted avg. price for Jan.–Sept. 1928 for
conversion iron, foundry iron, spiegeleisen, and
ferromanganese (*577*, 31, weighted by outputs
in *222*, 134) minus unit value of iron ore (see
series 704).

102 Rolled steel

Value of rolled steel (output times avg. price of
quality and ordinary rolled steel, *428*, 5, the
latter weighted by outputs derived from *222*,
133) minus value of steel ingots and castings
used in rolled steel (440.3 mill. rubles). The
latter derived as value of ingots and castings
(series 103) minus computed value of ingots not
used in rolled steel (price assumed same as for
foundry iron, *577*, 82; output as steel ingots and
castings minus rolled steel, derived from *222*,
133).

103 Steel ingots and castings

Value of gross turnover of ferrous metallurgy
(1286.7 mill. rubles, adjusted monthly data in
315, Oct. 1927–Sept. 1928) minus value of pig
iron (weighted avg. price of pig iron described
in series 101) and value of rolled steel (described
in series 102).

Steel ingots and castings

Unit value added. Value of steel ingots and
castings (see series 103) minus value of pig iron
(see series 101).

202 Copper

388, 1928, No. 11, 64. Avg. of prices for Oct.
1927 and 1928 at Uralmed factory.

203 Lead

388, 1928, No. 11, 64. Price for Oct. 1928 at
Altaipolimetal and Anegar plants.

204 Zinc

388, 1928, No. 11, 64. Price for Oct. 1928 at
Anegar plant.

301 Electric power

Value of sales divided by volume of sales (*186*,
II, 137).

301.1 Hydroelectric power

Value of sales divided by volume of sales to
industrial consumers (*186*, II, 136).

302 Anthracite

575, 58. Price.

303   Bituminous coal — Value of bituminous coal and anthracite (325, 856 th. rubles, Table C-2) minus value of anthracite (for price, see series 302).

303.1   Coke — Unit value (17.4 rubles/m. ton, from value and output, *186*, I, 12, 189) minus unit value of bituminous coal (see series 303).

304   Lignite — Avg. of prices for K, O (*186*, I, 195), and RM (*273*, 720).

305   Crude petroleum — Value and output (*186*, II, 56).

306   Natural gas — 1955 unit value (col. 3) times ratio for crude petroleum unit value of 1927/28 to 1955 (series 305, cols. 2 and 3).

307   Oil shale — Assumed same as for firewood (series 309).

308   Peat — Value and output (*186*, II, 77).

309   Firewood — *232*, 6,   Price for 1926/27.

401   Soda ash — *186*, I, 68.   Price for April 1928. Also, *273*, 711.

402   Caustic soda — *186*, I, 68.   Price for April 1928. Also, *273*, 711.

404   Sulfuric acid — *273*, 709.   Price converted from 52% basis to 100% basis.

404.1   Sulfuric acid not used in phosphoric fertilizer — Same as sulfuric acid.

405.1   Phosphoric fertilizer — *388*, 1928, No. 11, 65.   Price f.o.b. station sender converted into 18.7% P_2O. Given as rubles/100 kg., but assumed to be rubles/m. ton.

405.2   Ammonium sulfate — Planned value and planned output for 1932/33 in 1927/28 prices (*400*, 1931, No. 2, 126).

405.3   Potash fertilizer — Planned value and planned output for 1932/33 in 1927/28 prices (*400*, 1931, No. 2, 126). Reduced from 100% to 41.6% K_2O content.

406   Ground natural phosphate — 1955 price (col. 3) times ratio for phosphoric fertilizer price of 1927/28 to 1955 (series 405.1, cols. 2 and 3).

410   Red lead — *273*, 701.   Price.

411   Zinc oxide — *273*, 701.   Price.

412   Synthetic dyes — Weighted avg. price of azo, sulfur, and nigrosin dyes (6,170, 1,078, and 3,950 rubles/m. ton, respectively; outputs from *222*, 177). Price of azo dyes is weighted avg. of substantive, acid, and basic azo dyes (median prices in *273*, 707; outputs in *215*, 171). Price of sulfur dyes is weighted avg. of black and color sulfur dyes (median prices in *273*, 707; outputs in *215*, 171). Price of nigrosin dyes is median of prices in *273*, 707.

416   Paper — *370*, 1929, No. 8, 54.   Weighted avg. price.

417   Paperboard — *370*, 1929, No. 8, 54.   Weighted avg. price.

418   Motor vehicle tires — First quartile of prices for 33 types (*273*, 448 f).

501   Red bricks — *273*, 553.   Price.

505   Sand-lime, silica, and slag bricks — *273*, 552.   Price.

506   Cement — *388*, 1929, No. 11, 66.   Avg. price.

507   Construction gypsum — *388*, 553.   Price.

508   Construction lime — *273*, 553.   Avg. of 4 prices.

509   Industrial timber hauled — *232*, 6.   Median of prices for 13 types of industrial wood excl. firewood.

510   Lumber — Value and output (*103*, 494 f).

511   Plywood — 1926/27 value in 1927/28 prices; 1926/27 output (*185*, 234). 1926/27 value of lumber and

plywood (*185*, 233 f) times price index (1926/27 = 100, 1927/28 = 95.4, derived from *388*, 1928, No. 11, 66) minus 1926/27 value of lumber in 1927/28 prices (for unit value, see series 510; for output, *185*, 233).

512 Magnesite metallurgical powder — *273*, 551. Price.

513 Roll roofing — Weighted avg. price of rubberoid, pergamin, and tarpaper roofing, and tarpaper subroofing. Median prices for each in *273*, 549. Outputs of each (*186*, 105) converted from rolls into m² by factors derived from data for 1935 in *149*, 94 f, and *393*, 1937, No. 3, 3 (for details, see *567*, Part 3, notes to series 723.1).

514 Roofing iron — *430*, 28. Price for roofing and pickled iron.

Roofing iron — Unit value added. Unit value of roofing iron minus unit value of steel ingots and castings (see series 103).

516 Asbestos shingles — Value and output (*186*, II, 105).

518 Rails — *430*, 28. Price.

Rails — Unit value added. Unit value of rails minus unit value of steel ingots and castings (see series 103).

519 Window glass — *273*, 531. Derived from median price for case containing 11 m² of first-quality ordinary glass.

601 Crude alcohol (100%) — Price (35.57 rubles/hectoliter, converted from data for 40% alcohol in vedros, *166*, 294) times ratio of value added to value of crude alcohol. The former derived as value added of alcohol and vodka (164,741 th. rubles in Table C-2) minus value added of vodka (output times unit value added, for which see series 1518). The latter derived as value of alcohol and vodka (362,711 th. rubles in Table C-2) minus value of vodka (output times price, for which see 1518).

604 Hard leather — Median of prices for 28 kinds of 2nd sort (*273*, 597 f) times ratio of unit value added to unit value for all leather. Value and value added of all leather: 581,221 and 152,980 th. rubles in Table C-2.

605 Soft leather — Median of prices for 22 kinds (*273*, 598) times ratio of unit value added to unit value for all leather (see series 604).

704 Iron ore — Value and output (*186*, I, 234).

706 Manganese ore — Weighted avg. cost derived from data in *200*, 100 ff.

901 Automobiles — 1927/28 price of 1½-ton truck (9,200 rubles) times 1937 ratio of avg. price of GAZ-A and M-1 (*236*, 7) to price of 1½-ton truck (*236*, 7). 1927/28 price of 1½-ton truck derived from value of all trucks (for unit value, see series 902), outputs of trucks of 1½ tons and of over 4 tons (*222*, 165), and 1937 ratio of price of 1½-ton trucks to price of trucks over 4 tons (*236*, 7).

902 Trucks and buses — Value and output of trucks only (monthly data, *315*, Oct. 1927–Sept. 1928) since no buses were produced in 1927/28.

903 Diesel and electric locomotives — Assumed to be double the price of freight locomotives S.O. (118,700 rubles), approximate

		1945 ratio (*526*, 52 f). Price of S.O. derived as 1927/28 price of freight locomotive E. (*526*, 7) times 1949 price ratio of S.O. to E. (*526*, 55).
904	Steam locomotives	Weighted avg. price of locomotives E. (94,900 rubles, *526*, 7), O.V. (79,100), M. (79,100), and S.U. (116,600). Outputs in *222*, 163. Prices of O.V. and M. derived as 1927/28 price of E. times 1949 price ratio of N. (assumed to be same as prices of O.V. and M.) to E. (*526*, 55). Price of S.U. derived as 1927/28 price of E. times 1949 price ratio of S.U. to E. (*526*, 55).
905	Railroad freight cars	Weighted avg. price of 2-axle flat cars, 2- and 4-axle box cars (*370*, 1929, No. 19, 59), and tank cars (11,520 rubles). Outputs in *222*, 163 f. Price of tank cars is weighted avg. of prices of 2-axle tank cars (price of 2-axle flat cars times 1937 price ratio of 2-axle tank cars to 2-axle flat cars, *526*, 24) and 4-axle tank cars (price of 4-axle box cars times 1937 price ratio of 4-axle tank cars to 4-axle box cars, *526*, 24).
906	Railroad passenger cars	Weighted avg. price of 2- and 4-axle long-distance cars (*370*, 1929, No. 19, 61). Outputs in *222*, 164 (suburban cars counted as 2-axle long-distance cars).
907	Narrow-gauge railroad cars	Price of 2-axle flat cars (series 905) times 1937 price ratio of narrow-gauge flat cars with brakes to standard-gauge 2-axle flat cars (*236*, 9).
908	Street and subway cars	Price of 4-axle long-distance cars (series 906) times 1913 price ratio of street cars to 3rd class passenger cars (*28*, 12).
1001	Tractors	Value and output (*186*, I, 261).
1002	Plows, tractor-drawn	Price of horse-drawn plows (series 1004) times 1955 price ratio of tractor-drawn (col. 3) to horse-drawn plows (series 1004, col. 3).
1003	Paring plows, tractor-drawn	Price of horse-drawn plows (series 1004) times 1955 price ratio of tractor-drawn paring plows (col. 3) to horse-drawn plows (series 1004, col. 3).
1004	Plows, horse-drawn	Median of prices for 3 types (*273*, 499 f).
1005	Harrows, tractor-drawn	Median of prices for 8 imported disk types (*273*, 790).
1006	Harrows, horse-drawn	Median of prices for 32 types (*273*, 500 f).
1007	Cultivators, tractor-drawn	*273*, 790. Price of imported type.
1008	Cultivators, horse-drawn	Median of prices for 19 imported types (*273*, 790 f).
1009	Drills, tractor-drawn	*273*, 791. Price of imported type.
1010	Drills, horse-drawn	Median of prices for 27 types (*273*, 501).
1011	Combined plows and drills	Median of prices for 7 types (*273*, 502).
1019	Reapers, horse-drawn	Weighted avg. of median prices for nonraking and self-raking types (*273*, 502). Outputs in *222*, 162.
1021	Haymowers, tractor-drawn	Median of prices for 12 imported types (*273*, 793).
1022	Haymowers, horse-drawn	Avg. of prices for 2 types (*273*, 502).
1024	Rakers, horse-drawn	Median of prices for 7 imported types (*273*, 794).
1025	Threshers, tractor-drawn	Median of prices for 23 imported types (*59*, 786).

1026	Threshers, horse-drawn	Median of prices for 14 types (*273*, 502 f).
1028	Winnowers, horse-drawn	Assumed same price as for horse-driven threshers (series 1020).
1029	Horse drivings	*273*, 504. Price for no. 1 × 2.
1101	Steam boilers (capacity)	Price per boiler (11,156 rubles) divided by avg. capacity per boiler (calculated as 107.9 m² from *222*, 154). Price is linear interpolation (based on rated capacities) of prices for boilers of 100 and 120 m² capacities (*273*, 235) with pressure of 12 atmospheres, assuming avg. capacity of 107.9 m².
1102	Water turbines (capacity)	*525*, 137.
1103	Steam and gas turbines (capacity)	Unit value (72,133 rubles, derived from monthly values and outputs in *315*, Oct. 1927–Sept. 1928) divided by avg. capacity per unit (calculated as 2,100 kw from *222*, 154).
1104	Locomobiles (capacity)	Unit value (12,190 rubles, derived from monthly values and outputs in *315*, Oct. 1927–Sept. 1928) divided by avg. capacity per unit (calculated as 80.66 hp from *222*, 154).
1105	Diesel engines (capacity)	Unit value (37,250 rubles, derived from monthly values and outputs in *315*, Oct. 1927–Sept. 1928) divided by avg. capacity per unit (calculated as 193.53 hp from *222*, 154, and *312*, 1929, No. 2, 158.
1106	Other internal combustion engines (capacity)	Unit value (2,572 rubles, derived from monthly values and outputs in *315*, Oct. 1927–Sept. 1928) divided by avg. capacity per unit (calculated as 14.58 hp from *222*, 154).
1107	Turbogenerators (capacity)	Value and output (*186*, II, 134).
1108	Hydroelectric generators (capacity)	Unit value for turbogenerators (series 1107) times 1955 price ratio of hydroelectric generators in 1955 (col. 3) to turbogenerators (series 1107, col. 3).
1109	Electric motors, A.C. (capacity)	Unit value (791 rubles, derived from value and output in *186*, II, 134) divided by avg. capacity per unit (calculated as 7.81 kw from *221*, 45).
1110	Power transformers (capacity)	Unit value (2,509 rubles, derived from value and output in *186*, II, 134) divided by avg. capacity per unit (calculated as 133.3 kva from *222*, 155).
1210	Machine tools	Sum of monthly values divided by sum of monthly outputs (*315*, Oct. 1927–Sept. 1928).
1212	Spinning machines	*273*, 362. Midpoint of range of prices for 5 types.
1214	Looms	*273*, 362. Median of prices for 4 types.
1215	Cotton-carding machines	Sum of monthly values divided by sum of monthly outputs, both for carding machines (*315*, Oct. 1927–Sept. 1928).
1216	Knitting machines	*273*, 365. Midpoint of range of prices.
1219	Typesetting machines, linotype	*273*, 341. Median of prices for 6 types.
1220	Flat-bed printing presses	*273*, 341.
1221	Industrial sewing machines	*273*, 369. Median of prices for 6 types.
1222.1	Presses	*237*, 171. Median of prices (item 280). Rounded.
1301	Excavators	Unweighted avg. price of single-bucket (132,500 rubles) and multiple-bucket excavators (126,300 rubles). The latter are derived from 1955 prices (86,000 rubles for single-bucket, median

of 13 prices in *235*, II, 3 f; and 82,000 rubles for multiple-bucket, median of 11 prices in *235*, II, 10 f) divided by ratio (0.649) of 1955 to 1927/28 price for single-bucket internal combustion caterpillar excavators with capacity of 0.35 m². The ratio derived from relation of 1955 and 1949 prices (*235*, II, 10 f, and *527*, 20) and price index for road-building and construction machinery (1937 = 100, 1927/28 = 83.8, 1949 = 120.8, *527*, Table IV).

1302 Trench excavators — 1955 price (col. 3) divided by ratio of 1955 to 1927/28 price (derived as 0.649 in series 1301).

1303 Stone crushers — 1955 price (13,400 rubles, price for combined crushers in *235*, II, 24) divided by ratio of 1955 to 1927/28 price (derived as 0.649 in series 1301).

1304 Road graders — Weighted avg. price of medium (7,100 rubles) and light (5,800 rubles) road graders. Outputs from *222*, 166. Price of medium graders derived from price of heavy graders (9,300 rubles) times 1955 price ratio of medium to heavy graders (calculated as 0.7619 from *235*, II, 20). 1927/28 price of heavy graders derived from 1937 price (11,100 rubles in *527*, 20) times price index for road-building machinery (1937 = 100, 1927/28 = 83.8, *527*, Table IV, 20). Price of light graders derived from 1927/28 price of medium graders above times U.S. price ratio of light to medium graders (calculated as 0.82 from *467*, 103).

1306 Concrete mixers — *273*, 380. Midpoint of range of prices.

1401 Telephones — Avg. price of wall (no. 1145T) and table (no. 1405) hand-operated telephones (*237*, 110). No automatic telephones produced in 1927/28.

1402 Switchboards, hand-operated — Value (*186*, II, 135) and output (*222*, 165).

1403 Switchboards, automatic — *237*, 101. Price of 21,000 rubles given for exchange with 600 lines.

1405 Calculating machines — *273*, 443. Avg. price of 2 makes of 13-digit calculating machines.

1406 Typewriters — *237*, 18. Median of prices including delivery for 25 types.

1501 Flour — Value added from Table C-2.

1502 Macaroni — Avg. price (365 rubles/m. ton) presumably weighted by 1932 planned assortment (*166*, 294) minus value per unit of flour (109 rubles/m. ton, value from Table C-2).

1503 Butter — Price (2,145 rubles/m. ton) minus price of milk in butter (1,716 rubles/m. ton, from price of milk, *388*, 1929, No. 5, 29, and no. of liters of milk per kg. of butter in 1913, *138*, 90). Price of butter derived from 1926/27 price (2,000 rubles/m. ton, *233*, 37) times ratio of 1926/27 to 1927/28 prices (calculated as 1.0727 from *388*, 1929, No. 5, 29).

1504 Vegetable oil — Price (411 rubles/m. ton) times ratio of value added to value (0.992, from Table C-2). Price derived from 1927/28. Avg. price for 1932 planned product composition (414.38 rubles/m.

APPENDIX D

ton, *166*, 294) times ratio of avg. cost weighted by 1927/28 output mix to avg. cost weighted by 1932 planned mix (0.992, from *166*, 69, 294).

1504.1 Oleomargarine

Price (1,200 rubles/m. ton, assumed same as in 1926/27, *233*, 41) minus difference between price and unit value added of vegetable oil (see series 1504).

1504.2 Vegetable oil minus oleomargarine

Same as for vegetable oil (series 1504).

1506 Meat slaughtering

Price (827 rubles/m. ton) times 1934 ratio of wages to total cost in meat industry (0.125, *222*, 34). Price derived from 1926/27 price 840 rubles/m. ton) times ratio of 1927/28 to 1926/27 for avg. price of product marketed by agriculture (0.984, from *388*, 1929, No. 5, 29). 1926/27 price derived from 1926/27 price of beef (800 rubles/m. ton, *233*, 11) times 1926/27 ratio of avg. price of product marketed by agriculture to avg. price of beef (1.05, from *388*, 1929, No. 5, 29).

1507 Fish catch

166, 294. Avg. price weighted presumably by 1932 planned assortment.

1508 Soap (40%)

Assumed same as price in 1926/27 (*233*, 21).

1509 Salt

186, 69. Price for April 1928.

1510 Raw sugar consumption

Price excluding excise tax (302 rubles/m. ton, *186*, 69, 559) minus cost of raw materials (118 rubles/m.ton, *186*, 553).

1510.1 Refined sugar

Price excluding excise tax (364 rubles/m. ton, *186*, 69, 559) minus cost of raw materials (118 rubles/m. ton, *186*, 553).

1510.2 Raw sugar minus refined sugar and sugar in candy

Same as for raw sugar (series 1510).

1511 Starch and syrup

Price (315 rubles/m. ton) times ratio of value added to value of starch and syrup industry (0.33 from Table C-2). Price derived from avg. price for 1932 planned product composition (319 rubles/m. ton, *166*, 294) times ratio of avg. cost weighted by 1927/28 output mix to that weighted by 1932 planned mix (0.9866, from *166*, 220).

1513 Canned food

Avg. price weighted by output mix (0.252 rubles/can, *166*, 74) times 1934 ratio of wages to total cost in canned food industry (0.224, *215*, 216).

1514 Beer

Price (21.3 rubles/hectoliter, converted from vedros, *166*, 294) times ratio of value added to value of beer industry (0.628 from Table C-2).

1515 Cigarettes

Price (2.75 rubles/thous., f.o.b. receiving station, *166*, 294) times 1926/27 ratio of value added to value of large-scale industry (0.472, from *48*).

1516 Low-grade tobacco

Price (11.4 rubles/crate, *166*, 294) times ratio of value added to value of large-scale makhorka industry in 1926/27 (0.31, from *48*).

1517 Matches

186, 69. Price for April 1928.

1518 Vodka (40%)

Unit value (28.24 rubles/hectoliter, value and output in *186*, 577) minus price of crude

546

		alcohol (14.23 rubles/hectoliter, converted from vedros, *166*, 294).
1519	Candy	Price (1580 rubles/m. ton) times ratio of unit value added to price of raw sugar (see series 1510). Price of candy assumed to be 112% of price of all confectionery (1,407 rubles/m. ton, *166*, 294).
1601	Boots and shoes	Value added (Table C-2).
1602	Rubber footwear	Value and output (*103*, 494 f).
	Rubber footwear	Unit value (see series 1602) times 1932 ratio of wages to total cost in rubber industry (0.381, *215*, 174).
1604	Cotton fabrics	Value added of cotton industry including ginning (Table C-2).
1607	Linen fabrics	Value added of linen industry including primary processing (Table C-2). Output taken as 175.3 mill. m² from outputs for 1927 and 1928.
1609	Silk and rayon fabrics	Value added of silk industry (Table C-2).
1611	Woolen and worsted fabrics	Value added of woolen industry including washing (Table C-2).
1614	Felt footwear	Price of women's gray felt shoes in Yaroslav region (7 rubles/pair, *273*, 609) times ratio of value added to value for felt industry (0.743, from Table C-2).
1701	Bicycles	Avg. price presumably including delivery (175 rubles/bicycle, *237*, 143) minus value of 2 tires (4.4 rubles/tire, *273*, 449) and 2 inner tubes (1.85 rubles/inner tube, *273*, 443).
1702	Cameras	*273*, 437 f. Median of prices for 4 types.
1703	Electric light bulbs	Value and output (*186*, 134).
1704	Phonographs	Price of bicycle including tires (175 rubles/bicycle, *237*, 143) times 1937 price ratio of phonographs PT-3 to bicycles (1.412, from *443*, 11).
1705	Radios	*273*, 205. Median of prices for 4 types.
1707	Household sewing machines	Value and output (sums of monthly data in *315*, Oct. 1927–Sept. 1928).
1709	Motorcycles	*237*, 143. Median of prices, presumably including delivery, for 9 types.

Derivation of 1955 Soviet Weights (col. 3)

101	Pig iron	Weighted avg. price (345 rubles/m. ton) of conversion iron, foundry iron, ferromanganese, ferrosilicon, and spiegeleisen (*576*, 31, weighted by outputs in *180*, 109) minus price of iron ore (see series 704).
102	Rolled steel	Price (731 rubles/m. ton) times 1927/28 ratio of unit value added to unit value (0.271, see series 102, col. 2). Price is avg. of quality steel (1,173 rubles/m. ton) and ordinary steel (604 rubles/m. ton), weighted by outputs (*180*, 110). Price of quality steel is weighted price of carbon, alloyed, and spring engineering steel; carbon, alloyed, and high-speed tool steel; special and dynamo steel; and cold rolled steel (*576*, 30, weighted by outputs in *72*, 21 ff). Price of ordinary steel is weighted avg. of

547

prices in col. 3 below, weighted by output (*180*, 110):

	Un-weighted 1955 Price	1950 Ratio of Weighted to Un-weighted Price	Weighted 1955 Price
	(1)	(2)	(3)
a. Steel rims	722	0.892	644
b. Steel wire rods	559	1.101	616
c. Steel beams and channels (girders)	525	0.981	515
d. Rails	566	1.01	572
e. Steel bars	542	1.093	592
Rounds	542		
Squares	534		
Equal-leg angles	551		
L-bars	542		
f. Steel sheets			642
Plate	552	1.08	596
Thin sheet	653	1.101	719

Col. 1: *576*, 29; price for *e* is unweighted avg. of subgroups.
Col. 2: Ratio of weighted avg. price to unweighted avg. price (derived from *430*, 28, 55).
Col. 3: Col. 1 times col. 2 prices. Price for *f* is avg. of 2 subgroups weighted by 1950 planned percentage distribution of output (*12*, 33).

103 Steel ingots and castings	Value of steel not used in rolled steel (3,823.8 mill. rubles; output of steel ingots and castings minus output of rolled steel; price assumed same as for foundry iron, *576*, 31) plus value of steel used in rolled steel (18,835.7 mill. rubles; output of rolled steel; 1955 price of rolled steel minus unit value added of rolled steel, series 102).
Steel ingots and castings	Unit value added. Value (derived above) minus value of pig iron (for price, see series 101).
202 Copper	*576*, 35. Price.
203 Lead	*235*, I, v. Median of prices for 6 kinds.
204 Zinc	*235*, I, v. Median of prices for 6 kinds.
301 Electric power	Avg. cost to power station (0.0938 rubles/kwh, *576*, 48) times 1941 planned ratio of selling price to cost (1.464, derived from 1941 planned production and value, *505*, 11, and cost in 1941, *72*, 570).
301.1 Hydroelectric power	Assumed 60% of unit value of electric power (series 301).
302 Anthracite	*235*, I, 691 f. Median of prices for 8 kinds.
303 Bituminous coal	Value of all coal (29,034.5 mill. rubles; output, *180*, 144; price 74.2 rubles/m. ton) minus value of lignite (6,532.2 mill. rubles from price in

series 304 and output) and of anthracite (5,958.4 mill. rubles from price in series 302 and output). Price of all coal is weighted avg. for Moscow, Donets, Georgia, other regions of European Russia, Urals, Kuznets, Karaganda, other regions of Central Asia, Eastern Siberia, and the Far East (mostly medians in *235*, I, 691 ff; weighted by outputs mostly in *180*, 142).

303.1   Coke — Median of prices for 63 kinds and grades (174 rubles/m. ton in *235*, I. 696 ff) times 1927/28 ratio of unit value added to unit value (series 303.1, col. 2).

304   Lignite — *235*, I, 692 f. Median of 38 prices.

305   Crude petroleum — Value derived from as 3,684 mill. rubles from output in conventional tons (*180*, 133) and price per conventional ton (36.4 rubles/ton). The latter derived from value of a conven. ton of coal (93.4 rubles/ton, from output in conven. tons, *180*, 133, and value of all coal, series 303) times cost ratio for a conven. ton of petroleum to coal (0.3895, from index in *410*, 1956, No. 1, 23).

306   Natural gas — Value derived as 940.2 mill. rubles from output in conven. tons (*180*, 133) and price per conven. ton (82.47 rubles/ton). The latter derived from price of a conven. ton of coal (93.4 rubles/ton, series 305) times cost ratio for a conven. ton of natural gas to coal (0.883, from index in *410*, 1956, No. 1, 23).

307   Oil shale — Weighted avg. of median prices for Estonia, Leningrad, and Volga region (prices in *235*, I, 696, and outputs in *180*, 166).

308   Peat — Weighted avg. of medians of zonal prices for milled peat and lump peat (*235*, I, 700). For weighting, 61% of all peat is taken as milled (*395*, 1956, No. 2, 4).

309   Firewood — *576*, 52. Price for 1956.

401   Soda ash — *576*, 56. Price.

402   Caustic soda — *576*, 56. Price.

404   Sulfuric acid — *576*, I, 687. Price converted from 75% basis to 100% basis.

404.1   Sulfuric acid not used in phosphoric fertilizer — Same as for sulfuric acid.

405.1   Phosphoric fertilizer — Price of sulfuric acid (see series 404) times 1939 cost ratio of phosphoric fertilizer to sulfuric acid (0.749, from *318*, May 12, 1939).

405.2   Ammonium sulfate — 1927/28 price (see series 405.2, col. 2) times phosphoric fertilizer price ratio of 1955 to 1927/28 (3.4, see series 405.1).

405.3   Potash fertilizer — 1927/28 price (see series 405.3, col. 2) times phosphoric fertilizer price ratio of 1955 to 1927/28 (3.4, see series 405.1).

406   Ground natural phosphate — Price of phosphoric fertilizer (see series 405.1) times 1934 cost ratio of ground natural phosphate to phosphoric fertilizer (0.31 from adjusted data in *351*, 1935, No. 5, 38).

410   Red lead — *235*, I, 678. Price.

411	Zinc oxide	*235*, I, 678. Avg. price for 2 types.
416	Paper	*235*, I, 859 ff. Median of prices for 68 kinds.
417	Paperboard	*235*, I, 862. Median of prices for 21 kinds. For waterproof paperboard and electric insulated paperboard, only the median price for each group was taken.
418	Motor vehicle tires	*235*, I, 808 f. Median of 60 prices.
501	Red bricks	*235*, I, 9 ff. Median of 143 prices for brand no. 75.
502	Fire-clay bricks	*235*, I, 18. Median of 6 prices for first and second quality.
503	Magnesite bricks	*235*, I, 26 ff. Median of 72 prices for first and second quality.
504	Quartzite bricks	*235*, I, 24. Median of prices for 3 types.
505	Sand-lime, silica, and slag bricks	*235*, I, 12 f. Median of 33 prices for brand 100.
506	Cement	Weighted avg. price of Portland (avg. of Portland 300 and 400), Portland slag, puzzuolana, and all other cements (assumed to have same price as Portland 500). All prices in *576*, 72, and outputs in *180*, 278.
507	Construction gypsum	*235*, I, 4 f. Median of 57 prices for second quality.
508	Construction lime	*235*, I, 5 ff. Median of 110 prices for second quality.
509	Industrial timber hauled	Assumed to have same price as structural timber in 1956 (*576*, 52).
510	Lumber	*576*, 52. Price for 1956.
	Lumber	Unit value added. Price of lumber minus price of timber (series 509).
511	Plywood	*576*, 52. Price for 1956.
	Plywood	Unit value added. Price of plywood minus price of timber (series 509).
512	Magnesite powder	*235*, I, 31. Median of 3 prices.
513	Roll roofing	Weighted avg. of median prices for rubberoid, pergamin, and tarpaper roofing and tarpaper subroofing for zone 1 (*235*, I, 83 f). Outputs (*180*, 301) given for first 2 separately and for second 2 together; the latter broken down according to output of rubberoid and pergamin roofing.
514	Roofing iron	Unweighted avg. price (1,337 rubles/m. ton, *576*, 29) times 1950 ratio of weighted to unweighted avg. price (0.9333, *430*, 28, 78).
	Roofing iron	Unit value added. Price (series 514) minus price of steel ingots and castings (see series 103).
515	Roofing tiles	Weighted avg. of median prices for each republic. Prices in *235*, III, 387–514, and outputs in *180*, 307 ff.
516	Asbestos shingles	*235*, I, 48. Price for ordinary unpainted shingles for zone 1.
518	Rails	Unweighted avg. price (566 rubles/m. ton, *576*, 29) times 1950 ratio of weighted to unweighted avg. price (1.01, *430*, 28, 58).
	Rails	Unit value added. Price of rails minus price of steel ingots and castings (see series 103).
519	Window glass	*235*, I, 35. Zone I price for first quality 2-mm. glass sheets from 0.4 to 1 m².

601	Crude alcohol	Price of rye grain in alcohol (530 rubles/hecto-liter) times ratio of nonmaterial to material costs of alcohol (0.199, *180*, 371). Price of rye grain in alcohol derived as retail price of rye flour (2,100 rubles/m. ton, *458*, 377) times 0.8 to eliminate retailing and milling cost, the result divided by the amount of alcohol produced from one ton of rye grain (318 hectoliters, *180*, 406).
604	Hard leather	Price (36,000 rubles/m. ton) times 1934 ratio of wages to total cost in leather industry (0.249, *222*, 34). Price derived as 1927/28 price (2,850 rubles/m. ton, see series 604, col. 2) times ratio for shoes of 1955 price (80 rubles/pair, see series 1601) to 1927/28 unit value (6.3 rubles/pair, value from Table C-2).
605	Soft leather	Price (1,300 rubles/th. dcm², derived in same way as hard leather above, 1927/28 price 104.4 rubles/th. dcm², see series 605, col. 2) times 1934 ratio of wages to total cost in leather industry (0.249, *222*, 34).
704	Iron ore	*576*, 27. Avg. of range of prices for Krivoi Rog ore with iron content of 57–65%.
706	Manganese ore	Price of iron ore (see series 704) times 1927/28 ratio of manganese ore to iron ore (2.38, see series 704 and 706, col. 2).
901	Automobiles	*235*, II, 905. Price for Pobeda.
902	Trucks and buses	Weighted avg. price of trucks (13,700 rubles for 4-ton Zis truck 150 in *235*, II, 903) and buses (31,450 rubles, avg. of 2 prices in *235*, II, 904). Outputs in *138*, 57.
903	Diesel and electric locomotives	*235*, II, 878. Price for diesel locomotive.
904	Steam locomotives	*235*, II, 877. Price for type LV.
905	Railroad freight cars	Weighted avg. of median prices for flat cars, hopper cars, box cars, refrigerator cars, cars for cement, and oil tank cars (*235*, II, 879 ff). Outputs in *180*, 222.
906	Railroad passenger cars	Weighted avg. price of upholstered compartment cars, unupholstered cars without compartments, mail cars, and baggage cars (*235*, II, 882 f). Weighted arbitrarily by 3, 5, 1, and 1, respectively.
907	Narrow-gauge railroad cars	Median of prices for self-dumping hoppers, narrow-gauge flat cars, hoppers, and hoppers for peat (*235*, II, 882).
908	Street and subway cars	Weighted avg. price of streetcars (135,000 rubles, median of prices for 5 types in *235*, II, 883 f) and subway cars (220,700 rubles, assumed to be same as for unupholstered passenger cars without compartments in *235*, II, 882). Outputs in *180*, 220.
1001	Tractors	Weighted avg. price of DT-54, KD-35, KDP-35, Trelevoch, Belorus, Universal, and KhTZ tractors (*235*, II, 908). Outputs in *180*, 228 f.
1002	Plows, tractor-drawn	Median of prices for 14 types (*235*, III, 160).
1003	Paring plows, tractor-drawn	Avg. price of 2 types (*235*, III, 161).
1004	Plows, horse-drawn	*235*, III, 160. Price.
1005	Harrows, tractor-drawn	*235*, III, 161. Median of 3 prices.

APPENDIX D

1006	Harrows, horse-drawn	Assumed to be same as price of horse-drawn plows (series 1004).
1007	Cultivators, tractor-drawn	*235*, III, 161 f. Median of prices for 11 types.
1008	Cultivators, horse-drawn	*235*, III, 162. Median of prices for 3 types.
1009	Drills, tractor-drawn	*235*, III, 163. Median of prices for first 5 types.
1010	Drills, horse-drawn	*235*, III, 163. Price of grain drills.
1013	Potato planters, tractor-drawn	*235*, III, 164. Price.
1014	Machines for planting seedlings	*235*, III, 163. Avg. price for 2 types.
1016	Grain combines	*235*, III, 165. Avg. price for 2 types.
1017	All other combines	Weighted avg. price of beet-harvesting, corn-harvesting, potato-harvesting, and silage-harvesting combines (*235*, III, 165 ff). Outputs in *180*, 230.
1018	Windrowers	*235*, III, 166. Price.
1019	Reapers, horse-drawn	*235*, III, 166. Price for self-raking horse-drawn reapers.
1020	Cotton pickers	*235*, III, 168. Price.
1021	Haymowers tractor-drawn	*235*, III, 164. Median of prices for 4 types.
1022	Haymowers horse-drawn	*235*, III, 164. Price.
1023	Rakers, tractor-drawn	*235*, III, 164. Avg. price.
1024	Rakers, horse-drawn	*235*, III, 164. Avg. price.
1025	Threshers, tractor-driven	*235*, III, 167. Avg. price for 2 complex and semicomplex threshers.
1026	Threshers, horse-driven	Price of tractor-driven threshers (see series 1025) times 1927/28 price ratio of horse-driven to tractor-driven threshers (see series 1025 and 1026, col. 2).
1027	Grain-cleaning machines	*235*, III, 166. Avg. price.
1028	Winnowers, horse-drawn	*235*, III, 166. Price.
1029	Horse drivings	*235*, III, 166. Price.
1030	Chaff and silo cutters	*235*, III, 168. Avg. price.
1101	Steam boilers (capacity)	Median of prices for 3 types (29,200 rubles, *235*, II, 939) divided by corresponding capacity (161 m², *235*, II, 939).
1102	Water turbines (capacity)	Price of steam turbines (see series 1103) times 1927/28 price ratio of water turbines to steam turbines (1.37, from series 1102 and 1103, col. 2).
1103	Steam and gas turbines (capacity)	Weighted avg. of median prices of turbines of 100,000 kw and over, 500,000 kw, 25,000–49,000 kw, and up to 25,000 kw (*235*, II, 1072 f). Outputs in *180*, 216.
1104	Locomobiles (capacity)	Median of prices for 11 types of locomobiles (85,000 rubles, *235*, II, 991 ff) divided by corresponding capacity (125 hp, *235*, II, 939).
1105	Diesel engines (capacity)	Median of prices for 14 types (214,000 rubles, *235*, II, 983) divided by corresponding capacity (600 hp, *235*, II, 983).
1106	Other internal combustion engines (capacity)	Price (5,400 rubles, *235*, II, 989) divided by capacity (22 hp, *235*, II, 989).
1107	Turbogenerators (capacity)	Price of largest turbogenerator (481,000 rubles, *235*, II, 533) divided by its capacity (12,000 kw, *235*, II, 533).
1108	Hydroelectric generators (capacity)	Price of largest hydroelectric generator (432,400 rubles, *235*, II, 534) divided by its capacity (4,000 kw, *235*, II, 534).

1109 Electric motors, A.C. (capacity) — Weighted avg. price of motors under 100 kw (derived as 73.5 rubles/kw from median of 17 prices for 40 kw motors in *235*, II, 473 ff) and motors over 100 kw (derived as 215 rubles/kw from avg. price of 190 kw 3,000 volt motor and 180 kw 6,000 volt motor in *235*, II, 512). Outputs in *180*, 214 f.

1110 Power transformers (capacity) — Median of prices for 8 types (167,500 rubles, *235*, II, 686 ff) divided by corresponding capacity (15,000 kva, *235*, II, 686 ff).

1201 Coal-mining combines — *235*, III, 4 ff. Avg. price for Donbas-1 and UKMG-2M types.

1202 Coal-cutting machines — *235*, III, 6. Avg. price.

1203 Electric mining locomotives — *235*, III, 11. Median of 8 prices.

1204 Ore-loading machines — *235*, III, 7 f. Median of 6 prices.

1205 Deep-shaft pumps — *235*, III, 53 f. Median of 6 prices.

1206 Turbodrills — *235*, III, 49. Median of 5 prices.

1210 Machine tools — Weighted avg. of median prices for turret lathes, automatic and semi-automatic turret lathes, slotters, planers, milling machines, broaching machines, shapers, radial drilling machines, vertical drilling machines, boring machines, grinding machines, sharpening machines, gear-cutting machines, tool-grinding machines (*235*, II, 58–87) and bench and engine lathes (24,400 rubles). Price of bench and engine lathes is weighted avg. of median prices for bench lathes, screw-cutting lathes, boring and turning lathes, face and wheel lathes, and automatic and semi-automatic bench and engine lathes (prices in *235*, II, 56 ff; weighted by planned outputs for 1941 in *72*, 95). Outputs in *180*, 208 f.

1211 Electric furnaces — *235*, II, 758. Median of 5 prices.

1212 Spinning machines — Avg. price of water spinning machines (33,800 rubles, median of 27 prices in *235*, II, 220 ff) and water doubling frames (37,300 rubles, median of 14 prices in *235*, II, 223 f).

1213 Winding machines — *235*, II, 233 f. Median of 30 prices.

1214 Looms — *235*, II, 238 f. Median of 13 prices.

1215 Cotton-carding machines — *235*, II, 218 f. Median of 5 prices.

1216 Knitting machines — *235*, II, 252.

1217 Leather-spreading machines — *235*, II, 254. Median of 3 prices.

1218 Leather-dressing machines — *235*, II, 255 f. Avg. price.

1219 Typesetting, machines linotype — *235*, II, 288 f. Median of prices for 5 types.

1220 Flat-bed printing presses — *235*, II, 294. Median of 6 prices.

1221 Industrial sewing machines — *235*, II, 250 ff. Median of prices for heads only for 23 types.

1222.1 Presses — Price of machine tools (see series 1210) times 1927/28 price ratio of presses to machine tools (0.177 from series 1210 and 1222.1, col. 2).

1301 Excavators — Weighted avg. price of single-bucket (100,000 rubles, median of 15 prices in *235*, II, 3 f, 779) and multiple-bucket (82,000 rubles, median of 11 prices in *235*, II, 10 f) excavators. Outputs in *180*, 234 f.

1302 Trench excavators — *235*, II, 19. Median of 5 prices.

1303	Stone crushers	*235*, II, 24 f. Median of 17 prices.
1304	Road graders	*235*, II, 20. Price for medium road graders.
1305	Self-propelled road graders	*235*, II, 20. Median of 3 prices.
1306	Concrete mixers	*235*, II, 27 f. Median of 11 prices.
1307	Scrapers, tractor-driven	*235*, II, 19. Median of 3 prices.
1308	Bulldozers	*235*, II, 19 f, 53 f, 779. Median of prices.
1309	Railroad cranes, steam	*235*, II, 13 f. Median of 11 prices.
1310	Self-propelled cranes	*235*, II, 12, 14. Median of 11 prices.
1311	Overhead traveling cranes	Weighted avg. price of electric (99,750 rubles, median of 64 prices in *235*, II, 1001 ff) and hand-operated (8,610 rubles, avg. of median prices for single- and double-beam cranes in *235*, II, 997 ff) cranes. Weighted by 1935 output (*215*, 80).
1312	Tower cranes	*235*, II, 14 f. Median of 16 prices.
1313	Electric elevators	*235*, II, 45 f. Median of 8 prices.
1401	Telephones	Unweighted avg. price of hand-operated (102.5 rubles, avg. price for table and table-wall telephones in *235*, II, 816) and automatic (112.5 rubles, avg. price for table and wall telephones in *235*, II, 815) telephones.
1402	Switchboards, hand-operated	*235*, II, 817 f. Median of 9 prices.
1403	Switchboards, automatic	Price of an automatic switchboard (117,000 rubles, *235*, II, 819) divided by its no. of lines (600, *235*, II, 819).
1405	Calculating machines	*235*, II, 301 f. Median of 5 prices.
1501	Flour	Commercial cost of processing in large-scale flour and groats industry (3,454 mill. rubles, *133a*, 43) divided by corresponding output (19,702.4 th. m. tons, *133a*, 41). Data adjusted upward to account for higher costs in small-scale industry.
1502	Macaroni	Price (4,000 rubles/m. ton) minus price of flour (2,200 rubles/m. ton, see series 1501). Price derived as retail price (4.35 rubles/kg., *458*, 1955, No. 4, 377) times 0.9 to eliminate retailing mark-up.
1503	Butter	Price (25,000 rubles/m. ton) times ratio of wages to total cost in dairy products industry (0.078, *180*, 371). Price derived as 1953 (same as 1955) retail price (27.8 rubles/kg.) times 0.9 to eliminate retailing mark-up. Retail price is avg. price in 1952 (30.6 rubles/kg., *442*) times price ratio, 1953 to 1952 (0.090, *364*, 4/1/53).
1504	Vegetable oil	Price (12,700 rubles/m. ton) times 1934 ratio of wages to total cost in vegetable oil industry (0.126, *215*, 216). Price derived as 1927/28 price (411 rubles/m. ton, see series 1504, col. 2) times price ratio, 1955 to 1927/28 (30.88, derived from price index for sunflower oil for 1952 on 1927/28 = 100 in *441*, 152, and official price index for vegetable oil for 1955 on 1952 = 100 in *226*, 131).
1504.1	Oleomargarine	Price (13,700 rubles/m. ton) minus difference between price and unit value added of vegetable oil (11,100 rubles/m. ton, see series 1504).
1504.2	Vegetable oil minus oleomargarine	Same as for vegetable oil (series 1504).

1506 Meat slaughtering   Price (11,100 rubles/m. ton) times ratio of wages to total cost in meat industry (0.038, *180*, 371). Price derived as retail price (11,835 rubles/m. ton) times 0.935 (*133*, 112) to eliminate retailing mark-up. Retail price is weighted avg. price of beef, pork, lamb, and fowl (prices in *133*, 112; outputs in *180*, 378).

1507 Fish catch   Retail price (12,600 rubles/m. ton) times 0.5 (ratio of 1927/28 in col. 2 to avg. price paid by worker's family for fish, *422*) to eliminate trade mark-up, transportation, and spoilage. Retail price derived as weighted avg. 1952 retail price (14,000 rubles/m. ton) of fresh and frozen (pike, perch), salted (herring), and other fish (sturgeon) (prices in *442*; weighted by percentage distribution of 1955 production in *363*, 1956, No. 1, 85) times price ratio, 1955 to 1952 (0.9, *226*, 131). But see note b to this table.

1508 Soap (40%)   Price (3,400 rubles/m. ton) times 0.377 to eliminate turnover taxes (*594*, 131). Price derived as retail price (3,725 rubles/m. ton) times 0.9 to eliminate retailing mark-up. Retail price derived as value of sales of household and toilet soap (*226*, 68) divided by sales (assumed to be 90% of output).

1509 Salt   Price (200 rubles/m. ton) times 0.171 to eliminate turnover taxes (*594*, 131). Price derived as retail price (0.222 rubles/kg., derived as 1952 price in *442* times price ratio, 1955 to 1952, given as 0.66 in *408*, 1956, No. 5, 83) times 0.9 to eliminate retailing mark-up.

1510 Raw sugar consumption   Price (8,500 rubles/m. ton) times ratio of wages to total cost in sugar industry (0.097, *180*, 29, 371). Price is retail price for Sept. 1954 in Moscow (9.4 rubles/kg., *458*, 1955, No. 4, 377) times 0.9 to eliminate retailing mark-up. Price same in 1955 as 1954 (*408*, 1956, No. 5, 83).

1510.1 Refined sugar   Price (9,700 rubles/m. ton) times ratio of wages to total cost in sugar industry (0.097, *180*, 29, 371). Price is retail price for Sept. 1954 in Moscow (10.7 rubles/kg., *458*, 1955, No. 4, 377) times 0.9 to eliminate retailing mark-up. Price same in 1955 as 1954 (*408*, 1956, No. 5, 83).

1510.2 Raw sugar minus refined sugar and sugar in candy   Same as for raw sugar (series 1510).

1511 Starch and syrup   Price (1,900 rubles/m. ton) times 1927/28 ratio of unit value added to price (0.33, see series 1511, col. 2). Price derived as price of yeast (4,800 rubles/m. ton, *67*, 228) times 1927/28 price ratio of starch and syrup to yeast (0.4, from series 1511, col. 2, and *166*, 294).

1513 Canned food   Price (2.20 rubles/can) times 1934 ratio of wages to total cost in canned food industry (0.223, *215*, 216). Price derived as retail price (2.39 rubles/can, value of sales excl. canned milk in *226*, 40, divided by volume of sales, assumed to be 90% of output excl. canned milk in *180*, 399) times 0.9 to eliminate retailing mark-up.

1514 Beer	Price (338 rubles/hectoliter) times 1934 ratio of wages to total cost in beer and yeast industry (0.224, *215*, 216). Price is retail price for April 1954 (4.5 rubles/liter, *461*, 1955, No. 3, 111) times 1926/27 ratio of wholesale to retail price incl. excise and special tax (0.75 from data in *185*, 518).
1515 Cigarettes	Price (58 rubles/th.) times 1934 ratio of wages to total cost in tobacco industry (0.196, *215*, 216). Price is retail price (64 rubles/th.) times 0.9 to eliminate retailing mark-up. Retail price derived from sales (assumed to be 90% of output) and value of sales (11,423 mill. rubles, value of sales of cigarettes and makhorka in *226*, 42, minus value of sales of makhorka). Value of sales of makhorka (576 mill. rubles) derived as retail price of makhorka (see series 1516) times volume of sales of makhorka (assumed to be 90% of output).
1516 Low-grade tobacco	Price (220 rubles/20 kg.-crate) times 1934 ratio of wages to total cost in tobacco industry (0.196, *215*, 216). Price derived as retail price for Sept. 1954 (0.60 rubles/50 gms., *461*, 1955, No. 3, 112) times 0.9 to eliminate retailing mark-up.
1517 Matches	Price (75 rubles/crate) times ratio of wages to total cost in match industry (0.358, *180*, 245). Price derived as retail price (80 rubles/crate) times 0.9 to eliminate retailing mark-up. Retail price derived as 1952 retail price (*442*) times price ratio, 1955 to 1952 (0.68, from data in *226*, 131).
1518 Vodka (40%)	Price (3,500 rubles/hectoliter) times ratio of wages to total cost of alcohol industry (0.070, *180*, 371). Price is retail price (3,890 rubles/ hectoliter) times 0.9 to eliminate retailing mark-up. Retail price derived as 1952 retail price (*442*) times price ratio, 1953 to 1952 (1.11, *364*, 4/1/53).
1519 Candy	Price (24,600 rubles/m. ton) times ratio of wages to total cost in sugar industry (0.097, see series 1510, col. 3). Price derived as 1927/28 price (1,580 rubles/m. ton, see series 1519, col. 2) times price ratio for raw sugar of 1955 to 1927/28 (15.6, from series 1510, col. 3, and 1927/28 price incl. excise tax in *186*, 69).
1601 Boots and shoes	Price (80 rubles/pair) times ratio of wages to total cost in shoe industry (0.134, *180*, 322). Price is weighted avg. price of leather shoes (incl. shoes with rubber soles) and cloth shoes (outputs in *180*, 351). Price of cloth shoes derived as value of sales (*226*, 42) divided by sales (assumed to be same as output in *180*, 351). Price of leather shoes in 1952 weighted avg. price (110.8 rubles/pair) times price ratio, 1955 to 1952 (0.82, from data in *226*, 131). 1952 price is weighted avg. price of

women's and men's leather shoes and rubber-soled leather shoes (prices in *442*; weighted by 1955 percentage share of formed shoes [19%] and nonformed shoes [81%], *180*, 351).

1602 Rubber footwear — Price derived as retail price (37.7 rubles/pair) times 1927/28 ratio of wholesale to retail price (0.87, from wholesale price derived from output and value of output in *103*, 494 f, and retail price in *442*). 1955 price derived as value of sales (*226*, 42) divided by sales (assumed to be same as output).

Rubber footwear — Unit value added. Price (series 1602) times 0.14 to eliminate turnover tax (*594*, 131).

1604 Cotton fabrics — Price (7.5 rubles/meter) times ratio of wages to total cost in cotton industry (0.109, *180*, 322). Price derived as weighted avg. retail price for first quarter, 1956 (8.3 rubles/meter, *394*, 1956, No. 11, 60) times 0.9 to eliminate retailing mark-up.

1607 Linen fabrics — Price (11 rubles/meter) times ratio of wages to total cost in linen industry (0.094, *180*, 322). Price derived as weighted avg. retail price for first quarter, 1956 (12.2 rubles/meter, *394*, 1956, No. 11, 60) times 0.9 to eliminate retailing mark-up.

1609 Silk and rayon fabrics — Price (28.4 rubles/meter) times ratio of wages to total cost in silk industry (0.080, *180*, 322). Price derived as weighted avg. retail price for first half, 1956 (31.5 rubles/meter, *394*, 1956, No. 11, 60) times 0.9 to eliminate retailing mark-up.

1611 Woolen and worsted fabrics — Price (105 rubles/meter) times ratio of wages to cost in woolen industry (0.065, *180*, 322). Price derived as weighted avg. retail price for first half, 1956 (116.1 rubles/meter, *394*, 1956, No. 11, 60) times 0.9 to eliminate retailing mark-up.

1612 Knitted goods — Price (21 rubles/unit) times ratio of wages to total cost in knitted goods industry (0.22, *410*, 1957, No. 7, 34). Price derived as retail price (23.6 rubles/unit, from value of sales in *226*, 42, divided by sales, assumed to be 90% of output) times 0.9 to eliminate retailing mark-up.

1613 Hosiery — Price (55 rubles/pair) times ratio of wages to total cost in knitted goods industry (0.22, *410*, 1957, No. 7, 34). Price derived as retail price (6.13 rubles/pair, from value of sales in *226*, 42, divided by sales, assumed to be same as output) times 0.9 to eliminate retailing mark-up.

1614 Felt footwear — Price (85 rubles/pair) times 1927/28 ratio of value added to value in felt industry (0.743 from Table C-2). Price derived as retail price (88 rubles/pair, from value of sales in *226*, 42, divided by volume of sales, assumed to be 90% of output) times 0.95 to eliminate retailing mark-up.

1701 Bicycles — Retail price (645 rubles/unit in *442*) times price ratio, 1953 to 1952 (0.90, *364*, 4/1/53).

1702	Cameras	*458*, 1955, No. 4, 378. Price.
1703	Electric light bulbs	*458*, 1955, No. 4, 378. Price.
1704	Phonographs	*458*, 1955, No. 4, 378. Price.
1705	Radios	*585*, 48. Price for 3-tube radio in 1952. Price same in 1955 as 1952.
1707	Household sewing machines	Value of sales (1,120 mill. rubles) divided by sales (*408*, 1956, No. 5, 82). Value is sum of values for all republics except Karelo-Finnish (1,085 mill. rubles, *226*, 231 ff) times ratio for value of sales of all "other nonfood products" of USSR to USSR excl. Karelo-Finnish Republic (1.032, from data in *226*, 43, 231 ff).
1708	Clocks and watches	Value of sales (3,293 mill. rubles) divided by sales (*408*, 1956, No. 5, 82). Value is sum of values for all republics except Karelo-Finnish Republic (3,191 mill. rubles, *226*, 231 ff) times ratio described above (see series 1707).
1709	Motorcycles	Value of sales (871 mill. rubles) divided by volume of sales (*226*, 57). Value derived as summed values of bicycles and motorcycles (2,496 mill. rubles, *226*, 43) minus value of bicycles (sales in *226*, 57, and price in series 1701).

Derivation of 1914 U.S. Weights (col. 4)

103	Steel ingots and castings	*640*, 74. Avg. unit value of unrolled steel ingots produced for sale and interplant transfer. Also, *618*, 546.
202	Copper	*626*, 150. Also, *637*, 580.
203	Lead	*626*, 150.
204	Zinc	*626*, 150.
301.1	Hydroelectric power	Avg. price of electric power for 1912 and 1917 (derived from sales and value of sales to commercial and industrial consumers in *626*, 159).
302	Anthracite	*626*, 142.
303	Bituminous coal	*626*, 142.
304	Lignite	Unit value of bituminous coal in 1914 (see series 303) times 1929 ratio of unit value of lignite to bituminous coal (0.869, see series 303 and 304, col. 5).
305	Crude petroleum	*626*, 146. Converted from barrels at 1 barrel = 139.07 kg.
306	Natural gas	*626*, 146.
401	Soda ash	*655*, No. 493, 192. Price.
404	Sulfuric acid	*655*, No. 493, 186. Price. Converted from 66° Baumé basis to 100% H_2SO_4 basis with 66° Baumé = 93.19% H_2SO_4.
405.1	Phosphoric fertilizer	*618*, 498. Price. Converted from 16% P_2O_5 basis to 18.7% basis.
405.2	Ammonium sulfate	*655*, No. 473, 225. Price f.a.s. N.Y.
405.3	Potash fertilizer	*655*, No. 473, 225. War Industry Board avg. price for muriate of potash (80–85% K_2O) converted to 41.6% K_2O.
406	Ground natural phosphate	*626*, 148.
410	Red lead	*655*, No. 473, 204. Price of dry red lead in N.Y.
416	Paper	*618*, 481 f. Avg. unit value of all kinds excl. building paper.

417 Paperboard   *618*, 482.

418 Motor vehicle tires   *618*, 480. Pneumatic tires and casing (motor vehicle tires, excl. motorcycle and bicycle tires).

501 Red bricks   *618*, 522. Common brick.

505 Sand-lime, silica, and slag bricks   *618*, 533. Sand-lime brick.

506 Cement   *626*, 147. Converted from barrels at 1 barrel = 170.55 kg.

507 Construction gypsum   *640*, 74. Price of crude gypsum.

508 Construction lime   *626*, 147.

510 Lumber   *649*, 1923, 233. Avg. mill value for 1915. Also, *640*, 74. Converted from board ft. at 1 bd. ft. = 0.00236 m³.

512 Magnesite metallurgical powder   *626*, 148.

513 Roll roofing   *618*, 482. Building paper. Converted from short tons into metric tons and then into m² at 1 m² = 1.48 kg.

516 Asbestos shingles   1929 unit value (see series 516, col. 5) times unit value ratio for asbestos of 1915 to 1929 (0.4, from data in *649*, 1932, 693).

519 Window glass   *618*, 528.

601 Crude alcohol   Price of 188° denatured alcohol in N.Y. ($0.338/ gallon, *655*, No. 473, 212) times ratio of value added to value of distilled liquors, excl. internal revenue taxes (0.471, from *609*, 1939, II, part 1, 228). Also, *640*, 75.

604 Hard leather   Avg. price of 3 kinds (Hemlock middle, no. 1, oak, in Boston; scoured back, in Boston; and Union backs, steer, tannery run, in N.Y.— $0.398/lb. in *655*, No. 473, 124 f) times ratio of value added for leather, tanned, curried, and finished, to computed value of leather (0.577, from *640*, 75).

605 Soft leather   Avg. price of 2 kinds (chrome calf, grade B, in Boston; and side, black, chrome, tanned, grade B, in Boston—$0.274/ft.² in *655*, No. 473, 123 f) times ratio described above in series 604. Converted at 1 ft.² = 9.29 dcm².

1501 Flour   *640*, 75. Value added of flourmill and gristmill products and 2-year avg. output (1912 and 1913). Converted from barrels into m. tons at 1 barrel = 196 lbs.

1503 Butter   Avg. unit value ($0.284/lb. in *609*, 1914, 353, 349) times ratio for creamery butter of value added to value (0.1267, from *609*, 1939, II, part 1, 80).

1504 Vegetable oil   Value added of crude cottonseed oil (*609*, 1929, II, 709) and output (*640*, 70).

1506 Meat slaughtering   Avg. value per lb. of fresh meat, edible offal, and dressed poultry (value and output in *609*, 1914, II, 333) times ratio for slaughtering and meat packing of value added to value (0.1284, from *609*, 1914, II, 319).

1507 Fish catch   Avg. price of 3 kinds (pickled or cured cod, in Gloucester, Mass.; pickled herring, in N.Y.; and pickled, salted, and large mackerel, in Boston—in *655*, No. 473, 107).

559

1509	Salt	*626*, 148.
1510	Raw sugar consumption	Value added and output of beet sugar in *649*, 1923, 311, 213.
1511	Starch and syrup	Avg. price of 42° glucose and corn starch in N.Y. ($0.0418/lb., from *655*, No. 493, 86) times ratio for glucose and starch of value added to value (0.2358, from *609*, 1914, vol. II, 411).
1513	Canned food	Value added of canning and preserving (*609*, 1914, II, 363) and output of canned food excl. milk and meat products. Converted from lbs. into 400-gm. cans.
1514	Beer	Value added of malt liquors excl. internal revenue tax (*609*, 1939, II, part 1, 210) and 2-year (1914 and 1915 fiscal years) avg. output (*640*, 70). Converted from barrels into hectoliters at 1 barrel = 1.1735 hectoliters.
1515	Cigarettes	Value added excl. internal revenue tax (*609*, 1914, 1029) and output (*618*, 414).
1516	Low-grade tobacco	Value added excl. internal revenue tax of "other tobacco products" (*609*, 1914, 1029) and output (*618*, 415). Converted from lbs. into 20-kg. crates.
1604	Cotton fabrics	Avg. unit value of cotton woven goods excl. "other cotton products" (*609*, 1914, 32) times ratio for cotton manufactures of value added to value (0.3676, from *609*, 1914, 20). Converted from square yards to m²; then adjusted to linear meters, Soviet width (1.4286 linear meters = 1 m² from Appendix A, technical note 1).
1607	Linen fabrics	Avg. unit value (*609*, 1914, 152) times ratio for linen goods of value added to value (0.3837, from *609*, 1914, 148). Converted from square yards to m². No adjustment to linear meters necessary since avg. Soviet width is assumed to be 100 cm.
1609	Silk and rayon fabrics	Avg. unit value of broad woven silk (*609*, 1914, 138) times ratio for silk industry of value added to value (0.4314, from *609*, 1914, 125). Converted from yards to m²; then adjusted to linear meters, Soviet width, at 1.0753 linear meters = 1 m² (*265*, II, 124 ff).
1611	Woolen and worsted fabrics	Value added of woolen and worsted goods (*609*, 1914, 51) and output (*618*, 457). Converted from square yards to m²; adjusted to linear meters, Soviet width (0.7812 linear meters = 1 m² from *478*, 121).
1614	Felt footwear	Avg. value of 4 lbs. of saddle felt (*609*, 1914, 77, 4 lbs. of felt needed to produce a pair of Soviet felt shoes) times ratio for felt goods of value added to cost of materials (0.6529 from *609*, 1914, 51).

Derivation of 1929 U.S. Weights (col. 5)

103	Steel ingots and castings	*618*, 546.
202	Copper	*626*, 150. Also, *637*, 580.
203	Lead	*626*, 150.
204	Zinc	*626*, 150.

301.1 Hydroelectric power — 626, 159. Sales and value of sales of electric power to commercial and industrial consumers.

302 Anthracite — 626, 142.

303 Bituminous coal — 626, 142.

304 Lignite — 638, 797.

305 Crude petroleum — 626, 146. Converted from barrels at 1 barrel = 139.07 kg.

306 Natural gas — 626, 146.

401 Soda ash — 655, No. 521, 34. Price.

404 Sulfuric acid — 655, No. 521, 33. Price converted from 66° Baumé basis to 100% H_2SO_4 basis with 66° Baumé = 93.19% H_2SO_4.

405.1 Phosphoric fertilizer — 618, 498. Avg. price for nonammoniated superphosphate and concentrated phosphates. Converted from 16% P_2O_5 basis to 18.7% basis.

405.2 Ammonium sulfate — 655, No. 521, 35. Price in N.Y.

405.3 Potash fertilizer — 655, No. 521, 35. Price for muriate of potash (80–85%) in N. Y. converted to 41.6% K_2O.

406 Ground natural phosphate — 626, 148.

410 Red lead — 655, No. 521, 51. Price of dry red lead in N.Y.

416 Paper — 609, 1939, II, part 1, 643 f. Avg. unit value of all kinds excl. building paper.

417 Paperboard — 618, 482.

418 Motor vehicle tires — 618, 480. Pneumatic tires and casing (motor vehicle tires, excl. motorcycle and bicycle tires).

501 Red bricks — 618, 522. Common brick.

505 Sand-lime, silica, and slag brick — 618, 533. Sand-lime brick.

506 Cement — 626, 147. Converted from barrels at 1 barrel = 170.55 kg.

507 Construction gypsum — 610, 4. Value of shipment of primary product.

508 Construction lime — 626, 147.

510 Lumber — 649, 1938, 695.

512 Magnesite metallurgical powder — 626, 148.

513 Roll roofing — 618, 482. Building paper. Converted from short into m. tons, then into m² at 1 m² = 1.48 kg.

516 Asbestos shingles — 618, 520.

519 Window glass — 618, 528.

601 Crude alcohol — Price of denatured alcohol at works ($0.57/gallon, 655, No. 521, 33) times avg. ratio for distilled liquors in 1914 and 1939 of value added to value of product excl. internal revenue tax (0.482, from 609, 1939, II, part 1, 228).

604 Hard leather — Avg. price of 3 kinds (sole oak insides, scoured backs and sole, and Union backs—$0.50/lb. in 655, No. 521, 25) times avg. ratio for leather industry in 1914 and 1939 of value added to value of product (0.538, from 640, 75).

605 Soft leather — Avg. price of 2 kinds (chrome calf, grade B; and side black, chrome, tanned, grade B, in Boston—$0.342/sq. ft. in 655, No. 521, 25) times avg. ratio described above in series 604.

1501 Flour — Value added of flour and other grain mill products (609, 1929, II, 134) and output (605, 131, 128). Converted from barrels at 1 barrel = 196 lbs.

1503 Butter — Avg. price of creamery butter and whey ($0.437/lb. in 609, 1929, II, 71) times ratio of value

		added to value of product (0.1481, from *609*, 1929, II, 67).
1504	Vegetable oil	Value added to crude cottonseed oil (*609*, 1929, II, 709) and avg. output for 1929 and 1930 (*649*, 1938, 678).
1506	Meat slaughtering	Unit value of fresh meat (value and output in *609*, 1929, II, 176) times ratio for meat packing of value added to value (0.1341, from *609*, 1929, II, 173).
1507	Fish catch	Avg. price of 3 kinds (pickled or cured cod, in Gloucester, Mass.; pickled herring, in N.Y.; and salted mackerel, in N.Y.—in *655*, No. 521, 23).
1509	Salt	*626*, 148.
1510	Raw sugar consumption	Value added (*605*, 192) and output of beet sugar including molasses (*609*, 1929, II, 20).
1511	Starch and syrup	Avg. price of 42° mixing glucose and laundry starch in N.Y. ($0.0485/lb., from *655*, No. 521, 23, 37) times ratio for glucose and starch of value added to value (0.3717, from *609*, 1929, II, 121).
1513	Canned food	Value added of canning and preserving (*609*, 1929, II, 80) and output of canned food excl. milk and meat products. Converted from lbs. into 400-gm. cans.
1515	Cigarettes	Value added of cigar and cigarette industry incl. internal revenue tax (*609*, 1929, II, 1376) times ratio for tobacco industry of value added excl. and incl. tax (0.4682, from *626*, 302, and *609*, 1929, II, 1376). Output (*626*, 186).
1516	Low-grade tobacco	Value added incl. internal revenue tax for chewing and smoking tobacco (*609*, 1929, II, 1377) times ratio for tobacco industry of value added excl. and incl. tax (0.4682, from *626*, 302, and *609*, 1929, II, 1376). Output (*618*, 415). Converted from lbs. into 20-kg. crates.
1604	Cotton fabrics	Avg. unit value of woven goods over 12″ wide (*609*, 1929, II, 249) times ratio for cotton industry of value added to value (0.4108, from *609*, 1929, II, 247). Adjusted as in col. 4.
1607	Linen fabrics	Avg. unit value of linen and partly linen woven goods (*618*, 446) times ratio for linen goods of value added to value (0.4645, from *609*, 1929, II, 241). No width adjustment (see col. 4).
1609	Silk and rayon fabrics	Avg. unit value of broad woven silk goods excl. velvet, plush, upholstery, and tapestry (*609*, 1929, II, 339) times ratio for silk and rayon manufactures of value added to value (0.4363, from *609*, 1929, II, 337). Adjusted as in col. 4.
1611	Woolen and worsted fabrics	Avg. unit value (*609*, 1929, II, 415) times ratio for woolen and worsted goods industry of value added to value (0.3923, from *609*, 1929, II, 412). Adjusted as in col. 4.
1614	Felt footwear	Avg. value of 4 lbs. (see col. 4) of shoe and slipper felt (*609*, 1929, II, 425) times ratio for felt goods of value added to cost of materials (0.7406, from *609*, 1929, II, 424).

PRODUCTION INDEXES AND WEIGHTS

Derivation of 1939 U.S. Weights (col. 6)

103	Steel ingots and castings	640, 74.
202	Copper	626, 150.
203	Lead	626, 150.
204	Zinc	626, 150.
301.1	Hydroelectric power	626, 159. Sales and value of sales to commercial and industrial consumers.
302	Anthracite	626, 142.
303	Bituminous coal	626, 142.
304	Lignite	71, 12 A-4. Value of net shipments.
305	Crude petroleum	626, 146.
306	Natural gas	626, 146.
401	Soda ash	655, No. R 1069, 40. Price.
404	Sulfuric acid	655, No. R 1069, 39. Price. Converted from 66° Baumé basis to 100% H₂SO₄ basis unit 66° Baumé = 93.19% H₂SO₄.
405.1	Phosphoric fertilizer	609, 1939, II, part 1, 801. Unit value of non-ammoniated superphosphate incl. concentrated phosphates converted to 18.7% P₂O₅ basis. Converted from short to m. tons.
405.2	Ammonium sulfate	655, No. R 1069, 41. Price, bulk, ex vessel, port.
405.3	Potash fertilizer	655, No. R 1069, 41. Price for 80% muriate of potash converted to 41.6% K₂O basis.
406	Ground natural phosphate	626, 148.
410	Red lead	655, No. R 1069, 37. Price for dry red lead in N.Y.
416	Paper	609, 1939, II, part 1, 643 f. Avg. unit value of all kinds excl. building paper.
417	Paperboard	609, 1939, II, part 1, 644. Avg. unit value.
418	Motor vehicle tires	609, 1939, II, part 2, 21. Pneumatic tires and casings.
501	Red bricks	609, 1939, II, part 2. Red burning clay bricks, all sizes.
505	Sand-lime, silica, and slag bricks	655, No. R 1069, 36. Price of sand-lime brick.
506	Cement	626, 147. Converted from barrels at 1 barrel = 170.55 kg.
507	Construction gypsum	610, 4. Value of shipments of primary product.
508	Construction lime	626, 147.
510	Lumber	649, 1942, 823. Also, 640, 74. Converted from bd. ft. at 1 bd. ft. = 0.00236 m³.
512	Magnesite metallurgical powder	626, 148.
513	Roll roofing	609, 1939, II, part 1, 644. Building paper. Converted from short to m. tons and then to m² at 1 m² = 1.48 kg.
516	Asbestos shingles	655, No. R 1069, 38. Individual shingles, composite price, factory.
519	Window glass	609, 1939, II, part 2, 73.
601	Crude alcohol	Price at works ($0.299/gallon, 655, No. R 1069, 39) times ratio for distilled liquors of value added to value of excl. internal revenue tax (0.494, from 609, 1939, II, part 1, 228). Also, 640, 75.
604	Hard leather	Avg. price of 3 kinds (sole, oak scoured backs, and Union backs, steers—$0.349/lb., 655, No. R 1069, 24) times ratio of value added for leather, tanned, curried, and finished, to total

563

		computed value of leather (0.498, from *640*, 75).
605	Soft leather	Avg. price of 2 kinds (chrome calf, grade B, and side back, chrome, tanned, grade B, in Boston —$0.306/sq. ft., *655*, No. R 1069, 24) times ratio described above in series 604. Converted at 1 sq. ft.^{2} = 9.29 dcm^2.
1501	Flour	Value added of flour and other grain mill products *609*, 1939, II, part 1, 134) and output (*640*, 69). Converted from barrels (1 barrel = 196 lbs.) into m. tons.
1503	Butter	Avg. price of creamery butter (*609*, 1939, II, part 1, 83) times ratio for creamery butter of value added to value (0.1493, from *609*, 1939, II, part 1, 80).
1504	Vegetable oil	Value added of crude cottonseed oil and output (*609*, 1939, II, part 1, 28 G5, 28 G1).
1506	Meat slaughtering	Avg. unit value of fresh meat (value and output in *609*, 1939, II, part 1, 57) times ratio for meat packing of value added to value (0.1593, from *609*, 1939, II, part 1, 54).
1507	Fish catch	Avg. price of 3 kinds (pickled or cured cod, in Gloucester, Mass.; pickled herring, in N.Y.; and salted mackerel, in N.Y.—in *655*, No. R 1069, 23).
1509	Salt	*626*, 148.
1510	Raw sugar consumption	Value added and output of beet sugar including molasses (*609*, 1939, II, part 1, 178).
1511	Starch and syrup	Avg. price of 42° unmixed glucose and corn starch in N.Y. ($0.0375/lb. from *655*, No. R 1069, 22 f) times ratio for corn syrup, corn sugar, corn oil and starch of value added to value (0.4396, from *609*, 1939, II, part 1, 243).
1513	Canned food	Value added of canned fish, crustacea and mollusks, and canned and dried fruits and vegetables, incl. canned soups (*609*, 1939, II, part 1, 105, 111) and output of canned food excl. meat and milk products. Converted from lbs. into 400-gm. cans.
1514	Beer	Value added of malt liquors excl. internal revenue tax (*609*, 1939, II, part 1, 216) and output (*608*, 132). Converted from barrels into hectoliters at 1 barrel = 1.1735 hectoliters.
1515	Cigarettes	Value added excl. internal revenue tax for cigarettes (*609*, 1939, II, part 1, 271) and output (*626*, 186).
1516	Low-grade tobacco	Value added and output of chewing and smoking tobacco (*609*, 1939, II, part 1, 274). Converted from lbs. into 20-kg. crates.
1604	Cotton fabrics	Avg. unit value of woven goods over 12″ wide (*609*, 1939, II, part 1, 291) times ratio for cotton industry of value added to value (0.5042, from *609*, 1939, II, part 1, 287). Adjusted for width as in col 4.
1607	Linen fabrics	1937 avg. unit value (*609*, 1939, II, part 1, 392) times 1939 ratio for linen goods of value added to value (0.468, from *609*, 1939, II, part 1, 389). No width adjustment (see col. 4).

1609	Silk and rayon fabrics	Avg. unit value of rayon, silk, and silk mixtures, broad woven goods, over 12″ wide (*609*, 1939, II, part 1, 314) times ratio for rayon manufactures and silk manufactures of value added to value (0.3883, from *609*, 1939, II, part 1, 309). Adjusted for width as in col. 4.
1611	Woolen and worsted fabrics	Avg. unit value of woven woolen goods (*609*, 1939, II, part 1, 325) times ratio for woolen and worsted manufactures of value added to value (0.3866, from *609*, 1939, II, part 1, 322). Adjusted for width as in col. 4.
1614	Felt footwear	Avg. value of 4 lbs. (see col. 4) of boots, shoes, and slipper felt and linings (*609*, 1939, II, part 1, 376) times ratio for felt goods of value added to cost of materials (0.8067, from *609*, 1939, II, part 1, 375).

Derivation of 1954 U.S. Weights (col. 7)

103	Steel ingots and castings	*609*, 1954, II, part 2, 33A-14, 33A-19 ff. Avg. unit value of carbon, alloy, and stainless steel shipped for sale and interplant transfer weighted by total production of each.
202	Copper	*649*, 1957, 724.
203	Lead	*649*, 1957, 724.
204	Zinc	*649*, 1957, 724.
301.1	Hydroelectric power	*649*, 1957, 533.
302	Anthracite	*649*, 1957, 730.
303	Bituminous coal	*649*, 1957, 730.
304	Lignite	*610*, 12A-4. Total value of shipments.
305	Crude petroleum	*649*, 1957, 736.
306	Natural gas	*649*, 1957, 734. Value at wells.
401	Soda ash	*601*, 4. Code 06-11-65.
404	Sulfuric acid	*601*, 4. Code 06-11-09.
405.1	Phosphoric fertilizer	*601*, 4. Code 06-62-21.
405.2	Ammonium sulfate	*601*, 4. Code 06-61-16.
105.3	Potash fertilizer	*601*, 4. Code 06-63-11-0.1.
406	Ground natural phosphate	649, 1957, 723.
410	Red lead	1939 price (see col. 6) times white lead price ratio of 1954 to 1939 (1.37, from *601*, 4, code 06-22-16, and *655*, No. R 1069, 37).
416	Paper	*609*, 1954, II, part 1, 26 A-10-14. Avg. unit value of all kinds excl. construction paper and paperboard.
417	Paperboard	*609*, 1954, II, part 1, 26 A-14-16. Avg. unit value.
418	Motor vehicle tires	*609*, 1954, II, part 2, 30 A-12. Avg. unit value of pneumatic tires (casings) of passenger cars, trucks, and buses, incl. off-the-road.
501	Red bricks	*608*, 181. Wholesale price of common brick f.o.b. plant. Also, *601*, 9.
505	Sand-lime, silica, and slag bricks	*609*, 1954, II, part 2, 32 E-15. Avg. value per sand-lime brick.
506	Cement	*649*, 1957. 722. Converted from barrels at 1 barrel = 170.55 kg.
507	Construction gypsum	*649*, 1957, 722.
508	Construction lime	*649*, 1957, 722.
510	Lumber	1947 avg. mill unit value ($55/1,000 bd. ft. in *649*, 1957, 703) divided by price ratio, 1955 to

		1947 (1.241, from *608*, 29). Converted from bd. ft. at 1 bd. ft. = 0.00236 m³.
512	Magnesite metallurgical powder	*649*, 1957, 722.
513	Roll roofing	*609*, 1954, II, part 1, 26 A-16. Avg. value per short ton of construction paper converted into m² at 1 m² = 1.48 kg.
516	Asbestos shingles	*609*, 1954, II, part 2, 32 E-14. Avg. value per 100 ft.² of asbestos-cement shingles, clapboard, siding, and roofing shingles.
519	Window glass	*609*, 1954, II, part 2, 32 A-9. Avg. value per 1 ft.² of flat window glass, single strength.
601	Crude alcohol	Price of ethyl alcohol ($0.55/gallon, *601*, 4) times ratio for distilled liquors of value added to value (0.5015, from *609*, 1954, II, part 1, 20 G-3).
604	Hard leather	Avg. wholesale price of 3 kinds of sole leather (light bends, heavy bends, and bellies—$0.465/ lb., *601*, 3 ff) times 1939 ratio for leather of value added to value (0.498, *640*, 75).
605	Soft leather	Avg. price of 3 kinds (upper, smooth side; upper, kip side; and upper, chrome tanned—$0.613/ sq. ft., *601*, 3 ff) times 1939 ratio for leather of value added to value (0.498, *640*, 75).
1501	Flour	Avg. unit value of wheat flour, excl. blended or prepared ($5.98/cwt., *609*, 1954, II, part 1, 20 D-12) times ratio of value added to value (0.1695, from *609*, 1954, II, part 1, 20 D-3).
1503	Butter	Value added and total shipments (*609*, 1954, II, part 1, 20 B-1, 20 B-16).
1504	Vegetable oil	Value added and output of crude cottonseed oil (*609*, 1954, II, part 1, 28 G-5, 28 G-1).
1506	Meat slaughtering	Value added and live weight of slaughtered cattle, calves, hogs, sheep, and lambs (*609*, 1954, II, part 1, 20 H-4, 20 A-3).
1507	Fish catch	Value and output of cured, dried, pickled, salted, smoked, and kippered fish (*594*, 585).
1509	Salt	*649*, 1957, 723.
1510	Raw sugar consumption	Value added and output of refined raw sugar and beet syrup and molasses (*609*, 1954, II, part 1, 20 F-3, 20 F-104).
1511	Starch and syrup	Unit value of corn syrup, corn starch, other starch incl. reprocessed, starch reprocessed from purchased stock, and dextrin ($0.06717/ lb. from *609*, 1954, II, part 1, 20 H-15-16) times ratio for corn wet milling of value added to value (0.3854, from *609*, 1954, II, part 1, 20 H-4).
1513	Canned food	Avg. unit value of canned tomatoes, all kinds ($0.1419/lb., *609*, 1954, II, part 1, 20 C-19) times ratio for canned fruits and vegetables of value added to value (0.3725, from *609*, 1954, II, part 1, 20 C-4).
1514	Beer	Value added of beer and ale (*609*, 1954, II, part 1, 20 G-2) and output (*649*, 1957, 805). Converted from barrels into hectoliters at 1 barrel = 1.1735 hectoliters.
1515	Cigarettes	Value added and output (*609*, 1954, II, part 1, 21 A-3). Also *649*, 1957, 786, 807.

1516	Low-grade tobacco	Value added and output of chewing and smoking tobacco (*609*, 1954, II, part 1, 21 A-3).
1604	Cotton fabrics	Avg. unit value of cotton broad-woven fabrics, gray goods (*609*, 1954, II, part 1, 22 B-15 ff, code 2233) times ratio of value added to (0.4042, from *609* 1954, II, part 1, 22 B-5). Converted from yds to m²; then adjusted for width as in col. 4.
1607	Linen fabrics	Avg. unit value of flax or hemp woven goods and towels (*609*, 1954, II, part 1, 22 F-14) times ratio for linen goods of value added to value (0.4450, from *609*, 1954, II, part 1, 22 F-14). No adjustment for width (see col. 4).
1609	Silk and rayon fabrics	Avg. unit value of rayon and related broad woven fabrics, gray goods (*609*, 1954, II, part 1, 22 B-19) times ratio for synthetic broad woven fabrics of value added to value (0.37, from *609*, 1954, II, part 1, 22 B-5). For conversion and adjustment, see col. 4.
1611	Woolen and worsted fabrics	Avg. unit value of woolen and worsted apparel and nonapparel fabrics, excl. woven felt (*609*, 1954, II, part 1, 22 A-9) times ratio for woolen and worsted fabrics of value added to value (0.3546, from *609*, 1954, II, part 1, 22 A-3). Converted from yds to m²; then adjusted for width as in col. 4.
1614	Felt footwear	Avg. value of 4 lbs. (see col. 4) of industrial felt (*609*, 1954, II, part 1, 22 F-12) times ratio for felt goods of value added to cost of materials (0.8122, from *609*, 1954, II, part 1, 22 F-3).

TABLE D-9

VALUE-ADDED AND EMPLOYMENT WEIGHTS USED IN INDEXES FOR ALL CIVILIAN
INDUSTRIAL PRODUCTS

Code		Value Added, 1927/28 (mill. rubles) (1)	Value per Unit, 1927/28 (rubles) (2)	Employment, 1955 (per cent) (3)	Value per Unit, 1955 (rubles) (4)
Ferrous mining and metals					
101	Pig iron	⎫	52.5	⎫	316
102	Rolled steel	⎬ 286.8	47.7		198
103	Steel ingots and castings	⎭	70.9		246
704	Iron ore	27.6			
706	Manganese ore	6.8			
		321.2		⎬ 5.7	
Nonferrous mining and metals		18.2			
202	Copper		995		5,950
203	Lead		675		7,150
204	Zinc		700	⎭	3,150
Fuel and electricity					
301	Electric power	274.4		1.5	
302	Anthracite	⎫	10.8	⎫	98
303	Bituminous coal	⎬ 333.5	9.8		77
303.1	Coke		7.6		76
304	Lignite	⎭	6.9		57
305	Crude petroleum	⎫ 287.3	28.7	⎬ 7.7	52
306	Natural gas	⎭	0.058		0.105
307	Oil shale	n.i.			39.7
308	Peat	31.1			34
		926.3		9.2	
Chemicals (incl. rubber and paper)				5.5	
401	Soda ash	⎫	73		275
402	Caustic soda		195		1,100
404.1	Sulfuric acid		101.9		183
405.1	Phosphoric fertilizer	⎬ 25.5	39.9		135
405.2	Ammonium sulfate		100		340
405.3	Potash fertilizer		62.4		210
406	Ground natural phosphate	⎭	12		42
410	Red lead	1.7			7,300
412	Synthetic dyes	10.7		n.i.	
416	Paper	⎫ 63.9	444		1,900
417	Paperboard	⎭	275		1,780
418	Motor vehicle tires	⎫ 66.7	83		430
1602	Rubber footwear	⎭	3.1		33
		168.5			

(continued)

TABLE D-9 (continued)

e	Value Added, 1927/28 (mill. rubles) (1)	Value per Unit, 1927/28 (rubles) (2)	Employment, 1955 (per cent) (3)	Value per Unit, 1955 (rubles) (4)
struction materials			18.1	
1 Red bricks	⎤	38		205
5 Sand-lime, silica, and slag bricks	⎟	38		160
7 Construction gypsum	⎟	11		100
8 Construction lime	⎬ 88.8	15.4		100
2 Magnesite metall. powder	⎟	286.7		122
3 Roll roofing	⎟	0.355		1.035
6 Asbestos shingles	⎦	147		377
5 Cement	33.9			116
9 Industrial timber hauled	577.0			78
0 Lumber	⎫ 144.9	28.6		77
1 Plywood	⎭	131.9		822
4 Roofing iron	28.1			748
8 Rails	4.4			72
9 Window glass	58.7			6.0
2 Fire-clay bricks	n.i.			179
3 Magnesite bricks	n.i.			355
4 Quartzite bricks	n.i.			227
	935.8			
nsportation equipment	60.8		11.3	
1 Automobiles		10,800		12,100
2 Trucks and buses		11,258		14,150
3 Diesel and electric locomotives		235,000		1,040,000
4 Steam locomotives		100,100		890,000
5 RR freight cars		5,450		36,500
6 RR passenger cars		16,400		245,700
7 Narrow-gauge RR cars	n.i.			10,500
8 Street and subway cars	n.i.			146,900
icultural machinery	83.6		6.9	
1 Tractors		5,352		16,000
2 Plows, tractor-drawn		135		2,225
3 Paring plows, tractor-drawn		190		3,075
4 Plows, horse-drawn		21.5		350
5 Harrows, tractor-drawn		92.7		2,300
6 Harrows, horse-drawn		20.9		350
7 Cultivators, tractor-drawn		105		1,700
8 Cultivators, horse-drawn	n.i.			170
9 Drills, tractor-drawn		243.3		2,000
0 Drills, horse-drawn		150		1,000
3 Potato planters, tractor-drawn	n.i.			4,400

(continued)

TABLE D-9 (continued)

Code		Value Added, 1927/28 (mill. rubles) (1)	Value per Unit, 1927/28 (rubles) (2)	Employment, 1955 (per cent) (3)	Value per Unit, 1955 (rubles) (4)
1014	Machines for planting				
	seedlings	n.i.			7,350
1016	Grain combines	n.i.			20,500
1017	All other combines	n.i.			14,400
1018	Windrowers	n.i.			4,200
1019	Reapers, horse-drawn		163.3		840
1020	Cotton pickers	n.i.			22,700
1021	Haymowers, tractor-drawn		166		5,050
1022	Haymowers, horse-drawn		127.5		530
1023	Rakers, tractor-drawn	n.i.			2,680
1024	Rakers, horse-drawn		74		695
1025	Threshers, tractor-driven		2,272		6,055
1026	Threshers, horse-driven		245		650
1027	Grain-cleaning machines	n.i.			4,925
1028	Winnowers, horse-drawn		245		700
1029	Horse drivings		130		950
1030	Chaff and silo cutters	n.i.			1,455
	Miscellaneous machinery	45.4		9.7	
1101	Steam boilers (capacity)		103.4		181.4
1102	Water turbines (capacity)		46.9		120
1103	Steam and gas turbines				
	(capacity)		34.3		87
1104	Locomobiles (capacity)		151.1		680
1105	Diesel engines (capacity)		192.5		357
1106	Other internal combustion				
	engines		176.4		245
1107	Turbogenerators (capacity)		24.3		40
1108	Hydroelectric generators		66		108
1109	Electric motors, A.C.		101.3		109
1110	Power transformers		18.8		11.2
1201	Coal-mining combines	n.i.			56,200
1202	Coal-cutting machines	n.i.			32,100
1203	Electric mining locomotives	n.i.			22,500
1204	Ore-loading machines	n.i.			59,700
1205	Deep-shaft pumps	n.i.			465
1206	Turbodrills	n.i.			13,000
1210	Machine tools		2,549		17,600
1211	Electric furnaces	n.i.			10,300
1212	Spinning machines		12,000		35,600
1213	Winding machines	n.i.			26,800
1214	Looms		900		7,400
1215	Cotton-carding machines		5,900		11,400
1216	Knitting machines		1,100		5,800
1217	Leather-spreading machines	n.i.			15,900
1218	Leather-dressing machines	n.i.			16,200
1219	Typesetting machines,				
	linotype		10,700		31,000
1220	Flat-bed printing press		8,500		70,000

(continued)

TABLE D-9 (continued)

·de		Value Added, 1927/28 (mill. rubles) (1)	Value per Unit, 1927/28 (rubles) (2)	Employment, 1955 (per cent) (3)	Value per Unit, 1955 (rubles) (4)
21	Industrial sewing machines		132		890
22.1	Presses		400		3,100
01	Excavators		129,400		97,500
02	Trench excavators		18,200		12,000
03	Stone crushers		20,600		24,000
04	Road graders		5,900		8,000
05	Self-propelled road graders	n.i.			60,000
06	Concrete mixers		3,500		3,400
07	Scrapers, tractor-driven	n.i.			27,300
08	Bulldozers	n.i.			6,000
09	RR cranes, steam	n.i.			126,000
10	Self-propelled cranes	n.i.			48,000
11	Overhead traveling cranes	n.i.			95,100
12	Tower cranes	n.i.			55,000
13	Electric elevators	n.i.			5,300
01	Telephones		34		107.5
02	Switchboards, hand-operated		29		69
03	Switchboards, automatic		35		195
05	Calculating machines		400		1,400
06	Typewriters		500	n.i.	
	od and allied products			9.3	
01	Flour	511.5			178
02	Macaroni	⎫	256		1,800
03	Butter	⎬ 214.7	429		1,950
06	Meat	⎪	103		420
13	Canned food	⎭	0.0564		0.50
04	Vegetable oil	⎱ 71.9	120	n.i.	
04.1	Oleomargarine	⎰	909		2,600
04.2	Vegetable oil minus oleomargarine	n.i.			1,600
07	Fish catch	194.2			6,300
08	Soap	44.8			1,282
09	Salt	11.7			34.2
10	Raw sugar consumption	210.8		n.i.	
10.1	Refined sugar	n.i.			2,025
10.2	Raw sugar minus refined sugar and sugar in candy	n.i.			825
11	Starch and syrup	9.2			627
14	Beer	52.2			76
15	Cigarettes	⎱ 75.5	1.3		11
16	Low-grade tobacco	⎰	3.5		43
17	Matches	20.6			27
18	Vodka	⎱ 108.9	14		250
01	Crude alcohol	⎰			110
19	Candy	54.7	15.1		2,386
		———			
		1,580.7			

(continued)

TABLE D-9 (concluded)

Code		Value Added, 1927/28 (mill. rubles) (1)	Value per Unit, 1927/28 (rubles) (2)	Employment, 1955 (per cent) (3)	Value per Unit, 1955 (rubles) (4)
Textiles and allied products				17.0	
602	Ginned cotton	20.9		n.i.	
604	Hard leather	⎱ 153.0	750		8,900
605	Soft leather	⎰	27		300
1601	Boots and shoes	248.0			10.7
1604	Cotton fabrics	909.5			0.82
1607	Linen fabrics	102.3			1.0
1609	Silk and rayon fabrics	42.9			2.3
1611	Woolen and worsted fabrics	217.1			6.8
1612	Knitted goods	n.i.			4.6
1613	Hosiery	n.i.			1.2
1614	Felt footwear	81.2			63
		1,774.9			
Consumer durables		8.6		3.1	
1701	Bicycles		162.5		580
1702	Cameras		45		720
1703	Electric light bulbs		0.45		1.25
1704	Phonographs		247		340
1705	Radios		122		300
1707	Household sewing machines		30.3		680
1708	Clocks and watches	n.i.			171.6
1709	Motorcycles		1,600		4,000
Total:		5,924.0		95.8	

n.i.: not included.

Value Added, 1927/28 (col. 1)

In general, the value-added weights are taken from Table C-2. Value added for the following industrial categories was not used because no corresponding output series were available: petroleum refining; artificial gas; shipbuilding; metal products; extraction of minerals for the chemical, construction, and glass and china industries; pharmaceutical chemicals; china; extraction of all other minerals; miscellaneous wood products; primary processing of mixed fibers; hemp and jute products; knitted goods; garment industry; fur industry; printing, publishing, and stationery; "all others"; and district railroad repair shops. When the 1927/28 value of output as computed from outputs in Table B-2 and unit values in Table D-8 was within 10% of the value of output for that industry as given in Table C-2, the entire value added was used as a weight. When the computed value was not within this range, value added was multiplied by the ratio of computed to given (Table C-2) value of output. The following tabulation gives these ratios rounded to three decimal places:

Nonferrous mining and metallurgy	0.347
Electric power stations	2.241
Basic chemicals	0.591
Paints and varnishes	0.074
All other chemicals	0.228
Pulp and paper	0.723
Rubber	0.650
Glass	0.748
Electrical and industrial machinery	0.179
All other food	0.721
Grease, tallow, soap, and perfume	0.610
Beer and malt	0.857
Wine, yeast, and vodka	0.661
Confectionery	0.749
Felt products	0.837
Consumer durables	0.179

Value added for roofing iron and rails was computed as output (Table B-2) times unit value added (Table D-8).

Value added for tractors (derived as 3.1 mill. rubles from value of output times 0.45, the ratio for land transportation equipment of value added to value of output) was transferred from land transportation equipment to agricultural machinery.

Value added of electrical and industrial machinery was apportioned to miscellaneous machinery and consumer durables on the basis of computed value of output.

Value per Unit, 1927/28 (col. 2)

From Table D-8.

Employment, 1955 (col. 3)

Percentage breakdown of production workers (*180*, 24). The percentage for timber haulage, wood industry, and paper industry (14.7%) was apportioned as follows on the basis of computed value of output: (1) to the paper industry (2.3%), included under chemicals; (2) to timber, lumber, and plywood (12.2%), included under construction materials; and (3) to matches (0.2%), included under food and allied products. The percentage for machine building and metal products (31.0%) was apportioned as follows on the basis of computed value of output: (1) to transportation equipment (11.3%); (2) to agricultural machinery (6.9%); (3) to miscellaneous machinery (9.7%); and (4) to consumer durables (3.1%).

Value per Unit, 1955 (col. 4)

From Table D-8.

TABLE D-10
LIST OF SOVIET OUTPUT SERIES INCLUDED IN INDEXES OF INDUSTRIAL PRODUCTION, 1913–1955
(entry indicates indexes in which series is included[a])

Code	Indexes for Industrial Materials — Soviet Weights	U.S. Weights	Indexes for Finished Industrial Products	Indexes for All Industrial Products
Intermediate industrial products				
Ferrous metals				
101 Pig iron				Both
102 Rolled steel				Both
103 Steel ingots and castings	All	All		Both
704 Iron ore				Both
706 Manganese ore				Both
Nonferrous metals				
202 Copper	All	All		Both
203 Lead	All	All		Both
204 Zinc	All	All		Both
Fuel and electricity				
301 Electric power				Both
301.1 Hydroelectric power	B,C	All		
302 Anthracite	All	All		Both
303 Bituminous coal	All	All		Both
303.1 Coke				Both
304 Lignite	All	All		Both
305 Crude petroleum	All	All		Both
306 Natural gas	B,C	All		Both
307 Oil shale	B,C			C
308 Peat	All			Both
309 Firewood, consumption	All			
Chemicals				
401 Soda ash	All	All		Both
402 Caustic soda		°		Both
404 Sulfuric acid	All	All		
404.1 Sulfuric acid not used in phosphoric fertilizer				Both
405.1 Phosphoric fertilizer	All	All		Both
405.2 Ammonium sulfate	All	All		Both
405.3 Potash fertilizer	All	All		Both
406 Ground natural phosphate	All	All		Both
410 Red lead	All	All		Both
412 Synthetic dyes				B
416 Paper	All	All		Both
417 Paperboard	All	All		Both
418 Motor vehicle tires	All	All		Both
1602 Rubber footwear[b]			Both	Both
Construction materials				
501 Red bricks	All	All	Both	Both

(continued)

PRODUCTION INDEXES AND WEIGHTS

TABLE D-10 (continued)

Code	Indexes for Industrial Materials Soviet Weights	U.S. Weights	Indexes for Finished Industrial Products	Indexes for All Industrial Products
502 Fire-clay bricks			C	C
503 Magnesite bricks			C	C
504 Quartzite bricks			C	C
505 Sand-lime, silica, and			C	C
slag bricks	All	All	Both	Both
506 Cement	All	All	Both	Both
507 Construction gypsum	All	All	Both	Both
508 Construction lime	All	All	Both	Both
509 Industrial timber hauled				Both
510 Lumber	All	All	Both	Both
511 Plywood	All		Both	Both
512 Magnesite metallurgical powder	B,C	All	Both	Both
513 Roll roofing	All	All	Both	Both
514 Roofing iron			Both	Both
516 Asbestos shingles	B,C	All	Both	Both
518 Rails			Both	Both
519 Window glass	All	All	Both	Both

Machinery and equipment (excl. miscellaneous machinery)
Transportation equipment

Code			Finished	All
901 Automobiles			Both	Both
902 Trucks and buses			Both	Both
903 Diesel and electric locomotives			Both	Both
904 Steam locomotives, main-line			Both	Both
905 Railroad freight cars			Both	Both
906 Railroad passenger cars			Both	Both
907 Railroad cars, narrow-gauge[c]			Both	C
908 Street and subway cars[c]			Both	C

Agricultural machinery

1001 Tractors			Both	Both
1002 Tractor-drawn plows			Both	Both
1003 Tractor-drawn paring plows			Both	Both
1004 Horse-drawn plows			Both	Both
1005 Tractor-drawn harrows			Both	Both
1006 Horse-drawn harrows			Both	Both
1007 Tractor-drawn cultivators			Both	Both
1008 Horse-drawn cultivators[c]			Both	C
1009 Tractor-drawn drills			Both	Both
1010 Horse-drawn drills			Both	Both
1011 Combined plows and drills[c]			B	
1013 Tractor-drawn potato planters			C	C

(continued)

575

TABLE D-10 (continued)

Code		Indexes for Industrial Materials		Indexes for Finished Industrial Products	Indexes for All Industrial Products
		Soviet Weights	U.S. Weights		
1014	Machines for planting seedlings			C	C
1016	Grain combines			C	C
1017	Other combines			C	C
1018	Windrowers			C	C
1019	Horse-drawn reapers			Both	Both
1020	Cotton pickers			C	C
1021	Tractor-drawn haymowers			Both	Both
1022	Horse-drawn haymowers			Both	Both
1023	Tractor-drawn rakers			C	C
1024	Horse-drawn rakers			Both	Both
1025	Tractor-drawn threshers			Both	Both
1026	Horse-drawn threshers			Both	Both
1027	Grain-cleaning machines			C	C
1028	Horse-drawn winnowers			Both	Both
1029	Horse drivings			Both	Both
1030	Chaff and silo cutters			C	C
	Miscellaneous machinery[d]				
	Prime movers and electrical machinery				
1101	Steam boilers			Both	Both
1102	Water turbines			Both	Both
1103	Steam and gas turbines			Both	Both
1104	Locomobiles[c]			Both	Both
1105	Diesel engines			Both	Both
1106	Other internal combustion engines[c]			Both	Both
1107	Turbogenerators[c]			Both	Both
1108	Hydroelectric generators			Both	Both
1109	Electric motors, A.C.			Both	Both
1110	Power transformers			Both	Both
	Mining and industrial machinery				
1201	Coal-mining combines			C	C
1202	Coal-cutting machines			C	C
1203	Electric mining locomotives			C	C
1204	Ore-loading machines[c]			C	C
1205	Deep-shaft pumps[c]			C	C
1206	Turbodrills			C	C
1210	Machine tools			Both	Both
1211	Electric furnaces			C	C
1212	Spinning machines[c]			Both	Both
1213	Winding machines			C	C
1214	Looms			Both	Both
1215	Cotton-carding machines[c]			Both	Both
1216	Knitting machines[c]			Both	Both

(continued)

TABLE D-10 (continued)

Code		Indexes for Industrial Materials		Indexes for Finished Industrial Products	Indexes for All Industrial Products
		Soviet Weights	U.S. Weights		
1217	Leather-spreading machines			C	C
1218	Leather-dressing machines			C	C
1219	Typesetting machines, linotype			Both	Both
1220	Flat-bed printing presses			Both	Both
1221	Industrial sewing machines			Both	Both
1222.1	Presses			Both	Both
	Construction machinery				
1301	Excavators			Both	Both
1302	Trench excavators c			Both	Both
1303	Stone crushers c			Both	Both
1304	Road graders, not self-propelled c			Both	Both
1305	Self-propelled road graders			C	C
1306	Concrete mixers c			Both	Both
1307	Tractor-driven scrapers			C	C
1308	Bulldozers			C	C
1309	Railroad cranes, steam-operated			C	C
1310	Self-propelled cranes, not railroad cranes			C	C
1311	Overhead traveling cranes c			C	C
1312	Tower cranes			C	C
1313	Electric elevators c			C	C
	Machinery, n.e.c.				
1401	Telephones c			Both	Both
1402	Switchboards, hand-operated c			Both	Both
1403	Switchboards, automatic c			Both	Both
1405	Calculating machines c			Both	Both
1406	Typewriters c			B	B
Consumer goods					
	Food and allied products				
1501	Flour	All	All	Both	Both
1502	Macaroni			Both	Both
1503	Butter	All	All	Both	Both
1504	Vegetable oil	All	All		B
1504.1	Oleomargarine			Both	Both
1504.2	Vegetable oil minus oleomargarine			Both	C

(continued)

577

TABLE D-10 (concluded)

Code		Indexes for Industrial Materials		Indexes for Finished Industrial Products	Indexes for All Industrial Products
		Soviet Weights	U.S. Weights		
1506	Meat slaughtering	All	All	Both	Both
1507	Fish catch	All	All	Both	Both
1508	Soap			Both	Both
1509	Salt	All	All	Both	Both
1510	Raw sugar consumption	All	All		B
1510.1	Refined sugar			Both	C
1510.2	Raw sugar minus refined sugar and sugar in candy			Both	C
1511	Starch and syrup	All	All	Both	Both
1513	Canned food	All	All	Both	Both
1514	Beer	All	D,F,G	Both	Both
1515	Cigarettes	All	All	Both	Both
1516	Low-grade tobacco	All	All	Both	Both
1517	Matches			Both	Both
1518	Vodka			Both	Both
1519	Candy			Both	Both
601	Crude alcohol	All	All		Both
	Textiles and allied products				
1601	Boots and shoes			Both	Both
602	Ginned cotton				B
1604	Cotton fabrics	All	All	Both	Both
1607	Linen fabrics	All	All	Both	Both
1609	Silk and rayon fabrics	All	All	Both	Both
1611	Woolen and worsted fabrics	All	All	Both	Both
1612	Knitted goods[c]			C	C
1613	Hosiery[c]			C	C
1614	Felt footwear	All	All	Both	Both
604	Hard leather	All	All		Both
605	Soft leather	All	All		Both
	Consumer durables				
1701	Bicycles			Both	Both
1702	Cameras			Both	Both
1703	Electric light bulbs			Both	Both
1704	Phonographs			Both	Both
1705	Radios			Both	Both
1707	Household sewing machines			Both	Both
1708	Clocks and watches			C	C
1709	Motorcycles			Both	Both

[a] When series is included in all variants of the specified index, the word "all" or "both" is entered. Otherwise, variant in which series is included is indicated as follows: A, 1913 Soviet weights; B, 1928 Soviet weights; C, 1955 Soviet weights; D, 1914 U.S. weights; E, 1929 U.S. weights; F, 1939 U.S. weights; and G, 1954 U.S. weights.

[b] Rubber footwear was included in textiles in the index for finished industrial products.

[c] Output data missing for one or more benchmark years.

[d] These items are included in illustrative indexes only, not in the basic indexes.

TABLE D-11

LIST OF RUSSIAN OUTPUT SERIES INCLUDED IN PRODUCTION
INDEX FOR INDUSTRIAL MATERIALS, 1860–1913

Code		Period Covered
103	Steel ingots and castings	1860–1913
202	Copper	1860–1913
203	Lead	1860–1913
204	Zinc	1860–1913
305	Crude petroleum	1860–1913
310	Coal	1860–1913
401	Soda ash	1860–1913
404	Sulfuric acid	1860–1913
405.1	Phosphoric fertilizer	1860–1913
411	Zinc oxide	1860–1913[a]
420	White lead	1860–1913[a]
501	Red bricks	1890–1913[a]
506	Cement	1893–1913[a]
518	Rails	1878–1913[a]
519	Window glass	1900–1912[a]
601	Crude alcohol	1859/60–1912/13
602.1	Ginned cotton consumption	1860–1913
1501	Flour	1888–1912[a]
1504	Vegetable oil	1888–1913[a]
1509	Salt	1860–1913
1510	Raw sugar	1859/60–1912/13
1511	Starch and syrup	1888–1913[a]
1514	Beer	1896–1913[a]
1515	Cigarettes	1860–1913
1516	Low-grade tobacco	1881–1913[a]
1610	Woolen yarn	1893–1913[a]

[a] Output data missing for one or more benchmark
years.

APPENDIX E

Output Data for the United States

General Note

THE output series for the United States used in this study
are given in Tables E-1 and E-2 below. Since these data
were compiled in order to compare the growth of individual industries in the Soviet Union and the United
States, the basic U.S. data have, in some cases, been
adjusted to match counterpart Soviet data as closely as
possible in coverage and units of measurement. The
basic sources for the U.S. data are as follows: *598, 607,
608, 609, 613, 618, 619, 626, 634, 635, 636, 637, 638,
649, 652,* and *656.*

Additional sources, coverage that might be ambiguous,
and adjustments are briefly described in the notes following the tables. All data given in short tons or pounds in
the original source have been converted into metric tons.

TABLE E-1

OUTPUT SERIES: UNITED STATES, 1870–1955

	101 Pig Iron (th. m.t.)	102 Rolled Steel (mill. m.t.)	103 Steel Ingots and Castings (mill. m.t.)	201 Primary Aluminum (th. m.t.)	202 Copper (th. m.t.)
1870	1,692		0.070		12.80
1871	1,734		0.074		13.21
1872	2,590		0.145		12.70
1873	2,602		0.202		15.75
1874	2,440		0.219		17.78
1875	2,056		0.396		18.29
1876	1,899		0.542		19.30
1877	2,100		0.579		21.34
1878	2,338		0.744		21.85
1879	2,786		0.950		23.37
1880	3,897		1.27		27.43
1881	4,211		1.61		32.51
1882	4,697		1.76		41.57
1883	4,669		1.70	0.00004	53.14
1884	4,164		1.58	0.00007	67.04
1885	4,109	3.15	1.74	0.00013	77.55
1886	5,775	4.45	2.60	0.001	73.60
1887	6,520	5.32	3.39	0.008	84.02
1888	6,594	4.69	2.95	0.009	104.9
1889	7,726	5.32	3.44	0.021	105.2
1890	9,350	6.12	4.35	0.028	120.6
1891	8,413	6.49	3.97	0.068	134.2
1892	9,304	6.27	5.01	0.118	160.2
1893	7,239	5.06	4.08	0.098	154.1
1894	6,764	4.72	4.48	0.224	165.5
1895	9,598	6.29	6.21	0.227	175.1
1896	8,761	5.61	5.37	0.455	211.4
1897	9,808	7.11	7.27	1.08	229.6
1898	11,963	8.65	9.08	1.36	247.8
1899	13,839	10.46	10.81	1.48	268.7
1900	14,011	9.64	10.35	2.30	291.4
1901	16,133	12.55	13.69	2.60	302.1
1902	18,107	14.17	15.19	2.61	317.3
1903	18,298	13.42	14.77	3.01	331.1
1904	16.762	12.21	14.08	3.67	386.2
1905	23,361	17.11	20.35	4.90	461.3
1906	25,713	19.90	23.77	6.41	489.5
1907	26,195	20.18	23.74	7.40	468.3
1908	16,192	12.02	14.25	4.84	516.2
1909	26,209	19.96	24.34	13.19	716.7

(continued)

	101 Pig Iron (th. m.t.)	102 Rolled Steel (mill. m.t.)	103 Steel Ingots and Castings (mill. m.t.)	201 Primary Aluminum (th. m.t.)	202 Copper (th. m.t.)
1910	27,742	21.97	26.51	16.06	730.7
1911	24,029	19.35	24.06	17.42	747.5
1912	30,204	25.05	31.75	18.96	836.0
1913	31,463	25.19	31.79	21.45	856.4
1914	23,707	18.67	23.89	26.30	811.7
1915	30,396	24.78	32.67	41.05	919.2
1916	40,068	32.90	43.46	52.21	134.2
1917	39,241	33.60	45.78	58.90	1,446
1918	39,681	31.66	45.18	56.57	1,406
1919	31,513	25.51	35.23	58.28	1,063
1920	37,519	32.87	42.81	62.61	975.7
1921	16,956	15.01	20.10	24.74	628.4
1922	27,657	26.88	36.17	33.40	874.2
1923	41,009	33.81	45.66	58.36	1,271
1924	31,910	28.54	38.54	68.29	1,377
1925	37,289	33.92	46.12	63.56	1,381
1926	40,005	36.07	49.07	66.85	1,489
1927	37,152	33.41	45.66	74.21	1,500
1928	38,768	38.27	52.37	95.50	1,615
1929	43,298	41.73	57.34	103.4	1,811
1930	32,262	29.99	41.35	103.9	1,402
1931	18,722	19.48	26.36	80.53	995.8
1932	8,687	10.62	13.90	47.58	534.0
1933	13,236	17.00	23.61	38.61	643.1
1934	15,938	19.27	26.47	33.65	746.4
1935	21,161	24.35	34.64	54.11	941.4
1936	30,739	34.34	48.53	102.0	1,186
1937	36,725	37.36	51.38	132.8	1,451
1938	18,881	21.38	28.80	130.1	1,045
1939	31,575	35.44	47.90	148.4	1,369
1940	41,916	44.14	60.77	187.1	1,674
1941	49,973	56.54	75.15	280.4	1,925
1942	53,594	56.65	78.05	472.7	2,125
1943	55,125	57.42	80.59	834.8	2,236
1944	55,342	59.70	81.32	704.4	1,971
1945	48,284	54.26	72.30	449.1	1,919
1946	40,680	46.21	60.42	371.6	1,526
1947	52,914	60.06	77.01	518.7	1,925
1948	54,497	62.77	80.41	565.6	1,887
1949	48,374	55.23	70.74	547.5	1,489
1950	58,513	68.21	87.85	651.9	2,011
1951	63,755	74.31	95.44	759.2	1,941
1952	55,618	64.73	84.52	850.3	1,888
1953	67,906	77.97	101.3	1,136	2,043
1954	52,569	62.11	80.11	1,325	1,861
1955	70,524	82.24	106.2	1,420	2,088

(continued)

583

TABLE E-1 (continued)

	203 Lead (th. m.t.)	204 Zinc (th. m.t.)	301 Electric Power (mill. kwh)	303.1 Coke (mill. m.t.)
1870	16.18	4.90		
1871	18.12	6.26		
1872	23.33	7.08		
1873	38.05	8.71		
1874	46.48	11.88		
1875	53.15	15.15		
1876	57.10	15.42		
1877	72.92	14.15		
1878	80.86	17.78		
1879	82.41	19.32		
1880	86.84	22.77		3.0
1881	103.9	27.45		3.7
1882	117.7	30.63	0.80	4.4
1883	127.3	33.45		5.0
1884	123.7	34.97		4.4
1885	114.5	36.91		4.6
1886	119.9	38.68		6.2
1887	142.1	45.67		6.9
1888	159.7	50.71		7.7
1889	161.8	53.40		9.3
1890	143.2	57.77		10.4
1891	179.9	73.37		9.4
1892	188.9	79.16		10.9
1893	203.5	71.52		8.6
1894	193.8	68.34		8.3
1895	213.9	81.36		12.1
1896	233.6	73.93		10.7
1897	256.0	90.70		12.1
1898	274.1	104.7		14.5
1899	270.4	117.1		17.9
1900	333.6	112.4		18.6
1901	336.6	127.7		19.8
1902	333.7	142.4	5,969	23.0
1903	334.7	144.4		23.0
1904	356.9	169.4		21.5
1905	352.3	184.9		29.2
1906	367.2	203.9		33.0
1907	398.3	226.7	14,121	37.0
1908	376.5	190.9		23.6
1909	443.3	262.0		35.7

(continued)

OUTPUT DATA FOR THE UNITED STATES

TABLE E-1 (continued)

	203 Lead (th. m.t.)	204 Zinc (th. m.t.)	301 Electric Power (mill. kwh)	303.1 Coke (mill. m.t.)
1910	476.9	281.6		37.8
1911	491.0	296.7		32.3
1912	497.2	354.8	24,752	39.9
1913	485.6	359.9		42.0
1914	547.2	359.3		31.4
1915	570.6	492.1		37.7
1916	605.5	651.5		49.4
1917	638.9	635.9	43,429	50.4
1918	668.9	494.5		51.3
1919	548.2	458.7		40.1
1920	593.6	459.2	56,559	46.5
1921	501.1	212.6	53,125	23.0
1922	628.0	384.3	61,204	33.7
1923	737.4	522.2	71,399	51.7
1924	811.9	522.7	75,892	40.2
1925	901.6	575.5	84,666	46.5
1926	976.3	619.6	94,222	51.6
1927	973.0	596.3	101,390	46.4
1928	988.5	610.8	108,069	47.9
1929	984.9	626.7	116,747	54.3
1930	815.4	574.6	114,637	43.5
1931	614.6	363.4	109,373	30.4
1932	435.7	261.0	99,359	19.7
1933	442.9	396.4	102,655	33.2
1934	471.4	417.4	110,404	28.8
1935	539.7	499.7	118,935	31.8
1936	600.6	594.1	130,000	42.0
1937	673.5	657.3	146,476	47.4
1938	552.1	514.4	141,955	29.5
1939	658.2	647.9	161,308	40.2
1940	719.9	814.0	179,907	51.8
1941	878.5	1,003	208,306	59.1
1942	807.3	1,109	233,146	64.0
1943	736.4	1,189	267,540	65.0
1944	722.3	1,102	279,524	67.2
1945	731.7	1,021	271,254	61.1
1946	663.1	933.4	269,609	53.1
1947	864.5	1,010	307,400	66.7
1948	822.6	1,009	336,808	67.9
1949	807.0	954.9	345,066	57.7
1950	898.7	1,061	388,674	66.0
1951	848.9	1,085	433,358	71.9
1952	856.5	1,102	463,056	62.0
1953	866.1	1,098	514,164	71.5
1954	877.8	1,029	544,644	54.1
1955	891.9	1,223	629,010	68.2

(continued)

585

TABLE E-1 (continued)

	305 Crude Petroleum (th. m.t.)	306 Natural Gas (mill. m³)	310 Coal (mill. m.t.)	401 Soda Ash (th. m.t.)	402 Caustic Soda (th. m.t.)	404 Sulfuric Acid (th. m.t.)
1870	718		29.97			
1871	716		42.53			
1872	866		46.68			
1873	1,362		52.26			
1874	1,504		47.72			
1875	1,209		47.49			
1876	1,257		48.33			
1877	1,837		54.87			
1878	2,119		52.56			
1879	2,741		61.79	18.2		
1880	3,618		64.85			
1881	3,807		77.91			
1882	4,177	96	93.94			
1883	3,227	218	105.0			
1884	3,333	680	109.0			
1885	3,008	2,152	100.8			
1886	3,863	4,446	103.1			
1887	3,893	6,824	118.5			
1888	3,800	9,713	134.9			
1889	4,840	7,079	128.0	151.0		
1890	6,307	6,768	143.1			
1891	7,472	5,183	152.9			
1892	6,952	4,502	162.7			
1893	6,665	4,219	165.4			
1894	6,791	4,078	154.9			
1895	7,279	3,879	175.2			
1896	8,390	3,964	174.2			
1897	8,323	4,219	181.7			
1898	7,620	4,899	199.6			
1899	7,853	6,315	230.2	354.7	151.5	307
1900	8,756	6,711	244.7			
1901	9,550	7,476	266.1			
1902	12,217	7,957	273.6			
1903	13,826	8,438	324.2			
1904	16,114	8,778	319.2	470.8	78.7	611
1905	18,541	9,939	356.3			
1906	17,409	11,011	375.7			
1907	22,859	11,514	435.8			
1908	24,570	11,387	377.3			
1909	25,209	13,612	418.0	586.0	119.7	998

(continued)

TABLE E-1 (continued)

	305 Crude Petroleum (th. m.t.)	306 Natural Gas (mill. m³)	310 Coal (mill. m.t.)	401 Soda Ash (th. m.t.)	402 Caustic Soda (th. m.t.)	404 Sulfuric Acid (th. m.t.)
1910	28,841	14,418	455.0			
1911	30,340	14,526	450.3			
1912	30,682	15,920	484.9			
1913	34,193	16,478	517.1			
1914	36,576	16,760	465.9	848.2	193.2	1,690
1915	38,688	17,799	482.3			
1916	41,394	21,328	535.3			
1917	46,149	22,515	590.9			
1918	48,985	20,417	615.3			
1919	52,074	21,122	502.5	934.4	274.0	2,000
1920	60,959	22,603	597.2			
1921	64,985	18,747	459.4	704.0	209.6	1,810
1922	76,731	21,593	432.7			
1923	100,799	28,515	596.8	1,143	391.0	2,990
1924	98,258	32,324	518.6			
1925	105,112	33,657	527.9	1,243	441.8	2,980
1926	106,093	37,181	596.7			
1927	124,020	40,930	542.4	1,334	496.2	2,970
1928	124,067	44,405	522.6			
1929	138,635	54,303	552.3	1,672	657.7	3,880
1930	123,591	55,032	487.1			
1931	117,132	47,755	400.7	1,370	575.2	3,430
1932	108,059	44,061	326.2			
1933	124,643	44,046	347.6	1,497	585.1	2,390
1934	124,975	50,142	377.9			
1935	137,159	54,272	385.1	1,696	653.2	3,630
1936	151,347	61,386	447.9			
1937	176,047	68,177	451.2	2,105	813.7	4,490
1938	167,128	65,003	358.0			3,720
1939	174,093	70,134	404.9	2,564	948.0	4,350
1940	186,239	75,330	464.7			5,180
1941	192,985	79,646	517.6	3,272	1,296	6,140
1942	190,840	86,465	583.3	3,437	1,428	7,030
1943	207,213	96,694	590.4	3,999	1,614	7,660
1944	230,925	105,086	619.9	4,117	1,697	8,380
1945	235,846	110,965	573.8	3,969	1,691	8,640
1946	238,637	114,135	539.3	3,886	1,699	8,350
1947	255,572	129,753	624.0	4,100	1,936	9,590
1948	278,033	145,777	595.7	4,150	2,156	10,400
1949	253,501	153,471	436.0	3,553	2,017	10,370
1950	271,618	177,889	508.4	3,621	2,278	11,820
1951	309,346	211,170	522.8	4,620	2,818	12,130
1952	315,144	226,917	460.3	4,030	2,750	12,070
1953	324,399	237,776	442.9	4,426	2,959	12,700
1954	318,606	247,563	380.2	4,265	3,079	12,700
1955	341,938	264,484	448.5	4,451	3,542	14,296

(continued)

TABLE E-1 (continued)

	405 Mineral Fertilizer (th. m.t.)	412 Synthetic Dyes (m.t.)	416 Paper (th. m.t.)	418 Motor Vehicle Tires (millions)	506 Cement (mill. m.t.)
1870	79.9				
1871	59.0				
1872	45.0				
1873	96.3				
1874	105.6				
1875	93.9				
1876	97.0				
1877	104.8				
1878	156.0				
1879	137.4		392.0		
1880	331.4				0.35
1881	461.9				0.43
1882	516.8				0.55
1883	567.6				0.71
1884	562.2				0.68
1885	557.0				0.71
1886	568.7				0.77
1887	575.7				1.18
1888	675.7				1.11
1889	839.7		724.1		1.17
1890	669.4				1.33
1891	784.9				1.40
1892	641.8				1.49
1893	867.0				1.36
1894	837.8				1.43
1895	865.6				1.49
1896	850.1				1.62
1897	916.5				1.88
1898	141.2				2.11
1899	132.0	3,492	1,604		2.70
1900	1,768			0.016	2.94
1901	1,581				3.42
1902	1,406				4.39
1903	1,590				5.10
1904	2,000	4,826	2,310		5.40
1905	1,823				6.84
1906	2,056				8.70
1907	2,189				8.91
1908	2,096				9.02
1909	2,290		2,938		11.37

(continued)

	405 Mineral Fertilizer (th. m.t.)	412 Synthetic Dyes (m.t.)	416 Paper (th. m.t.)	418 Motor Vehicle Tires (millions)	506 Cement (mill. m.t.)
1910	2,875				13.27
1911	3,125				13.57
1912	3,071				14.22
1913	2,959				15.85
1914	2,973	2,994	3,504	8.00	15.19
1915	2,596				14.79
1916	2,837				15.75
1917	4,010	20,865			15.94
1918	3,991	26,535			12.20
1919	3,102	28,758	3,716	32.8	13.87
1920	5,040	40,052			17.19
1921	2,253	17,690	3,259	27.3	16.95
1922	2,891	29,302			19.72
1923	3,735	42,502	4,609	45.4	23.66
1924	3,775	31,162			25.72
1925	4,903	39,145	5,181	58.8	27.87
1926	4,703	39,916			28.42
1927	4,322	43,182	5,654	63.5	29.90
1928	5,120	43,817			30.44
1929	5,056	50,530	6,069	68.7	29.49
1930	5,360	39,236		51.0	27.80
1931	3,594	37,875	5,018	48.7	21.60
1932	2,436	32,341		40.1	13.17
1933	3,452	45,813	4,636	45.3	10.91
1934	3,743	39,553		47.2	13.37
1935	4,069	46,221	5,242	49.4	13.26
1936	4,767	54,204		56.3	19.52
1937	5,881	55,429	6,384	53.3	20.14
1938	5,302	37,104		40.9	18.28
1939	5,677	54,522	6,718	57.6	21.27
1940	6,421	57,969		59.2	22.64
1941	7,233	76,521		61.5	28.47
1942	7,786	68,901	6,963	15.3	31.61
1943	9,259	65,317	6,923	20.4	23.07
1944	10,314	68,810	6,765	33.4	15.72
1945	10,873	65,862	6,963	44.5	17.79
1946	12,030	84,504	8,059	82.3	28.40
1947	14,836	96,298	8,810	95.6	32.31
1948	15,299	91,354	9,155	81.3	35.63
1949	15,523	63,231	8,523	76.4	36.31
1950	17,314	88,768	9,926	92.8	39.27
1951	18,164	84,867	10,706	83.4	42.55
1952	19,371	65,862	10,033	90.4	43.09
1953	19,525	75,206	10,468	96.1	45.64
1954	19,952		10,676	89.1	46.90
1955	19,698		11,698	112.2	51.32

(continued)

TABLE E-1 (continued)

	507 Construction Gypsum (th. m.t.)	508 Lime (th. m.t.)	510 Lumber (mill. m³)	518 Rails (th. m.t.)	519 Flat Glass (mill. m²)	704 Iron Ore (mill. m.t.)
1870				563		3.89
1871				704		3.88
1872				907		5.63
1873				808		5.49
1874				661		5.00
1875				719		4.08
1876				798		3.72
1877				694		4.06
1878				801		4.46
1879			42.77	1,010	8.75	5.24
1880	81.6	2,540		1,326		7.24
1881	77.1	2,722		1,673		7.23
1882	90.7	2,812		1,532		9.14
1883	81.6	2,903		1,235		8.54
1884	81.6	3,357		1,038		8.33
1885	81.6	3,629		993		7.72
1886	86.2	3,855		1,627		10.16
1887	86.2	4,241		2,174		11.48
1888	99.8	4,453		1,427		12.26
1889	243.1		63.80	1,546	18.36	14.75
1890	166.0			1,915		16.29
1891	188.7			1,328		14.83
1892	232.2			1,577		16.56
1893	230.4			1,154		11.77
1894	216.8			1,038		12.07
1895	241.3			1,329		16.21
1896	203.2			1,140		16.26
1897	262.2			1,674		17.80
1898	264.9			2,013		19.75
1899	440.9		82.77	2,309	21.73	25.08
1900	538.9			2,424		28.00
1901	575.2			2,921		29.35
1902	740.3			2,995		36.13
1903	945.3			3,040		35.58
1904	853.7	2,457	101.5	2,322	25.08	28.09
1905	946.2	2,707	102.7	3,430		43.21
1906	1,398	2,901	108.5	4,042		48.52
1907	1,589	2,806	108.5	3,692		52.55
1908	1,562	2,510	99.15	1,952		36.56
1909	2,044	3,161	105.0	3,073	36.55	52.12

(continued)

	507 Construction Gypsum (th. m.t.)	508 Lime (th. m.t.)	510 Lumber (mill. m³)	518 Rails (th. m.t.)	519 Flat Glass (mill. m²)	704 Iron Ore (mill. m.t.)
1910	2,158	3,181	105.0	3,694		57.93
1911	2,108	3,078	101.5	2,868		44.58
1912	2,269	3,201	106.2	3,381		56.04
1913	2,359	3,261	103.8	3,559		62.98
1914	2,246	3,067	95.58	1,976	42.86	42.11
1915	2,221	3,287	87.34	2,239		56.42
1916	2,502	3,695	93.94	2,901		76.37
1917	2,446	3,435	84.55	2,991		76.50
1918	1,867	2,908	75.29	2,582		70.78
1919	2,195	3,021	81.55	2,239	39.55	61.94
1920	2,839	3,239	82.59	2,646		68.69
1921	2,623	2,297	68.43	2,214	29.38	29.96
1922	3,429	3,302	83.28	2,207		47.89
1923	4,312	3,698	96.75	2,952	56.18	70.46
1924	4,575	3,694	93.21	2,472		55.14
1925	5,151	4,156	96.75	2,830	63.56	62.90
1926	5,112	4,137	93.80	3,270		68.71
1927	4,851	4,005	87.91	2,851	55.65	62.73
1928	4,629	4,044	86.72	2,689		63.20
1929	4,550	3,874	91.43	2,766	51.24	74.20
1930	3,149	3,073	69.28	1,903		59.35
1931	2,321	2,457	30.67	1,177	32.07	31.63
1932	1,285	1,778	31.91	409		10.01
1933	1,211	2,058	40.47	423	32.73	17.84
1934	1,393	2,175	44.43	1,026		24.98
1935	1,727	2,710	54.14	723	56.29	31.03
1936	2,461	3,401	65.19	1,240		49.57
1937	2,774	3,741	68.44	1,469	80.91	73.25
1938	2,435	3,036	58.58	633		28.90
1939	2,927	3,859	67.85	1,191	68.2	52.56
1940	3,356	4,433	73.53	1,523		74.88
1941	4,345	5,515	86.22	1,749		93.89
1942	4,262	5,538	85.74	1,902		107.2
1943	3,518	5,985	80.91	1,929		102.9
1944	3,412	5,873	77.72	2,260		95.63
1945	3,458	5,371	66.36	2,194		89.80
1946	5,107	5,437	80.50	1,783		71.98
1947	5,632	6,150	83.55	2,215	115.6	94.59
1948	6,582	6,590		2,003		102.6
1949	5,995	5,732	75.93	1,724		86.30
1950	7,433	6,784	89.69	1,677		99.62
1951	7,862	7,490	86.72	1,683		118.4
1952	7,323	7,324	88.83	1,335		99.49
1953	7,483	7,581	86.71	1,798		119.9
1954	8,219	6,799	88.09	1,063	142.2	79.11
1955	9,592	8,373	92.27	1,114		106.1

(continued)

TABLE E-1 (continued)

	901 Automobiles (thousands)	902 Trucks and Buses (thousands)	905 Railroad Freight Cars (units)	906 Railroad Passenger Cars (units)	1001 Tractors (thousands)
1870					
1871					
1872					
1873					
1874					
1875					
1876					
1877					
1878					
1879					
1880			14,098	308	
1881			22,496	351	
1882			20,671	344	
1883			13,683	455	
1884			7,468	321	
1885			3,802	262	
1886			12,937	397	
1887			23,775	561	
1888			71,719	1,954	
1889			70,546		
1890			103,774	1,654	
1891			95,514	1,640	
1892			93,293	2,195	
1893			56,900	1,986	
1894			17,029	516	
1895			38,100	430	
1896			51,189	474	
1897			43,588	494	
1898			99,809	699	
1899			119,886	1,305	
1900	4.19		115,631	1,636	
1901	7.00		136,950	2,055	
1902	9.00		162,599	1,948	
1903	11.24		152,801	2,007	
1904	22.13	0.70	60,806	2,144	
1905	24.25	0.75	165,155	2,551	
1906	33.2	0.80	240,503	3,167	
1907	43.0	1.00	284,188	5,457	
1908	63.5	1.50	76,555	1,716	
1909	124.0	3.30	93,570	2,849	2.00

(continued)

	901 Automobiles (thousands)	902 Trucks and Buses (thousands)	905 Railroad Freight Cars (units)	906 Railroad Passenger Cars (units)	1001 Tractors (thousands)
1910	181.0	6.00	180,945	4,412	4.00
1911	199.3	10.68	72,161	3,688	7.00
1912	356.0	22.00	152,429	2,774	11.00
1913	461.5	23.50	190,501	3,003	7.00
1914	548.1	24.90	101,027	3,703	10.00
1915	895.9	74.00	71,933	1,540	21.00
1916	1,526	92.13	128,663	1,423	29.67
1917	1,746	128.2	139,743	1,735	62.74
1918	943	227.3	109,896	841	132.7
1919	1,652	224.7	155,145	226	164.6
1920	1,906	321.8	75,557	966	203.2
1921	1,468	148.1	45,643	1,210	73.20
1922	2,274	270.0	67,688	1,133	98.79
1923	3,625	409.3	177,714	2,079	131.9
1924	3,186	416.6	115,295	2,571	116.8
1925	3,735	530.7	108,812	2,470	164.1
1926	3,784	516.9	91,307	2,925	178.1
1927	2,937	464.8	63,837	2,129	194.9
1928	3,775	583.3	47,513	1,692	171.5
1929	4,455	881.9	85,038	2,583	223.1
1930	2,787	575.4	76,021	1,574	196.3
1931	1,948	432.3	13,613	343	69.03
1932	1,104	228.3	3,336	77	41.98
1933	1,561	329.2	2,202	9	14.94
1934	2,161	576.2	25,267	290	85.40
1935	3,274	697.4	8,778	205	155.9
1936	3,679	782.2	47,135	191	221.3
1937	3,929	891.0	78,819	629	272.4
1938	2,020	488.8	17,081	434	189.3
1939	2,889	700.4	25,513	276	205.7
1940	3,717	754.9	64,075	285	274.2
1941	3,780	1,061	83,009	363	342.1
1942	222.9	818.7	71,402	429	201.7
1943	0.14	699.7	74,953	706	134.7
1944	0.61	737.5	81,762	1,003	294.0
1945	69.53	655.7	54,522	931	289.3
1946	2,149	940.9	59,975	1,372	284.2
1947	3,558	1,239	96,243	887	470.6
1948	3,909	1,376	114,885	9᾿6	569.0
1949	5,119	1,134	95,172	1,013	600.1
1950	6,666	1,337	44,209	964	542.5
1951	5,338	1,427	96,043	311	617.1
1952	4,321	1,218	79,398	128	467.3
1953	6,117	1,206	83,811	391	445.3
1954	5,559	1,042	38,451	585	288.0
1955	7,920	1,249	42,042	983	377.1

(continued)

TABLE E-1 (continued)

	1002 Tractor-Drawn Plows (thousands)	1007 Tractor-Drawn Cultivators (thousands)	1016 Grain Combines (thousands)	1105 Diesel Engines (th. hp)	1109 Electric Motors (A.C.) (th. kw)
1870					
1871					
1872					
1873					
1874					
1875					
1876					
1877					
1878					
1879					
1880					
1881					
1882					
1883					
1884					
1885					
1886					
1887					
1888					
1889					
1890					
1891					
1892					
1893					
1894					
1895					
1896					
1897					
1898					
1899					
1900					
1901					
1902					
1903					
1904					
1905					
1906					
1907					
1908					
1909			0.54		

(continued)

	1002 Tractor-Drawn Plows (thousands)	1007 Tractor-Drawn Cultivators (thousands)	1016 Grain Combines (thousands)	1105 Diesel Engines (th. hp.)	1109 Electric Motors (A.C.) (th. kw)
1910					
1911					
1912					
1913					
1914			0.27		1,194
1915					
1916					
1917					
1918					
1919			2.39		2,280
1920					
1921	34.13	1.61	5.03	89	2,308
1922	52.54	1.56	2.85		
1923	76.40	2.09	4.01	198	3,021
1924	47.96		5.83		
1925	71.29	1.70	5.13	409	1,041
1926	112.9	10.40	11.76		
1927	106.6	10.21	18.31	368	3,260
1928	129.1	12.86	25.39		
1929	154.7	34.63	36.96	455	4,255
1930	154.9	56.25	24.41		
1931	35.58	15.63	5.91	264	1,546
1932					
1933		3.37	0.35	139	822.1
1934					
1935	88.35	54.50	3.87	650	1,591
1936	153.4	116.0	16.98		
1937	207.6	127.2	29.40	1,449	2,644
1938	152.6	90.76	48.05		
1939	130.8	63.55	41.54	1,911	
1940	220.5	104.3	46.55		
1941	241.7	272.8	54.30		
1942	176.9	141.7	41.72		
1943	72.78	83.80	29.22		
1944	172.7	181.5	44.70		
1945	229.7	191.3	51.42		
1946	216.0	151.5	48.81		
1947	340.1	245.7	76.64	10,620	9,962
1948	441.5	359.1	90.67		
1949	476.3	327.3	104.9		
1950	443.9	247.5	116.14	15,732	
1951	448.3	288.3	109.02	20,616	
1952	360.9	259.0	81.51	16,474	
1953	219.4	147.1	79.42	15,374	
1954			58.13	12,170	12,552
1955			63.89		

(continued)

595

TABLE E-1 (continued)

	1501 Flour (mill. m.t.)	1503 Butter (th. m.t.)	Cottonseed Oil (th. m.t.)	1504 Vegetable Oil (th. m.t.)	1504.1 Oleomargarine (th. m.t.)
1870					
1871					
1872			7.26		
1873			7.26		
1874			9.98		
1875			11.34		
1876			16.78		
1877			13.61		
1878			20.41		
1879			24.49		
1880			32.21		
1881		26.8	24.95		
1882		29.9	39.92		
1883		41.3	53.52		
1884		47.4	53.98		
1885		56.8	68.04		
1886		62.4	78.93		
1887		69.2	94.35		9.8
1888		75.5	112.0		15.6
1889		97.3	107.9		16.1
1890		99.1	118.8		14.7
1891		104.5	139.3		20.1
1892		103.5	145.6		22.0
1893		109.2	142.9		30.5
1894		112.8	194.6		31.6
1895		140.0	228.2		25.9
1896		177.7	195.0		23.0
1897		184.4	221.3		20.7
1898		182.8	285.8		26.1
1899	11.54	190.9	320.2		37.7
1900		201.2	317.5		48.5
1901		212.6	328.9		47.6
1902		209.0	403.7		57.3
1903		234.0	418.2		33.2
1904	11.56	242.0	414.6		22.8
1905		272.2	455.4		24.0
1906		269.8	427.7		25.1
1907		255.2	523.0		32.4
1908		283.6	350.6		37.0
1909	12.22	284.5	499.4		52.6

(continued)

TABLE E-1 (continued)

	1501 Flour (mill. m.t.)	1503 Butter (th. m.t.)	Cottonseed Oil (th. m.t.)	1504 Vegetable Oil (th. m.t.)	1504.1 Oleomargarine (th. m.t.)
1910		287.0	445.4		66.7
1911		314.1	571.5		47.6
1912		327.3	685.8		64.4
1913		347.9	631.9		68.9
1914	12.10	356.5	657.7		64.0
1915		353.8	779.7		64.4
1916		374.2	568.3		85.1
1917		380.0	638.7		130.3
1918		377.4	595.1		159.0
1919	13.01	425.7	601.0	1,050	167.3
1920		421.5	549.3	862.0	167.6
1921	11.00	513.3	593.7	915.5	97.5
1922		556.5	421.8	792.4	83.8
1923	11.44	598.6	454.9	918.7	103.2
1924		652.8	444.5	1,008	105.1
1925	11.24	662.0	636.8	1,202	106.1
1926		697.1	733.5	1,328	110.0
1927	11.57	709.5	856.4	1,382	125.8
1928		697.1	670.0	1,241	143.6
1929	11.85	734.0	727.6	1,339	161.6
1930		724.7	713.1	1,233	147.7
1931	10.61	756.3	654.1	1,152	104.3
1932		768.4	768.4	1,079	92.2
1933	9.50	799.5	655.9	1,087	111.3
1934		768.7		975.3	119.9
1935	9.91	740.4		1,065	173.1
1936		739.1		1,165	178.3
1937	10.10	796.6		1,393	180.3
1938		810.2		1,382	174.7
1939	10.71	808.2		1,396	136.4
1940		833.2		1,447	145.3
1941		849.2		1,700	166.7
1942		800.2		1,698	193.1
1943		759.2		1,883	278.6
1944		675.2		1,802	266.8
1945		618.6		1,785	278.5
1946		531.3		1,725	259.6
1947	14.79	602.9		2,019	338.4
1948		549.0		2,253	411.9
1949		640.5		2,515	390.9
1950		628.9		2,537	425.0
1951		545.7		2,591	472.1
1952		538.9		2,553	583.3
1953		640.4		2,618	586.0
1954	11.13	657.3		2,667	618.8
1955		627.0		2,756	604.8

(continued)

TABLE E-1 (continued)

	1505 Cheese (th. m.t.)	1506 Meat Slaughtering (th. m.t.)	1506.1 Sausages (th. m.t.)	1507 Fish Catch (th. m.t.)	1508 Soap (th. m.t.)
1870	57.6				
1871	54.4				
1872	64.0				
1873	74.8				
1874	74.8				
1875	86.6				
1876	72.6				
1877	91.6				
1878	120.2				
1879	98.0				377
1880	109.3	1,473		732.5	
1881	123.8	1,402		711.2	
1882	107.0	1,315		689.9	
1883	116.1	1,423		669.1	
1884	113.9	1,430		647.7	
1885	108.4	1,602		628.2	
1886	102.5	1,677		606.5	
1887	112.5	1,641		585.1	
1888	121.1	1,787		651.4	
1889	127.9	2,048	178.7	724.8	
1890	132.0	2,521		760.2	
1891	124.7	2,427		733.0	
1893	135.6	2,473		723.5	
1893	108.0	2,259		713.9	
1894	109.8	2,548		708.5	
1895	99.8	2,466		702.6	
1896	102.5	2,548		701.7	
1897	132.9	2,786		700.8	
1898	120.2	3,021		731.6	
1899	128.4	3,099	348.4	791.1	
1900	139.3	3,174		831.4	
1901	156.0	3,318		871.3	
1902	137.4	3,102		885.0	
1903	139.7	3,313		872.7	
1904	143.8	3,428	388.4	870.9	1,110
1905	142.4	3,624		855.9	
1906	127.5	3,694		856.8	
1907	125.2	3,770		857.7	
1908	137.4	3,966		858.7	
1909	141.1	3,700	542.2	874.1	1,438

(continued)

	1505 Cheese (th. m.t.)	1506 Meat Slaughtering (th. m.t.)	1506.1 Sausages (th. m.t.)	1507 Fish Catch (th. m.t.)	1508 Soap (th. m.t.)
1910	161.0	3,450		889.5	
1911	156.0	3,862		904.9	
1912	149.2	3,703		920.3	
1913	143.3	3,741		935.8	
1914	171.5	3,604	571.6	968.4	1,824
1915	203.2	3,959		992.0	
1916	194.6	4,471		994.7	
1917	216.4	4,381		1,008	
1918	181.4	5,158		1,026	
1919	215.5	4,891	822.6	1,017	1,824
1920	196.0	4,779		1,005	1,836
1921	192.3	4,825	449.1	979.8	1,849
1922	196.9	5,122		931.2	1,980
1923	206.4	5,832	597.7	941.7	2,113
1924	213.2	5,368		941.2	2,049
1925	224.5	5,070	672.0	996.5	1,937
1926	215.3	5,149		966.6	2,029
1927	203.8	5,112	683.3	1,268	2,119
1928	218.3	5,132		1,398	2,186
1929	221.0	5,072	595.6	1,618	2,252
1930	227.0	4,985		1,491	2,259
1931	223.3	5,055	549.1	1,205	2,265
1932	219.5	4,878		1,186	2,160
1933	246.6	5,284	521.7	1,330	2,053
1934	262.7	5,271		1,841	2,068
1935	281.7	4,246	605.0	1,844	2,081
1936	291.5	5,164		2,159	2,302
1937	294.4	4,676	722.3	1,974	3,075
1938	328.6	4,981		1,929	2,353
1939	321.5	5,264	759.1	2,015	2,496
1940	356.3	5,830		1,842	2,391
1941	433.9	6.092		2,223	2,884
1942	504.9	7,009		1,759	2,692
1943	451.6	7,632		1,906	2,574
1944	462.6	8,127		2,043	3,079
1945	507.5	6,965		2,076	2,672
1946	501.8	6,256		2,021	2,111
1947	536.6	7,363	1,069	1,970	2,616
1948	498.2	6,676		2,075	2,244
1949	544.0	7,089		2,175	2,089
1950	540.4	7,274		2,215	2,083
1951	526.6	7,205		2,002	1,628
1952	530.8	7,619		1,950	1,434
1953	610.0	8,248		2,023	1,215
1954	614.0	8,447	1,282	2,132	994
1955	613.9	9,128		2,175	

(continued)

TABLE E-1 (continued)

	1509 Salt (th.m.t.)	1510 Raw Sugar Consumption (th.m.t.)	1513 Canned Food (mill. cans)	1514 Beer (mill. hectol.)	1515 Cigarettes (millions)
1870		582.8		7.74	
1871		655.8		9.03	
1872		750.3		10.21	
1873		762.3		11.26	
1874		812.4		11.26	
1875		783.9		11.15	
1876		748.5		11.62	
1877		839.7		11.50	
1878		766.7		11.97	
1879		942.4	501	13.02	
1880	757.5	906.8		15.61	533
1881	787.4	1,008.4		16.78	595
1882	814.7	978.5		19.95	599
1883	786.5	1,114		20.89	844
1884	827.4	1,384		22.29	920
1885	893.6	1,333		22.53	1,080
1886	978.9	1,354		24.29	1,607
1887	1,017	1,503		27.10	1,865
1888	1,023	1,385		28.98	2,212
1889	1,017	1,409	835	29.45	2,413
1890	1,128	1,462		32.38	2,505
1891	1,268	1,809		35.79	3,137
1892	1,486	1,791		37.43	3,282
1893	1,511	1,951		40.60	3,661
1894	1,647	2,246		39.19	3,621
1895	1,736	1,974		39.42	4,238
1896	1,759	2,055		42.12	4.967
1897	2,029	2,546		40.48	4,927
1898	2,237	1,568		44.00	4,843
1899	2,503	2,134	1,451	43.06	4,367
1900	2,651	2,045		46.35	3,870
1901	2,612	2,627		47.64	3,503
1902	3,029	2,311		52.33	3,647
1903	2,409	2,921		54.80	3,959
1904	2,798	2,593	2,169	56.67	4,170
1905	3,298	2,830		58.08	4,477
1906	3,578	3,120		64.18	5,502
1907	3,773	3,213		68.76	6.345
1908	3,661	2,972		68.99	6,833
1909	3,824	3,425	2,803	66.06	7,880

(continued)

	1509 Salt (th.m.t.)	1510 Raw Sugar Consumption (th.m.t.)	1513 Canned Food (mill. cans)	1514 Beer (mill. hectol.)	1515 Cigarettes (millions)
1910	3,849	3,360	3,082	69.81	9,782
1911	3,961	3,396	3,479	74.27	11,700
1912	4,232	3,695	4,095	72.98	14,239
1913	4,369	3,801	4,028	76.62	16,530
1914	4,422	4,012	4,349	77.68	17.944
1915	4,855	4,308	3,966	70.17	18,945
1916	5,773	4,327	4,665	68.76	26,203
1917	6,330	4,357	5,542	71.34	36,323
1918	6,567	3,926	6,433	59.02	47,528
1919	6,244	4,432	6,074	32.50	53,865
1920	6,205	5,443	5,706	10.79	48,091
1921	4,519	4,990	4,232	10.79	52,770
1922	6,163	5,701	5,109	7.39	56,413
1923	6,469	5,879	6,449	6.22	67,239
1924	6,172	5,413	6.202	5.75	73,256
1925	6,711	5,967	7,421	5.98	82,712
1926	6,688	6,272	6,684	5.75	92,523
1927	6,867	6,167	6.962	5.16	100,260
1928	7,326	5,987	7,201	4.93	109,131
1929	7,751	6,568	8,711	4.58	122,822
1930	7,307	6,009	8,783	4.34	124,193
1931	6,675	5,770	7.607	3.64	117,407
1932	5,813	6,128	6,712	3.17	106,915
1933	6,899	6,058	7,183	11.50	115,087
1934	6,906	5,459	8,481	44.21	130,287
1935	7,191	6,033	10,429	53.07	140,147
1936	8,010	5,973	10.873	60.79	159,076
1937	8,384	5,606	12,175	68.93	170,171
1938	7,281	6,019	12,435	66.11	171,842
1939	8,417	6,449	11,670	63.21	180,828
1940	9,399	6,417	14,065	64.41	189,508
1941	11,541	7,128	17,520	64.79	218,083
1942	12,422	5,192	20,522	74.76	257,657
1943	13,803	5,823	19,884	83.33	296,305
1944	14,259	6,315	20,869	95.89	323,734
1945	13,965	6,005	21,881	101.6	332,345
1946	13,734	5,568	24,141	99.71	350,132
1947	14,564	7,842	20,017	103.1	369,763
1948	14,881	6,260	20,274	107.1	386,916
1949	14,127	7,056	19,593	105.3	385,046
1950	15,087	7,652	20,554	104.2	392,025
1951	18,332	6,905		104.4	418,872
1952	17,731	7,269		106.2	435,616
1953	18,860	7,623		108.1	423,129
1954	18,751	7,765		104.0	401,928
1955	20,597	7,699	19,360	105.9	412,323

(continued)

TABLE E-1 (continued)

	1601 Boots and Shoes (mill. pairs)	1602 Rubber Footwear (th. pairs)	1604 Cotton Fabrics (mill. m)	1609.1 Pure Silk and Nylon Fabrics (mill. m)	1609.2 Rayon and Mixed Fabrics (mill. m)
1870				5	
1871					
1872					
1873					
1874					
1875					
1876					
1877					
1878					
1879			2,910	15	
1880					
1881					
1882					
1883					
1884					
1885					
1886					
1887					
1888					
1889	173.9		3,515	37	
1890					
1891					
1892					
1893					
1894					
1895					
1896					
1897					
1898					
1899	212.6	49,832	4,610	75	32
1900					
1901					
1902					
1903					
1904	233.5		5,090	108	42
1905					
1906					
1907					
1908					
1909	265.1		6,621	126	92

(continued)

	1601 Boots and Shoes (mill. pairs)	1602 Rubber Footwear (th. pairs)	1604 Cotton Fabrics (mill. m)	1609.1 Pure Silk and Nylon Fabrics (mill. m.)	1609.2 Rayon and Mixed Fabrics (mill. m.)
1910					
1911					
1912					
1913					
1914	292.7	61,220	7,041	157	109
1915					
1916					
1917					
1918					
1919	331.2	96,388	8,263	271	94
1920					
1921	305.1	78,930	7,690	245	75
1922					
1923	373.5	95,315	9,355	280	141
1924					
1925	344.2	82,078	8,726	424	105
1926					
1927	367.1	105,749	10,052	425	44
1928					
1929	361.4	100,765	9,783	468	
1930	304.2				
1931	316.2	57,198	7,949	425	87
1932	313.3				
1933	349.4	65,295	9,008	221	295
1934	357.1				
1935	383.8	64,793	8,173	263	674
1936	415.2				
1937	412.0	77,002	11,087	120	920
1938	390.7				
1939	424.1	62,847	10,609		
1940	404.1				
1941	498.4		13,310		
1942	483.9		14,220		
1943	465.4		13,535		
1944	462.6		12,223	73	
1945	486.2		11,164	50	
1946	529.0		11,705	34	
1947	468.1	79,359	12,568	35	2,201
1948	479.6		12,341		
1949	475.6		10,760		
1950	522.5		12,837	152	2,709
1951	481.9		12,975		
1952	533.2		12,181	345	2,173
1953	532.0		13,062	382	2,257
1954	524.0	75,518	12,512	408	2,048
1955	577.0		12,929	437	2,384

(continued)

TABLE E-1 (continued)

	1611 Woolen and Worsted Fabrics (mill. m.)	1613 Hosiery (mill. pairs)	1701 Bicycles (thousands)	1704 Phonographs (thousands)
1870				
1871				
1872				
1873				
1874				
1875				
1876				
1877				
1878				
1879	245.0			
1880				
1881				
1882				
1883				
1884				
1885				
1886				
1887				
1888				
1889	250.4	288.1		
1890				
1891				
1892				
1893				
1894				
1895				
1896				
1897				
1898				
1899	272.0	359.1	1,183	151
1900				
1901				
1902				
1903				
1904	322.3	530.2	250	
1905				
1906				
1907				
1908				
1909	363.8	753.9	234	345

(continued)

604

	1611 Woolen and Worsted Fabrics (mill. m.)	1613 Hosiery (mill. pairs)	1701 Bicycles (thousands)	1704 Phonographs (thousands)
1910				
1911				
1912				
1913				
1914	359.9	902.0	399	514
1915				
1916				
1917				
1918				
1919	341.4	1,016	479	2,230
1920				
1921	314.7	963.1	216	596
1922				
1923	400.1	1,169	486	997
1924				
1925	369.5	1,197	303	642
1926				
1927	355.4	1,320	255	1,050
1928				
1929	327.5	1,408	308	755
1930				
1931	248.5	1,341	260	
1932				
1933	272.0	1,233	320	
1934				
1935	356.1	1,398	657	
1936				
1937	373.1	1,507	1,131	
1938				
1939	374.0	1,828	1,253	
1940				
1941		1,800		
1942	530.9	1,775		
1943	539.6	1,791		
1944	531.1	1,697		
1945	496.3	1,630		
1946	607.2	1,889		
1947	518.9	1,795	2,875	5,444
1948	503.4	1,764	2,795	
1949	416.8	1,734	1,483	
1950	473.2	1,926	1,964	
1951	377.6	1,857	1,880	
1952	353.4	1,959		2,713
1953	339.9	1,905		3,663
1954	281.8		1,746	
1955	312.0			3,123

(continued)

TABLE E-1 (continued)

	1705 Radios (thousands)	1706 Television Sets (thousands)	1707 Household Sewing Machines (thousands)
1870			
1871			
1872			
1873			
1874			
1875			
1876			
1877			
1878			
1879			
1880			
1881			
1882			
1883			
1884			
1885			
1886			
1887			
1888			
1889			
1890			
1891			
1892			
1893			
1894			
1895			
1896			
1897			
1898			
1899			748
1900			
1901			
1902			
1903			
1904			
1905			
1906			
1907			
1908			
1909			

(continued)

TABLE E-1 (concluded)

	1705 Radios (thousands)	1706 Television Sets (thousands)	1707 Household Sewing Machines (thousands)
1910			
1911			
1912			
1913			
1914			
1915			
1916			
1917			
1918			
1919			
1920			
1921			
1922	100		
1923	250		
1924	1,500		
1925	2,000		
1926	1,750		
1927	1,350		764
1928	3,281		
1929	4,428		669
1930	3,788		
1931	3,594		232
1932	2,446		
1933	4,157		128
1934	4,478		
1935	6,030		343
1936	8,249		
1937	8,083		548
1938	7,142		
1939	10,763	4.1	457
1940	11,831		
1941	13,643		
1942			
1943			
1944			
1945			
1946	15,955	7.0	
1947	20,000	178.8	626
1948	16,500	975.6	
1949	11,400	3,000	
1950	14,590	7,464	
1951	12,628	5,384	
1952	10,934	6,096	
1953	13,680	7,216	
1954	10,400	7,346	676
1955	14,529	7,757	

APPENDIX E

TABLE E-2
OUTPUT SERIES: UNITED STATES, 1799–1869

	101 Pig Iron (th.m.t.)	103 Steel Ingots and Castings (mill.m.t.)	202 Copper (th.m.t.)	203 Lead (th.m.t.)	204 Zinc (th.m.t.)	305 Crude Petroleum (th.m.t.)	310 Coal (mill.m.t.)	416 Paper (th.m.t.)	510 Lumb (mill.n
1799									0.71
1808				0.9					
1809									0.94
1810	54.8								
1813				1.4					
1818				1.4					
1819									1.30
1820	20.3								
1821				1.72					
1822				1.72					
1823				1.88					
1824				1.80					
1825				2.02					
1826				2.16					
1827				4.07					
1828	132.1			6.76					
1829	144.3			7.78					2.01
1830	167.6			7.26					
1831	194.1			6.80					
1832	203.2			9.07					
1833				9.98					
1834				10.89					
1835				11.79					
1836				13.61					
1837				12.24					
1838				13.61					
1839				15.88					3.79
1840	291.5			15.42			1.88		
1841	286.5			18.60			2.08		
1842	281.5			21.77			2.37		
1843	405.5			22.68			2.78		
1844	529.4			23.59			3.34		
1845	653.4		0.10	27.22			3.91		
1846	777.3		0.15	25.40			4.41		
1847	812.8		0.30	25.40			4.80		
1848	812.8		0.51	22.68			3.45		
1849	660.4		0.71	21.32			5.85		12.72
1850	572.8		0.66	19.96			6.37		
1851	540.4		0.91	16.78			7.92		
1852	508.0		1.12	14.24			8.91		
1853	588.0		2.03	15.24			9.59		

(continued)

TABLE E-2 (concluded)

	101 Pig Iron (th.m.t.)	103 Steel Ingots and Castings (mill.m.t.)	202 Copper (th.m.t.)	203 Lead (th.m.t.)	204 Zinc (th.m.t.)	305 Crude Petroleum (th.m.t.)	310 Coal (mill.m.t.)	416 Paper (th.m.t.)	510 Lumber (mill.m³)
4	667.9		2.29	14.97			10.87		
5	711.4		3.05	14.33			11.73		
6	801.1		4.06	14.51			12.29		
7	724.1		4.88	14.33			12.10		
8	639.7		5.59	13.88	0.02		12.68		
9	762.6		6.40	14.88	0.05	0.3	14.18	103.8	18.95
0	834.4		7.32	14.15	0.73	69	13.25		
1	663.6		7.62	12.79	1.36	291	14.96		
2	714.6		9.60	12.88	1.36	421	15.86		
3	859.6		8.64	13.43	1.54	359	19.34		
4	1,030.6		8.13	13.88	1.63	291	21.41		
5	845.1		8.64	13.34	1.91	344	21.58		
6	1,225		9.04	14.61	1.81	495	26.31		
7	1,326	0.020	10.16	13.79	2.90	461	27.87		
8	1,454	0.027	11.79	14.88	3.36	502	29.81		
9	1,739	0.032	12.70	15.88	3.90	580	29.85		30.10

	518 Rails (th.m.t.)	704 Iron Ore (mill.m.t.)	1505 Cheese (th.m.t.)	1513 Canned Food (mill.cans)	1604 Cotton Fabrics (mill.m)	1611 Woolen and Worsted Fabrics (mill.m)
9					977.6	82.7
0						
1						
2						
3						
4						
5						
6						
7						
8						
9					1,470	148.5
0		2.92				
1		2.24				
2		2.33				
3		2.70				
4		3.11				
5		2.45				
6		3.41				
7	420	3.53				
8		3.70				
9		4.21	49.4	167	1,455	247.6

APPENDIX E

Notes to Tables E-1 and E-2

102 *Rolled steel*

1946–1955: *601a*, 1955, 65.

103 *Steel ingots and castings*

1946–1955: *601a*, 1955, 51.

202 *Copper*

1845–1881: Primary copper from domestic ores.
1882–1908: Primary copper from domestic and foreign ores.
1909–1955: Sum of refinery production from foreign and domestic ores, secondary copper from primary refineries, new copper scrap, and old copper scrap.

203 *Lead*

1808, 1813, 1818, 1821–1906: Refined lead from domestic and foreign ore and base bullion. For first three dates, centered annual average of five-year output. For 1907, output was 375 th. m. tons.
1907–1955: Sum of refined lead from domestic and foreign ore and base bullion, secondary lead, and lead in alloys. For 1955, the last 2 are taken to be the same fraction of the total as in 1954.

204 *Zinc*

1858–1908: Slab zinc from domestic and foreign ores (for 1858–1879, from *642a*, Table 11, 19). For 1909, output was 232 th. m. tons.
1909–1928: Sum of slab zinc from domestic and foreign ores and secondary zinc recovered unalloyed (except for zinc dust).
1929–1955: Sum of (1) slab zinc from domestic and foreign ores, (2) secondary zinc recovered unalloyed (except for zinc dust), and (3) zinc in alloys other than brass, zinc in brass and bronze, zinc recovered in chemical products, and secondary zinc dust. For 1955, the last 2 are taken to be the same fraction of the total as in 1954.

301 *Electric power*

1882: *593*, 965. Converted from hp into kwh.

306 *Natural gas*

1882–1955: Converted from cubic feet into cubic meters.

401 *Soda ash*

1904–1955: *611*, Part V.

404 *Sulfuric acid*

1938, 1940: *611*, Part V.

405 *Mineral fertilizer*

1870–1879: Superphosphate (converted from 16 to 18.7% P_2O_5).
1880–1914: Sum of superphosphate (as above) and ammonium sulfate (20.5% N).
1915–1951: Sum of superphosphate (as above), ammonium sulfate (20.5% N), and potash (41.6% K_2O). Potash for 1915–1950 is taken from *611*, Part VII, series 726.21.
1952–1955: Extrapolated by fertilizer consumption from *649*, 1958, 641.

412 *Synthetic dyes*

1914–1953: *611*, Part V, series 520.31.

610

418 *Motor vehicle tires*

1900: Output of automobiles times four.

506 *Cement*

1880–1955: Sum of natural, masonry, puzzolan, and Portland cements. For 1955, the first 3 cements are estimated from their ratios to total in 1954.

510 *Lumber*

All years: Converted from board feet into cubic meters.

518 *Rails*

1867: *634a*, 247.
1940–1945: *601a*, 1948, 46.
1946–1955: *601a*, 1955, p. 77.

519 *Flat glass*

All years: Sum of window glass and plate glass (polished). Not strictly comparable to Soviet counterpart because U.S. product is at least 35% thicker (see Chapter 3). For some years, output of plate glass has been estimated from other data.

901 *Automobiles*

1900–1904: *602*, 4.

902 *Trucks and buses*

1953–1954: *602*, 4.

905 *Railroad freight cars*

1880–1898: *646*, January issue of each year.
1899–1912: *647*, January 1934. For 1905–1912, includes Canadian output.
1913–1954: *645*. Cars delivered to domestic and foreign receivers. Includes cars built in railroad and private line shops.
1955: American Railway Car Institute, unpublished data.

906 *Railroad passenger cars*

1880–1912: National Bureau of Economic Research files.
1913–1953: *645*, 50.
1954–1955: American Railway Car Institute, unpublished data.

1001 *Tractors*

All years: Wheel-type and track-laying tractors, excluding garden tractors.
1909–1921: Department of Agriculture, "Circular 212," April 1922.

1002 *Tractor-drawn plows*

All years: Includes listers, whose production was interpolated when data were not available.

1109 *Electric motors*

All years: Sum of synchronous, single-phase, polyphase, and capacitor type motors.
1954: Extrapolated from 1947 by production index with cross weights (*609*, 1954, IV, 11).

1504 *Vegetable oil*

1872–1933: Cottonseed oil. For 1872–1874, from *607*, 298. For 1875–1933, from *654*, 314–315, year ending July 31. Crude oil produced.
1919–1955: Vegetable oil.

611

1504.1 *Oleomargarine*

1901–1908:	*615*, 3.
1909–1948:	*612*, Table 57C, 159.

1506 *Meat slaughtering*

All years:
Federally inspected production, dressed weight, beef, veal, pork, lamb, and mutton.

1880–1898:
Number slaughtered (each of above categories) times average dressed weight (for each category) as of 1900, the results summed. Number slaughtered from *607*.

1508 *Soap*

All years:
Total production of soap minus toilet soap. When data on toilet soap were not available, they were estimated from total production in given year and ratio of toilet soap to total soap in 1923 (given in *609*, 1929, II, 736). All figures were multiplied by 1.875 to adjust to Soviet fatty acid content of 40%.

1914–1931 (census years),
1935–1952:
611, Part V, series 590.31.

1510 *Raw sugar consumption*

All years:
Consumption of raw, cane, and beet sugar. Includes Puerto Rico after 1898, Hawaii after 1896, the Virgin Islands after 1928, and the Philippines from 1898 through 1940 and in 1945.

1513 *Canned food*

All years:
Converted into standard cans of 400 grams. Details available on request.

1869–1899
(census years):
Canned vegetables only.

1904, 1909–1920:
Sum of canned milk (condensed, evaporated, dry whole, and dry skim milk), fruit, fruit juices, vegetables (including vegetable juices), and meat. Canned meat from *618*, 404. All the others from *612*, 154.

1921–1950:
Sum of canned fish, milk (as above), fruit, fruit juices, vegetables, baby foods, soups, and meat. Canned fish given in or derived from *621* and *649*, 1954, 738. All others from above sources and *598*, 1945 and 1954.

1955:
Extrapolated from 1950 by production in cases. Averages of two adjoining canning years.

1601 *Boots and Shoes*

1919–1927
(census years):
633, Table 14, 49.

1604 *Cotton fabrics*

All years:
All data were multiplied by 1.4 to adjust for difference in average width between Soviet and U.S. fabrics.

1941–1953:
611, Part V.

1609.1 *Pure silk and nylon fabrics*

All years:
All data were multiplied by 1.2 to adjust for difference in average width between Soviet and U.S. fabrics.

1870, 1879, 1889:
Extrapolated by silk imports.

1609.2 *Rayon and mixed fabrics*

All years:
Adjusted as pure silk and nylon fabrics above.

1611 *Woolen and worsted fabrics*

Before 1921: Excludes upholstery materials.

From 1951 on: Excludes products with 25 to 50% wool content. All data were multiplied by 1.1 to adjust for difference in average width between Soviet and U.S. fabrics.

1613 *Hosiery*

1941–1946: *616*, 394.

1701 *Bicycles*

1947–1951: Shipments from *604*.

1705 *Radios*

1922–1948: *644*, 26–27. Domestic set sales.

Official Soviet Data on Industrial Production

THE basic Soviet accounts of aggregate industrial production are kept in the form of gross value of industrial production, in both current and "constant" rubles. The comprehensive accounts have not been published for any year, and the few figures that have been made public refer to the interwar period. The data shown here (Tables F-1 and F-3) have generally been reconstructed from the few available figures, some derived indirectly, and published index numbers (Table F-2) or other relationships.

The nature of the Soviet production accounts has been carefully described elsewhere[1] and cannot be given satisfactorily in brief compass. The few notes written here are intended merely to highlight some of the considerations needed to interpret the assembled data.

Major Categories of Gross Production

Following Marxian doctrine, industrial products are broken down into two primary categories: Group "A" and Group "B," sometimes referred to rather inaccurately as "producer goods" and "consumer goods." The former represent goods—and some services—used to produce other goods; the latter, goods used to produce services in households and other "nonproductive" sectors of the economy (as education, health services, government). This formal dichotomy leaves room for trouble in deciding where specific items should be entered, and we know from the Soviet literature on the subject that a number of arbitrary decisions are made. In the absence of detailed published accounts, we are left in the dark, however, on how some of the more important issues are resolved.

For example, where are military products recorded? In principle, they would seem to belong in Group "B," but they could hardly have been recorded there as late as 1945 since they undoubtedly exceeded "B" goods in gross value that year (see Table F-1). As we shall discuss further below, some important changes were apparently made in the production accounts at the time of the shift from "1926/27" prices to "1952" prices, and the change in the gross value for machine building, taken together with the data on "tools of labor" (*orudiia truda*), suggests

---

[1] See, e.g., an excellent article by Alec Nove (*538*). See also our discussion of official production indexes in Chapter 5 and the references given there.

TABL

S<small>ELECTED</small> O<small>FFICIAL</small> D<small>ATA</small> <small>ON</small> V<small>ALUE</small> <small>OF</small> G<small>ROSS</small> P<small>RODUCTIO</small>

		"*1926/27*" Prices							
		1913	1928	1932	1937	1940	1945	1946	195(
1.	All industry	16.4	21.6	43.7	96.2	139.3	128.0	106.9	241.
2	Group "A"	5.5	8.5	23.3	55.6	85.3	95.8	70.4	175.
3.	Group "B"	10.9	13.1	20.4	40.6	54.0	32.2	36.5	66.
4.	Large-scale industry	11.1	16.9	39.0	90.5	130.0	120.4	98.5	229.
5.	Small-scale industry	(5.3)	(4.7)	(4.6)	(5.7)	(9.3)	(7.6)	(8.1)	(12.
6.	Machine building and metalworking	1.3	2.4	9.7	27.5	48.4	62.4		104.
7.	Machine building		1.4	7.4	22.7	40.3	52.8		94.
8.	Metal products		0.8	(1.7)	(2.6)	(8.1)	(9.6)		(9.
9.	Repair shops		0.2	0.6	2.2				
	Group "A"								
10.	Tools of labor[c]								
11.	Materials[d]								
12.	Category I								
13.	Category II								
14.	Military products[e]				8.5	24.6	(44.6)	(6.8)	(17

Figures in parentheses are residuals or indirect estimates.

Sums and detail may not agree because of rounding.

[a] Excludes turnover taxes, except those levied on industrial materials consumed within industry. See Table F-3 and text.

[b] Prices of January 1, 1952, and July 1, 1955, with important exceptions. See text.

[c] *Orudiia truda.* This seems to be machinery and equipment plus repair shops minus

1

SOVIET INDUSTRY, BENCHMARK YEARS (billion rubles)

	"1952" Prices[b]			*"1955" Prices*[b]		
1950B	1953	1955A	1955B	1956	1957	1958
(451)	(655)	(834)	(766)	(847)	(932)	(1,030)
(310)	(453)	(589)	(540)	(600)	(664)	(740)
(141)	(202)	(248)	(226)	(247)	(268)	(290)
(192)	(302)	(417)	(384)	(436)	(494)	(562)
(73)	(123)	(177)	(163)	(190)	(221)	(253)
(107)⎫ (12)⎭	(179)	⎰(223) ⎱ (17)	(205)⎫ (16)⎭	(246)	(273)	(309)
(81)	(131)	(183)	(167)	(198)	(232)	(266)
(229)	(322)	(406)	(373)	(402)	(432)	(474)
(149)	(213)	(271)	(248)	(264)	(286)	(311)
(81)	(109)	(135)	(124)	(138)	(146)	(163)
(16)	(39)	(44)	(42)			

consumer durables. If this interpretation is correct, the latter would be about 4 billion rubles for 1950 and about 12 billion for 1955, in "1952" and "1955" prices, respectively.

d *Predmety truda.*

e Estimated earmarked expenditures on military products, excluding such things as atomic energy. Over 1950–1955, estimates are probably too high in view of recent information (see annex to technical note 3, Appendix A).

NOTES TO TABLE F-1

Line 1

1913–1950A: Value in 1933 (45,955 million rubles as given in *241*, 7–11, and *362*, 1935, No. 7, 41–49) extrapolated by index (see Table F-2 and, for 1933, *180*, 32).

1955A, B: Gross production less turnover taxes (800 billion current rubles from Table F-3) corrected by price index. We assume that half the volume of production occurred before July 1, 1955, when the "1955" prices became effective. Since "1955" prices were apparently 0.92 of "1952" prices when properly weighted (*580*, 1956, 1-4), gross industrial production may be estimated as follows (billion rubles):

	Current Prices	"1952" Prices	"1955" Prices
First half, 1955	417	417	383
Second half, 1955	383	417	383
Total	800	834	766

1950B, 1953: 1955A extrapolated by index (see Table F-2).

1956–1958: 1955B extrapolated by index (see Table F-2). The figure for 1958 checks roughly with the statement by Khrushchev, *364*, 1/28/59 (*451*, XI, 3, 6) that an increase in gross industrial production by 1% in 1959 would amount to more than 11 billion rubles.

Lines 2 and 3

1913–1940, 1946,
1950B–1955: Line 1 times percentages in *180*, 13.

1945, 1950A: 1932 extrapolated by index in *180*, 33. See text for reason in case of 1950A.

1956–1958: Line 1 times percentages in *141*, 147.

Line 4

1928–1950A: 1932 extrapolated by index (see Table F-2). 1932 derived from 1933 value (42,261 million rubles as given in *241*, 7–11) and 1933 as per cent of 1932 (105% as given in *180*, 33).

Line 5

1928–1950A: Residual, all industry (line 1) minus large-scale industry (line 4).

Line 6

1913–1932,
1940–1950A: 1937 extrapolated by index (see Table F-2).

1937: *490*, 86.

1955A, B: Machine building and metalworking are stated (*34*, 35) to account for about 50% of gross industrial production in 1954–55. This figure is explicitly identified as an estimate. The same source gives the share for 1940 as 31%, which is less than our implied estimate of 35% or the figure of 36.3% given by Voznesensky (*292*, 45). It may be that repair shops are excluded in the Soviet estimate.

1950B, 1953: 1955A extrapolated by index (see Table F-2).

1956–1958: 1955B extrapolated by index (see Table F-2).

Line 7

1928: 1928/29 in current prices from Table C-2. This year is used because current data for it are consistent with the implied official 1928 figure for machine building and metalworking in "1926/27" prices. The alternative would have been to estimate a current value for 1928 and translate it into "1926/27" prices. Both adjustments would have been largely arbitrary.

1932:   Large-scale value multiplied by ratio of total to large-scale in 1933. For basic data, see *467*, 340, series excluding repair shops.

1937:   Large-scale value (*467*, 340) plus estimated small-scale value. The latter (565 million rubles) is taken to be 10.0 per cent of total value of small-scale industry, the percentage for 1933. For 1933 data on small-scale sectors, see *467* and *362*, 1935, No. 7, 41–49.

1940:   Machine building and metalworking times 0.833, interpolated ratio between 1937 and 1941 Plan. For 1941 Plan data, see *490*, 181.

1945–1950A: 1940 extrapolated by index (see Table F-2).
1950B, 1953:   1955A extrapolated by index (see Table F-2).
1955A: Taken as same ratio to line 6 as for 1955B.
1955B–1957:   1958 extrapolated by index (see Table F-2).
1958:   Based on line 1 and statement (*410*, 1959, No. 8, 11) that machine building accounted for 25% of gross industrial production.

Line 8
1928:   1928/29 from Table C-2. See line 7, same year.
1932 and 1937:   Residual, line 6 minus lines 7 and 9.
1940–1950A, 1953,
1956–1958:   Residual, combined with repair shops, line 6 minus line 7.
1950B, 1955;   Combined residual (line 6 minus line 7) for metal products and repair shops distributed on the basis of the following indexes of gross production (*180*, 203):

	1955 as Per Cent of 1950
Metal products	209
Repair shops	141

Line 9
1928–1937:   *467*, 340. Difference between series including and excluding repair shops.
1940–1958:   See line 8.

Line 10–13
1950B–1957:   Group "A" (line 2) broken down by percentage distribution (*180*, 13; *141*, 148; and *141a*, 149).

Line 14
1937:   Table A-9, note to 1937.
1940:   Estimated value in current rubles (31.0 billion from Table A-9) divided by 1.26 (see same table, note to 1937).
1945–1950A: Estimated value in current rubles, assumed to be the same as "1926/27." From Table A-9, col. 2.
1950B, 1953, 1955A: Estimated value in current rubles (Table A-9) deflated by price index for basic industrial materials (estimate A, Table A-10).
1955B: From Table A-9, col. 2.

TABLE F-2

Selected Official Indexes of Gross Production in Soviet Industry, Benchmark Years

	1913	1928	1932	1937	1940	1945	1946	1950	1953	1955	1956	1957	1958
								Index (1928 = 100)					
1. All industry	76	100	202	446	646	593	495	1,119	1,626	2,069	2,288	2,517	2,776
2. Group "A"	65	100	273	652	1,000	1,122	824	2,049	2,992	3,895	4,335	4,812	5,361
3. Group "B"	83	100	156	311	415	246	279	510	736	899	982	1,063	1,149
4. Large-scale industry	66	100	232	537	771	714	584	1,355	2,004	2,576			
5. Small-scale industry	(113)	(100)	(98)	(121)	(198)	(162)	(172)	(270)					
6. Machine building and metalworking	56	100	399	1,128	1,982	2,553		4,252	6,699	9,235	10,505	11,892	13,533
7. Machine building		(100)	(529)	(1,621)	(2,879)	3,771		6,737	11,401	16,439	19,174	22,312	25,503
8,9. Metal products and repair shops		(100)	(230)	(480)	(810)	(960)		(970)	(1,500)	(1,960)	(2,010)	(2,230)	(2,524)
								Index (1950 = 100)					
Group "A"	3.2	4.9	13	32	49	55	40	100	146	190	212	235	263
10. Tools of labor								100	(160)	227	(270)	306	354
11. Materials								100	(140)	177	(190)	211	231
12. Category I								100	(150)	183	(200)	219	242
13. Category II								100	(130)	167	(190)	197	213
14. Military products				(50)	(210)	(265)	(40)	100	(244)	(275)			
Group "B"	16	19	31	61	81	48	55	100	144	176	193	209	225
15. Light industry	14	21	31	54	89			100	143	178	190	200	216
16. Food industry	22	22	35	67	103			100	138	160	175	192	203

Note: In some cases, published indexes with differing base years have been linked together. Figures in parentheses have been derived from estimates of gross production (see Table F-1), and not from official indexes. For notes on coverage, see Table F-1.

NOTES TO TABLE F-2

Line 1

1913:	*180*, 9.
1928–1955:	*180*, 32.
1956–1957:	*141*, 60. Index with 1913 = 100.
1958:	*141a*, 141. Index with 1913 = 100.

Lines 2 and 3

1913:	*180*, 9.
1928–1955:	*180*, 32.
1956–1957:	*141*, 60. Index with 1913 = 100.
1958:	*141a*, 141. Index with 1913 = 100.

Line 4

1913–1955:	*180*, 31.

Line 5

1913–1950B:	Derived from gross production estimates in Table F-1.

Line 6

1913:	*180*, 203.
1928–1950, 1955:	*180*, 10.
1953, 1956–1957:	*141*, 52 f, 229. Index with 1913 = 100.
1958:	*141a*, 146. Index with 1940 = 100.

Line 7

1928–1940:	Derived from gross production estimates in Table F-1.
1945–1955:	*180*, 203. Index with 1940 = 100.
1956–1957:	*141*, 135. Index with 1940 = 100.
1958:	*141a*, 146. Index with 1940 = 100.

Line 8 and 9

1928–1958:	Derived from gross production estimates in Table F-1.

Line 10–13

1950, 1955:	*180*, 13.
1953, 1956:	Derived from gross production estimates in Table F-1.
1957:	*141*, 148.
1958:	*141a*, 149.

Line 14

1937–1955:	Derived from gross production estimates in Table F-1.

Lines 15 and 16

1913–1937:	*180*, 319, 367. Index with 1955 as per cent of these years.
1940–1957:	*141*, 139 f. Index with 1940 = 100.
1958:	*141a*, 146. Index with 1940 = 100.

TABLE F-3
ESTIMATED SOVIET INDUSTRIAL PRODUCTION ACCOUNT, 1955
(billion current rubles)

1.	Gross production	1,040
2.	Turnover taxes	242
3.	Profits (incl. subsidized losses)	72
4.	"Commercial" outlays and misc. charges	27
5.	Production outlays	700
6.	Cost of materials consumed	530
7.	Raw and basic materials	420
8.	Auxiliary materials	38
9.	Fuel	31
10.	Power	13
11.	Amortization	24
12.	Employee compensation (incl. social insurance deductions)	150
13.	Unallocated outlays	22
14.	Net production	500
15.	Turnover taxes	242
16.	Profits (incl. subsidized losses)	72
17.	Net "commercial" outlays and misc. charges	21
18.	Employee compensation (incl. social insurance deductions)	150
19.	Net unallocated outlays	17

General Note: Sums and detail may not be consistent because of rounding. The concepts of gross and net production are intended to be those on a "commercial cost" basis outlined by Nove in *538*. We are also indebted to Nove for bringing important source materials to our attention, as indicated below.

Line 1:   Net production (line 14) divided by its share in gross production (given as 0.48 by Notkin in *410*, 1956, No. 9, 6). From the context it seems clear that Notkin refers to magnitudes in "realized" prices, i.e., including turnover taxes. He also seems to refer to current prices, since he gives national income as 50% of aggregate social product, a fraction identified elsewhere (*363*, 1957, No. 8, 76) as applying to current prices. Gross production as derived here is not entirely consistent with the statement (*364*, 5/31/57) that Ukrainian gross production (**preliminarily estimated as 177 billion in** *365*, 1/19/56) was "almost a fifth" of Soviet gross production. These sources were brought to our attention by Nove.

Line 2:   *141a*, 799. We assume all turnover taxes are assigned to industry in official Soviet national income accounts. Note that some of these taxes are double-counted to an unknown extent in lines 4, 6–11, and 13, since turnover taxes are levied on some of the intermediate products consumed within industry.

Line 3:   Sum of net profits of state enterprises and industrial cooperatives (*141a*, 799) plus estimate of 5 billion rubles for subsidized losses. The latter seems consistent with estimates of subsidized losses in *491*, 143.

Lines 4–13:   Mutually determined on the basis of the following relations. Production outlays (*P*) plus "commercial" outlays (*C*) are equal to gross production minus the sum of turnover taxes and profits. Employee compensation (*E*) plus "commercial" and unallocated outlays (*U*), both net of materials consumed, are equal to net

that military products may have been transferred at that time to Group "B."

Recent statistical sources have published a percentage breakdown of Group "A" goods into tools of labor and materials of labor (*predmety truda*), the latter being further broken down into materials used in making "A" goods (materials of category I) and "B" goods (materials of category II). The classification "tools of labor" apparently covers machinery and equipment (including repairs carried out in repair shops) except consumer durables. Most military equipment may also be excluded, as noted below. This interpretation is supported by the movement of the Group "B" official production index relative to the official indexes for the light and food industries.

Another major category for which data on gross production can be reconstructed is "machine building and metalworking." This category overlaps all the others discussed to this point. Its three main subdivisions are machine building, metal products, and repair shops. Machine building apparently includes machinery and equipment of all kinds— hence both "A" and "B" goods—except that, as we have noted, military

---

Notes to Table F–2 (continued)

production minus the sum of turnover taxes and profits (*538*, 265 f). For unallocated outlays, materials consumed are taken in Soviet statistics as 24% of the outlays (*538*); we assume the same percentage holds for "commercial" outlays. The percentage distribution of production outlays is given (*180*, 29) for cost of materials (*M*) and its components, employee compensation, and unallocated outlays. Hence we have the following equations whose solution is given in the body of the table:

$$P + C = 725 \text{ billion rubles}$$
$$E + 0.76 \,(C + U) = 185 \text{ billion rubles}$$
$$M = 0.757 \, P$$
$$E = 0.212 \, P$$
$$U = 0.031 \, P$$

It should be noted that all items involving materials (lines 4, 6–11, and 13) include such turnover taxes as were levied on those materials, with an unknown extent of doublecounting.

Line 14: Estimated national income (928 billion rubles) times 0.54, the fraction accounted for by industry (*363*, 1957, No. 8, 76 f). National income is Nove's estimate of 1,100 billion rubles for 1957 (based on seemingly firm evidence summarized in *538a*) extrapolated to 1955 by the official index (*141*, 95). Since the latter is in terms of "constant" prices, this calculation is subject to undeterminable error.

Lines 15, 16, and 18: Lines 2–4 and 12.
Lines 17 and 19: 76% of lines 4 and 13.

equipment may have been removed at the time of the shift from "1926/27" to "1952" prices and placed with metal products. Metal products also fall into both "A" and "B" categories, and they include intermediate materials as well as final products. Finally, repair shops are apparently those specialized establishments that repair and rebuild machinery and equipment of various kinds; the value of their activity seems to be counted entirely within the "A" category.

For some years, statistics can also be broken down for large- and small-scale industry. This classification is explained in some detail in Chapter 7, and it seems better to refer to that discussion than to attempt a brief and inadequate summary.

Role of Turnover Taxes

A special problem in interpreting Soviet data on the value of industrial output is created by the treatment of turnover taxes, which have their primary incidence on "B" goods. According to established Soviet doctrine, turnover taxes—including those levied on agricultural products —represent the product of all industry that is transferred to the state, being collected for financial convenience from certain industries. In national product accounts, turnover taxes are therefore included in the product attributed to industry. A case in point is the total gross production shown in line 1 of Table F-3, which also includes an undeterminable amount of double counting of turnover taxes to the extent that they are levied on intermediate products consumed within industry. That is to say, some of the turnover taxes (line 2 of Table F-3) attributed to the gross production of industry are already included, perhaps several times, in the gross production "net" of turnover taxes (line 1 minus line 2) to the extent that they appear in the prices of intermediate products consumed within industry.

In internal industrial accounts, gross production is recorded "net" of turnover taxes, in the sense just explained. That is, output of each good is evaluated at its price net of the turnover tax levied on it, so that turnover taxes are included only to the extent that they are levied on materials consumed within industry. For example, the gross value of shoes does not include the turnover tax on shoes, but it does include any turnover tax on the leather used in making shoes—and on things used in making leather, and so on. The gross production of industry used in these accounts would be the sum of lines 3–5 in Table F-3. The accounts reconstructed in Table F-1 and F-2 were presumably calculated in this way, except that they are expressed in "constant" prices.

Net Production

The net production of industry, though calculated by Soviet statisticians as part of national income, has not been published since the mid-thirties, and it cannot be derived from the accounts thus far discussed. Using indirect procedures, we have estimated net production, as defined in Soviet national income accounts, for 1955 in current rubles (Table F-3). The Soviet concept of net production differs somewhat from the U.S. concept of value added in that the former is net of amortization charges, but these charges are generally small, much smaller than depreciation calculated under U.S. accounting practices. A more important difference arises from the inclusion of turnover taxes in the Soviet concept. While it is true that business taxes are also included in U.S. value added, they are relatively so much smaller that they are not at all comparable.

The comparability of Soviet net production with U.S. value added is perhaps best examined by considering the share of employee compensation in each. For 1955, employee compensation accounted for 55 per cent of value added in U.S. manufacturing; if income of unincorporated enterprises is added to employee compensation, the fraction is 56 per cent.[2] We see from Table F-3 that employee compensation accounted for only 30 per cent of Soviet net industrial production in the same year if turnover taxes are included, but for 58 per cent if they are excluded. For Soviet net production including turnover taxes to be comparable with U.S. value added in coverage, the share of production attributable to capital would have to be half again as large in the Soviet Union as it is in the United States, which seems unlikely. It would therefore seem that value added as measured in the United States is approximately equivalent to Soviet net production excluding turnover taxes, or at least a very large part of them.[3]

Industrial Production Account for 1955 in Current Rubles

The production account in Table F-3 is erected, by means of various internal relations revealed here and there in the Soviet literature, on independent estimates of net production, profits, and turnover taxes.

---

[2] *649*, 1958, 493, 774.

[3] In a recent article, Academician S. G. Strumilin presents some estimates of net production for industry in "1926/27" prices (see *256a*, 233–242). Among other things, it is interesting to note that he considers employee compensation to be 57 per cent of net production, a fraction he treats as constant over the Plan period, and net production in 1955 to be 30.6 per cent of gross production. If gross and net production are both taken as excluding turnover taxes, the corresponding fractions derived from Table F-3 are 58 and 32.3 per cent.

Thus, net production is derived as a percentage of national income; gross production is derived as a percentage of net production; and the items within gross production (except, of course, profits and turnover taxes) are mutually derived from a set of relations explained in that table.

If the production account has been properly reconstructed (there is room for error), our interpretation of the Soviet treatment of turnover taxes outlined above seems to be confirmed. Note that net production is estimated at about 500 billion rubles, and that the gross production of about 1,040 billion rubles is derived from net production. Similarly, cost of materials is derived from gross production minus turnover taxes and profits. Both net and gross production are known to include turnover taxes, but it is not entirely clear from Soviet sources to what extent those taxes are included. This seems to become clear from the reconstructed production account. If we subtract from net production the total amount of turnover taxes paid to the government, we are left with 258 billion rubles. Similarly, if we subtract the same amount from gross production, we derive the cost of materials as 536 billion rubles. Gross production then consists of the following items (billion rubles):

Net production excluding turnover taxes	258
Cost of materials consumed in "commercial" and production outlays	536
Turnover taxes	242
Total (rounded)	1,040

The three items are consistent with each other, and this would not be the case if only a fraction of turnover taxes were considered as included in net and gross production: the total derived here would come out larger than the independently derived 1,040 billion rubles, because cost of materials would be larger.

It is very difficult to check the accuracy of the reconstructed account in any other way, since, to our knowledge, none of the components has been independently published. A partial check is provided by various indirect estimates of employee compensation, usually in the form of average annual or hourly earnings, made by Soviet and Western economists; but they extend over a wide range, often apply to the wrong year, and usually cover a broader sector of the economy than industry alone. In other words, they do not seem to be inherently more reliable than the estimate that we have reconstructed. It is nevertheless important to see how they compare with ours.

On the Soviet side, Academician Strumlin has estimated that average hourly earnings, apparently in industry only, were 4 rubles an hour around 1955.[4] This implies aggregate employee compensation of 160 to 170 billion rubles (see our estimate of annual hours worked in Table A-23), or 10 to 20 billion more than our estimate. On the Western side, a figure somewhat lower than this is implied by Janet Chapman's estimate that 1952 average annual earnings of workers and employees were 8,050 rubles in the nonagricultural sector and 7,800 rubles in the economy as a whole,[5] if we assume that the average had not changed significantly by 1955 and that it applied to the 17.4 million wage and salary earners, with the 2 to 3 million other workers—members of producer cooperatives and collective farms—earning substantially less (for employment data, see Table C-1). An even lower figure for aggregate employee compensation, perhaps about equal to ours, is implied by the BLS estimate that average annual earnings of all workers and employees was about 7,200 rubles in 1953.[6] Finally, a figure below ours is implied by Solomon Schwarz's estimate of 5,200 to 5,400 rubles for average annual earnings of all workers and employees in 1951.[7] It therefore seems that our estimate of employee compensation is bracketed by those made by prominent scholars in the field of Soviet labor.

Data in "Constant" Prices

Since the characteristics of Soviet gross production in "constant" prices are discussed in Chapter 5, we shall confine ourselves here to a few comments on some of the apparent revisions made in the series on two occasions, when the system of price weights was changed. Through 1950 the series was expressed in so-called "1926/27" prices. For the succeeding two years, it was temporarily extended by a link based on current prices, a revised link being calculated later when 1952 prices were adopted as the unit of measure. The data continued to be expressed in "1952" prices through 1955, when a new link was established using "1955" prices. The latter have continued in effect up to the present.

From internal evidence it is seen that Soviet production accounts were substantially revised in connection with the shift from "1926/27" to "1952" prices, though the exact nature of the revision can only be surmised. We note, first of all, that for 1950 the percentage breakdown of gross production into "A" and "B" goods is different in the two sets of

[4] In 367, 11/4/54, as cited in 529a, 361.
[5] 441, 144.
[6] 529a, 361.
[7] 555a, 253.

prices. This may be seen by comparing published index numbers for "A" and "B" goods based on "1926/27" prices with the published percentage breakdown of gross production into the two categories.[8] For benchmark years within the period 1913–1946, the two sets of data are consistent; that is, the same values of gross production are derived for "A" and "B" goods either by extrapolating base figures by the indexes or by multiplying total gross production by the given percentages. For 1950, two different sets of figures are derived as follows (billion "1926/27" rubles):

	From Indexes	From Percentage Breakdown
Group "A"	175.0	166.3
Group "B"	66.7	75.4
Total	241.7	241.7

Since the figures derived from indexes based on "1926/27" prices sum to the known total for gross industrial production in "1926/27" prices, we may infer that the percentage breakdown implied by those figures (72.4 and 27.6 per cent) refers to values in "1926/27" prices, while the published percentage breakdown underlying the figures in the second column above (68.8 and 31.2 per cent) refers to values in "1952" prices.

The question next arises whether this revision reflects merely changes in relative prices—a raising of "B" prices relative to "A" prices—or a reclassification of goods as well. There is some internal evidence to suggest that the latter may have been the case, if the reconstruction of accounts in Table F-1 is essentially correct. Note that, according to those reconstructed data, the gross production of machine building in 1950 was reduced from 94 to 73 billion rubles, or by 21 billion rubles, while the gross production of metal products and repair shops was raised from 10 to about 120 billion rubles, or by 110 billion rubles. Although there is good reason to believe that the gross value of machinery and equipment in "1926/27" rubles was not less than the gross value in either current or "1952" rubles, it seems unlikely that the former actually exceeded the latter by 29 per cent, as would be implied if the entire adjustment were in prices alone.

A possible and plausible explanation is that conventional military products formerly classified under machine building were transferred to metal products and that the prices of machinery and equipment were not

[8] *180*, 9–13, 31–33; *141*, 60, 137.

628

changed. Our estimate of 1950 expenditures on conventional military products in current rubles, about the same as "1926/27" rubles, is 17 billion rubles, which differs insignificantly from the calculated 21 billion rubles by which machine building was reduced in view of probable estimating errors and of double counting in the latter item. If this explanation seems reasonable, one may also infer that military products were simultaneously shifted from "A" to "B" goods, because the values for machine building and tools of labor are consistent in "1952" prices (see Table F-1), and also because the official index for "B" goods shows a sharper rise over most years after 1950 than either of the indexes for the component light and food industries, a condition that does not apply to the prewar period (see Table F-2). Following these suppositions, we could reconstruct the 1950 accounts in "1926/27" prices to make them approximately comparable in coverage with those in "1952" prices. This is done in the following table (billion rubles for 1950):

	"1926/27" Prices	"1952" Prices
Group "A"	154	310
Tools of labor	81	81
Materials	73	229
Group "B"	88	141
Machine building	73	73
Metal products and repair shops	31	119

We may now compare the price changes for 1950 implied by these revised accounts with those implied by the accounts as given in Table F-1:

	Value in "1952" Prices as % of Value in "1926/27" Prices	
	Accounts in Table F-1	Revised Accounts
Group "A"	177	201
Tools of labor	71	100
Materials	376	314
Group "B"	211	160
Machine building	71	100
Metal products and repair shops	1,227	384

For the first column, we have taken the implied price change for machine building as applying to tools of labor as well, and from this we have derived a value in "1926/27" rubles for both the latter and materials (114 and 61 billion rubles, respectively). The pattern of price changes seems to be more plausible and consistent in the second column than in the first. It seems particularly odd and inconsistent to find the price level for metal products and repair shops shown as multiplying twelve times, while the price level for machine building—a related classification—is shown as declining and that for materials—another related classification—as multiplying less than four times. We conclude that some reclassification of products, such as supposed for the second column, took place in connection with the shift from "1926/27" to "1952" prices.

In passing, we should note one important difficulty in comparing data for machine building and metalworking with data for military products. The former refer to gross value and hence include double counting of products to the extent that enterprises classified within that category specialize in particular stages for fabrication. The latter refer to expenditures on end products only and hence exclude double counting. We may presume that industrial specialization has increased over the years so that there has been an upward trend in double counting. The figures as given therefore understate the relative importance of military production more for 1955 than for 1950 or earlier years. It may even be that some of the increase in gross production of metal products that accompanied the shift from "1926/27" to "1952" prices is attributable to a reorganization of statistical recording of output leading to more double counting.

We should also note that atomic energy is probably included in the category of machine building, since it is administratively organized under a special Ministry for Medium Machine Building. Inclusion of atomic energy, together with growing specialization, could help to explain the fact that gross production in machine building shows a much sharper percentage rise between 1950 and 1955 than can be accounted for by civilian machinery (see the indexes in Table A-8).

By contrast, the change-over from "1952" to "1955" prices seems to have involved few adjustments. For one thing, there was no change in the relative prices of "A" and "B" goods. This is shown by the fact that the published percentage breakdowns for 1955 and later years coincide with the ones derived from production indexes. We therefore infer that values for "A" and "B" goods were multiplied by the same factor (0.92) in shifting from "1952" to "1955" prices.[9]

[9] Two sources (*580*, 1956, 1–4; and *423*, 56 f) suggest that prices fell more relatively for "A" than for "B" goods. If this was so, as it well may have been, Soviet statistical authorities apparently did not adjust the accounts for 1955 accordingly.

Early Data on Machinery

The data for large-scale production of machine building in the late 1920's, as published in the interwar period, apparently included metal products as well as machinery and equipment, as may be seen by comparing those data[10] with figures taken from our Table C-2 (million rubles):

	Machine Building Interwar Sources, "1926/27" Prices	Table C-2, Current Prices	Machine Building and Metal Products, Table C-2, Current Prices
1926/27		925	1,369
1927	1,226		
1927/28		917	1,431
1928	1,545		
1928/29		1,352	1,936
1929	2,117		

Since wholesale industrial prices fell gradually and slightly during the years in question,[11] the figures in the first column seem to refer to the same products as those in the third. The apparent inclusion of metal products in the early official figures may explain why no index for machine building is given in postwar statistical sources for years before 1940.

Annex: Data Published in 1960

The Soviet statistical handbook published in 1960[12] contains some important information on industry that, because of its late appearance, could not be carefully analyzed and integrated into this study, though minor revisions were made where possible and appropriate. We present here, with a brief commentary, some additional data bearing most directly on the estimates of gross and net industrial production given in the main body of this appendix.

For the first time in postwar years, a percentage breakdown has been given for gross social product and national income, both according to their Soviet definitions. These breakdowns may be combined with other information in a recent speech by Khrushchev to reproduce estimated

[10] *467*, 340, series excluding repair shops.
[11] See *498*, 784.
[12] *141a*.

absolute magnitudes for 1959 in "1958" rubles (see Table F-4). The resulting estimates for gross and net industrial production are derived essentially independently of each other, enabling us to construct a

TABLE F-4

OFFICIAL DATA ON SOVIET GROSS SOCIAL PRODUCT AND NATIONAL INCOME, 1959

	Per Cent		Billion "1958" Rubles	
	Gross Social Product	National Income	Gross Social Product	National Income
Total	100.0	100.0	2,430	1,330
Industry	61.3	52.7	1,490	700
Agriculture	17.5	20.9	425	280
Construction	10.5	10.2	255	135
Transportation and communication	4.1	4.8	100	60
Others	6.6	11.4	160	90

GENERAL NOTE: The percentage distributions are given in *141a*, 78. The fact that the accounts are in "1958" rubles is indicated in *141a*, 829. The items for gross social product in rubles are derived from gross industrial production (including turnover taxes) and the percentage distribution; the items for national income in rubles, from total national income and the percentage distribution. Gross industrial production was said by Khrushchev in his speech of May 5, 1960, to the Supreme Soviet (*451*, XII, 18, p. 11) to be "already approaching 1,500 billion rubles." National income is derived from the following information in the same source: (a) the increase in 1959 was 8 per cent or 100 billion rubles (p.11); and (b) national income planned for 1960 is about 1,450 billion rubles, an increase of 9 per cent (p. 5). We have interpreted the following statements in the same source as applying to gross industrial production *net* of turnover taxes: (a) "a rise in labor productivity of just 1 per cent in the current year [1960] would yield the country's industry as a whole additional output of almost 13,000,000,000 rubles" (p. 11); and (b) the increase in 1959 was more than 11 per cent instead of the planned 7.7 per cent, or 50 billion rubles more than planned (p. 5).

seemingly more reliable production account for 1959 (see Table F-5) than for 1955. On the basis of those two accounts, one can compare percentage increases in official figures for gross and net industrial production.

In current prices ("1958" prices for 1959), gross production excluding turnover taxes rose by 48 per cent over 1955–1959 (Tables F-3 and F-5). This is about the same as the growth of 49 per cent shown by the official index in "1955" prices,[13] which provides some ground for confidence in this part of the reconstructed accounts. Net production excluding turnover taxes rose by 51 per cent, or somewhat more. (Net production

[13] *141a*, 141, 145.

including turnover taxes rose by 40 per cent, or substantially less.) However, there was a significant shift in the structure of net production over this period, the percentage share rising for profits and falling for

TABLE F-5

ESTIMATED SOVIET INDUSTRIAL PRODUCTION ACCOUNT, 1959
(billion current rubles)

1.	Gross production	1,490[a]
2.	Turnover taxes	311
3.	Profits (incl. subsidized losses)	130
4.	"Commercial" outlays and misc. charges	60
5.	Production outlays	990
6.	Cost of materials consumed	770
7.	Raw and basic materials	630
8.	Auxiliary materials	48
9.	Fuel	36
10.	Power	17
11.	Amortization	35
12.	Employee compensation (including social insurance deductions)	190
13.	Unallocated outlays	32
14.	Net production	700[a]
15.	Turnover taxes	311
16.	Profits (incl. subsidized losses)	130
17.	Net "commercial" outlays and misc. charges	46
18.	Employee compensation (including social insurance deductions)	190
19.	Net unallocated outlays	24

[a] "1958" rubles.
GENERAL NOTE: See general note to Table F-3.
Line 1:   From Table F-4.
Line 2:   *141a*, 799.
Line 3:   Sum of net profits of state enterprises and producer cooperatives (*141a*), plus estimate of 5 billion rubles for subsidized losses.
Lines 4–13: See Table F-3, same lines. Percentage distribution of productive outlays from *141a*, 161. The following equations are solved simultaneously:

$$P + C = 1,049 \text{ billion rubles}$$
$$E + 0.76 \ (C + U) = 259 \text{ billion rubles}$$
$$M = 0.775 \ P$$
$$E = 0.193 \ P$$
$$U = 0.032 \ P$$

Line 14:   From Table F-4.
Lines 15, 16, and 18: Lines 2–4 and 12.
Lines 17 and 19:   76% of lines 4 and 13.

turnover taxes and employee compensation. Such a change could have been effected solely for fiscal convenience—for example, to facilitate a switch from turnover to profits taxes—and may have no relation to economic factors. Employee compensation accounted for 58 per cent of net production (excluding turnover taxes) in 1955 but for only 49 per cent in 1959. Put another way, employee compensation rose by only 27 per cent while net production (excluding turnover taxes) rose by 51 per cent. Under such circumstances, it is hardly possible to know what is a proper measure of net production. Incidentally, the figure of 190 billion rubles for employee compensation in 1959, if more or less accurate, suggests that the figure of 150 billion rubles for 1955 is not seriously in error.

The latest statistical handbook also publishes the results of the large-scale revaluation of capital in the Soviet economy at replacement cost as of January 1, 1960.[14] We may note here that the replacement cost of industrial capital (including inventory but excluding land, depreciated assets, and fiduciary assets) comes to about 600 billion rubles.[15] Unfortunately, this figure cannot be directly compared with estimates of capital in U.S. industry[16] because of important differences in the definition of capital.

[14] *141a*, 65 ff.
[15] *141a*, 67, 75.
[16] See, e.g., *614a*.

Bibliography

Sources for Russian and Soviet Data

A. RUSSIAN BOOKS AND PAMPHLETS (1–302)

1. Abramov, I. V. *Puti tekhnicheskogo progressa v sovetskom mashinostroenii* [Technical Progress in Soviet Machine Building]. Moscow, 1948.
2. Anisimov, N. I. *Pobeda sotsialisticheskogo sel'skogo khoziaistva* [The Victory of Socialist Agriculture]. Moscow, 1947.
3. ———. *Razvitie sel'skogo khoziaistva v pervoi poslevoennoi piatiletke* [Development of Agriculture in the First Postwar Five Year Plan]. Moscow, 1952.
4. *Annuaire Statistique de la Lettonie, 1939.* Riga, 1939.
5. *Annuaire Statistique de la Lithuanie, 1938.* Kaunas, 1939.
6. Arakelian, A. *Osnovnye zadachi poslevoennoi piatiletki* [The Basic Tasks of the Postwar Five Year Plan]. Moscow, 1946.
7. Bakulev, G. D. *Voprosy ekonomiki topliva v SSSR* [Economic Problems of the Fuel Industry in the USSR]. Moscow, 1957.
8. Bakulin, Iu. A. *Sovetskoe khlopkovodstvo v piatoi piatiletke* [Soviet Cotton Growing in the Fifth Five Year Plan]. Moscow, 1953.
9. ———, and Mishustin, D. D. *Vneshniaia torgovlia SSSR za 20 let, 1918–1937* [Twenty Years of USSR Foreign Trade, 1918–1937]. Moscow, 1939.
10. *Balans narodnogo khoziaistva na 1923/24 god* [Balance of the National Economy in 1923/24]. Moscow, 1926.
11. Balzak, S. S.; Vasyutin, V. F.; and Feigin, Ya. G. (eds.). *Economic Geography of the USSR* (translated from the Russian). New York, 1952.
12. Bardin, I. P., and Bannyi, N. P. *Chernaia metallurgiia v novoi piatiletke* [Ferrous Metallurgy in the New Five Year Plan]. Moscow and Leningrad, 1947.
13. Benenson, G. M. *Drevesina v narodnom khoziaistve SSSR* [Timber in the USSR National Economy]. Moscow and Leningrad, 1947.
14. Betekhtin, A. G., *et al. Kurs mestorozhdenii poleznykh iskopaemykh* [Textbook on Deposits of Mineral Resources]. 2nd ed. Moscow, 1946.
15. Blinkov, B. S. *Khimicheskaia promyshlennost' SSSR* [The Chemical Industry of the USSR]. Moscow, 1932.
16. ———, and Burov, M. N. (eds.). *Khimicheskaia promyshlennost' SSSR* [The Chemical Industry of the USSR]. Volume I. Moscow and Leningrad, 1933.
17. *Bol'shaia sovetskaia entsiklopediia* [The Great Soviet Encyclopedia]. 1st ed. Moscow, 1926–1947. 2nd ed. Moscow, 1950–.
18. *Bol'shaia sovetskaia entsiklopediia, SSSR* [The Great Soviet Encyclopedia, the USSR]. Supplementary volume. Moscow, 1947.
19. Brianskii, A. M. *Statistika zhivotnovodstva* [Statistics on Animal Husbandry]. Moscow, 1956.
20. Burov, M. N. *Khimicheskaia pererabotka burykh uglei SSSR* [The Chemical Processing of USSR Brown Coals]. Moscow, 1938.
21. But, A. I. *Planirovanie v tsvetnoi metallurgii* [Planning in Nonferrous Metallurgy]. Moscow, 1946.

635

22. Buznikov, V. I. *Lesotekhnicheskie produkty* [Wood Chemical Products]. Petrograd, 1922.

23. Buzyrev, V. M. *Vosstanovitel'nye raboty i ikh finansirovanie* [Restoration Work and Its Financing]. Moscow, 1945.

24. Chastnyi kapital v narodnom khoziaistve SSSR [Private Capital in the USSR National Economy]. Moscow and Leningrad, 1927.

25. *Chernaia metallurgiia SSSR v pervoi piatiletke* [Ferrous Metallurgy in the USSR in the First Five Year Plan]. Moscow, 1935.

26. Den, V. E. *Istochniki vazhneishikh otraslei khoziaistvennoi statistiki SSSR* [Sources for the Most Important Branches of Economic Statistics in the USSR]. Leningrad, 1929.

27. *Dinamika rossiiskoi i sovetskoi promyshlennosti v sviazi s razvitiem narodnogo khoziaistva za sorok let, 1887–1926* [Dynamics of Russian and Soviet Industry During Forty Years of the Development of the National Economy, 1887–1926]. Parts I–III. Moscow, 1929–1930.

28. *Dinamika tsen na glavneishie izdeliia fabrichno-zavodskoi promyshlennosti za period 1913–1918* [Dynamics of Prices for the Main Products of Factory Industry for 1913–1918]. Moscow, 1926.

29. *Direktivy XIX s'ezda partii po piatomu planu razvitiia SSSR na 1951–1955 godu* [Directives of the XIX Party Congress on the Fifth Five Year Plan for the Development of the USSR from 1951 to 1955]. Moscow, 1952.

30. *Doklad Vysochaishei Uchrezhdennoi Kommissi* [Report of the Imperial Special Commission]. Supplement. St. Petersburg, 1873.

31. *Dostizheniia sovetskoi vlasti za 40 let v tsifrakh* [The Achievements of the Soviet Regime During Forty Years, in Figures]. Moscow, 1957.

32. *Dvadtsat' let sovetskoi vlasti* [Twenty Years of Soviet Power]. Moscow, 1937.

33. Egorov, A. P., *et al. Kurs tekhnologii mineral'nykh veshchestv* [Textbook on the Technology of Minerals]. Moscow, 1944.

34. *Ekonomicheskoe sotrudnichestvo i vzaimopomoshch' mezhdu Sovetskim Soiuzom i evropeiskimi stranami narodnoi demokratii* [Economic Cooperation and Mutual Aid Between the Soviet Union and the European People's Democracies]. Moscow, 1958.

35. *Ekonomika promyshlennosti SSSR* [Economics of USSR Industry]. Moscow, 1956.

36. *Ekonomika sotsialisticheskikh promyshlennykh predpriiatii* [Economics of Socialist Industrial Enterprises]. Moscow, 1956.

37. *Eksportno-importnyi slovar'* [Export-Import Dictionary]. Moscow, 1952.

38. *Electric Power Development in the USSR.* Moscow and New York, 1936.

39. *Entsiklopediia sovetskogo eksporta* [Encyclopedia of Soviet Exports]. Volume II. Moscow, 1932.

40. *Estestvennye proizvoditel'nye sily Rossii* [Natural Resources of Russia]. Volume IV. Petrograd, 1917–1923.

41. *Estonian Economic Yearbook.* Tallinn, 1938.

42. *Ezhegodnik khlebnoi torgovli, 1925/26–1926/27* [Grain Trade Yearbook, 1925/26–1926/27]. Moscow, 1928.

43. *Ezhegodnik khlebooborota, 1928/29* [Grain Trade Yearbook, 1928/29]. Moscow and Leningrad, 1931.

BIBLIOGRAPHY

44 ——, *1929/30–1930/31.* Moscow, 1932.

45. *Ezhegodnik Ministerstva Finansov* [Yearbook of the Ministry of Finances]. Issues II–XXIII and issues for 1900–1914. St. Petersburg, 1871–1914.

46. *Fabrichno-zavodskaia promyshlennost' i torgovlia Rossii* [Factory Industry and Trade in Russia]. St. Petersburg, 1896.

47. *Fabrichno-zavodskaia promyshlennost' SSSR, 1926/27* [Factory Industry in the USSR, 1926/27]. Moscow, 1929.

48. —— *v evropeiskoi Rossii za 1910–1912.* Petrograd, 1914.

49. —— *v period 1913–1918.* Moscow, 1926.

50. —— *za 1922 god.* Moscow, 1924.

51. —— *za 1923 khoziaistvennyi god.* Moscow, 1925.

52. —— *za 1924 khoziaistvennyi god.* Moscow, 1926.

53. Fersman, A. E. *Novyi promyshlennyi tsentr SSSR za poliarnym krugom* [A New Soviet Industrial Center Beyond the Arctic Circle]. Leningrad, 1931.

54. ——, and Betekhtin, A. G. (eds.). *Khromity SSSR* [USSR Chromites]. Moscow, 1937.

54a. *Finansy i kredit SSSR* [Finance and Credit in the USSR]. Moscow, 1958.

55. *Five Year Plan for the Rehabilitation and Development of the National Economy of the USSR, 1946–1950.* London, 1946.

56. *Fulfillment of the USSR State Plan for 1949.* London, 1950.

57. Gatovskii, L. *Ekonomicheskaia pobeda sovetskogo soiuza v velikoi otechestvennoi voine* [Economic Victory of the Soviet Union in the Great Patriotic War]. Moscow, 1946.

58. *Geologicheskaia izuchennost' i mineral'no-syrevaia baza SSSR k XVIII s'ezdu VKP (b)* [Geological Research and the Mineral Raw Material Resources of the USSR at the XVIII Party Congress]. Moscow and Leningrad, 1939.

59. *Geologorazvedochnye raboty vo vtorom piatiletii. Materialy konferentsii 12–24 aprelia 1932* [Geological Prospecting in the Second Five Year Plan. Materials for a Conference, April 12–24, 1932]. Issues 1–6. Moscow, 1932.

60. Gerashchenko, B. *Novyi moshchnyi pod'em narodnogo khoziaistva SSSR v pervoi poslevoennoi piatiletke* [Great New Upsurge of the USSR National Economy in the First Postwar Five Year Plan]. Moscow, 1951.

61. Gessen, Iu. Iu. *Ocherki istorii proizvodstva sody* [Essays on the History of the Production of Soda]. Moscow, 1951.

62. Gilels, G. G. *Osnovy organizatsii pishchevogo proizvodstva* [The Fundamentals of the Organization of Food Production]. Moscow, 1948.

63. Gimmelfarb, B. M., and Unaniants, T. P. *Syr'evaia baza tukovoi promyshlennosti SSSR* [Raw Materials for the USSR Fertilizer Industry]. Moscow and Leningrad, 1937.

64. Glivits, I. *Zheleznaia promyshlennost' Rossii* [The Iron Industry of Russia]. St. Petersburg, 1911.

65. *Godovoi obzor mineral'nykh resursov SSSR za 1925/26 god* [Annual Survey of the Mineral Resources of the USSR for 1925/26]. Leningrad, 1927.

66. —— *1926/27 god.* Leningrad, 1928.

67. Gorelik, S. A. *Statistika* [Statistics]. Moscow, 1956.

68. *Gornaia promyshlennost' SSSR* [The USSR Mining Industry]. Volumes I and II. Moscow and Leningrad, 1932.

69. Gornostai-Pol'skii, A. M. *Osnovy ekonomiki kozhevenno-obuvnoi promyshlennosti* [The Economics of the Shoe and Leather Industry]. Moscow and Leningrad, 1947.

70. *Gornozavodskaia proizvoditel'nost' Rossii v 1885 godu* [Mining Productivity in Russia in 1885]. St. Petersburg, 1888.

71. *O gosudarstvennom plane SSSR na 1947 god* [On the USSR State Plan for 1947]. Moscow, 1947.

72. *Gosudarstvennyi plan razvitiia narodnogo khoziaistva SSSR na 1941 god* [The State Plan for the Development of the USSR National Economy for 1941]. Moscow, 1941 (reprinted by the American Council of Learned Societies, 1948).

73. Granovskii, E. L., *et al. Tekhnicheskaia rekonstruktsiia narodnogo khoziaistva SSSR v pervoi piatiletke* [The Technical Reconstruction of the USSR National Economy in the First Five Year Plan]. Moscow, 1934.

74. ——, and Markus, B. L. *Ekonomika sotsialisticheskoi promyshlennosti* [The Economics of Socialist Industry]. Moscow, 1940.

75. Grinko, G. F. "The Financial Program for 1935" in *Soviet Union 1935*. Moscow and Leningrad, 1935.

76. ——, "The Financial Program of the USSR for 1936" in *Second Session of the Central Executive Committee of the USSR*. Moscow, 1936.

77. Iakobi, A. (ed.). *Zheleznye dorogi SSSR v tsifrakh* [USSR Railroads in Figures]. Moscow, 1935.

78. Ioffe, Ia. A. *Ob osnovnoi ekonomicheskoi zadache SSSR* [On the Main Economic Task of the USSR]. Moscow, 1941.

79. ——. *SSSR i kapitalicheskie strany, 1913–1937* [The USSR and the Capitalist Countries, 1913–1937]. Moscow, 1939.

80. ——. *SSSR i kapitalicheskii mir* [The USSR and the Capitalist World]. Moscow and Leningrad, 1934.

81. —— (ed.). *Strany sotsializma i kapitalizma v tsifrakh* [Socialist and Capitalist Countries in Figures]. Moscow, 1957.

82. Itin and Gornostai-Pol'skii, A. M. *Ekonomika kozhevennoi-obuvnoi promyshlennosti* [The Economics of the Shoe and Leather Industry]. Moscow, 1940.

83. *Ob itogakh vypolneniia chetvertogo (pervogo poslevoennogo) piatiletnego plana SSSR na 1946–1950 gody* [On the Fulfillment of the USSR Fourth (First Postwar) Five Year Plan for 1946–1950]. Moscow, 1951.

84. *Itogi desiatiletiia sovetskoi vlasti v tsifrakh, 1917–1927* [Ten Years of Soviet Power in Figures, 1917–1927]. Moscow, 1927.

85. *Itogi perepisi zaboev i oborudovaniia ugol'noi promyshlennosti* [Census of Mines Operations and Equipment in the Coal Industry]. Moscow, 1936.

86. *Itogi vypolneniia pervogo piatiletnego plana razvitiia narodnogo khoziaistva Soiuza SSR* [The Fulfillment of the First Five Year Plan for the Development of the USSR National Economy]. Moscow, 1933.

87. *Itogi vypolneniia vtorogo piatiletnego plana razvitiia narodnogo khoziaistva SSSR* [The Fulfillment of the Second Five Year Plan for the Development of the USSR National Economy]. Moscow, 1939.

88. Iulin, A. I. *Sovetskaia khimicheskaia promyshlennost'* [The Soviet Chemical Industry]. Leningrad, 1928.

BIBLIOGRAPHY

89. *Kalendar' spravochnik, 1948 god* [Almanac for 1948]. Moscow, 1948.
90. Kasperovich, G. *Zhelezodelatel'naia promyshlennost' Rossii za poslednee 10-letie, 1903–1912* [The Russian Iron Industry During the Last 10 Years, 1903–1912]. St. Petersburg, 1913.
91. Keppen, A. *Mining and Metallurgy.* St. Petersburg, 1893.
92. ———. *Statisticheskie tablitsy po gornoi promyshlennosti Rossii* [Statistical Tables on the Russian Mining Industry]. St. Petersburg, 1879.
93. Khazan, D. *Light Industries of the USSR.* Moscow, 1939.
94. Khromov, P. A. *Amortizatsiia v promyshlennosti SSSR* [Depreciation in USSR Industry]. Moscow, 1939.
95. ———. *Ekonomicheskoe razvitie Rossii v XIX-XX vekakh* [The Economic Development of Russia in the 19th and 20th Centuries]. Moscow, 1950.
96. ———. *Ocherki ekonomiki tekstil'noi promyshlennosti SSSR* [Essays on the Economics of the USSR Textile Industry]. Moscow and Leningrad, 1946.
97. Kiriukhin, A. M. *Traktory shestoi piatiletki* [Tractors of the Sixth Five Year Plan]. Moscow, 1956.
98. Kondrashev, S. K. *Oroshaemoe zemledelie* [Irrigation for Farming]. Moscow, 1948.
99. Kondrat'ev, N. D. (ed.). *Mirovoe khoziaistvo* [World Economy]. Moscow, 1926.
100. *Kontrol'nye tsifry narodnogo khoziaistva SSSR na 1925/26* [Control Figures for the USSR National Economy]. Moscow and Leningrad, 1925.
101. ——— *1926/27.* Moscow, 1927.
102. ——— *1927/28.* Moscow, 1928.
103. ——— *1928/29.* Moscow, 1929.
104. ——— *1929/30.* Moscow, 1930.
105. ——— *1930/31.* Moscow, 1931.
106. *Kontrol'nye tsifry piatiletnego plana narodnogo khoziaistva i sotsial'no-kul'turnogo stroitel'stva RSFSR, 1928/29–1932/33* [Control Figures for the Five Year Plan for the National Economy and the Social and Cultural Development of the Russian Republic, 1928/29–1932/33]. Moscow, 1929.
107. Koshelev, F. P. *Novyi etap v razvitii narodnogo khoziaistva SSSR* [New Stage in the Development of the USSR National Economy]. Moscow, 1954.
108. ———. *Osnovnye itogi vypolneniia pervoi poslevoennoi stalinskoi piatiletki* [Main Results of the First Postwar Stalin Five Year Plan]. Moscow, 1951.
109. Kovalevskii, N. *Problemy planovogo regulirovaniia narodnogo khoziaistva* [Problems of the Planned Management of the National Economy]. Moscow and Leningrad, 1928.
110. Kurov, A. A. *Avtomobil'* [Motor Vehicles]. Moscow, 1938.
111. Kuznetsov, V. I. *Dostizheniia v oblasti tekhnicheskogo progressa v SSSR* [Technical Progress in the USSR]. Moscow, 1951.
112. *The Land of Socialism Today and Tomorrow. Reports and Speeches at the 18th Party Congress.* Moscow, 1939.
113. Lauer, G. (ed.). *Chernaia metallurgiia, zheleznorudnaia, margantsevaia, koksovaia promyshlennost' SSSR, 1928–1934* [Ferrous Metallurgy, the Iron Ore, Manganese, and Coke Industry of the USSR, 1928–1934]. Moscow, 1935.
114. *Lesnaia promyshlennost'* [The Timber Industry]. Moscow, 1958.

115. Livshits, R. S. *Ocherki po razmeshcheniiu promyshlennosti SSSR* [Essays on Location of Industry in the USSR]. Moscow, 1954.
116. Loevetskii, D. A. *Valiutnaia politika SSSR* [USSR Currency Policy]. Moscow, 1926.
117. Lokshin, E. Iu. *Promyshlennost' SSSR v novoi stalinskoi piatiletke* [USSR Industry in the New Stalin Five Year Plan]. Moscow, 1946.
118. ———. *Promyshlennost' SSSR v pervoi piatiletke* [USSR Industry in the First Five Year Plan]. Moscow, 1934.
119. ———. *Promyshlennost' SSSR za XV let* [Fifteen Years of USSR Industry]. Moscow, 1932.
120. ———. *Tiazhelaia industriia v tret'em godu piatiletki* [Heavy Industry in the Third Year of the Five Year Plan]. Moscow and Leningrad, 1932.
121. Lukashkin, N. I. *Industrializatsiia stroitel'stva promyshlennykh predpriiatii SSSR v piatoi piatiletke* [Industrializing Construction of Industrial Enterprises in the USSR in the Fifth Five Year Plan]. Moscow, 1953.
122. Luk'ianov, P. M. *Istoriia khimicheskikh promyslov i khimicheskoi promyshlennosti Rossii do kontsa 19go veka* [History of the Chemical Trades and the Chemical Industry of Russia up to the End of the 19th Century]. Moscow, 1948.
123. *Malaia sovetskaia entsiklopediia* [The Concise Soviet Encyclopedia]. 1st ed. Moscow, 1928–1931.
124. Margolis, I. A. *Produkty zhivotnovodstva* [Livestock Products]. Moscow and Leningrad, 1925.
125. *Mashinostroenie* [Machine Building]. Volume II. Moscow, 1947.
126. *Materialy dlia statistiki khlopchatobumazhnogo proizvodstva v Rossii* [Statistics on the Cotton Industry in Russia]. St. Petersburg, 1901.
127. Matveev, G. A. *Istoriia otechestvennogo kotlostroeniia* [History of Domestic Boiler Construction]. Moscow, 1950.
128. *Melkaia i kustarno-remeslennaia promyshlennost' Soiuza SSR v 1925 godu* [Small-Scale, Cottage, and Handicraft Industry of the USSR in 1925]. Moscow, 1926.
129. *Melkaia promyshlennost' SSSR po dannym vsesoiuznoi perepisi 1929 goda* [Small-Scale Industry in the USSR According to Data from the All-Union Census of 1929]. Moscow, 1932–1933.
130. Mezhlauk, V. I. (ed.). *Metallopromyshlennost' SSSR v 1924/25 operatsionnom godu* [The Metal Industry in the USSR in 1924/25]. Moscow and Leningrad, 1925.
131. Mikoyan, A. I. *Pishchevaia industriia Sovetskogo Soiuza* [The Food Industry of the Soviet Union]. Moscow, 1936.
132. *Mineral'no-syrevaia baza SSSR* [Mineral Raw Material Resources of the USSR]. Moscow, 1935–1936.
133. Motov, S., and Shul'ts. *Finansovoe planirovanie v sovkhozakh* [Financial Planning on State Farms]. Moscow, 1956.
133a. *Mukomol'naia, krupnaia, i kombikormovaia promyshlennost' v SSSR, 1917–1957* [Flour, Groats, and Fodder in the USSR, 1917–1957]. Moscow, 1958.
134. *Narodne gospodarstvo Ukrains'koi RSR* [The National Economy of the Ukrainian Republic]. Kiev, 1957.
135. *Narodnoe khoziaistvo Rossii za 1921 god* [The Russian National Economy in 1921]. Berlin, 1922.

130. *Narodnoe khoziaistvo RSFSR* [The National Economy of the RSFSR]. Moscow, 1957.
137. *Narodnoe khoziaistvo SSSR* [The USSR National Economy]. Moscow, 1932.
138. ———. Moscow, 1956.
139. *Narodnoe khoziaistvo SSSR na poroge tret'ego goda piatiletki i kontrol'nye tsifry na 1931* [The USSR National Economy on the Threshold of the Third Year of the Five Year Plan and Control Figures for 1931]. Moscow and Leningrad, 1931.
140. *Narodnoe khoziaistvo SSSR v 1956 godu* [The USSR National Economy in 1956]. Moscow, 1957.
141. ——— *1958 godu.* Moscow, 1959.
141a. ——— *1959 godu.* Moscow, 1960.
142. *Narodnoe khoziaistvo v 1914 godu* [The National Economy in 1914]. Petrograd, 1916.
143. ——— *1916 godu.* Issue IV. Petrograd, 1921.
144. ——— *1916 godu.* Issue VII. Petrograd, 1922.
145. *Narodnoe khoziaistvo v tsifrakh* [The National Economy in Figures]. Moscow, 1925.
146. *Narodno-khoziaistvennyi plan na 1935 god* [The National Economic Plan for 1935]. Moscow, 1935.
147. ———. 2nd ed. Moscow, 1935.
148. ——— *1936 god.* Moscow, 1936.
149. ——— *1937 god.* Moscow, 1937.
150. *Nemetallicheskie iskopaemye SSSR* [Nonmetallic Minerals of the USSR]. Volume I, edited by N. P. Gorbunov, Moscow, 1936. Volume II, edited by A. E. Fersman, Moscow, 1943.
151. Nifontov, V. P. *Produktsiia zhivotnovodstva* [Livestock Production]. Moscow, 1937.
152. ———. *Zhivotnovodstvo SSSR v tsifrakh* [USSR Animal Husbandry in Figures] Moscow, 1932,
153. Nikitin, P. V. *Mashinostroenie SSSR v poslevoennoi stalinskoi piatiletke* [USSR Machine Building in the Postwar Stalin Five Year Plan]. Moscow, 1949.
154. Notkin, A. I. *Ocherki teorii sotsialisticheskogo vosproizvodstva* [Essays on the Theory of Socialist Reproduction]. Moscow, 1948.
155. *Obshchii obzor glavnykh otraslei gornoi i gornozavodskoi promyshlennosti* [General Survey of the Main Branches of the Mining and Metallurgical Industry]. Petrograd, 1915.
156. *Obshchii svod po Imperii resultatov razrabotki dannykh pervoi vseobshchei perepisi naseleniia* [General Empire Summary of the Data of the First General Population Census]. St. Petersburg, 1905.
157. *Obzor deiatel'nosti Ministerstva Finansov v tsarstvovanie imperatora Aleksandra III, 1881–1894* [Survey of the Work of the Ministry of Finances During the Reign of Emperor Alexander III, 1881–1894]. St. Petersburg, 1902.
158. *Obzor mineral'nykh resursov SSSR* [Survey of the Mineral Resources of the USSR]. Leningrad, n.d.
159. *Obzory glavneishikh otraslei promyshlennosti i torgovli* [Surveys of the Main Branches of Industry and Trade]. Volume II. St. Petersburg, 1910.

641

160. Omarovskii, A. *Sovetskoe stankostroenie i ego rol' v industrializatsii strany* [Soviet Machine Tool Building and Its Part in the Industrialization of the Country]. Moscow, 1948.

161. Pavlov, M. A. *Metallurgiia chuguna* [The Metallurgy of Pig Iron]. Moscow, 1945.

162. Perevalov, V. I. *Tekhnologiia ogneuporov* [The Technology of Refractory Materials]. Moscow, 1944.

163. *Perspektivy razvertyvaniia narodnogo khoziaistva SSSR na 1926/27–1930/31* [Prospects for the Development of the USSR National Economy over 1926/27—1930/31]. Moscow, 1927.

164. Peterburgskii, A. V. *Znachenie kalinykh udobrenii v povyshenii urozhai* [The Importance of Potash Fertilizer in Increasing the Yield]. Moscow, 1953.

165. *Piatiletnii plan narodno-khoziaistvennogo stroitel'stva SSSR* [Five Year Plan for the Development of the USSR National Economy]. Volume II, Part I. 3rd ed. Moscow, 1930.

166. *Piatiletnii plan sel'sko-khoziaistvennoi i pishchevoi promyshlennosti VSNKh SSSR na 1928/29–1932/33 gody* [Five Year Plan for Agriculture and the Food Industry for 1928/29–1932/33]. Moscow, 1930.

167. *Politicheskaia ekonomika, uchebnik* [Political Economy, A Textbook]. Moscow, 1954.

168. Pomus, M. I. *Buriat-Mongol'skaia ASSR* [The Buriat Mongolian ASSR]. Moscow, 1937.

169. Prianishnikov, D. N. *Agrokhimiia* [Agrochemistry]. 3rd ed. Moscow, 1940.

170. ———. *Azot v zhizn rastenii i v zemledelii SSSR* [Nitrogen in the Life of Plants and in Agriculture in the USSR]. Moscow and Leningrad, 1935.

171. *Problemy ekonomiki truda* [Problems of Labor Economics]. Moscow, 1957.

172. Probst, A. E. *Osnovnye problemy geograficheskogo razmeshcheniia toplivnogo khoziaistva SSSR* [Basic Problems in the Geographic Distribution of the USSR Fuel Industry]. Moscow, 1939.

173. ———. *Toplivo i otechestvennaia voina* [Fuel and World War II]. Moscow, 1945.

174. *Produktsiia fabrichno-zavodskoi promyshlennosti za 1912, 1920, i 1921 gody* [Output of Factory Industry for 1912, 1920, and 1921]. Moscow, 1922.

175. *Proekt vtorogo piatiletnego plana razvitiia narodnogo khoziaistva SSSR, 1933–1937* [Draft of a Second Five Year Plan for the Development of the USSR National Economy, 1933–1937]. Moscow, 1934.

176. *Proizvoditel'nost' truda v promyshlennosti SSSR* [Labor Productivity in USSR Industry]. Moscow and Leningrad, 1940.

177. Prokopovich, S. N. (ed.). *Biulleten' ekonomicheskogo kabineta Prof. S. N. Prokopovicha* [Prof. S. N. Prokopovich's Economic Research Bulletin]. Prague, 1934.

178. ———. *Die Vierte Fünfjahrplan der Sowjetunion.* Zurich and Vienna, 1948.

179. *Promyshlennost' Narkomlesa SSSR* [The Industry of the USSR People's Commissariat of Timber]. Moscow and Leningrad, 1935.

180. *Promyshlennost' SSSR* [Industry of the USSR]. Moscow, 1957.

181. *Promyshlennost' SSSR v eksporte i importe* [USSR Industry: Export and Import]. Moscow and Leningrad, 1930.

182. *Promyshlennost' SSSR v 1924 godu* [USSR Industry in 1924]. Moscow, 1925.
183. ———— *1925 g.* Moscow and Leningrad, 1926.
184. ———— *1925/26 g.* Moscow and Leningrad, 1927.
185. ———— *1926/27 g.* Moscow, 1928.
186. ———— *1927/28 g.* Moscow, 1930.
187. *Puti razvitiia lesnoi promyshlennosti SSSR* [Development of the USSR Timber Industry]. Moscow, 1933.
188. Rabinovich, M., and Khodzhaev, T. *Plan Goelro i ego osushchestvlenie* [The Goelro Plan and Its Fulfillment]. Moscow, 1952.
189. *Resolutions at the 19th Congress of the Communist Party.* Moscow, 1952.
190. Rogovoi, M. I., and Ryss, M. B. *Stroitel'naia keramika* [Mineral Building Materials]. Moscow, 1945.
191. Rotshtein, A. I. *Osnovy statistiki sotsialisticheskoi promyshlennosti* [Principles of Statistics of Socialist Industry]. Moscow, 1932–1934.
192. *Russkaia promyshlennost' v 1921 godu i ee perspektivy* [Russian Industry in 1921 and Its Prospects]. Moscow, n.d.
193. ———— *1922 g.* Petrograd, n.d.
194. Saburov, M. *Doklad o direktivakh 19-go s'ezda partii po piatomu piatiletnemu planu razvitiia SSSR na 1951–1955 gody* [Report on the Directives of the 19th Party Congress on the Fifth Five Year Plan for the Development of the USSR, 1951–1955]. Moscow, 1952.
195. Savinskii, D. V. *Kurs promyshlennoi statistiki* [Textbook on Industrial Statistics]. Moscow, 1954.
196. *Sbornik statisticheskikh svedenii o gornozavodskoi promyshlennosti Rossii* [Statistical Summary of the Russian Mining and Metallurgical Industry]. Issues for 1887–1910. St. Petersburg, 1890–1911.
197. *Sbornik statisticheskikh svedenii po gornoi i gornozavodskoi promyshlennosti SSSR za 1911–1924/25 gg.* [Statistical Summary of the USSR Mining and Metallurgical Industry for 1911–1924/25]. Edited by M. N. Jackson and A. N. Flerov. Leningrad, 1928.
198. ———— *za 1925/26 god.* Leningrad, 1928.
199. ———— *za 1926/27 god.* Leningrad, 1929.
200. ———— *za 1927/28 god.* Moscow and Leningrad, 1930.
201. *Sbornik statisticheskikh svedenii po Soiuzu SSR, 1918–1923* [Statistical Summary for the USSR for 1918–1923]. Moscow, 1924.
202. Seliber, B. *Lesa i lesnaia promyshlennost'* [Forestry and the Timber Industry]. Leningrad, 1933.
203. *Sel'skoe khoziaistvo na putiakh vosstanovleniia* [Agriculture on the Road to Recovery]. Moscow, 1925.
204. *Sel'skoe khoziaistvo SSSR, ezhegodnik 1935* [USSR Agricultural Yearbook for 1935]. Moscow, 1936.
205. *Sel'skokhoziaistvennaia entsiklopediia* [Agricultural Encyclopedia]. Moscow, 1932–1935.
206. Sen'ko, A., and Afanas'ev. *Mestnaia promyshlennost' i promyslovaia kooperatsiia v 3ei piatiletke* [Local Industry and Producer Cooperatives in the Third Five Year Plan]. Moscow, 1939.

207. Serebrovskii, A. P. *Zolotaia promyshlennost'* [The Gold Industry]. Leningrad, 1935.

208. Shereshevskii, A. I.; Sokolovskii, A. A.; and Derevitskii, P. F. *Proizvodstvo fosfornykh udobrenii* [The Production of Phosphoric Fertilizer]. Moscow, 1938.

209. Shershov, S. F. *Leninsko-Stalinskaia elektrifikatsiia SSSR* [The Lenin-Stalin Electrification of the USSR]. Moscow and Leningrad, 1951.

210. Shul'kin, L. P. *Potreblenie chernykh metallov v SSSR* [The Consumption of Ferrous Metals in the USSR]. Moscow, 1940.

211. Sivolap, Iu. K. *Za sozdanie obiliia produktov pitaniia v SSSR* [For an Abundance of Food Products in the USSR]. Moscow, 1954.

212. ———, and Shakhtan, A. S. *Pishchevaia promyshlennost' SSSR* [The USSR Food Industry]. Moscow, 1957.

213. *Sliudy SSSR* [Micas of the USSR]. Leningrad and Moscow, 1937.

214. *Slovar'-spravochnik po sotsial'no-ekonomicheskoi statistike* [Handbook on Social-Economic Statistics]. Moscow, 1948.

215. *Socialist Construction in the USSR.* Moscow, 1936.

216. *Soiuznaia promyshlennost' v tsifrakh* [USSR Industry in Figures]. Moscow, 1929.

217. Sokolov, V., and Nazarov, R. *Sovetskaia torgovlia v poslevoennyi period* [Postwar Soviet Trade]. Moscow, 1954.

218. *Sotsialisticheskoe sel'skoe khoziaistvo, 1935* [Socialist Agriculture in 1935]. Moscow, 1936.

219. ———, *1938.* Moscow, 1939.

220. *Sotsialisticheskoe stroitel'stvo SSSR* [Socialist Construction in the USSR]. Moscow, 1934.

221. ———. Moscow, 1935.

222. ———. Moscow, 1936.

223. ———, *1933–1938.* Moscow, 1939.

224. *Sovetskaia khimiia za 25 let* [Twenty-Five Years of Soviet Chemistry]. Moscow, 1947.

225. *Sovetskaia sotsialisticheskaia ekonomika, 1917–1957* [The Soviet Socialist Economy, 1917–1957]. Moscow, 1957.

226. *Sovetskaia torgovlia* [Soviet Trade]. Moscow, 1956.

227. *Soskvetaia torgovlia za 30 let* [Thirty Years of Soviet Trade]. Moscow, 1947.

228. *Soviet Union, 1935.* Moscow and Leningrad, 1935.

229. *Sozdanie i razvitie promyshlennosti nemetallicheskikh iskopaemykh* [The Origin and Development of the Nonmetallic Minerals Industry]. Moscow, 1933.

230. *Spravochnik komsomol'skogo propagandista i agitatora* [Reference Book for the Young Communist Propagandist and Agitator]. Moscow, 1957.

231. *Spravochnik metallurga po tsvetnym metallam* [Handbook for a Metallurgist of Nonferrous Metals]. Volume I. 2nd ed. Moscow, 1953.

232. *Spravochnik neizmennykh tsen 1926/27 g. na produktsiiu otraslei lesnoi promyshlennosti* [Handbook of Fixed 1926/27 Prices for Products of the Timber Industry]. Moscow, 1935.

233. *Spravochnik neizmennykh tsen 1926/27 g. na produktsiiu pishchevoi promyshlennosti* [Handbook of Fixed 1926/27 Prices for Products of the Food Industry]. Moscow and Leningrad, 1935.

234. *Spravochnik tsen dovoennogo vremeni* [Handbook of Prewar Prices]. Moscow, 1923.

235. *Spravochnik tsen na stroitel'nye materialy i oborudovanie deistvuiushchikh s 1 iiulia 1955 g.* [Handbook of Prices for Building Materials and Equipment Effective July 1, 1955]. Moscow, 1956.

236. *Spravochnik tsennik* [Price Handbook]. Moscow, 1936.

237. *Spravochnik-ukazatel' tsen i srednikh srokov sluzhby* [Handbook of Prices and Average Duration of Usage]. Moscow, 1929.

238. *Sputnik rabochego bumazhnika* [Handbook of the Paper Worker]. Leningrad, 1935.

239. *SSSR—strana sotsializma* [USSR—Country of Socialism]. Moscow, 1936.

240. *SSSR stroit sotsializm* [The USSR Is Building Socialism]. Moscow, 1933.

241. *SSSR v tsifrakh* [The USSR in Figures]. Moscow, 1935.

242. *Statisticheskii ezhegodnik Rossii* [Russian Statistical Yearbook]. Issues for 1904–1913. St. Petersburg, 1904–1913.

243. *Statisticheskii ezhegodnik na 1914 god* [Statistical Yearbook for 1914]. St. Petersburg, 1914.

244. —— *1918–1920 gg.* Moscow, 1922.

245. —— *1921 g.* Moscow, 1922.

246. —— *1922/23 g.* Moscow, 1924.

247. *Statisticheskii sbornik za 1913–1917* [Statistical Summary for 1913–1917]. Moscow, 1921–1922.

248. *Statisticheskii spravochnik SSSR za 1927 god* [Statistical Handbook of the USSR for 1927]. Moscow, 1927.

249. —— *1928 god.* Moscow, 1929.

250. *Statistika bumagopriadil'nogo i tkatskogo proizvodstva za 1900–1910 gg.* [Statistics on Cotton Spinning and Weaving from 1900 to 1910]. St. Petersburg, 1911.

251. *Statistika privoza inostrannykh tovarov i proizvodstva sootvetstvuiushchikh tovarov v Rossii za 1910–1912 gg.* [Statistics on Imports of Foreign Goods and the Production of the Same Goods in Russia from 1910 to 1912]. Petrograd, 1916.

252. *Statistika proizvodstv, oblagaemykh aktsizom* [Statistics on Industries Subject to Excise Tax]. Issues for 1900, 1909, and 1914. St. Petersburg, 1902 and 1911; Petrograd, 1916.

253. *Statistika Rossiiskoi Imperii* [Statistics of the Russian Empire]. Issues for 1890 and 1896. St. Petersburg, 1890 and 1897.

254. *Statistiko-ekonomicheskii spravochnik* [Handbook of Economic Statistics]. Moscow, 1936.

255. Stepanov, P. N. *Geografiia promyshlennosti SSSR* [The Geography of USSR Industry]. Moscow, 1955.

256. Stoklitskii, A. V. (ed.). *L'novodstvo SSSR i ego perspektivy* [Flax Cultivation in the USSR and Its Prospects]. Moscow, 1926.

256a. Strumilin, S. *Ocherki sotsialisticheskoi ekonomiki SSSR* [Essays on the USSR Socialist Economy]. Moscow, 1959.

257. ——. "Rabochee vremia v promyshlennosti SSSR" [Working Hours in Soviet Industry] in *Problemy ekonomiki truda.* Moscow, 1957.

258. *Svod dannykh o fabrichno-zavodskoi promyshlennosti Rossii* [Summary Data on

Russian Factory Industry]. Issues for 1888–1893 and 1897. St. Petersburg, 1891–1900.

259. *Svod tovarnykh tsen na fabrichno-zavodskie izdeliia za 1913 god* [Price List of Factory Products in 1913]. Petrograd, 1914.

260. *Tekhnicheskaia entsiklopediia* [Technical Encyclopedia]. Moscow, 1934.

261. *Ten Years of Soviet Power in Figures, 1917–1927.* Moscow, 1927.

262. Tigranov, G. F., and Ol', P. V. *Dragotsennye metally* [Precious Metals]. Moscow, 1925.

263. Timiriazev, D. A. *Istoriko-statisticheskii obzor promyshlennosti Rossii* [A Historical and Statistical Survey of Russian Industry]. St. Petersburg, Volume I, 1892; Volume II, 1896.

264. *Torgovo-promyshlennyi i finansovyi slovar'* [Trade, Industrial, and Financial Dictionary]. Leningrad, 1925.

265. *Tovarovedenie promyshlennykh tovarov* [Commercial Specifications of Industrial Goods]. Moscow, 1954.

266. *Trebovaniia promyshlennosti k kachestve mineral'nego syr'ia* [Industrial Quality Requirements for Mineral Raw Materials]. Moscow, 1946.

267. *Tretii piatiletnii plan razvitiia narodnogo khoziaistva Soiuza SSR, 1938–1942* [Third Five Year Plan for the Development of the USSR National Economy, 1938–1942]. Moscow, 1939.

268. *Trud v SSSR* [Labor in the USSR]. Moscow, 1934.

269. ———. Moscow, 1936.

270. Tsylko, F. A. *Puti razvitiia sel'skogo khoziaistva v blizhaishie piat let* [Ways of Developing Agriculture in the Next Five Years]. Moscow and Leningrad, n.d.

271. Tugan-Baranovskii, M. *Russkaia fabrika v proshlom i nastoiashchem* [Russian Factories in the Past and in the Present]. St. Petersburg, 1898.

272. *Ugol'naia promyshlennost'* [The Coal Industry]. Moscow, 1957.

273. *Universal'nyi spravochnik tsen* [General Price Handbook]. Moscow and Leningrad, 1928.

274. *Valsts statistika parvalde Rupiuecipas statistika, 1937* [Statistical Yearbook of Latvia, 1937]. Riga, 1939.

275. Vasil'ev, P., and Nevzorov, N. *Lesnoe khoziaistvo i lesnaia promyshlennost' SSSR* [Forestry and the Timber Industry in the USSR]. Moscow, 1948.

276. Vasilevskii, P. I., and Shlifshtein, E. I. *Ocherki kustarnoi promyshlennosti SSSR* [Essays on the USSR *Kustar'* Industry]. Moscow, 1930.

277. *Vazhneishie resheniia po sel'skomu khoziaistvu za 1938–1946 gg.* [Important Agricultural Resolutions from 1938 to 1946]. Moscow, 1948.

278. Veingarten, S. M. *Ocherki ekonomiki sovetskoi chernoi metallurgi* [Essays on the Economics of Soviet Ferrous Metallurgy]. Leningrad, 1933.

279. Veits, V. I. *Ot plana Goelro k velikim stroikam kommunizma* [From the Goelro Plan to the Great Construction Works of Communism]. Moscow, 1952.

280. *Velikie stroiki kommunizma* [The Great Construction Works of Communism]. Moscow, 1951.

281. Velikovskii, A. S. (ed.). *Sovetskie nefti* [Soviet Oils]. Moscow, 1947.

282. Vikent'ev, A. *Ocherki razvitiia sovetskoi ekonomiki v chetvertoi piatiletke* [Essays on the Development of Soviet Economic Structure in the Fourth Five Year Plan]. Moscow, 1952.

283. *Vneshniaia torgovlia Soiuza SSR za period 1918–1927/28 gody* [USSR Foreign Trade from 1918 to 1927/28]. Moscow, 1931.

284. Volf, M. B., and Mebus, G. A. *Statisticheskii spravochnik po ekonomicheskoi geografii SSSR i drugikh gosudarstv* [A Statistical Handbook on the Economic Geography of the USSR and Other Countries]. 3rd ed. Moscow and Leningrad, 1926.

285. ———. 4th ed. Moscow and Leningrad, 1928.

286. Volkov, E. Z. *Dinamika narodonaseleniia SSSR va 80 let* [Dynamics of the USSR Population During Eighty Years]. Moscow, 1930.

287. Volodarskii, L. M. *Razvitie promyshlennosti SSSR v piatoi piatiletke* [Development of USSR Industry in the Fifth Five Year Plan]. Moscow, 1953.

288. *Voprosy ekonomiki zheleznodorozhnogo transporta* [Problems of Railroad Transportation]. Moscow, 1948.

289. *Voprosy koniunktury* [Problems of the Economic Situation]. Moscow, 1926.

290. *Voprosy organizatsii i ratsionalizatsii proizvodstva vo vtorom piatiletke* [Problems of the Efficient Organization of Production in the Second Five Year Plan]. Moscow, 1933.

291. Voznesenskii, N. *Economic Results of the USSR in 1940 and the Plan of National Economic Development for 1941.* Moscow, 1941.

292. ———. *The Economy of the USSR During World War II* (translated from the Russian). Washington, 1948.

293. ———. *Voennaia ekonomika SSSR v period otechestvennoi voiny* [The Economy of the USSR During World War II]. Moscow, 1947.

294. *Vtoroi piatiletnii plan razvitiia narodnogo khoziaistva SSSR, 1933–1937* [The Second Five Year Plan for the Development of the USSR National Economy, 1933–1937]. Moscow, 1934.

295. Vyshinskii, A. *Sovetskoe gosudarstvo v otechestvennoi voine* [The Soviet State in World War II]. Moscow, 1944.

296. Winter, A. V. *Soviet Electric Power Development.* Moscow, 1952.

297. Yerhov, A. *Soviet Statistics.* Moscow, 1957.

298. *Zakon o piatiletnem plane vosstanovleniia i razvitiia narodnogo khoziaistva SSSR na 1946–1950 gg.* [Decree on the Five Year Plan for the Rehabilitation and Development of the USSR National Economy, 1946–1950]. Moscow, 1946.

299. Zhemchuzhina, P. S. *The Food Industry of the USSR.* Moscow, 1939.

300. Zotov, V. P. *Pishchevaia promyshlennost' Sovetskogo Soiuza* [The Soviet Food Industry]. Moscow, 1958.

301. ———. *Razvitie pishchevoi promyshlennosti v novoi piatiletke* [Development of the Food Industry in the New Five Year Plan]. Moscow, 1947.

302. Zvorykin, A. A. *Ocherki po istorii sovetskoi gornoi tekhniki* [Essays on the History of Soviet Mining Technology]. Moscow and Leningrad, 1950.

B. RUSSIAN JOURNALS AND NEWSPAPERS (303–419)

303. *Anilinokrasochnaia promyshlennost'* [The Aniline Dye Industry]. All-Union State Trust of the Aniline Dye Industry.

  1931: Dubov, P. I. "Anilino-krasochnaia promyshlennost'—rychag khimizatsii" [The Crucial Role of Aniline Dye Production in the Development of the Chemical Industry]. No. 1, 5–7.

1934: "XVII let sovetskoi anilinokrasochnoi promyshlennosti" [Seventeen Years of the Soviet Aniline Dye Industry]. No. 8, 457–459.

304. *Avtomobil'naia promyshlennost'* [The Automobile Industry]. Now called: *Avtomobil'naia i traktornaia promyshlennost'* [The Automobile and Tractor Industry]. USSR Ministry of the Automobile Industry.

1947: "Povyshenie proizvoditel'nosti truda—vazhneishee uslovie vypolneniia plana" [Increasing Labor Productivity Is the Most Important Condition Necessary to Fulfill the Plan]. No. 3, 1–3.

1955: "Za dosrochnoe vypolnenie piatogo piatiletnego plana avtomobil'noi i traktornoi promyshlennost'iu!" [For the Preschedule Fulfillment of the Fifth Five Year Plan for the Automobile and Tractor Industry]. No. 1, 1–2.

305. *Biulleten' ekonomicheskogo i finansovogo zakonodatel'stva* [Bulletin of Economic and Financial Legislation].

306. *Biulleten' Sakharotresta* [Bulletin of the Sugar Trust].

1925: Nepomniashchii, L., and Myslitskii, N. G. "Perspektivy sbyta sakhara v 1925/26 operativnom godu" [Sugar Supply Outlook for 1925/26]. No. 9, 8–18.

307. *Bol'shevik* [The Bolshevik]. Central Committee of the Communist Party.

1944: Granovskii, E. "Sila i zhiznesposobnost' ekonomicheskoi osnovy sovetskogo gosudarstva" [The Strength and Vital Capacity of the Economic Foundation of the Soviet State]. No. 22, 19–29.

1951: Zhimerin, D. "Stroitel'stvo elektroenergeticheskoi bazy kommunizma" [Building of the Electric Power Base of Communism]. No. 8, 25–37.

1952: Malenkov, G. M. "Otchetnyi doklad XIX s'ezdu partii o rabote Tsentral'nogo Komiteta VKP (b)" [Report to the XIX Party Congress on the Work of the Party Central Committee]. No. 19, 5–63.

308. *Bumazhnaia promyshlennost'* [The Paper Industry]. Technical-Economic Council of the Paper Industry.

1923: Zherebov, L. P. "Lesnye kontsessii v Rossii" [Timber Concessions in Russia]. No. 4, 342–364.

1927: Nikitin, A. A. "Bumazhnaia promyshlennost' SSSR za 10 let" [Ten Years of the USSR Paper Industry]. No. 11–12, 709–717.

1935: Shusser, M. I. "Sostoianie mirovogo bumazhnogo rynka i bumazhnoi promyshlennosti" [The State of the World Paper Market and the USSR Paper Industry]. No. 7, 82–90.

1937: Bobrov, F. F., and Vilenchik, S. B. "20 let raboty" [Twenty Years of Work]. No. 8, 6–12.

1938: Kazarnovskii, Sh. S. "Bumazhnaia promyshlennost' v pervom godu tret'ei piatiletki" [The Paper Industry in the First Year of the Third Five Year Plan]. No. 2, 8–12.

1939: ———. "Bumazhnaia promyshlennost' v 1938 i 1939 godakh" [The Paper Industry in 1938 and 1939]. No. 4, 70–75.

1940: Nazarov, A. I. "K voprosam stroitel'stva novykh kartonnykh fabrik" [On the Construction of New Cardboard Factories]. No. 10, 62–65.

1946: "Dvigat' vpered nauku i tekhniku proizvodstva" [Make Progress in the Science and Technology of Production]. No. 1–2, 3–5.

1946: "Pretvorim v zhizn' Stalinskii plan" [Put the Stalin Plan into Action].
No. 3–4, 7–8.

1946: "Postanovlenie VIII plenuma Tsentral'nogo Komiteta profsoiuza
rabochikh bumazhnoi promyshlennosti SSSR [Resolution of the VIII
Plenary Session of the Central Committee of the Trade Union of USSR
Paper Industry Workers]. No. 3–4, 9–13.

1946: "K novomu pod'emu izobretatel'stva i ratsionalizatsii" [For More
Inventions and Innovations]. No. 7–8, 3–4.

1947: "K novym pobedam!" [On to New Victories!]. No. 6, 3–6.

1947: Vilenchik, S. B. "Piatiletka—v chetyre goda!" [The Five Year Plan
in Four Years!]. No. 7, 7–9.

1951: "Za vysokoe ispol'zovanie tekhniki" [For the Greater Use of
Technology]. No. 2, 3–5.

309. *Derevo-obrabatyvaiushchaia i leso-khimicheskaia promyshlennost'* [The Wood
Processing and Wood Chemical Processing Industry]. USSR Ministry of
the Paper and Wood Processing Industry.

310. *Ekonomicheskaia zhizn'* [Economic Life]. USSR Ministry of Finances and
the USSR State Bank.

1935: "Doklad V. V. Kuibysheva na III Moskovskom oblastnom s'ezde
sovetov" [V. V. Kuibyshev's Report at the III Moscow Oblast Congress
of Soviets]. Jan. 12, 2–4.

1935: "Otchetnyi doklad Narodnogo Komissara Tiazheloi Promyshlennosti
SSSR G. K. Ordzhonikidze" [Report of G. K. Ordzhonikidze, People's
Commissar of USSR Heavy Industry]. Feb. 2, 1–3, and Feb. 4, 2–4.

311. *Ekonomicheskii biulleten'* [Economic Bulletin]. Conjuncture Institute.

312. *Ekonomicheskoe obozrenie* [Economic Survey].

1926: Gradov, M. "Rybnoe khoziaistvo SSSR i ego organizatsionnye
zadachi" [The USSR Fishing Industry and Its Organizational Tasks].
No. 2, 112–119.

1926: Savinskii, D, "Krupnaia gosudarstvennaia promyshlennost' "
[Large-Scale State Industry]. No. 12, 64–81.

1928: Dobrovol'skii, B. M. "Metallopromyshlennost' v 1927/28 godu i
perspektivy na 1928/29 god" [The Metal Industry in 1927/28 and the
Outlook for 1928/29]. No. 10, 132–148.

1929: Savinskii, D. "Krupnaia promyshlennost' v SSSR v 1927/28 g."
[Large-Scale Industry in the USSR in 1927/28]. No. 2, 144–166.

1929: Ulitskii, Ia. "Promyshlennost' v pervom polugodii" [Industry in
the First Half Year]. No. 5, 120–139.

1929: "Pokazateli sostoianiia narodnogo khoziaistva" [Indicators of the
State of the National Economy]. No. 6, 148–176.

1929: Kachanov, I. Z. "O kachestve potrebitel'skikh tovarov" [The
Quality of Consumer Goods]. No. 10, 23–39.

1929: Roze, A. "Sostoianie sel'sko-khoziaistvennogo mashinostroeniia i
sel'skokhoziaistvennogo mashinosnabzheniia v SSSR" [The State of Agricultural Machine Building and Supply in the USSR]. No. 12, 138–151.

1930: Volkov, I. "Metalloobrabatyvaiushchaia promyshlennost' " [The
Metalworking Industry]. No. 2, 116–127.

313. *Elektricheskie stantsii* [Power Plants]. USSR Ministry of Power Plants.
1949: "Za dosrochnoe vypolnenie poslevoennoi stalinskoi piatiletki" [For the Preschedule Fulfillment of the Stalin Postwar Five Year Plan]. No. 1, 5–8.
1953: "Za novyi pod'em sovetskoi energetiki" [For New Advances in Power Engineering]. No. 1, 3–5.
1954: "Zadachi energetikov na 1954 god" [Tasks of Power Plant Workers in 1954]. No. 1, 3–5.
1954: "Podniat' tempy stroitel'stva energeticheskikh predpriiatii" [Increase the Rate of Construction of Power Stations]. No. 6, 3–5.
1955: "Leninskaia elektrifikatsiia strany sovetov" [The Leninist Electrification of the Country of the Soviets]. No. 4, 3–5.
1955: "K novym pobedam Leninskoi elektrifikatsii" [On to New Victories of Leninist Electrification]. No. 12, 1–5.
1956: "K novym uspekham energetiki" [On to New Successes in Power Engineering]. No. 1, 1–4.

314. *Elektrichestvo* [Electricity]. USSR Academy of Sciences, USSR Ministry of Power Stations, and USSR Ministry of the Electrical Engineering Industry.
1940: Pervukhin, M. G. "K piatidesiatiletiiu Viacheslava Mikhailovicha Molotova" [On the Fiftieth Anniversary of V. M. Molotov]. No. 3, 1–2.
1955: Loginov, F. G. "Razvitie sovetskoi energetiki i zadachi energeticheskogo stroitel'stva v 1955 g." [The Development of Soviet Power Engineering and Tasks of Power Plant Construction in 1955]. No. 7, 11–16.

315. *Ezhemesiachnyi statisticheskii biulleten'* [Monthly Statistical Bulletin]. Chief Economic Agency, Central Statistical Section of *VSNKh*. 1923/24–1927/28.

316. *Gornyi zhurnal* [Journal of Mining]. All-Union Scientific Engineering and Mining Society.
1936: Voitsekhovskii, A. E. "Kaoliny SSSR" [Kaolins of the USSR]. No. 10, 53–61.
1938: Karasik, M. "Syr'evaia baza ogneupornoi promyshlennosti" [Raw Material Base of the Refractory Materials Industry]. No. 1, 24–38.
1938: "Plan ugol'noi i rudnoi promyshlennosti na 1938 god—boevoe zadanie" [The 1938 Plan for the Coal and Ore Industry Is an Urgent Task]. No. 3, 5–8.
1938: Gorodetskii, P. I. "Rudospusknye ustroistva i kapital'naia shtol'nia apatitovogo rudnika imeni S. M. Kirova" [Ore Chutes and the Main Drift of the Kirov Apatite Mine]. No. 8–9, 38–46.
1939: Troitskii, A. V., and Fishman, M. A. "Obzor deiatel'nosti obogatitel'-nykh fabrik Glavtsinksvintsa za 1938 g." [Survey of the Work of the Concentration Plants of the Chief Administration of Zinc and Lead in 1938]. No. 3, 57–64, and No. 4–5, 99–103.
1939: Voitsekhovskii, A. E. "Puti razvitiia kaolinovoi promyshlennosti SSSR" [The Development of the USSR Kaolin Industry]. No. 9 31–36.

1939: "Zhelezurudnaia promyshlennost' k XXII godovshchine Velikoi Oktiabr'skoi Sotsialisticheskoi Revoliutsii" [The Iron Ore Industry on the 22nd Anniversary of the Great October Socialist Revolution]. No. 10–11, 1–2.

1947: Zvorykin, A. A. "Tekhnicheskoe perevooruzhenie i razvitie gorno-rudnoi promyshlennosti" [The Technical Re-Equipment and Develop-ment of the Ore Mining Industry]. No. 11, 3–8.

1947: Kassiura, K. G. "Osvoenie Severoural'skikh boksitovykh rudnikov" [Mastering the Production Processes in the Northern Urals Bauxite Mines]. No. 12, 14–18.

317. *Gudok* [Whistle]. USSR Ministry of Communications and Central Committee of Trade Union Workers.

318. *Industriia* [Industry]. USSR Ministries of the Fuel Industry, of Power Stations and the Electrical Industry, and of the Chemical Industry.

1939: Gimmel'farb, B.; Kurman, I.; and Ul'ianov, N. "Vnimanie fosfatnomu syr'iu" [More Attention to Phosphate Raw Materials]. Jan. 6.

1939: Rabinovich, M. "Puti razvitiia sodovoi promyshlennosti" [The Development of the Soda Industry]. Feb. 3.

1939: Denisov, M. "Prevratit' khimicheskuiu promyshlennost' v odnu iz vedushchikh otraslei" [Transform the Chemical Industry into One of the Leading Industries]. Feb. 22.

1939: Dubovitskii, A. "Kak razmestit' promyshlennost' mineral'nykh udobrenii" [How to Locate the Mineral Fertilizer Industry]. March 3.

1939: Samokhvalov, A. "Zadachi tsvetnoi metallurgii" [The Tasks of Nonferrous Metallurgy]. March 4, 3.

1939: Pshenitsyn, V. "Segodnia i zavtra Kol'skogo poluostrova" [The Present and the Future of the Kola Peninsula]. May 9.

1939: Gofshtein, M. "Puti pod'ema asbestovoi promyshlennosti" [Ways of Developing the Asbestos Industry]. May 10, 2.

1939: Shegov, B. "Sebestoimost' tonny superfosfata" [The Cost of a Ton of Superphosphate]. May 12.

1939: "Sozdat' bol'shuiu slantsevuiu promyshlennost' " [Create a Larger Slate Industry]. June 9, 1.

1939: Pshenitsyn, V. "Volkhovskii aliuminievyi zavod perekhodit na nefeliny" [The Volkhov Aluminum Plant Is Being Converted to Nephe-line]. June 23.

1939: Kholmianskii, I. "Tsvetnaia metallurgiia za 5 mesiatsev 1939 goda" [Nonferrous Metallurgy During Five Months of 1939]. June 24, 2.

1939: Zabelyshinskii, I. "Aliuminievaia promyshlennost' za granitsei i u nas" [The Aluminum Industry at Home and Abroad]. Sept. 21, 2.

319. *Iskusstvennoe volokno* [Synthetic Fibers]. All-Union Synthetic Fiber Industry.

320. *Istoriia SSSR* [History of the USSR]. Academy of Sciences.

1959: Khavin, A. F. "Razvitie tiazheloi promyshlennosti v tretei piatiletke" [The Development of Heavy Industry in the Third Five Year Plan]. No. 1, 10–35.

321. *Izvestia* [News]. USSR Council of Deputies.

   1941: "Mestnye udobreniia—na polia!" [Local Fertilizer onto the Fields!]. Feb. 14.

   1941: Malenkov, G. M. "O zadachakh partiinykh organizatsii v oblasti promyshlennosti i transporta" [On the Task of Party Organizations in Industry and Transportation]. Feb. 16, 1–3.

   1941: "Rech' tov. Tevosiana na XVIII Vsesoiuznoi konferentsii VKP (b)" [Comrade Tevosian's Speech at the XVIII All-Union Party Conference]. Feb. 21, 2–3.

   1941: "Rech' Denisova" [Denisov's Speech]. Feb. 27.

   1946: Lomako, P. "Novyi pod'em tsvetnoi metallurgii" [New Advances in Nonferrous Metallurgy]. April 2, 2.

   1947: Lokshin, E. "Tiazhelaia industriia—osnova razvitiia narodnogo khoziaistva SSSR" [Heavy Industry Is the Basis of the Development of the USSR National Economy]. April 7, 2.

   1950: Aleksenko, G. "Dostizheniia otechestvennoi radiopromyshlennosti" [Achievements of Our Native Radio Industry]. May 7, 1.

   1951: Kostousov, A. "Za dal'neishii pod'em sovetskogo stankostroeniia" [For Further Progress in Soviet Machine Tool Building]. April 20, 2.

   1952: Kostousov, A. "V bor'be za dal'neishii tekhnicheskii progress" [For Further Technical Progress]. Jan. 30, 2.

322. *Izvestia Akademii Nauk SSSR—Otdelenie ekonomiki i prava* [News of the USSR Academy of Sciences—Economics and Law Division].

   1951: Badzhadze, I.; Kakabadze, A.; and Nutsubidze, A. "Rastsvet ekonomiki Sovetskoi Gruzii" [The Economic Prosperity of Soviet Georgia]. No. 3, 172–185.

323. *Izvestia tekstil'noi promyshlennosti i torgovli* [News of the Textile Industry and Trade]. All-Union Textile Syndicate.

   1930: Kudriavtsev, A. "O kachestve khlopchatobumazhnykh tkanei" [On the Quality of Cotton Fabrics]. No. 3, 19–23.

   1931: Andreev, D. G. "O kontrol'nykh tochkakh na 1932 god po khlopchatobumazhnoi promyshlennosti" [On the Control Points in 1932 in the Cotton Industry]. No. 10–11, 5–7.

324. *Kauchuk i rezina* [Rubber]. Chief Administration of the Rubber Industry.

   1937: Zmii, P. "Sovetskoe shinnoe proizvodstvo za 20 let" [Soviet Tire Production During 20 Years]. No. 11, 57–62.

   1937: Eremeev, Iu. "Rezino-obuvnaia promyshlennost' SSSR k 20-letiiu Oktiabria" [The USSR Rubber Shoe Industry on the 20th Anniversary of the October Revolution]. No. 11, 68–76.

325. *Kazakhstanskaia pravda* [Kazakhstan Truth]. Communist Party of Kazakhstan.

326. *Keramika i steklo* [Ceramics and Glass]. Now called *Steklo i keramika* (see 391).

   1932: Reingerts, M. D. "Stekol'no-farforovaia promyshlennost' za 15 let—1917–1932" [Fifteen Years of the Glass and Porcelain Industry—1917–1932]. No. 11, 3–11.

327. *Khimicheskaia promyshlennost'* [The Chemical Industry]. Ministry of the Chemical Industry.

BIBLIOGRAPHY

1944: Dubovitskii, A. M. "Fosfority Kara-Tau" [Phosphorites of Kara-Tau]. No. 2–3.

1947: Pervukhin, M. G. "Rasshirit' proizvodstvo, povysit' kachestvo mineral'nykh udobrenii i khimikatov dlia sel'skogo khoziaistva" [Increase the Production and Improve the Quality of Mineral Fertilizers and Chemicals for Agriculture]. No. 4, 1–4.

1947: "Tridtsat' let sovetskoi khimicheskoi promyshlennosti" [Thirty Years of the Soviet Chemical Industry]. No. 11, 1–7.

1954: Kuritsyn, P. V. "Udovletvorim potrebnost' v tovarakh shirokogo potrebleniia, vyrabatyvaemykh na predpriatiiakh MKhP" [Let Us Meet the Demand for Consumer Goods Produced at the Ministry of the Chemical Industry Enterprises]. No. 1, 8–12.

1954: Garbar, M. I. "Rasshirenie vypuska i uluchshenie kachestva predmetov narodnogo potrebleniia iz plasticheskikh mass" [Increase and Improvement in Plastic Consumer Goods]. No. 3, 1–5.

1955: Mel'nik, B. D. "Rabota zavodov sernoi kisloty i fosfornykh udobrenii v 1954 godu i ocherednye zadachi" [The Work of the Sulfuric Acid and Phosphate Fertilizer Plants in 1954 and Their Future Tasks]. No. 1, 1–10.

1955: Ul'ianov, N. S. "Blizhaishie zadachi gornokhimicheskoi promyshlennosti" [Urgent Tasks of the Chemical Ore Industry]. No. 6, 1–4.

1955: Unaniants, T. P. "Ob uvelichenii proizvodstva fosforitnoi muki iz nizkoprotsentnykh fosforitov" [Increasing the Production of Ground Phosphate from Low-Grade Phosphorites]. No. 6, 30–31.

1955: Andreichev, A. N. "Puti dal'neishego vnedreniia novoi tekhniki na gornykh predpriatiakh MKhP" [Means of Introducing New Technology in the Mining Enterprises of the Ministry of the Chemical Industry]. No. 7, 13–18.

328. *Khimiia i khoziaistvo* [Chemistry and the National Economy]. Committee for the Introduction of Chemistry in the USSR National Economy.

1930: Gavrilov, N. "Khimicheskaia promyshlennost' pered 3-m godom piatiletki" [The Chemical Industry Before the Third Year of the Five Year Plan]. No. 4, 5–14.

1930: Kaktyn', A., and Chuchupal, A. "K khimizatsii sel'skogo khoziaistva" [The Introduction of Chemistry into Agriculture]. No. 4, 26–43.

329. *Khimiia i sotsialisticheskoe khoziaistvo* [Chemistry and Socialist Economy]. Committee for the Introduction of Chemistry into the USSR National Economy.

1931: Dubov, P. "Neotlozhnye voprosy osnovnoi khimicheskoi promyshlennosti" [Vital Problems of the Heavy Chemical Industry]. No. 1, 20–28.

330. *Khimizatsiia sotsialisticheskogo zemledeliia* [Introduction of Chemistry in Socialist Agriculture]. All-Union Scientific Research Institute of Fertilizers and Soil Improvement.

1932: Tolochko, P. F. "Effektivnost' fosforitnoi muki na Ukraine" [The Effectiveness of Ground Phosphate in the Ukraine]. No. 11–12.

1939: Petrov, N. G. "Udobrenie sakharnoi svekly v kolkhozakh SSSR" [Fertilization of Sugar Beets on USSR Collective Farms]. No. 6.

653

331. *Khlopchatobumazhnaia promyshlennost'* [The Cotton Industry]. USSR Ministry of the Textile Industry.

332. *Koks i khimiia* [Coke and Chemistry]. Ministry of Ferrous Metallurgy.
   1939: Zarovnyi, P. B. "Sdelat' sovetskuiu koksokhimiiu samoi peredovoi v mire" [Let Us Make the Soviet Chemical Coke Processing Industry the Most Advanced in the World]. No. 2, 9–11.
   1939: "Stalinskim putem k novym pobedam!" [On to New Victories the Stalinist Way!]. No. 4–5, 1–2.
   1939: Gimel'stein, T. E., and Gorzon, R. D. "Puti pererabotki kamennougol'noi smoly" [Ways of Reprocessing Coal Tar]. No. 4–5, 68–69.
   1940: Levin, Iu. I. "Obraztsovo podgotovit'sia k letu" [Prepare for Summer in an Exemplary Fashion]. No. 3, 2–3.

333. *Kommunist* [The Communist]. Central Committee of the Communist Party.
   1953: Malenkov, G. M. "Rech' na piatoi sessii Verkhovnogo Soveta SSSR" [Speech at the Fifth Session of the USSR Supreme Soviet]. No. 12, 12–34.
   1953: Kosygin, A. "Programma krutogo pod'ema proizvodstva promyshlennykh tovarov shirokogo potrebleniia" [A Program for a Sharp Increase in the Production of Industrial Consumer Goods]. No. 18, 19–34.
   1957: Starovskii, V. "Novye zadachi sovetskoi statistiki" [New Tasks for Soviet Statistics]. No. 14, 61–73.

334. *Konservnaia promyshlennost'* [The Canning Industry]. Chief Administration of the Canning Industry.
   1930: Kirillov, A. "K voprosu o piatiletnem plane konservnoi promyshlennosti" [On the Five Year Plan for the Canning Industry]. No. 1, 3–7.
   1931: Mikoyan, A. "Za moshchnuiu pishchevuiu industriiu" [For a Bigger and Better Food Industry]. No. 10–12, 1–2.

335. *Kozhevenno-obuvnaia promyshlennost' SSSR* [The Shoe and Leather Industry of the USSR]. In early years, called: *Vestnik kozhevenno-obuvnoi promyshlennosti* [Bulletin of the Shoe and Leather Industry] and *Vestnik kozhevenno-obuvnoi promyshlennosti i torgovli* [Bulletin of the Shoe and Leather Industry and Trade]. All-Union Agency of the Leather Industry.
   1932: Eskin, A. "Itogi raboty kozhevennoi promyshlennosti i nashi zadachi v 1932 godu" [Results of the Leather Industry and Our Tasks for 1932]. No. 1, 4–6.

336. *Krasnaia zvezda* [Red Star]. Soviet Army.

337. *Krasnyi flot* [Red Fleet]. Soviet Navy.

338. *Legkaia industriia* [Light Industry].

339. *Legkaia promyshlennost'* [Light Industry]. USSR Ministry of Light Industry.
   1939: "K novomu pod'emu" [Toward New Advances]. No. 1, 5–6.
   1939: Obukhov, N. S. "Dadim strane bol'she obuvi" [Let Us Give the Country More Shoes]. No. 12, 50–53.
   1945: "Prevzoiti dovoennyi uroven'" [Surpass the Prewar Level]. No. 10–11, 1–3.
   1947: Kostenko, D. G. "Vosstanovlenie i razvitie kozhevenno-obuvnoi promyshlennosti" [The Restoration and Development of the Leather and Shoe Industry]. No. 1, 7–9.

1947: Chesnokov, N. E. "Legkaia promyshlennost' Soiuza SSR za 30 let" [Thirty Years of Light Industry in the USSR]. No. 11, 1–5.

1948: "Tretii god Stalinskoi piatiletki" [The Third Year of the Stalin Five Year Plan]. No. 1, 1–3.

1952: "Uluchshit' kachestvo i rasshirit' assortiment obuvi" [Improve the Quality and Increase the Variety of Shoes]. No. 8, 1–2.

1956: Goriachkin, A. V. "Bol'shie zadachi" [Great Tasks]. No. 3, 4–10.

340. *Les* [Timber]. Chief Timber Supply under USSR Council of Ministers.

1946: Reinberg, S. A. "Ob urovne proizvodstva lesnoi produktsii" [On the Level of Production in the Timber Industry]. No. 1, 22–26.

1946: Benenson, G. M. "Polnost'iu snabdit' shpalami zheleznodorozhnyi transport" [Supply the Railroads Fully with Cross Ties]. No. 1, 32–37.

1946: Vekshegonov, V. Ia. "Syr'evye resursy lesosnabzheniia v chetvertom piatiletii" [Raw Materials for Lumber Supply in the Fourth Five Year Plan]. No. 2–3, 7–11.

1947: Lopukhov, E. I. "Les i bumaga" [Timber and Paper]. No. 1, 4–13.

341. *Lesnaia industriia* [The Timber Industry]. USSR Ministry of the Timber Industry.

1937: Benenson, G. M., and Gugel', G. L. "Snabzhenie lesom narodnogo khoziaistva vo vtorom i v tret'em piatiletii" [The Supply of Timber for the National Economy in the Second and Third Five Year Plan]. No. 5, 2–9.

342. *Lesnaia promyshlennost'* [The Timber Industry]. USSR Ministry of the Lumber Industry.

1946: Popov, V. A. "Na novom etape" [At a New Stage]. No. 6–7, 4–10.

1946: Gaitsgori, Sh. Z. "Spichechnaia promyshlennost' SSSR" [The USSR Match Industry]. No. 6–7, 12–15.

1946: Saltykov, M. I. "Lesnaia promyshlennost' v IV piatiletii" [The Lumber Industry in the IV Five Year Plan]. No. 8–9, 1–5.

1947: "Lesnaia promyshlennost' za 30 let" [Thirty Years of the Lumber Industry]. No. 10, 5–14.

1947: Zinov'ev, V. V. "Fanernaia promyshlennost' SSSR" [The USSR Plywood Industry]. No. 10, 14–15.

343. *Lesnaia promyshlennost'* [The Timber Industry]. Newspaper.

344. *Lesnoe khoziaistvo* [Forestry]. USSR Ministry of Forestry.

345. *Lesokhimicheskaia promyshlennost'* [Chemical Wood Processing Industry]. Chief Administration of the Chemical Wood Processing Industry.

1932: Ozolin, K. M. "Resul'taty dvuletnikh opytov dlitel'noi podsochki sosny v razlichnykh raionakh Soiuza SSR" [Results of Two-Year Experiments with Prolonged Tapping of Pine Trees in Different Regions of the USSR]. No. 5–6, 45–55.

1936: Veitsman, A. I. "Desiat' let promyshlennogo terpentinnogo khoziaistva v Sovetskom Soiuze" [Ten Years of Industrial Turpentine Production in the Soviet Union]. No. 1, 19–21.

1936: "Podsochku 1936 goda provedem po-stakhanovski" [We Shall Tap Trees in a Stakhanovite Way in 1936]. No. 4, 1–2.

1939: Tuliakov, V. B. "Puti razvitiia lesokhimicheskoi promyshlennosti" [The Development of the Chemical Wood Processing Industry]. No. 9.

346. *Mashinostroenie* [Machine Building]. Ministry of Machine Building and Ministry of Defense.

1938: Nelidov, I. "Somnitel'nye metody planirovaniia" [Doubtful Planning Methods]. Sept. 30.

1939: "Elektrifikatsiia sovetskoi strany" [Electrification of the Soviet Union]. Jan. 21, 3.

1939: Gorin, A. "Ogromny reservy vagonostroeniia" [Sizable Potentialities in Railroad Car Construction]. July 15, 2.

347. *Masloboino-zhirovoe delo* [The Oil and Fat Industry]. All-Union Scientific Research Institute of Fats.

1927: "Zhirovaia promyshlennost' SSSR k desiatiletiiu Oktiabria" [The Soviet Fat Industry on the Tenth Anniversary of the October Revolution]. No. 11, 23–33.

1927: "Syr'evaia baza masloboinoi promyshlennosti SSSR" [The Raw Material Base of the Soviet Oil Industry]. No. 11, 33–38.

1934: Margolin, G., and Dizhur, M. "Margarinovaia promyshlennost' v bor'be za kachestvo" [The Margarine Industry in Its Struggle for Quality]. No. 11, 4–6.

1934: Murin, G. "Zhirovaia promyshlennost' k VII s'ezdu sovetov" [The Fat Industry at the Time of the VIIth Congress of Soviets]. No. 12, 48–50.

348. *Miasnaia industriia SSSR* [The USSR Meat Industry].

1954: "Neotlozhnye zadachi miasnoi promyshlennosti" [Urgent Tasks of the Meat Industry]. No. 3, 1–5.

349. *Miasnaia promyshlennost'* [The Meat Industry].

1932: Babich, V. "Sovetskaia miasnaia promyshlennost' na poroge 15 godovshchiny Oktiabria" [The Soviet Meat Industry on the Threshold of the 15th Anniversary of the October Revolution]. No. 11, 9–15.

350. *Mineral'noe syr'e* [Mineral Raw Materials]. Institute of Applied Mineralogy.

1934: Arzhekaev, S. A. "Mineral'nosyr'evaia baza SSSR k nachalu vtorogo piatiletiia i ee udel'nyi ves v mirovykh resursakh" [The Mineral and Raw Material Resources of the USSR at the Beginning of the Second Five Year Plan and Their Share in World Resources]. No. 2, 1–13.

1934: Fedorovskii, N. M., and Diukalov, N. A. "Promyshlennost' nemetallicheskikh iskopaemykh na sluzhbu vtoroi piatiletki" [The Nonmetallic Minerals Industry Serving the Second Five Year Plan]. No. 3, 1–16.

1935: Bagratuni, E. G. "Sernokolchedannye mestorozhdeniia Zakavkaz'ia i ikh real'nye perspektivy" [Sulfur Pyrites Deposits in Transcaucasia and Their Potentialities]. No. 6.

351. *Mineral'nye udobreniia i insektofungisidy* [Mineral Fertilizers and Pesticides].

1935: Manchev, V. P. "Osnovnye zadachi promyshlennosti insektofungisidov" [The Basic Tasks of the Pesticide Industry]. No. 1, 82–89.

1935: Kazakov, A. V. "Problema fosforitnoi muki" [The Problem of Ground Phosphate]. No. 5, 31–40.

1935: Smirnov, N. D. "Ispol'zovanie nefelinovykh porod v kachestve udobrenii" [The Use of Nepheline Rock as Fertilizer]. No. 5, 81–88.

352. *Molochnoe khoziaistvo* [The Dairy Industry]. All-Russian Union of Dairy Cooperatives.

1927: Liubimov, N. "Dal'she vpered" [Forward]. No. 20–21, 12–17.

353. *Mulochnaia promyshlennost' SSSR* [The USSR Dairy Industry]. USSR Ministry of the Meat and Dairy Industry.
   1940: "Desiat' let gosudarstvennoi molochnoi promyshlennosti" [Ten Years of the State Dairy Industry]. No. 2–3, 1–14.

354. *Mukomol'e i elevatorno-skladskoe khoziaistvo* [Flour Milling and Storage]. USSR Ministry of Procurements.
   1939: "Mukomol'naia promyshlennost' dolzhna stat' peredovoi otrasl'iu pishchevoi industrii" [The Flour Milling Industry Should Become a Leading Branch of the Food Industry]. No. 1, 3–4.

355. *Narodnoe khoziaistvo* [National Economy]. Supreme Soviet of the National Economy.
   1922: Morgenshtern, V. "Melkaia promyshlennost' v 1921 godu" [Small-Scale Industry in 1921]. No. 4, 42–53.

356. *Nashe stroitel'stvo* [Our Construction]. USSR State Planning Office.
   1935: Kuznetsov, V. "Razvitie shifernoi promyshlennosti v SSSR" [The Development of the Slate Industry in the USSR]. No. 21, 13–15.
   1937: Gorskii, D. V. "Tsementnaia promyshlennost'" [The Cement Industry]. No. 21, 71–73.
   1937: Kriuchkovich, A. I. "Kirpichnaia promyshlennost'" [The Brick Industry]. No. 21, 74–76.

357. *Neftianoe khoziaistvo* [The Petroleum Industry]. USSR Ministry of the Fuel Industry.
   1928: Baliabo, I. "Itogi razvitiia neftianoi promyshlennosti v 1926/27 operatsionnom godu" [Results of the Development of the Oil Industry in 1926/27]. No. 1, 116–127.
   1939: Trebin, F. A. "Neftedobyvaiushchaia promyshlennost' SSSR mezhdu XVII i XVIII s'ezdami VKP (b)" [The USSR Oil Extraction Industry Between the XVII and XVIII Party Congresses]. No. 3, 8–9.
   1955: Baibakov, N. K. "Itogi 1954 goda i zadachi neftianoi promyshlennosti na 1955 god" [The Oil Industry: Results in 1954 and Tasks for 1955]. No. 1, 1–12.

358. *Nerudnye iskopaemye* [Nonmetallic Minerals]. USSR Academy of Sciences.

359. *Ogneupory* [Refractory Materials]. USSR Ministry of Ferrous Metallurgy.
   1947: Gol'din, Ia. A. "Ogneupornaia promyshlennost' k tridtsatiletiui Oktiabria" [The Refractory Materials Industry on the Thirtieth Anniversary of the October Revolution]. No. 11, 485–493.

360. *Pishchevaia industriia* [The Food Industry]. USSR Ministry of the Food Industry.
   1938: "O proizvodstvennom plane Narodnogo Komissariata pishchevoi promyshlennosti SSSR na 1938 god" [On the 1938 Production Plan of the People's Commissariat of the Food Industry]. Feb. 26, 1–2.
   1938: Gilinskii, A. "Pishchevaia promyshlennost' Sovetskogo Soiuza v 1938 godu" [The Soviet Food Industry in 1938]. March 22, 2–3.

361. *Pishchevaia promyshlennost'* [The Food Industry]. USSR Ministry of Supply.
   1926: Brif, E. M. "Perspektivy pishchevoi promyshlennosti na 1926/27 operatsionnyi god" [The Outlook for the Food Industry for 1926/27]. No. 7–8, 256–262.

657

1929: Priselkov, A. "Predvaritel'nye itogi raboty pishchevoi promyshlennosti v 1928/29 godu" [Preliminary Results of the Food Industry in 1928/29]. No. 11–12, 593–601.

1930: Frumkin, L., and Moizhes, M. "K voprosu o postroike kukuruznogo krakhmalo-patochnogo zavoda na Ukraine" [On the Construction of a Corn Starch and Corn Syrup Factory in the Ukraine]. No. 1, 3–8.

1932: Malinin, A. "Plan 1932" [The 1932 Plan]. No. 1–2, 8–18.

1932: Shase, M. "Za industriiu sotsialisticheskogo obshchestva" [For Industry in the Socialist Society]. No. 11–12, 3–7.

362. *Plan* [Plan]. USSR State Planning Office.

1934: Malinin, A. "Pishchevaia promyshlennost' vo vtoroi piatiletke" [The Food Industry in the Second Five Year Plan]. No. 1, 41–43.

1934: Ponorovskii, I. "Protiv izvrashchenii v planirovanii kozhevennoi promyshlennosti" [Against Distortion in the Planning of the Leather Industry]. No. 4, 11–14.

1935: Malinin, A. "Pishchevaia promyshlennost' na pod'eme" [The Food Industry on the Rise]. No. 2–3, 42–45.

1935: "Itogi registratsii promyshlennykh predpriatii SSSR v 1933 godu" [The Results of the 1933 Census of USSR Industrial Enterprises]. No. 7, 41–49.

1935: Demichoglian, I. "Nekotorye itogi perepisi promyshlennosti SSSR za 1933 god" [Some Results of the 1933 Industrial Census in the USSR]. No. 8.

1936: Smilga, P. "Za organizatsionno-khoziaistvennoe ukreplenie promkooperatsii" [For the Organizational and Economic Strengthening of Producer Cooperatives]. No. 1.

1936: Malinin, A. "Pishchevoi industrii—novyi moshchnyi razbeg [Let Us Give the Food Industry a New Impetus]. No. 2, 13–16.

1936: Lomov, F. "Vazhneishie zadachi sovetskoi torgovli" [The Most Important Tasks of Soviet Trade]. No. 2, 29–32.

1936: Chadaev, Ia., and Tsibul'skii, G. "Ukreplenie syr'evoi bazy i ispol'zovanie syr'ia v legkoi promyshlennosti" [Strengthening of the Raw Material Base and Utilization of Raw Materials in Light Industry]. No. 14, 8–11.

1937: Fridlender, L. "Legkaia promyshlennost' v zavershaiushchem godu vtoroi piatiletki" [Light Industry in the Last Year of the Second Five Year Plan]. No. 3, 17–22.

1937: Malinin, A. "Pishchevaia promyshlennost' v plane 1937 goda" [The Food Industry in the 1937 Plan]. No. 4, 22–27.

363. *Planovoe khoziaistvo* [Planned Economy]. USSR State Planning Office.

1925: Strumilin, S. "Nash dovoennyi tovarooborot" [Our Prewar Commodity Turnover]. No. 1.

1934: Kurskii, A. "Rekonstruktsiia legkoi i pishchevoi promyshlennosti SSSR" [Reconstruction of Light Industry and the Food Industry in the USSR]. No. 1, 97–124.

1936: Mikoyan, A. "Nekotorye zametki o pishchevoi promyshlennosti" [A Few Notes on the Food Industry]. No. 6.

1936: "Chrezvychainyi VIII s'ezd Sovetov SSSR" [The Extraordinary 8th Congress of Soviets of the USSR]. No. 11.

1936: Strumilin, S. "Sovetskaia promyshlennost' za desiat' let" [Soviet Industry During Ten Years]. No. 11.

1937: Peters, Ia. "Kachestvo i assortiment v tekstil'noi promyshlennosti v 1937 g." [Quality and Assortment in the Textile Industry in 1937]. No. 2, 62.

1937: Egorov, V. "Sovetskaia torgovlia v poslednem godu vtoroi piatiletki" [Soviet Trade in the Last Year of the Second Five Year Plan]. No. 2, 91–108.

1937: Voinilovich, F., and Khvilivitskii, T. "Syr'evaia baza i puti razvitiia promyshlennosti mineral'nykh solei v tret'ei piatiletke" [Raw Material Resources and the Development of the Mineral Salts Industry in the Third Five Year Plan]. No. 3.

1937: "Dvadtsat' let sovetskoi vlasti" [Twenty Years of Soviet Power]. No. 8, 178–207.

1937: Vitin, G. "Puti razvitiia transportnogo mashinostroeniia SSSR" [Ways of Developing USSR Transportation Machinery Building]. No. 11–12, 57–77.

1938: Erlikh, D. "Boevye zadachi tekstil'nogo mashinostroeniia" [Fighting Tasks of Textile Machine Building]. No. 10, 32–48.

1938: Volikov, S. "Potreblenie i perevozki chernogo metalla po raionam SSSR" [The Demand for and Transportation of Ferrous Metals by Region of the USSR]. No. 11, 84–99.

1938: Balbashevskii, Iu. "Voprosy razmeshcheniia ogneupornoi promyshlennosti" [Problems of the Allocation of the Refractory Materials Industry]. No. 12, 36–47.

1939: Shneider, V., and Brodskii, G. "Itogi i perspektivy razmeshcheniia tsementnoi promyshlennosti" [Location of the Cement Industry—Past and Future]. No. 2, 81–98.

1939: Chizh, G. "Uzkie mesta lesnoi promyshlennosti" [Bottlenecks in the Lumber Industry]. No. 2, 99–116.

1939: Kravtsev, G. "Vedushchaia otrasl' v tekhnicheskom vooruzhenii narodnogo khoziaistva" [A Leading Sector in the Technological Reorganization of the National Economy]. No. 3, 68–79.

1939: Sheremet'ev, A. "Tret'ia piatiletka—piatiletka spetsial'nykh stalei" [The Third Five Year Plan—a Plan for Special Steels]. No. 3, 80–87.

1939: Kukoev, A., and Onufriev, N. "Tret'ia piatiletka—piatiletka khimii" [The Third Five Year Plan—a Plan for Chemistry]. No. 3, 88–93.

1939: "Osnovnye pokazateli itogov vtoroi piatiletki" [Basic Data on the Second Five Year Plan]. No. 5, 155–178.

1940: Lerner, D. "Zameniteli kozhi" [Leather Substitutes]. No. 3, 85–91.

1940: Sukharevskii, B. "Mashinostroenie i osnovnaia ekonomicheskaia zadacha SSSR" [Machine Building and the Main Economic Task of the USSR]. No. 6, 12–29.

1940: Erlikh, D. "Khlopchatobumazhnaia promyshlennost' i osnovnaia ekonomicheskaia zadacha SSSR" [The Cotton Industry and the Main Economic Task of the USSR]. No. 9, 78–93.

1940: Petrovskii, V. "Bor'ba za kachestvo metalla" [The Struggle for Quality in Metal]. No. 12, 22–29.

1941: Brodskii, G. "Otstavanie promyshlennosti stroimaterialov i puti ego likvidatsii" [The Lag in the Building Materials Industry and Means of Overcoming It]. No. 3, 87–99.

1945: Vol'vunovich, S. "Novye ressursy tukovoi promyshlennosti" [New Resources in the Fertilizer Industry]. No. 5.

1946: Eremenko, N. "Vosstanovlenie i razvitie chernoi metallurgii v novoi piatiletke" [The Reconstruction and Development of Ferrous Metallurgy in the New Five Year Plan]. No. 2, 89–99.

1946: Korobov, A. "Stroitel'naia programma novoi piatiletki" [The Building Program in the New Five Year Plan]. No. 3.

1947: Dmitriev, V. "Pod'em kul'tury zemledeliia i voprosy povysheniia urozhainosti" [Improvement of Cultivation and Problems of Increasing the Yield]. No. 3, 26–40.

1951: "Soobshchenie Gosplana SSSR i TsSU SSSR" [Reports of the USSR State Planning Office and the Central Statistical Administration]. No. 2, 3–13.

1951: Sivolap, I. "Na putiakh k izobiliiu pishchevykh produktov" [Toward an Abundance of Food Products]. No. 5, 38–52.

1952: Sudnitsyn, I., and Solov'ev, N. "Reshaiushchie usloviia vypolneniia plana lesnoi promyshlennosti" [Indispensable Conditions for the Fulfillment of the Lumber Industry Plan]. No. 3, 35–44.

1952: "Direktivy XIX s'ezda partii po piatomu piatiletnemu planu razvitiia SSSR na 1951–1955 gody." [Directives of the XIX Party Congress on the Fifth Five Year Plan for 1951–1955]. No. 4, 4–25.

1952: Sorokin, G. "Sotsialisticheskaia promyshlennost' v piatoi piatiletke" [Socialist Industry in the Fifth Five Year Plan]. No. 5, 47–60.

1954: Volosatov, N., and Kaganov, S. "Osnovnye zadachi razvitiia promyshlennosti stroitel'nykh materialov" [The Main Tasks for the Development of the Building Materials Industry]. No. 1, 82–92.

1957: Strukov, A. "Planirovanie natsional'nogo dokhoda v SSSR" [Planning the National Income in the USSR]. No. 8, 75–81.

364. *Pravda* [Truth]. Central Committee of the Communist Party.

1946: "Metall—osnova industrial'noi moshchi strany" [Metal—the Basis of the Industrial Power of the Country]. Feb. 17, 1.

1946: Voznesenskii, N. A. "Doklad na pervoi sessii Verkhovnogo Soveta SSSR o piatiletnem plane vosstanovleniia i razvitiia narodnogo khoziaistva SSSR na 1946–1950 gg" [Report on the First Session of the USSR Supreme Soviet on the Five Year Plan for the Restoration and Development of the USSR National Economy, 1946–1950]. March 16, 1–4.

1946: "Doklad predsedatelia Gosplana SSSR N. A. Voznesenskogo na pervoi sessii Verkhovnogo Soveta SSSR" [Report of N. A. Voznesensky, Chairman of USSR State Planning Committee, at the First Session of the USSR Supreme Soviet]. March 16, 2–4.

1946: "Rech' M. G. Pervukhina v pervoi sessii Verkhovnogo Soveta SSSR" [M. G. Pervukhin's Speech at the First Session of the USSR Supreme Soviet]. March 18, 2–3.

1946: Belopol'skii, S. "Sibir' dolzhna imet' svoiu sodu i mineral'nye udobreniia" [Siberia Should Have Its Own Soda and Mineral Fertilizer]. March 29.

1946: Mel'nik, B. "Mineral'nye udobreniia—zalog vysokikh urozhaev" [Mineral Fertilizer—a Guarantee of High Yields]. April 18.

1946: Zhikharev, N. "Kak v Ministerstve resinovoi promyshlennosti zanimaiutsia proizvodstvom resiny" [How the Ministry of the Rubber Industry Manages the Production of Rubber]. July 5, 2.

1947: Pervukhin, M. "Uvelichim vypusk mineral'nykh udobrenii i khimikatov dlia sel'skogo khoziaistva" [Let Us Increase the Output of Mineral Fertilizers and Chemicals for Agriculture]. April 3, 2.

1947: Tevosian, I. "Neotlozhnaia zadacha sovetskikh metallurgov" [Urgent Task of Soviet Metallurgists]. April 24, 2.

1949: Evseev, P. "Vsemerno uluchshit' kachestvo i assortiment tovarov legkoi promyshlennosti" [Improve the Quality and Increase the Variety of Light Industry Goods in Every Way]. Jan. 11, 2.

1952: "Doklad sekretaria TsK VKP (b) G. M. Malenkova XIX s'ezdu partii [Report of G. M. Malenkov, Secretary of the Party Central Committee at the XIX Party Congress]. Oct. 6, 2–9.

1952: "Rech' Kosygina na XIX s'ezde VKP (b)" [Kosygin's Speech at the XIX Party Congress]. Oct. 13, 6.

1953: Tikhomirov, S. "Dadim legkoi promyshlennosti bol'she prochnykh i iarkikh krasitelei" [Give Light Industry More Lasting and Colorful Dyes]. Nov. 12, 2.

1954: "Rech' M. G. Pervukhina na sobranii izbiratelei Tbilisskogo-Kalininskogo izbiratel'nogo okruga" [M. G. Pervukhin's Speech at a Meeting of Voters from the Tbilisi-Kalinin Electoral District]. March 12, 4.

1954: Moskovskii, V. "Partiia i narod" [The Party and the People]. March 11, 2.

1954: "Rech' predsedatelia Soveta Ministrov SSSR deputata G. M. Malenkova na zasedanii Verkhovnogo Soveta SSSR" [Speech of Deputy G. M. Malenkov, Chairman of the USSR Council of Ministers, at a Session of the USSR Supreme Soviet]. April 27, 5–6.

1954: "Preodelet' otstavanie lesnoi promyshlennosti" [Eliminate the Lag in the Lumber Industry]. Sept. 9, 1.

1954: "Doklad M. Z. Saburova na zasedanii Moskovskogo Soveta" [M. Z. Saburov's Report at a Meeting of the Moscow Soviet]. Nov. 7, 1–2.

1956: "Doklad N. S. Khrushcheva na XX-om s'ezde Kommunisticheskoi Partii Sovetskogo Soiuza" [N. S. Khrushchev's Report at the XXth Party Congress]. Feb. 15, 1–11.

1956: "Ob itogakh vypolneniia piatogo piatiletnego plana razvitiia SSSR na 1951–1955 gody" [Fulfillment of the Fifth Five Year Plan for the Development of the USSR, 1951–1955]. April 25, 1–3.

365. *Pravda Ukrainy* [Pravda of the Ukraine]. Communist Party of the Ukraine.
366. *Problemy ekonomiki* [Problems of Economics]. Communist Academy, Economics Institute.
    1935: Strumilin, S. "Khimicheskaia promyshlennost' SSSR" [The USSR Chemical Industry]. No. 2, 118–131.
    1935: Pivovarov, I. "Sovetskoe stankostroenie" [Soviet Machine-Tool Building]. No. 4, 189–206.
    1940: Sergievskii, A. "O ratsionalizatsii perevozok massovykh tovarov lichnogo potrebleniia" [On Efficient Shipping of Mass-Produced Consumer Goods]. No. 11–12, 182–190.
367. *Promyshlenno-ekonomicheskaia gazeta* [Industrial Economic Gazette]. State Scientific and Technical Committee of the USSR Council of Ministers.
368. *Promyshlennost' organicheskoi khimii* [The Organic Chemistry Industry]. USSR Ministry of the Chemical Industry.
    1936: Kamernitskii, V. I. "Organicheskaia khimicheskaia promyshlennost' v chetvertom godu vtoroi piatiletki" [The Organic Chemistry Industry in the Fourth Year of the Second Five Year Plan]. No. 1, 7–12.
    1936: Ravdel', A. "Anilinokrasochnaia promyshlennost' v 1936 godu" [The Aniline Dye Industry in 1936]. No. 4, 193–195.
    1936: Kamernitskii, V. I. "Aromaticheskie i geterotsiklicheskie soedineniia kak syr'evaia baza promyshlennosti organicheskogo sinteza" [Aromatic and Heterocyclic Compounds as Raw Material Resources for the Organic Chemistry Industry]. No. 11.
    1936: Lukovskii, S. "Lakokrasochnaia promyshlennost' na pod'eme" [The Paint and Varnish Industry on the Rise]. No. 19, 317–321.
    1937: Bukstein, V., and Smirnov, A. "Nekotorye voprosy razvitiia anilino-krasochnoi promyshlennosti v tret'em piatiletii" [Some Aspects of the Development of the Aniline Dye Industry in the Third Five Year Plan]. No. 14, 120–121.
    1938: Segalovskii, M. B. "Krasochnaia promyshlennost' k XXI godovshchine Oktiabria" [The Paint Industry on the XXI Anniversary of the October Revolution]. No. 11, 663–666.
    1939: Kuritsyn, P. V. "O nekotorykh syr'evykh voprosakh promyshlennosti plastmass i voprosakh ee tekhnologii" [Obtaining and Utilizing Raw Materials for the Plastic Industry]. No. 4–5, 201–202.
    1939: Golosenko, E. N. "Puti razvitiia anilinokrasochnoi promyshlennosti v 3-em piatiletii" [The Development of the Aniline Dye Industry in the Third Five Year Plan]. No. 6, 289–293.
    1939: "Vsemerno ispol'zovat' ogromnye rezervy sovetskoi khimii" [Make Every Possible Use of the Huge Resources of Soviet Chemistry]. No. 8, 417–419.
369. *Promyshlennost' stroitel'nykh materialov* [The Building Materials Industry]. USSR Ministry of the Building Materials Industry.
370. *Puti industrializatsii* [Means of Industrialization]. Presidium of *VSNKh*.
    1929: Azarkh, B. "Problema ispol'zovaniia syr'ia l'nianoi promysh-lennost'iu [Utilization of Raw Materials for the Linen Industry]. No. 2, 52–63.

1929: Grintser, A. "Voprosy kachestva promyshlennykh izdelii v khoziaist-
vennom plane na 1929/30 god" [The Quality of Industrial Products in
the Economic Plan for 1929/30]. No. 17–18, 77–98.

1929: Mar. "Osnovnye pokazateli dinamiki promyshlennogo proizvodstva
za 1925/26–1928/29 gg." [The Basic Data on Industrial Production from
1925/26–1928/29]. No. 23–24, 127–128.

371. *Rybnoe khoziaistvo* [The Fishing Industry]. Chief Administration of the
Fishing Industry.

    1946: Ishkov, A. A. "Piatiletnii plan razvitiia rybnoi promyshlennosti"
[The Five Year Plan for the Development of the Fishing Industry].
No. 1, 4–8.

    1946: Bogdanov, A. S. "Rybnaia promyshlennost' Kuril'skikh ostrovov"
[The Fishing Industry of the Kurile Islands]. No. 8, 3–16.

    1946: Cherfas, B. I. "Rybnaia promyshlennost' Iuzhnogo Sakhalina"
[The Fishing Industry of Southern Sakhalin]. No. 10–11, 16–25.

    1949: "Likvidirovat' otstavanie predpriatii!" [Eliminate the Lag in Enter-
prises]. No. 2, 1–2.

    1953: Obukhov, A. K. "Za pod'em rybnoi promyshlennosti" [For an
Increase in the Output of the Fishing Industry]. No. 12, 1–19.

372. *Sakharnaia promyshlennost'* [The Sugar Industry]. Chief Administration of
the Sugar Industry under the USSR Ministry of the Food Industry.

    1947: Nikolaev, M. V. "Tekhnicheskaia baza sovetskoi sakharnoi promy-
shlennosti" [The Technological Resources of the Sugar Industry].
No. 11, 13–18.

373. *Sel'khozmashina* [Agricultural Machinery]. USSR Ministry of Machine
Building.

    1953: "Sel'skokhoziaistvennoe mashinostroenie k 36-i godovshchine Velikoi
Oktiabr'skoi sotsialisticheskoi revoliutsii" [Agricultural Machine Building
on the 36th Anniversary of the Great October Socialist Revolution].
No. 11, 1 3.

374. *Sel'skoe khoziaistvo* [Agriculture]. USSR Ministries of Agriculture and of
State Farms.

375. *Shelk* [Silk]. Chief Administration of the Silk Industry.

376. *Sherstianoe delo* [The Wool Industry]. All-Union Wool Society.

    1925: Voronov, N. "Perspektivy sherstianoi promyshlennosti v otnoshenii
assortimenta" [On the Assortment of Goods in the Wool Industry].
No. 11, 16–21.

    1926: Gusev, V. A. "Uplotnenie rabochei sily v sherstianoi promyshlen-
nosti" [Increase in Labor Productivity in the Wool Industry]. No. 1, 68–77.

    1927: Riaben'kii, S. A. "K voprosu o tselesoobraznosti sushchestvuiushchei
shiriny nashikh tkanei" [On the Usefulness of the Present Width of Our
Fabrics]. No. 4–5, 15–16.

    1931: Deich, M. A. "Po-novomu rabotat' v sherstianoi promyshlennosti"
[Reorganize Work in the Wool Industry]. No. 9, 3–9.

    1939: Skulanov, S. M. "Ocherednye zadachi sherstianoi promyshlennosti
po vypolneniiu plana 1939 goda" [The Current Tasks of the Wool
Industry for the Fulfillment of the 1939 Plan]. No. 1, 6–8.

377. *Sotsialisticheskaia rekonstruktsiia i nauka* [Socialist Reconstruction and Science].
USSR Ministry of Heavy Industry.
1932: Prianishnikov, D. N. "Osnovnye zadachi v oblasti khimizatsii
zemledeliia" [Essential Conditions for the Utilization of Chemicals in
Agriculture]. No. 8.

378. *Sotsialisticheskaia rekonstruktsiia sel'skogo khoziaistva* [Socialist Reconstruction
of Agriculture]. USSR Ministry of Agriculture.
1937: "Likvidirovat' politicheskuiu bespechnost', po bol'shevistski vypolnit'
plan 1937 goda" [Put an End to Political Laxity, Fulfill the 1937 Plan
in a Bolshevist Style]. No. 3.
1938: Morozov, G. "Itogi 1937 goda i zadachi khlopkovodstva v 1938
godu" [Cotton Growing: Results in 1937 and Tasks for 1938]. No. 3.

379. *Sotsialisticheskoe sel'skoe khoziaistvo* [Socialist Agriculture]. USSR Ministry of
Agriculture.
1941: Mamchenkov, I., and Romashkevich, I. "O ratsional'nom ispol'-
zovanii navoza i drugikh mestnykh udobrenii" [On the Efficient Use of
Manure and Other Local Fertilizers]. No. 3, 61–72.

380. *Sotsialisticheskii trud* [Socialist Labor]. USSR Council of Ministers
Committee on Labor and Wages.
1960: Krasnovskii, V. "Issledovanie po voprosam mekhanizatsii truda"
[Research on the Mechanization of Labor]. No. 2, 151–154.

381. *Sovetskaia geologiia* [Soviet Geology]. Committee on Geological Affairs.
1939: "Itogi i perspektivy geologo-razvedochnykh rabot v SSSR" [Results
and Outlook of Geological Prospecting in the USSR]. No. 3, 3–16.
1939: "Stalinskii plan stroitel'stva kommunizma" [The Stalin Plan for
Building Communism]. No. 4–5, 3–13.
1939: "Osnovnye zadachi v oblasti nemetallicheskogo mineral'nogo syr'ia
v tret'ei piatiletke" [Basic Tasks in the Extraction of Nonmetallic Mineral
Raw Materials in the Third Five Year Plan]. No. 9, 12–25.
1939: "Vpered, k novym pobedam!" [On to New Successes]. No. 10–11,
3–11.
1939: Rozin, M. S. "Mineral'nye resoursy Zapadnoi Ukrainy" [Mineral
Resources of Western Ukraine]. No. 12, 5–14.

382. *Sovetskaia metallurgiia* [Soviet Metallurgy]. State Institute for Planning
Metallurgical Plants and All-Union Scientific and Engineering Society of
Metallurgists.

383. *Sovetskaia torgovlia* [Soviet Trade]. USSR Ministry of Trade.
1937: Lomov, F. "Pishchevaia promyshlennost' SSSR v poslednem godu
vtoroi piatiletki" [The Food Industry of the USSR in the Last Year of the
Second Five Year Plan]. No. 1, 33–41.
1937: Zberzhkovskii, G. "Plan tovarooborota 1937 goda" [The Plan for the
Commodity Turnover in 1937]. No. 2, 13–22.
1937: Menakhovskii, S. "Priblizit' rabotu promkooperatsii k trebovaniiam
torgovli" [Bring the Work of the Producer Cooperatives Closer to Trade
Requirements]. No. 4, 38–47.
1937: Gerasimov, I., and Bulanov, V. "Torguiushchie organizatsii i
voprosy assortimenta i kachestva trikotazhnykh tovarov" [Trading

Organizations and Problems of the Assortment and Quality of Knitted Goods]. No. 5, 38–44.

1937: Grigor'ev, S., and Dement'ev, A. "Likvidirovat' posledstviia vreditel'stva v planirovanii obshchestvennogo pitaniia" [Eliminate the Consequences of Wrecking in the Planning of Public Eating Places]. No. 7, 24–30.

1937: Dukel'skii, S. "Gosudarstvennaia torgovlia molokom i molochnymi produktami vo vtoroi piatiletke" [State Trade in Milk and Dairy Products in the Second Five Year Plan]. No. 7, 50–56.

1954: Shmidt, A. "Produktsiia margarinovoi promyshlennosti" [The Production of the Margarine Industry]. No. 8, 28–32.

384. *Sovetskaia zolotaia promyshlennost'* [The Soviet Gold Industry]. Chief Gold Administration.

1935: Shchuka, P. V. "Zolotaia promyshlennost' dosrochno vypolnila godovoi plan zolotodobychi" [The Gold Industry Fulfilled the Annual Plan for Gold Mining Ahead of Schedule]. No. 12, 8–12.

385. *Sovetskii sakhar* [Soviet Sugar]. Chief Sugar Administration.

1936: Odintsov, S. S. "Piatiletka v chetyre goda" [The Five Year Plan in Four Years]. No. 1, 1–8.

386. *Stal'* [Steel]. Ministry of Ferrous Metallurgy.

1947: Pisarevskii, M. V. "Tridtsat' let sovetskoi koksokhimii" [Thirty Years of the Soviet Chemical Coke Processing Industry]. No. 11.

387. *Stanki i instrument* [Tools and Instruments]. USSR Ministry of the Machine-Building Industry.

1949: Zhed', M. S., and Levin, I. M. "Nekotorye itogi raboty stanko-stroitel'noi promyshlennosti v 1948 g." [Some Results of the Work of the Machine-Building Industry in 1948]. No. 1, 4–6.

388. *Statisticheskoe obozrenie* [Statistical Review]. USSR Central Statistical Administration.

1927: Vasil'ev, G. M. "Dinamika gruzooborota glavneishikh tovarov" [The Dynamics of the Freight Turnover of the Most Important Goods]. No. 8, 71–74.

1928: Stelletskii, S. "Tsenzovaia promyshlennost' v 1926/27 godu" [The Census Industry in 1926/27]. No. 1, 30–43.

1928: Loginov, Z. "Promyshlennost' stroitel'nykh materialov mineral'nogo proiskhozhdeniia" [The Industry of Mineral Building Materials]. No. 4, 47–56.

1928: Batsofen, S. I. "Dinamika fizicheskogo ob'ema promyshlennykh produktsii 1924/25–1926/27" [The Physical Volume of Industrial Production, 1924/25–1926/27]. No. 5, 31–44.

1929: Debiuk, A. "Udel'nyi ves melkoi promyshlennosti Soiuza SSR v obshchem promyshlennom proizvodstve" [The Share of Small-Scale Industry in Total Industrial Production in the USSR]. No. 2, 28–32.

1929: "Pokazateli narodnogo khoziaistva SSSR. Itogi proizvodstva fabrichnozavodskoi promyshlennosti SSSR za 1928/29 i za IV kv. 1928/29 goda" [Data on the USSR National Economy. Output of the

USSR Factory Industry in 1928/29 and the Fourth Quarter of 1928/29]. No. 12, 88–93.

1930: Tsigel'nitskii, M. "Fabrichno-zavodskaia (tsenzovaia) promyshlennost' v 1928/29" [The Factory (Census) Industry in 1928/29]. No. 1, 31–43.

389. *Statistika i narodnoe khoziaistvo* [Statistics and the National Economy]. Central Statistical Administration.

1929: Kokshaiskii, I. "Organizovannoe snabzhenie gorodskogo naseleniia RSFSR miasom" [Organized Supply of Meat to the Urban Population of the RSFSR]. No. 4.

1929: Sereda, S. "Ob organizatsii sotsialisticheskoi statistiki" [On the Organization of Socialist Statistics]. No. 9.

390. *Statistika truda* [Labor Statistics]. Central Bureau of Labor Statistics.

1928: "Sostav fabrichno-zavodskogo personala po polu i vozrastu po dannym ucheta na 1 ianvaria 1928 g. po SSSR" [The Composition of Factory Personnel by Sex and Age According to Accounting Data on Jan. 1, 1928, for the USSR]. No. 8, 12–13.

391. *Steklo i keramika* [Glass and Ceramics]. Previously called *Keramika i steklo* (see 326). USSR Ministry of the Building Materials Industry.

1949: Potanin, D. N. "K novym proizvodstvennym pobedam!" [On to New Industrial Successes]. No. 1, 1–2.

1950: "Na poroge 34-go goda Velikoi Oktiabr'skoi sotsialisticheskoi revoliutsii" [On the Threshold of the 34th Anniversary of the Great October Socialist Revolution]. No. 11, 1–2.

1951: "Itogi i zadachi" [Results and Tasks]. No. 1, 1–2.

392. *Stroitel'naia i keramicheskaia promyshlennost'* [The Building and Ceramics Industry].

393. *Stroitel'nye materialy* [Building Materials].

1930: Gurari, M. D.; Sebekin, I. I.; and Sudnitsin, I. I. "Asbo-shifernoe proizvodstvo" [Asbestos Slate Production]. No. 1, 65–68.

1930: Kuznetsov, P. "Stroitel'stvo shifernykh zavodov" [The Construction of Slate Factories]. No. 2, 93–96.

1930: Ponomarev, A. F. "Sostoianie melo-izvestkovoi-alebastrovoi promyshlennosti" [The State of the Chalk, Lime, and Alabaster Industry]. No. 2, 104–109.

1931: Loginov, Z. "Sostoianie kirpichnoi promyshlennosti SSSR" [The State of the USSR Brick Industry]. No. 8, 143–157.

1932: Zharenov, A. S. "Peresmotr standartov na karton tolevyi i tol' krovel'nyl" [Review of the Standards for Tar Paper and Tar Paper Roofing]. No. 7, 128–132.

1933: ———. "O zadachakh promyshlennosti krovel'nykh materialov" [The Tasks of the Roofing Materials Industry]. No. 4, 12–18.

1937: Smurov, A. "Promyshlennost' krovel'nykh materialov" [The Roofing Materials Industry]. No. 3, 1.

1937: Lipshits, L. L. "Izvestkovaia i alebastrovaia promyshlennost' na poroge tret'ei piatiletki" [The Lime and Alabaster Industry on the Threshold of the Third Five Year Plan]. No. 11, 24–28.

1937: Vorob'ev, V. A. "Tolevo-ruberoidnaia promyshlennost' za dvadtsat let" [The Tar Paper and Rubberoid Industry During Twenty Years]. No. 11, 29–31.

394. *Tekstil'naia promyshlennost'* [The Textile Industry]. USSR Ministry of the Textile Industry.

1945: Gamburg, Ia. Iu., and Maiants, M. L. "Zadachi sherstianoi promyshlennosti na puti k dal'neishemu razvitiiu" [The Tasks of the Wool Industry for its Further Development]. No. 11–12, 9–11.

1946: Glazov, Ia. I. "Osnovnye napravleniia novogo piatiletnego plana. Khlopchatobumazhnaia promyshlennost'" [The Main Trends of the New Five Year Plan. The Cotton Goods Industry]. No. 7–8, 3–4.

1947: "Bol'she tovarov shirokogo potrebleniia" [More Consumer Goods]. No. 1, 2–4.

1947: Rodichev, S. D. "Tekstil'noi promyshlennosti—krepkuiu syr'evuiu bazu" [Supply the Textile Industry Adequately with Raw Materials]. No. 4, 2–4.

1947: "Narashchivanie novykh moshchnostei—vazhneishaia zadacha stroitelei tekstil'noi promyshlennosti" [Increasing Industrial Capacities Is the Most Important Job of Textile Industry Builders]. No. 7, 2–4.

1947: Lavrent'ev, M. "Vsemerno udovletvorim spros potrebitelia" [Satisfy the Consumers' Demands in Every Possible Way]. No. 10, 4.

1947: Khazan, D. M. "30 let sovetskoi tekstil'noi promyshlennosti" [Thirty Years of the Soviet Textile Industry]. No. 11, 4–7.

1947: Glazov, Ia.I., and Velikovskii, A. S. "Tekhnicheskoe perevooruzhenie khlopchatobumazhnoi promyshlennosti" [The Technical Reequipment of the Cotton Goods Industry]. No. 11, 31–34.

1947: Gamburg, Ia. Iu. "Sovershenstvuem tekhniku sherstianoi promyshlennosti" [Let Us Perfect the Technology of the Wool Industry]. No. 11, 35–38.

1947: Tarasov, S. V. "Na puti tekhnicheskogo progressa l'nianoi promyshlennosti" [Toward Technical Progress in the Linen Industry]. No. 11, 38–40.

1947: "Za dal'neishee razvertyvanie tekstil'noi promyshlennosti" [For the Further Development of the Textile Industry]. No. 12, 2–4.

1948: "Tretii reshaiushchii god novoi stalinskoi piatiletki" [The Third and Decisive Year of the New Stalin Five Year Plan]. No. 5, 2–5.

1950: Ushakov, G. "Za dal'neishee uluchshenie assortimenta khlopchato-bumazhnykh tkanei" [For the Further Improvement of the Assortment of Cotton Fabrics]. No. 7, 7–9.

1952: "Moguchaia postup' stalinskikh piatiletok" [The Great Advance of the Stalin Five Year Plans]. No. 10, 1–4.

395. *Torfianaia promyshlennost'* [The Peat Industry]. USSR Ministry of Power Stations.

1947: Bausin, A. F. "Torfianaia promyshlennost' za 30 let" [Thirty Years of the Peat Industry]. No. 11, 4–8.

1947: Olenin, A. S. "Razvedka i kadastr torfianogo syr'ia za 30 let" [Thirty Years of Peat Prospecting]. No. 11, 22–24.

1951: Bausin, A. F. "Torfianaia promyshlennost' Ministerstva elektrostantsii SSSR za 1946–1950 gg" [The Peat Industry Under the USSR Ministry of Power Stations from 1946 to 1950]. No. 1, 1–5.

1952: "Torfianaia promyshlennost' k XXXV godovshchine Velikoi Oktiabr'skoi sotsialisticheskoi revoliutsii" [The Peat Industry on the 35th Anniversary of the Great October Socialist Revolution]. No. 11, 1–4.

1954: "XXXVII godovshchina Velikoi Oktiabr'skoi sotsialisticheskoi revoliutsii" [The 37th Anniversary of the Great October Socialist Revolution]. No. 7, 1–4.

1955: Bausin, A. F. "O rabote i zadachakh torfianoi promyshlennosti MES" [On the Work and the Tasks of the Peat Industry Under the Ministry of Power Stations]. No. 2, 1–4.

396. *Trud* [Labor]. Trade Unions.

397. *Trudy Vsesoiuznogo nauchno-issledovatel'skogo instituta mineral'nogo' syr'ia* [Works of the All-Union Scientific Research Institute of Mineral Raw Materials].

398. *Tsement* [Cement]. Cement Union.

1934: Kazanskii, A. M. "Predvaritel'nye itogi raboty tsempromyshlennosti za 1934 god i perspektivy na 1935 god" [Preliminary Results of the Cement Industry in 1934 and Its Outlook for 1935]. No. 10, 6–10.

1936: ———. "Plan 1936 goda" [The 1936 Plan]. No. 1, 33–37.

1936: "Plan i zadachi tsementnoi promyshlennosti na 1936 god" [The Plan and Tasks of the Cement Industry for 1936]. No. 3, 2–5.

1938: Shatalov, E. S. "Zadachi tsementnoi promyshlennosti" [The Tasks of the Cement Industry]. No. 4, 9–14.

1938: Brodskii, G. S. "Geografiia potrebleniia tsementa v SSSR" [The Geography of Consumption of Cement in the USSR]. No. 6, 5–15.

399. *Tsvetnye metally* [Nonferrous Metals]. Ministry of Ferrous and Nonferrous Metallurgy.

1932: But, A. I. "Programma vyplavki medi na 1932 god" [Copper-Smelting Plan for 1932]. No. 3, 430–437.

1933: Rozin, S. E. "Shestnadtsat' let Oktiabria i tsvetnaia metallurgiia" [Sixteen Years After the October Revolution and Nonferrous Metallurgy]. No. 8–9, 3–7.

1934: Smirnov-Verin, S. S. "K perestroike oloviannoi promyshlennosti" [On the Reorganization of the Tin Industry]. No. 3, 24–32.

1936: But, A. I. "Rabota tsvetnoi metallurgii v 1935 godu" [Nonferrous Metallurgy in 1935]. No. 3, 3–15.

1937: Popov, G. N. "Rudnaia promyshlennost' tsvetnoi metallurgii do i posle oktiabr'skoi revoliutsii" [The Nonferrous Metallurgical Ore Industry Before and After the October Revolution]. No. 11, 38–43.

1938: Puchkov, S. G. "Nekotorye itogi raboty aliuminevoi promyshlennosti v 1937 godu i zadachi na 1938 god" [Some Results of the Aluminum Industry in 1937 and Its Tasks for 1938]. No. 6, 3–8.

1938: Zabelyshinskii, I. M. "Nikelevaia promyshlennost' Sovetskogo Soiuza" [The Nickel Industry of the Soviet Union]. No. 9, 10–16.

1938: ———. "Tekhniko-ekonomicheskie zadachi oloviannoi promyshlennosti" [The Technical and Economic Tasks of the Tin Industry]. No. 11, 7–12.

1939: ———. "Rezervy proizvoditel'nosti truda v tsvetnoi metallurgii" [Potentialities for Increasing Labor Productivity in Nonferrous Metallurgy]. No. 9, 3–10.

1939: ———. "Za dal'neishii pod'em tsvetnoi metallurgii" [For Further Advances in Nonferrous Metallurgy]. No. 10–11, 4–14.

400. *Udobrenie i urozhai* [Fertilizer and Harvest]. Committee for the Development of Applied Chemistry and Scientific Institute of Fertilizers.

1929: Dalenko, N. "Proizvodstvo i vvoz mineral'nykh udobrenii v SSSR v 1927/28 g." [Production and Import of Mineral Fertilizers in the USSR in 1927/28]. No. 2, 127.

1930: Gorianov, A. "O piatiletnem plane potrebleniia khimicheskikh sredstv v bor'be s vrediteliami" [The Five Year Plan for the Use of Weed Killers and Pesticides]. No. 3.

1931: Kochetkov, V. P. "K opredeleniiu plana potrebnosti sel'skogo khoziaistva SSSR v mineral'nykh udobreniiakh" [On Planning the Mineral Fertilizer Requirements of Soviet Agriculture]. No. 2, 124–134.

1931: Korkhov, V. "Mirovoe proizvodstvo azota" [World Production of Nitrogen]. No. 10, 943–949.

1931: Sokolovskii, A. "Tekushchie voprosy udobreniia" [Current Problems in Fertilization]. No. 10, 973–974.

1931: Tsyrlin, D. A. "Snabzhenie sel'skogo khoziaistva mineral'nymi udobreniiami v 1932 godu" [The Supply of Mineral Fertilizers to Agriculture in 1932]. No. 11–12, 984–988.

401. *Ugol'* [Coal]. USSR Ministry of the Coal Industry.

1955: "Za dal'neishii pod'em dobychi uglia" [For a Further Increase in Coal Mining]. No. 1, 1–6.

402. *Uspekhi khimii* [Progress in Chemistry].

1939: Iakhontov, A. P. "Tezisy doklada V. M. Molotova na 18 s'ezde VKP (b) i razvitie promyshlennosti organicheskogo sinteza v tret'em piatiletii" [V. M. Molotov's Report at the 18th Party Congress and the Development of the Organic Chemistry Industry in the Third Five Year Plan]. No. 2.

403. *USSR Information Bulletin.* USSR Embassy in Washington.

1946: Pervukhin, M. G. "Chemical Industry to Develop Under New Five Year Plan." July 24, 8–9.

404. *Vecherniaia Moskva* [Evening Moscow].

405. *Vestnik finansov* [Financial Courrier]. Ministry of Finances.

1925: Buznikov, I. V. "Sovremennoe sostoianie nashei zolotopromyshlennosti i ee perspektivy" [The Present Situation and Future Outlook of Our Gold Industry]. No. 11–12, 184–188.

1926: ———. "Mirovoi rynok zolota" [The World Gold Market]. No. 11, 79–90.

406. *Vestnik metallopromyshlennosti* [Bulletin of the Metal Industry]. Chief Administrations of the Metal Industry and of the War Industry.

669

1922: Veitsman, S. E. "Sovremennoe sostoianie metallopromyshlennosti" [The Present State of the Metal Industry]. No. 10–12, 65–86.

1927: "Obzor vazhneishikh dostizhenii metallopromyshlennosti SSSR za pervoe desiatiletie" [Review of the Main Achievements of the USSR Metal Industry for the First Ten Years]. No. 10, 5–20.

407. *Vestnik promyslovoi kooperatsii* [Bulletin of Producer Cooperatives]. All-Russian Union of Producer Cooperatives.

1931: Tikhomirov, V. A. "Promyslovaia kooperatsiia na sovremennom etape" [Producer Cooperatives at the Present Stage]. No. 8, 3–7, and No. 9, 5–9.

408. *Vestnik statistiki* [Statistical Bulletin]. Central Statistical Administration under the USSR Council of Ministers.

1923: Vorob'ev, N. V. "Izmeneniia v russkoi promyshlennosti v period voiny i revoliutsii" [Changes in Russian Industry During the War and Revolution]. No. 4–6.

1955: "Soveshchanie nachal'nikov statisticheskikh upravlenii soiuznykh respublik" [Conference of Heads of Statistical Agencies of the Union Republics]. No. 1, 80–91.

409. *Vneshniaia torgovlia* [Foreign Trade]. USSR Ministry of Foreign Trade.

1954: Borisov, G. "Sovetskie metalloobrabatyvaiushchie stanki" [Soviet Metalworking Machine Tools]. No. 10, 10–20.

410. *Voprosy ekonomiki* [Problems of Economics]. USSR Academy of Sciences, Economics Institute.

1950: Venzher, V. "Vedushchaia rol' mashino-traktornykh stantsii v razvitii kolkhoznogo sel'skogo khoziaistva" [The Leading Role of the Machine and Tractor Stations in the Development of Collective Farm Agriculture]. No. 5, 38–52.

1951: Opatskii, L. "Pod'em zhiznennogo urovnia sovetskogo naroda v poslevoennyi period" [The Rise in the Soviet Standard of Living After the War]. No. 4, 3–18.

1951: "Ob itogakh vypolneniia chetvertogo (pervogo poslevoennogo) piatiletnego plana SSSR na 1946–1950 gody" [Fulfillment of the Fourth (First Postwar) Five Year Plan of the USSR for 1946–1950]. No. 5, 3–13.

1952: "Ob itogakh vypolneniia gosudarstvennogo plana razvitiia narodnogo khoziaistva SSSR v 1951 godu" [Fulfillment of the State Plan for the Development of the USSR National Economy in 1951]. No. 2, 3–12.

1953: Khromov, P. "Pod'em promyshlennosti SSSR v novoi piatiletke" [The Rise of Soviet Industry in the New Five Year Plan]. No. 1, 46–57.

1953: Golubkov, P. "Voprosy razvitiia sel'skogo khoziaistva SSSR v piatoi stalinskoi piatiletke" [Problems in the Development of Soviet Agriculture in the Fifth Stalin Five Year Plan]. No. 2, 41–56.

1953: Orekhovich, P. "Nekotorye voprosy struktury tovarooborota sovetskoi torgovli" [Some Problems in the Composition of Commodity Turnover in Soviet Trade]. No. 8, 19–33.

1953: Shabalin, N. "O znachenii sovremennoi tekhniki dlia rosta sel'sko-khoziaistvennogo proizvodstva v SSSR" [The Importance of Modern

Technology for the Growth of Agricultural Production in the USSR]. No. 8, 45–56.

1954: Dmitriev, M. "O putiakh snizheniia sebestoimosti produktsii promyshlennosti tovarov shirokogo potrebleniia" [Means of Reducing the Production Cost of Consumer Goods]. No. 7, 33–45.

1954: Napol'skii, M., and Grigor'ev, V. "Vsesoiuznaia sel'skokhoziaist-vennaia vystavka—smotr dostizhenii sotsialisticheskogo sel'skogo khoziaistva" [The All-Union Agricultural Exhibit Is a Survey of the Achievements of Socialist Agriculture]. No. 7, 53–61.

1954: Roitburd, L. "Puti povysheniia proizvoditel'nosti truda v chernoi metallurgii SSSR" [Means of Increasing Labor Productivity in Soviet Ferrous Metallurgy]. No. 11, 40–52.

1955: Kirichenko, V. "Kniga o razvitii neftianoi promyshlennosti v Rossii" [A Book on the Development of the Oil Industry in Russia]. No. 3, 123–127.

1955: Mikhailov, S. "Puti pod'ema rybnoi promyshlennosti" [Means of Expanding the Fishing Industry]. No. 7, 56–67.

1955: Shteingauz, E. "Nekotorye voprosy razvitiia energetiki SSSR" [Some Problems in the Development of Soviet Power Engineering]. No. 8, 26–37.

1956: Probst, A. "Voprosy razvitiia toplivnogo khoziaistva SSSR" [Problems in the Development of the Soviet Fuel Industry]. No. 1, 17–32.

1956: Korneev, A. "K voprosu o proizvodstve i potreblenii tekstil'nykh izdelii v SSSR" [On the Production and Consumption of Textiles in the USSR]. No. 7, 43–58.

1956: Notkin, A. "Proizvoditel'nost' obshchestvennogo truda i nekotory voprosy ee izmereniia i planirovaniia" [The Productivity of Social Labor and a Few Problems Involved in Measuring and Planning It]. No. 9, 3–18.

1956: Serebrennikov, P. "O prekrashchenii raskhoda pishchevogo syr'ia na tekhnicheskie tseli" [On Stopping the Use of Edible Raw Materials for Technical Purposes]. No. 10.

1958: Sokolova, E. "O strukture toplivnogo balansa SSSR" [Breakdown of Fuel Produced in the USSR]. No. 5, 56–65.

1958: Kvasha, Ia., and Krasovskii, V. "Kapitaloemkost' proizvodstva i rezervy ee snizheniia" [Means of Reducing Capital-Intensive Production]. No. 8, 3–16.

411. *Voprosy sovetskoi torgovli* [Problems of Soviet Trade]. USSR Ministry of Trade.

1938: Smirnov, M. P. "Osnovnye zadachi sovetskoi torgovli" [Essential Tasks of Soviet Trade]. No. 1–2.

1938: Tsimbal, G. "Tipy predpriiatii obshchestvennogo pitaniia na fabrikakh i zavodakh" [Types of Public Eating Places at Factories and Plants]. No. 3.

1938: Sen'ko, A. "Polnost'iu ispol'zovat' rezervy promkooperatsii [Make Full Use of the Capacities of Producer Cooperatives]. No. 8–9.

1939: Merenkov, I. "Tovarooborot vo vtorom godu tret'ei piatiletki"

[Commodity Turnover in the Second Year of the Third Five Year Plan]. No. 3–4, 104–113.

1940: Garfinkel', L., and Kabachnik, Ia. "Voprosy organizatsii kolkhoznoi bazarnoi torgovli" [Problems in the Organization of Collective Farm Market Trade]. No. 9–10.

1940: Dukel'skii, S. "O tovarnoi produktsii, sezonnosti zagotovok i realizatsii moloka i masla" [Market Production, Seasonal Changes in Deliveries, and Consumption of Milk and Butter]. No. 11.

412. *Voprosy truda* [Labor Questions]. Ministry of Labor.

1932: Berlin, I., and Mebel', Ia. "Strukturnye sdvigi v naselenii i proletariate" [Structural Changes in the Population and the Proletariat]. No. 11/12, 17–23.

413. *Za industrializatsiiu* [For Industrialization]. Since 1938, called *Industriia* (see 318). Ministry of Heavy Industry.

414. *Za pishchevuiu industriiu* [For the Food Industry]. Since 1938, called *Pishchevaia industriia* (see 360). Ministry of the Food Industry.

1935: Bronshtein, G. "Molochnaia promyshlennost' za piat let" [The Dairy Industry During Five Years]. Feb. 28.

1935: Giber, B. "Shestoi god promyshlennogo maslodeliia" [The Sixth Year of the Industrial Production of Butter]. March 4, 2.

1935: Rozengol'ts, A. "Nash eksport korov'ego masla" [Our Butter Exports]. March 10.

1935: Stepanov, M. "Drozhzhi" [Yeast]. March 28, 3.

1935: Gilinskii, A. "Ovladet' kul'turoi i traditsiami krupnoi promyshlennosti" [Master the Technique of Large-Scale Industry]. April 2.

415. *Za rekonstruktsiiu tekstil'noi promyshlennosti* [For the Reconstruction of the Textile Industry]. Scientific Research Institute of the Textile Industry.

1933: Lebedev, G. "Za povyshenie kachestva produktsii" [For an Improvement in the Quality of Production]. No. 12, 1–7.

416. *Za sotsialisticheskoe rybnoe khoziaistvo* [For a Socialist Fishing Industry]. Chief Administration of the Fishing Industry.

417. *Zhurnal khimicheskoi promyshlennosti* [Journal of the Chemical Industry]. Council of the Chemical Industry.

1925: Vol'fkovich, S. I. "Sovremennoe polozhenie i dostizheniia v oblasti proizvodstva fosfornokislykh tukov za desiatiletie 1914–1924 gg." [The Production of Phosphate Fertilizer: Now and from 1914 to 1924]. No. 3 9–20.

1925: Gurvich, M. N. "Khimugol'—ego dostizheniia i blizhaishie perspektivy" [The Chemical Coal Processing Trust—Achievements and Prospects]. No. 3, 43–45.

1928: Korchagin, A. A. "Trest Lakokraska" [The Paint and Varnish Trust]. No. 1–4, 63–65.

1928: Vorozhtsov, N. N. "K voprosu o razvitii anilinokrasochnoi promyshlennosti v SSSR" [On the Development of the Soviet Aniline Dye Industry]. No. 9–10, 389–397.

1929: Blinkov, B. S. "Pervaia piatiletka bol'shoi khimii" [The First Five Year Plan of Heavy Chemistry]. No. 5, 240–250.

1929: Belovitskii, V. A., and Solov'eva, V. A. "Promyshlennost' insektisidov zagranitsei i v SSSR" [The Insecticide Industry in the USSR and Abroad]. No. 11, 786–792, and No. 13, 945–955.

1929: Belovitskii, V. A., and Lavit, I. Ia. "Mineral'noe syr'e dlia osnovnoi khimicheskoi promyshlennosti na blizhaishee piatiletie" [Mineral Raw Materials for the Basic Chemical Industry in the Next Five Years]. No. 14, 1034–1037.

1929: Gavrilov, N. V. "Kontrol'nye tsifry khimpromyshlennosti 1929/30 g. i voprosy khimicheskoi piatiletki" [The Chemical Industry: Control Figures for 1929/30 and Problems in the Five Year Plan]. No. 15, 1103–1110, and No. 16, 1179–1188.

1929: Soloveichik, M. T. "Kontrol'nye tsifry khimpromyshlennosti na 1929/30 g." [Control Figures for the Chemical Industry for 1929/30]. No. 22, 1668–1671.

1929: Korchagin, A. A. "Khimpromyshlennost' v pervom godu piatiletki [The Chemical Industry in the First Year of the Five Year Plan]. No. 23–24, 1759–1765.

1931: Tyshkovskii, Ia. D. "Dvizhenie zavodskoi sebestoimosti kaltsinirovannoi i kausticheskoi sody" [Movement of the Factory Cost of Soda Ash and Caustic Soda]. No. 1, 57–65.

1932: Kalistratov, Iu. "K probleme khimizatsii sotsialisticheskogo sel'skogo khoziaistva" [The Problem of Using Chemicals in Socialist Agriculture]. No. 3, 12–16.

1932: Blinkov, B. S. "Piatnadtsat' let" [Fifteen Years]. No. 10, 1–16.

1932: Rytslin, E. "Problema mineral'nykh solei vo 2-oi piatiletke" [Mineral Salts in the Second Five Year Plan]. No. 11, 8–15.

1933: Blinkov, B. S. "Na rubezhe piatiletii" [On the Borderline Between Five Year Plans]. No. 1, 1–4.

1933: Vaisbein, S. A. "Kontrol'nye tsifry khimicheskoi promyshlennosti na 1933 god" [Control Figures for the Chemical Industry for 1933]. No. 2, 8–12.

1933: Braginskii, L. P. "Itogi i perspektivy osnovnoi khimii" [Results and Prospects of Basic Chemistry]. No. 2.

1933: Rukavishnikov, V. N. "Promyshlennost' plasticheskikh mass SSSR" [The Soviet Plastics Industry]. No. 3, 4–8.

1933: Sass-Tisovskii, B. A. "Novyi sodovyi zavod v Slavianske" [A New Soda Plant in Slaviansk]. No. 3.

1934: Tyshkovskii, Ia. D. "Nekotorye itogi i perspektivy organicheskoi khimii" [Some Results and Prospects of Organic Chemistry]. No. 3, 4–10.

1934: Volkovysskii, S., and Shvaitser, I. "Osnovnye zadachi tekhnicheskoi rekonstruktsii lakokrasochnoi promyshlennosti vo vtorom piatiletii" [The Main Tasks in the Technical Reconstruction of the Paint and Varnish Industry in the Second Five Year Plan]. No. 3, 10–17.

1934: Denkin, D. Ia. "Puti rekonstruktsii Chernorechenskogo khimicheskogo zavoda" [The Reconstruction of the Chernorech'e Chemical Plant]. No. 3.

1934: Rytslin, E. I. "Osnovnaia khimicheskaia promyshlennost' vo vtoroi piatiletke" [The Basic Chemical Industry in the Second Five Year Plan]. No. 7, 4–15.

1934: Tyshkovskii, Ia. D. "Promyshlennost' organicheskoi khimii vo 2-oi piatiletke" [The Organic Chemistry Industry in the Second Five Year Plan]. No. 7, 15–30.

1935: Rytslin, E. I. "K itogam raboty khimicheskoi promyshlennosti v 1934 godu" [Results of the Chemical Industry in 1934]. No. 3, 226–236.

1935: Levitan, L. B. "Struktura izderzhek sodovogo proizvodstva" [Components of Cost of Soda Production]. No. 6.

1935: Vostokov, N. A. "Problema krasnoural'skogo Khimkombinata" [The Problem of the Krasnouralsk Chemical Combine]. No. 8.

1935: Liubimov, A. L. "Puti razvitiia baritovoi promyshlennosti SSSR" [The Development of the Soviet Barite Industry]. No. 9.

1935: Rytslin, E. I. "Mobilizatsiia rezervov—osnova rentabel'nosti v khimicheskoi promyshlennosti" [The Mobilization of Reserves Is Essential to Make the Chemical Industry Profitable]. No. 10.

1935: Ioffe, Ia. "Dovoennaia khimicheskaia promyshlennost' Rossii" [The Russian Chemical Industry Before the War]. No. 11, 1114–1125.

1936: "Obespechim sotsialisticheskie polia mineral'nymi udobreniiami [Secure Mineral Fertilizer for the Socialist Fields]. No. 3.

1936: Rytslin, E. I. "Nekotorye itogi osnovnoi khimicheskoi promyshlennosti na 1935 god" [Some Results of the Basic Chemical Industry in 1935]. No. 4, 195–203.

1936: "Stakhanovskoe dvizhenie v khimicheskoi promyshlennosti" [The Stakhanovite Movement in the Chemical Industry]. No. 9.

1936: Malin, K. M. "Zadachi issledovatel'skoi raboty po proizvodstvu sernoi kisloty" [Research Problems in the Production of Sulfuric Acid]. No. 21.

1936: Boguslavskii, I. M.; Ben'kovskii, S. V.; and Sinchuk, V. E. "Poluchenie edkogo natra i sernoi kisloty iz mirabilita" [Obtaining Caustic Soda and Sulfuric Acid from Mirabilite]. No. 24.

1937: Sandler, I., and Andreev, A. "Tekhniko-ekonomicheskoe sravnenie pechei dlia obzhiga kolchedana" [A Technical and Economic Comparison of Furnaces for Burning Pyrites]. No. 6.

1937: "Razvitie khimicheskoi promyshlennosti v tret'em piatiletii" [The Development of the Chemical Industry in the Third Five Year Plan]. No. 11–12, 791–794.

1937: Korolev, L. I. "Agrokhimicheskie soobrazheniia k planu razvitiia tukovoi promyshlennosti v tret'em piatiletii" [Agrochemical Considerations in the Plan for the Development of the Fertilizer Industry in the Third Five Year Period]. No. 11–12.

1937: "Puti razvitiia proizvodstva mineral'nykh udobrenii v tret'ei piatiletke" [The Development of the Production of Mineral Fertilizer in the Third Five Year Plan]. No. 11–12.

1937: Malin, K. M. "Zadachi sernokislotnoi promyshlennosti v tret'em piatiletii" [The Tasks of the Sulfuric Acid Industry in the Third Five Year Plan]. No. 14.

1937: Pevtsov, A. I. "Pokonchit' v tret'ei piatiletke s disproportsiei v tarnom khoziaistve khimicheskoi promyshlennosti" [During the Third Five Year Plan Eliminate the Shortage of Packing Materials for the Chemical Industry]. No. 17–18.

1937: Kalmykov, N., and Rybin, I. "Dvadtsat' let sovetskoi khimicheskoi promyshlennosti" [Twenty Years of the Soviet Chemical Industry]. No. 21–22.

1938: Grachev, D. G., and Mazaeva, M. M. "Poteri mineral'nykh udobrenii pri transportirovanii" [Loss of Mineral Fertilizer in Transportation]. No. 1.

1938: Melkumian, B. "Syr'evaia baza Allaverdskogo sernokislotnogo zavoda" [The Raw Material Base of the Allaverdsk Sulfuric Acid Plant]. No. 1.

1938: Vaisbein, S. A. "Osnovnye zadachi khimicheskoi promyshlennosti v 1938 godu" [The Main Tasks of the Chemical Industry in 1938]. No. 3, 2–4.

1938: ———. "Itogi raboty osnovnoi khimicheskoi promyshlennosti za 1937 god" [The Achievements of the Basic Chemical Industry in 1937]. No. 4, 4–8.

1938: Berlin, L. E. "O proizvodstve bornoi kisloty i bury" [On the Production of Boric Acid and Borax]. No. 6, 20–23.

1938: "Nashi zadachi" [Our Tasks]. No. 6.

1939: "Osnovnaia khimicheskaia promyshlennost' k 18-mu s'ezdu VKP (b) i ocherednye zadachi na 1939 god" [The Basic Chemical Industry at the 18th Party Congress and Its Tasks for 1939]. No. 3, 3–7.

1939: Dunaevskii, E. I., and Rozenberg, B. S. "Ekonomiia sernoi kisloty pri proizvodstve udobrenii" [Economizing Sulfuric Acid in the Production of Fertilizer]. No. 3.

1939: Vaisbein, S. A. "Itogi raboty khimicheskoi promyshlennosti v 1-om polugodii 1939 goda" [Results of the Chemical Industry in the First Half of 1939]. No. 8, 1–4.

1939: Sass-Tisovskii, B. A. "Sodovaia i khlornaia promyshlennost' kapitalisticheskikh stran" [The Soda and Chlorine Industry in Capitalist Countries]. No. 8.

1939: "Khimicheskaia promyshlennost' k 22-oi godovshchine Velikoi Oktiabr'skoi Revoliutsii i osnovnye zadachi 1940 goda" [The Chemical Industry on the 22nd Anniversary of the Great October Revolution and Its Main Tasks for 1940]. No. 10, 1–5.

1940: Kalmykov, N. N., and Vaisbein, S. A. "Khimicheskaia promyshlennost' v tret'ei piatiletke" [The Chemical Industry in the Third Five Year Plan]. No. 7, 1–11.

1940: Tsyrlin, D. "O proizvodstve dvoinogo superfosfata" [On the Production of Triple Superphosphate]. No. 7.

1940: Graevskii, Ia. S., and Tiurnikov, M. D. "Uporiadochenie tarnogo khoziaistva v khimicheskoi promyshlennosti" [Organize the Production of Packing Materials in the Chemical Industry]. No. 8.

1940: Malin, K. M. "Neobkhodimye meropriiatiia dlia sokrashcheniia raskhoda kolchedana i azotnoi kisloty na bashennykh sernokislotnykh sistemakh" [Necessary Measures to Reduce Expenditure of Pyrites and Nitric Acid in Sulfuric Acid Tower Installations]. No. 8.

1940: Khlebnikov, B. Ia. "Meropriiatiia dlia uvelicheniia vyrabotki prirodnoi sery" [Measures to Increase the Production of Natural Sulfur]. No. 9.

1940: Turgin, F. V. "Effektivnost' kaliinykh udobrenii dlia osnovnykh sel'skokhoziaistvennykh kul'tur SSSR" [The Effect of Potash Fertilizer on the Main Agricultural Crops of the USSR]. No. 12.

1940: "Osnovnye zadachi khimicheskoi promyshlennosti v 1941 godu" [The Main Tasks of the Chemical Industry in 1941]. No. 12.

418. *Zhurnal prikladnoi khimii* [The Journal of Applied Chemistry]. USSR Academy of Sciences.

1947: Vol'fkovich, S. I., and Dubovitskii, A. M. "Tekhnologiia udobrenii i sernoi kisloty v SSSR za 30 let" [Technological Means of Producing Fertilizer and Sulfuric Acid in the USSR for 30 Years]. No. 11, 1053–1082.

419. *Zhurnal rezinovoi promyshlennosti* [Journal of the Rubber Industry]. Chief Administration of the Rubber and Technical Fabrics Industry.

C. NON-RUSSIAN BOOKS AND ARTICLES (420–596)

420. *Armaments Year-Book*. League of Nations. Geneva, 1933.

421. Auer, Jaako. *Suomen Sotarkorvaustoimitukset Neuvostoliitolle* [The Finnish War Reparations Deliveries to the Soviet Union]. Helsinki, 1956.

421a. Balassa, Bela. *The Hungarian Experience in Economic Planning*. New Haven, 1959.

422. Baster, Nancy. "Russian Budget Studies" (mimeographed). National Bureau of Economic Research working memorandum. New York, 1955.

423. Becker, Abraham S. "Prices of Producers' Durables in the United States and the USSR in 1955" (mimeographed). RAND Corporation, RM-2432. Santa Monica, 1959.

424. Bergson, Abram. "A Problem in Soviet Statistics," *Review of Economic Statistics*, November 1947, 234–242.

425. ———. "Reliability and Usability of Soviet Statistics," *The American Statistician*, June-July 1953, 13–16.

426. ———. *Soviet National Income and Product, 1937*. New York, 1953.

427. ———, and Bernaut, Roman. "Prices of Basic Chemical Products in the Soviet Union, 1928–1950" (mimeographed). RAND Corporation, RM-920. Santa Monica, 1952.

428. ———, and Turgeon, Lynn. "Prices of Iron and Steel Products in the Soviet Union, 1928–1950: A Summary Report" (mimeographed). RAND Corporation, RM-802. Santa Monica, 1952.

429. ———, and Heymann, Hans. *Soviet National Income and Product, 1940–1948*. New York, 1954.

430. ———. "Prices of Ordinary Rolled Steel in the Soviet Union, 1928–1950" (mimeographed). RAND Corporation, RM-767. Santa Monica, 1952.

431. ———, et al. "Postwar Economic Reconstruction and Development in the U.S.S.R.," *Annals of the American Academy of Political and Social Sciences*, May 1949, 52–72.

432. ———, et al. "Prices of Basic Industrial Products in the USSR, 1928–1950," *Journal of Political Economy*, August 1956, 303–328.

433. Berliner, Joseph. *Factory and Manager in the USSR*. Cambridge, Mass., 1957.

434. Bernaut, Roman, and Bergson, Abram. "Prices of Cement in the Soviet Union, 1928–1950" (mimeographed). RAND Corporation, RM-1136. Santa Monica, 1953.

435. ———. "Prices of Fuelwood and Wood Products in the USSR, 1928–1950" (mimeographed). RAND Corporation, RM-1421. Santa Monica, 1955.

436. ———. "Prices of Paints in the Soviet Union, 1928–1950" (mimeographed). RAND Corporation, RM-1071. Santa Monica, 1953.

437. Betts, R. R. (ed). *Central and South East Europe, 1945–1948*. London, 1950.

438. Carter, C. F.; Reddaway, W. B.; and Stone, R. *The Measurement of Production Movements*. London, 1947.

439. ———, and Robson, M. "A Test of the Accuracy of a Production Index," *Journal of the American Statistical Association*, March 1956, 17–23.

440. Chamberlin, William Henry. *Soviet Russia*. Boston, 1930.

441. Chapman, Janet. "Real Wages in the Soviet Union, 1928–1952," *Review of Economics and Statistics*, May 1954, 134–156.

442. ———. "Retail Prices of Goods and Services Included in the Cost of Living Index, Official Prices, Moscow, 1928, 1937, 1948, and 1952" (unpublished appendix).

443. ———. "Retail Prices of Manufactured Consumer Goods in the USSR, 1937–1948" (mimeographed). RAND Corporation RM-803-1. Santa Monica, 1952.

444. Clark, Colin. *The Conditions of Economic Progress*. 2nd ed. London, 1951.

445. ———. *A Critique of Russian Statistics*. London, 1939.

446. Clark, Gardner. *The Economics of Soviet Steel*. Cambridge, Mass., 1956.

447. *Comparisons of the United States and Soviet Economies*. Joint Economic Committee, Congress of the United States. Washington, 1959.

448. *Concise Statistical Yearbook of Poland, 1938*. Warsaw, 1938.

449. *Concise Statistical Yearbook of Poland, September 1939 to June 1941*. Glasgow, 1941.

450. Crankshaw, Edward. *Russia without Stalin*. New York, 1956.

451. *Current Digest of the Soviet Press*. New York, 1950–1960.

452. DeMille, John B. *Strategic Minerals*. New York and London, 1947.

453. Devons, Ely. *Planning in Practice*: *Essays in Aircraft Planning in Wartime*. Cambridge, Eng., 1950.

454. Dewitt, Nicholas. "Cement, Brick, and Other Mineral Construction Materials Industries in the USSR" (mimeographed). Council for Economic and Industry Research report A-18. Washington, 1955.

455. Dobb, Maurice. "Further Appraisals of Russian Economic Statistics—A Comment on Soviet Statistics," *Review of Economic Statistics*, February 1948, 34–38.

456. Dodge, Norton T. "The Tractor Industry of the USSR" (mimeographed). Council for Economic and Industry Research report A-31. Washington, 1955.

457. Dolina, J. "Foreign Trade" in *East-Central Europe under the Communists: Poland*. Edited by O. Halecki. New York, 1957.

458. *Etudes et Conjoncture.* Paris, 1955.
459. *Finland Yearbook, 1939/40.* Helsinki, 1939.
460. Florinsky, M. T. *Russia: A History and an Interpretation.* New York, 1953.
461. "Les Fluctuations des Prix de Détail en l'Union Soviétique" in *Conjoncture et Etudes Economiques.* Paris, 1955.
462. Friedensburg, Ferdinand, *Die Bergwirtschaft des Erde.* Stuttgart, 1948.
463. Friedman, Elisha M. *Russia in Transition.* London, 1933.
464. *From the First to the Second Five Year Plan* (translated from the Russian). New York, 1933.
465. Galenson, Walter. *Labor Productivity in Soviet and American Industry.* New York, 1955.
466. Gerschenkron, Alexander, "Comment on Naum Jasny's 'Soviet Statistics,' " *Review of Economics and Statistics,* August 1950, 250–251.
467. ———. *A Dollar Index of Soviet Machinery Output, 1927–28 to 1937.* Santa Monica, 1951.
468. ———. "The Rate of Industrial Growth in Russia since 1885" in *The Tasks of Economic History,* supplement VII to *Journal of Economic History,* 1947.
469. ———. "Reliability of Soviet Industrial and National Income Statistics," *The American Statistician,* June–July 1953, 18–21.
470. ———. "The Soviet Indices of Industrial Production," *Review of Economic Statistics,* November 1947, 217–226.
471. ———, and Nimitz, Nancy. "A Dollar Index of Soviet Iron and Steel Output" (mimeographed). RAND Corporation, RM-1055. Santa Monica, 1954.
472. ———. "A Dollar Index of Soviet Petroleum Output, 1927–28 to 1937" (mimeographed). RAND Corporation, RM-804. Santa Monica, 1952.
473. Goldsmith, Raymond W. "The Economic Growth of Russia, 1860–1913" (mimeographed). National Bureau of Economic Research working memorandum. New York, 1955.
474. Granick, David. "Are Adjusted Rubles Rational? A Comment," *Soviet Studies,* July 1956, 46–49.
475. ———. *Management of the Industrial Firm in the U.S.S.R.* New York, 1954.
476. Greenslade, R. V., and Wallace, Phyllis A. "Industrial Growth in the Soviet Union: Comment," *American Economic Review,* September 1959, 687–695.
477. Grossman, Gregory. "Discussion," *American Economic Review, Papers and Proceedings,* May 1957, 643–652.
478. ———. *Soviet Statistics of Physical Output of Industrial Commodities: Their Compilation and Quality.* Princeton for National Bureau of Economic Research, 1960.
479. ———. "Steel, Planning, and War Preparedness in the USSR" *Explorations in Entrepreneurial History,* Vol. IX, No. 4.
480. Grund, Herbert. *Die Energiewirtschaft der Sowjetunion.* Berlin, 1952.
481. Guderian, General Heinz. *Panzer Leader.* New York, 1952.
482. *Handbuch der Internationalen Kali-Stickotoff und Phosphorsaüre Industrie, 1938–39.* Berlin, 1938.
483. Harcave, S. *Russia: A History.* 3rd ed. Philadelphia, 1956.

484. Hardt, John Pearce. "Economics of the Soviet Electric Power Industry" (processed). Air University, Alabama, 1955.

485. Hassmann, Heinrich. *Oil in the Soviet Union*. Princeton, 1953.

486. *Hearings, November 13–20, 1959*. Joint Economic Committee, Congress of the United States. Washington, 1960.

487. Heymann, Hans, Jr. "Discussion," *American Economic Review, Papers and Proceedings*, May 1958, 422–427.

488. Hirsch, Alcan. *Industrialized Russia*. New York, 1934.

489. Hodgman, Donald R. "Measuring Soviet Industrial Expansion: A Reply," *Soviet Studies*, July 1956, 34–35.

490. ———. *Soviet Industrial Production, 1928–1951*. Cambridge, Mass., 1954.

491. Hoeffding, Oleg, and Nimitz, Nancy. "Soviet National Income and Product, 1949–1955" (mimeographed). RAND Corporation, RM-2101. Santa Monica, 1959.

492. Holzman, Franklyn. *Soviet Taxation: The Fiscal and Monetary Problems of a Planned Economy*. Cambridge, Mass., 1955.

493. Hoover, Calvin B. *The Economic Life of Soviet Russia*. New York, 1931.

494. *International Yearbook of Agriculture, 1940–41*. Rome, 1941.

495. Jasny, Naum. "Indices of Soviet Industrial Production, 1928–1954" (mimeographed). Council for Economic and Industry Research report A-46. Washington, 1955.

496. ———. "International Organizations and Soviet Statistics," *Journal of the American Statistical Association*, March 1950, 48–64.

497. ———. "Intricacies of Russian National Income Statistics," *Journal of Political Economy*, August 1947, 299–322.

498. ———. *The Socialized Agriculture of the USSR*. Stanford, 1949.

499. ———. *The Soviet Economy during the Plan Era*. Stanford, 1951.

500. ———. *Soviet Prices of Producers' Goods*. Stanford, 1952.

501. ———. *Soviet Price System*. Stanford, 1951.

502. ———. *The Soviet 1956 Statistical Handbook: A Commentary*. East Lansing, 1957.

503. ———. "Soviet Statistics," *Review of Economics and Statistics*, February 1950, 92–99.

504. Kaplan, Norman, and Moorsteen, Richard. "An Index of Soviet Industrial Output," *American Economic Review*, June 1960, 295–318.

504a. ———. "Indexes of Soviet Industrial Output" (mimeographed). RAND Corporation, RM-2495. Santa Monica, 1960.

505. ———, *et al.* "A Tentative Input-Output Table for the USSR, 1941 Plan" (mimeographed). RAND Corporation, RM-924. Santa Monica, 1952.

506. Kaufman, Adam. "Small-Scale Industry in the Soviet Union" National Bureau of Economic Research (in press).

507. Kazakov, George. *Soviet Peat Resources: A Descriptive Study*. New York, 1953.

508. Kiesenwetter, Bruno. *Statistiken zur Wirtschaft Ost und Südosteuropas*. Berlin, 1955.

509. Kivinen, L. "Finland's War Reparations Payments" in *The Finland Yearbook, 1947*. Helsinki, 1948.

510. ———. "The Payment of War Reparations to the Soviet Union" in *Finland: an Economic Survey*, supplement to *The Statist*, April 1955.

511. Kournakoff, S. N. *Russia's Fighting Forces*. New York, 1942.

512. Kravchenko, Victor. *I Chose Freedom*. New York, 1952.

513. Lamer, Mirko. "Fertilizers in the USSR," *Agricultural and Food Chemistry*, June 1955, 409–495.

514. ———. "The Timber Industry of the USSR" (mimeographed). Council for Economic and Industry Research report A-36. Washington, 1955.

515. ———. "Wood Pulp and Paper Industry of the USSR" (mimeographed). Council for Economic and Industry Research report A-38. Washington, 1955.

516. ———. "Woodworking Industries of the USSR" (mimeographed). Council for Economic and Industry Research report A-37. Washington, 1955.

517. Lange, Oscar. "The Economic Laws of Socialist Society in the Light of Joseph Stalin's Last Work," *International Papers*, 1954, No. 4.

517a. ———. "For a New Economic Program," *Zycie Gospodarcze*, July 16, 1956.

518. *The Leather and Shoe Industry in the Soviet Union*. Department of State. Washington, n.d.

519. Leimbach, Werner. *Die Sowjetunion: Natur, Volk und Wirtschaft*. Stuttgart, 1950.

520. Lorimer, Frank. *The Population of the Soviet Union: History and Prospects*. Geneva, 1946.

521. Lounasman, O. "Finnish War Reparations," *Bank of Finland Monthly Bulletin*, November-December 1952.

522. Marczewski, J. *Planifications et croissance économique des démocraties populaires*. Paris, 1956.

523. Meisner, M. *Die Versorgung der Weltwirtschaft mit Bergwerkereugnissen*. Stuttgart, 1925–1939.

524. Mikolajczyk, S. *The Rape of Poland*. New York, 1948.

525. Moorsteen, Richard. "Prices of Prime Movers, USSR, 1927/28–1949" (mimeographed). RAND Corporation, RM-1225. Santa Monica, 1954.

526. ———. "Prices of Railroad Rolling Stock, USSR, 1927/28–1949" (mimeographed). RAND Corporation, RM-1258. Santa Monica, 1954.

527. ———. "Prices of Road Building and Construction Machines, USSR, 1928–1949" (mimeographed). RAND Corporation, RM-1037. Santa Monica, 1953.

528. ———. "Prices of Tractors, Trucks, and Automobiles, USSR, 1928–1949" (mimeographed). RAND Corporation, RM-1121. Santa Monica, 1953.

529. Nash, Edmund. "Hours of Work and Leave Provisions in the USSR," *Monthly Labor Review*, September 1957, 1069–1073.

529a. ———. "Purchasing Power of Workers in the U.S.S.R.," *Monthly Labor Review*, April 1960, 359–364.

530. *Nazi-Soviet Relations, 1939–1941*. Department of State. Washington, 1948.

531. Nettle, P. *The Eastern Zone and Soviet Policy in Germany, 1945–1950*. New York, 1951.

532. *New York Times*.

533. Nimitz, Nancy. "A Dollar Index of Soviet Coal Output, 1927/28–1937" (mimeographed). RAND Corporation, RM-1042. Santa Monica, 1953.

534. ———. "Prices of Refined Petroleum Products in the USSR, 1928–1950" (mimeographed). RAND Corporation, RM-1497. Santa Monica, 1955.

535. Nove, A. "'1926/27' and All That," Soviet Studies, October 1957, 117–130.

536. ———. "The Pace of Soviet Economic Development," Lloyds Bank Review, April 1956, 1–23.

537. ———. "The Problem of Success Indicators in Soviet Industry," Economica, February 1958, 1–13.

538. ———. "Soviet National Income Statistics," Soviet Studies, January 1955, 247–264.

538a. ———, and Zauberman, Alfred. "A Soviet Disclosure of Ruble National Income," Soviet Studies, October 1959, 195–202.

539. Nutter, G. Warren. "On Measuring Economic Growth," Journal of Political Economy, February 1957, 51–63.

540. ———. "Reply," American Economic Review, September 1959, 695–701.

541. ———. Some Observations on Soviet Industrial Growth. National Bureau of Economic Research Occasional Paper 55. New York, 1957.

542. Ostland in Zahlen. Riga, 1942.

543. Pares, Bernard. A History of Russia. Rev. ed. New York, 1944.

544. Redding, David. "USSR Industrial Employment and Its Distribution" (mimeographed). Council for Economic and Industry Research report A-8. Washington, 1955.

544a. A Report on USSR Electric Power Development, 1958–1959. Edison Electric Institute. New York, 1960.

544b. A Report on the Visit of an American Delegation to Observe Concrete and Prestressed Concrete Engineering in the U.S.S.R. Portland Cement Association. Chicago, 1959.

544c. Report on Visit of U.S.A. Plastics Industry Exchange Delegation to U.S.S.R., June 2 to June 28, 1958. Society of the Plastics Industry. New York, n.d.

545. Rice, Stuart A. "Statistical Concepts in the Soviet Union Examined from Generally Accepted Scientific Viewpoints," Review of Economic Statistics, February 1952, 82–86.

546. ———. "Statistics in the Soviet Union," Bulletin of the Atomic Scientists, June 1952, 159–162.

547. Robinson, Joan. "Mr. Wiles' Rationality: A Comment," Soviet Studies, January 1956, 269–273.

548. The Russian Iron and Steel Industry. Iron and Steel Institute Special Report No. 57. London, 1956.

548a. "Russian Metallurgy," Journal of Metals, March 1958.

549. "The Russian Steel Industry," Steel Review, April 1956, 24–28.

549a. Rzezpospolita. Warsaw.

550. Schelling, T. International Economics. Boston, 1958.

551. Schwalberg, Barney K. Industrial Employment in the USSR, 1933, 1937, 1950, and 1955. Bureau of the Census. Series P-95, No. 55. Washington, 1960.

552. Schwartz, Harry. "On the Use of Soviet Statistics," Journal of the American Statistical Association, September 1947, 401–406.

553. ———. "The Organization and Operation of the Soviet Statistical Apparatus," *The American Statistician*, April-May 1952, 9–13.

554. ———. *Russia's Soviet Economy*. 2nd ed. New York, 1954.

555. ——— (ed.). *Statistical Handbook of the USSR*. New York, 1957.

555a. Schwarz, Solomon. *Labor in the Soviet Union*. New York, 1951.

556. Schwind, Martin. *Die Gestaltung Karafutos zum Japanischen Raum*. Gotha, 1942.

557. Scott, John. *Beyond the Urals*. Cambridge, Mass., 1942.

558. Seton, Francis. "An Estimate of Soviet Industrial Expansion," *Soviet Studies*, October 1955, 128–142.

559. ———. "The Tempo of Soviet Industrial Expansion," *Manchester Statistical Society*, January 1957, 1–39.

560. Shabad, Theodore. *Geography of the USSR*. New York, 1951.

561. Shimkin, Demitri B. *Minerals—a Key to Soviet Power*. Cambridge, Mass., 1953.

562. ———, and Leedy, F. A. "Soviet Industrial Growth," *Automotive Industries*, January 1, 1958, 4–35.

562a. "Soviet Computing Technology—1959," *Transactions*, Institute of Radio Engineers, March 1960, and *Communications*, Association for Computing Machinery, March 1960.

563. *Soviet Economic Growth: A Comparison with the United States*. Joint Economic Committee, Congress of the United States. Washington, 1957.

564. *Soviet Railroad Equipment Industry*. Institute for Research and Social Science, University of North Carolina. Chapel Hill, 1954.

565. Spulber, N. *The Economics of Communist Eastern Europe*. Cambridge, Mass., 1957.

566. Starlinger, Wilhelm. *Grenzen der Sowjetmacht*. Würzburg, 1955.

567. *Statistical Abstract of Industrial Output in the Soviet Union*. Parts 1–5 and Supplement. National Bureau of Economic Research. New York, 1956 and 1957.

568. *Statistical Yearbook of the League of Nations, 1941/42*. Geneva, 1943.

569. *Statystyka Przemyslowa* [Industrial Statistics]. Warsaw, 1938.

569a. *Steel in the Soviet Union*. American Iron and Steel Institute. New York, 1959.

570. Tolpin, J. G. "The Growth of Industry in the USSR," *Chemical Engineering News*, February 1943.

571. *Treaties and Other International Acts Series*. Department of State. Washington, 1947–1948.

572. Tsonev, V. "Falsification of Soviet Industrial Statistics" (unpublished manuscript). Research Program on the USSR. New York, 1953.

573. Turgeon, Lynn. "Cost-Price Relationships in Basic Industries during the Soviet Planning Era," *Soviet Studies*, October 1957, 143–177.

574. ———. "On the Reliability of Soviet Statistics," *Review of Economics and Statistics*, February 1952, 75–76.

575. ———. "Prices of Coal and Peat in the Soviet Union" (mimeographed). RAND Corporation, RM-1423. Santa Monica, 1955.

576. ———, and Bergson, Abram. "Prices of Basic Industrial Goods in the

USSR, 1950 to 1956," (mimeographed). RAND Corporation, RM-1919. Santa Monica, 1957.

577. ———; Bernaut, Roman; and Bergson, Abram. "Prices of Miscellaneous Basic Industrial Products, USSR, 1928–1950" (mimeographed). RAND Corporation, RM-1482. Santa Monica, 1955.

578. United Nations. *Bulletin of Coal Statistics for Europe.* Geneva, 1954.

579. ———. *Competition between Steel and Aluminum.* Geneva, 1954.

580. ———. *Economic Survey of Europe.* Issues for 1950, 1953–1956. Geneva, 1951–1957.

581. ———. *Economic Survey of Europe since the War.* Geneva, 1953.

582. ———. *Monthly Bulletin of Statistics.* New York.

583. ———. *Statistical Yearbook.* Issues for 1953–1959. New York.

583a. Vannah, William E. "A Team Reports on Control Inside Russia," *Control Engineering*, November 1958.

584. Vernadsky, G. *A History of Russia.* New Haven, 1951.

584a. Wagenführ, Rolf. "Der Wettlauf der Grossmächte," *Frankfurter Allgemeine Zeitung*, July 23, 1960.

585. Wainstein, E. S. "A Comparison of Soviet and United States Retail Prices for Manufactured Goods and Services in 1950" (mimeographed). RAND Corporation, RM-1606. Santa Monica, 1954.

586. Wiles, P. J. D. "Are Adjusted Rubles Rational?" *Soviet Studies*, October 1955, 143–160.

587. ———. "A Rejoinder to All and Sundry," *Soviet Studies*, October 1956, 134–143.

588. Williams, Ernest. "Transportation in the Soviet Union." National Bureau of Economic Research working memorandum. New York, 1957.

589. ———. *Freight Transportation in the Soviet Union: A Comparison with the United States.* National Bureau of Economic Research Occasional Paper 65. New York, 1959.

590. Winston, V. "The Soviet Satellites—Economic Liability?" *Problems of Communism.* Washington, 1958.

591. Wolff, R. *Balkans in Our Time.* Cambridge, Mass., 1956.

592. Wool, Harold. "Statistics of Population, Labor Force, and Employment in the Soviet Union" (mimeographed). National Bureau of Economic Research working memorandum. New York, 1958.

593. Woytinsky, W. S. and E. S. *World Population and Production.* New York, 1953.

594. Yugow, A. *Russia's Economic Front for War and Peace* (translated from the Russian). New York and London, 1942.

595. Zamoyski, T., and Checinski, T. "Przemysl chemiczny" [The Chemical Industry], *Przeglad Gospodarczy*, No. 2, 1938.

596. Zec, George C. "Aluminum Industry of the USSR and Satellite Nations" (mimeographed). Council for Economic and Industry Research report A-2. Washington, 1955.

Sources for U.S. Data (597–656)

597. *Abstract of the Census of Manufactures, 1919.* Washington, 1923.

598. *Agricultural Statistics.* Issues for 1942–1957. Washington, 1942–1957.

599. *American Cotton Handbook.* New York, 1941.

600. *Annual Abstract of Statistics, No. 90.* London, 1953.

601. *Annual Average Price Relatives and Prices, 1954 and 1955.* Bureau of Labor Statistics, Washington, 1956.

601a. *Annual Statistical Report.* American Iron and Steel Institute, New York, 1948 and 1955.

602. *Automobile Facts and Figures.* Detroit, 1955.

603. Barger, Harold, and Schurr, Sam H. *The Mining Industries, 1899–1939.* National Bureau of Economic Research. New York, 1944.

604. *Bicycles and Parts, Report on the Escape Clause Investigations.* Tariff Commission, Washington, 1952.

605. *Biennial Census of Manufactures, 1931.* Washington, 1935.

606. Borenstein, Israel. *Capital and Output Trends in Mining Industries, 1870–1948.* National Bureau of Economic Research Occasional Paper 45. New York, 1954.

607. Burns, Arthur F. *Production Trends in the United States since 1870.* National Bureau of Economic Research. New York, 1934.

608. *Business Statistics, 1955.* Office of Business Economics, Washington, 1955.

609. *Census of United States Manufactures.* Issues for 1914, 1920, 1929, 1939, 1947, and 1954. Washington, 1919–1957.

610. *Census of Mineral Industries, 1954.* Washington, 1957.

611. *Chemical Economic Handbook,* Stanford, 1957.

612. *Consumption of Food in the U.S., 1909–1948.* Agricultural Economics Bureau, Washington, 1949.

613. *Continuation to 1952 of Historical Statistics of the United States, 1789–1945.* Washington, 1954.

614. *Cotton from Field to Fabric.* National Cotton Council of America, Memphis, 1951.

614a. Creamer, D.; Dobrovolsky, S. P.; and Borenstein, I. *Capital in Manufacturing and Mining, Its Formation and Financing.* Princeton for National Bureau of Economic Research, 1960.

614b. *A Critique of the United States Income and Product Accounts.* Studies in Income and Wealth 22. Princeton for National Bureau of Economic Research, 1958.

615. Dewees, Anne. *Oleomargarine Statistics of Production, Materials Used in Manufacture, Consumption, Trade and Prices.* Department of Agriculture, Washington, 1938.

616. *The Economic Almanac.* New York, 1956.

617. *Economic Report of the President.* Washington, 1957.

618. Fabricant, Solomon. *The Output of Manufacturing Industries, 1899–1937.* National Bureau of Economic Research. New York, 1940.

619. *Facts for Industry.*

620. *Federal Reserve Bulletin.*

621. *Fishery Industries of the U.S., 1927–1937.* Fish and Wildlife Service, Washington.

622. Frickey, Edwin. *Production in the United States, 1860–1914.* Cambridge, Mass., 1947.

623. Garfield, Frank R. "Measurement of Industrial Production since 1939," *Journal of the American Statistical Association*, December 1944, 439–454.

624. Goldsmith, Raymond W.; Brady, D. S.; and Mendershausen, H. *A Study of Saving in the United States*. Princeton, 1958.

625. Gould, Jacob Martin. *Output and Productivity in the Electric and Gas Utilities, 1899–1942*. National Bureau of Economic Research. New York, 1946.

626. *Historical Statistics of the United States, 1789–1945*. Washington, 1949.

626a. *Historical Statistics of the United States, Colonial Times to 1957*. Washington, 1960.

626b. *Industrial Production, 1959 Revision*. Federal Reserve System. Washington, 1960.

626c. *Industrial Production Indexes for 1959*. Federal Reserve System. Washington, 1960.

627. Kendrick, John W. "Measurement of Real Product" in *A Critique of the United States Income and Product Accounts*, Studies in Income and Wealth 22. Princeton for National Bureau of Economic Research, 1958.

628. ———. *Productivity Trends in the United States*. Princeton for National Bureau of Economic Research, 1961.

629. Kuznets, Simon. *National Income and Its Composition, 1919–1938*. National Bureau of Economic Research. New York, 1941.

630. ———. *Secular Movements in Production and Prices*. New York, 1930.

631. ———, and Rubin, Ernest. *Immigration and the Foreign Born*. National Bureau of Economic Research Occasional Paper 46. New York, 1954.

632. Leong, Y. S. "Index of the Physical Volume Production of Minerals, 1880–1948," *Journal of the American Statistical Association*, March 1950, 15–29.

633. Mack, Ruth. *Consumption and Business Fluctuations: A Case Study of the Shoe, Leather, Hide Sequence*. National Bureau of Economic Research. New York, 1956.

634. *Manufacture and Sale of Farm Equipment*. Federal Trade Commission, Washington.

634a. *Metal Statistics*. American Metal Markets, 1955.

635. *Mineral Facts and Problems*. Bureau of Mines, Washington, 1956.

636. *Mineral Industries, 1939*. Bureau of Mines, Washington, 1944.

637. *Mineral Resources of the United States*. Issues for 1913 and 1929. Bureau of Mines, Washington, 1914 and 1932.

638. *Minerals Yearbook*. Issues for 1940, 1951–1953. Bureau of Mines, Washington, 1940–1956.

639. Moore, Geoffrey H. "Accuracy of Government Statistics," *Harvard Business Review*, Spring 1947, 306–317.

640. ———. *Production of Industrial Materials in World Wars I and II*. National Bureau of Economic Research Occasional Paper 18. New York, 1944.

641. *1950 Bituminous Coal Annual*. Bituminous Coal Institute, Washington, 1950.

642. Persons, Warren M. *Forecasting Business Cycles*. New York, 1931.

642a. Peterson, Elmer W. *Summarized Data of Zinc Production*. Washington, 1929.

643. Putman, P. C. *Energy in the Future*, New York, 1953.

644. *Radio Retailing*. January 1938.

645. *Railroad Car Facts, 1954.* New York, 1955.

646. *Railroad Gazette.*

647. *Railway Age.*

648. Rostas, L. *Comparative Productivity in British and American Industry.* Cambridge, 1948.

649. *Statistical Abstract of the United States.* Issues for 1923–1958. Washington, 1924–1958.

650. *Statistics of Electric Utilities in the U.S., Privately Owned Companies.* Federal Power Commission, Washington.

651. *Statistics of Electric Utilities in the U.S., Publicly Owned.* Federal Power Commission, Washington.

652. *Survey of Current Business.*

653. *U.S. Income and Output.* Washington, 1958.

654. Weber, G. M., and Alsbery, C. L. *The American Vegetable-Shortening Industry.* Washington, 1934.

655. *Wholesale Prices.* Bureau of Labor Statistics, Washington 1913–1939.

656. *Yearbook of Agriculture.* Issues for 1910–1932. Washington, 1910–1932.

INDEX

INDEX

U.S. data and comparisons, 246, 282, 371, 598 f, 609

Chemicals:
employment, 171, 346 ff, 390, 499, 505 f, 508
labor productivity, 172, 174, 199, 234, 243, 387
list of products, 404
plan data, 206, 397, 399 ff
price index, 341 f
production index, 115, 128, 166, 186 f, 195 f, 217, 222, 234, 310 f, 336, 339, 348, 525, 527
growth rate, 165, 198 f
weights, 530 f, 568
production indexes included in, 574
weights, 314, 316, 334, 568
retardation in growth, 106
ruble-dollar ratio, 379
U.S. data and comparisons, 234, 243, 250, 252 f, 362 f, 385 ff
value data, 511

China and pottery, 362, 378, 390, 503, 512

Cigarettes:
output, 37, 193, 303, 415, 454, 496
growth rate, 85, 90, 96
plan, 398
production indexes included in, 578 f
weights, 120 f, 535, 571
Russian term for, 409
turnover tax, adjustment for, 123 n
U.S. data and comparisons, 94, 104, 245, 263, 273 f, 276, 280, 360, 365, 600 f
value data, 300, 364

Clark, Colin, 26 n, 158

Clocks and watches:
output, 37, 302, 459, 495
growth rate, 85, 96
production indexes included in, 578
weights, 536, 572
Russian term for, 410

Coal:
employment, 347, 499
output, 35, 302, 412
growth rate, 85, 96
plan, 223, 397
production indexes included in, 570
weights, 530
quality of, 65, 75
Russian term for, 404
thermal content, 372, 376
U.S. data and comparisons, 94, 104, 244, 262, 273 f, 276, 280, 356, 363, 586 f, 608 f

value data, 300, 362, 509
See also Anthracite; Bituminous coal; Lignite

Coal-cutting machines:
output, 36, 442
production indexes included in, 576
weights, 534
Russian term for, 407

Coal-mining combines:
output, 441
production indexes included in, 576
weights, 533
Russian term for, 407

Coke:
employment, 499
output, 35, 302, 421, 495
growth rate, 85, 90, 96
plan, 397
production indexes included in, 574
weights, 530, 568
Russian term for, 404
U.S. data and comparisons, 94, 104, 244, 262, 273 f, 276, 356, 362, 584 f
value data, 300, 362, 509

Combines, all other:
output, 437
production indexes included in, 576
weights, 533, 570
Russian term for, 406

Combines, grain:
output, 36, 436
plan, 398
production indexes included in, 576
weights, 533, 570
Russian term for, 406
U.S. data and comparisons, 246, 264, 282, 370, 594 f

Comparisons, U.S. and Soviet Union, 225 ff, 288 ff, 354 ff
aggregate production, 237 ff, 248 ff, 290
capital inputs, 236
comparable periods, 256 ff, 291
employee compensation, 241, 625
employment, 238, 252 f, 291 f
hypothetical future performance, 269 ff
labor productivity, 232 ff, 289 f
lags in Soviet output behind U.S., 258 f, 261, 271 ff
military production, 255 f, 268, 290
output of individual industries, 355 ff
growth rates, 244 ff, 262 ff
population, 230, 238, 289
production index, 227, 231, 233 ff
growth rate, 229, 243, 248
ruble-dollar price ratios, 377 ff
shortcomings of, 243 n, 246 n, 267 f, 272

689